Fodor's 2014

NORTHERN CALIFORNIA

D0000217

Portions of this book appear in *Fodor's California 2014.*

WELCOME TO NORTHERN CALIFORNIA

It's easy to tap into the good life in Northern California. Between rounds of golf at Pebble Beach, winding drives along the iconic Big Sur coast, or scenic treks through Yosemite National Park, you can indulge in a wealth of top-notch outdoor activities. In Napa and Sonoma, eating and drinking are cultivated as high arts. You can sip wine at picturesque vineyards and then dine at stellar locavore restaurants. Urban pleasures await in San Francisco, too, where cable cars zip through vibrant neighborhoods lined with chic boutiques and cutting-edge museums.

TOP REASONS TO GO

★ **San Francisco:** This diverse city beguiles with natural beauty and contagious energy.

★ **Wine Country:** Top-notch whites and reds in Napa, Sonoma, and beyond.

★ **Feasts:** Cutting-edge cuisine, food trucks, fusion flavors, farmers' markets.

★ **Stunning Scenery:** Picture-perfect backdrops from the Golden Gate Bridge to redwoods.

★ **Outdoor Adventures:** National park excursions, hiking, and golfing are all excellent.

★ **Road Trips:** The Pacific Coast Highway offers spectacular views and thrills aplenty.

Fodor's NORTHERN CALIFORNIA 2014

Publisher: Amanda D'Acierno, *Senior Vice President*

Editorial: Arabella Bowen, *Executive Editorial Director*; Linda Cabasin, *Editorial Director*

Design: Fabrizio La Rocca, *Vice President, Creative Director*; Tina Malaney, *Associate Art Director*; Chie Ushio, *Senior Designer*; Ann McBride, *Production Designer*

Photography: Melanie Marin, *Associate Director of Photography*; Jessica Parkhill and Jennifer Romains, *Researchers*

Maps: Rebecca Baer, *Senior Map Editor*; Mark Stroud (Moon Street Cartography), David Lindroth, *Cartographers*

Production: Linda Schmidt, *Managing Editor*; Evangelos Vasilakis, *Associate Managing Editor*; Angela L. McLean, *Senior Production Manager*

Sales: Jacqueline Lebow, *Sales Director*

Marketing & Publicity: Heather Dalton, *Marketing Director*; Katherine Fleming, *Senior Publicist*

Business & Operations: Susan Livingston, *Vice President, Strategic Business Planning*; Sue Daulton, *Vice President, Operations*

Fodors.com: Megan Bell, *Executive Director, Revenue & Business Development*; Yasmin Marinaro, *Senior Director, Marketing & Partnerships*

Copyright © 2014 by Fodor's Travel, a division of Random House LLC.

Writers: Michele Bigley, Christine Ciarmello, Cheryl Crabtree, Denise M. Leto, Daniel Mangin, Fiona G. Parrott, Reed Parsell, Jerry James Stone, Christine Vovakes, Bobbi Zane

Editors: Luke Epplin (lead project editor), Salwa Jabado, Amanda Sadlowski

Editorial Contributors: Linda Cabasin, Debbie Harmsen, Daniel Mangin, Maria Teresa Hart

Production Editor: Evangelos Vasilakis

ISBN 978-0-7704-3266-9

ISSN 1543–1045

All details in this book are based on information supplied to us at press time. Always confirm information when it matters, especially if you're making a detour to visit a specific place. Fodor's expressly disclaims any liability, loss, or risk, personal or otherwise, that is incurred as a consequence of the use of any of the contents of this book.

SPECIAL SALES

This book is available at special discounts for bulk purchases for sales promotions or premiums. For more information, e-mail specialmarkets@randomhouse.com

PRINTED IN CHINA

10 9 8 7 6 5 4 3 2 1

CONTENTS

Fodor's Features

MAPS

ABOUT
THIS GUIDE

Fodor's Recommendations

Everything in this guide is worth doing—we don't cover what isn't—but exceptional sights, hotels, and restaurants are recognized with additional accolades. **Fodor's Choice★** indicates our top recommendations; and **Best Bets** call attention to notable hotels and restaurants in various categories. Care to nominate a new place? Visit Fodors.com/contact-us.

Trip Costs

We list prices wherever possible to help you budget well. Hotel and restaurant price categories from **$** to **$$$$** are noted alongside each recommendation. For hotels, we include the lowest cost of a standard double room in high season. For restaurants, we cite the average price of a main course at dinner or, if dinner isn't served, at lunch. For attractions, we always list adult admission fees; discounts are usually available for children, students, and senior citizens.

Hotels

Our local writers vet every hotel to recommend the best overnights in each price category, from budget to expensive. Unless otherwise specified, you can expect private bath, phone, and TV in your room. For expanded hotel reviews, facilities, and deals visit Fodors.com.

Restaurants

Unless we state otherwise, restaurants are open for lunch and dinner daily. We mention dress code only when there's a specific requirement and reservations only when they're essential or not accepted. To make restaurant reservations, visit Fodors.com.

Credit Cards

The hotels and restaurants in this guide typically accept credit cards. If not, we'll say so.

Top Picks
★ Fodor'sChoice

Listings
⊠ Address
✉ Branch address
☎ Telephone
🖷 Fax
🌐 Website
✍ E-mail
🎫 Admission fee
🕓 Open/closed times
Ⓜ Subway
✛ Directions or Map coordinates

Hotels & Restaurants
🛏 Hotel
🛌 Number of rooms
🍽 Meal plans
✗ Restaurant
🍸 Reservations
👔 Dress code
▭ No credit cards
ⓢ Price

Other
⇨ See also
☞ Take note
🏌 Golf facilities

1

EXPERIENCE NORTHERN CALIFORNIA

WHAT'S NEW IN NORTHERN CALIFORNIA

Foodie's Paradise

Great dining is a staple of the California lifestyle, and a new young generation of chefs is challenging old ideas about preparing and presenting great food. Food-truck frenzy has created a movable feast up and down the state. Esteemed chefs and urban foodies follow the trucks on Twitter as they move around cities 24/7 purveying delicious, cheap, fresh meals. The Spencer on the Go truck hangs out in SoMa in San Francisco, dishing such delicacies as escargot puff lollipops. California chefs continue to shop locally for produce and farmer-sourced meat.

Grape Expectations

California wine culture is alive and well and continues to grow beyond the traditional wine country of Napa and Sonoma. Winemaking is expanding in the Central Valley and Shasta Cascade areas. The Turkovich Family Winery opened in the Central Valley town of Winters just west of Sacramento. The Truckee River Winery, near Lake Tahoe, claims to be the highest and coldest winery in the nation.

Suite Dreams

Hotels are coming back to life in a big way. Visitors to Yountville in the Napa Valley have another lodging choice, the Bardessono, a LEED-certified hotel that sports an eco spa and an underground geothermal system.

All Aboard

Riding the rails can be a satisfying experience, particularly in California where the distances between destinations sometimes run into the hundreds of miles. The best trip is on the luxuriously appointed Coast Starlight, a long-distance train with sleeping cars that runs between Seattle and Los Angeles, passing some of California's most beautiful coastline as it hugs the beach. For the best surfside viewing, get a seat or a room on the left side of the train and ride south to north from San Diego to Oakland.

Head for the Hills

Things are looking up for visitors to California's alpine recreation areas, thanks to a host of enhancements. Yosemite National Park observed its 120th birthday in late 2011 with some new ways to see the park. Yosemite Guide Service offers guided day hikes, customized driving tours, and backpacking trips. You can also take Yosemite Audio Adventures CD tours with you as you explore the park.

It's Easy Being Green

The Golden State is glowing green all over. It's the only state in the nation to mandate green building codes for all new construction to reduce greenhouse emissions. Santa Barbara's car-free program can save you up to 50% on lodging, meals, and, of course, transportation.

Homegrown Hospitality

Agritourism in California isn't new (remember, Knott's Berry Farm once *was* a berry farm), but it is on the rise, with farm tours and agricultural festivals sprouting up everywhere.

Wine country is a particularly fertile area—spurred by the success of vineyards, the area's lavender growers and olive-oil producers have started welcoming visitors. Sonoma Farm Trail Tours include walking the land and a farm-driven dinner with paired wines.

In the Central Valley, America's number-one producer of stone fruit, you can travel themed tourist routes (like Fresno County's Blossom Trail) and tour herb gardens, fruit orchards, organic dairies, and pumpkin patches.

WHEN TO GO

Because it offers activities indoors and out, San Francisco rates as all-season destinations. Early spring—when the gray-whale migration overlaps with the end of the elephant-seal breeding season and the start of the bird migration—is the optimal time to visit Point Reyes National Seashore. Yosemite is ideal in the late spring because roads closed in winter are reopened, and the park's waterfalls—swollen with melting snow—run fast. Autumn is "crush time" in all the wine destinations, from Napa/Sonoma in the north and the central coast. Snowfall makes winter peak season for skiers in Mammoth Mountain and Lake Tahoe, where runs typically open around Thanksgiving. (They sometimes remain in operation into June.)

Climate

It's difficult to generalize much about the state's weather beyond saying that precipitation comes in winter and summer is dry in most places. As a rule, inland regions are hotter in summer and colder in winter, compared with coastal areas, which are relatively cool year-round. Fog is a potential hazard any day of the year in coastal regions. As you climb into the mountains, seasonal variations are more apparent: winter brings snow (at elevations above 3,000 feet), autumn is crisp, spring can go either way, and summer is sunny and warm, with only an occasional thundershower in the southern part of the state.

Microclimates

Mountains separate the California coastline from the state's interior, and the weather can sometimes vary dramatically within a 15-minute drive. On a foggy summer day in San Francisco, you'll be grateful for a sweater—but head 50 miles north inland to Napa Valley, and you'll likely be content in short sleeves. Day and nighttime temperatures can also vary greatly. Temperature swings elsewhere can be even more extreme. Take Sacramento: On August afternoons the mercury hits the 90s and occasionally exceeds 100°F. Yet as darkness falls, it sometimes plummets to 40°F.

Forecasts

National Weather Service
⊕ *www.wrh.noaa.gov.*

WHAT'S WHERE

The following numbers refer to chapters.

2 The Central Coast.
Three of the state's top stops—swanky Santa Barbara, Hearst Castle, and Big Sur—sit along the scenic 200-mile route.

3 Monterey Bay Area.
Postcard-perfect Monterey, Victorian-flavored Pacific Grove, and exclusive Carmel all share this stretch of California coast. To the north, Santa Cruz boasts a boardwalk, a UC campus, ethnic clothing shops, and plenty of surfers.

4 San Francisco. To see why so many have left their hearts here, you need to the city's iconic neighborhoods—posh Pacific Heights, the Hispanic Mission, and gay-friendly Castro.

5 The Bay Area. The area that rings San Francisco is nothing like the city—but it is home to some of the nation's great universities, fabulous bay views, and Alice Waters' Chez Panisse.

6 The Wine Country.
Napa and Sonoma counties retain their title as the California Wine Country, by virtue of award-winning vintages, luxe lodgings, and epicurean eats.

7 The North Coast.
The star attractions here are the natural ones, from the secluded beaches and wave-battered bluffs of Point Reyes National Seashore to the towering redwood forests.

8 Redwood National Park. More than 200 miles of trails, ranging from easy to strenuous, allow visitors to see these spectacular trees in their primitive environments.

9 The Southern Sierra.
In the Mammoth Lakes region, sawtooth mountains and deep powdery snowdrifts combine to create the state's premier conditions for skiing and snowboarding.

10 Yosemite National Park. The views immortalized by photographer Ansel Adams—of towering granite monoliths, verdant glacial valleys, and lofty waterfalls—are still camera-ready.

11 Sequoia and Kings Canyon National Parks. The sight of ancient redwoods towering above jagged mountains will take your breath away.

12 Sacramento and the Gold Country. The 1849 gold rush that built San Francisco and Sacramento began here, and the former mining camps strung along 185 miles of Highway 49 replay their past to the hilt.

13 Lake Tahoe. With miles of crystalline water reflecting the peaks of the High Sierra, Lake Tahoe is the perfect setting for activities like hiking and golfing in summer and skiing and snowmobiling in winter.

14 The Far North. California's far northeast corner is home to snowcapped Mount Shasta, the pristine Trinity Wilderness, and abundant backwoods character that appeals to outdoorsy types.

Crescent
City
Yreka
Klamath
*Redwood
National Park*
Mt. Shasta
Burney
Alturas
Arcata
Eureka
Weaverville
Redding
*Shasta
Lake*
14
*Lassen Volcanic
National Park*
Susanville
Ferndale
Red Bluff
Garberville
Chico
Paradise
*Pyramid
Lake*
NEVADA
Leggett
Willows
Oroville
Fort Bragg
Willits
Grass
Valley
Truckee
Reno
Mendocino
Ukiah
Yuba City
49
13
CARSON CITY
Boonville
*Clear
Lake*
Auburn
*Lake
Tahoe*
Point Arena
Gualala
7
Woodland
Placerville
South Lake
Tahoe
Jenner
Healdsburg
6
★ SACRAMENTO
Santa Rosa
Napa
Elk Grove
12
*Yosemite
National
Park*
Bridgeport
Novato
Sonoma
Fairfield
Lodi
*Point Reyes
National Seashore*
4
Berkeley
Stockton
Sonora
10
Mono
Lake
9
SAN FRANCISCO
Oakland
Modesto
Yosemite
Village
Mammoth
Lakes
5
Fremont
Turlock
Palo
Alto
San Jose
Merced
Bishop
Santa Cruz
Gilroy
Chowchilla
Castroville
*San Luis
Res.*
Los Banos
Madera
*Kings Canyon
National
Park*
*PACIFIC
OCEAN*
Monterey
Salinas
Fresno
Big Pine
Pacific Grove
Carmel
3
Soledad
Visalia
11
China
Lake
Big Sur
Coalinga
Porterville
*Sequoia
National
Park*
San Simeon
Paso Robles
Kernville
Ridgecrest
Bakersfield
San Luis
Obispo
McKittrick
*Tulare
Lake Bed*
TEHACHAPI MTS.
Santa Maria
*Tejon
Pass*
Lancaster
Lompoc
2
Santa
Barbara
Ojai
Pasadena
*Santa Barbara
Channel*
Ventura
Oxnard

CASCADE RANGE

Sacramento Valley

Eel R.

San Joaquin Valley

SIERRA NEVADA

0   75 mi

0   75 km

NORTHERN CALIFORNIA PLANNER

Car Travel

Driving may be a way of life in California, but it isn't cheap (gas prices here are usually among the highest in the nation). It's also not for the fainthearted; you've surely heard horror stories about California's freeways, but even the state's scenic highways and byways have their own hassles. For instance, on the dramatic coastal road between San Simeon and Carmel, twists, turns, and divinely distracting vistas frequently slow traffic; in rainy season, mud slides can close the road altogether. ⚠ Never cross the double line to pass a slower car ahead of you. If you see that cars are backing up behind you, stop at the first available pullout to allow faster drivers to pass.

On California's notorious freeways, other rules apply. Nervous Nellies must resist the urge to stay in the two slow-moving lanes on the far right, used primarily by trucks. To drive at least the speed limit, get yourself in a middle lane. If you're ready to bend the rules a bit, the second (lanes are numbered from 1 starting at the center) lane moves about 5 mph faster. But avoid the far-left lane (the one next to the carpool lane), where speeds range from 75 mph to 90 mph.

Air Travel

Air travelers beginning or ending their vacation in San Francisco have two main airports to choose from: San Francisco International (SFO) or Oakland International (OAK) across the bay. The former lands you closer to the city core (ground transportation will take about 20 minutes versus 35), but the latter is less heavily trafficked and less prone to pesky fog delays. BART, the Bay Area's affordable rapid-transit system, serves both airports. So your decision will probably rest on which one has the best fares and connections for your particular route.

If your final destination is Monterey or Carmel, San Jose International Airport (SJC), about 40 miles south of San Francisco, is another alternative.

FAQ

I'm not particularly active. Will I still enjoy visiting a national park? Absolutely, the most popular parks have something for everyone. In Yosemite the ultrafit embark on 12-hour trail treks and mere mortals can hike Cook's Meadow—an easy 1-mile loop that's also wheelchair accessible. Or just hop on a free shuttle or drive yourself to sites.

What's the single best place to take the kids? For its sheer smorgasbord of activities, San Francisco is hard to beat. A cable-car ride is a no-brainer—but be sure to also take a spin on the historic F-line trolleys. Other classic kid-friendly SF sights include the Exploratorium, the San Francisco Zoo, Alcatraz, the Ferry Building, and the California Academy of Sciences. Or head to Musée Mécanique to see what kids played way before Nintendo's Wii came out.

California sounds expensive. How can I save on sightseeing? CityPass (☎ 888/330–5008 ⊕ www.citypass.com) includes admission and some upgrades for main attractions in San Francisco. Also, many museums set aside free-admission days. Prefer the great outdoors? An America the Beautiful annual pass (☎ 888/275–8747 ⊕ www.nps.gov) admits you to every site under the National Park Service umbrella. Better yet, depending on the property, passengers in your vehicle get in free, too.

NORTHERN CALIFORNIA'S TOP EXPERIENCES

Hit the Road

Kings Canyon Highway, Redwood Highway, Tioga Pass, 17-Mile Drive, the Lake Tahoe loop: California has some splendid and challenging roads. You'll drive through a tunnel formed by towering redwood trees on the Redwood Highway. If you venture over the Sierras by way of Tioga Pass (through Yosemite in summer only), you'll see emerald green meadows, gray granite monoliths, and pristine blue lakes—and very few people.

Pan for Gold

Though California's gold rush ended more than a hundred years ago, you can still feel the '49er fever on the western face of the Sierra Nevada in Columbia, a well-preserved town populated by costumed interpreters, where you can pan for gold or tour a mine. Or visit Bodie, an eerie ghost town in the eastern Sierra that remains in a state of "arrested decay."

Think Globally, Eat Locally

Over the years California cuisine has evolved from a mere trend into a respected gastronomic tradition: one that pairs local, often organic or sustainable, ingredients with techniques inspired by European, Asian, and, increasingly, Indian and Middle Eastern cookery.

See Eccentric Architecture

California has always drawn creative and, well, eccentric people. And all that quirkiness has left its mark in the form of oddball architecture that makes for some fun sightseeing. Begin by touring Hearst Castle—the beautifully bizarre estate William Randolph Hearst built above San Simeon. And Lake Tahoe's Vikingsholm (a re-created Viking castle) is equally odd.

Be Transported

San Franciscans take cable cars seriously—and riding on one is a must-do. You may even want to visit the (free!) Cable Car Museum to get a handle on the inner workings or just ring a gripman's bell. *(See the Cable Car feature in the San Francisco chapter.)*But the city's options for vintage public transport doesn't end there: the lesser known F line streetcars are every bit as photogenic, and they have shorter lines.

Go Wild

California communities host hundreds of annual events, but some of the best are organized by Mother Nature. The most famous is the "miracle migration" that sees swallows flock back to Mission San Juan Capistrano each March. In Pacific Grove masses of monarch butterflies reliably arrive for their winter vacation every year in October. If you can't make it there, visit the butterfly sanctuary in the California Academy of Sciences in San Francisco.

People-Watch

Opportunities for world-class people-watching abound in California. Just saunter the rainbow-flagged streets of San Francisco's Castro neighborhood or the century-old boardwalk in time-warped, resiliently boho Santa Cruz.

NORTHERN CALIFORNIA TODAY

The People

California is as much a state of mind as a state in the union—a kind of perpetual promised land that has represented many things to many people. In the 18th century, Spanish missionaries came seeking converts and gold. In the 19th, miners rushed here to search for gold. And, in the years since, a long line of Dust Bowl farmers, land speculators, Haight-Ashbury hippies, migrant workers, dotcommers, real estate speculators, and would-be actors has come chasing their own dreams.

The result is a population that leans toward idealism—without necessarily being as liberal as you might think. (Remember, this is Ronald Reagan's old stomping ground.) And despite the stereotype of the blue-eyed, blond surfer, California's population is not homogeneous either. Ten million people who live here (more than 28% of Californians) are foreign born—including former Governor Schwarzenegger. Almost half hail from Latin American countries; another third emigrated from Asia, following the waves of Chinese workers who arrived in the 1860s to build the railroads and subsequent waves of Indochinese refugees from the Vietnam War.

The Politics

What's blue and red and green all over? California: a predominantly Democratic state with an aggressive "go green" agenda. Democratic Governor Jerry Brown, who was elected to the office for the second time in 30 years, is moving the progressive agenda ahead with policies that make California the greenest state in the nation supporting more green construction, wind farms, and solar panels.

The Economy

Leading all other states in terms of the income generated by agriculture, tourism, entertainment, and industrial activity, California has the country's most diverse state economy. Moreover, with a gross state product of more than $2 trillion, California would be one of the top 10 economies *in the world* if it were an independent nation. But due to its wealth ($65,476 median household income) and productivity, California took a large hit in the recession that began in 2007. This affected all levels of government from local to statewide and resulted in reduction of services that Californians have long taken for granted.

But the Golden State's economic history is filled with boom and bust cycles—beginning with the mid-19th-century gold rush that started it all. Optimists already have their eyes on the next potential boom: high-tech and bio research, "green companies" focused on alternative energy, renewables, electric cars, and the like.

The Culture

Cultural organizations thrive in California. San Francisco—a city with only about 812,000 residents—has well-regarded ballet, opera, and theater companies, and is home to one of the continent's most noteworthy orchestras. Museums like San Francisco Museum of Modern Art (SFMOMA) and the de Young also represent the city's ongoing commitment to the arts. Art and culture thrive farther south in San Diego as well. Balboa Park alone holds 15 museums, opulent gardens, and three performance venues, in addition to the San Diego Zoo. And L.A. and its environs are the chief arbiters of movies, TV, and video production. Capitol Records set up shop in L.A. in the

1940s, and this area has been instrumental in the music industry ever since. And now websites are coming to thrive in that creative landscape—Facebook, YouTube, and Google are California companies.

The Parks and Preserves

Cloud-spearing redwood groves, snow-tipped mountains, canyon-slashed deserts, primordial lava beds, and a seemingly endless coast: California's natural diversity is staggering—and efforts to protect it started early. The first national park here was established in 1890, and the National Park Service now oversees 30 sites in California (more than in any other state). When you factor in 278 state parks—which encompass underwater preserves, historic sites, wildlife reserves, dune systems, and other sensitive habitats—the number of acres involved is almost as impressive as the topography itself.

Due to encroaching development and pollution, keeping these natural treasures in pristine condition is an ongoing challenge. For instance, Sequoia and Kings Canyon (which is plagued by pesticides and other agricultural pollutants blown in from the San Joaquin Valley) has been named America's "smoggiest park" by the National Parks Conservation Association, and the Environmental Protection Agency has designated it as an "ozone non-attainment area with levels of ozone pollution that threaten human health."

There is no question that Californians love their 278 state parks. Nearly every park has its grass-roots supporters, who volunteer to raise money, volunteer as rangers, and work other jobs to keep the parks open.

The Cuisine

California gave us McDonald's, Denny's, Carl's Jr., Taco Bell, and, of course, In-N-Out Burger. Fortunately for those of us with fast-clogging arteries, the state also kick-started the organic food movement. Back in the 1970s, California-based chefs put American cuisine on the culinary map by focusing on freshly prepared seasonal ingredients.

Today, this focus has spawned the "locavore" or sustainable food movement—followers try to only consume food produced within a 100-mile radius of where they live, since processing and refining food and transporting goods over long distances is bad for both the body and the environment. This isn't much of a restriction in California, where a huge variety of crops grow year-round. Some 350 cities and towns have certified farmers' markets—and their stalls are bursting with a variety of goods. California has been America's top agricultural producer for the last 50 years, growing more fruits and vegetables than any other state. Dairies and ranches also thrive here, and fishing fleets harvest fish and shellfish from the rich waters offshore.

NORTHERN CALIFORNIA TOP ATTRACTIONS

Yosemite National Park
(A) Nature looms large here, both literally and figuratively. In addition to hulking Half Dome, the park is home to El Capitan (the world's largest exposed granite monolith, rising 3,593 feet above the glacier-carved valley floor) and Yosemite Falls (North America's tallest cascade). In Yosemite's signature stand of giant sequoias—the Mariposa Grove—even the trees are Bunyanesque. Needless to say, crowds can be supersize, too.

San Francisco
(B) Population-wise, San Francisco is smaller than Indianapolis. But when it comes to sites (and soul), this city is a giant. Start working through the standard travelers' "to do" list by strolling across the Golden Gate Bridge, taking a ferry to Alcatraz, and hopping on the Powell–Hyde cable car. Just leave enough time to explore the diverse neighborhoods where San Francisco's distinctive personality—an amalgam of gold-rush history, immigrant traditions, counterculture proclivities, and millennial materialism—is on display.

Wine Country
(C) Although the vineyard-blanketed hills of California's original Wine Country are undeniably scenic, the wine itself (preferably accompanied by the area's famed cuisine) remains the big draw here. Budding oenophiles can educate their palettes on scores of tours and tasting sessions.

Point Reyes National Seashore
(D) Aside from the namesake seashore, this Marin County preserve encompasses ecosystems that range from woodlands and marshlands to heathlike grasslands. The range of wildlife here is equally diverse—depending on when you visit, expect to see gray whales, rare Tule elk, and almost 500 species of birds. December through March you can also see male elephant seals compete for mates.

Lake Tahoe

(E) Deep, clear, and intensely blue, this forest-rimmed body of water straddling the California–Nevada border is one of the continent's prettiest alpine lakes. That environmental controls can keep it that way is something of a miracle, given Tahoe's popularity. Throngs of outdoor adventurers flock to the California side to ski, hike, bike, and boat. On the Nevada side, where casinos are king, gambling often wins out over fresh-air activities—but natural wonders are never far away.

Gold Country

(F) California's gold rush was one of the most significant events in U.S. history. It saved the Union and helped open the western frontier, when Argonauts flooded a 300-mile-long stretch of the Sierra foothills. Remnants of the gold rush remain to this day in the towns, diggings, trains, museums, and culture that you'll encounter along historic Highway 49; it runs north to south from Loyalton near the Nevada border to Oakhurst, just south of Yosemite. Towns along the way, mostly updated and renovated, allow you to dig into the past and discover what the excitement was all about.

QUINTESSENTIAL NORTHERN CALIFORNIA

The Wine

If California were a country, it would rank as the world's fourth-largest wine producer, after Italy, France, and Spain. In those countries, where vino is barely considered an alcoholic beverage, wine drinking has evolved into a relaxing ritual best shared with friends and family. A modern, Americanized version of that mentality integrates wine into daily life in California, and there are many places to sample it. The Napa and Sonoma valleys come to mind first. However, there are other destinations for oenophiles who want a vintage vacation. You can find great wineries around Monterey Bay and Gold Country's Amador County, too. All are respected appellations, and their winery tours and tastings will show you what all the buzz is about.

The Beach

California's beach culture is, in a word, legendary. Of course, it only makes sense that folks living in a state with a 1,264-mile coastline (a hefty portion of which sees the sun upward of 300 days a year) would perfect the art of beach-going. True aficionados begin with a reasonably fit physique, plus a stylish wardrobe consisting of flip-flops, bikinis, wet suits, and such. Mastery of at least one beach skill—surfing, boogie boarding, kayaking, Frisbee tossing, or looking fab while catching rays—is also essential. As a visitor, though, you need only a swimsuit and some rented equipment for most sports. You can then hit the beach almost anywhere, thanks to the California belief in coastal access as a birthright. The farther south you go, the wider, sandier, and sunnier the beaches become; moving north they are rockier and foggier, with colder and rougher surf.

Californians live in such a large and splashy state that they sometimes seem to forget about the rest of the country. They've developed a distinctive culture all their own, which you can delve into by doing as the locals do.

The Outdoors

One of California's greatest assets—the mild year-round weather enjoyed by most of the state—inspires residents to spend as much time outside as they possibly can. They have a tremendous enthusiasm for every imaginable outdoor sport, and, up north especially, fresh-air adventures are extremely popular (which may explain why everyone there seems to own at least one pair of hiking boots). But the California-alfresco creed is more broadly interpreted, and the general rule when planning any activity is "if it can happen outside, it will!" *Plein air* vacation opportunities include dining on patios, decks, and wharves; shopping in street markets or elaborate open-air malls; hearing almost any kind of music at moonlight concerts; touring the sculpture gardens that grace major art museums; and celebrating everything from gay pride to garlic at outdoor fairs.

The Automobile

Americans may have a love affair with the automobile, but Californians have an out-and-out obsession. Even when gas prices rev up and freeway traffic slows down, their passion burns as hot as ever. You can witness this ardor any summer weekend at huge classic- and custom-car shows held statewide. Even better, you can feel it yourself by taking the wheel. Trace an old stagecoach route through the mountains above Santa Barbara on Highway 154; track migrating whales up the coast to Big Sur; or take 17-Mile Drive along the precipitous edge of the Monterey Peninsula. Glorious for the most part, but authentically congested in some areas in the south, Highway 1 runs almost the entire length of the state, hugging the coast most of the way.

GREAT ITINERARIES

SIERRA RICHES: YOSEMITE, GOLD COUNTRY, AND TAHOE, 10 DAYS

This tour will show you why Tony Bennett left his heart in San Francisco. It also includes some of the most beautiful places is a very scenic state, plus gold-rush-era history, and a chance to hike a trail or two.

Day 1: San Francisco

Straight from the airport, drop your bags at the lighthearted **Hotel Monaco** near **Union Square** and request a goldfish for your room. A Union Square stroll packs a wallop of people-watching, window-shopping, and architecture viewing. **Chinatown**, chock-full of dim sum shops, storefront temples, and open-air markets, promises unfamiliar tastes for lunch. Catch a Powell Street **cable car** to the end of the line and get off to see the bay views and the antique arcade games at **Musée Mécanique**, the hidden gem of otherwise mindless **Fisherman's Wharf**. No need to go any farther than cosmopolitan North Beach for cocktail hour, dinner, and live music.

Day 2: Golden Gate Park

In **Golden Gate Park**, linger amid the flora of the **Conservatory of Flowers** and the **San Francisco Botanical Garden at Strybing Arboretum**, soak up some art at the **de Young Museum**, and find serene refreshment at the **San Francisco Japanese Tea Garden**. The Pacific surf pounds the cliffs below the **Legion of Honor** art museum, which has an exquisite view of the **Golden Gate Bridge**—when the fog stays away. Sunset cocktails at the circa-1909 **Cliff House** include a prospect over Seal Rock (actually occupied by sea lions). Eat dinner elsewhere: Pacific Heights, the Mission, and SoMa teem with excellent restaurants.

Day 3: Into the High Sierra

First thing in the morning, pick up your rental car and head for the hills. A five-hour drive due east brings you to **Yosemite National Park**, where **Bridalveil Fall** and **El Capitan**, the 350-story granite monolith, greet you on your way to **Yosemite Village**. Ditch the car and pick up information and refreshment before hopping on the year-round shuttle to explore. Justly famous sights cram Yosemite Valley: massive **Half Dome** and **Sentinel Dome**, thundering **Yosemite Falls**, and wispy **Ribbon Fall** and **Nevada Fall**. Invigorating short hikes off the shuttle route lead to numerous vantage points. Celebrate your arrival in one of the world's most sublime spots with dinner in the dramatic **Ahwahnee Hotel Dining Room** and stay the night there (reserve well in advance).

Day 4: Yosemite National Park

Ardent hikers consider **John Muir Trail to Half Dome** a must-do, tackling the rigorous 12-hour round-trip to the top of Half Dome in search of life-changing vistas. The merely mortal hike downhill from Glacier Point on Four-Mile Trail or **Panorama Trail**, the latter an all-day trek past waterfalls. Less demanding still is a drive to Wawona for a stroll in the **Mariposa Grove of Big Trees** and lunch at the 19th-century **Wawona Hotel Dining Room**. In bad weather, take shelter in the Ansel Adams Gallery and Yosemite Museum; in fair conditions, drive up to **Glacier Point** for a breathtaking sunset view.

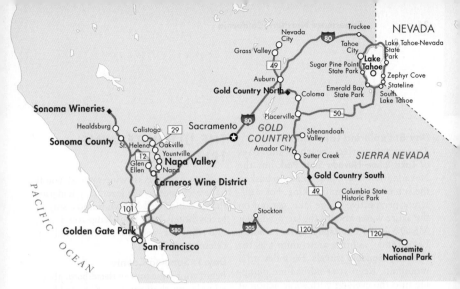

Day 5: Gold Country South

Highway 49 traces the mother lode that yielded many fortunes in gold in the 1850s and 1860s. Step into a living gold-rush town at **Columbia State Historic Park**, where you can ride a stagecoach and pan for riches. **Sutter Creek's** well-preserved downtown bursts with shopping opportunities, but the vintage goods displayed at **Monteverde Store Museum** are not for sale. A different sort of vintage powers the present-day bonanza of **Shenandoah Valley**, heart of the Sierra Foothills Wine Country. Taste your way through Rhône-style blended Zinfandels and Syrahs at boutique wineries such as **Shenandoah Vineyards** and **Sobon Estate**. Amador City's 1879 **Imperial Hotel** places you firmly in the past for the night.

Day 6: Gold Country North

In **Placerville**, a mineshaft invites investigation at **Hangtown's Gold Bug Mine**, while **Marshall Gold Discovery State Historic Park** encompasses most of **Coloma** and preserves the spot where James Marshall's 1849 find set off the California gold rush. Old Town **Auburn**, with its museums and courthouse, makes a good lunch stop, but if you hold out until you reach Grass Valley you can try authentic miners' pasties. A tour of **Empire Mine State Historic Park** takes you into a mine, and a few miles away horse-drawn carriages ply the narrow, shop-lined streets of downtown **Nevada City**. Both Nevada City and **Grass Valley** hold a collection of bed-and-breakfast inns that date back to gold-rush days. For more contemporary accommodations backtrack to Auburn or Placerville.

Day 7: Lake Tahoe

Jewel-like **Lake Tahoe** is a straight shot east of Placerville on Highway 50; stop for picnic provisions in commercial **South Lake Tahoe**. A stroll past the three magnificent estates in **Pope-Baldwin Recreation Area** hints at the sumptuous lakefront summers once enjoyed by the elite. High above a glittering cove, **Emerald Bay State Park** offers one of the best lake views as well as a steep hike down to (and back up from) **Vikingsholm**, a replica 9th-century Scandinavian castle. Another fine, old mansion—plus a nature preserve and many hiking trails—lies in **Sugar Pine Point State Park**. Tahoe City offers more history and ample dining and lodging choices.

Day 8: Exploring Lake Tahoe

The picture-perfect beaches and bays of **Lake Tahoe–Nevada State Park** line the Nevada shoreline, a great place to bask in the sun or go mountain biking. For a different perspective of the lake, get out on the azure water aboard the stern-wheeler MS *Dixie II* from **Zephyr Cove**. In South Lake Tahoe, another view unfurls as the **Heavenly Gondola** travels 2½ miles up a mountain. Keep your adrenaline pumping into the evening with some action at the massive casinos clustered in Stateline, Nevada.

Day 9: Return to San Francisco

After a long (five hours) morning of driving, return your rental car in San Francisco and soak up some more urban excitement. Good options include a late lunch at the **Ferry Building**, followed by a visit to the **San Francisco Museum of Modern Art**, or lunch in **Japantown** followed by shopping in **Pacific Heights**. People-watching excels in the late afternoon bustle of the **Castro** and the **Haight**. Say good-bye to Northern California at one of the plush lounges or trendy bars in the downtown hotels.

Day 10: Departure

Check the weather and your flight information before you start out for the airport: Fog sometimes causes delays at SFO. On a clear day, your flight path might give you one last fabulous glimpse of the City by the Bay.

THE ULTIMATE WINE TRIP, 5 DAYS

In these five days of wine tasting, you'll have a chance to see legendary wineries that produce well-known brands, stay in lovely hotels with knowledgeable hosts, and dine at restaurants operated by celebrity chefs.

Day 1: Sonoma County

Begin your wine tour in **Healdsburg,** about 65 miles north of San Francisco on Highway 101. Healdsburg was named one of the Top Small Towns in America by Fodor's editors in 2013 for its charming atmosphere, great restaurants, and lovely B&Bs. The best choices to overnight at are **The Honor Mansion** or **Hotel Healdsburg**. Take your pick of the trendy restaurants that ring the plaza. Stellar choices are **Cyrus** and **Bovolo**. End the day with a stroll around the plaza.

Day 2: Sonoma Wineries

You won't have to travel far to begin your day of wine tasting. Many local wineries have tasting rooms within walking distance of the Healdsburg plaza. You'll find some of the most interesting wineries in the countryside surrounding the town, including **Preston Vineyards, Francis Ford Coppola Winery,** and **Dry Creek Vineyard.** All produce wonderful Cabernet Sauvignon, Chardonnay, and Zinfandel. Most have picnic areas where you can savor a bite while sampling the grape. In the afternoon head south on Highway 101 to scenic Highway 12. Take a break at **Glen Ellen** to visit **Jack London State Historic Park,** the memorabilia-filled home of the famed writer.

Day 3: Napa Valley

Plan to spend two nights in the same lodging in the **Napa Valley,** in the city of **Napa** or a few miles north in **Yountville.** For your Day 3 tasting schedule head north to **Saint Helena,** which has the largest concentration of wineries, like the **Beringer Vineyards, John Phelps Vineyards,** and **Spring Mountain Vineyard,** and most of the well-known names in the region plus the **Culinary Institute of America** and **Wine Spectator Greystone Restaurant.** Yountville has **V Marketplace** where you'll find **NapaStyle,** a luxury food market and deli, and celebrity chef Michael Chiarello's **Bottega** restaurant.

Day 4: North on Hwy 29

After breakfast, head north on Highway 29 to **Oakville,** home of the oldest continually operating grocery store in California, the **Oakville Grocery. Calistoga,** a few miles up the road, dates back more than 100 years and is known for its hot-spring spas. Robert Louis Stevenson and his bride spent their honeymoon in 1880 here. Head south for dinner at one of the Napa Valley's celebrity restaurants.

Day 5: Carneros to San Francisco

Your final day in the Wine Country includes a couple of stops in the Carneros Wine District on the way back to San Francisco. Stop at **Domaine Carneros,** a Taittinger brand that creates perfectly dry sparkling wine in the French tradition. The art-stuffed **di Rosa** preserve nearby is worth a stop as well. Give yourself plenty of time to get to your departure airport; traffic is generally heavy as you close in on the Bay Area.

TIPS

Parking in San Francisco is expensive and scarce. When you fly in, take a shuttle or taxi from the airport to the city, and then use the excellent public transportation to get around.

Try to time your trip for late spring or early fall to avoid the worst of the crowds and the road-closing snowfalls in Yosemite and around Lake Tahoe. Yosemite's falls peak in spring and early summer, while fall brings the grape harvest in the Sierra Nevada foothills.

For a visit in any season, reserve your hotel or campground accommodations in Yosemite as far in advance as possible—up to a year ahead.

THE ULTIMATE ROAD TRIP

CALIFORNIA'S LEGENDARY HIGHWAY 1

by Cheryl Crabtree

One of the world's most scenic drives, California's State Route 1 (also known as Highway 1, the Pacific Coast Highway, the PCH) stretches along the edge of the state for nearly 660 miles, from Southern California's Dana Point to its northern terminus near Leggett, about 40 miles north of Fort Bragg. As you travel south to north, the water's edge transitions from long, sandy beaches and low-lying bluffs to towering dunes, craggy cliffs, and ancient redwood groves. The ocean changes as well; the relatively tame and surfable swells lapping the Southern California shore give way to the frigid, powerful waves crashing against weatherbeaten rocks in the north.

○ Ft. Bragg
○ Mendocino

SONOMA COUNTY

MARIN COUNTY

Point Reyes National Seashore ○

Marin Headlands ○

○ Sacramento

○ San Francisco

○ Santa Cruz

17-Mile Drive ○ Monterey
○ Carmel

Big Sur

○ Fresno

Hearst San Simeon State Historical Monument ○

○ San Luis Obispo

Santa Barbara ○

Santa Monica ○
Los Angeles ○
Long Beach ○

HIGHWAY 1 TOP 10

- Santa Monica
- Santa Barbara
- Hearst San Simeon State Historical Monument
- Big Sur
- Carmel
- 17-Mile Drive
- Monterey
- San Francisco
- Marin Headlands
- Point Reyes National Seashore

Give yourself lots of extra time to pull off the road and enjoy the scenery

STARTING YOUR JOURNEY

You may decide to drive the road's entire 660-mile route, or bite off a smaller piece. In either case, a Highway 1 road trip allows you to experience California at your own pace, stopping when and where you wish. Hike a beachside trail, dig your toes in the sand, and search for creatures in the tidepools. Buy some artichokes and strawberries from a roadside farmstand. Talk to people along the way (you'll run into everyone from soul-searching meditators, farmers, and beatniks to city-slackers and working-class folks), and take lots of pictures. Don't rush—you could easily spend a lifetime discovering secret spots along this route.

To help you plan your trip, we've broken the road into three regions (Santa Monica to Carmel, Carmel to San Francisco, and San Francisco to Fort Bragg); each region is then broken up into smaller segments—many of which are suitable for a day's drive. If you're pressed for time, you can always tackle a section of Highway 1, and then head inland to U.S. 101 or I-5 to reach your next destination more quickly.

WHAT'S IN A NAME?

Though it's often referred to as the Pacific Coast Highway (or PCH), sections of Highway 1 actually have different names. The southernmost section (Dana Point to Oxnard) is the Pacific Coast Highway. After that, the road becomes the Cabrillo Highway (Las Cruces to Lompoc), the Big Sur Coast Highway (San Luis Obispo County line to Monterey), the North Coast Scenic Byway (San Luis Obispo city limit to the Monterey County line), the Cabrillo Highway again (Santa Cruz County line to Half Moon Bay), and finally the Shoreline Highway (Marin City to Leggett). To make matters more confusing, smaller chunks of the road have additional honorary monikers.

Just follow the green triangular signs that say "California 1."

HIGHWAY 1 DRIVING

- Rent a convertible. (You will not regret it.)
- Begin the drive north from Santa Monica, where congestion and traffic delays pose less of a problem.
- Take advantage of turnouts. Let cars pass you as you take in the ocean view and snap a picture.
- Mind your manners: Don't tailgate or glare at other drivers.
- If you're prone to motion sickness, take the wheel yourself. Focusing on the landscape outside should help you feel less queasy.
- If you're afraid of heights, drive from south to north so you'll be on the mountain rather than the cliff side of the road.
- Driving PCH is glorious during winter, but check weather conditions before you go as landslides are frequent after storms.

HIGHWAY 1: SANTA MONICA TO BIG SUR

Hearst Castle

THE PLAN

Distance: approx. 335 mi

Time: 3-5 days

Good Overnight Options: Malibu, Santa Barbara, Pismo Beach, San Luis Obispo, Cambria, Carmel

For more information on the sights and attractions along this portion of Highway 1, please see the Central Coast chapter.

SANTA MONICA TO MALIBU (approx. 26 mi)

Highway 1 begins in Dana point, but it seems more appropriate to begin a PCH adventure in **Santa Monica.** Be sure to experience the beach culture, then balance the tacky pleasures of Santa Monica's amusement pier with a stylish dinner in a neighborhood restaurant.

MALIBU TO SANTA BARBARA (approx. 70 mi)

The PCH follows the curve of Santa Monica Bay all the way to **Malibu** and **Point Mugu,**

near **Oxnard.** Chances are you'll experience *déjà vu* driving this 27-mile stretch: mountains on one side, ocean on the other, opulent homes perched on hillsides; you've seen this piece of coast countless times on TV and film. Be sure to walk out on the **Malibu Pier** for a great photo opp, then check out **Surfrider Beach,** with three famous points where perfect waves ignited a worldwide surfing rage in the 1960s.

After Malibu you'll drive through miles of protected, largely unpopulated coastline. Ride a wave at **Zuma Beach**, scout for offshore whales at **Point Dume State Preserve,** or hike the trails at **Point Mugu State Park.** After skirting Point Mugu, Highway 1 merges with U.S. 101 for about 70 mi before reaching **Santa Barbara.** A mini-tour of the city includes a real Mexican lunch at **La Super-Rica,** a visit to the magnificent Spanish **Mission Santa Barbara,** and a walk down hopping **State Street to Stearns Wharf.**

SANTA BARBARA TO SAN SIMEON (approx. 147 mi)

North of Santa Barbara, Highway 1 morphs into the Cabrillo Highway, separating

Santa Barbara

from and then rejoining U.S. 101. The route winds through rolling vineyards and rangeland to **San Luis Obispo,** where any legit road trip includes a photo stop at the quirky **Madonna Inn.** Be sure to also climb the humungous dunes at **Guadalupe-Nipomo Dunes Preserve.**

In downtown San Luis Obispo, the **Mission San Luis Obispo de Tolosa** stands by a tree-shaded creek edged with shops and cafés. Highway 1 continues to **Morro Bay** and up the coast. About 4 mi north of Morro Bay, you'll reach **Cayucos,** a classic old California beach town with an 1875 pier, restaurants, taverns, and shops in historic buildings. The road continues through **Cambria** to solitary **Hearst San Simeon State Historical Monument**—the art-filled pleasure palace at **San Simeon.** Just four miles north of the castle, elephant seals grunt and cavort at the

Santa Monica

Big Sur

TOP 5 PLACES TO LINGER

- Point Dume State Preserve
- Santa Barbara
- Hearst San Simeon State Historical Monument
- Big Sur/Julia Pfeiffer Burns State Park
- Carmel

Piedras Blancas Elephant Seal Rookery, just off the side of the road.

SAN SIMEON TO CARMEL (approx. 92 mi) Heading north, you'll drive through **Big Sur,** a place of ancient forests and rugged shoreline stretching 90 mi from San Simeon to **Carmel.** Much of Big Sur lies within several state parks and the 165,000-acre **Ventana Wilderness,** itself part of the **Los Padres National Forest.** This famously scenic stretch of the coastal drive, which twists up and down bluffs above the ocean, can last hours. Take your time.

At **Julia Pfeiffer Burns State Park** one easy but rewarding hike leads to an iconic waterfall off a beach-front cliff. When you reach lovely **Carmel,** stroll around the picture-perfect town's mission, galleries, and shops.

HIGHWAY 1: CARMEL TO SAN FRANCISCO

San Francisco

THE PLAN

Distance: approx. 123 mi

Time: 2-4 days

Good Overnight Options: Carmel, Monterey, Santa Cruz, Half Moon Bay, San Francisco

For more information on the sights and attractions along this portion of Highway 1, please see chapters Monterey Bay, San Francisco, and Bay Area.

CARMEL TO MONTEREY
(approx. 4 mi)

Between **Carmel** and **Monterey,** Highway 1 cuts across the base of the Monterey Peninsula. Pony up the toll and take a brief detour to follow famous **17-Mile Drive,** which traverses a surf-pounded landscape of cypress trees, sea lions, gargantuan estates, and the world famous **Pebble Beach Golf Links.** Take your time here as well, and be sure to allow lots of time for pulling off to enjoy the gorgeous views.

If you have the time, spend a day checking out the sights in **Monterey,** especially the kelp forests and bat rays of the **Monterey Bay Aquarium** and the adobes and artifacts of **Monterey State Historic Park.**

MONTEREY TO SANTA CRUZ (approx. 42 mi)

From Monterey the highway rounds the gentle curve of Monterey Bay, passing through sand dunes and artichoke fields on its way to **Moss Landing** and the **Elkhorn Slough National Estuarine Marine Preserve.** Kayak near or walk through the protected wetlands here, or board a pontoon safari boat—don't forget your binoculars. The historic seaside villages of **Aptos, Capitola,** and **Soquel,** just off the highway near the bay's midpoint, are ideal stopovers for beachcombing, antiquing, and hiking through redwoods. In boho **Santa Cruz,** just 7 mi north, walk along the **wharf,** ride the historic roller coaster on the **boardwalk,** and perch on the cliffs to watch surfers peel through tubes at **Steamer Lane.**

SANTA CRUZ TO SAN FRANCISCO (approx. 77 mi)

Highway 1 hugs the ocean's edge once again as it departs Santa Cruz and runs

Davenport cliffs, Devenport

northward past a string of secluded beaches and small towns. Stop and stretch your legs in the tiny, artsy town of **Davenport,** where you can wander through several galleries and enjoy sumptuous views from the bluffs. At **Año Nuevo State Reserve,** walk down to the dunes to view gargantuan elephant

FRIGID WATERS

If you're planning to jump in the ocean in Northern California, wear a wetsuit or prepare to shiver. Even in summer, the water temperatures warm up to just barely tolerable. The fog tends to burn off earlier in the day at relatively sheltered beaches near Monterey Bay's midpoint, near Aptos, Capitola and Santa Cruz. These beaches also tend to attract softer waves than those on the bay's outer edges.

Half Moon Bay

TOP 5 PLACES TO LINGER

- 17-Mile Drive
- Monterey
- Santa Cruz
- Año Nuevo State Reserve
- Half Moon Bay

seals lounging on shore, then break for a meal or snack in **Pescadero** or **Half Moon Bay**.

From Half Moon Bay to **Daly City,** the road includes a number of shoulderless twists and turns that demand slower speeds and nerves of steel. Signs of urban development soon appear: mansions holding fast to Pacific cliffs and then, as the road veers slightly inland to merge with Skyline Boulevard, boxlike houses sprawling across **Daly City** and **South San Francisco.**

Golden Gate Nat'l. Recreation Area
San Francisco
Daly City
San
Pacifica
South San Francisco
Francisco Bay
Moss Beach
San Mateo
Pillar Point
Half Moon Bay
El Granada
Hayward
Half Moon Bay
Belmont
San Gregorio
Palo Alto
Pescadero Point
Pescadero
Mountain View
Santa Clara
Bolsa Point
Pigeon Point
Año Nuevo State Reserve
Saratoga
San Jose
Point Año Nuevo
Boulder Creek
Los Gatos
Pacific Coast Highway
The Forest of Nisene Marks State Park
Davenport
Santa Cruz
Soquel
Capitola
Aptos
Watsonville
Monterey Bay
Elkhorn Slough National Estuarine Marine Preserve
Moss Landing
Castroville
17-Mile Drive
Pacific Grove
Cypress Point
Salinas
Pebble Beach
Carmel Bay
Monterey
Carmel
Carmel Valley
0   10 mi
0   10 km
Point Sur
Big Sur

HIGHWAY 1: SAN FRANCISCO TO FORT BRAGG

Mendocino Coast Botanical Garden

THE PLAN

Distance: 177 mi

Time: 2-4 days

Good Overnight Options: San Francisco, Olema, Bodega Bay, Gualala, Mendocino, Fort Bragg

For more information on the sights and attractions along this portion of Highway 1, please see San Francisco, Bay Area, and North Coast chapters

SAN FRANCISCO

The official Highway 1 heads straight through **San Francisco** along 19th Avenue through **Golden Gate Park** and the **Presidio** toward the **Golden Gate Bridge.** For a more scenic tour, watch for signs announcing exits for 35 North/Skyline Boulevard, then Ocean Beach/The Great Highway (past Lake Merced). The Great Highway follows the coast along the western border of San Francisco; you'll cruise past entrances to the **San Francisco Zoo, Golden Gate Park,** and the **Cliff**

Golden Gate Bridge

House. Hike out to **Point Lobos** or **Land's End** for awesome vistas, then drive through **Lincoln Park** and the **Palace of the Legion of Honor** and follow El Camino del Mar/Lincoln Boulevard all the way to the Golden Gate Bridge.

The best way to see San Francisco is on foot and public transportation. A **Union Square** stroll—complete with people-watching, window-shopping, and architecture-viewing—is a good first stop. In **Chinatown,** department stores give way to storefront temples, open-air markets, and delightful dim-sum shops. After lunch in one, catch a **Powell Street cable car** to the end of the line and get off to see the bay views and the antique arcade games at **Musée Mécanique** (the gem of otherwise mindless **Fisherman's Wharf**). For dinner and live music, try cosmopolitan **North Beach.**

SAN FRANCISCO TO OLEMA

(approx. 37 mi)

Leaving the city the next day, your drive across the Golden Gate Bridge and a stop at a **Marin Headlands** overlook will yield memorable views (if fog hasn't socked in the bay). So will a hike in **Point Reyes National Seashore,** farther up Highway 1 (now

Point Reyes National Seashore

called Shoreline Highway). On this wild swath of coast you'll likely be able to claim an unspoiled beach for yourself. You should expect company, however, around the lighthouse at the tip of Point Reyes because year-round views—and seasonal elephant seal– and whale-watching—draw crowds. If you have time, poke around tiny **Olema,** which has some excellent restaurants, and is home to the historic Olema Inn & Restaurant.

OLEMA TO MENDOCINO

(approx. 131 mi)

Passing only a few minuscule towns, this next stretch of Highway 1 showcases the northern coast in all its rugged glory. The reconstructed compound of eerily foreign buildings at **Fort Ross State Historic Park** recalls the era of Russian fur trading in California. Pull into **Gualala** for an espresso, a sandwich, and a little human contact

Point Reyes National Seashore

TOP 5 PLACES TO LINGER

- San Francisco
- Marin Headlands
- Point Reyes National Seashore
- Fort Ross State Historic Park
- Mendocino

before rolling onward. After another 50 mi of tranquil state beaches and parks you'll return to civilization in **Mendocino.**

MENDOCINO TO FORT BRAGG

(approx. 9 mi)

Exploring Mendocino you may feel like you've fallen through a rabbit hole: the weather screams Northern California, but the 19th-century buildings—erected by homesick Yankee loggers—definitely say New England. Once you've browsed around the artsy shops, continue on to the **Mendocino Coast Botanical Gardens;** then travel back in time on the **Skunk Train,** which follows an old logging route from **Fort Bragg** deep into the redwood forest.

THE CENTRAL COAST

From Ventura to Big Sur

WELCOME TO THE CENTRAL COAST

TOP REASONS TO GO

★ **Incredible nature:** Much of the Central Coast looks as wild and wonderful as it did centuries ago. The area is home to Channel Islands National Park, two national marine sanctuaries, state parks and beaches, and the vast and rugged Los Padres National Forest.

★ **Edible bounty:** Land and sea provide enough fresh regional foods to satisfy even the most sophisticated foodies—grapes, strawberries, seafood, olive oil…the list goes on and on. Get your fill at countless farmers' markets, wineries, and restaurants.

★ **Outdoor activities:** Kick back and revel in the casual California lifestyle. Surf, golf, kayak, hike, play tennis—or just hang out and enjoy the gorgeous scenery.

★ **Small-town charm, big-city culture:** Small, friendly, uncrowded towns offer amazing cultural amenities. With all the art and history museums, theater, music, and festivals, you might start thinking you're in L.A. or San Francisco.

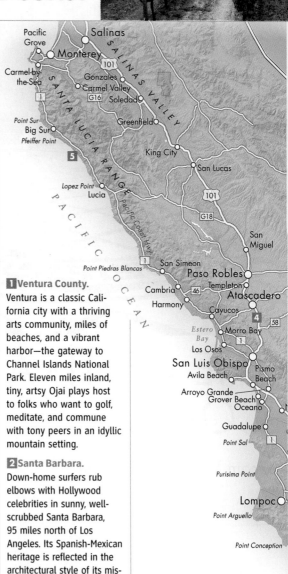

1 Ventura County.
Ventura is a classic California city with a thriving arts community, miles of beaches, and a vibrant harbor—the gateway to Channel Islands National Park. Eleven miles inland, tiny, artsy Ojai plays host to folks who want to golf, meditate, and commune with tony peers in an idyllic mountain setting.

2 Santa Barbara.
Down-home surfers rub elbows with Hollywood celebrities in sunny, well-scrubbed Santa Barbara, 95 miles north of Los Angeles. Its Spanish-Mexican heritage is reflected in the architectural style of its mission, courthouse, and many homes and public buildings.

3 **Santa Barbara County.** Wineries, ranches, and small villages dominate the quintessentially Californian landscape here.

4 **San Luis Obispo County.** Friendly college town San Luis Obispo serves as the hub of a burgeoning wine region that stretches nearly 100 miles from Pismo Beach north to Paso Robles; the 230-plus wineries here have earned reputations for high-quality vintages that rival those of Northern California.

5 **The Big Sur Coastline.** Rugged cliffs meet the Pacific for more than 60 miles—one of the most scenic and dramatic drives in the world.

6 **Channel Islands National Park.** Home to 145 species of plants and animals found nowhere else on Earth, this relatively undiscovered gem of a park encompasses five islands and a mile of surrounding ocean.

GETTING ORIENTED

The Central Coast region begins about 60 miles north of Los Angeles, near the seaside city of Ventura. North along the sinuous coastline from here lie the cities of Santa Barbara and San Luis Obispo, and beyond them the smaller towns of Morro Bay, Cambria, and Big Sur. The nearly 300-mile drive through this region, especially the section of Highway 1 from San Simeon to Big Sur, is one of the most scenic in the state.

Updated by Cheryl Crabtree

Balmy weather, glorious beaches, crystal clear air, and serene landscapes have lured people to the Central Coast since prehistoric times. It's an ideal place to relax, slow down, and appreciate the good things in life.

Along the Pacific coast, the scenic variety is stunning—everything from dramatic cliffs and grass-tufted bluffs to wildlife estuaries and miles of dunes. Offshore, a pristine national park and a vast marine sanctuary protect the wild, wonderful underwater resources of this incredible corner of the planet. But not all of the Central Coast's top attractions are natural: Ventura, Santa Barbara, and San Luis Obispo are filled with sparkling examples of Spanish-Mediterranean architecture, bustling shopping districts, and first-rate restaurants showcasing regional foods and wines.

PLANNING

WHEN TO GO

The Central Coast climate is mild year-round. If you like to swim in warmer (if still nippy) ocean waters, July and August are the best months to visit. Be aware that this is also high season. Fog often rolls in along the coastal areas in early summer; you'll need a jacket, especially after sunset, close to the shore. It usually rains from December through March. From April to early June and in early fall the weather is almost as fine as in high season, and the pace is less hectic.

GETTING HERE AND AROUND

AIR TRAVEL

Alaska Air, American, Frontier, United, and US Airways fly to Santa Barbara Airport (SBA), 9 miles from downtown. United and US Airways provide service to San Luis Obispo County Regional Airport (SBP), 3 miles from downtown San Luis Obispo.

Santa Barbara Airbus shuttles travelers between Santa Barbara and Los Angeles for $48 one-way and $90 round-trip. The Santa Barbara Metropolitan Transit District Bus 11 ($1.75) runs every 30 minutes from the airport to the downtown transit center. A taxi between the airport and the hotel districts costs between $20 and $38.

Airport Contacts San Luis Obispo County Regional Airport ⊠ 903 Airport Dr., off Hwy. 227, San Luis Obispo ☎ 805/781–5205 ⊕ www.sloairport.com. Santa Barbara Airport ⊠ 500 Fowler Rd., off U.S. 101 Exit 104B, Santa Barbara ☎ 805/683–4011 ⊕ www.flysba.com. Santa Barbara Airbus ☎ 805/964–7759, 800/423–1618 ⊕ www.sbairbus.com. Santa Barbara Metropolitan Transit District ☎ 805/963–3366 ⊕ www.sbmtd.gov.

BUS TRAVEL

Greyhound provides service from Los Angeles and San Francisco to San Luis Obispo, Ventura, and Santa Barbara. Local transit companies serve these three cities and several smaller towns. Buses can be useful for visiting some urban sights, particularly in Santa Barbara; they're less so for rural ones.

Bus Contact Greyhound ☎ 800/231–2222 ⊕ www.greyhound.com.

CAR TRAVEL

Driving is the easiest way to experience the Central Coast. U.S. 101 and Highway 1, which run north–south, are the main routes to and through the Central Coast from Los Angeles and San Francisco. Highly scenic Highway 1 hugs the coast, and U.S. 101 runs inland. Between Ventura County and northern Santa Barbara County, the two highways are the same road. Highway 1 again separates from U.S. 101 north of Gaviota, then rejoins the highway at Pismo Beach. Along any stretch where these two highways are separate, U.S. 101 is the quicker route.

The most dramatic section of the Central Coast is the 70 miles between San Simeon and Big Sur. The road is narrow and twisting, with a single lane in each direction. In fog or rain the drive can be downright nerve-racking; in wet seasons mudslides can close portions of the road.

Other routes into the Central Coast include Highway 46 and Highway 33, which head, respectively, west and south from Interstate 5 near Bakersfield.

Road Conditions Caltrans ☎ 800/427–7623, 888/836–0866 Hwy. 1 Visitor Hotline (Cambria north to Carmel) ⊕ www.dot.ca.gov.

TRAIN TRAVEL

The Amtrak Coast Starlight, which runs between Los Angeles and Seattle via Oakland, stops in Paso Robles, San Luis Obispo, Santa Barbara, and Oxnard. Amtrak runs several Pacific Surfliner trains and buses daily between San Luis Obispo, Santa Barbara, Los Angeles, and San Diego. Metrolink Regional Rail Service trains connect Ventura and Oxnard with Los Angeles and points between.

Train Contacts Amtrak ☎ 800/872–7245, 805/963–1015 in Santa Barbara, 805/541–0505 in San Luis Obispo ⊕ www.amtrak.com. Metrolink ☎ 800/371–5465 ⊕ www.metrolinktrains.com.

RESTAURANTS

The cuisine in Ventura and Santa Barbara is every bit as eclectic as it is in California's bigger cities; fresh seafood is a standout. A foodie renaissance has overtaken the entire region from Ventura to Paso Robles, spawning dozens of new restaurants touting locavore cuisine made with fresh organic produce and meats. Dining attire on the Central Coast is generally casual, though slightly dressy casual wear is the custom at pricier restaurants. *Prices in the reviews are the average cost of a main course at dinner or, if dinner is not served, at lunch.*

HOTELS

Lodging options abound in the Central Coast, but expect to pay top dollar for rooms along the shore, especially in summer. Moderately priced hotels and motels do exist—most just a short drive inland from their higher-price counterparts. Make your reservations as early as possible and take advantage of midweek specials to get the best rates. It's common for lodgings to require two-day minimum stays on holidays and some weekends, especially in summer, and to double rates during festivals and other events. Hot Spots provides room reservations and tourist information. *Prices in the reviews are the lowest cost of a standard double room in high season. For expanded reviews, facilities, and current deals, visit Fodors.com.*

Hot Spots ☎ *800/793–7666, 805/564–1637* ⊕ *www.hotspotsusa.com.*

TOUR OPTIONS

Central Coast Food Tours conducts walking tours ($69) of shops, restaurants, wineries, and other food-oriented spots in downtown San Luis Obispo, Paso Robles, and other Central Coast destinations. Cloud Climbers Jeep and Wine Tours offers four types of daily tours ($89–$129): wine tasting, mountain, sunset, and a discovery tour for families. These trips to the Santa Barbara/Santa Ynez mountains and Wine Country are conducted in open-air, six-passenger jeeps. The company also offers a four-hour All Around Ojai Tour ($109) and arranges biking, horseback riding, and trap-shooting tours and Paso Robles wine tours.

Wine Edventures operates guided wine tours ($105) in the Santa Ynez Valley in vans, minicoaches, and other vehicles. The Grapeline Wine Country Shuttle leads daily wine and vineyard picnic tours ($99–$119) in Paso Robles and the Santa Ynez Valley.

Santa Barbara Wine Country Cycling Tours leads half- and full-day tours ($80–$120) of the Santa Ynez wine region. The company also conducts half-day hiking tours ($100–$110) and custom and multiday cycling tours. Spencer's Limousine & Tours offers customized tours of Santa Barbara and the Wine Country via sedan, limousine, or van. A five-hour basic tour with at least four participants costs about $90 per person. Stagecoach Wine Tours runs daily wine-tasting excursions ($129) through the Santa Ynez Valley in vans, minicoaches, and SUVs. Sustainable Vine Wine Tours specializes in eco-friendly wine tours ($125) of the valley in nine-passenger Mercedes Sprinter vans. Trips include tastings at green-minded wineries, and a gourmet organic picnic lunch.

Many of the tour companies described above will pick you up at your hotel or central locations; ask about this when booking.

Tour Contacts Central Coast Food Tours ☎ *800/979–3370, 212/209–3370* ⊕ *www.centralcoastfoodtours.com.* **Cloud Climbers Jeep and Wine Tours** ☎ *805/646–3200* ⊕ *www.ccjeeps.com.* **The Grapeline Wine Country Shuttle** ☎ *888/894–6379* ⊕ *www.gogrape.com.* **Santa Barbara Wine Country Cycling**

Tours ✉ *3630 Sagunto St., Santa Ynez* ☎ *888/557-8687, 805/686-9490* ⊕ *www.winecountrycycling.com.* **Spencer's Limousine & Tours** ☎ *805/884-9700* ⊕ *www.spencerslimo.com.* **Stagecoach Wine Tours** ✉ *Solvang* ☎ *805/686-8347* ⊕ *www.winetourssantaynez.com.* **Sustainable Vine Wine Tours** ☎ *805/698-3911* ⊕ *www.sustainablevine.com.* **Wine Edventures** ✉ *Santa Barbara* ☎ *805/965-9463* ⊕ *www.welovewines.com.*

VISITOR INFORMATION

Contact **Central Coast Tourism Council** ⊕ *www.centralcoast-tourism.com.*

VENTURA COUNTY

Ventura County was first settled by the Chumash Indians. Spanish missionaries were the first Europeans to arrive, followed by Americans and other Europeans, who established bustling towns, transportation networks, and highly productive farms. Since the 1920s, agriculture has been steadily replaced as the area's main industry—first by the oil business and more recently by tourism.

VENTURA

60 miles north of Los Angeles.

Like Los Angeles, the city of Ventura enjoys gorgeous weather and sun-kissed beaches—but without the smog and congestion. The miles of beautiful beaches attract athletes—bodysurfers and boogie boarders, runners and bikers—and those who'd rather doze beneath an umbrella all day. Ventura Harbor is home to myriad fishing boats, restaurants, and water-activity centers where you can rent boats and take harbor cruises. Foodies can get their fix all over Ventura—dozens of upscale cafés and wine and tapas bars have opened in recent years. Arts and antiques buffs have long trekked downtown to browse the galleries and shops there.

GETTING HERE AND AROUND

Amtrak and Metrolink trains serve the area from Los Angeles area. Greyhound buses stop in Ventura; Gold Coast Transit serves the city and the rest of Ventura County.

U.S. 101 is the north–south main route into town, but for a scenic drive, take Highway 1 north from Santa Monica. The highway merges with U.S. 101 just south of Ventura. ■ TIP→ **Traveling north to Ventura from Los Angeles on weekdays it's best to depart before 6 am, between 10 and 2, or after 7, or you'll get caught in the extended rush-hour traffic. Coming south from Santa Barbara, depart before 1 or after 6.** On weekends, traffic is generally fine except southbound on U.S. 101 between Santa Barbara and Ventura.

ESSENTIALS

Bus Contact Gold Coast Transit ☎ *805/643-3158* ⊕ *www.goldcoasttransit.org.*

Visitor Information Ventura Visitors and Convention Bureau ✉ *Downtown Visitor Center, 101 S. California St.* ☎ *805/648-2075, 800/483-6214* ⊕ *www.ventura-usa.com.*

EXPLORING

FAMILY **Lake Casitas Recreation Area.** Lunker largemouth bass, rainbow trout, crappie, redears, and channel catfish live in the waters at this park, one of the country's best bass-fishing areas. Nestled below the Santa Ynez Mountains' Laguna Ridge, Lake Casitas is also a beautiful spot for pitching a tent or having a picnic. The Casitas Water Adventure, which has two water playgrounds and a lazy river for tubing and floating, provides kids with endless diversions in summer. ⊠ *11311 Santa Ana Rd., off Hwy. 33, 13 miles northwest of Ventura* ☎ *805/649–2233, 805/649–1122 campground reservations* ⊕ *www.casitaswater.org* ⊠ *$10–$15 per vehicle, $13 per boat; Water Adventure $12 ($6 5–7 pm)* ☉ *Daily.*

Mission San Buenaventura. The ninth of the 21 California missions, Mission San Buenaventura was established in 1782 but burned to the ground in the 1790s. It was rebuilt and rededicated in 1809. A self-guided tour takes you through a small museum, a quiet courtyard, and a chapel with 250-year-old paintings. ⊠ *211 E. Main St., at Figueroa St.* ☎ *805/643–4318* ⊕ *www.sanbuenaventuramission.org* ⊠ *$4* ☉ *Weekdays 10–5, Sat. 9–5, Sun. 10–4.*

Museum of Ventura County. Exhibits in a contemporary complex of galleries and a sunny courtyard plaza tell the story of Ventura County from prehistoric times to the present. A highlight is the gallery that contains Ojai artist George Stuart's historical figures, dressed in exceptionally detailed, custom-made clothing reflecting their particular eras. In the courtyard, eight panels made with 45,000 pieces of cut glass form a historical timeline. ⊠ *100 E. Main St., at S. Ventura Ave.* ☎ *805/653–0323* ⊕ *venturamuseum.org* ⊠ *$4, free first Sun. of the month* ☉ *Tues.–Sun. 11–5.*

Ventura Oceanfront. Four miles of gorgeous coastline stretch from the county fairgrounds at the northern border of the city of San Buenaventura, through San Buenaventura State Beach, down to Ventura Harbor in the south. The main attraction here is the San Buenaventura City Pier, a landmark built in 1872 and restored in 1993. Surfers rip the waves just north of the pier, and sunbathers relax on white-sand beaches on either side. The mile-long promenade and the Omer Rains Bike Trail north of the pier attract scores of joggers, surrey cyclers, and bikers throughout the year. ⊠ *California St., at ocean's edge.*

WHERE TO EAT

$$ ✕ **Brophy Bros.** The Ventura outpost of this wildly popular Santa Barbara
SEAFOOD   restaurant provides the same fresh seafood-oriented meals in a spacious second-story setting overlooking the harbor. Feast on everything from fish and chips and crab cakes to chowder and delectable fish—often straight from the boats moored below. ⑤ *Average main: $22* ⊠ *1559 Spinnaker Dr., in Ventura Harbor Village* ☎ *805/639–0865* ⊕ *www. brophybros.com* ⚓ *Reservations not accepted.*

$ ✕ **Lure Fish House.** Fresh, sustainably caught seafood charbroiled over a
SEAFOOD   mesquite grill, a well-stocked oyster bar, specialty cocktails, and a wine list heavy on local vintages lure diners into this slick, nautical-themed space downtown. The menu, which changes daily, centers on the mostly local catch and organic veggies, and also includes tacos, sandwiches, and salads. Grilled entrées come with a choice of unusual farm-to-table

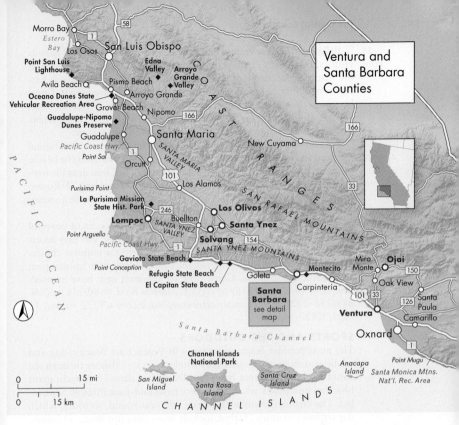

Ventura and
Santa Barbara
Counties

sides: quinoa salad, sweet-potato fries, pineapple cole slaw. The regulars rave about the shrimp-and-chips, cioppino, and citrus crab-cake salad. $ *Average main: $15* ✉ *60 S. California St.* ☎ *805/567-4400* ⊕ *www. lurefishhouse.com.*

WHERE TO STAY

For expanded reviews, facilities, and current deals, visit Fodors.com.

$$
HOTEL

🏨 **Crowne Plaza Ventura Beach.** A 12-story hotel with an enviable location on the beach and next to a historic pier, the Crowne Plaza is also within walking distance of downtown restaurants and nightlife. **Pros:** on the beach; near downtown; steps from waterfront. **Cons:** early-morning train noise; waterfront crowded in summer; most rooms on the small side. $ *Rooms from: $169* ✉ *450 E. Harbor Blvd.* ☎ *800/842–0800, 805/648–2100* ⊕ *cpventura.com* ➥ *254 rooms, 4 suites* ⊘ *No meals.*

$$
RESORT

🏨 **Four Points by Sheraton Ventura Harbor Resort.** An on-site restaurant, spacious rooms, and a slew of amenities make this 17-acre property—which includes sister hotel Holiday Inn Express—a popular and practical choice for Channel Islands visitors. **Pros:** close to island transportation; mostly quiet; short drive to historic downtown. **Cons:** not in the heart of downtown; noisy seagulls sometimes congregate nearby. $ *Rooms from: $145* ✉ *1050 Schooner Dr.* ☎ *805/658–1212* ⊕ *www. fourpoints.com/ventura* ➥ *102 rooms, 4 suites* ⊘ *No meals.*

$$ 🏨 **Holiday Inn Express Ventura Harbor.** A favorite among Channel Islands
HOTEL visitors, this quiet, comfortable, lodge-inspired property sits right at
the Ventura Harbor entrance. **Pros:** quiet at night; easy access to har-
bor restaurants and activities; five-minute drive to downtown. **Cons:**
busy area on weekends; complaints of erratic service. $ *Rooms from:*
$130 ⊠ *1080 Navigator Dr.* ☎ *805/856–9533, 800/315–2621* ⊕ *www.*
holidayinnexpress.com/venturaca ⇔ *69 rooms* ⧁ *Breakfast.*

$$ 🏨 **Pierpont Inn.** Back in 1910, Josephine Pierpont-Ginn built the original
HOTEL Pierpont Inn on a hill overlooking Ventura Beach. **Pros:** near the beach;
lush gardens; Tempur-Pedic mattresses and pillows. **Cons:** near the freeway and train tracks; difficult to walk downtown from here. $ *Rooms*
from: $125 ⊠ *550 Sanjon Rd.* ☎ *805/643–6144* ⊕ *www.pierpontinn.*
com ⇔ *65 rooms, 9 suites, 2 cottages* ⧁ *No meals.*

$$$ 🏨 **Ventura Beach Marriott.** Spacious, contemporary rooms, a peaceful
HOTEL location just steps from San Buenaventura State Beach, and easy access
to downtown arts and culture make the Marriott a popular choice.
Pros: walk to beach and biking/jogging trails; a block from historic pier;
great value for location. **Cons:** close to highway; near busy intersec-
tion. $ *Rooms from: $189* ⊠ *2055 E. Harbor Blvd.* ☎ *805/643–6000,*
888/236–2427 ⊕ *www.marriottventurabeach.com* ⇔ *272 rooms, 12*
suites ⧁ *No meals.*

SPORTS AND THE OUTDOORS

The most popular outdoor activities in Ventura are beach-going and
whale-watching. California gray whales migrate offshore through the
Santa Barbara Channel from late December through March; giant
blue and humpback whales feed here from mid-June through Septem-
ber. The channel teems with marine life year-round, so tours, which
depart from Ventura Harbor, include more than just whale sightings.
To learn about the spectacular hiking trails on the five islands that
comprise Channel Islands National Park, check out its visitor center,
also at the harbor.

Island Packers. A cruise through the Santa Barbara Channel with Island
Packers will give you the chance to spot dolphins and seals—and some-
times even whales—throughout the year. ⊠ *Ventura Harbor, 1691 Spin-*
naker Dr. ☎ *805/642–1393* ⊕ *www.islandpackers.com.*

OJAI

15 miles north of Ventura.

The Ojai Valley, which director Frank Capra used as a backdrop for
his 1936 film *Lost Horizon,* sizzles in the summer when temperatures
routinely reach 90°F. The acres of orange and avocado groves here
evoke postcard images of long-ago agricultural Southern California.
Many artists and celebrities have sought refuge from life in the fast
lane in lush Ojai.

GETTING HERE AND AROUND

From northern Ventura, Highway 33 veers east from U.S. 101 and
climbs inland to Ojai. From Santa Barbara, exit U.S. 101 at Highway
150 in Carpinteria, then travel east 20 miles on a twisting, two-lane

road that is not recommended at night or during poor weather. You can also access Ojai by heading west from Interstate 5 on Highway 126. Exit at Santa Paula and follow Highway 150 north for 16 miles to Ojai. Gold Coast Transit provides service to Ojai from Ventura.

Ojai can be easily explored on foot; you can also hop on the Ojai Trolley ($1, or $2 day pass), which until about 5 pm follows two routes around Ojai and neighboring Miramonte on weekdays and one route on weekends. Tell the driver you're visiting and you'll get an informal guided tour.

ESSENTIALS
Bus Contacts Gold Coast Transit ☎ *805/643–3158* ⊕ *www.goldcoasttransit. org.* **Ojai Trolley** ☎ *805/646–5581* ⊕ *www.ojaitrolley.com.*

Visitor Information Ojai Visitors Bureau ✉ *206 N. Signal St., at E. Ojai Ave.* ☎ *888/652–4669* ⊕ *www.ojaivisitors.com* ⊙ *Weekdays 9–4.*

EXPLORING
Ojai Art Center. California's oldest nonprofit, multipurpose arts center exhibits visual art from various disciplines and presents theater, dance, and other performances. ✉ *113 S. Montgomery St., near E. Ojai Ave.* ☎ *805/646–0117* ⊕ *www.ojaiartcenter.org* ⊙ *Tues.–Sun. noon–4.*

Ojai Avenue. The work of local artists is displayed in the Spanish-style shopping arcade along the avenue downtown. Organic and specialty growers sell their produce on Sundays between 9 and 1 at the outdoor market behind the arcade.

Ojai Valley Museum. The museum has many Native American artifacts and mounts exhibits documenting local history. Walking tours of Ojai depart from here. ✉ *130 W. Ojai Ave.* ☎ *805/640–1390* ⊕ *www. ojaivalleymuseum.org* 🎟 *Musuem $4, walking tour $5* ⊙ *Tues.–Sat. 10–4, Sun. noon–4; tour Oct.–July, Sat. 10:30.*

Ojai Valley Trail. The 18-mile trail is open to pedestrians, joggers, equestrians, bikers, and others on nonmotorized vehicles. You can access it anywhere along its route. ✉ *Parallel to Hwy. 33 from Soule Park in Ojai to ocean in Ventura* ☎ *888/652–4669* ⊕ *www.ojaivisitors.com.*

WHERE TO EAT
$$$
MEDITERRANEAN
✕ **Azu.** Delectable tapas, a full bar, slick furnishings, and piped jazz music draw diners to this artsy Mediterranean bistro. You can also order soups, salads, and bistro fare such as steak frites and paella. Save room for the homemade gelato. ⑤ *Average main: $24* ✉ *457 E. Ojai Ave.* ☎ *805/640–7987* ⊕ *www.azuojai.com.*

$
ITALIAN
✕ **Boccali's.** Edging a ranch, citrus groves, and a seasonal garden that provides produce for menu items, the modest but cheery Boccali's attracts many loyal fans. When it's warm, you can dine alfresco in the oak-shaded patio and lawn area and sometimes listen to live music. The family-run operation, best known for hand-rolled pizzas and home-style pastas (don't miss the eggplant lasagna), also serves a popular seasonal strawberry shortcake. ⑤ *Average main: $15* ✉ *3277 Ojai Ave., about 2 miles east of downtown* ☎ *805/646–6116* ⊕ *www.boccalis.com* ▭ *No credit cards* ⊙ *No lunch Mon. and Tues.*

$$$ ✕ **The Ranch House.** This elegant yet laid-back eatery has been around
AMERICAN   for decades. Main dishes such as the broiled-and-roasted rack of lamb
with pineapple guava chutney and the grilled diver scallops with cur-
ried sweet-corn sauce are not to be missed. The verdant patio is a
wonderful place to have Sunday brunch. ⑤ *Average main: $29* ⊠ *500
S. Lomita Ave.* ☎ *805/646–2360* ⊕ *www.theranchhouse.com* ⊘ *Closed
Mon. No lunch.*

$$$ ✕ **Suzanne's Cuisine.** Peppered filet mignon, linguine with steamed clams,
EUROPEAN   and pan-roasted salmon with a roasted mango sauce are among the
offerings at this European-style restaurant. Game, seafood, and vegetarian dishes dominate the dinner menu, and salads and soups star
at lunchtime. All the breads and desserts are made on the premises.
⑤ *Average main: $24* ⊠ *502 W. Ojai Ave.* ☎ *805/640–1961* ⊕ *www.
suzannescuisine.com* ⊘ *Closed Tues.*

WHERE TO STAY

For expanded reviews, facilities, and current deals, visit Fodors.com.

$$ ⛺ **The Blue Iguana Inn & Suites.** Artists run this Southwestern-style hotel,
B&B/INN   and their work (which is for sale) decorates the rooms. **Pros:** colorful
art everywhere; secluded. **Cons:** 2 miles from downtown; on a highway;
small. ⑤ *Rooms from: $129* ⊠ *11794 N. Ventura Ave.* ☎ *805/646–
5277* ⊕ *www.iguanainnsofojai.com* ⮎ *4 rooms, 8 suites, 8 cottages*
� ⦿ *Breakfast.*

$$$ ⛺ **Oaks at Ojai.** Rejuvenation is the name of the game at this destination
RESORT   spa. **Pros:** great place to get fit; peaceful retreat; healthful meals. **Cons:**
basic rooms; on main highway through town. ⑤ *Rooms from: $199*
⊠ *122 E. Ojai Ave.* ☎ *805/646–5573, 800/753–6257* ⊕ *www.oaksspa.
com* ⮎ *44 rooms, 2 suites* ⦿ *All meals* ⌑ *2-night minimum stay.*

$$$$ ⛺ **Ojai Valley Inn & Spa.** This outdoorsy, golf-oriented resort and spa
RESORT   is set on beautifully landscaped grounds, with hillside views in nearly
Fodor's Choice   all directions. **Pros:** gorgeous grounds; exceptional outdoor activities;
★   romantic yet kid-friendly. **Cons:** expensive; areas near restaurants can
be noisy. ⑤ *Rooms from: $400* ⊠ *905 Country Club Rd.* ☎ *805/646–
1111, 888/697–8780* ⊕ *www.ojairesort.com* ⮎ *231 rooms, 77 suites*
⦿ *No meals.*

$$$ ⛺ **Su Nido Inn.** A short walk from downtown Ojai sights and restau-
B&B/INN   rants, this posh Mission revival–style inn sits in a quiet neighborhood
a few blocks from Libbey Park. **Pros:** walking distance from down-
town; homey feel. **Cons:** no pool; can get hot during summer. ⑤ *Rooms
from: $189* ⊠ *301 N. Montgomery St.* ☎ *805/646–7080, 866/646–7080*
⊕ *www.sunidoinn.com* ⮎ *3 rooms, 9 suites* ⦿ *No meals* ⌑ *2-night
minimum stay on weekends.*

SANTA BARBARA

27 miles northwest of Ventura and 29 miles west of Ojai.

Santa Barbara has long been an oasis for Los Angelenos seeking respite from big-city life. The attractions begin at the ocean and end in the foothills of the Santa Ynez Mountains. A few miles up the coast east and west—but still very much a part of Santa Barbara—are the exclusive residential districts of Montecito and Hope Ranch. Santa Barbara is on a jog in the coastline, so the ocean is actually to the south, instead of the west; for this reason, directions can be confusing. "Up" the coast toward San Francisco is west, "down" toward Los Angeles is east, and the mountains are north.

GETTING HERE AND AROUND

U.S. 101 is the main route into Santa Barbara. If you're staying in town, a car is handy but not essential; the beaches and downtown are easily explored by bicycle or on foot. Visit the Santa Barbara Car Free website for bike-route and walking-tour maps and car-free vacation packages with substantial lodging, dining, activity, and transportation discounts.

Santa Barbara Metropolitan Transit District's Line 22 bus serves major tourist sights. Several bus lines connect with the very convenient electric shuttles that cruise the downtown and waterfront every 10 to 15 minutes (50¢ each way).

Santa Barbara Trolley Co. operates a motorized San Francisco–style cable car that loops past major hotels, shopping areas, and attractions from 10 to 4. Get off whenever you like, and pick up another trolley (they come every hour) when you're ready to move on. The fare is $19 for the day.

TOURS

Land and Sea Tours. This outfit conducts 90-minute narrated tours in an amphibious 49-passenger vehicle nicknamed the Land Shark. The adventure begins with a drive through the city, followed by a plunge into the harbor for a cruise along the coast. ⊠ *State St., at Stearns Wharf* ☎ *805/683-7600* ⊕ *www.out2seesb.com* ⊠ *$25* ☉ *Tours May–Oct., daily noon, 2, and 4; Nov.–Apr., daily noon and 2.*

Segway Tours of Santa Barbara. After a brief training session, a guide leads you around town on electric-powered personal balancing transporters. Tour options include the waterfront (1¼ hours), Butterfly Beach and Montecito (2 hours), historic downtown Santa Barbara (2½ hours), and through town to the mission (3 hours). This outfit also rents electric bikes. ⊠ *16 Helena Ave., at Cabrillo Blvd.* ☎ *805/963-7672* ⊕ *www. segwayofsb.com* ⊠ *$65–$110.*

ESSENTIALS

Transportation Contacts Santa Barbara Car Free ☎ *805/696-1100* ⊕ *www.santabarbaracarfree.org.* **Santa Barbara Metropolitan Transit District** ☎ *805/963-3366* ⊕ *www.sbmtd.gov.* **Santa Barbara Trolley Co.** ☎ *805/965-0353* ⊕ *www.sbtrolley.com.*

Visitor Information Santa Barbara Visitor Center ⊠ *1 Garden St., at Cabrillo Blvd.* ☎ *805/965-3021, 805/568-1811* ⊕ *www.sbchamber.org* ☉ *Mon.–Sat. 9–5, Sun. 10–5.* **Santa Barbara Conference and Visitors Bureau** ⊠ *500 E. Montecito St.* ☎ *805/966-9222* ⊕ *www.santabarbaraca.com.*

Continued on page 54

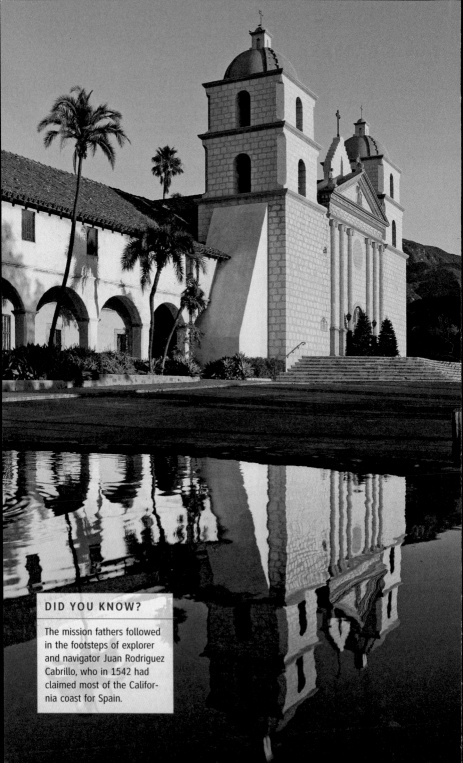

ON A MISSION

Their soul may belong to Spain, their heart to the New World, but the historic missions of California, with their lovely churches, beckon the traveler on a soulful journey back to the very founding of the American West.

by Cheryl Crabtree and Robert I.C. Fisher

California history changed forever in the 18th century when Spanish explorers founded a series of missions along the Pacific coast. Believing they were following God's will, they wanted to spread the gospel and convert as many natives as possible. The process produced a collision between the Hispanic and California Indian cultures, resulting in one of the most striking legacies of Old California: the Spanish mission churches. Rising like mirages in the middle of desert plains and rolling hills, these saintly sites transport you back to the days of the Spanish colonial period.

GOD AND MAN IN CALIFORNIA

The Alta California territory came under pressure in the 1760s when Spain feared foreign advances into the territory explorer Juan Rodríguez Cabrillo had claimed for the Spanish crown back in 1542. But how could Spain create a visible and viable presence halfway around the world? They decided to build on the model that had already worked well in Spain's Mexico colony. The plan involved establishing a series of missions, to be operated by the Catholic Church and protected by four of Spain's *presidios* (military outposts). The native Indians— after quick conversion to Christianity—would provide the labor force necessary to build mission towns.

FATHER OF THE MISSIONS

Father Junípero Serra is an icon of the Spanish colonial period. At the behest of the Spanish government, the diminutive padre—then well into his fifties, and despite a chronic leg infection— started out on foot from Baja California to search for suitable mission sites, with a goal of reaching Monterey. In 1769 he helped establish Alta California's first mission in San Diego and continued his travels until his death, in 1784, by which time he had founded eight more missions.

The system ended about a decade after the Mexican government took control of Alta California in the early 1820s and began to secularize the missions. The church lost horses and cattle, as well as vast tracts of land, which the Mexican government in turn granted to private individuals. They also lost laborers, as the Indians were for the most part free to find work and a life beyond the missions. In 1848, the Americans assumed control of the territory, and California became part of the United States. Today, these missions stand as extraordinary monuments to their colorful past.

Mission Santa Barbara Museum

MISSION ACCOMPLISHED

California's Mission Trail is the best way to follow in the fathers' footsteps. Here, below, are its 21 settlements, north to south.

Amazingly, all 21 Spanish missions in California are still standing—some in their pristine historic state, others with modifications made over the centuries. Many are found on or near the "King's Road"—El Camino Real—which linked these mission outposts. At the height of the mission system the trail was approximately 600 miles long, eventually extending from San Diego to Sonoma. Today the road is commemorated on portions of routes 101 and 82 in the form of roadside bell markers erected by CalTrans every one to two miles between San Diego and San Francisco.

San Francisco Solano, Sonoma (1823; this was the final California mission constructed.)

San Rafael, San Rafael (1817)

San Francisco de Asís (aka Mission Dolores), San Francisco (1776). Situated in the heart of San Francisco,

Mission Santa Clara de Asís

these mission grounds and nearby Arroyo de los Dolores (Creek of Sorrows) are home to the oldest intact building in the city.

Santa Clara de Asís, Santa Clara (1777). On the campus of Santa Clara University, this beautifully restored mission contains original paintings, statues, a bell, and hundreds of artifacts, as well as a spectacular rose garden.

San José, Fremont (1797)

Santa Cruz, Santa Cruz (1791)

San Juan Bautista, San Juan Bautista (1797). Immortalized in Hitchcock's *Vertigo*, this remarkably preserved pueblo contains the largest church of all the California missions, as well as 18th- and 19th-century buildings and a sprawling plaza.

San Carlos Borromeo del Río Carmelo, Carmel (1770). Carmel Mission was head-

quarters for the California mission system under Father Serra and the Father Presidents who succeeded him; the on-site museum includes Serra's tiny sleeping quarters (where he died in 1784).

Nuestra Señora de la Soledad, Soledad (1791)

San Antonio de Padua, Jolon (1771)

San Miguel Arcángel, San Miguel (1797). San Miguel boasts the only intact original interior wall painting in any of the missions, painted in 1821 by Native American converts under the direction of Spanish artist Esteban Muras.

Painting from 1818, San Juan Bautista.

Mission Santa Inés

San Luis Obispo de Tolosa, San Luis Obispo (1772). Bear meat from grizzlies captured here saved the Spaniards from starving, which helped convince Father Serra to establish a mission.

La Purísima Concepción, Lompoc (1787). La Purísima is the nation's most completely restored mission complex. It is now a living-history museum with a church and nearly forty craft and residence rooms.

Santa Inés, Solvang (1804). Home to one of the most significant pieces of religious art created by a California mission Indian.

Santa Bárbara, Santa Barbara (1786). The "Queen of the Missions" has twin bell towers, gorgeous gardens with heirloom plant varietals, a massive collection of rare artworks and artifacts, and lovely stonework.

San Buenaventura, Ventura (1782). This was the last mission founded by Father Serra; it is still an active parish in the Archdiocese of Los Angeles.

Mission San Fernando Rey de España

San Fernando Rey de España, Mission Hills (1797)

San Gabriel Arcángel, San Gabriel (1771)

San Luis Rey de Francia, Oceanside (1798)

San Juan Capistrano, San Juan Capistrano (1776). This mission is famed for its Saint Joseph's Day (March 19) celebration of the return of swallows in the springtime. The mission's adobe walls enclose acres of lush gardens and historic buildings.

San Diego de Alcalá, San Diego (1769). This was the first California missions constructed, although the original was destroyed in 1775 and rebuilt over a number of years.

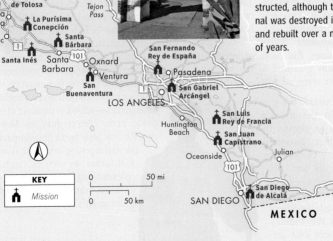

Coalinga

Paso Robles

San Miguel Arcángel

McKittrick

San Luis Obispo

San Luis Obispo de Tolosa

Tejon Pass

Santa Maria

La Purísima Conepción

Lompoc

Santa Bárbara

Santa Inés

Santa Barbara

Oxnard

Ventura

San Buenaventura

LOS ANGELES

San Fernando Rey de España

Pasadena

San Gabriel Arcángel

Huntington Beach

San Luis Rey de Francia

San Juan Capistrano

Oceanside

Julian

San Diego de Alcalá

SAN DIEGO

MEXICO

KEY	
✝	*Mission*

0   50 mi

0   50 km

SPANISH MISSION STYLE

(left) Mission San Luis Rey de Francia; (right) Mission San Antonio de Padua

The Spanish mission churches derive much of their strength and enduring power from their extraordinary admixture of styles. They are spectacular examples of the combination of races and cultures that bloomed along Father Serra's road through Alta California.

SPIRIT OF THE PLACE
In building the missions, the Franciscan padres had to rely on available resources. Spanish churches back in Europe boasted marble floors and gilded statues. But here, whitewashed adobe walls gleamed in the sun and floors were often merely packed earth.

However simple the structures, the art within the mission confines continued to glorify the Church. The padres imported much finery to decorate the churches and perform the mass—silver, silk and lovely paintings to teach the life of Christ to the Indians and soldiers and settlers. Serra himself commissioned fine artists in Mexico to produce custom works using the best materials and according to exact specifications. Sculptures of angels, Mary, Joseph, Jesus and the Franciscan heroes and saints—and of course the Stations of the Cross—adorned all the missions.

AN ENDURING LEGACY
Mission architecture reflects a gorgeous blend of European and New World influences. While naves followed the simple forms of Franciscan Gothic, cloisters (with beautiful arcades) adopted aspects of the Romanesque style, and ornamental touches of the Spanish Renaissance—including red-tiled roofs and wrought-iron grilles—added even more elegance. In the 20th century, the Mission Revival Style had a huge impact on architecture and design in California, as seen in examples ranging from San Diego's Union Station to Stanford University's main quadrangle.

Father Junípero Serra statue at Mission San Gabriel

FOR WHOM THE BELLS TOLLED

Perhaps the most famous architectural motif of the Spanish Mission churches was the belltower. These took the form of either a campanile—a single tower called a campanario—or, more spectacularly, of an open-work espedaña, a perforated adobe wall housing a series of bells (notable examples of this form are at San Miguel Arcángel and San Diego de Alcalá). Bells were essential to maintaining the routines of daily life at the missions.

MISSION LIFE

Morning bells summoned residents to chapel for services; noontime bells introduced the main meal, while the evening bells sounded the alert to gather around 5 pm for mass and dinner. Many of the natives were happy with their new faith, and even enjoyed putting in numerous hours a week working as farmers, soapmakers, weavers, and masons.

Others, however, were less willing to abandon their traditional culture, but were coerced to abide by the new Spanish laws and mission rules. Natives were sometimes mistreated by the friars, who used a system of punishments to enforce submission to the new culture.

NATIVE TRAGEDY

In the end, mission life proved extremely destructive to the Native Californian population. European diseases and contaminated water caused the death of nearly a third, with some tribes—notably the Chumash—being virtually decimated.

Despite these losses, small numbers did survive. After the Mexican government secularized the missions in 1833, a majority of the native population was reduced to poverty. Some stayed at the missions, while others went to live in the pueblos, ranchos, and countryside.

Many Native Californian people today still work and live near the missions that are monuments to their artistry skills.

FOR MORE INFORMATION

California Missions Foundation

✉ 26555 Carmel Rancho Blvd., Ste. 7 Carmel, CA 93923

☎ 831/622-7500

🌐 www.california missionsfoundation.org

Top, Mission San Gabriel Arcángel
Bottom, Mission San Miguel Arcángel

EXPLORING

Santa Barbara's waterfront is beautiful, with palm-studded promenades and plenty of sand. In the few miles between the beaches and the hills are downtown, the old mission, and the botanic gardens.

EXPLORING

TOP ATTRACTIONS

El Presidio State Historic Park. Founded in 1782, El Presidio was one of four military strongholds established by the Spanish along the coast of California. The park encompasses much of the original site in the heart of downtown. El Cuartel, the adobe guardhouse, is the oldest building in Santa Barbara and the second oldest in California. ⊠ *123 E. Canon Perdido St., at Anacapa St.* ☎ *805/965–0093* ⊕ *www.sbthp.org* ☞ *$5* ⊗ *Daily 10:30–4:30.*

FAMILY
Fodor'sChoice
★
Lotusland. The 37-acre estate called Lotusland once belonged to the Polish opera singer Ganna Walska, who purchased it in the late 1940s and lived here until her death in 1984. Many of the exotic trees and other subtropical flora were planted in 1882 by horticulturist R. Kinton Stevens. On the two-hour guided tour—the only option for visiting unless you're a member; reserve well ahead in summer—you'll see an outdoor theater, a topiary garden, a huge collection of rare cycads (an unusual plant genus that has been around since the time of the dinosaurs), and a lotus pond. ■TIP→ **Child-friendly family tours are available for groups with children under the age of 10; contact Lotusland for scheduling.** ⊠ *695 Ashley Rd., off Sycamore Canyon Rd. (Hwy. 192), Montecito* ☎ *805/969–9990* ⊕ *www.lotusland.org* ☞ *$35* ⊗ *Mid-Feb.–mid-Nov., Wed.–Sat. at 10 and 1:30 by appointment only.*

Fodor'sChoice
★
Mission Santa Barbara. Widely referred to as the "Queen of Missions," this is one of the most beautiful and frequently photographed buildings in coastal California. Dating to 1786, the architecture evolved from adobe-brick buildings with thatch roofs to more permanent edifices as the mission's population burgeoned. An earthquake in 1812 destroyed the third church built on the site. Its replacement, the present structure, is still a functioning Catholic church. Mission Santa Barbara has a splendid Spanish/Mexican colonial art collection, as well as Chumash sculptures and the only Native American–made altar and tabernacle left in the California missions. Docents lead 90-minute tours ($8 adult) Thursday and Friday at 11 and Saturday at 10:30. ⊠ *2201 Laguna St., at E. Los Olivos St.* ☎ *805/682–4149, 805/682–4713* ⊕ *www.santabarbaramission.org* ☞ *$5* ⊗ *Daily 9:30–4:30.*

Santa Barbara Botanic Garden. Scenic trails meander through the garden's 78 acres of native plants. The Mission Dam, built in 1806, stands just beyond the redwood grove and above the restored aqueduct that once carried water to Mission Santa Barbara. More than a thousand plant species thrive in various themed sections, including mountains, deserts, meadows, redwoods, and Channel Islands. ⊠ *1212 Mission Canyon Rd., north of Foothill Rd. (Hwy. 192)* ☎ *805/682–4726* ⊕ *www.sbbg.org* ☞ *$8* ⊗ *Mar.–Oct., daily 9–6; Nov.–Feb., daily 9–5. Guided tours weekends at 11 and 2, Mon. at 2.*

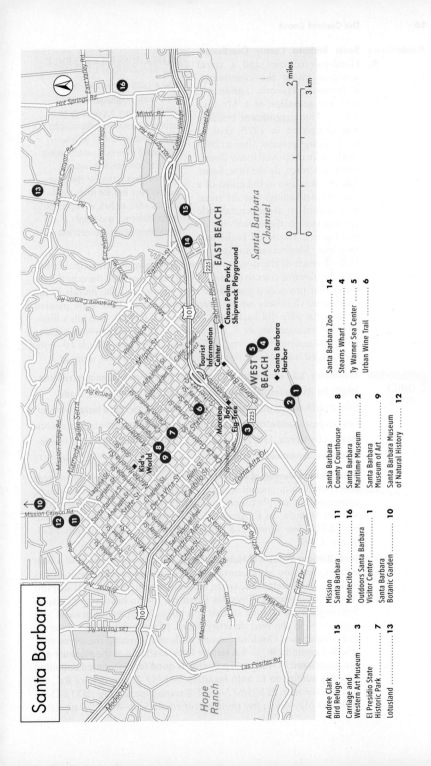

Santa Barbara

Andree Clark
Bird Refuge **15**
Carriage and
Western Art Museum **3**
El Presidio State
Historic Park **7**
Lotusland **13**

Mission
Santa Barbara **11**
Montecito **16**
Outdoors Santa Barbara
Visitor Center **1**
Santa Barbara
Botanic Garden **10**

Santa Barbara
County Courthouse **8**
Santa Barbara
Maritime Museum **2**
Santa Barbara
Museum of Art **9**
Santa Barbara Museum
of Natural History **12**

Santa Barbara Zoo **14**
Stearns Wharf **4**
Ty Warner Sea Center ... **5**
Urban Wine Trail **6**

Fodor's Choice
★

Santa Barbara County Courthouse. Hand-painted tiles and a spiral staircase infuse the courthouse, a National Historic Landmark, with the grandeur of a Moorish palace. This magnificent building was completed in 1929, part of a rebuilding process after a 1925 earthquake destroyed many downtown structures. At the time, Santa Barbara was also in the midst of a cultural awakening, and the trend was toward an architectural style appropriate to the area's climate and history. The result is the harmonious Mediterranean–Spanish

---

SANTA BARBARA STYLE

After a 1925 earthquake demolished many buildings, the city seized a golden opportunity to assume a Spanish-Mediterranean style. It established an architectural board of review, which, along with city commissions, created strict building codes for the downtown district: red tile roofs, earthtone facades, arches, wrought-iron embellishments, and height restrictions (about four stories).

---

look of much of the downtown area, especially the municipal buildings. An elevator rises to an arched observation area in the courthouse tower that provides a panoramic view of the city. The murals in the ceremonial chambers on the courthouse's second floor were painted by an artist who did backdrops for some of Cecil B. DeMille's films. ⊠ *1100 Anacapa St., at E. Anapamu St.* ☎ *805/962–6464* ⊕ *www.santabarbaracourthouse.org* ☉ *Weekdays 8–4:45, weekends 10–4:30. Free guided tours Mon., Tues., Weds., and Fri. at 10:30, daily at 2.*

QUICK BITES

Jeannine's. Take a break from State Street shopping at Jeannine's, revered locally for its wholesome sandwiches, salads, and baked goods, made from scratch with organic and natural ingredients. Pick up a turkey berry or chicken pesto sandwich to go, and picnic in the courthouse gardens a block away. ⊠ *La Arcada, 15 E. Figueroa St., at State St.* ☎ *805/687–8701* ⊕ *jeannines.com/downtown* ☉ *Daily 6:30–3:30.*

Santa Barbara Museum of Art. The highlights of this museum's permanent collection include ancient sculpture, Asian art, impressionist paintings, contemporary art, photography, and American works in several media. ⊠ *1130 State St., at E. Anapamu St.* ☎ *805/963–4364* ⊕ *www.sbma. net* ⊠ *$10, free Thurs. 5–8* ☉ *Tues., Wed., Fri. and weekends 11–5, Thurs. 11–8.*

FAMILY

Santa Barbara Museum of Natural History. The gigantic skeleton of a blue whale greets you at the entrance of this complex. The major draws include the planetarium, space lab, and a gem and mineral display. A room of dioramas illustrates Chumash Indian history and culture. Startlingly alive-looking stuffed specimens, complete with nests and eggs, roost in the bird diversity room. Many exhibits have interactive components. Outdoors, nature trails wind through the serene oakstudded grounds. ■TIP➔ A Nature Pass, available at the museum and the associated Ty Warner Sea Center, is good for discounted unlimited two-day admission to both facilities. ⊠ *2559 Puesta del Sol Rd., off E. Los Olivos St.* ☎ *805/682–4711* ⊕ *www.sbnature.org* ⊠ *$12 Oct.–Apr., $13 May–Sept.; free third Sun. of month Sept.–May* ☉ *Daily 10–5.*

2

FAMILY **Santa Barbara Zoo.** The grounds of this smallish zoo are so gorgeous people book their weddings here long in advance. The palm-studded lawns on a hilltop overlooking the beach are perfect spots for family picnics. The natural settings of the zoo shelter elephants, gorillas, exotic birds like the California condor, and big cats such as the rare snow leopard, a thick-furred, high-altitude dweller from Asia. For small children, there's a scenic railroad and barnyard petting zoo. Duncan, an amazingly lifelike dinosaur, stars in the live stage show *How to Train Your Dinosaur* (free with zoo admission, daily in summer, on weekends the rest of the year). Duncan, designed by one of Hollywood's top creature shops, demonstrates the special techniques trainers use to care for animals. ⊠ *500 Niños Dr., off El Cabrillo Blvd.* ☎ *805/962–5339 main line, 805/962–6310 information* ⊕ *www.santabarbarazoo.org* ⊠ *Zoo $14, parking $6* ⊙ *Daily 10–5.*

Stearns Wharf. Built in 1872, Stearns Wharf is Santa Barbara's most visited landmark. Expansive views of the mountains, cityscape, and harbor unfold from every vantage point on the three-block-long pier. Although it's a nice walk from the Cabrillo Boulevard parking areas, you can also park on the pier and then wander through the shops or stop for a meal at one of the wharf's restaurants. ⊠ *Cabrillo Blvd. and State St.* ⊕ *www.stearnswharf.org.*

FAMILY **Ty Warner Sea Center.** A branch of the Santa Barbara Museum of Natural History, the center specializes in Santa Barbara Channel marine life and conservation. Though small compared to aquariums in Monterey and Long Beach, this is a fascinating, hands-on marine science laboratory that lets you participate in experiments, projects, and exhibits, including touch tanks. Two-story glass walls here open to stunning ocean, mountain, and city views. You can purchase a Nature Pass, which includes discounted two-day admission to the natural history museum and the Sea Center. Ty Warner, the Beanie Baby mogul and a local resident, is a major donor. ⊠ *211 Stearns Wharf* ☎ *805/962–2526* ⊕ *www.sbnature. org* ⊠ *$8* ⊙ *Daily 10–5.*

WORTH NOTING

Andree Clark Bird Refuge. This peaceful lagoon and its gardens sit north of East Beach. Bike trails and footpaths, punctuated by signs identifying native and migratory birds, skirt the lagoon. ⊠ *1400 E. Cabrillo Blvd., near the zoo* ⊠ *Free.*

FAMILY **Carriage and Western Art Museum.** The country's largest collection of old horse-drawn vehicles—painstakingly restored—is exhibited here, everything from polished hearses to police buggies to old stagecoaches and circus vehicles. In August the Old Spanish Days Fiesta borrows many of the vehicles for a jaunt around town. This is one of the city's hidden gems. ⊠ *Pershing Park, 129 Castillo St.* ☎ *805/962–2353* ⊕ *www. carriagemuseum.org* ⊠ *Free* ⊙ *Weekdays 9–3, 3rd Sun. of month 1–4 for docent tours.*

Montecito. Since the late 1800s the tree-studded hills and valleys of this town have attracted the rich and famous: Hollywood icons, business tycoons, dot-commers who divested before the crash, and old-money families who installed themselves here years ago. Shady roads wind through the community, which consists mostly of gated estates. Swank boutiques line **Coast Village Road,** where well-heeled residents such as Oprah Winfrey sometimes browse for truffle oil, picture frames, and designer jeans. Residents also hang out in the Upper Village, a chic shopping area with restaurants and cafés at the intersection of San Ysidro and East Valley roads. ⊠ *3 miles east of Santa Barbara off U.S. 101.*

Outdoors Santa Barbara Visitor Center. The small office provides maps and information about Channel Islands National Park, Channel Islands National Marine Sanctuary, and the Santa Barbara Maritime Museum, which occupies the same harbor building. ⊠ *113 Harbor Way, off Shoreline Dr.* ☎ *805/884–1475* ⊕ *outdoorsb.noaa.gov* ⊠ *Free* ☉ *Daily 11–5.*

FAMILY **Santa Barbara Maritime Museum.** California's seafaring history is the focus here. High-tech, hands-on exhibits, such as a sportfishing activity that lets participants catch a "big one" and a local surfing history retrospective make this a fun stop for families. On display beginning fall 2013 is the museum's shining star: an extremely rare, 17-foot-tall First Order Fresnel lens from the historic Point Conception Lighthouse. ⊠ *113 Harbor Way, off Shoreline Dr.* ☎ *805/962–8404* ⊕ *www.sbmm.org* ⊠ *$7* ☉ *June–Aug., Thurs.–Tues. 10–6; Sept.–May, Thurs.–Tues. 10–5.*

Urban Wine Trail. More than a dozen winery tasting rooms form the Urban Wine Trail; most are within walking distance of the waterfront and the lower State Street shopping and restaurant district. **Santa Barbara Winery,** at 202 Anacapa Street, and **Au Bon Climat,** at 813 Anacapa Street, are good places to start your oenological trek. ⊕ *urbanwinetrailsb.com.*

BEACHES

Santa Barbara's beaches don't have the big surf of the shoreline farther south, but they also don't have the crowds. You can usually find a solitary spot to swim or sunbathe. In June and July, fog often hugs the coast until about noon.

Arroyo Burro Beach. The beach's usually gentle surf makes it ideal for families with young children. It's a local favorite, since you can walk for miles in both directions when tides are low. Leashed dogs are allowed on the main stretch of beach and westward; they are allowed to romp off-leash east of the slough at the beach entrance. The parking lots fill early on weekends and throughout the summer, but the park is relatively quiet at other times. Walk along the beach just a few hundreds yards away from the main steps at the entrance to escape crowds on warm-weather days. Surfers, swimmers, standup paddlers, and boogie boarders regularly ply the waves, and photographers come often to catch the vivid sunsets. **Amenities:** food and drink; lifeguard in summer; parking; showers, toilets. **Best for:** sunset; surfing; swimming; walking. ⊠ *Cliff Dr. and Las Positas Rd.* ⊕ *www.countyofsb.org/parks.*

FAMILY **East Beach.** The wide swath of sand at the east end of Cabrillo Boulevard is a great spot for people-watching. East Beach has sand volleyball courts, summertime lifeguard and sports competitions, and arts-and-crafts shows on Sundays and holidays. You can use showers, a weight

Santa Barbara's downtown is attractive, but be sure also to visit its beautiful—and usually uncrowded—beaches.

room, and lockers (bring your own towel) and rent umbrellas and boogie boards at the Cabrillo Bathhouse. Next door, there's an elaborate jungle-gym play area for kids. **Amenities:** food and drink; lifeguards in summer; parking (fee); showers; toilets; water sports. **Best for:** surfing; swimming; walking. ⊠ *1118 Cabrillo Blvd., at Ninos Dr.* ☎ *805/897–2680.*

WHERE TO EAT

$$ ✕**Arigato Sushi.** You might have to wait for a table at this trendy, two-story restaurant and sushi bar—locals line up early for the wildly creative combination rolls and other delectables. Fans of authentic Japanese food sometimes disagree about the quality of the seafood, but all dishes are fresh and artfully presented. The menu includes traditional dishes as well as innovative creations such as shellfish sushi pizza and Hawaiian sashimi salad. Ⓢ *Average main: $22* ⊠ *1225 State St., near W. Victoria St.* ☎ *805/965–6074* ⊕ *www.arigatosantabarbara. com* ⌂ *Reservations not accepted* ☉ *No lunch.*

JAPANESE

$$ ✕**Brophy Bros.** The outdoor tables at this casual harborside restaurant have perfect views of the marina and mountains. Staffers serve enormous, exceptionally fresh fish dishes—don't miss the seafood salad and chowder—and provide guests with a pager if there's a long wait for a table. Stroll along the waterfront until the beep lets you know your table's ready. Hugely popular, Brophy Bros. can be crowded and loud, especially on weekend evenings. Ⓢ *Average main: $22* ⊠ *119 Harbor Way, off Shoreline Dr.* ☎ *805/966–4418* ⊕ *www.brophybros.com.*

SEAFOOD

$ ╳ **Flavor of India.** Feast on authentic
INDIAN northern Indian dishes like tandoori
chicken, lamb biryani, and a host
of curries at this local favorite in a
residential neighborhood. Best bets
include the combination dinners
served in a traditional Indian tray and
the all-you-can-eat lunch buffet ($9).
⑤ *Average main: $13* ⊠ *3026 State
St., at De La Vina St.* ☎ *805/682–
6561* ⊕ *www.flavorofindiasb.com*
⊘ *Closed Sun.*

$$$ ╳ **The Hungry Cat.** The hip Santa
SEAFOOD Barbara sibling of a famed Holly-
wood eatery, run by chefs David
Lentz and his wife Suzanne Goin,
dishes up savory seafood in a small
but lively nook in the downtown

arts district. Feast on sea urchin, addictive peel-and-eat shrimp, and
creative cocktails made from farmers' market fruits and veggies. A busy
nightspot on weekends, the Cat also awakens for a popular brunch on
Sunday. Night or day, come early or be prepared for a wait. ⑤ *Average
main: $30* ⊠ *1134 Chapala St., near W. Figueroa St.* ☎ *805/884–4701*
⊕ *www.thehungrycat.com* ⊘ *Closed Mon. Sept.–April.*

$ ╳ **La Super-Rica.** Praised by Julia Child, this food stand on the east side
MEXICAN of town serves some of the spiciest and most authentic Mexican dishes
between Los Angeles and San Francisco. Fans fill up on the soft tacos
served with yummy spicy or mild sauces and legendary beans. Three
specials are offered daily. Portions are on the small side; order sev-
eral dishes and share. ⑤ *Average main: $10* ⊠ *622 N. Milpas St., at
Alphonse St.* ☎ *805/963–4940* ▭ *No credit cards* ⊘ *Closed Wed.*

$$$ ╳ **Olio e Limone.** Sophisticated Italian cuisine (with an emphasis on Sic-
ITALIAN ily) is served at this restaurant near the Arlington Center. The juicy
veal chop is popular, but surprises abound here; be sure to try unusual
dishes such as ribbon pasta with quail and sausage in a mushroom
ragout, or the duck ravioli. Tables are placed close together, so this may
not be the best spot for intimate conversations. Next door is the more
casual Olio Pizzeria, a combination pizzeria and wine bar. ⑤ *Average
main: $30* ⊠ *17 W. Victoria St., at State St.* ☎ *805/899–2699* ⊕ *www.
olioelimone.com* ⊘ *No lunch Sun.*

$$$ ╳ **Palace Grill.** Mardi Gras energy, team-style service, lively music, and
SOUTHERN great food have made the Palace a Santa Barbara icon. Acclaimed for its
Cajun and creole dishes such as blackened redfish and jambalaya with
dirty rice, the Palace also serves Caribbean fare, including a delicious
coconut-shrimp dish. If you're spice-phobic, you can choose pasta, soft-
shell crab, or filet mignon. Be prepared to wait for a table on Friday and
Saturday nights (when reservations are taken for a 5:30 seating only),
though the live entertainment and free appetizers, sent out front when
the line is long, will whet your appetite for the feast to come. ⑤ *Aver-*

age main: $29 ⊠ 8 E. Cota St., at State St. ☎ 805/963–5000 ⊕ www. palacegrill.com.

$$$
ECLECTIC
✕ **Roy.** Owner-chef Leroy Gandy serves a fixed-price dinner (selections $25 and $30)—a real bargain—that includes a small salad, fresh soup, homemade organic bread, and a rotating selection of contemporary American main courses. If you're lucky, the entrée choices might include grilled local fish with a mandarin beurre blanc, or bacon-wrapped filet mignon. You can also choose from an à la carte menu of inexpensive appetizers and entrées, plus local wines. Roy is a favorite spot for late-night dining—it's open until midnight and has a full bar. $ *Average main: $25 ⊠ 7 W. Carrillo St., near State St.* ☎ *805/966–5636 ⊕ www.restaurantroy.com ⊗ No lunch.*

$$$$
AMERICAN
Fodor'sChoice
★
✕ **The Stonehouse.** The elegant Stonehouse is inside a century-old granite former farmhouse at the San Ysidro Ranch resort. Executive chef Matt Johnson creates outstanding regional cuisine centered around herbs and veggies from the on-site garden and top-quality local ingredients. The menu changes constantly but typically includes favorites such as crab cake with persimmon relish appetizer and local spiny lobster with mascarpone risotto. Dine on the radiant-heated ocean-view deck with stone fireplace, next to a fountain under a canopy of loquat trees, or in the romantic, candlelit dining room overlooking a creek. The Plow & Angel pub, downstairs, offers more casual bistro fare. $ *Average main: $48 ⊠ 900 San Ysidro La., off San Ysidro Rd., Montecito* ☎ *805/565–1700 ⊕ www. sanysidroranch.com* ⚲ *Reservations essential ⊗ No lunch Sun.–Wed.*

$$$
AMERICAN
✕ **Wine Cask.** A reinvention of a same-named local favorite that closed a few years back, the Wine Cask serves bistro-style meals—many of them made with ingredients from a nearby farmers' market—in a comfortable and classy dining room. The dishes are paired with wines from Santa Barbara's most extensive wine list. The more casual bar-café, Intermezzo, across the courtyard, serves pizzas, salads, small plates, wines, and cocktails and is open late. $ *Average main: $29 ⊠ El Paseo, 813 Anacapa St., at E. De La Guerra St.* ☎ *805/966–9463 ⊕ www.winecask. com* ⚲ *Reservations essential.*

> **BEST VIEWS**
>
> Drive along Alameda Padre Serra, a hillside road that begins near the mission and continues to Montecito, to feast your eyes on spectacular views of the city and the Santa Barbara Channel.

2

WHERE TO STAY

For expanded reviews, facilities, and current deals, visit Fodors.com.

$$$$
RESORT
▦ **Bacara Resort & Spa.** A luxury resort with four restaurants and a 42,000-square-foot spa and fitness center with 36 treatment rooms, the Bacara provides a gorgeous setting for relaxing retreats. **Pros:** serene natural setting; nature trails; first-rate spa; three zero-edge pools. **Cons:** pricey; not close to downtown; sand on beach not pristine enough for some. $ *Rooms from: $450 ⊠ 8301 Hollister Ave., Goleta* ☎ *805/968–0100, 877/422–4245 toll-free reservations ⊕ www.bacararesort.com* ⬦ *306 rooms, 45 suites* ⊚| *No meals.*

$$$$ **Canary Hotel.** The only full-service hotel in the heart of downtown,
HOTEL this Kimpton property blends a casual, beach-getaway feel with urban
sophistication. **Pros:** easy stroll to museums, shopping, dining; friendly,
attentive service; adjacent fitness center. **Cons:** across from transit center; some rooms feel cramped. ⑤ *Rooms from: $450* ✉ *31 W. Carrillo
St.* ☎ *805/884–0300, 877/468–3515* ⊕ *www.canarysantabarbara.com*
↩ *77 rooms, 20 suites* ⦿*No meals.*

$$$$ **El Encanto.** Stunning vistas magically unfold from nearly every vantage point at this luxurious getaway in the hills above Mission Santa
HOTEL Barbara. **Pros:** serene residential setting; authentic historic restoration;
lavish spa facility. **Cons:** long walk to downtown; pricey. ⑤ *Rooms
from: $595* ✉ *800 Alvarado Pl.* ☎ *805/845–5800, 800/393–5315*
⊕ *elencanto.com* ↩ *70 rooms, 22 suites* ⦿*No meals.*

$$$$ **Four Seasons Resort The Biltmore Santa Barbara.** Surrounded by lush,
RESORT perfectly manicured gardens and across from the beach, Santa Barbara's
Fodor'sChoice grande dame has long been a favorite for quiet, California-style luxury.
★ **Pros:** first-class resort; historic Santa Barbara character; personal service; steps from the beach. **Cons:** back rooms are close to train tracks;
expensive. ⑤ *Rooms from: $425* ✉ *1260 Channel Dr.* ☎ *805/969–2261,
800/332–3442* ⊕ *www.fourseasons.com/santabarbara* ↩ *181 rooms,
26 suites* ⦿*No meals.*

$$ **Franciscan Inn.** Part of this Spanish-Mediterranean motel, a block
HOTEL from the harbor and West Beach, dates back to the 1920s. **Pros:** walking distance from waterfront and harbor; family-friendly; great value.
Cons: busy lobby; pool can be crowded. ⑤ *Rooms from: $160* ✉ *109
Bath St.* ☎ *805/963–8845, 800/663–5288* ⊕ *www.franciscaninn.com*
↩ *48 rooms, 5 suites* ⦿*Breakfast.*

$$$ **Hotel Indigo.** The closest hotel to the train station, artsy Hotel Indigo
HOTEL (opened in 2012) is a great choice for travelers who appreciate contemporary art and want easy access to dining, nightlife, and the beach. **Pros:**
multilingual staff; a block from Stearns Wharf; great value for location.
Cons: showers only (no bathtubs); train whistles early morning; rooms
on small side. ⑤ *Rooms from: $189* ✉ *121 State St.* ☎ *805/966–6586,
877/270–1392 toll-free* ⊕ *www.indigosantabarbara.com* ↩ *41 rooms*
⦿*No meals.*

$$$ **Hyatt Santa Barbara.** A complex of four buildings on three landscaped
HOTEL acres, the Hyatt provides an appealing lodging option in a prime location right across from East Beach. **Pros:** steps from the beach; many
room types and rates; walk to the zoo and waterfront shuttle. **Cons:**
motelish vibe; busy area in summer. ⑤ *Rooms from: $229* ✉ *1111 E.
Cabrillo Blvd.* ☎ *805/882–1234, 800/643–1994* ⊕ *www.santabarbara.
hyatt.com* ↩ *171 rooms, 3 suites* ⦿*No meals.*

$ **Motel 6 Santa Barbara Beach.** A half block from East Beach amid fancier hotels sits this basic but comfortable motel, which was the first
HOTEL Motel 6 in existence. **Pros:** very close to zoo and beach; friendly staff;
clean. **Cons:** no frills; motel-style rooms; no breakfast. ⑤ *Rooms from:
$119* ✉ *443 Corona Del Mar Dr.* ☎ *805/564–1392, 800/466–8356*
⊕ *www.motel6.com* ↩ *51 rooms* ⦿*No meals.*

$$$$
RESORT
Fodor's Choice
★
🏨 **San Ysidro Ranch.** At this romantic hideaway on an historic property in the Montecito foothills—where John and Jackie Kennedy spent their honeymoon and Oprah sends her out-of-town visitors—guest cottages are scattered among groves of orange trees and flower beds. **Pros:** ultimate privacy; surrounded by nature; celebrity hangout; pet-friendly. **Cons:** very expensive; too remote for some. ⑤ *Rooms from: $695* ✉ *900 San Ysidro La., Montecito* ☎ *805/565–1700, 800/368–6788* ⊕ *www. sanysidroranch.com* ➥ *23 rooms, 4 suites, 14 cottages* 🍽 *No meals* ⌇ *2-day minimum stay on weekends, 3 days on holiday weekends.*

$$$$
B&B/INN
Fodor's Choice
★
🏨 **Simpson House Inn.** If you're a fan of traditional B&Bs, this property, with its beautifully appointed Victorian main house and acre of lush gardens, is for you. **Pros:** impeccable landscaping; walking distance from everything downtown; ranked among the nation's top B&Bs. **Cons:** some rooms in main building are small; two-night minimum stay on weekends. ⑤ *Rooms from: $255* ✉ *121 E. Arrellaga St.* ☎ *805/963– 7067, 800/676–1280* ⊕ *www.simpsonhouseinn.com* ➥ *11 rooms, 4 cottages* 🍽 *Breakfast.*

$$$$
B&B/INN
🏨 **Spanish Garden Inn.** A half block from the Presidio in the heart of downtown, this elegant Spanish-Mediterranean retreat celebrates Santa Barbara style, from the tile floors, wrought-iron balconies, and exotic plants, to the original art by local plein-air artists. **Pros:** walking distance from downtown; classic Spanish-Mediterranean style; caring staff. **Cons:** far from the beach; not much here for kids. ⑤ *Rooms from: $369* ✉ *915 Garden St.* ☎ *805/564–4700, 866/564–4700* ⊕ *www. spanishgardeninn.com* ➥ *23 rooms* 🍽 *Breakfast.*

NIGHTLIFE AND THE ARTS

Most major hotels present entertainment nightly during the summer and on weekends all year. The bar, club, and live-music scene centers on lower State Street, between the 300 and 800 blocks. The thriving arts district, with theaters, restaurants, and cafés, starts around the 900 block of State Street and continues north to the Arlington Center for the Performing Arts, in the 1300 block. The proximity to the University of California at Santa Barbara assures an endless stream of visiting artists and performers. To see what's scheduled around town, pick up a copy of the free weekly *Santa Barbara Independent* newspaper or visit its website ⊕ *www.independent.com.*

NIGHTLIFE

Blue Agave. Leather couches, a crackling fire in chilly weather, a cigar balcony, and pool tables draw a fancy crowd here for good food and designer martinis. ✉ *20 E. Cota St., near State St.* ☎ *805/899–4694* ⊕ *www.blueagavesb.com.*

Dargan's. Lively Dargan's pub has pool tables, great draft beers and Irish whiskeys, and serves a full menu of traditional Irish dishes. ✉ *18 E. Ortega St., at Anacapa St.* ☎ *805/568–0702* ⊕ *darganssb.com.*

James Joyce. A good place to have a few beers and while away an evening, the James Joyce sometimes hosts folk and rock performers. ✉ *513 State St., at W. Haley St.* ☎ *805/962–2688* ⊕ *www.sbjamesjoyce.com.*

Joe's Cafe. Steins of beer accompany hearty bar food at Joe's. It's a fun, if occasionally rowdy, collegiate scene. ⊠ *536 State St., at E. Cota St.* ☎ *805/966–4638* ⊕ *www.joescafesb.com.*

Lucky's. A slick sports bar attached to an upscale steak house owned by the maker of Lucky Brand dungarees, this place attracts hip patrons hoping to see and be seen. ⊠ *1279 Coast Village Rd., near Olive Mill Rd., Montecito* ☎ *805/565–7540* ⊕ *www.luckys-steakhouse.com/bar.*

Milk & Honey. Artfully prepared tapas, coconut-mango mojitos, and exotic cocktails lure trendy crowds to swank M&H, despite high prices and a reputation for inattentive service. ⊠ *30 W. Anapamu St., at State St.* ☎ *805/275–4232* ⊕ *milknhoneytapas.com.*

SOhO. A hip restaurant, bar, and music club, SOhO books bands, from jazz to blues to rock, nightly. ⊠ *1221 State St., at W. Victoria St.* ☎ *805/962–7776* ⊕ *www.sohosb.com.*

THE ARTS

Arlington Theatre. This Moorish-style auditorium hosts events during the two-week Santa Barbara International Film Festival every winter and presents touring performers and films throughout the year. ⊠ *1317 State St., at Arlington Ave.* ☎ *805/963–4408* ⊕ *www.thearlingtontheatre.com.*

Granada. A restored, modernized landmark that dates to 1924, the Granada hosts Broadway touring shows and dance, music, and other cultural events. ⊠ *1214 State St., at E. Anapamu St.* ☎ *805/899–2222 box office* ⊕ *www.granadasb.org.*

Lobero Theatre. A state landmark, the Lobero hosts community theater groups and touring professionals. ⊠ *33 E. Canon Perdido St., at Anacapa St.* ☎ *805/963–0761* ⊕ *www.lobero.com.*

Santa Barbara International Film Festival. The hottest ticket in town in late January, the 11-day festival attracts film enthusiasts and major stars to various downtown venues for screenings, industry panels, and celebrity tributes. ⊕ *sbiff.org.*

SPORTS AND THE OUTDOORS

BICYCLING

Cabrillo Bike Lane. The level, two-lane, 3-mile Cabrillo Bike Lane passes the Santa Barbara Zoo, the Andree Clark Bird Refuge, beaches, and the harbor. There are restaurants along the way, and you can stop for a picnic along the palm-lined path looking out on the Pacific.

Wheel Fun Rentals. You can rent bikes, quadricycles, and skates here. ⊠ *23 E. Cabrillo Blvd.* ☎ *805/966–2282* ⊕ *www.wheelfunrentalssb.com.*

BOATS AND CHARTERS

Channel Islands Outfitters. A full-service paddle sports center in the harbor, this outfit rents kayaks, stand-up paddleboards, surfboards, boogie boards, and watersports gear, and conducts guided tours and excursions. ⊠ *117 B Harbor Way, off Shoreline Dr.* ☎ *805/899–4925* ⊕ *www. channelislandso.com.*

Condor Express. From SEA Landing, the *Condor Express*, a 75-foot high-speed catamaran, whisks up to 149 passengers toward the Channel Islands on dinner cruises, whale-watching excursions, and pelagic-bird trips. ☏ 805/882–0088, 888/779–4253 ⊕ condorexpress.com.

Santa Barbara Sailing Center. The center offers sailing instruction, rents and charters sailboats, and organizes dinner and sunset champagne cruises, island excursions, and whale-watching trips. ✉ Santa Barbara Harbor launching ramp ☏ 805/962–2826, 800/350–9090 ⊕ www.sbsail.com.

FAMILY **Santa Barbara Water Taxi.** Children beg to ride Lil' Toot, a cherry yellow water taxi that cruises from the harbor to Stearns Wharf and back again. The fare for kids is $1 each way. ✉ Santa Barbara Harbor and Stearns Wharf ☏ 805/896–6900, 888/316–9363 ⊕ sbwatertaxi.com ☒ $4 one-way ☉ June–Aug., daily noon–6, Sept.–May, Fri.–Sun. noon–sunset.

Truth Aquatics. Truth runs kayaking, paddle boarding, hiking, and scuba excursions to the National Marine Sanctuary and Channel Islands National Park. ✉ Departures from SEA Landing, Santa Barbara Harbor ☏ 805/962–1127 ⊕ www.truthaquatics.com.

> **EARTH DAY**
>
> In 1969, 200,000 gallons of crude oil spilled into the Santa Barbara Channel, causing an immediate outcry from residents. The day after the spill, Get Oil Out (GOO) was established; the group helped lead the successful fight for legislation to limit and regulate offshore drilling in California. The Santa Barbara spill also spawned Earth Day, which is still celebrated across the nation today.

GOLF

Sandpiper Golf Club. This super-scenic course sits on the ocean bluffs and combines stunning views with a challenging game. ✉ 7925 Hollister Ave., 14 miles north of downtown off U.S. 101 ☏ 805/968–1541 ⊕ www.sandpipergolf.com ⚑ 18 holes. 7,000 yds. Par 72. Greens fees: $139/$159 ☞ Facilities: Driving range, putting green, pitching area, golf carts, rental clubs, pro shop, lessons, restaurant, bar.

Santa Barbara Golf Club. The well-maintained public club—among the area's most affordable—occupies a hilltop site with sweeping views of mountains, ocean, and islands. Hotel guests receive greens-fee discounts by showing a room keycard. ✉ 3500 McCaw Ave., at Las Positas Rd. ☏ 805/687–7087 ⊕ www.thesantabarbaragolfclub.com ⚑ 18 holes. 6,037 yds. Par 70. Greens fees: $48/$58 ☞ Facilities: Driving range, putting green, pitching area, golf carts, pull carts, rental clubs, pro shop, lessons, restaurant, bar.

TENNIS

Many hotels in Santa Barbara have courts.

City of Santa Barbara Parks and Recreation Department. The City of Santa Barbara Parks and Recreation Department operates public courts with lighted play until 9 pm weekdays. You can purchase day permits ($8) at the courts, or call the department. ☏ 805/564–5573 ⊕ www.santabarbaraca.gov/visitor.

Municipal Tennis Center. The center's 12 hard courts include an enclosed stadium court and three that are lighted on weekdays. ⊠ *1414 Park Pl., near Salinas St. and U.S. 101.*

Pershing Park. The eight lighted courts here are available for public play after 5 pm weekdays and all day on weekends and some holidays. ⊠ *100 Castillo St., near Cabrillo Blvd.*

SHOPPING

SHOPPING AREAS

Brinkerhoff Avenue. Antiques and gift shops are clustered in restored Victorian buildings on Brinkerhoff Avenue. ⊠ *2 blocks west of State St., at W. Cota St.*

El Paseo. Shops, art galleries, and studios share the courtyard and gardens of El Paseo, a historic arcade. ⊠ *Canon Perdido St., between State and Anacapa Sts.*

State Street. State Street, roughly between Cabrillo Boulevard and Sola Street, is a shopper's paradise. Chic malls, quirky storefronts, antiques emporia, elegant boutiques, and funky thrift shops abound here. You can shop on foot or ride a battery-powered trolley (50¢) that runs between the waterfront and the 1300 block. Nordstrom and Macy's anchor **Paseo Nuevo**, an open-air mall in the 700 block. Shops, restaurants, galleries, and fountains line the tiled walkways of **La Arcada**, a small complex of landscaped courtyards in the 1100 block designed by famed architect Myron Hunt in 1926.

Summerland. Serious antiques hunters head southeast of Santa Barbara to Summerland, which is full of shops and markets. Several good ones are along Lillie Avenue and Ortega Hill Road. ⊠ *Summerland.*

BOOKS

Book Den. Bibliophiles have browsed for new, used, and out-of-print books at this independent shop since 1933. ⊠ *15 E. Anapamu St., at State St.* ☎ *805/962–3321* ⊕ *www.bookden.com.*

Chaucer's Bookstore. This well-stocked independent shop is a favorite bookstore of many residents. ⊠ *Loreto Plaza, 3321 State St., at Los Positas Rd.* ☎ *805/682–6787* ⊕ *www.chaucersbooks.com.*

CLOTHING

Diani. This upscale, European-style women's boutique dresses clients in designer clothing from around the world. A sibling shoe shop is nearby. ⊠ *1324 State St., at Arlington Ave.* ☎ *805/966–3114, 805/966–7175 shoe shop* ⊕ *www.dianiboutique.com.*

Surf N Wear's Beach House. This shop carries surf clothing, gear, and collectibles; it's also the home of Santa Barbara Surf Shop and the exclusive local dealer of Surfboards by Yater. ⊠ *10 State St., at Cabrillo Blvd.* ☎ *805/963–1281* ⊕ *surfnwear.com.*

Wendy Foster. This store sells casual-chic women's fashions. ⊠ *833 State St., at W. Canon Perdido St.* ☎ *805/966–2276* ⊕ *www.wendyfoster.com.*

WORD OF MOUTH

"California's Central Coast is a popular place for surfers and windsurfers. If you're not up to surfing yourself, spend some time relaxing on the beach and watching the action." —photo by Doreen Miller, Fodors.com member

EN ROUTE If you choose to drive north via U.S. 101 without detouring to the Solvang/Santa Ynez area, you will drive right past some good beaches. In succession from east to west, **El Capitan, Gaviota, and Refugio state beaches** all have campsites, picnic tables, and fire rings.

SANTA BARBARA COUNTY

Residents refer to the glorious 30-mile stretch of coastline from Carpinteria to Gaviota as the South Coast. The Santa Ynez Mountains divide the county geographically; U.S. 101 passes through a mountain tunnel leading inland. Northern Santa Barbara County used to be known for its sprawling ranches and strawberry and broccoli fields. Today its 100-plus wineries and 22,000 acres of vineyards dominate the landscape from the Santa Ynez Valley in the south to Santa Maria in the north. The hit film *Sideways* was filmed almost entirely in the North County Wine Country; when the movie won Golden Globe and Oscar awards in 2005, it sparked national and international interest in visits to the region.

GETTING HERE AND AROUND

Two-lane Highway 154 over San Marcos Pass is the shortest and most scenic route from Santa Barbara into the Santa Ynez Valley. You can also drive along U.S. 101 north 43 miles to Buellton, then 7 miles east through Solvang to Santa Ynez. Santa Ynez Valley Transit shuttle buses serve Santa Ynez, Los Olivos, Ballard, Solvang, and Buellton. COLT Wine Country Express buses connect Lompoc, Buellton, and Solvang weekdays except holidays.

ESSENTIALS

Bus Contacts COLT Wine Country Express ✉ *Lompoc* ☎ *805/736–7666* ⊕ *www.cityoflompoc.com/transit.* **Santa Ynez Valley Transit** ☎ *805/688–5452* ⊕ *www.syvt.com.*

Visitor Information Santa Barbara County Vintners' Association ☎ *805/688–0881* ⊕ *www.sbcountywines.com.* **The Santa Barbara Conference & Visitors Bureau** ☎ *805/966–9222* ⊕ *www.santabarbaraca.com.* **Santa Ynez Valley Visitors Association** ☎ *805/686–0053* ⊕ *www.visitthesantaynezvalley.com.*

SANTA YNEZ

31 miles north of Goleta.

Founded in 1882, the tiny town of Santa Ynez still has many of its original frontier buildings. You can walk through the three-block downtown area in a few minutes, shop for antiques, and hang around the old-time saloon. At some of the eponymous valley's best restaurants, you just might bump into one of the celebrities who own nearby ranches.

GETTING HERE AND AROUND

Take Highway 154 over San Marcos Pass or U.S. 101 north 43 miles to Buellton, then 7 miles east.

WHERE TO EAT AND STAY

For expanded reviews, facilities, and current deals, visit Fodors.com.

\$\$ ✕ **Trattoria Grappolo.** Authentic Italian fare, an open kitchen, and festive,
ITALIAN family-style seating make this trattoria equally popular with celebrities
from Hollywood and ranchers from the Santa Ynez Valley. Thin-crust
pizza, homemade ravioli, risottos, and seafood linguine are among
the menu favorites. The noise level tends to rise in the evening, so
this isn't the best spot for a romantic getaway. $ *Average main: $22*
⊠ *3687-C Sagunto St.* ☎ *805/688–6899* ⊕ *www.trattoriagrappolo.com*
⊗ *No lunch Mon.*

\$\$\$ 🏠 **Santa Ynez Inn.** This posh two-story Victorian inn in downtown
B&B/INN Santa Ynez was built from scratch in 2002, and the owners have
furnished all the rooms with authentic historical pieces. **Pros:** near
restaurants; unusual antiques; spacious rooms. **Cons:** high price for
location; building not historic. $ *Rooms from: $245* ⊠ *3627 Sagunto
St.* ☎ *805/688–5588, 800/643–5774* ⊕ *www.santaynezinn.com* ⇲ *20
rooms* ⎟⍥⎟ *Breakfast.*

LOS OLIVOS

4 miles north of Santa Ynez.

This pretty village was once on Spanish-built El Camino Real (Royal
Road) and later a stop on major stagecoach and rail routes. It's so sleepy
today, though, that the movie *Return to Mayberry* was filmed here.
Tasting rooms, art galleries, antiques stores, and country markets line
Grand Avenue and intersecting streets for several blocks.

GETTING HERE AND AROUND

From U.S. 101 north or south, exit at Highway 154 and drive east about
8 miles. From Santa Barbara, travel 30 miles northwest on Highway 154.

EXPLORING

Carhartt Vineyard Tasting Room. Pinot Noir, Sauvignon Blanc, and Syrah
are among the small-lot vintages produced by owner-winemakers Mike
and Brooke Carhartt. You'll often find the duo pouring at their intimate tasting room. ⊠ *2990-A Grand Ave.* ☎ *805/693–5100* ⊕ *www.
carharttvineyard.com* 🍷 *Tasting $10* ⊗ *Daily 11–5:30.*

Daniel Gehrs Tasting Room. Heather Cottage, built in the early 1900s as
a doctor's office, houses winemaker Gehrs's tasting room, where you
can sample Chenin Blanc, Pinot Gris, Pinot Noir, and other small-lot
wines. ⊠ *2939 Grand Ave.* ☎ *805/693–9686* ⊕ *www.danielgehrswines.
com* 🍷 *Tasting $10* ⊗ *Sun.–Thurs. 11–5, Fri. and Sat. 11–6.*

Firestone Vineyard. Heirs to the Firestone tire fortune developed (but no
longer own) this winery known for Chardonnay, Gewürztraminer, Merlot, Riesling, and Syrah—and for the fantastic valley views from its tasting room and picnic area. The tour here is highly informative. ⊠ *5000
Zaca Station Rd., off U.S. 101* ☎ *805/688–3940* ⊕ *www.firestonewine.
com* 🍷 *Tastings $10–$15* ⊗ *Daily 10–5; tours 11:15, 1:15, and 3:15.*

WHERE TO EAT AND STAY

For expanded hotel reviews, visit Fodors.com.

$$ ✕ **Los Olivos Cafe.** Part wine store and part social hub, this café that
AMERICAN   appeared in the film *Sideways* focuses on wine-friendly fish, pasta, and
meat dishes, plus salads, pizzas, and burgers. Don't miss the home-
made muffuletta and olive tapenade spreads. Other house favorites
include an artisanal cheese plate, baked Brie with honey-roasted hazel-
nuts, and braised short ribs with smashed potatoes. $ *Average main:*
$21 ✉ *2879 Grand Ave.* ☎ *805/688–7265, 888/946–3748* ⊕ *www.*
losolivoscafe.com.

$$$ ✕ **Sides Hardware & Shoes: A Brothers Restaurant.** After renovating a his-
AMERICAN   toric Los Olivos storefront, brothers Matt and Jeff Nichols shuttered
their highly popular Brothers restaurant and began serving comfort
food prepared with their inimitable panache. Popular breakfast dishes
include cooked-to-order beignets and eggs Benedict with house-made
bacon steak. The Kobe-style burgers make a great lunch, and the dinner
favorites include fried chicken and lamb sirloin with herbed gnocchi.
$ *Average main: $24* ✉ *2375 Alamo Pintado Ave.* ☎ *805/688–4820*
⊕ *www.brothersrestaurant.com* ☽ *No breakfast Mon.–Thurs.*

$$$ ⊞ **The Ballard Inn & Restaurant.** Set among orchards and vineyards in
B&B/INN   the tiny town of Ballard, 2 miles south of Los Olivos, this inn makes
an elegant Wine Country escape. **Pros:** exceptional food; attentive
staff; secluded. **Cons:** some baths could use updating. $ *Rooms from:*
$245 ✉ *2436 Baseline Ave., Ballard* ☎ *805/688–7770, 800/638–2466*
⊕ *www.ballardinn.com* ⇆ *15 rooms* ◐ *Breakfast.*

$$$$ ⊞ **Fess Parker's Wine Country Inn and Spa.** This luxury inn includes an
B&B/INN   elegant, tree-shaded French country–style main building and an equally
attractive annex across the street with a pool and day spa. **Pros:** conve-
nient wine-touring base; walking distance from restaurants and galler-
ies; well-appointed rooms. **Cons:** pricey; staff attention is inconsistent.
$ *Rooms from: $345* ✉ *2860 Grand Ave.* ☎ *805/688–7788, 800/446–*
2455 ⊕ *www.fessparker.com* ⇆ *15 rooms, 4 suites* ◐ *Breakfast.*

SOLVANG

5 miles south of Los Olivos.

You'll know you've reached the town of Solvang when the architecture
suddenly changes to half-timber buildings and windmills. The town
was settled in 1911 by Danish educators—the flatlands and rolling
green hills reminded them of home—and even today, more than half
the residents are of Danish descent. Although Solvang has attracted
tourists for decades, it's lately become more sophisticated, with gal-
leries, upscale restaurants, and wine-tasting rooms. To get your bear-
ings, park your car in one of the free public lots and stroll the town.
The visitor center on Copenhagen Drive has walking-tour maps (also
available online). The "Sweet Treats" tour covers the town's bakeries,
confectionary stores, and ice-cream parlors, all well worth investigating.

GETTING HERE AND AROUND

Highway 246 West (Mission Drive) traverses Solvang, connecting with U.S. 101 to the west and Highway 154 to the east. Alamo Pintado Road connects Solvang with Ballard and Los Olivos to the north. Santa Ynez Valley Transit shuttle buses run between Solvang and nearby towns.

TOURS

Segway Tours of Solvang. After a brief training session, tool around Solvang on a guided tour via electric-powered personal balancing transporters. This company also offers off-road wine tours, twilight adventures, and trips high up Figueroa Mountain. ☎ 805/688–8899 ⊕ *www. advoutwest.com* ☒ *$85* ⊙ *Nov.–Mar.: tours at 11, 1, and 3. Apr.–Oct.: tours at 9, 11, 1, 3, and 5.*

ESSENTIALS

Visitor Information Solvang Conference & Visitors Bureau ☒ *1639 Copenhagen Dr., at 2nd St.* ☎ *805/688–6144* ⊕ *www.solvangusa.com.*

EXPLORING

Lafond Winery and Vineyards. A rich, concentrated Pinot Noir is the main attention-getter at this winery that also produces noteworthy Chardonnays and Syrahs. Bottles with Lafond's SRH (Santa Rita Hills) label are an especially good value. ☒ *6855 Santa Rosa Rd., west off U.S. 101 Exit 139, Buellton* ☎ *805/688–7921* ⊕ *www.lafondwinery.com* ☒ *Tasting $5 weekdays, $10 weekends (includes logo glass)* ⊙ *Daily 10–5.*

Mission Santa Inés. The mission holds an impressive collection of paintings, statuary, vestments, and Chumash and Spanish artifacts in a serene bluff-top setting. Take a self-guided tour through the museum, sanctuary, and gardens. ☒ *1760 Mission Dr., at Alisal Rd.* ☎ *805/688–4815* ⊕ *www.missionsantaines.org* ☒ *$5* ⊙ *Daily 9–4:30.*

Rideau Vineyard. This winery celebrates its locale's rich history—the King of Spain himself once owned this land, and the tasting room occupies a former guest ranch inn—but fully embraces the area's wine-making present. The Rhone varietals Marsanne, Mourvèdre, Roussanne, Syrah, and Viognier are the specialty. ☒ *1562 Alamo Pintado Rd., 2 miles north of Hwy. 246* ☎ *805/688–0717* ⊕ *www.rideauvineyard.com* ☒ *Tasting $12* ⊙ *Sun.–Fri. 11–4:30, Sat. 11–5.*

WHERE TO EAT

$$
SCANDINAVIAN
✕ **Bit O' Denmark.** Perhaps the most authentic Danish eatery in Solvang, this restaurant occupies an old-beam building that was a church until 1929. Two specialties of the house are the *Frikadeller* (meatballs with pickled red cabbage, potatoes, and thick brown gravy) and the *Medisterpølse* (Danish beef and pork sausage with cabbage). ⑤ *Average main: $18* ☒ *473 Alisal Rd., at Park Way* ☎ *805/688–5426* ⊕ *www. bitodenmark.com.*

$$$
AMERICAN
✕ **The Hitching Post II.** You'll find everything from grilled artichokes to quail at this casual eatery just outside Solvang, but most people come for the wonderful smoky Santa Maria–style barbecue. Be sure to try a glass of owner-chef-winemaker Frank Ostini's signature Highliner Pinot Noir, a star in the film *Sideways.* ⑤ *Average main: $29* ☒ *406 E. Hwy. 246, off U.S. 101* ☎ *805/688–0676* ⊕ *www.hitchingpost2.com* ⊙ *No lunch.*

$$$

AMERICAN

Fodor's Choice

★

✕ **Root 246.** The chefs at this chic restaurant tap local purveyors and shop for organic ingredients at farmers' markets before deciding on the day's menu. Depending on the season, you might feast on local squid with sweet baby prawns, rib-eye steak grilled over an oak fire and served with root vegetable gratin, or rhubarb and polenta upside-down cake. The well-informed wait staff can recommend regional wines from the restaurant's 1,800-bottle selection. Root 246's gorgeous design incorporates wood, stone, tempered glass, and leather elements in several distinct areas, including a slick 47-seat dining room, a more casual bar with sofas and chairs, and a hip lounge. ⑤ *Average main: $26* ⊠ *Hotel Corque, 420 Alisal Rd., at Molle Way* ☎ *805/686–8681* ⊕ *www.root-246.com* ☺ *No lunch. Closed Mon. and Tues.*

WHERE TO STAY

For expanded hotel reviews, visit Fodors.com.

$$$$

RESORT

▥ **Alisal Guest Ranch and Resort.** Since 1946 this 10,000-acre ranch has been popular with celebrities and plain folk alike. **Pros:** Old West atmosphere; tons of activities; ultraprivate. **Cons:** isolated; cut off from high-tech world; some units aging. ⑤ *Rooms from: $515* ⊠ *1054 Alisal Rd.* ☎ *805/688–6411, 800/425–4725* ⊕ *www.alisal.com* ⇆ *36 rooms, 37 suites* ❙⓪❙ *Some meals.*

$$$

HOTEL

▥ **Hotel Corque.** Sleek, stunning Hotel Corque—the Santa Ynez Valley's largest hotel—provides a full slate of upscale amenities. **Pros:** front desk staff are trained concierges; short walk to shops, tasting rooms and restaurants; smoke-free. **Cons:** no kitchenettes or laundry facilities; pricey. ⑤ *Rooms from: $239* ⊠ *400 Alisal Rd.* ☎ *805/688–8000, 800/624–5572* ⊕ *www.hotelcorque.com* ⇆ *122 rooms, 10 suites* ❙⓪❙ *No meals.*

$$

B&B/INN

▥ **Petersen Village Inn.** The canopy beds here are plush, the bathrooms small but sparkling, and the rates include a European buffet breakfast. **Pros:** in the heart of Solvang; easy parking; comfy beds. **Cons:** on highway; some find atmosphere too traditional. ⑤ *Rooms from: $150* ⊠ *1576 Mission Dr.* ☎ *805/688–3121, 800/321–8985* ⊕ *www.peterseninn.com* ⇆ *37 rooms, 1 suite* ❙⓪❙ *Breakfast.*

$

B&B/INN

▥ **Solvang Gardens Lodge.** The lush gardens with fountains and waterfalls and the cheery English-country-theme rooms make for a peaceful retreat just a few blocks—but worlds away—from Solvang's main tourist area. **Pros:** homey; family-friendly; colorful gardens. **Cons:** some rooms tiny; some need upgrades. ⑤ *Rooms from: $119* ⊠ *293 Alisal Rd.* ☎ *805/688–4404, 888/688–4404* ⊕ *www.solvanggardens.com* ⇆ *16 rooms, 8 suites* ❙⓪❙ *Breakfast.*

LOMPOC

20 miles west of Solvang.

Known as the flower-seed capital of the world, Lompoc is blanketed with vast fields of brightly colored flowers that bloom from May through August.

2

GETTING HERE AND AROUND
Driving is the easiest way to get to Lompoc. From Santa Barbara, follow U.S. 101 north to Highway 1 exit off Gaviota Pass, or Highway 246 west at Buellton.

ESSENTIALS
Visitor Information Lompoc Valley Chamber of Commerce & Visitors Bureau ⊠ *111 S. I St., at Hwy. 246* ☎ *805/736–4567, 800/240–0999* ⊕ *www.lompoc.com.*

EXPLORING

FAMILY **La Purisima Mission State Historic Park.** The state's most fully restored mission, founded in 1787, stands in a stark and still remote location that powerfully evokes the lives and isolation of California's Spanish settlers. Docents lead tours every afternoon, and vivid displays illustrate the secular and religious activities that formed mission life. Special events include crafts demonstrations by costumed docents. ⊠ *2295 Purisima Rd., off Hwy. 246* ☎ *805/733–3713* ⊕ *www.lapurisimamission.org* ⊠ *$6 per vehicle* ☉ *Daily 9–5; tour daily at 1.*

Lompoc Wine Ghetto. Nearly 20 laid-back tasting rooms with premium wines from the surrounding Santa Rita Hills appellation—among them Loring Wine Company and Longoria (both known for stellar Pinot Noirs)—cluster in a downtown industrial park. ⊠ *Take 7th St. north from Hwy. 1/246 and turn east (right), 200 N. 9th St.* ☎ *805/735–8937* ⊕ *www.lompocghetto.com* ⊠ *Tasting fee varies, some free* ☉ *Most rooms open Thurs.–Sun., 11 or noon until 4 or 5; some also Mon. and by appointment* ☉ *Closed Tues. and Wed.*

EN ROUTE **Guadalupe-Nipomo Dunes Preserve.** This spectacular preserve straddles the coast for 18 miles between Santa Barbara and San Luis Obispo counties. California's largest and most ecologically diverse dune system, this habitat shelters more than 200 species of birds as well as sea otters, black bears, bobcats, coyotes, and deer. The 1,500-foot Mussel Rock is the highest beach dune in the western states. About two dozen movies have been filmed here, including Cecil B. DeMille's 1923 silent epic *The Ten Commandments.* At the **Dunes Center** (⊠ *1065 Guadalupe Street*) in downtown Guadalupe, you can get nature information and view an exhibit about DeMille's movie set. ⊠ *Hwy. 166/Main St., west 5 miles from Hwy. 1, Guadalupe* ☎ *805/343–2455* ⊕ *www.dunescenter. org* ⊠ *Free* ☉ *Dunes daily sunrise–sunset; center weekends 10–4, weekdays by appointment.*

SAN LUIS OBISPO COUNTY

San Luis Obispo County's pristine landscapes and abundant wildlife areas, especially those around Morro Bay and Montaña de Oro State Park, have long attracted nature lovers. In the south, Pismo Beach and other coastal towns have great sand and surf; inland, a booming wine region stretches from the Edna, Arroyo Grande, and Avila valleys and Nipomo in the south to Paso Robles in the north. With historical attractions, a photogenic downtown, and busy shops and restaurants, the college town of San Luis Obispo is at the heart of the county.

GETTING HERE AND AROUND

San Luis Obispo Regional Transit Authority operates buses in San Luis Obispo and serves Paso Robles as well as Pismo Beach and other coastal towns.

ESSENTIALS

Transportation Contact San Luis Obispo Regional Transit Authority ☎ 805/541–2228 ⊕ www.slorta.org.

Visitor Information Visit San Luis Obispo County ✉ 811 El Capitan Way, Suite 200, San Luis Obispo ☎ 805/541–8000, 800/634–1414 ⊕ www.visitsanluisobispocounty.com. **WineCoastCountry** ✉ San Luis Obispo ⊕ winecoastcountry.com.

PISMO BEACH

40 miles north of Lompoc.

About 20 miles of sandy shoreline—nicknamed the Bakersfield Riviera for the throngs of vacationers who come here from the Central Valley—begins at the town of Pismo Beach. The southern end of town runs along sand dunes, some of which are open to cars and off-road vehicles. Sheltered by the dunes, a grove of eucalyptus trees attracts thousands of migrating monarch butterflies from November through February. A long, broad beach fronts the center of town, where a municipal pier extends into the sea at the foot of shop-lined Pomeroy Street. To the north, hotels and homes perch atop chalky oceanfront cliffs. Fewer than 10,000 people live in this quintessential surfer haven, but Pismo Beach has a slew of hotels and restaurants with great views of the Pacific Ocean.

GETTING HERE AND AROUND

Pismo Beach straddles both sides of U.S. 101. If you're coming from the south and have time for a scenic drive, exit U.S. 101 in Santa Maria and take Highway 166 west for 8 miles to Guadalupe and follow Highway 1 north 16 miles to Pismo Beach. South County Area Transit (SCAT; ⊕ *www.slorta.org*) buses run throughout San Luis Obispo and connect the city with nearby towns. On summer weekends, the free Avila Trolley extends service to Pismo Beach.

ESSENTIALS

Visitor Information California Welcome Center ✉ 333 Five Cities Dr. ☎ 805/773–7924. **Pismo Beach Visitors Information Center** ✉ Dolliver St./ Hwy. 1, at Hinds Ave. ☎ 800/443–7778 visitor center, 805/773–7034 visitor information ⊕ classiccalifornia.com ⊙ Weekdays 9–5, Sat. 11–4.

BEACHES

Fodor'sChoice **Oceano Dunes State Vehicular Recreation Area.** Part of ⇨ *Guadalupe-*
★ *Nipomo Dunes,* the largest and most ecologically diverse dunes complex in California, this popular state park offers a huge array of activities in a 3,600-acre coastal playground. This is one of the only places in California where you can drive or ride off-highway vehicles on the beach and sand dunes (1,500 acres are open to OHVs.) Hike, ride horses, kiteboard, join a Hummer tour, or rent an ATV or a dune buggy

and cruise up the white-sand peaks for spectacular views. At **Oso Flaco Lake Nature Area**—3 miles west of Highway 1 on Oso Flaco Road—a 1½-mile boardwalk over the lake leads to a platform with views up and down the coast. Leashed dogs are allowed in much of the park except Oso Flaco and Pismo Dunes Natural Reserve. **Amenities:** food and drink; lifeguards (seasonal); parking (fee); showers; toilets; water sports. **Best for:** sunset; surfing; swimming; walking. ⊠ *West end of Pier Ave., off Hwy. 1, Oceano* ☎ *805/473–7220* ⊕ *www.parks.ca.gov* ⊠ *$5 per vehicle* ⊗ *Daily 6 am–11 pm; Oso Flaco Lake sunrise to sunset.*

> **VOLCANOES?**
>
> Those funny looking, sawed-off peaks along the drive from Pismo Beach to Morro Bay are the Seven Sisters—a series of ancient volcanic plugs. Morro Rock, the northernmost sibling and a state historic monument, is the most famous and photo-graphed of the clan.

Pismo State Beach. One of the busiest state beaches in the county, Pismo offers a slew of activities along the 17-mile western edges of Oceano, Grover Beach, and Pismo Beach. Hike, surf, golf, ride horses, swim, fish in a lagoon or off the pier, and dig for Pismo clams. From November through late February, one of the nation's largest colonies of monarch butterflies rests in a grove of eucalyptus and Monterey pine trees (Hwy. 1, 3 miles north of Pier Ave.). Entrances to day use parking areas are off Hwy. 1 (milepost 8) and at Pier Ave. in the south. **Facilities:** food and drink; lifeguards (seasonal); parking (fee); showers; toilets; water sports. **Best for:** sunset; surfing; swimming; walking. ⊠ *555 Pier Ave., Oceano* ☎ *805/489–1869* ⊕ *www.parks.ca.gov* ⊠ *Day use $5 per vehicle if parking at the beach* ⊗ *Day use 6 am–11 pm.*

WHERE TO EAT

$$$
SEAFOOD
✕ **Cracked Crab.** This traditional New England–style crab shack imports fresh seafood daily from Australia, Alaska, and the East Coast. Fish is line-caught, much of the produce is organic, and everything is made from scratch. For a real treat, don a bib and sample a bucket of steamed shellfish with Cajun sausage, potatoes, and corn on the cob, all dumped right onto your table. ⑤ *Average main: $24* ⊠ *751 Price St., near Main St.* ☎ *805/773–2722* ⊕ *www.crackedcrab.com* ⚞ *Reservations not accepted.*

$$
ITALIAN
✕ **Giuseppe's Cucina Italiana.** The classic flavors of southern Italy are highlighted at this lively downtown spot. Most recipes originate from Bari, a seaport on the Adriatic; the menu includes breads and pizzas baked in the wood-burning oven, hearty dishes such as osso buco and lamb, and homemade pastas. The wait for a table can be long at peak dinner hours, but sometimes an accordion player gets the crowd singing. ⑤ *Average main: $22* ⊠ *891 Price St., at Pismo Ave.* ☎ *805/773–2870* ⊕ *www.giuseppesrestaurant.com* ⚞ *Reservations not accepted* ⊗ *No lunch weekends.*

$
SEAFOOD
✕ **Splash Café.** Folks stand in line down the block for clam chowder served in a sourdough bread bowl at this wildly popular seafood stand. You can also order beach food such as fresh steamed clams, burgers, and fried calamari at the counter (no table service). The grimy, cramped,

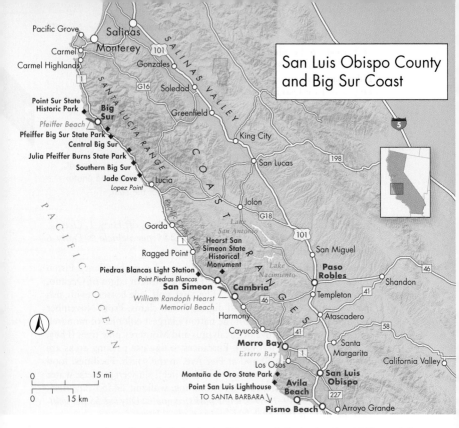

San Luis Obispo County and Big Sur Coast

but cheery hole-in-the-wall is open daily for lunch and dinner (plus a rock-bottom basic breakfast), but closes early on weekday evenings during low season. $ *Average main: $8* ⊠ *197 Pomeroy St., at Cypress St.* ☎ *805/773–4653* ⊕ *www.splashcafe.com.*

WHERE TO STAY

For expanded hotel reviews, visit Fodors.com.

$$$ 🖼 **The Cliffs Resort.** Perched dramatically on an oceanfront cliff, this
RESORT full-service resort is surrounded by lawns and palm trees; the pool, with a cascading fountain, overlooks the sea. **Pros:** beach access via short downhill path; oceanfront restaurant and lounge; blufftop walking trail. **Cons:** not close to downtown; rooms near service areas and elevator can be noisy. $ *Rooms from: $189* ⊠ *2757 Shell Beach Rd.* ☎ *805/773–5000, 800/826–7827* ⊕ *www.cliffsresort.com* 🛏 *160 rooms* ⫶⃝ *No meals.*

$$$ 🖼 **Pismo Lighthouse Suites.** Each of the well-appointed two-room, two-
HOTEL bath suites at this oceanfront resort has a private balcony or patio. **Pros:** lots of space for families and groups; nice pool area. **Cons:** not easy to walk to main attractions; some units are next to busy road. $ *Rooms from: $239* ⊠ *2411 Price St.* ☎ *805/773–2411, 800/245–2411* ⊕ *www. pismolighthousesuites.com* 🛏 *70 suites* ⫶⃝ *Breakfast.*

$$$ ▦ **Sea Venture Resort.** The bright, homey rooms at this hotel all have
HOTEL fireplaces and featherbeds; most have balconies with private hot tubs,
and some have beautiful ocean views. **Pros:** on the beach; excellent
food; romantic rooms. **Cons:** touristy area; some rooms and facilities
are beginning to age; dark hallways. Ⓢ *Rooms from: $179* ⊠ *100 Ocean
View Ave.* ☎ *805/773–4994, 800/662–5545* ⊕ *www.seaventure.com*
⤳ *50 rooms* ♚ *No meals.*

$ ▦ **Shell Beach Inn.** Just 2½ blocks from the beach, this basic but cozy
HOTEL motor court is a great bargain for the area. **Pros:** walking distance from
the beach; clean rooms; friendly and dependable service. **Cons:** sits on
a busy road; small rooms; tiny pool. Ⓢ *Rooms from: $100* ⊠ *653 Shell
Beach Rd.* ☎ *805/773–4373, 800/549–4727* ⊕ *www.shellbeachinn.com*
⤳ *10 rooms* ♚ *No meals.*

AVILA BEACH

4 miles north of Pismo Beach.

FAMILY Because the village of Avila Beach and the sandy, cove-front shoreline
for which it's named face south into the Pacific Ocean, they get more
sun and less fog than any other stretch of coast in the area. With its
fortuitous climate and protected waters, Avila's public beach draws sun-
bathers and families; weekends are very busy. Downtown Avila Beach
has a lively seaside promenade and some shops and hotels, but for real
local color, head to the far end of the cove and watch the commercial
fishers offload their catch on the old Port San Luis wharf. A few sea-
food shacks and fish markets do business on the pier while sea lions
congregate below. On Friday from mid-April through mid-September,
a fish and farmers' market livens up the beach area with music, fresh
local produce and seafood, and children's activities.

GETTING HERE AND AROUND

Exit U.S. 101 at Avila Beach Drive and head 3 miles west to reach the
beach. The free Avila Trolley operates weekends year-round, plus Friday
afternoon/evenings from April to September. The minibuses connect
Avila Beach and Port San Luis to Shell Beach, with multiple stops along
the way. Service extends to Pismo Beach in summer.

ESSENTIALS

Visitor Information Avila Beach Tourism Alliance ⊕ *visitavilabeach.com.*

EXPLORING

Avila Beach Sea Life Center. You'll learn all about local marine plants
and animals from the hands-on exhibits at this science center next
to the main beach. ⊠ *50 San Juan St., at 1st St., off Avila Beach Dr.*
☎ *805/595–7280* ⊕ *www.sealifecenter.org* ☜ *$5* ⊙ *Weekends 10–4.*

Avila Valley Barn. An old-fashioned, family-friendly country store jam-
packed with local fruits and veggies, prepared foods and gift items,
Avila Valley Barn also gives visitors a chance to experience rural Ameri-
can traditions. Pet farm animals, savor home-made ice cream and pies;
on weekends, ride a hay wagon out to the fields to pick your own farm-
fresh produce. ⊠ *560 Avila Beach Dr., San Luis Obispo* ☎ *805/595–
2810, 805/595–2816* ⊕ *avilavalleybarn.com* ⊙ *Daily 9–5.*

FAMILY   **Point San Luis Lighthouse.** Docents lead guided hikes along scenic Pecho
Coast Trail (3½ miles round-trip) to see the historic 1890 lighthouse
and its rare Fresnel lens. If you'd prefer a lift out to the lighthouse,
join a trolley tour. Both tours require reservations. ⊠ *Point San
Luis, 1¾ miles west of Harford Pier, Port San Luis* ☎ *805/540–5771*
⊕ *www.sanluislighthouse.org* ✉ *Trolley tours $20; hikes free ($5 to
enter lighthouse)* ⊙ *Trolley tours Sat. noon, 1, and 2; hikes Wed.
and Sat. at 9.*

BEACHES

FAMILY   **Avila State Beach.** At the edge of a sunny cove next to downtown shops
and restaurants, Avila's ½-mile stretch of white sand lures scores of
beachgoers on weekends year-round and daily in summer. It's especially family-friendly, with a playground, barbecue and picnic tables,
volleyball and basketball courts, and lifeguards on watch in summer
and on many holiday weekends. Limited free beachfront parking is
available but fills up fast; otherwise park in a nearby pay lot ($5 for
the day, $1 after 4 pm). Dogs are not allowed on the beach from 10
to 5. **Facilities:** food and drink; lifeguards (seasonal); parking; showers; toilets; water sports. **Best for:** sunset; surfing; swimming; walking. ⊠ *Avila Beach Dr., at 1st St.* ⊕ *www.visitavilabeach.com* ✉ *Free*
⊙ *6 am–10 pm.*

WHERE TO STAY

For expanded hotel reviews, visit Fodors.com.

$$$$ ⚇ **Avila La Fonda.** Modeled after a village in early California's Mexican
HOTEL   period, Avila La Fonda surrounds guests with rich jewel tones, fountains, and upscale comfort. **Pros:** one-of-a-kind theme and artwork;
flexible room combinations; a block from the beach. **Cons:** pricey;
most rooms don't have an ocean view. ⑤ *Rooms from: $300* ⊠ *101
San Miguel St.* ☎ *805/595–1700* ⊕ *www.avilalafondahotel.com* ⮐ *28
rooms, 1 suite* ⦿ *No meals.*

$$$$ ⚇ **Avila Lighthouse Suites.** Families, honeymooners, and business travel-
HOTEL   ers all find respite at this two-story, all-suite luxury hotel. **Pros:** directly
across from sand; easy walk to restaurants and shops; free underground
parking. **Cons:** noise from passersby can be heard in room; some
ocean-view rooms have limited vistas. ⑤ *Rooms from: $289* ⊠ *550
Front St.* ☎ *805/627–1900, 800/372–8452* ⊟ *805/627–1909* ⊕ *www.
avilalighthousesuites.com* ⮐ *54 suites* ⦿ *Breakfast.*

$$ ⚇ **Sycamore Mineral Springs Resort.** This wellness resort's hot mineral
RESORT   springs bubble up into private outdoor tubs on an oak-and-sycamore-
forest hillside. **Pros:** great place to rejuvenate; nice hiking; incredible
spa services. **Cons:** rooms vary in quality; 2½ miles from the beach.
⑤ *Rooms from: $169* ⊠ *1215 Avila Beach Dr., San Luis Obispo*
☎ *805/595–7302, 800/234–5831* ⊕ *www.sycamoresprings.com* ⮐ *26
rooms, 50 suites* ⦿ *No meals.*

SAN LUIS OBISPO

8 miles north of Avila Beach.

About halfway between San Francisco and Los Angeles, San Luis Obispo—nicknamed SLO—spreads out below gentle hills and rocky extinct volcanoes. Its main appeal lies in its architecturally diverse, pedestrian-friendly downtown, which bustles with shoppers, restaurant goers, and students from California Polytechnic State University, known as Cal Poly. On Thursday evenings from 6 to 9 a farmers' market fills Higuera Street with local produce, entertainment, and food stalls. A Saturday-morning market in the Cost Plus World Market parking lot includes organic meats and wine tasting.

The wineries of the Edna Valley and Arroyo Grande Valley wine regions lie just south of the city off Highway 227, the parallel (to the east) Orcutt Road, and connecting roads. Wine-touring maps are available around town.

GETTING HERE AND AROUND

U.S. 101/Highway 1 traverses the city for several miles. From the north, Highway 1 merges with U.S. 101 when it reaches the city limits. SLO City Transit buses operate daily; Regional Transit Authority (SLORTA) buses connect with north county towns. The Downtown Trolley provides evening service to the city's hub every Thursday, on Fridays from June to early September, and on Saturdays from April through October.

ESSENTIALS

Visitor Information San Luis Obispo Chamber of Commerce ⊠ *895 Monterey St.* ☎ *805/781–2777* ⊕ *www.visitslo.com.* **San Luis Obispo City Visitor Information** ⊕ *www.sanluisobispovacations.com.* **San Luis Obispo Vintners Association** ☎ *805/541–5868* ⊕ *www.slowine.com.*

EXPLORING
TOP ATTRACTIONS

FAMILY **History Center of San Luis Obispo County.** Across the street from the old Spanish mission, the center presents exhibits that survey topics such as Native American life in the county, the California ranchos, and the impact of railroads. On the center's website are links to free downloadable video-podcast walking tours of historic San Luis Obispo. ⊠ *696 Monterey St., at Broad St.* ☎ *805/543–0638* ⊕ *historycenterslo.org* ⌦ *Free* ⊙ *Daily 10–4.*

Mission San Luis Obispo de Tolosa. Sun-dappled Mission Plaza fronts the fifth mission established in 1772 by Franciscan friars. A small museum exhibits artifacts of the Chumash Indians and early Spanish settlers. ⊠ *751 Palm St., at Chorro St.* ☎ *805/543–6850* ⊕ *www.missionsanluisobispo.org* ⌦ *$3* ⊙ *Early Mar.–early Nov. daily 9–5, early Nov.–early Mar. daily 9–4.*

San Luis Obispo Museum of Art. The permanent collection here focuses on the artistic legacy of the Central Coast. Temporary exhibits include traditional and cutting-edge arts and crafts by Central Coast, national, and international artists. ⊠ *Mission Plaza, 1010 Broad St., at Monterey St.* ☎ *805/543–8562* ⊕ *www.sloma.org* ⊙ *Early Sept.–early July, Wed.–Mon. 11–5; early July–early Sept., daily 11–5.*

2

WORTH NOTING

Baileyana Winery. A refurbished 1909 schoolhouse serves as tasting room for this winery that produces mostly Chardonnays, Pinot Noirs, and Syrahs. Four sister wineries share the facility. ⊠ *5828 Orcutt Rd., at Righetti Rd.* ☎ *805/269–8200* ⊕ *www. baileyana.com* 🍷 *Tasting $8–$12* ⊙ *Daily 10–5.*

> **DEEP ROOTS**
>
> Way back in the 1700s, the Spanish padres who accompanied Father Junípero Serra planted grapevines from Mexico along California's Central Coast, and began using European wine-making techniques to turn the grapes into delectable vintages.

Claiborne & Churchill. An eco-friendly winery built from straw bales, C&C makes small lots of exceptional Alsatian-style wines such as dry Riesling and Gewürztraminer, plus Pinot Noir and Chardonnay. ⊠ *2649 Carpenter Canyon Rd., at Price Canyon Rd.* ☎ *805/544–4066* ⊕ *www.claibornechurchill. com* 🍷 *Tasting $10* ⊙ *Daily 11–5.*

Edna Valley Vineyard. For sweeping valley views and crisp Sauvignon Blancs and Chardonnays, head to the modern tasting bar here. The reserve tasting ($15) is the best option. ⊠ *2585 Biddle Ranch Rd., off Edna Rd.* ☎ *805/544–5855* ⊕ *www.ednavalleyvineyard.com* 🍷 *Tastings $10–$15* ⊙ *Daily 10–5.*

Old Edna. This peaceful, 2-acre site once *was* the town of Edna. Browse local art and antiques, peek at the vintage 1897 and 1908 farmhouse cottages, taste wines, pick up sandwiches at the gourmet deli, and stroll along Old Edna Lane. ⊠ *1655 Old Price Canyon Rd., at Hwy. 227* ☎ *805/544–8062* ⊕ *www.oldedna.com.*

FAMILY **San Luis Obispo Children's Museum.** Activities at this delightful facility geared to kids under age eight include an "imagination-powered" elevator that transports visitors to a series of underground caverns. Elsewhere, simulated lava and steam sputter from an active volcano. Kids can pick rubber fruit at a farmers' market and race in a fire engine to fight a fire. ⊠ *1010 Nipomo St., at Monterey St.* ☎ *805/545–5874* ⊕ *www.slocm.org* 🍷 *$8* ⊙ *May–Aug.: Mon.–Wed. 10–3, Thurs.–Sat. 10–5, Sun. and some holidays 11–5; Sept.–Apr.: Tues. and Wed. 10–3, Thurs.–Sat. 10–5, Sun. and some holidays 1–5.*

Fodor'sChoice **Talley Vineyards.** Acres of Chardonnay and Pinot Noir, plus smaller lots
★ of Sauvignon Blanc, Syrah, and other varietals blanket Talley's mountain-ringed dell in the Arroyo Grande Valley. The estate tour, worth a splurge, includes wine and cheese, a visit to an 1860s adobe, and barrel-room tastings of upcoming releases. ⊠ *3031 Lopez Dr., off Orcutt Rd., Arroyo Grande* ☎ *805/489–0446* ⊕ *www.talleyvineyards.com* 🍷 *Tastings $8–$12; basic tour $15, estate tour $25 or $35 (includes tasting)* ⊙ *Daily 10:30–4:30; tour by appointment.*

WHERE TO EAT

$$ ✕ **Big Sky Café.** Family-friendly Big Sky turns local and organically
ECLECTIC grown ingredients into global dishes, starting with breakfast. Just pick your continent: Brazilian churrasco chicken breast, Thai catfish, North African vegetable stew, Maryland crab cakes. Vegetarians have

ample choices. ⑤ *Average main: $17* ✉ *1121 Broad St., at Higuera St.* ☎ *805/545–5401* ⊕ *www.bigskycafe.com* ⚫ *Reservations not accepted.*

$$
ITALIAN

✕ **Buona Tavola.** Homemade pasta with river shrimp in a creamy tomato sauce and porcini-mushroom risotto are among the northern Italian dishes served at this casual spot. Daily fresh fish and salad specials and an impressive wine list attract a steady stream of regulars. In good weather you can dine on the flower-filled patio. The Paso Robles branch is equally enjoyable. ⑤ *Average main: $22* ✉ *1037 Monterey St., near Osos St.* ☎ *805/545–8000* ⊕ *www.btslo.com* ☉ *No lunch weekends.*

$$
NORTHERN
ITALIAN

✕ **Café Roma.** Authentic northern Italian cuisine is the specialty at this Railroad Square restaurant. Beneath a mural of Tuscany or out on the covered patio, you can dine on squash-filled ravioli with a sage-and-butter sauce or filet mignon glistening with porcini butter and a Pinot Noir reduction. ⑤ *Average main: $19* ✉ *1020 Railroad Ave., at Osos St.* ☎ *805/541–6800* ⊕ *www.caferomaslo.com* ☉ *No lunch weekends.*

$$$
INTERNATIONAL

✕ **Luna Red.** A spacious, contemporary space with a festive outdoor patio, this restaurant near Mission Plaza serves creative tapas and cocktails. The small plates include wild-boar spare ribs, prawns adobo, skillet cornbread with honey-masala butter, and potstickers filled with red cabbage and carrot and served with a coconut-curry sauce. Among the large plates are saffron-onion shellfish stew and roasted chicken with dried summer fruit. ⑤ *Average main: $25* ✉ *1023 Chorro St., Monterey St.* ☎ *805/540–5243* ⊕ *www.lunaredslo.com.*

$
SOUTHERN

✕ **Mo's Smokehouse BBQ.** Barbecue joints abound on the Central Coast, but this one excels. Various Southern-style sauces season tender hickory-smoked ribs and shredded-meat sandwiches. Sides such as baked beans, coleslaw, homemade potato chips, and garlic bread extend the pleasure. ⑤ *Average main: $11* ✉ *1005 Monterey St., at Osos St.* ☎ *805/544–6193* ⊕ *www.smokinmosbbq.com.*

$$
ECLECTIC

✕ **Novo Restaurant & Lounge.** In the colorful dining room or on the large creek-side deck, this animated downtown eatery will take you on a culinary world tour. The salads, small plates, and entrées come from nearly every continent. The wine and beer list also covers the globe and includes local favorites. ⑤ *Average main: $19* ✉ *726 Higuera St., at Broad St.* ☎ *805/543–3986* ⊕ *www.novorestaurant.com.*

$$
MODERN
AMERICAN

✕ **Sidecar.** This hip eatery serves farm-fresh meals and small plates along with classic cocktails and 16 mostly local beers on tap. Burger patties made from grass-fed beef, free-range chicken, or housemade veggies are served on a brioche bun with inventive sauces such as bacon-maple ketchup. The menu includes many vegetarian and vegan options, among them the raw "green zebra" lasagna, made of basil-pistachio pesto, tomato sauce, and pine-nut "ricotta." Happy hour (daily from 4 to 6) and Sunday brunch (live jazz, five types of eggs Benedict) are very popular here. ⑤ *Average main: $16* ✉ *1127 Broad St., at Marsh St.* ☎ *805/540–5340* ⊕ *sidecarslo.com.*

2

WHERE TO STAY

For expanded hotel reviews, visit Fodors.com.

$$$
HOTEL
⚏ **Apple Farm.** Decorated to the hilt with floral bedspreads and water-colors by local artists, this Wine Country–theme hotel is highly popular. **Pros:** flowers everywhere; convenient to Cal Poly and U.S. 101; creek-side setting. **Cons:** hordes of tourists during the day; too floral for some people's tastes. ⑤ *Rooms from: $219* ⊠ *2015 Monterey St.* ☎ *800/255–2040, 805/544-2040* ⊕ *www.applefarm.com* 🛏 *104 rooms* ¶⊙¶ *No meals.*

$$$
B&B/INN
⚏ **Garden Street Inn.** From this fully restored 1887 Italianate Queen Anne downtown, you can walk to many restaurants and attractions. **Pros:** classic B&B; convenient location; wine-and-cheese reception. **Cons:** city noise filters into some rooms; not great for families. ⑤ *Rooms from: $182* ⊠ *1212 Garden St.* ☎ *805/545–9802, 800/488–2045* ⊕ *www.gardenstreetinn.com* 🛏 *9 rooms, 4 suites* ¶⊙¶ *Breakfast.*

$$$
HOTEL
⚏ **Madonna Inn.** From its rococo bathrooms to its pink-on-pink frou-frou steak house, the Madonna Inn is fabulous or tacky, depending on your taste. **Pros:** fun, one-of-a-kind experience. **Cons:** rooms vary widely; must appreciate kitsch. ⑤ *Rooms from: $189* ⊠ *100 Madonna Rd.* ☎ *805/543–3000, 800/543–9666* 🖶 *805/543–1800* ⊕ *www.madonnainn.com* 🛏 *106 rooms, 4 suites* ¶⊙¶ *No meals.*

$
HOTEL
⚏ **Peach Tree Inn.** Extra touches such as rose gardens, a porch with rockers, and flower-filled vases turn this modest, family-run motel into a relaxing creek-side haven. **Pros:** bargain rates; cozy rooms; decent breakfast. **Cons:** near a busy intersection; basic amenities. ⑤ *Rooms from: $99* ⊠ *2001 Monterey St.* ☎ *805/543–3170, 800/227–6396* ⊕ *www.peachtreeinn.com* 🛏 *37 rooms* ¶⊙¶ *Breakfast.*

$$
B&B/INN
⚏ **Petit Soleil.** A cobblestone courtyard, country-French custom furnishings, and Gallic music piped through the halls evoke a Provençal mood at this cheery inn on upper Monterey Street's motel row. **Pros:** French details throughout; scrumptious breakfasts; cozy rooms. **Cons:** sits on a busy avenue; cramped parking. ⑤ *Rooms from: $169* ⊠ *1473 Monterey St.* ☎ *805/549–0321, 800/676–1588* ⊕ *www.psslo.com* 🛏 *15 rooms, 1 suite* ¶⊙¶ *Breakfast.*

NIGHTLIFE AND THE ARTS

NIGHTLIFE

SLO's club scene is centered on Higuera Street off Monterey Street.

Koberl at Blue. A trendy crowd hangs out at this upscale restaurant's slick bar to sip on exotic martinis and the many local and imported beers and wines. ⊠ *998 Monterey St., at Osos St.* ☎ *805/783–1135* ⊕ *www.epkoberl.com.*

Linnaea's Cafe. A mellow java joint, Linnaea's sometimes hosts poetry readings, as well as blues, jazz, and folk music performances. ⊠ *1110 Garden St., at Higuera St.* ☎ *805/541–5888* ⊕ *linnaeas.com.*

MoTav. Chicago-style MoTav draws crowds with good pub food and live entertainment in a turn-of-the-20th-century setting (complete with antique U.S. flags and a wall-mounted moose head). ⊠ *725 Higuera St., at Broad St.* ☎ *805/541–8733* ⊕ *www.motherstavern.com.*

SLO Brew. Handcrafted microbrews, live music most nights, and a rooftop patio make for a winning combination at this downtown watering hole and restaurant. ⊠ *736 Higuera St.* ☎ *805/543–1843* ⊕ *www. slobrewingco.com.*

THE ARTS

Performing Arts Center, San Luis Obispo. The center hosts live theater, dance, and music performances by artists from around the world. ⊠ *Cal Poly, 1 Grand Ave., off U.S. 101* ☎ *805/756–7222, 805/756–2787 box office, 888/233–2787 toll-free* ⊕ *www.pacslo.org.*

OFF THE BEATEN PATH

Montaña de Oro State Park. West of San Luis Obispo, Los Osos Valley Road winds past farms and ranches to this state park whose miles of nature trails traverse rocky shoreline, wild beaches, and hills overlooking dramatic scenery. Check out the tide pools, watch the waves roll into the bluffs, and picnic in the eucalyptus groves. From Montaña de Oro you can reach Morro Bay by following the coastline along South Bay Boulevard 8 miles through the quaint residential villages of Los Osos and Baywood Park. ⊠ *West about 13 miles from downtown San Luis Obispo on Madonna Rd., to Los Osos Valley Rd., to Pecho Valley Rd.; to continue on to Morro Bay, backtrack east to Los Osos Valley Rd., then head north on S. Bay Blvd., and west on State Park Rd.* ☎ *805/528–0513, 805/772–7434* ⊕ *www.parks.ca.gov.*

MORRO BAY

14 miles north of San Luis Obispo.

Commercial fishermen slog around Morro Bay in galoshes, and beatup fishing boats bob in the bay's protected waters. Nature-oriented activities take center stage here: kayaking, hiking, biking, fishing, and wildlife watching around the bay and national marine estuary and along the state beach.

GETTING HERE AND AROUND

From U.S. 101 south or north, exit at Highway 1 in San Luis Obispo and head west. Scenic Highway 1 passes through the eastern edge of town. From Atascadero, two-lane Highway 41 West treks over the mountains to Morro Bay. San Luis Obispo RTA Route 12 buses travel year-round between Morro Bay, San Luis Obispo, Cayucos, Cambria, San Simeon, and Hearst Castle. The Morro Bay Shuttle picks up riders throughout the town from Friday through Monday in summer ($1.25 one-way, $3 day pass).

ESSENTIALS

Visitor Information Morro Bay Visitors Center ⊠ *255 Morro Bay Blvd., at Morro Ave.* ☎ *805/225–1633, 800/231–0592* ⊕ *www.morrobay.org* ☾ *Daily 9–5.*

EXPLORING

Embarcadero. The center of the action on land is the Embarcadero, where vacationers pour in and out of souvenir shops and seafood restaurants and stroll or bike along the scenic half-mile Harborwalk to Morro Rock. From here, you can get out on the bay in a kayak or tour boat. ⊠ *On waterfront from Beach St. to Tidelands Park.*

FAMILY **Morro Bay State Park Museum of Natural History.** Entertaining interactive exhibits at this spiffy museum explain the natural environment and how to preserve it—in the bay and estuary and on the rest of the planet. ⊠ *State Park Rd., south of downtown* ☎ *805/772–2694* ⊕ *www.ccnha. org/morrobay* ⊠ *$3* ☉ *Daily 10–5.*

Morro Rock. At the mouth of Morro Bay stands 576-foot-high Morro Rock, one of nine small volcanic peaks, or morros, in the area. A short walk leads to a breakwater, with the harbor on one side and crashing ocean waves on the other. You may not climb the rock, where endangered falcons and other birds nest. Sea lions and otters often play in the water below the rock. ⊠ *Northern end of Embarcadero.*

WHERE TO EAT

$$ ✕ **Dorn's Original Breakers Cafe.** This restaurant overlooking the harbor has
SEAFOOD satisfied local appetites since 1948. In addition to straight-ahead dishes such as cod or shrimp fish-and-chips or calamari steaks sautéed in butter and wine, Dorn's serves breakfast. ⑤ *Average main: $22* ⊠ *801 Market Ave., at Morro Bay Blvd.* ☎ *805/772–4415* ⊕ *www.dornscafe.com.*

$ ✕ **Taco Temple.** This family-run diner serves some of the freshest food
SOUTHWESTERN around. The seafood-heavy menu includes salmon burritos, superb fish tacos with mango salsa, and other dishes hailing from somewhere between California and Mexico. This gem is in a supermarket parking lot on the frontage road parallel to Highway 1, just north of the Highway 41 junction. ⑤ *Average main: $14* ⊠ *2680 Main St., at Elena St.* ☎ *805/772–4965* ⚠ *Reservations not accepted* ▭ *No credit cards* ☉ *Closed Tues.*

$$$ ✕ **Windows on the Water.** Diners at this second-floor restaurant view the
SEAFOOD sunset through giant picture windows. Meanwhile, fresh fish and other dishes based on local ingredients emerge from the wood-fired oven in the open kitchen, and oysters on the half shell beckon from the raw bar. The California-centric wine list includes about 20 selections poured by the glass. ⑤ *Average main: $28* ⊠ *699 Embarcadero, at Pacific St.* ☎ *805/772–0677* ⊕ *www.windowsmb.com* ☉ *No lunch.*

WHERE TO STAY

For expanded hotel reviews, visit Fodors.com.

$$$ ⊞ **Anderson Inn.** Friendly, personalized service and an oceanfront set-
B&B/INN ting keep loyal patrons returning to this Embarcadero inn. **Pros:** walk
Fodor'sChoice to restaurants and sights; nice rooms; attentive service. **Cons:** not low-
★ budget; waterfront area can get crowded. ⑤ *Rooms from: $239* ⊠ *897 Embarcadero* ☎ *805/772–3434, 866/950–3434 toll-free reservations* ⊕ *www.andersoninnmorrobay.com* ⤵ *8 rooms* ⊚ *No meals.*

$$$ ⊞ **Cass House.** In tiny Cayucos, 4 miles north of Morro Bay, a ship-
B&B/INN ping pioneer's 1867 home is now a luxurious B&B surrounded by rose
Fodor'sChoice and other gardens. **Pros:** historic property; some ocean views; excellent
★ meals. **Cons:** away from nightlife and attractions; not good for families. ⑤ *Rooms from: $200* ⊠ *222 N. Ocean Ave., Cayucos* ☎ *805/995–3669* ⊕ *casshouseinn.com* ⤵ *5 rooms* ⊚ *Breakfast.*

$$ ⊞ **Embarcadero Inn.** The rooms at this waterfront hotel are cheery
HOTEL and welcoming, and many have fireplaces. **Pros:** right across from the waterfront. **Cons:** tiny lobby; no pool. ⑤ *Rooms from: $145*

✉ *456 Embarcadero* ☎ *805/772–2700, 800/292–7625* ⊕ *www. embarcaderoinn.com* ⇨ *29 rooms, 4 suites* ⦿ *Breakfast.*

$$
RESORT
⌂ **The Inn at Morro Bay.** Surrounded by eucalyptus trees, this inn abuts a heron rookery and Morro Bay State Park. **Pros:** great for wildlife enthusiasts; stellar views from restaurant and some rooms. **Cons:** some rooms on the small side; birds and seals can wake you early. ⑤ *Rooms from: $169* ✉ *60 State Park Rd.* ☎ *805/772–5651, 800/321–9566* ⊕ *innatmorrobay.com* ⇨ *97 rooms, 1 cottage* ⦿ *No meals.*

SPORTS AND THE OUTDOORS

Kayak Horizons. This outfit rents kayaks and gives lessons and guided tours. ✉ *551 Embarcadero, near Marina St.* ☎ *805/772–6444* ⊕ *www. kayakhorizons.com.*

Sub-Sea Tours. You can view sea life aboard this outfit's glass-bottom boat, watch whales from its catamaran, or rent a kayak or canoe. ✉ *699 Embarcadero* ☎ *805/772–9463* ⊕ *subseatours.com.*

Virg's Landing. Virg's conducts deep-sea-fishing and whale-watching trips. ✉ *1215 Embarcadero* ☎ *805/772–1222* ⊕ *www.virgs.com.*

PASO ROBLES

30 miles north of San Luis Obispo; 25 miles northwest of Morro Bay.

In the 1860s tourists began flocking to this dusty ranching outpost to "take the cure" in a luxurious bathhouse fed by underground mineral hot springs. An Old West town, complete with opera house, emerged, and grand Victorian homes went up, followed in the 20th century by Craftsman bungalows. A 2003 earthquake demolished or weakened several beloved downtown buildings, but historically faithful reconstruction has helped the district retain its character.

More than 200 wineries pepper the wooded hills of Paso Robles west of U.S. 101 and blanket the flatter, more open land on the east side. The region's brutally hot summer days and cool nights yield stellar grapes that produce robust Cabernet Sauvignon, Merlot, Syrah, and Zinfandel. Pinot Noir does well in some of the cooler, more fog-heavy western sections. Chardonnay, Sauvignon Blanc, and Viognier are among stellar white-wine grapes grown here. Small-town friendliness prevails at most wineries, especially smaller ones. Pick up a regional wine-touring map at lodgings, wineries, and attractions around town. Many lodgings pass out coupons good for discount tastings. Most tasting rooms close at 5 pm; many charge a small fee.

But more attracts people to the Paso Robles area than fine wine and fancy tasting rooms. Golfers play the four local courses and spandex-clad bicyclists race along the winding back roads. Down-home and upmarket restaurants, bars, antiques stores, and little shops fill the streets around oak-shaded City Park, where special events of all kinds—custom car shows, an olive festival, Friday-night summer concerts—take place on many weekends. Despite its increasing sophistication, Paso (as the locals call it) more or less remains cowboy country. Each year in late July and early August, the city throws the two-week California Mid-State Fair, complete with livestock auctions, carnival rides, and corn dogs.

2

GETTING HERE AND AROUND

U.S. 101 runs through the city of Paso Robles. Highway 46 West links Paso Robles to Highway 1 and Cambria on the coast. Highway 46 East connects Paso Robles with Interstate 5 and the San Joaquin Valley. Public transit is not convenient for wine touring and sightseeing.

ESSENTIALS

Visitor Information Travel Paso Robles Alliance ⊠ *1225 Park St., near 12th St.* ☎ *888/988–7276, 805/238–0506* ⊕ *www.travelpaso.com.* **Paso Robles Wine Country Alliance** ☎ *805/239–8463* ⊕ *www.pasowine.com.*

EXPLORING

TOP ATTRACTIONS

Eberle Winery. Even if you don't drink wine, stop at Eberle for a fascinating tour of the huge wine caves beneath the vineyards here. Gary Eberle, one of Paso wine's founding fathers, is obsessed with Cabernet Sauvignon. ⊠ *3810 Hwy. 46 E, 3½ miles east of U.S. 101* ☎ *805/238–9607* ⊕ *www.eberlewinery.com* ⌷ *Tasting and tour free* ⊙ *Apr.–Sept. daily 10–6, Oct.–Mar. daily 10–5.*

FAMILY **Estrella Warbirds Museum.** An entertaining homage to fighter planes, flyboys, and flygirls, this museum maintains indoor exhibits about wartime aviation and displays retired specimens (of planes) outdoors and in repair shops. Bonus attraction: a huge building with spruced-up autos, drag racers, and "funny cars." ⊠ *4251 Dry Creek Rd., off Airport Rd., north off Hwy. 46E* ☎ *805/227–0440* ⊕ *www.ewarbirds.org* ⌷ *$10* ⊙ *Thurs.–Sun. 10–4 and Mon. legal holidays.*

Firestone Walker Brewing Company. At this working craft brewery you can sample medal winners such as the Double Barrel Ale and learn about the beer-making process on 30-minute guided tours of the brew house and cellar. ⊠ *1400 Ramada Dr., east side of U.S. 101; exit at Hwy. 46 W/Cambria, but head east* ☎ *805/225–5591* ⊕ *www.firestonebeer. com* ⌷ *Tasting $1.50–$3 per sample, tour free* ⊙ *Daily 10–5; tours on the half hour Fri.–Sun. 10:30–3:30 and Mon.–Thurs. by appointment.*

Justin Vineyards & Winery. Swank Justin built its reputation—and, claim some, the Paso Robles wine region's as well—on Isosceles, a hearty Bordeaux blend, usually of Cabernet Sauvignon, Cabernet Franc, and Merlot. Justin's Cabernet Sauvignon is also well regarded. Tastings here take place in an elegant room; outside are gardens with flowers and grapevines of major varietals. ⊠ *11680 Chimney Rock Rd., 15 miles west of U.S. 101's Hwy 46 E exit; take 24th St. west and follow road (name changes along the way) to Chimney Rock Rd.* ☎ *805/238–6932, 800/726–0049* ⊕ *www.justinwine.com* ⌷ *Tasting $10, tour $10, tour and tasting $15* ⊙ *Daily 10–4:30.*

Fodor's Choice **Pasolivo.** While touring the idyllic west side of Paso Robles, take a break
★ from wine by stopping at Pasolivo. Find out how the artisans here make their Tuscan-style olive oils on a high-tech Italian press, and taste the acclaimed results. ⊠ *8530 Vineyard Dr., west off U.S. 101 (Exit 224) or Hwy. 46 W (Exit 228)* ☎ *805/227–0186* ⊕ *www.pasolivo.com* ⌷ *Free* ⊙ *Daily 11–5.*

River Oaks Hot Springs & Spa. The lakeside spa, on 240 hilly acres near the intersection of U.S. 101 and Highway 46 E, is a great place to relax after wine tasting or festival going. Soak in a private indoor or outdoor hot tub fed by natural mineral springs, or indulge in a massage or facial. ⊠ *800 Clubhouse Dr., off River Oaks Dr.* ☎ *805/238–4600* ⊕ *www. riveroakshotsprings.com* 🖃 *$20–$24 per hr* ⊙ *Tues.–Sun. 9–9.*

Tablas Creek Vineyard. Tucked in the far-west hills of Paso Robles, Tablas Creek Vineyard makes some of the area's finest wine by blending organically grown, hand-harvested Rhône varietals such as Syrah, Grenache, Roussanne, and Viognier. Tours include a chance to graft your own grapevine; call to reserve space. There's a fine picnic area here. ⊠ *9339 Adelaida Rd., west of Vineyard Dr.* ☎ *805/237–1231* ⊕ *www. tablascreek.com* 🖃 *Tasting $10* ⊙ *Daily 10–5.*

WORTH NOTING

Paso Robles Pioneer Museum. The museum's one-room schoolhouse and its displays of ranching paraphernalia, horse-drawn vehicles, hot-springs artifacts, and photos evoke Paso's rural heritage. ⊠ *2010 Riverside Ave., at 21st St.* ☎ *805/239–4556* ⊕ *www.pasoroblespioneermuseum. org* 🖃 *Free* ⊙ *Sep.–May Thurs.–Sun. 1–4; Jun.–Aug. Thurs., Fri. and Sun. 1–4, Sat. 10–4.*

Paso Wine Centre. Four dozen local wines are available for tasting via enomatic dispensers at this downtown space that's furnished with comfy sofas and hand-hewn oak tables. ⊠ *1240 Park St., at 13th St.* ☎ *805/239–9156* ⊕ *www.pasowinecentre.com.*

WHERE TO EAT

$$$
AMERICAN
✕ **Artisan.** Innovative variations on traditional American comfort foods, well-chosen regional wines, and a sophisticated urban vibe have made this family-run American bistro such a hit with winemakers, locals, and tourists that it recently relocated to larger quarters. Chef Chris Kobayashi, a James Beard–award nominee, uses local, organic, wild-caught ingredients to put a superfresh spin on dishes such as wild boar tenderloin and pig cheek, which he serves with fennel risotto, and scallops with shrimp, mussels, clams, Spanish chorizo, and saffron. Save room for chef's home-style desserts: sundaes, puddings, cakes, cookies, and other sweet delights. ⑤ *Average main: $28* ⊠ *843 12th St., at Pine St.* ☎ *805/237–8084* ⊕ *www.artisanpasorobles.com.*

$$$
FRENCH
✕ **Bistro Laurent.** Owner-chef Laurent Grangien's handsome, welcoming French bistro occupies an 1890s brick building across from City Park. He focuses on traditional dishes such as duck confit, rack of lamb, and onion soup, but always prepares a few au courant daily specials as well. The wines, sourced from the adjacent wine shop, come from around the world. ⑤ *Average main: $28* ⊠ *1202 Pine St., at 12th St.* ☎ *805/226–8191* ⊕ *www.bistrolaurent.com* ⊙ *Closed Sun. and Mon.*

$$$
AMERICAN
✕ **McPhee's Grill.** Just south of Paso Robles in tiny Templeton, this casual chophouse in an 1860s wood-frame storefront serves sophisticated, contemporary versions of traditional Western fare such as oak-grilled filet mignon and cedar-planked salmon. The house-label wines, made especially for the restaurant, are quite good. ⑤ *Average main: $25* ⊠ *416*

S. Main St., at 5th St., Templeton ☎ *805/434–3204* ⊕ *mcpheesgrill. com* ☼ *No lunch Sun.*

$ ✕**Panolivo Family Bistro.** Scrump-
FRENCH tious, affordable French fare draws patrons to this cheery café just north of the town square. For breakfast, try a fresh pastry or quiche, or build your own omelet. Lunch and dinner choices include sandwiches, salads, and fresh pastas—including can-nelloni stuffed with vegetables or house-made beef—along with tra-ditional dishes like snails baked in garlic-butter sauce or beef bourgui-gnon. ⑤ *Average main: $15* ☒ *1344 Park St., at 14th St.* ☎ *805/239–3366* ⊕ *www.panolivo.com.*

$$ ✕**Thomas Hill Organics Market Bis-**
MODERN **tro & Wine Bar.** Off a tiny alley, Joe
AMERICAN and Debbie Thomas serve inven-tive locavore cuisine. Much of the produce comes from their nearby 10-acre organic farm, and the meats and fish—even the olive oil, cheeses, not to mention the wines—come mostly from local providers as well. ■**TIP➔ When the weather's fine, ask for a table in the outdoor courtyard.** ⑤ *Average main: $16* ☒ *1305 Park St., at 13th St., Temple-ton* ☎ *805/226–5888* ⊕ *thomashillorganics.com* ☼ *Closed Tues.*

$$$ ✕**Villa Creek.** With a firm nod to the Rancho and Mission cuisine of
SOUTHWESTERN California's early settlers, chef Tom Fundero conjures distinctly modern magic with local, organic ingredients. The seasonal menu has included butternut-squash enchiladas, braised lamb shank with pumpkin risotto, fennel-crusted salmon, and duck breast with sweet-potato latkes. Cen-tral Coast selections dominate the wine list. All brick and bare wood, the dining room can get loud, but the atmosphere is always festive. For lighter appetites or wallets, the bar serves smaller plates—and killer margaritas. ⑤ *Average main: $26* ☒ *1144 Pine St., at 12th St.* ☎ *805/238–3000* ⊕ *www.villacreek.com* ☼ *No lunch.*

WHERE TO STAY
For expanded hotel reviews, visit Fodors.com.

$ ⬚ **Adelaide Inn.** Family-owned and -managed, this clean, friendly oasis
HOTEL with meticulous landscaping offers spacious rooms and everything you need: coffeemaker, iron, hair dryer, and peace and quiet. **Pros:** great bargain; attractive pool area; ideal for families. **Cons:** not a romantic retreat; near a busy intersection. ⑤ *Rooms from: $99* ☒ *1215 Ysabel Ave.* ☎ *805/238–2770, 800/549–7276* ⊕ *www.adelaideinn.com* ⇄ *108 rooms* ⦿| *Breakfast.*

$$$$ ⬚ **Hotel Cheval.** Equestrian themes surface throughout this intimate,
HOTEL European-style inn a half-block from the main square and near some of Paso's best restaurants. **Pros:** near downtown restaurants; sophisticated;

LAID-BACK WINE COUNTRY

Hundreds of vineyards and wineries dot the hillsides from Paso Robles to San Luis Obispo, through the scenic Edna Valley and south to northern Santa Barbara County. The wineries offer much of the variety of northern California's Napa and Sonoma valleys—without the glitz and crowds. Since the early 1980s the region has developed an interna-tional reputation for high-quality wines, most notably Pinot Noir, Chardonnay, and Zinfandel. Winer-ies here tend to be small, but most have tasting rooms (some have tours), and you'll often meet the winemakers themselves.

personal service. **Cons:** views aren't great; no pool or hot tub. ⑤ *Rooms from: $330* ⊠ *1021 Pine St.* ☎ *805/226–9995, 866/522–6999* ⊕ *www. hotelcheval.com* ⌁ *16 rooms* ⦿ *Breakfast.*

$$
HOTEL

⛺ **La Bellasera Hotel & Suites.** The swankest full-service hotel for miles around, La Bellasera caters to those looking for high-tech amenities and easy access to major Central Coast roadways. **Pros:** new property; tons of amenities. **Cons:** far from downtown; at a major intersection. ⑤ *Rooms from: $169* ⊠ *206 Alexa Court* ☎ *805/238–2834, 866/782–9669* ⊕ *www.labellasera.com* ⌁ *35 rooms, 25 suites* ⦿ *No meals.*

$$$
HOTEL

⛺ **Paso Robles Inn.** On the site of an old spa hotel of the same name, the inn is built around a lush, shady garden with a pool. **Pros:** private spring-fed hot tubs; historic property; across from town square. **Cons:** fronts a busy street; rooms vary in size and quality. ⑤ *Rooms from: $183* ⊠ *1103 Spring St.* ☎ *805/238–2660, 800/676–1713* ⊕ *www. pasoroblesinn.com* ⌁ *92 rooms, 6 suites* ⦿ *No meals.*

THE ARTS

Vina Robles Ampitheatre. At this 3,300-seat, Mission-style venue that opened in summer 2013, you can wine, dine, and listen to acclaimed musicians in concert. ⊠ *Vina Robles winery, 3800 Mill Rd., off Hwy. 46* ☎ *805/227–4812* ⊕ *www.vinarobles.com* ☉ *May–Nov.*

CAMBRIA

28 miles west of Paso Robles; 20 miles north of Morro Bay.

Cambria, set on piney hills above the sea, was settled by Welsh miners in the 1890s. In the 1970s, the gorgeous, isolated setting attracted artists and other independent types; the town now caters to tourists, but it still bears the imprint of its bohemian past. Both of Cambria's downtowns, the original East Village and the newer West Village, are packed with art and crafts galleries, antiques shops, cafés, restaurants, and B&Bs. Late-Victorian homes stand alongside streets, and the hills are filled with redwood-and-glass residences. If you're driving north up Highway 1 from Morro Bay, make a quick stop 7 miles south of Cambria at the cute former dairy town of Harmony, population 18, to visit its glassworks, pottery, and other enterprises.

GETTING HERE AND AROUND

Highway 1 leads to Cambria from the north and south. Highway 246 West curves from U.S. 101 through the mountains to Cambria. San Luis Obispo RTA Route 12 buses stop in Cambria (and Hearst Castle).

ESSENTIALS

Visitor Information Cambria Chamber of Commerce ☎ *805/927–3624* ⊕ *www.cambriachamber.org.*

EXPLORING

Fiscalini Ranch Preserve. Walk along a mile-long coastal bluff trail to spot migrating whales, otters, and shore birds at this 450-acre public open space. Miles of additional scenic trails crisscross the protected habitats of rare and endangered species of flora and fauna, including a Monterey pine forest, western pond turtles, monarch butterflies, and burrowing owls. Dogs are permitted on-leash everywhere and off-leash on all trails except the bluff. ⊠ *Hwy. 1, between Cambria Rd. and Main St. to the north, and Burton Dr. and Warren Rd. to the south; access either end of bluff trail off Windsor Blvd.* ☎ *805/927–2856* ⊕ *www.ffrpcambria.org.*

Leffingwell's Landing. A state picnic ground, the landing is a good place for examining tidal pools and watching otters as they frolic in the surf. ⊠ *North end of Moonstone Beach Dr.* ☎ *805/927–2070.*

Moonstone Beach Drive. The drive runs along a bluff above the ocean, paralleled by a 3-mile boardwalk that winds along the beach. On this fine walk—a great photo op—you might glimpse sea lions and sea otters, and perhaps a gray whale during winter and spring. Year-round, birds aplenty fly about, and tiny creatures scurry amid the tidepools. ⊠ *Off Hwy. 1.*

Nitt-Witt Ridge. Arthur Beal (aka Captain Nitt-Witt, Der Tinkerpaw) spent 51 years building a home out of all kinds of collected junk: beer cans, rocks, abalone shells, car parts, TV antennas—you name it. The site, above Cambria's West Village, is a state landmark. You can drive by and peek in—from the 700 block of Main Street, head southeast on Cornwall Street and east on Hillcrest Drive. Better yet, schedule a guided tour. ⊠ *881 Hillcrest Dr.* ☎ *805/927–2690* ⊡ *$10* ⊙ *Tour daily by appointment.*

WHERE TO EAT

$$$
AMERICAN
✕ **Black Cat Bistro.** Jazz wafts through the several small rooms of this intimate East Village bistro where stylish cushions line the banquettes. Start with an order of the fried olives stuffed with Gorgonzola, accompanied by a glass of local or imported wine. Mains on offer might include chipotle linguini (vegetarian or with shrimp) or breast of pheasant stuffed with caramelized apples. ⑤ *Average main: $24* ⊠ *1602 Main St.* ☎ *805/927–1600* ⊕ *www.blackcatbistro.com* ⚶ *Reservations essential* ⊙ *Closed Tues. and Wed. No lunch.*

$
CAFÉ
✕ **French Corner Bakery.** Place your order at the counter and then sit outside to watch the passing East Village scene. The rich aroma of coffee and fresh breakfast pastries makes mouths water in the morning; for lunch, try a quiche with flaky crust or a sandwich on house-baked bread. ⑤ *Average main: $8* ⊠ *2214 Main St.* ☎ *805/927–8227* ⚶ *Reservations not accepted* ⊙ *No dinner.*

$$
AMERICAN
FAMILY
✕ **Linn's Restaurant.** Homemade olallieberry pies, soups, potpies, and other farmhouse comfort foods share the menu with fancier dishes such as free-range chicken cordon bleu at this spacious East Village restaurant. Also on-site are a bakery, a café serving more casual fare (take-out available), and a gift shop that sells gourmet foods. ⑤ *Average main: $18* ⊠ *2277 Main St.* ☎ *805/927–0371* ⊕ *www.linnsfruitbin.com.*

$$
ECLECTIC
✕ **Robin's.** A multiethnic, vegetarian-friendly dining experience awaits you at this cozy East Village cottage. At dinner, choose from lobster enchiladas, five-spice duck breast, Thai green-curry chicken, and more. Lunchtime's extensive salad and sandwich menu embraces burgers and tofu alike. ■TIP➔ **Unless it's raining, ask for a table on the secluded (heated) garden patio.** ⑤ *Average main: $22* ⊠ *4095 Burton Dr., at Center St.* ☎ *805/927–5007* ⊕ *www.robinsrestaurant.com.*

$$$ ✕ **Sea Chest Oyster Bar and Restaurant.** Cambria's best place for seafood
SEAFOOD fills up soon after it opens at 5:30. Those in the know grab seats at the oyster bar and take in spectacular sunsets while watching the chefs broil fresh halibut, steam garlicky clams, and fry crispy calamari steaks. If you arrive to a wait, play cribbage or checkers in the game room. $⑤ Average main: $26 ✉6216 Moonstone Beach Dr., near Weymouth St. ☎805/927–4514 ⊕ www.seachestrestaurant.com ⚲ Reservations not accepted ▬ No credit cards ⊙ Closed Tues. mid-Sept.–May. No lunch.*

WHERE TO STAY

For expanded hotel reviews, visit Fodors.com.

$ ▦ **Bluebird Inn.** This sweet motel in Cambria's East Village sits amid
HOTEL beautiful gardens along Santa Rosa Creek. **Pros:** excellent value; well-kept gardens; friendly staff. **Cons:** few frills; basic rooms; on Cambria's main drag; not on beach. $⑤ Rooms from: $78 ✉1880 Main St. ☎805/927–4634, 800/552–5434 ⊕ bluebirdmotel.com ⬩37 rooms* ⦿*No meals.*

$$ ▦ **Cambria Pines Lodge.** This 25-acre retreat up the hill from the East
RESORT Village is a good choice for families. **Pros:** short walk from downtown; many recreational facilities; verdant gardens; spacious grounds. **Cons:** service and housekeeping not always top-quality; some units need updating. $⑤ Rooms from: $169 ✉2905 Burton Dr. ☎805/927–4200, 800/966–6490 ⊕ www.cambriapineslodge.com ⬩77 rooms, 75 suites* ⦿*Breakfast.*

$$ ▦ **J. Patrick House.** Monterey pines and flower gardens surround this
B&B/INN Irish-theme inn, which sits on a hilltop above Cambria's East Village. **Pros:** fantastic breakfasts; friendly innkeepers; quiet neighborhood. **Cons:** few rooms; fills up quickly. $⑤ Rooms from: $165 ✉2990 Burton Dr. ☎805/927–3812, 800/341–5258 ⊕ www.jpatrickhouse.com ⬩8 rooms* ⦿*Breakfast.*

$$ ▦ **Moonstone Landing.** Friendly staff, lots of amenities, and reasonable
HOTEL rates make this up-to-date motel a top pick of readers who like to stay right on Moonstone Beach. **Pros:** sleek furnishings; across from the beach; cheery lounge. **Cons:** narrow property; some rooms overlook a parking lot. $⑤ Rooms from: $125 ✉6240 Moonstone Beach Dr. ☎805/927–0012, 800/830–4540 ⊕ www.moonstonelanding.com ⬩29 rooms* ⦿*Breakfast.*

SAN SIMEON

9 miles north of Cambria; 65 miles south of Big Sur.

Whalers founded San Simeon in the 1850s but had virtually abandoned the town by the time Senator George Hearst reestablished it 20 years later. Hearst bought up most of the surrounding ranch land, built a 1,000-foot wharf, and turned San Simeon into a bustling port. His son, William Randolph Hearst, further developed the area during the construction of Hearst Castle. Today the town, 4 miles south of the entrance to Hearst San Simeon State Historical Monument, is basically a strip of gift shops and mediocre motels along Highway 1.

GETTING HERE AND AROUND

Highway 1 is the only way to reach San Simeon. Connect with the highway off U.S. 101 directly or via rural routes such as Highway 41 West (Atascadero to Morro Bay) and Highway 46 West (Paso Robles to Cambria).

EXPLORING

Hearst Castle. Officially known as "Hearst San Simeon State Historical Monument," Hearst Castle sits in solitary splendor atop La Cuesta Encantada (the Enchanted Hill). Its buildings and gardens spread over 127 acres that were the heart of newspaper magnate William Randolph Hearst's 250,000-acre ranch. Hearst devoted nearly 30 years and about $10 million to building this elaborate estate. He commissioned renowned California architect Julia Morgan, but he was very much involved with the final product, a blend of Italian, Spanish, and Moorish styles. The 115-room main building and three huge "cottages" are connected by terraces and staircases and surrounded by pools, gardens, and statuary. In its heyday the castle was a playground for Hearst and his guests—Hollywood celebrities, political leaders, scientists, and other well-known figures. Construction began in 1919 and was never officially completed. Work was halted in 1947 when Hearst had to leave San Simeon because of failing health. The Hearst family donated the property to the State of California in 1958.

Access to the castle is through the visitor center at the foot of the hill, which contains a collection of Hearst memorabilia and a giant-screen theater that shows a 40-minute film giving an overview of Hearst's life and of the castle's construction. Buses from the visitor center zigzag up to the neoclassical extravaganza, where guides conduct three different daytime tours of parts of the estate: grand rooms, upstairs suites, and cottages and kitchen. Daytime tours take about two hours and include the movie and time at the end to explore the castle exteriors. In spring and fall, docents in period costume portray Hearst's guests and staff for the slightly longer evening tour, which begins at sunset. Reservations are recommended for all the tours, which include a ½-mile walk and between 150 and 400 stairs. ⊠ *San Simeon State Park, 750 Hearst Castle Rd.* ☎ *800/444–4445* ⊕ *www.hearstcastle.com* ☞ *Daytime tours $25, evening tours $36* ⊙ *Tours daily 9–3:20, later in summer; additional tours take place most Fri. and Sat. evenings Mar.–May and Sept.–Dec.*

Old San Simeon. Turn west from Highway 1 across from the Hearst Castle entrance to see Old San Simeon, an 1850s whaling village that morphed into an outpost for Hearst employees. There's a one-room schoolhouse and Spanish-style buildings; don't miss Sebastian's General Store in an 1852 building. Now a state historic landmark, Sebastian's houses a store, a wine-tasting room, and a café that serves excellent sandwiches and salads. ⊠ *West of Hwy. 1, across from Hearst Castle entrance.*

FAMILY **Piedras Blancas Elephant Seal Rookery.** A large colony of elephant seals (at last count 15,000 members) gathers every year at Piedras Blancas Elephant Seal Rookery, on the beaches near Piedras Blancas Lighthouse. The huge males with their pendulous, trunklike noses typically start appearing on shore in late November, and the females begin to arrive in December to give birth—most babies are born in the last two weeks of January. The newborn pups spend about four weeks nursing before their mothers head out to sea, leaving them on their own; the "weaners" leave the rookery when they are about 3½ months old. The seals return in the spring and summer months to molt or rest, but not en masse as in winter. You can watch them from a boardwalk along the bluffs just a few feet above the beach; do not attempt to approach them, as they are wild animals. The nonprofit Friends of the Elephant Seal runs a small visitor center and gift shop at 250 San Simeon Avenue in San Simeon. ⊠ *Off Hwy. 1, 4½ miles north of Hearst Castle, just south of Piedras Blancas Lighthouse* ☎ *805/924–1628* ⊕ *www.elephantseal.org.*

Piedras Blancas Light Station. If you think traversing craggy, twisting Highway 1 is tough, imagine trying to navigate a boat up the rocky coastline (piedras blancas means "white rocks" in Spanish) near San Simeon before lighthouses were built. Captains must have cheered wildly when the beam began to shine here in 1875. Try to time a visit to include a morning tour (reservations not required). ■**TIP→ Do not meet at the gate to the lighthouse—you'll miss the tour. Meet your guide instead at the former Piedras Blancas Motel, a mile and a half north of the light station.** ☎ *805/927–7361* ⊕ *piedrasblancas.org* ☞ *$10* ⊙ *Tours at 9:45, mid-June–Aug. Mon–Sat.; Sept.–mid-June Tues., Thurs., and Sat.; no tours on national holidays* ☞ *No pets allowed.*

BEACHES

William Randolph Hearst Memorial Beach. A popular destination on weekends and sunny summer days, this wide, sandy beach edges a protected cove on both sides of San Simeon Pier. Fish from the pier or from a charter boat, picnic and barbecue on the bluffs, or boogie board or body surf on relatively gentle waves. In summer, you can rent a kayak and paddle out into the bay for close encounters with marine life and sea caves. The Coastal Discovery Center here offers guided walks and special programs. **Amenities:** food and drink; parking; toilets; water sports. **Best for:** sunset; swimming; walking. ⊠ *750 Hearst Castle Rd., off Hwy. 1 directly west of the Hearst Castle entrance* ☎ *805/927–2020* ⊕ *slostateparks.com* ☞ *Free* ⊙ *Daily sunrise–sunset.*

WHERE TO STAY

For expanded hotel reviews, visit Fodors.com.

$$
HOTEL
🖥 **Best Western Cavalier Oceanfront Resort.** Reasonable rates, an oceanfront location, evening bonfires, and well-equipped rooms—some with wood-burning fireplaces and private patios—make this motel a great choice. **Pros:** on the bluffs; fantastic views; close to Hearst Castle. **Cons:** room amenities and sizes vary; pools are small and sometimes crowded. ⑤ *Rooms from: $169* ⊠ *9415 Hearst Dr.* ☎ *805/927–4688, 800/826–8168* ⊕ *www.cavalierresort.com* ⇶ *90 rooms* ⊙❘ *No meals.*

$$
HOTEL
🖥 **The Morgan San Simeon.** On Highway 1's ocean side, the Morgan offers motel-style rooming options in two Asian-inspired buildings. **Pros:** fascinating artwork; easy access to Hearst Castle; some ocean views. **Cons:** not right on beach; no fitness room or laundry facilities. ⑤ *Rooms from: $149* ⊠ *9135 Hearst Dr.* ☎ *805/927–3878, 800/451–9900* ⊕ *www.hotel-morgan.com* ⇶ *54 rooms, 1 suite* ⊙❘ *Breakfast.*

BIG SUR COASTLINE

Long a retreat of artists and writers, Big Sur is a place of ancient forests and rugged shoreline, stretching 90 miles from San Simeon to Carmel. Residents have protected it from overdevelopment, and much of the region lies within several state parks and the more than 165,000-acre Ventana Wilderness, itself part of the Los Padres National Forest.

ESSENTIALS

Visitor Information Big Sur Chamber of Commerce ☎ *831/667–2100* ⊕ *www.bigsurcalifornia.org.*

SOUTHERN BIG SUR

Hwy. 1 from San Simeon to Julia Pfeiffer Burns State Park.

This especially rugged stretch of oceanfront is a rocky world of mountains, cliffs, and beaches.

GETTING HERE AND AROUND

Highway 1 is the only major access route from north or south. From the south, access Highway 1 from U.S. 101 in San Luis Obispo. From the north, take rural route Highway 46 West (Paso Robles to Cambria) or Highway 41 West (Atascadero to Morro Bay). Nacimiento-Fergusson Road snakes through mountains and forest from U.S. 101 at Jolon about 25 miles to Highway 1 at Kirk Creek, about 4 miles south of Lucia; this curving, at times precipitous road is a motorcyclist favorite, not recommended for the faint of heart or during inclement weather.

EXPLORING

Fodor's Choice ★ **Highway 1.** One of California's most spectacular drives, Highway 1 snakes up the coast north of San Simeon. Numerous pullouts along the way offer tremendous views and photo ops. On some of the beaches, huge elephant seals lounge nonchalantly, seemingly oblivious to the attention of rubberneckers. Heavy rain sometimes causes mudslides that block the highway north and south of Big Sur. ☎ *888/836–0866 for Hwy. 1 conditions between Cambria and Carmel* ⊕ *www.dot.ca.gov.*

Jade Cove. In Los Padres National Forest just north of the town of Gorda is Jade Cove, a well-known jade-hunting spot. Rock hunting is allowed on the beach, but you may not remove anything from the walls of the cliffs. ⊠ *Hwy. 1, 34 miles north of San Simeon.*

Julia Pfeiffer Burns State Park. The park provides fine hiking, from an easy ½-mile stroll with marvelous coastal views to a strenuous 6-mile trek through redwoods. The big draw here, an 80-foot waterfall that drops into the ocean, gets crowded in summer; still, it's an astounding place to contemplate nature. Migrating whales, harbor seals, and sea lions can sometimes be spotted just offshore. ⊠ *Hwy. 1, 15 miles north of Lucia* ☎ *831/667–2315* ⊕ *www.parks.ca.gov* ⊠ *$10* ☉ *Daily sunrise–sunset.*

WHERE TO STAY

For expanded hotel reviews, visit Fodors.com.

$$
HOTEL

⚇ **Ragged Point Inn.** At this cliff-top resort—the only inn and restaurant for miles around—glass walls in most rooms open to awesome ocean views. **Pros:** on the cliffs; great food; idyllic views. **Cons:** busy road stop during the day; often booked for weekend weddings. Ⓢ *Rooms from: $169* ⊠ *19019 Hwy. 1, 20 miles north of San Simeon, Ragged Point* ☎ *805/927–4502, 805/927–5708 restaurant* ⊕ *raggedpointinn. com* ⌇ *39 rooms* ⏐◎⏐ *No meals.*

$$$
RESORT

⚇ **Treebones Resort.** Perched on a hilltop, surrounded by national forest and stunning, unobstructed ocean views, this yurt resort provides a stellar back-to-nature experience along with creature comforts. **Pros:** 360-degree views; spacious pool area; comfortable beds. **Cons:** steep paths; no private bathrooms; not good for families with young children. Ⓢ *Rooms from: $199* ⊠ *71895 Hwy. 1, Willow Creek Rd., 32 miles north of San Simeon, 1 mile north of Gorda* ☎ *805/927–2390, 877/424–4787* ⊕ *www.treebonesresort.com* ⌇ *16 yurts, 5 campsites, 1 human nest w/campsite* ⏐◎⏐ *Breakfast* ⌇ *Two-night minimum on weekends and Apr.–Oct.*

CENTRAL BIG SUR

Hwy. 1, from Partington Cove to Bixby Bridge.

The countercultural spirit of Big Sur—which instead of a conventional town is a loose string of coast-hugging properties along Highway 1—is alive and well today. Its few residents include the very wealthy, the enthusiastically outdoorsy, and the thoroughly evolved: since the 1960s the Esalen Institute, a center for alternative education and East–West philosophical study, has attracted seekers of higher consciousness and devotees of the property's hot springs. Today, posh and rustic resorts hidden among the redwoods cater to visitors drawn from near and far by the extraordinary scenery and serene isolation.

GETTING HERE AND AROUND

From the north, follow Highway 1 south from Carmel. From the south, continue the drive north from Julia Pfeiffer Burns State Park *(above)* on Highway 1. Monterey-Salinas Transit operates the Line 22 Big Sur bus from Monterey and Carmel to Central Big Sur (the last top is Nepenthe), daily from late May to early September and weekends only the rest of the year.

Bus Contact Monterey-Salinas Transit ☎ *888/678–2871* ⊕ *www.mst.org.*

EXPLORING

Bixby Creek Bridge. The graceful arc of Bixby Creek Bridge is a photographer's dream. Built in 1932, the bridge spans a deep canyon, more than 100 feet wide at the bottom. From the north-side parking area you can admire the view or walk the 550-foot structure. ⊠ *Hwy. 1, 6 miles north of Point Sur State Historic Park, 13 miles south of Carmel.*

Pfeiffer Big Sur State Park. Among the many hiking trails at Pfeiffer Big Sur, a short route through a redwood-filled valley leads to a waterfall. You can double back or continue on the more difficult trail along the valley wall for views over miles of treetops to the sea. ⊠ *47225 Hwy. 1* ☎ *831/667–2315* ⊕ *www.parks.ca.gov* 🎫 *$10 per vehicle* ☉ *Daily sunrise–sunset.*

Point Sur State Historic Park. An 1889 lighthouse still stands watch from atop a large volcanic rock at this state park. Four lighthouse keepers lived here with their families until 1974, when the light station became automated. Their homes and working spaces are open to the public only on 2½- to 3-hour ranger-led tours. Considerable walking, including up two stairways, is involved. Strollers are not allowed. ⊠ *Hwy. 1, 7 miles north of Pfeiffer Big Sur State Park* ☎ *831/625–4419* ⊕ *www.pointsur. org* 🎫 *$12* ☉ *Tours generally Nov.–Mar., weekends at 10, Wed. at 1; Apr.–Oct., Sat. and Wed. at 10 and 2, Sun. at 10; call to confirm.*

BEACHES

Pfeiffer Beach. Through a hole in one of the gigantic boulders at secluded Pfeiffer Beach, you can watch the waves break first on the sea side and then on the beach side. Keep a sharp eye out for the unsigned, ungated road to the beach: it branches west of Highway 1 between the post office and Pfeiffer Big Sur State Park. The 2-mile, one-lane road descends sharply. **Amenities:** parking (fee); toilets. **Best for:** solitude; sunset. ⊠ *Off Hwy. 1, 1 mile south of Pfeiffer Big Sur State Park* 🎫 *$5 per vehicle* ☉ *Daily 9–8.*

WHERE TO EAT

$$$
AMERICAN
✕ **Deetjen's Big Sur Inn.** The candle-lighted, creaky-floor restaurant in the main house at the historic inn of the same name is a Big Sur institution. It serves spicy seafood paella, steak, and rack of lamb for dinner and wonderfully flavorful eggs Benedict for breakfast. The chef sources most ingredients from purveyors known for sustainable practices. 💲 *Average main: $30* ⊠ *Hwy. 1, 3½ mile south of Pfeiffer Big Sur State Park* ☎ *831/667–2377* ⊕ *www.deetjens.com* ☉ *No lunch.*

$$$
AMERICAN
✕ **Nepenthe.** It may be that no other restaurant between San Francisco and Los Angeles has a better coastal view than this one. The food and drink are overpriced but good; there are burgers, sandwiches, and sal-ads for lunch, and fresh fish and hormone-free steaks for dinner. For the real show, settle on the terraced deck in the late afternoon, order a glass from the extensive wine list, and watch the sun slip into the Pacific Ocean. The less expensive, outdoor Café Kevah serves brunch and lunch. 💲 *Average main: $30* ⊠ *Hwy. 1, 2½ miles south of Big Sur Station* ☎ *831/667–2345* ⊕ *www.nepenthebigsur.com.*

$$$$
AMERICAN
✕ **The Restaurant at Ventana.** The redwood, copper, and cedar elements at the Ventana Inn's restaurant pay tribute to the historic natural set-ting, while gleaming fixtures and dining accoutrements place the facility firmly in the 21st century. Chef Truman Jones's seasonal menu show-cases meat, fish, and produce—such as rabbit loin, California white sea bass, artichokes, and abalone—grown or caught in California. A full slate of regional and international wines complements his dishes. The restaurant is also open for lunch. ■TIP→ **If the day is sunny, ask for a table on the outdoor terrace and take in the ocean views.** 💲 *Average main: $36* ⊠ *Hwy. 1, 1½ miles south of Pfeiffer Big Sur State Park* ☎ *831/667–2242* ⊕ *www.ventanainn.com* ⚶ *Reservations essential.*

$$$$

AMERICAN

✕ **Sierra Mar.** Ocean-view dining doesn't get much better than this. At cliff's edge 1,200 feet above the Pacific at the ultra-chic Post Ranch Inn, Sierra Mar serves cutting-edge American food made from mostly organic, seasonal ingredients. The four-course prix-fixe option always shines. The nine-course Taste of Big Sur menu centers around ingredients grown and foraged on the property or sourced locally. The restaurant's wine list is among the nation's most extensive. $ *Average main: $50* ⊠ *Hwy. 1, 1½ miles south of Pfeiffer Big Sur State Park* ☎ 831/667–2800 ⊕ *www. postranchinn.com/dining* ⚘ *Reservations essential.*

WHERE TO STAY

For expanded hotel reviews, visit Fodors.com.

$$$

HOTEL

Big Sur Lodge. Modern motel-style cottages with Mission-style furnishings and vaulted ceilings sit in a meadow, surrounded by trees and flowering shrubbery. **Pros:** near trailheads; good camping alternative. **Cons:** basic rooms; walk to main lodge. $ *Rooms from: $204* ⊠ *Pfeiffer Big Sur State Park, 47225 Hwy. 1* ☎ 831/667–3100, 800/424–4787 ⊕ *www.bigsurlodge.com* ⋗ *61 rooms* ⦿ *No meals.*

$$

B&B/INN

Deetjen's Big Sur Inn. This historic 1930s Norwegian-style property is endearingly rustic, especially if you're willing to go with a camplike flow. **Pros:** tons of character; wooded grounds. **Cons:** thin walls; some rooms don't have private baths. $ *Rooms from: $160* ⊠ *Hwy. 1, 3½ miles south of Pfeiffer Big Sur State Park* ☎ 831/667–2377 ⊕ *www. deetjens.com* ⋗ *20 rooms, 15 with bath* ⦿ *No meals.*

$$$$

HOTEL

Glen Oaks Big Sur. At this rustic-modern cluster of adobe-and-redwood buildings, you can choose between motel-style rooms, cabins, and cottages in the woods. **Pros:** in the heart of town; walking distance of restaurants. **Cons:** near busy road and parking lot; no TVs. $ *Rooms from: $275* ⊠ *Hwy. 1, 1 mile north of Pfeiffer Big Sur State Park* ☎ 831/667–2105 ⊕ *www.glenoaksbigsur.com* ⋗ *16 rooms, 2 cottages, 7 cabins* ⦿ *No meals.*

$$$$

RESORT

Fodor's Choice

★

Post Ranch Inn. This luxurious retreat, designed exclusively for adult getaways, has remarkably environmentally conscious architecture. **Pros:** world-class resort; spectacular views; gorgeous property with hiking trails. **Cons:** expensive; austere design; not a good choice if heights scare you. $ *Rooms from: $675* ⊠ *Hwy. 1, 1½ miles south of Pfeiffer Big Sur State Park* ☎ 831/667–2200, 888/524–4787 ⊕ *www.postranchinn.com* ⋗ *39 units* ⦿ *Breakfast.*

$$$$

HOTEL

Fodor's Choice

★

Ventana. Hundreds of celebrities, from Oprah Winfrey to Sir Anthony Hopkins, have escaped to Ventana, a romantic resort on 243 tranquil acres 1,200 feet above the Pacific. **Pros:** nature trails everywhere; great food; secluded. **Cons:** simple breakfast; some rooms have no ocean view. $ *Rooms from: $650* ⊠ *Hwy. 1, almost 1 mile south of Pfeiffer Big Sur State Park* ☎ 831/667–2331, 800/628–6500 ⊕ *www.ventanainn.com* ⋗ *25 rooms, 31 suites* ⦿ *Breakfast.*

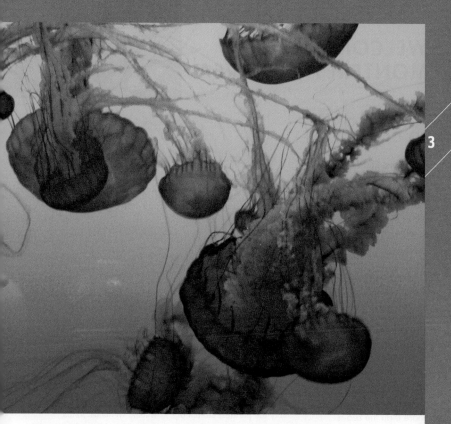

THE MONTEREY BAY AREA

From Carmel to Santa Cruz

WELCOME TO THE MONTEREY BAY AREA

TOP REASONS TO GO

★ **Marine life:** Monterey Bay is the location of the world's third-largest marine sanctuary, home to whales, otters, and other underwater creatures.

★ **Getaway central:** For more than a century, urbanites have come to the Monterey Bay area to unwind, relax, and have fun. It's a great place to browse unique shops and galleries, ride a giant roller coaster, or play a round of golf on a world-class course.

★ **Nature preserves:** More than the sea is protected here—the region boasts nearly 30 state parks, beaches, and preserves, fantastic places for walking, jogging, hiking, and biking.

★ **Wine and dine:** The area's rich agricultural bounty translates to abundant fresh produce, great wines, and fabulous dining. It's no wonder more than 300 culinary events take place here every year.

★ **Small-town vibes:** Even the cities here are friendly, walkable places where you'll feel like a local.

1 Carmel and Pacific Grove. Exclusive Carmel-by-the-Sea and Carmel Valley Village burst with historic charm, fine dining, and unusual boutiques that cater to celebrity residents and well-heeled visitors. Nearby 17-Mile Drive—quite possibly the prettiest stretch of road you'll ever travel—runs between Carmel-by-the-Sea and Victorian-studded Pacific Grove, home to thousands of migrating monarch butterflies between October and February.

2 Monterey. A former Spanish military outpost, Monterey's well-preserved historic district is a hands-on history lesson. Cannery Row, the former center of Monterey's once-thriving sardine industry, has been reborn as a tourist attraction with shops, restaurants, hotels, and the Monterey Bay Aquarium.

3 Around Monterey Bay. Much of California's lettuce, berries, artichokes, and Brussels sprouts come from Salinas and Watsonville. Salinas is also home to the National Steinbeck Center, and Moss Landing and Watsonville encompass pristine wildlife wetlands. Aptos, Capitola, and Soquel are former lumber towns that became popular seaside resorts more than a century ago. Today they're filled with antiques shops, restaurants, and wine-tasting rooms; you'll also find some of the bay's best beaches along the shore here.

4 Santa Cruz. Santa Cruz shows its colors along an old-time beach boardwalk and municipal wharf. A University of California campus imbues the town with arts and culture and a liberal mind-set.

Santa Cruz

GETTING ORIENTED

North of Big Sur the coastline softens into lower bluffs, windswept dunes, pristine estuaries, and long, sandy beaches, bordering one of the world's most amazing marine environments—the Monterey Bay. On the Monterey Peninsula, at the southern end of the bay, are Carmel-by-the-Sea, Pacific Grove, and Monterey; Santa Cruz sits at the northern tip of the crescent. In between, Highway 1 cruises along the coastline, passing windswept beaches piled high with sand dunes. Along the route are wetlands, artichoke and strawberry fields, and workaday towns such as Castroville and Watsonville.

The Forest of Nisene Marks State Park

Soquel

Capitola — Soquel Cove

Aptos

Rio del Mar

Freedom

Watsonville

Pajaro

Las Lomas

MONTEREY BAY

Moss Landing

Prunedale

Castroville

Salinas R.

SALINAS VALLEY

Marina

Salinas

G17

Spreckels

Point Pinos

Pacific Grove

Spanish Bay

17-Mile Dr.

Seaside

Sand City

Monterey

Del Rey Oaks

Pebble Beach

Cypress Point

Carmel

SIERRA DE SALINAS

Carmel Bay

Point Lobos

Carmel Valley Rd.

Carmel River

Carmel Highlands

Carmel Valley

Updated
by Cheryl
Crabtree

Natural beauty is at the heart of this region's enormous appeal—you sense it everywhere, whether you're exploring one of Monterey Bay's attractive coast-side towns, relaxing at a luxurious resort, or touring the coast on the lookout for marine life.

It's been this way for a long time: an abiding current of plenty runs through the region's history. Military buffs see it in centuries' worth of battles for control of the rich territory. John Steinbeck saw it in the success of a community built on the elbow grease of farm laborers in the Salinas Valley and fishermen along Cannery Row. Biologists see it in the ocean's potential as a more sustainable source of food.

Downtown Carmel-by-the-Sea and Monterey are walks through history. The bay itself is protected by the Monterey Bay National Marine Sanctuary, the nation's largest undersea canyon—bigger and deeper than the Grand Canyon. And of course, the backdrop of natural beauty is still everywhere to be seen.

PLANNING

WHEN TO GO

Summer is peak season; mild weather brings in big crowds. In this coastal region, a cool breeze generally blows and fog often rolls in from offshore; you will frequently need a sweater or windbreaker. Off-season, from November through April, fewer people visit and the mood is mellower. Rainfall is heaviest in January and February, but autumn through spring days are crystal clear more often than in summer.

GETTING HERE AND AROUND

AIR TRAVEL

Monterey Regional Airport, 3 miles east of downtown Monterey off Highway 68, is served by Alaska, Allegiant, American Eagle, and United. Taxi service to downtown runs about $15 to $17; to Carmel the fare is $23 to $32. To and from San Jose International Airport and San Francisco International Airport, Monterey Airbus starts at $40 and the Early Bird Airport Shuttle runs $75 to $190.

Airport Contacts Monterey Regional Airport ✉ *200 Fred Kane Dr., at Olmsted Rd., off Hwy. 68, Monterey* ☎ *831/648-7000* ⊕ *www.montereyairport.com.*

Ground Transportation Central Coast Cab Company ☎ *831/626-3333.* **Early Bird Airport Shuttle** ☎ *831/462-3933* ⊕ *www.earlybirdairportshuttle.com.* **Monterey Airbus** ☎ *831/373-7777* ⊕ *www.montereyairbus.com.* **Yellow Cab** ☎ *831/333-1234.*

BUS TRAVEL

Greyhound serves Santa Cruz and Salinas from San Francisco and San Jose. The trips take about 3 and 4½ hours, respectively. Monterey-Salinas Transit (MST) provides frequent service in Monterey County (fares $1.50 to $3.50; day pass $10), and Santa Cruz METRO ($2; day pass $6 to $10) buses operate throughout Santa Cruz County. You can switch between the two lines in Watsonville, in southern Santa Cruz County.

Bus Contacts Greyhound ☎ *800/231-2222* ⊕ *www.greyhound.com.* **Monterey-Salinas Transit** ☎ *888/678-2871* ⊕ *www.mst.org.*

CAR TRAVEL

Highway 1 runs south–north along the coast, linking the towns of Carmel-by-the-Sea, Monterey, and Santa Cruz; some sections have only two lanes. The freeway, U.S. 101, lies to the east, roughly parallel to Highway 1. The two roads are connected by Highway 68 from Pacific Grove to Salinas; Highway 156 from Castroville to Prunedale; Highway 152 from Watsonville to Gilroy; and Highway 17 from Santa Cruz to San Jose. ⚠ **Traffic near Santa Cruz can crawl to a standstill during commuter hours. In the morning, avoid traveling between 7 and 9; in the afternoon avoid traveling between 4 and 7.**

The drive south from San Francisco to Monterey can be made comfortably in three hours or less. The most scenic way is to follow Highway 1 down the coast past flower, pumpkin, and artichoke fields and small seaside communities. Unless you drive on sunny weekends when locals are heading for the beach, the two-lane coast highway may take no longer than the freeway. A sometimes-faster route is Interstate 280 south from San Francisco to Highway 17, north of San Jose.

From Los Angeles the drive to Monterey can be made in five to six hours by heading north on U.S. 101 to Salinas and then west on Highway 68. You can also follow Highway 1 all or part of the way north from Southern California.

TRAIN TRAVEL

Amtrak's *Coast Starlight* runs between Los Angeles, Oakland, and Seattle. From the train station in Salinas, you can connect with buses serving Carmel, Monterey, and Santa Cruz.

Train Contacts Amtrak ☎ *800/872-7245* ⊕ *www.amtrak.com.*

RESTAURANTS

The Monterey Bay area is a culinary paradise. The surrounding waters are full of fish, wild game roams the foothills, and the inland valleys are some of the most fertile in the country—local chefs draw on this bounty for their fresh, truly Californian cuisine. Except at beachside stands and inexpensive eateries, where anything goes, casual but neat dress is the norm. *Prices in the restaurant reviews are the average cost of a main course at dinner or, if dinner is not served, at lunch (excluding sales tax).*

HOTELS

Accommodations in the Monterey area range from no-frills motels to luxurious hotels. Pacific Grove, amply endowed with ornate Victorian houses, is the region's B&B capital; Carmel also has charming inns. Lavish resorts cluster in exclusive Pebble Beach and pastoral Carmel Valley.

High season runs from April through October. Rates in winter, especially at the larger hotels, may drop by 50% or more, and B&Bs often offer midweek specials. Whatever the month, some properties require a two-night stay on weekends. *Prices in the hotel reviews are the lowest cost of a standard double room in high season. For expanded reviews, facilities, and current deals, visit Fodors.com.* ⚠ **Many of the fancier accommodations aren't suitable for children; if you're traveling with kids, ask before you book.**

Lodging Contact Bed and Breakfast Inns of Santa Cruz County. This association of innkeepers can help you find a bed-and-breakfast. ⊕ *www.santacruzbnb.com.*

TOUR OPTIONS

California Parlor Car Tours operates motor-coach tours from San Francisco that include one or two days in Monterey and Carmel. Ag Venture Tours runs wine-tasting, sightseeing, and agricultural tours to several towns.

Tour Contacts Ag Venture Tours ☎ *831/761–8463* ⊕ *www.agventuretours.com.* **California Parlor Car Tours** ☎ *415/474–7500, 800/227–4250* ⊕ *www.calpartours.com.*

VISITOR INFORMATION

Contacts Monterey County Convention & Visitors Bureau ☎ *877/666–8373* ⊕ *www.seemonterey.com.* **Monterey County Vintners and Growers Association** ☎ *831/375–9400* ⊕ *www.montereywines.org.* **Santa Cruz County Conference and Visitors Council** ⊠ *303 Water St., #100, Santa Cruz* ☎ *831/425–1234, 800/833–3494* ⊕ *www.santacruz.org.* **Santa Cruz Mountain Winegrowers Association** ⊠ *725 Front St., #112, Santa Cruz* ☎ *831/685–8463* ⊕ *www.scmwa.com.*

CARMEL AND PACIFIC GROVE

As Highway 1 swings inland about 30 miles north of Big Sur, historic Carmel-by-the Sea anchors the southern entry to the Monterey Peninsula—a gorgeous promontory at the southern tip of Monterey Bay. Just north of Carmel along the coast, the legendary 17-Mile Drive wends its way through private Pebble Beach and the town of Pacific Grove. Highway 1 skirts the peninsula to the east with more direct access to Pebble Beach and Pacific Grove.

CARMEL-BY-THE-SEA

26 miles north of Big Sur on Hwy. 1.

Although the community has grown quickly through the years and its population quadruples with tourists on weekends and in summer, Carmel-by-the-Sea, commonly referred to as Carmel, retains its identity as a quaint village. Self-consciously charming, the town is populated by many celebrities, major and minor, and has its share of quirky ordinances. For instance, women wearing high heels do not have the right to pursue legal action if they trip and fall on the cobblestone streets, and drivers who hit a tree and leave the scene are charged with hit-and-run.

Buildings have no street numbers (street names are written on discreet white posts) and consequently no mail delivery (if you want to see the locals, go to the post office). Artists started this community, and their legacy is evident in the numerous galleries.

GETTING HERE AND AROUND

From north or south follow Highway 1 to Carmel. Head west at Ocean Avenue to reach the main village hub. In summer the MST Carmel-by-the-Sea Trolley loops around town to the beach and mission every 30 minutes or so.

TOURS

For insight into Carmel's history and culture, join a guided two-hour Carmel Walks tour through hidden courtyards, gardens, and pathways. Tours ($25) depart from the Pine Inn courtyard on Lincoln Street. Call to reserve a spot.

ESSENTIALS

Tour Contacts Carmel Walks ⊠ *Lincoln St. at 6th Ave.* ☎ *831/642–2700* ⊕ *www.carmelwalks.com* ⊗ *Tues.–Fri. at 10, Sat. at 10 and 2.*

Visitor Information Carmel Chamber of Commerce ⊠ *Visitor Center, San Carlos, between 5th and 6th* ☎ *831/624–2522, 800/550–4333* ⊕ *www.carmelcalifornia.org* ⊗ *Daily 10–5.*

EXPLORING

TOP ATTRACTIONS

Carmel Mission. Long before it became a shopping and browsing destination, Carmel was an important religious center during the establishment of Spanish California. That heritage is preserved in the Mission San Carlos Borroméo del Rio Carmelo, more commonly known as the Carmel Mission. Founded in 1771, it served as headquarters for the mission system in California under Father Junípero Serra. Adjoining the stone church is a tranquil garden planted with California poppies. Museum rooms at the mission include an early kitchen, Serra's spartan sleeping quarters, and the first college library in California. ⊠ *3080 Rio Rd., at Lasuen Dr.* ☎ *831/624–1271* ⊕ *www.carmelmission.org* ⊠ *$6.50* ⊗ *Museum: Mon.–Sun. 9:30–4:45, store open until 5.*

Fodor'sChoice ★ **Point Lobos State Reserve.** A 350-acre headland harboring a wealth of marine life, this reserve lies a few miles south of Carmel. The best way to explore here is to walk along one of the many trails. The Cypress Grove

Trail leads through a forest of Monterey cypress (one of only two natural groves remaining), which clings to the rocks above an emerald green cove. Sea Lion Point Trail is a good place to view sea lions. From those and other trails you may also spot otters, harbor seals, and (in winter and spring) migrating whales. An additional 750 acres of the reserve is an undersea marine park open to qualified scuba divers. ■TIP→ Arrive early (or in late afternoon) to avoid crowds; the parking lots fill up. No pets are allowed. Only California state park annual passes are accepted. ⊠ *Hwy. 1* ☎ *831/624–4909, 831/624–8413 for scuba-diving reservations* ⊕ *www.pointlobos.org* ⊡ *$10 per vehicle* ⊙ *Daily 8 am–½ hr after sunset in winter, 8 am–7 pm spring–fall.*

WORTH NOTING

Carmel Plaza. In the east end of the village proper, Carmel Plaza holds nearly 50 shops and restaurants. ⊠ *Ocean Ave. and Mission St.* ☎ *831/624–1385 concierge, 831/624–0137 shopping line* ⊕ *www. carmelplaza.com.*

Carmel Wine Walk By-the-Sea. Park the car and sample local wines at tasting rooms and shops in downtown Carmel, all within a few blocks of each other. Purchase a Wine Walk Passport, good for flights in seven tasting rooms and free corkage at local restaurants. There's no expiration date—participating venues will stamp it each time you visit. ⊠ *Carmel*

Chamber of Commerce Visitor Center, San Carlos St., between 5th and 6th Aves. ☎ *831/624–2522, 800/550–4333* ⊕ *www.carmelcalifornia.org* ⌨ *$50.*

Ocean Avenue. Downtown Carmel's chief lure is shopping, especially along its main street, Ocean Avenue, between Junipero Avenue and Camino Real. The architecture here is a mishmash of ersatz Tudor, Mediterranean, and other styles.

Tor House. Scattered throughout the pines in Carmel-by-the-Sea are houses and cottages originally built for the writers, artists, and photographers who discovered the area decades ago. Among the most impressive dwellings is Tor House, a stone cottage built in 1919 by poet Robinson Jeffers on a craggy knoll overlooking the sea. Portraits, books, and unusual art objects fill the low-ceiling rooms. The highlight of the small estate is Hawk Tower, a detached edifice set with stones from the Carmel coastline—as well as one from the Great Wall of China. The docents who lead tours (six people maximum) are well informed about the poet's work and life. Reservations for tours, via e-mail at ✎ *thf@torhouse.org*, are recommended. ✉ *26304 Ocean View Ave.* ☎ *831/624–1813, 831/624–1840 direct docent office line, available Fri. and Sat. only* ⊕ *www.torhouse.org* ⌨ *$10* ☉ *Hourly tours Fri. and Sat. 10–3* ⌕ *No children under 12.*

BEACHES

Carmel Beach. Carmel-by-the-Sea's greatest attraction is its rugged coastline, with pine and cypress forests and countless inlets. Carmel Beach, an easy walk from downtown shops, has sparkling white sands and magnificent sunsets. ■**TIP**→ **Dogs are allowed to romp off-leash here.** **Amenities:** parking (no fee); toilets. **Best for:** sunset; surfing; walking. ✉ *End of Ocean Ave.*

Carmel River State Beach. This sugar-white beach, stretching 106 acres along Carmel Bay, is adjacent to a bird sanctuary, where you might spot pelicans, kingfishers, hawks, and sandpipers. **Amenities:** none. **Best for:** sunrise; sunset; walking. ✉ *Off Scenic Rd., south of Carmel Beach* ☎ *831/624–4909, 831/649–2836* ⊕ *www.parks.ca.gov* ⌨ *Free* ☉ *Daily 8 am–½ hr after sunset in winter; 8 am–7 pm spring–fall.*

WHERE TO EAT

$$$ ✕ **Andre's Bouchée.** The food here presents an innovative bistro-style take
FRENCH on local ingredients. A Monterey Bay sea scallop reduction adorns pan-seared veal tenderloin; grilled rib-eye steaks are topped with a shallot–Cabernet Sauvignon sauce. With its copper wine bar, the dining room feels more urban than most of Carmel; perhaps that's why this is the "cool" place in town to dine. The stellar wine list sources the selection at the in-house wine shop. ⑤ *Average main: $28* ✉ *Mission St., between Ocean and 7th Aves.* ☎ *831/626–7880* ⊕ *www.andresbouchee. com* ⌨ *Reservations essential* ☉ *No lunch Mon. and Tues.*

$$$
EUROPEAN
✕ **Anton and Michel.** Carefully prepared European cuisine is the draw at this airy restaurant. The rack of lamb is carved at the table, the grilled Halloumi cheese and tomatoes are meticulously stacked and served with basil and kalamata olive tapenade, and the desserts are set aflame before your eyes. $ *Average main: $30* ⊠ *Mission St. and 7th Ave.* ☎ *831/624–2406* ⊕ *www.antonandmichel.com* ⌕ *Reservations essential.*

$$$
MEDITERRANEAN
✕ **Casanova.** This cozy restaurant inspires European-style celebration and romance—accordions hang from the walls, and tiny party lights dance along the low ceilings. The food consists of delectable seasonal dishes from southern France and northern Italy. Private dining and a special menu are offered at Van Gogh's Table, a special table imported from France's Auberge Ravoux, the artist's final residence. $ *Average main: $30* ⊠ *5th Ave., between San Carlos and Mission Sts.* ☎ *831/625–0501* ⊕ *www.casanovarestaurant.com* ⌕ *Reservations essential.*

$
AMERICAN
✕ **The Cottage Restaurant.** This family-friendly spot serves sandwiches, pizzas, and homemade soups at lunch and simple entrées at dinner, but the best meal is breakfast (good thing it's served all day). The menu offers six variations on eggs Benedict, and all kinds of sweet and savory crepes. $ *Average main: $14* ⊠ *Lincoln St., between Ocean and 7th Aves.* ☎ *831/625–6260* ⊕ *www.cottagerestaurant.com* ⊘ *No dinner Sun.–Wed.*

$$$
SEAFOOD
✕ **Flying Fish Grill.** Simple in appearance yet bold with its flavors, this Japanese–California seafood restaurant is one of Carmel's most inventive eateries. Among the best entrées is the almond-crusted sea bass served with Chinese cabbage and rock shrimp stir-fry. The warm, wood-lined dining room is broken up into very private booths. $ *Average main: $26* ⊠ *Carmel Plaza, Mission St., between Ocean and 7th Aves.* ☎ *831/625–1962* ⊕ *www.flyingfishgrill.com* ⊘ *No lunch.*

$$$
AMERICAN
✕ **Grasing's Coastal Cuisine.** Chef Kurt Grasing draws from fresh Carmel Coast and Central Valley ingredients to whip up contemporary adaptations of European-provincial and American cooking. Longtime menu favorites include artichoke lasagna in a roasted tomato sauce, duck with fresh cherries and green peppercorns in a red wine sauce, a savory paella, and grilled steaks and chops. $ *Average main: $30* ⊠ *6th Ave. and Mission St.* ☎ *831/624–6562* ⊕ *www.grasings.com* ⌕ *Reservations essential.*

$
AMERICAN
✕ **Jack London's.** This pub-like local hangout is one of the only Carmel restaurants to serve food late at night, often until 11 pm or midnight. The menu includes everything from nachos to steaks. $ *Average main: $15* ⊠ *Su Vecino Court, Dolores St., between 5th and 6th Aves.* ☎ *831/624–2336* ⊕ *www.jacklondons.com.*

$$$
FRENCH
✕ **L'Escargot.** Chef-owner Kericos Loutas personally sees to each plate of food served at this romantic, unpretentious French restaurant. Order the pan-roasted duck breast or the cassoulet de Toulouse; or, if you can't decide, choose the three-course prix-fixe dinner. $ *Average main: $30* ⊠ *Mission and 4th Ave.* ☎ *831/620–1942* ⊕ *www.escargot-carmel.com* ⌕ *Reservations essential* ⊘ *No lunch.*

$$
TAPAS
✕ **Mundaka.** Traditional Spanish-style tapas made with fresh local ingredients, a full bar, and live music seven nights a week attract legions of locals to this cozy downtown eatery. The menu changes weekly,

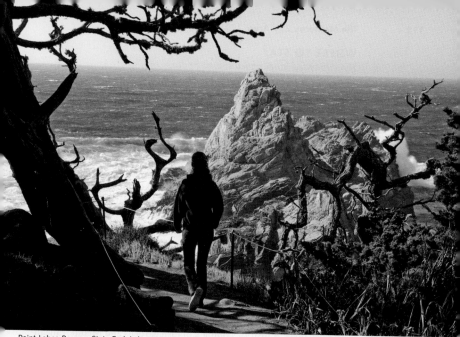

Point Lobos Reserve State Park is home to one of the only two natural stands of Monterey Cypress in the world.

but longtime favorites include the Angus beef slider with Spanish blue cheese and truffle fries, the authentic Valencian paella, and a platter of housemade charcuterie. Come early in the evening for a more intimate experience—music starts at 9:30 pm on weekends, while mellower music entertains diners starting at 7:30 other nights. The breakfast menu includes Spanish tortillas, plus Belgian waffles and homemade baked goods; for lunch, choose among sandwiches, panini, and salads. ⑤ *Average main: $21* ⊠ *San Carlos St., between Ocean and 7th Aves.* ☎ *831/624–7400* ⊕ *www.mundakacarmel.com.*

$
AMERICAN
✕ **Tuck Box.** This bright little restaurant is in a cottage right out of a fairy tale, complete with stone fireplace. Handmade scones, good for breakfast or afternoon tea, are the specialty. ⑤ *Average main: $12* ⊠ *Dolores St., between Ocean and 7th Aves.* ☎ *831/624–6365* ⊕ *www.tuckbox. com* ⌂ *Reservations not accepted* ☐ *No credit cards* ⊗ *No dinner.*

$$$
ITALIAN
✕ **Vesuvio.** Chef and restaurateur Rich Pèpe heats up the night with his latest venture, a lively trattoria downstairs and a swinging rooftop terrace, Starlight Lounge 65°. Pèpe's elegant take on traditional Italian cuisine yields dishes such as wild-boar Bolognese pappardelle, lobster ravioli, and velvety limoncello mousse cake. Pizzas and small plates are served in the restaurant and two bars. Upstairs, relax in comfy chairs by fire pits and enjoy bird's-eye views of the village and, most nights in summer, take in live music. ⑤ *Average main: $24* ⊠ *6th and Junipero Aves.* ☎ *831/625–1766 ext. 2* ⊕ *www.vesuviocarmel.com* ⊗ *No lunch.*

WHERE TO STAY

For expanded hotel reviews, visit Fodors.com.

$$$　**Cypress Inn.** A top-to-bottom redecorating project in 2013 gave this
B&B/INN　luxurious inn a fresh Mediterranean air with Moroccan touches. **Pros:**
luxury without snobbery; popular lounge; traditional British-style after-
noon tea. **Cons:** not for the pet-phobic. $ *Rooms from: $235* ⊠ *Lincoln
St. and 7th Ave.* 🕾 *831/624–3871, 800/443–7443* ⊕ *www.cypress-inn.
com* 🛏 *39 rooms, 5 suites* ⊙∣ *Breakfast.*

$$$$　**Hyatt Carmel Highlands.** High on a hill overlooking the Pacific, this
HOTEL　place has superb views; accommodations include king rooms with fire-
places, suites with personal Jacuzzis, and full town houses with all the
perks. **Pros:** killer views; romantic getaway; great food. **Cons:** thin
walls; must drive to Carmel. $ *Rooms from: $369* ⊠ *120 Highlands
Dr.* 🕾 *831/620–1234, 800/233–1234* ⊕ *carmelhighlands.hyatt.com*
🛏 *46 rooms, 2 suites.*

$$$$　**L'Auberge Carmel.** Stepping through the doors of this elegant inn is
B&B/INN　like being transported to a little European village. **Pros:** in town but off
Fodor's Choice　the main drag; four blocks from the beach; full-service luxury. **Cons:**
★　touristy area; not a good choice for families. $ *Rooms from: $425*
⊠ *Monte Verde, at 7th Ave.* 🕾 *831/624–8578* ⊕ *www.laubergecarmel.
com* 🛏 *20 rooms* ⊙∣ *Breakfast.*

$$$$　**La Playa Hotel.** A historic complex of lush gardens and Mediterranean-
HOTEL　style buildings, La Playa reopened in 2012 after a $3.5 million renova-
tion. **Pros:** residential neighborhood; manicured gardens; two blocks
from the beach. **Cons:** four stories (no elevator); busy lobby; some
rooms are on the small side. $ *Rooms from: $279* ⊠ *Camino Real, at
8th Ave.* 🕾 *831/293–6100, 800/582–8900* ⊕ *www.laplayahotel.com*
🛏 *75 rooms* ⊙∣ *Breakfast.*

$$　**Mission Ranch.** Movie star Clint Eastwood owns this sprawling prop-
HOTEL　erty whose accommodations include rooms in a converted barn, and
several cottages, some with fireplaces. **Pros:** farm setting; pastoral views;
great for tennis buffs. **Cons:** busy parking lot; must drive to the heart
of town. $ *Rooms from: $140* ⊠ *26270 Dolores St.* 🕾 *831/624–6436,
800/538–8221, 831/625–9040 restaurant* ⊕ *www.missionranchcarmel.
com* 🛏 *31 rooms* ⊙∣ *Breakfast.*

$$$　**Sea View Inn.** In a residential area a few hundred feet from the beach,
B&B/INN　this restored 1905 home has a double parlor with two fireplaces, orien-
tal rugs, canopy beds, and a spacious front porch. **Pros:** quiet; private;
close to the beach. **Cons:** small building; uphill trek to the heart of
town. $ *Rooms from: $200* ⊠ *Camino Real, between 11th and 12th
Aves.* 🕾 *831/624–8778* ⊕ *www.seaviewinncarmel.com* 🛏 *8 rooms, 6
with private bath* ⊙∣ *Breakfast.*

$$$$　**Tickle Pink Inn.** Atop a towering cliff, this inn has views of the Big
B&B/INN　Sur coastline, which you can contemplate from your private balcony.
Pros: close to great hiking; intimate; dramatic views. **Cons:** close to a
big hotel; lots of traffic during the day. $ *Rooms from: $289* ⊠ *155
Highland Dr.* 🕾 *831/624–1244, 800/635–4774* ⊕ *www.ticklepink.com*
🛏 *23 rooms, 10 suites, 1 cottage* ⊙∣ *Breakfast.*

$$$　**Tradewinds Carmel.** This converted motel with sleek decor inspired
B&B/INN　by the South Seas encircles a courtyard with waterfalls, a meditation

garden, and a fire pit. **Pros:** serene; within walking distance of restaurants; friendly service. **Cons:** no pool; long walk to the beach. ⑤ *Rooms from: $250* ✉ *Mission St., at 3rd Ave.* ☎ *831/624–2776* ⊕ *www. tradewindscarmel.com* ⮑ *26 rooms, 2 suites* ❍❙ *Breakfast.*

SHOPPING

ART GALLERIES

Carmel Art Association. The association exhibits the original paintings and sculptures of local artists. ✉ *Dolores St., between 5th and 6th Aves.* ☎ *831/624–6176* ⊕ *www.carmelart.org.*

Galerie Plein Aire. The gallery showcases the oil paintings of a group of local artists. ✉ *Dolores St., between 5th and 6th Aves.* ☎ *831/625–5686* ⊕ *www.galeriepleinaire.com.*

Gallery Sur. Fine art photography of the Big Sur Coast and the Monterey Peninsula, including scenic shots and golf images, is the focus here. ✉ *6th Ave., between Dolores and Lincoln Sts.* ☎ *831/626–2615* ⊕ *www.gallerysur.com.*

Richard MacDonald/Dawson Cole Fine Art. Amazing images of dancers, athletes, and other humans in motion come to life in this gallery that is devoted to the artworks of Monterey Bay resident Richard MacDonald, one of the most famed figurative sculptors of our time. ✉ *Lincoln St., at 6th Ave.* ☎ *800/972–5528* ⊕ *www.dawsoncolefineart.com* ☾ *Mon.–Sat. 10–6, Sun. 10–5:30.*

Weston Gallery. Run by the family of the late Edward Weston, this is hands down the best photography gallery around, with contemporary color photography complemented by classic black-and-whites. ✉ *6th Ave., between Dolores and Lincoln Sts.* ☎ *831/624–4453* ⊕ *www. westongallery.com.*

SPECIALTY SHOPS

Avant Garden & Home. An eclectic array of art, jewelry, home furnishings, garden accents, and handmade gift items from around the world are on display at this small, family-run shop. ✉ *San Carlos St., at 7th Ave.* ☎ *831/626–9899* ⊕ *www.avantgardenandhome.com.*

Bittner. The shop carries a fine selection of collectible and vintage pens from around the world. ✉ *Ocean Ave., between Mission and San Carlos Sts.* ☎ *831/626–8828* ⊕ *www.bittner.com.*

Intima. Find European lingerie here that ranges from lacy to racy. ✉ *San Carlos St., between Ocean and 6th Aves.* ☎ *831/625–0599* ⊕ *www. intimacarmel.com.*

Jan de Luz. This shop monograms and embroiders fine linens (including bathrobes) while you wait. ✉ *Dolores St., between Ocean and 7th Aves.* ☎ *831/622–7621* ⊕ *www.jandeluz.com.*

Madrigal. Sportswear, sweaters, and accessories for women are the specialties here. ✉ *Carmel Plaza and Mission St.* ☎ *831/624–3477.*

CARMEL VALLEY

10 miles east of Carmel, Hwy. 1 to Carmel Valley Rd.

Carmel Valley Road, which heads inland from Highway 1 south of Carmel, is the main thoroughfare through this valley, a secluded enclave of horse ranchers and other well-heeled residents who prefer the area's sunny climate to coastal fog and wind. Once thick with dairy farms, the valley has evolved into an esteemed wine appellation. Carmel Valley Village has crafts shops, art galleries, and the tasting rooms of numerous local wineries.

GETTING HERE AND AROUND

From U.S. 101 north or south, exit at Highway 68 and head west toward the coast. Scenic, two-lane Laureles Grade winds west over the mountains to Carmel Valley Road north of the village.

TOURS

The Carmel Valley Grapevine Express, aka MST's Line 24 bus, travels between downtown Monterey and Carmel Valley Village, with stops near wineries, restaurants, and shopping centers. At $10 for a ride-all-day pass, it's an incredible bargain.

Bus Contact Carmel Valley Grapevine Express ☎ *888/678–2871* ⊕ *www.mst.org.*

EXPLORING

Bernardus Tasting Room. At this tasting room you can sample many of Bernardus Winery's offerings, including older vintages and reserve wines. ⊠ *5 W. Carmel Valley Rd., at El Caminito Rd.* ☎ *831/298–8021, 800/223–2533* ⊕ *www.bernardus.com* ⊗ *Daily 11–5.*

Château Julien. The expansive winery, recognized internationally for its Chardonnays and Merlots, offers tours by appointment only, but the tasting room is open daily. ⊠ *8940 Carmel Valley Rd., at Schetter Rd.* ☎ *831/624–2600* ⊕ *www.chateaujulien.com* ⊗ *Mon.–Fri. 8–5, Sat.–Sun. 11–5; tours Mon.–Fri. at 10:30 and 2:30, Sat.–Sun. at 12:30 and 2:30, by appointment.*

Cowgirl Winery. Taste Chardonnay, Cabernet Sauvignon, Rosé, and blends in a hip, cowgirl-chic main building or at outdoor tables amid chickens, a tractor, and a rustic flatbed truck. Order woodfired pizzas from sister business Corkscrew Café down the block for delivery to your tasting table. ⊠ *25 Pilot Rd.* ☎ *831/298–7030* ⊗ *Apr.–Oct., Sun.–Fri. 11:30–5, Sat. 11:30–6. Nov.–Mar., Wed.–Fri. 11:30–5, Sat. 11:30–6.*

Earthbound Farm. Pick up fresh veggies, ready-to-eat meals, gourmet groceries, flowers, and gifts at Earthbound Farm, the world's largest grower of organic produce. You can also take a romp in the kid's garden, cut your own herbs, and stroll through the chamomile aromatherapy labyrinth. Special events, on Saturdays from April through December, include bug walks and garlic-braiding workshops. ⊠ *7250 Carmel Valley Rd.* ☎ *831/625–6219* ⊕ *www.ebfarm.com* ⊠ *Free* ⊗ *Mon.–Sat. 8–6:30, Sun. 9–6.*

Garland Ranch Regional Park. Hiking trails stretch across much of this park's 4,500 acres of meadows, forested hillsides, and creeks. ⊠ *Carmel Valley Rd., 9 miles east of Carmel-by-the-Sea* ☎ *831/659–4488* ⊕ *www.mprpd.org.*

WHERE TO EAT

$$
EUROPEAN
✕ **Café Rustica.** European country cooking is the focus at this lively road-house. Specialties include roasted meats, seafood, pastas, and thin-crust pizzas from the wood-fired oven. It can get noisy inside; for a quieter meal, request a table outside. $ *Average main: $20* ✉ *10 Delfino Pl., at Pilot Rd., off Carmel Valley Rd.* ☎ *831/659–4444* ⊕ *www. caferusticavillage.com* ⚘ *Reservations essential* ⊙ *Closed Mon.*

$$
MODERN
AMERICAN
✕ **Corkscrew Café.** Take a break from wine touring and fill up on farm-fresh wine-country food at this casual, Old Monterey-style bistro. Herbs and seasonal produce come from their own organic gardens; fish comes from local waters, meats are hormone-free. Popular dishes include the homemade chicken salad, fish tacos, and woodfired pizzas with classic toppings and more unusual combinations (Meyer lemon and prosciutto). Dine indoors near the open kitchen or in the garden patio, and check out the collection of corkscrews from their beginnings in 17th-century Europe to the present. $ *Average main: $22* ✉ *55 W. Carmel Valley Rd., at Pilot Rd.* ☎ *831/659–8888* ⊕ *www.corkscrewcafe.com.*

$
AMERICAN
✕ **Wagon Wheel Coffee Shop.** This local hangout decorated with wagon wheels, cowboy hats, and lassos serves terrific hearty breakfasts, including oatmeal and banana pancakes, eggs Benedict, and biscuits and gravy. The lunch menu includes a dozen different burgers and other sandwiches. $ *Average main: $11* ✉ *Valley Hill Center, 7156 Carmel Valley Rd., next to Quail Lodge* ☎ *831/624–8878* ▬ *No credit cards* ⊙ *No dinner.*

$$$
AMERICAN
✕ **Will's Fargo.** Around since the 1920s, this restaurant calls itself a "dressed-up saloon." Steer horns and gilt-frame paintings adorn the walls of the Victorian-style dining room; you can also eat on the patios. The menu is mainly seafood and steaks, including a 20-ounce porter-house. $ *Average main: $28* ✉ *16 E. Carmel Valley Rd.* ☎ *831/659–2774* ⊕ *www.bernardus.com* ⊙ *No lunch.*

WHERE TO STAY

For expanded hotel reviews, visit Fodors.com.

$$$$
RESORT
Fodor's Choice
★
⌗ **Bernardus Lodge.** The spacious guest rooms at this luxury spa resort have vaulted ceilings, featherbeds, fireplaces, patios, and bathtubs for two. **Pros:** exceptional personal service; outstanding food and wine. **Cons:** pricey; some guests can seem snooty. $ *Rooms from: $455* ✉ *415 W. Carmel Valley Rd.* ☎ *831/658–3400, 888/648–9463* ⊕ *www. bernardus.com* ⇥ *56 rooms, 1 suite.*

$$$$
RESORT
⌗ **Carmel Valley Ranch.** Hotel scion John Pritzker bought this 500-acre all-suites resort in 2009 and committed more than $30 million to transform the property into an upscale experiential getaway. **Pros:** stunning natural setting; tons of activities; state-of-the-art amenities. **Cons:** must drive several miles to shops and nightlife; pricey. $ *Rooms from: $375* ✉ *1 Old Ranch Rd.* ☎☎ *831/625–9500* ⊕ *www.carmelvalleyranch.com* ⇥ *139 suites.*

$$$
HOTEL
FAMILY
⌗ **Quail Lodge & Golf Club.** A sprawling collection of California ranch-style buildings on 850 acres of lush meadows, fairways, and lakes, Quail Lodge offers luxury rooms and outdoor activities at surprisingly affordable rates. **Pros:** on the golf course; two on-site restaurants;

Land Rover Driving School on property. **Cons:** extra fees for athletic club passes and some services; 5 miles from the beach and Carmel Valley Village. Ⓢ *Rooms from: $225* ✉ *8205 Valley Greens Dr.* ☎ *831/624–2888* 🖷 *866/675–1101* ⊕ *www.quaillodge.com* ⤳ *77 rooms, 16 suites* ⦿ *Breakfast.*

$$$$
RESORT
Fodor'sChoice
★

🖹 **Stonepine Estate Resort.** Set on 330 pastoral acres, this former estate of the Crocker banking family has been converted to a luxurious inn. **Pros:** supremely exclusive. **Cons:** difficult to get a reservation; far from the coast. Ⓢ *Rooms from: $300* ✉ *150 E. Carmel Valley Rd.* ☎ *831/659–2245* ⊕ *www.stonepineestate.com* ⤳ *10 rooms, 2 suites, 3 cottages.*

SPAS

Refuge. Relax and recharge in a coed, European-style relaxation center on 2 serene acres—without breaking the bank. Heat up in the eucalyptus steam room or cedar sauna, plunge into cold pools, and relax indoors in zero-gravity chairs or outdoors in Adirondack chairs around fire pits. Repeat the cycle a few times, then lounge around the thermal waterfall pools. Talk is not allowed, and bathing suits are required. Optional 50-minute massages ($60) are available. ✉ *27300 Rancho San Carlos Rd., south off Carmel Valley Rd.* ☎ *831/620–7360* ⊕ *www. refuge.com* 🖾 *$39* ⊗ *Daily 10–10.*

SPORTS AND THE OUTDOORS
GOLF

Quail Lodge & Golf Club. The championship course here incorporates several lakes into its design. ✉ *8000 Valley Greens Dr.* ☎ *831/620–8808 golf shop, 831/620–8866 club concierge* ⊕ *www.quaillodge.com* ⅃ *18 holes. 5,478 yds. Par 71. Greens fees: $125/$150* ⌖ *Driving range, putting green, pitching area, golf carts, pull carts, rental clubs, pro shop, golf academy, lessons, restaurant, bar.*

Rancho Cañada Golf Club. Some of the holes at this public course with 36 holes overlook the Carmel River. ✉ *4860 Carmel Valley Rd., 1 mile east of Hwy. 1* ☎ *831/624–0111, 800/536–9459* ⊕ *www.ranchocanada. com* ⅃ *East Course: 18 holes. 6,125 yds. Par 71. Greens fee: $70. West Course: 18 holes. 6,357 yds. Par 71. Greens fee: $70* ⌖ *Driving range, putting green, pitching area, golf carts, pull carts, rental clubs, pro shop, golf lessons, restaurant, bar.*

PEBBLE BEACH

Off North San Antonio Rd. in Carmel-by-the-Sea or off Sunset Dr. in Pacific Grove.

Fodor'sChoice
★

In 1919 the Pacific Improvement Company acquired 18,000 acres of prime land on the Monterey Peninsula, including the entire Pebble Beach coastal region and much of Pacific Grove. Pebble Beach Golf Links and the Lodge at Pebble Beach opened the same year, and the private enclave evolved into a world-class golf destination with three posh lodges, five golf courses, and some of the West Coast's ritziest homes.

GETTING HERE AND AROUND

If you drive south from Monterey on Highway 1, exit at 17-Mile-Drive/Sunset Drive in Pacific Grove to find the northern entrance gate. Coming from Carmel, exit at Ocean Avenue and follow the road almost to the beach; turn right on North San Antonio Road to the Carmel Gate. You can also enter through the Highway 1 Gate at Scenic Drive/Sunridge Road. Monterey–Salinas Transit buses provide regular service in and around Pebble Beach.

EXPLORING

17-Mile Drive. Primordial nature resides in quiet harmony with palatial estates along 17-Mile Drive, which winds through an 8,400-acre microcosm of the Pebble Beach coastal landscape. Dotting the drive are rare Monterey cypress, trees so gnarled and twisted that Robert Louis Stevenson described them as "ghosts fleeing before the wind." Some sightseers balk at the $9.75-per-car collected at the gates to drive on the private roads, but most find the drive well worth the price. An alternative is to grab a bike; cyclists tour for free. ■ TIP→ **Visitors who spend at least $25 on dining or shopping in Pebble Beach receive a fee refund if they show a receipt at the exit gate.**

Bird Rock. Bird Rock, the largest of several islands at the southern end of the Monterey Peninsula Country Club's golf course, teems with harbor seals, sea lions, cormorants, and pelicans.

Crocker Marble Palace. Many of the stately homes along 17-Mile Drive reflect the classic Monterey or Spanish Mission style typical of the region. A standout is the Crocker Marble Palace, about a mile south of the Lone Cypress (⇨ *below*). It's a private waterfront estate inspired by a Byzantine castle, easily identifiable by its dozens of marble arches.

The Lone Cypress. The most-photographed tree along 17-Mile Drive is the weather-sculpted Lone Cypress, which grows out of a precipitous outcropping above the waves about 1½ miles up the road from Pebble Beach Golf Links. You can't walk out to the tree, but you can stop for a view of the Lone Cypress at a small parking area off the road.

Seal Rock. Sea creatures and birds—as well as some very friendly ground squirrels—make use of Seal Rock, the largest of a group of islands about 2 miles north of Lone Cypress.

WHERE TO STAY

For expanded hotel reviews, visit Fodors.com.

$$$$
RESORT
Fodor's Choice
★
🗑 **Casa Palmero.** This exclusive boutique hotel evokes a stately Mediterranean villa, where rooms are decorated with sumptuous fabrics and fine art and each has a wood-burning fireplace and heated floor; some have private outdoor patios with in-ground whirlpools. **Pros:** ultimate in pampering; more private than sister resorts; right on the golf course. **Cons:** pricey; may be *too* posh for some. ⑤ *Rooms from: $885* ✉ *1518 Cypress Dr.* ☎ *831/622–6650, 800/654–9300* ⊕ *www.pebblebeach.com* ⊃ *20 rooms, 4 suites.*

$$$$
RESORT
🗑 **The Inn at Spanish Bay.** This resort sprawls across a breathtaking stretch of shoreline and has lush, 600-square-foot rooms. **Pros:** attentive service; tons of amenities; spectacular views. **Cons:** huge hotel; 4 miles from other Pebble Beach Resorts facilities. ⑤ *Rooms from:*

$625 ⊠ 2700 17-Mile Dr. ☎ 831/647–7500, 800/654–9300 ⊕ www. pebblebeach.com ⚲ 252 rooms, 17 suites.

$$$$
RESORT
🍽 **Lodge at Pebble Beach.** All rooms have fireplaces and many have wonderful ocean views at this circa-1919 resort. **Pros:** world-class golf; borders the ocean and fairways; fabulous facilities. **Cons:** some rooms are on the small side; very pricey. ⑤ *Rooms from: $725 ⊠ 1700 17-Mile Dr. ☎ 831/624–3811, 800/654–9300 ⊕ www.pebblebeach.com ⚲ 142 rooms, 19 suites.*

SPORTS AND THE OUTDOORS

GOLF

Links at Spanish Bay. This course, which hugs a choice stretch of shoreline, is designed in the rugged manner of a traditional Scottish course, with sand dunes and coastal marshes interspersed among the greens. Nonguests can reserve tee times up to two months in advance. ⊠ *17-Mile Dr., north end* ☎ *800/654–9300* ⊕ *www.pebblebeach.com* 🏌 *18 holes. 6,821 yds. Par 72. Greens fee: $265 ☞ Putting green, pitching area, golf carts, caddies, rental clubs, pro shop, golf academy, lessons, restaurant, bar.*

Fodor's Choice
★
Pebble Beach Golf Links. This club attracts golfers from around the world. The ocean plays a major role in the 18th hole of the famed links. Each February the course is the main site of the AT&T Pebble Beach Pro-Am, where show-business celebrities and golf pros team up for one of the nation's most glamorous tournaments. Tee times are available to guests who book a minimum two-night stay. Nonguests can reserve a tee time only one day in advance on a space-available basis (up to a year for groups); resort guests can reserve up to 18 months in advance. ⊠ *17-Mile Dr., near Lodge at Pebble Beach* ☎ *800/654–9300* ⊕ *www.pebblebeach.com* 🏌 *18 holes. 6,828 yds. Par 72. Greens fee: $495 ☞ Driving range, putting green, pitching area, golf carts, caddies, rental clubs, pro shop, golf academy, lessons, restaurant, bar.*

Peter Hay. This 9-hole, par-3 course has attracted golfers of all skill levels since 1957. ⊠ *17-Mile Dr.* ☎ *831/622–8723* ⊕ *www.pebblebeach.com* 🏌 *9 holes. 725 yds. Par 27. Greens fee: $30 ☞ Rental clubs, pro shop, golf academy, lessons, restaurant, bar.*

Spyglass Hill. This course is among the most challenging Pebble Beach courses. With the first five holes bordering on the Pacific and the other 13 reaching deep into the Del Monte Forest, the course is tricky, but oh, the views! Reservations are essential and may be made up to one month in advance (18 months for resort guests). ⊠ *Stevenson Dr. and Spyglass Hill Rd.* ☎ *800/654–9300* ⊕ *www.pebblebeach.com* 🏌 *18 holes. 6,960 yds. Par 72. Greens fee: $370 ☞ Driving range, putting green, pitching area, golf carts, caddies, rental clubs, pro shop, golf academy, lessons, restaurant, bar.*

PACIFIC GROVE

3 miles north of Carmel-by-the-Sea on Hwy. 68.

This picturesque town, which began as a summer retreat for church groups more than a century ago, recalls its prim and proper Victorian heritage in its host of tiny board-and-batten cottages and stately mansions. However, long before the church groups flocked here the area received thousands of annual pilgrims—in the form of bright orange-and-black monarch butterflies. They still come, migrating south from Canada and the Pacific Northwest to take residence in pine and eucalyptus groves from October through March. In Butterfly Town USA, as Pacific Grove is known, the sight of a mass of butterflies hanging from the branches like a long, fluttering veil is unforgettable.

A prime way to enjoy Pacific Grove is to walk or bicycle the 3 miles of city-owned shoreline along Ocean View Boulevard, a cliff-top area landscaped with native plants and dotted with benches meant for sitting and gazing at the sea. You can spot many types of birds here, including the web-footed cormorants that crowd the massive rocks rising out of the surf. Two Victorians of note along Ocean View are the Queen Anne–style Green Gables, at No. 301—erected in 1888, it's now a B&B—and the 1909 Pryor House, at No. 429, a massive, shingled, private residence with a leaded- and beveled-glass doorway.

GETTING HERE AND AROUND

Reach Pacific Grove via Highway 68 off Highway 1, just south of Monterey. From Cannery Row in Monterey, head north until the road merges with Ocean Boulevard and follow it along the coast. MST buses travel within Pacific Grove and surrounding towns.

EXPLORING

FAMILY **Lovers Point Park.** The coastal views are gorgeous from this waterfront park whose sheltered beach has a children's pool and a picnic area. The main lawn has a volleyball court and a snack bar. ⊠ *Ocean View Blvd. northwest of Forest Ave.* ☎ *831/648–5730.*

FAMILY **Monarch Grove Sanctuary.** This sanctuary is a fairly reliable spot for viewing the butterflies between October and February. ⊠ *1073 Lighthouse Ave., at Ridge Rd.* ⊕ *www.pgmuseum.org.*

Pacific Grove Museum of Natural History. Contact the museum for the latest information about the butterfly population. Year-round, you can view the well-crafted butterfly tree exhibit here. ⊠ *165 Forest Ave., at Central Ave.* ☎ *831/648–5716* ⊕ *www.pgmuseum.org* ⌷ *$3 suggested donation; $5 per family* ⊙ *Tues.–Sun. 10–5.*

FAMILY **Point Pinos Lighthouse.** At this 1855-vintage lighthouse, the oldest continuously operating lighthouse on the West Coast, you can learn about the lighting and foghorn operations and wander through a small museum containing U.S. Coast Guard memorabilia. ⊠ *Asilomar Ave., between Lighthouse Ave. and Del Monte Blvd.* ☎ *831/648–3176* ⊕ *www.pointpinos.org* ⌷ *$2 suggested donation* ⊙ *Thur.–Mon. 1–4.*

BEACHES

Asilomar State Beach. A beautiful coastal area, Asilomar State Beach stretches between Point Pinos and the Del Monte Forest. The 100 acres of dunes, tidal pools, and pocket-size beaches form one of the region's richest areas for marine life—including surfers, who migrate here most winter mornings. Leashed dogs are allowed on the beach. **Amenities:** none. **Best for:** sunrise; sunset; surfing; walking. ⊠ *Sunset Dr. and Asilomar Ave.* ☎ *831/646–6440* ⊕ *www.parks.ca.gov.*

WHERE TO EAT

$$$
MEDITERRANEAN

✕ **Fandango.** The menu here is mostly Mediterranean and southern French, with such dishes as calves' liver and onions and paella served in a skillet. The decor follows suit: stone walls and country furniture give the restaurant the earthy feel of a European farmhouse. This is where locals come when they want to have a big dinner with friends, drink wine, have fun, and generally feel at home. $ *Average main: $26* ⊠ *223 17th St., south of Lighthouse Ave.* ☎ *831/372–3456* ⊕ *www.fandangorestaurant.com.*

$$
SEAFOOD

✕ **Fishwife.** Fresh fish with a Latin accent makes this spot a favorite of locals for lunch or a casual dinner. Standards are the sea garden salads topped with your choice of fish and the fried seafood plates with fresh veggies. Diners with large appetites appreciate the fisherman's bowls— fresh fish served with rice, black beans, spicy cabbage, salsa, vegetables, and crispy tortilla strips. $ *Average main: $22* ⊠ *1996½ Sunset Dr., at Asilomar Blvd.* ☎ *831/375–7107* ⊕ *www.fishwife.com.*

$$$
ITALIAN

✕ **Joe Rombi's La Mia Cucina.** Pasta, fish, steaks, and chops are the specialties at this modern trattoria, which is the best in town for Italian food. The look is spare and clean, with colorful antique wine posters decorating the white walls. Next door, Joe Rombi's La Piccola Casa Pizzeria & Coffee House serves breakfast (baked goods) and lunch daily, plus early dinner Wednesday through Sunday. $ *Average main: $23* ⊠ *208 17th St., at Lighthouse Ave.* ☎ *831/373–2416* ⊕ *www.joerombi.com* ⊙ *Closed Mon. and Tues. No lunch.*

$$$
MODERN
AMERICAN

✕ **Passionfish.** South American artwork and artifacts decorate the walls, and Latin and Asian flavors infuse the dishes. Chef Ted Walter shops at local farmers' markets several times a week to find the best produce, fish, and meat available, then pairs them with creative sauces. The menu might include sea scallops with tomato-truffle butter and savory rice pudding. $ *Average main: $23* ⊠ *701 Lighthouse Ave., at Congress Ave.* ☎ *831/655–3311* ⊕ *www.passionfish.net* ⊙ *No lunch.*

$
MEXICAN

✕ **Peppers Mexicali Cafe.** This cheerful white-walled storefront serves traditional dishes from Mexico and Latin America, with an emphasis on fresh seafood. Excellent red and green salsas are made throughout the day, and there's a large selection of beers, along with fresh lime margaritas. $ *Average main: $15* ⊠ *170 Forest Ave., between Lighthouse and Central Aves.* ☎ *831/373–6892* ⊕ *www.peppersmexicalicafe.com* ⊙ *Closed Tues. No lunch Sun.*

$$
AMERICAN

✕ **Red House Café.** When it's nice out, sun pours through the big windows of this cozy restaurant and across tables on the porch; when fog rolls in, the fireplace is lighted. The American menu changes with the seasons but typically includes grilled lamb fillets atop mashed potatoes for dinner and Dungeness crab cakes over salad for lunch. Breakfast on weekends is a local favorite. $ *Average main: $20* ⊠ *662 Lighthouse Ave., at 19th St.* ☎ *831/643–1060* ⊕ *www.redhousecafe.com* ☾ *Closed Mon.*

$$ ✕**Taste Café and Bistro.** Grilled marinated rabbit, roasted half chicken,
AMERICAN filet mignon, and other meats are the focus at this café, which serves hearty European-inspired food in a casual, open-kitchen setting. $ *Average main: $20* ⊠ *1199 Forest Ave.* ☎ *831/655–0324* ⊕ *www. tastecafebistro.com* ☾ *Closed Sun.–Mon.*

WHERE TO STAY

For expanded hotel reviews, visit Fodors.com.

$$ 📷 **Green Gables Inn.** Stained-glass windows and ornate interior details
B&B/INN compete with spectacular ocean views at this Queen Anne–style mansion, built by a businessman for his mistress in 1888. **Pros:** exceptional views; impeccable attention to historic detail. **Cons:** some rooms are small; thin walls. $ *Rooms from: $145* ⊠ *301 Ocean View Blvd.* ☎ *831/375–2095, 800/722–1774* ⊕ *www.greengablesinnpg.com* ⤴ *10 rooms, 7 with bath; 1 suite* ⎮○⎮ *Breakfast.*

$$ 📷 **Lighthouse Lodge and Cottages.** Near the tip of the peninsula, this basic
HOTEL complex straddles Lighthouse Avenue—the lodge is on one side, the all-suites facility on the other. **Pros:** near lighthouse and 17-Mile Drive; friendly reception; many room options. **Cons:** next to a cemetery; lodge rooms are basic. $ *Rooms from: $139* ⊠ *1150 and 1249 Lighthouse Ave.* ☎ *831/655–2111, 800/858–1249* ⊕ *www.lighthouselodgecottages. com* ⤴ *64 rooms, 31 suites* ⎮○⎮ *Breakfast.*

$$$ 📷 **Martine Inn.** The glassed-in parlor and many guest rooms at this 1899
B&B/INN Mediterranean-style villa have stunning ocean views, and thoughtful details such as robes and rocking chairs create an ambience of luxuriant comfort. **Pros:** romantic; fancy breakfast; ocean views. **Cons:** not child-friendly; sits on a busy thoroughfare. $ *Rooms from: $199* ⊠ *255 Ocean View Blvd.* ☎ *831/373–3388, 800/852–5588* ⊕ *www. martineinn.com* ⤴ *25 rooms* ⎮○⎮ *Breakfast.*

MONTEREY

2 miles southeast of Pacific Grove via Lighthouse Ave.; 2 miles north of Carmel-by-the-Sea via Hwy. 1.

Early in the 20th century Carmel Martin, the first mayor of the city of Monterey, saw a bright future for his town: "Monterey Bay is the one place where people can live without being disturbed by manufacturing and big factories. I am certain that the day is coming when this will be the most desirable place in the whole state of California." His Honor was not far off the mark.

GETTING HERE AND AROUND

From San Jose or San Francisco, take U.S. 101 south to Highway 156 West at Prunedale. Head west about 8 miles to Highway 1 and follow it about 15 miles south. From San Luis Obispo, take U.S. 101 north to Salinas and drive west on Highway 68 about 20 miles.

Many MST bus lines connect at the Monterey Transit Center, at Pearl Street and Munras Avenue. In summer (daily from 10 until at least 7), the free

MST Monterey Trolley travels from downtown Monterey along Cannery Row to the Aquarium and back.

TOURS

Monterey Movie Tours. Board a customized motorcoach and relax while a film-savvy local takes you on a scenic tour of the Monterey Peninsula enhanced by film clips shown on overhead monitors. More than 200 movies have been shot in the area, and scenes with Marilyn Monroe, Clint Eastwood, Tom Hanks, and other stars play when the tour passes through the exact film locations. The three-hour adventure travels a 32-mile loop through Monterey, Pacific Grove, and Carmel, with stops along 17-Mile Drive and at Pebble Beach Lodge. The tour departs from the Monterey Conference Center; free pickup and return is available at some hotels. ☎ *831/372–6278, 800/343–6437* ⊕ *www.montereymovietours. com* ⊠ *$55* ⊘ *Daily at 1 pm.*

Old Monterey Walking Tour. Learn all about Monterey's storied past by joining a guided walking tour through the historic district. Tours begin at Custom House Plaza, across from Fisherman's Wharf. ⊠ *$5, includes admission to Custom House and Pacific House* ⊘ *Fri.–Sun. at 10:30, noon, and 2.*

ESSENTIALS

Visitor Information Monterey County Convention & Visitors Bureau ☎ *877/666–8373* ⊕ *www.seemonterey.com.*

> **JOHN STEINBECK'S CANNERY ROW**
>
> "Cannery Row in Monterey in California is a poem, a stink, a grating noise, a quality of light, a tone, a habit, a nostalgia, a dream. Cannery Row is the gathered and scattered, tin and iron and rust and splintered wood, chipped pavement and weedy lots and junk heaps, sardine canneries of corrugated iron, honky tonks, restaurants and whore houses, and little crowded groceries, and laboratories and flophouses."
>
> —John Steinbeck, *Cannery Row*

EXPLORING

TOP ATTRACTIONS

Cannery Row. When John Steinbeck published the novel *Cannery Row* in 1945, he immortalized a place of rough-edged working people. The waterfront street, edging a mile of gorgeous coastline, once was crowded with sardine canneries processing, at their peak, nearly 200,000 tons of the smelly silver fish a year. During the mid-1940s, however, the sardines disappeared from the bay, causing the canneries to close. Through the years the old tin-roof canneries have been converted into restaurants, art galleries, and malls with shops selling T-shirts, fudge, and plastic sea otters. Recent tourist development along the row has been more tasteful, however, and includes several stylish inns and hotels, wine tasting rooms, and upscale specialty shops. ⊠ *Cannery Row, between Reeside and David Aves.* ⊕ *www.canneryrow.com.*

Colton Hall. A convention of delegates met here in 1849 to draft the first state constitution. The stone building, which has served as a school, a

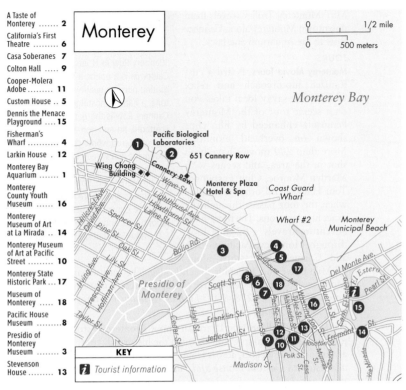

courthouse, and the county seat, is a city-run museum furnished as it was during the constitutional convention. The extensive grounds outside the hall surround the Old Monterey Jail. ⊠ *570 Pacific St., between Madison and Jefferson Sts.* ☎ *831/646–5640* ⊕ *www.monterey.org/ museums* ⊠ *Free* ⊙ *Daily 10–4; Tues. and Sun. noon–3 in winter.*

Cooper-Molera Adobe. The restored 2-acre complex includes a house dating from the 1820s, a gift shop, and a large garden enclosed by a high adobe wall. The mostly Victorian-era antiques and memorabilia that fill the house provide a glimpse into the life of a prosperous sea merchant's family. If the house is closed, you can still stop by the Cooper Store and pick up walking-tour maps and stroll the grounds. ⊠ *Monterey State Historic Park, Polk and Munras Sts.* ☎ *831/649–7111* ⊕ *www.parks. ca.gov/mshp* ⊠ *$5* ⊙ *Store, daily 10–4; gardens, daily 9–4; tours, Fri.– Sun 10:30 and 1:30.*

Custom House. Built by the Mexican government in 1827 and now California's oldest standing public building, the Custom House was the first stop for sea traders whose goods were subject to duties. In 1846, Commodore John Sloat raised the American flag over this adobe structure and claimed California for the United States. The lower floor displays cargo from a 19th-century trading ship. If the house is closed, you can visit the cactus gardens and stroll the plaza. ⊠ *Monterey State*

Historic Park, 1 Custom House Plaza, across from Fisherman's Wharf ☎ *831/649–7118* ⊕ *www.parks.ca.gov/mshp* 🖃 *$3 (also includes admission to Pacific House)* ⊘ *Fri.–Mon. 10–4.*

FAMILY **Fisherman's Wharf.** The mournful barking of sea lions provides a steady soundtrack all along Monterey's waterfront, but the best way to actually view the whiskered marine mammals is to walk along one of the two piers across from Custom House Plaza. Lined with souvenir shops, the wharf is undeniably touristy, but it's lively and entertaining. At Wharf No. 2, a working municipal pier, you can see the day's catch being unloaded from fishing boats on one side and fishermen casting their lines into the water on the other. The pier has a couple of low-key restaurants, from whose seats lucky customers may spot otters and harbor seals. ✉ *At end of Calle Principal* ⊕ *www.montereywharf.com.*

FAMILY **Monterey Bay Aquarium.** The minute you hand over your ticket at this
Fodor'sChoice extraordinary aquarium you're surrounded by sea creatures; right at
★ the entrance, you can see dozens of them swimming in a three-story-tall, sunlit kelp forest tank. The beauty of the exhibits here is that they are all designed to give a sense of what it's like to be in the water with the animals—sardines swim around your head in a circular tank, and jellyfish drift in and out of view in dramatically lighted spaces that suggest the ocean depths. A petting pool gives you a hands-on experience with bat rays, and the million-gallon Open Seas tank shows the vast variety of creatures (from sharks to placid-looking turtles) that live in the eastern Pacific. At the Splash Zone, which has 45 interactive bilingual exhibits, kids (and kids at heart) can commune with sea dragons, potbellied seahorses, and other fascinating creatures. The only drawback to the experience is that it must be shared with the throngs of people that crowd the place daily; most think it's worth it. ■**TIP→ To avoid the crowds, arrive as soon as the aquarium opens or visit after 2 pm.** Weekend evenings in summer, the aquarium stays open later and is usually less crowded during the extended hours. ■**TIP→ Reserve a lunch table at the aquarium's restaurant, perched on the ocean's edge. Otters and other sea creatures often frolic just outside the floor-to-ceiling windows.** ✉ *886 Cannery Row, at David Ave.* ☎ *831/648–4800 info, 866/963–9645 for advance tickets* ⊕ *www.montereybayaquarium. org* 🖃 *$35* ⊘ *Daily 10–6. Summer/holidays 9:30–6; summer weekends 9:30–8; winter daily 10–5.*

Monterey State Historic Park. You can glimpse Monterey's early history in the well-preserved adobe buildings scattered along several city blocks. Far from being a hermetic period museum, the park facilities are an integral part of the day-to-day business life of the town—within some of the buildings are a store, a theater, and government offices. At some of the historic houses, the gardens (open daily 10 to 5 in summer, 10 to 4 the rest of the year) are worthy sights themselves. ■**TIP→ At this writing, some buildings are closed and tours are on hiatus due to state park budget cuts. Private tours of some adobes are available by reservation. Cell phone tours are available 24/7—dial (831) 998–9498, followed by a stop number (401–410). Visit the park's website for up-to-date information.** ✉ *20 Custom House Plaza* ☎ *831/649–7118* ⊕ *www.parks. ca.gov/mshp* 🖃 *Free* ⊘ *Call for hrs.*

Trained "seals" that perform in circuses are actually California sea lions—intelligent, social animals that live (and sleep) close together in groups.

Museum of Monterey. The former Monterey Maritime Museum still displays maritime artifacts but has expanded its focus to include art, photography, and costumes from Monterey's earliest days to the present. The jewel in the museum's crown remains the enormous Fresnel lens from the Point Sur Light Station. ⊠ *Stanton Center, 5 Custom House Plaza* ☎ *831/372–2608* ⊕ *www.museumofmonterey.org* ✉ *$5. Free first Wed. of month 1–5* ⊙ *May–Aug. Tues.–Sat. 10–7, Sun. noon–5; Sept.– Apr. Wed.–Sat. 10–5, Sun. noon–5.*

WORTH NOTING

A Taste of Monterey. Without driving the back roads, you can taste the wines of more than 90 area vintners while taking in fantastic bay views. Purchase a few bottles and pick up a map and guide to the county's wineries and vineyards. ⊠ *700 Cannery Row, Suite KK* ☎ *831/646–5446, 888/646–5446* ⊕ *www.atasteofmonterey.com* ✉ *Wine tastings $8–$15* ⊙ *Sun.–Wed. 11–6, Thurs.–Sat. 11–7.*

California's First Theatre. This adobe began its life in 1846 as a saloon and lodging house for sailors. Four years later stage curtains were fashioned from army blankets, and some U.S. officers staged plays to the light of whale oil lamps. As of this writing, the building is open only for private tours, but you can stroll in the garden. ⊠ *Monterey State Historic Park, Scott and Pacific Sts.* ☎ *831/649–7118* ⊕ *www.parks. ca.gov/mshp* ✉ *Free* ⊙ *Call for hrs.*

Casa Soberanes. A classic low-ceiling adobe structure built in 1842, this was once a Custom House guard's residence. Exhibits at the house survey life in Monterey from the era of Mexican rule to the present. The building is open only for private tour requests, but you can visit the peaceful rear garden and its rose-covered arbor. ⊠ *Monterey State Historic Park, 336 Pacific St., at Del Monte Ave.* ☎ *831/649–7118* ⊕ *www.parks. ca.gov/mshp* ✉ *Free.*

FAMILY **Dennis the Menace Playground.** This play area was designed by the late cartoonist Hank Ketcham. The equipment is on a grand scale and made for Dennis-like daredevils: there's a roller slide, a clanking suspension bridge, and a real Southern Pacific steam locomotive.

> ### FORMER CAPITAL OF CALIFORNIA
>
> In 1602 Spanish explorer Sebastián Vizcaíno stepped ashore on a remote California peninsula. He named it after the viceroy of New Spain—Count de Monte Rey. Soon the Spanish built a military outpost, and the site was the capital of California until the state came under American rule.

You can rent a rowboat or a paddleboat for cruising around U-shaped Lake El Estero, populated with an assortment of ducks, mud hens, and geese. ⊠ *El Estero Park, Pearl St. and Camino El Estero* ☎ *831/646– 3866* ⊕ *www.monterey.org/Departments/MontereyRecreation/Parks andBeaches/ElEsteroParkComplex.aspx* ☉ *Daily 10–dusk in summer* ☉ *Closed Tues., Sept.–May.*

Larkin House. A veranda encircles the second floor of this 1835 adobe, whose design bears witness to the Mexican and New England influences on the Monterey style. Many of the antiques inside were brought from New Hampshire by the building's namesake, Thomas O. Larkin, an early California statesman. The building is open only for special tour requests, but you can peek in the windows and stroll the gardens. ⊠ *Monterey State Historic Park, 464 Calle Principal, between Jefferson and Pacific Sts.* ☎ *831/649–7118* ⊕ *www.parks.ca.gov/mshp.*

FAMILY **Monterey County Youth Museum (MY Museum).** Monterey Bay comes to life from a child's perspective in this fun-filled, interactive indoor exploration center. The seven exhibit galleries showcase the science and nature of the Big Sur coast, theater arts, Pebble Beach golf, and beaches. There's also a live performance theater, a creation station, a hospital emergency room, and an agriculture corner where kids follow artichokes, strawberries, and other fruits and veggies on their evolution from sprout to harvest to farmers' markets. ⊠ *425 Washington St., between E. Franklin St. and Bonifacio Pl.* ☎ *831/649–6444* ⊕ *www.mymuseum.org* ✉ *$7* ☉ *Tues.–Sat. 10–5, Sun. noon–5.*

Monterey Museum of Art at La Mirada. Asian and European antiques fill this 19th-century adobe house. A newer 10,000-square-foot gallery space, designed by Charles Moore, houses Asian and California regional art. Outdoors are magnificent rose and rhododendron gardens. ⊠ *720 Via Mirada, at Fremont St.* ☎ *831/372–3689* ⊕ *www.montereyart. org* ✉ *$10, also good for admission to museum's Pacific Street facility* ☉ *Wed.–Sat. 11–5, Sun. 1–4.*

Monterey Museum of Art at Pacific Street. Photographs by Ansel Adams and Edward Weston, as well as works by other artists who have spent time on the peninsula, are on display here, along with international folk art, from Kentucky hearth brooms to Tibetan prayer wheels. ⊠ *559 Pacific*

St., across from Colton Hall ☎ *831/372–5477* ⊕ *www.montereyart. org* ✉ *$10, also good for admission to museum's La Mirada facility* ☉ *Wed.–Sat. 11–5, Sun. 1–4.*

Pacific House Museum. Once a hotel and saloon, this visitor center and museum now commemorates early-California life with gold-rush relics and photographs of old Monterey. The upper floor displays Native American artifacts, including gorgeous baskets and pottery. ✉ *Monterey State Historic Park, 10 Custom House Plaza* ☎ *831/649–7118* ⊕ *www.parks.ca.gov/mshp* ✉ *$3 (includes admission to Custom House)* ☉ *Fri.–Sun. 10–4.*

Presidio of Monterey Museum. This spot has been significant for centuries. Its first incarnation was as a Native American village for the Rumsien tribe. The Spanish explorer Sebastián Vizcaíno landed here in 1602, and Father Junípero Serra arrived in 1770. Notable battles fought here include the 1818 skirmish in which the corsair Hipólito Bruchard conquered the Spanish garrison that stood on this site and claimed part of California for Argentina. The indoor museum tells the stories; plaques mark the outdoor sites. ✉ *Presidio of Monterey, Corporal Ewing Rd., off Lighthouse Ave.* ☎ *831/646–3456* ⊕ *www.monterey.org/museums* ✉ *Free* ☉ *Mon. 10–1, Thurs.–Sat. 10–4, Sun. 1–4.*

Stevenson House. This house was named in honor of author Robert Louis Stevenson, who boarded here briefly in a tiny upstairs room. Items from his family's estate furnish Stevenson's room; period-decorated chambers elsewhere in the house include a gallery of memorabilia and a children's nursery stocked with Victorian toys and games. The house is open only for special tour requests, but you can stroll around the gardens. ✉ *Monterey State Historic Park, 530 Houston St., near Pearl St.* ☎ *831/649–7118* ⊕ *www.parks.ca.gov/mshp* ☉ *Daily 9–5, gardens only.*

WHERE TO EAT

$$ ✕ **Monterey Fish House.** Casual yet stylish and always packed, this sea-
SEAFOOD food restaurant is removed from the hubbub of the wharf. If the dining room is full, you can wait at the bar and savor deliciously plump oysters on the half shell. The bartenders and waitstaff will gladly advise you on the perfect wine to go with your poached, blackened, or oak-grilled seafood. ⑤ *Average main: $21* ✉ *2114 Del Monte Ave., at Dela Vina Ave.* ☎ *831/373–4647* ⟲ *Reservations essential* ☉ *No lunch Sat.–Sun.*

$$$ ✕ **Montrio Bistro.** This quirky, converted firehouse, with its rawhide walls
AMERICAN and iron indoor trellises, has a wonderfully sophisticated menu. Chef
Fodor's Choice Tony Baker uses organic produce and meats and sustainably sourced
★ seafood to create imaginative dishes that reflect local agriculture, such as baby artichoke risotto fritters, and pesto-rubbed prime sirloin with marinated prawns, spinach, and a red wine–veal reduction sauce. The wine list also draws primarily on California—Monterey-area wineries are well represented—and signature cocktails are infused with local fruits, herbs, and veggies. ⑤ *Average main: $24* ✉ *414 Calle Principal, at W. Franklin St.* ☎ *831/648–8880* ⊕ *www.montrio.com* ⟲ *Reservations essential* ☉ *No lunch.*

CLOSE UP

The Underwater Kingdom

Although Monterey's coastal landscapes are stunning, their beauty is more than equaled by the wonders that lie offshore. The huge Monterey Bay National Marine Sanctuary—which stretches 276 miles, from north of San Francisco almost all the way down to Santa Barbara—teems with abundant life, and has topography as diverse as that aboveground.

The preserve's 5,322 square miles include vast submarine canyons, which reach down 10,663 feet at their deepest point. They also encompass dense forests of giant kelp—a kind of seaweed that can grow more than a hundred feet from its roots on the ocean floor. These kelp forests are especially robust off Monterey.

The sanctuary was established in 1992 to protect the habitat of the many species that thrive in the bay. Some animals can be seen quite easily from land. In summer and winter you might glimpse the offshore spray of gray whales as

they migrate between their summer feeding grounds in Alaska and their breeding grounds in Baja. Clouds of marine birds—including white-faced ibis, three types of albatross, and more than 15 types of gull—skim the waves, or roost in the rock islands along 17-Mile Drive. Sea otters dart and gambol in the calmer waters of the bay; and of course, you can watch the sea lions—and hear their round-the-clock barking—on the wharves in Santa Cruz and Monterey.

The sanctuary supports many other creatures, however, that remain unseen by most on-land visitors. Some of these are enormous, such as the giant blue whales that arrive to feed on plankton in summer; others, like the more than 22 species of red algae in these waters, are microscopic. So whether you choose to visit the Monterey Bay Aquarium, take a whale-watch trip, or look out to sea with your binoculars, remember you're seeing just a small part of a vibrant underwater kingdom.

3

$$$
SEAFOOD
✕ **Old Fisherman's Grotto.** Watch otters and seals frolic in the water while savoring seafood, steak, and pasta at this family-owned and operated eatery, established in 1950 in the midsection of Fisherman's Wharf. The founder's son and current owner, Chris Shake, has updated the decor and menu while retaining the classic 1950s nautical style. Famed for its creamy clam chowder, the restaurant also serves a huge range of dishes, from seafood paella and sand dabs to filet mignon and teriyaki chicken. ■TIP➔ Reserve a windowside table for the best views. $ *Average main: $25* ✉ *39 Fisherman's Wharf* ☎ *831/375–4604* ⊕ *www.oldfishermansgrotto.com.*

$
AMERICAN
✕ **Old Monterey Café.** Breakfast here gets constant local raves. The café's fame rests on familiar favorites: a dozen kinds of omelets, and pancakes from blueberry to cinnamon-raisin-pecan. For lunch are good soups, salads, and sandwiches. This is a fine place to relax with an afternoon cappuccino. $ *Average main: $12* ✉ *489 Alvarado St., at Munras Ave.* ☎ *831/646–1021* ⌦ *Reservations not accepted* ☾ *No dinner.*

$$$$ ✕ **Restaurant 1833.** Housed in the historic Stokes Adobe, built in 1833,
MODERN this überpopular restaurant and bar showcases the region's colorful his-
AMERICAN tory and local bounty in one of the most unusual settings anywhere.
Fodor's Choice The two-story structure, a national heritage site, was once the home of
★ the mayor of Monterey. Today it includes seven distinct dining rooms;
each honors an era and characters from the adobe's storied past. Sit in a
leather booth on the Founder's Balcony for a bird's-eye view of the rocking bar scene below, or outdoors by the fire pits in the courtyard, near
giant oak, redwood, palm, and magnolia trees. The casual menu changes
daily and centers around seasonal local ingredients. Regular stars include
bacon-cheddar biscuits with maple-chili butter and soy-glazed quail, pan-
roasted mahi mahi, and bacon-wrapped pork loin. The cocktail menu
pays tribute to the adobe's 1840s-era apothecary business with four categories: Pain Killers, Stress Relievers, Elixirs, and Aphrodisiacs, which,
along with the extensive wine list, fuel a lively atmosphere indoors and
out, especially on weekend nights. ⑤ *Average main: $32* ⊠ *500 Hartnell
St.* ☎ *831/643–1833* ⊕ *www.restaurant1833.com* ☻ *No lunch.*

$$ ✕ **Tarpy's Roadhouse.** Fun, dressed-up American favorites—a little some-
AMERICAN thing for everyone—are served in this renovated early-1900s stone
farmhouse several miles east of town. The kitchen cranks out every-
thing from Cajun-spiced prawns to meat loaf with marsala-mushroom
gravy to grilled ribs and steaks. Eat indoors by a fireplace or outdoors
in the courtyard. ⑤ *Average main: $22* ⊠ *2999 Monterey–Salinas Hwy.,
Hwy. 68* ☎ *831/647–1444* ⊕ *www.tarpys.com.*

WHERE TO STAY

For expanded hotel reviews, visit Fodors.com.

$$$ 🏨 **Best Western Beach Resort Monterey.** With a great waterfront loca-
RESORT tion about 2 miles north of Monterey—with views of the bay and the
city skyline—and a surprising array of amenities, this hotel is one of
the area's best values. **Pros:** on the beach; great value; family-friendly.
Cons: several miles from major attractions; big-box mall neighborhood. ⑤ *Rooms from: $189* ⊠ *2600 Sand Dunes Dr.* ☎ *831/394–3321,
800/242–8627* ⊕ *www.montereybeachresort.com* ☂ *196 rooms.*

$$ 🏨 **Hotel Abrego.** In central Monterey just a half-block from the transit
HOTEL center and a 15-minute walk to Fisherman's Wharf, this full-service
hotel offers six different room types in four Mission-style buildings.
Pros: central location; near public transit; range of room options. **Cons:**
not on waterfront; pool and exercise room on the small side; some
rooms near busy street. ⑤ *Rooms from: $139* ⊠ *755 Abrego St., at
Fremont St.* ☎ *831/372–7551, 800/982–1986 reservations* 🖷 *831/324–
4625* ⊕ *www.hotelabrego.com* ☂ *93 rooms* ⦿ *No meals.*

$$$ 🏨 **InterContinental The Clement Monterey.** Spectacular bay views, assiduous
HOTEL service, a slew of upscale amenities, and a superb waterfront location next
FAMILY to the aquarium propelled this full-service luxury hotel to immediate star-
dom. **Pros:** a block from the aquarium; fantastic views from some rooms;
great for families. **Cons:** a tad formal; not budget-friendly. ⑤ *Rooms
from: $195* ⊠ *750 Cannery Row* ☎ *831/375–4500, 866/781–2406 toll
free* ⊕ *www.ictheclementmonterey.com* ☂ *192 rooms, 16 suites.*

$$ ▦ **Monterey Bay Lodge.** Location
HOTEL (on the edge of Monterey's El
Estero Park) and superior ameni-
ties give this cheerful facility an
edge over other motels in town.
Pros: within walking distance of
beach and playground; quiet at
night; good family choice. **Cons:**
near busy boulevard. ⑤ *Rooms
from: $130* ✉ *55 Camino Aguajito*
☎ *831/372–8057, 800/558–1900*
⊕ *www.montereybaylodge.com*
⟿ *43 rooms, 3 suites.*

> ### THE FIRST ARTICHOKE QUEEN
>
> Castroville, a tiny town off High-
> way 1 between Monterey and
> Watsonville, produces about 95%
> of U.S. artichokes. Back in 1948,
> the town chose its first queen
> to preside during its Artichoke
> Festival—a beautiful young
> woman named Norma Jean
> Mortenson, who later changed her
> name to Marilyn Monroe.

$$$$ ▦ **Monterey Plaza Hotel & Spa.** This
HOTEL hotel commands a waterfront loca-
tion on Cannery Row, where you can see frolicking sea otters from
the wide outdoor patio and many room balconies. **Pros:** on the ocean;
lots of amenities; attentive service. **Cons:** touristy area; heavy traffic.
⑤ *Rooms from: $269* ✉ *400 Cannery Row* ☎ *831/646–1700, 800/334–
3999* ⊕ *www.montereyplazahotel.com* ⟿ *280 rooms, 10 suites.*

$$$$ ▦ **Old Monterey Inn.** This three-story manor house was the home of Mon-
B&B/INN terey's first mayor, and today it remains a private enclave within walk-
Fodor's Choice ing distance of downtown, set off by lush gardens shaded by huge old
★ trees and bordered by a creek. **Pros:** gorgeous gardens; refined luxury;
serene. **Cons:** must drive to attractions and sights; fills quickly. ⑤ *Rooms
from: $289* ✉ *500 Martin St.* ☎ *831/375–8284, 800/350–2344* ⊕ *www.
oldmontereyinn.com* ⟿ *6 rooms, 3 suites, 1 cottage* ⑪ *Breakfast.*

$$$ ▦ **Spindrift Inn.** This boutique hotel on Cannery Row has beach access
HOTEL and a rooftop garden that overlooks the water. **Pros:** close to aquarium;
steps from the beach; friendly staff. **Cons:** throngs of visitors outside;
can be noisy; not good for families. ⑤ *Rooms from: $209* ✉ *652 Can-
nery Row* ☎ *831/646–8900, 800/841–1879* ⊕ *www.spindriftinn.com*
⟿ *45 rooms* ⑪ *Breakfast.*

NIGHTLIFE

Cibo. An Italian restaurant with a big bar area, Cibo brings live jazz,
Latin, soul, and more to downtown Tuesday through Sunday. ✉ *301
Alvarado St., at Del Monte Ave.* ☎ *831/649–8151* ⊕ *www.cibo.com.*

Bruce Ariss Wharf Theater (*The New Wharf Theatre*). American musicals
past and present are the focus here, with dramas and comedies also in
the mix. ✉ *One Fisherman's Wharf* ☎ *831/649–2332.*

Dixieland Monterey. Traditional jazz bands play at waterfront venues
during this festival, held on the first full weekend of March. ☎ *831/675–
0298, 888/349–6879* ⊕ *www.dixieland-monterey.com.*

Monterey Jazz Festival. The world's oldest jazz festival attracts top-name
performers to the Monterey Fairgrounds on the third full weekend
of September. ☎ *888/248–6499 ticket office, 831/373–3366* ⊕ *www.
montereyjazzfestival.org.*

SPORTS AND THE OUTDOORS

Throughout most of the year, the Monterey Bay area is a haven for those who love tennis, golf, surfing, fishing, biking, hiking, scuba diving, and kayaking. In the rainy winter months, when the waves grow larger, adventurous surfers flock to the water.

BICYCLING

Adventures by the Sea, Inc. You can rent surreys plus tandem and standard bicycles from Adventures by the Sea, which also offers bike tours. ⊠ *299 Cannery Row* ☎ *831/372–1807* ⊕ *www.adventuresbythesea. com* ⊠ *210 Alvarado Mall* ⊠ *Stillwater Cove, 17-Mile Drive, Pebble Beach* ⊠ *Beach at Lovers Point, Pacific Grove.*

Bay Bikes. For bicycle and surrey rentals and tours, visit Bay Bikes' main location or its second shop at 486 Washington St. ⊠ *585 Cannery Row* ☎ *831/655–2453* ⊕ *www.baybikes.com.*

FISHING

Randy's Fishing and Whale Watching Trips. Family-run Randy's has been in business since 1949. ⊠ *66 Fisherman's Wharf* ☎ *831/372–7440, 800/251–7440* ⊕ *www.randysfishingtrips.com.*

SCUBA DIVING

Monterey Bay waters never warm to the temperatures of their Southern California counterparts (the warmest they get is the low 60s), but that's one reason why the marine life here is among the world's most diverse.

Aquarius Dive Shop. Staffers at Aquarius give diving lessons and tours, and rent equipment. The diving-conditions information line is updated daily. ⊠ *2040 Del Monte Ave.* ☎ *831/375–1933, 831/657–1020 diving conditions* ⊕ *www.aquariusdivers.com.*

Monterey Bay National Marine Sanctuary. The sanctuary, home to mammals, seabirds, fishes, invertebrates, and plants, encompasses a 276-mile shoreline and 5,322 square miles of ocean. Ringed by beaches and campgrounds, it's a place for kayaking, whale-watching, scuba diving, and other water sports. ☎ *831/647–4201* ⊕ *www.montereybay.noaa.gov.*

WALKING

Monterey Bay Coastal Trail. From Custom House Plaza, you can walk along the coast in either direction on this 29-mile-long trail for spectacular views of the sea. The trail runs from north of Monterey to Pacific Grove, with sections continuing around Pebble Beach. ☎ *831/372–3196* ⊕ *www.mtycounty.com/pgs-parks/bike-path.html.*

WHALE-WATCHING

Thousands of gray whales pass close by the Monterey Coast on their annual migration between the Bering Sea and Baja California. The gigantic creatures are sometimes visible through binoculars from shore, but a whale-watching cruise is the best way to get a close look at these magnificent mammals. The migration south takes place from December through March; January is prime viewing time. The whales migrate north from March through June. In addition, some 2,000 blue whales and 600 humpbacks pass the coast and are easily spotted in late summer and early fall.

Monterey Bay Whale Watch. The marine biologists here lead three- to five-hour whale-watching tours. ⊠ *84 Fisherman's Wharf* ☎ *831/375–4658* ⊕ *www.montereybaywhalewatch.com.*

Princess Monterey Whale Watching. Tours are offered daily on a 150-passenger high-speed cruiser and a large 75-foot boat. ⊠ *96 Fisherman's Wharf #1* ☎ *831/372–2203, 831/205–2370 reservations, 888/223–9153 international reservations* ⊕ *www.montereywhalewatching.com.*

AROUND MONTEREY BAY

As Highway 1 follows the curve of the bay between Monterey and Santa Cruz, it passes through a rich agricultural zone. Opening right onto the bay, where the Salinas and Pajaro rivers drain into the Pacific, a broad valley brings together fertile soil, an ideal climate, and a good water supply to create optimum growing conditions for crops such as strawberries, artichokes, Brussels sprouts, and broccoli. Several beautiful beaches line this part of the coast. Salinas and Moss Landing are in Monterey County; the other cities and towns covered here are in Santa Cruz County.

GETTING HERE AND AROUND

All the towns in this area are on or just off Highway 1. MST buses serve Monterey County destinations, connecting in Watsonville with Santa Cruz METRO buses, which operate throughout Santa Cruz County.

SALINAS

17 miles east of Monterey on Hwy. 68.

Salinas, a hard-working city surrounded by vineyards and fruit and vegetable fields, honors the memory and literary legacy of John Steinbeck, its most famous native, with the National Steinbeck Center. The facility spurred the revival of Old Town Salinas, where renovated turn-of-the-20th-century stone buildings house shops and restaurants. Stop at the California Welcome Center, newly opened in 2012, for visitor information on the Salinas Valley and Monterey Bay region.

ESSENTIALS

Transportation Information Salinas Amtrak Station ⊠ *11 Station Place, Salinas* ☎ *800/872–7245.*

Visitor Information California Welcome Center ⊠ *1213 N. Davis Rd., west of Hwy. 101 exit #330, Salinas* ☎ *831/757–8687* ⊕ *www.visitcwc.com/Salinas* ⊙ *Open daily 9–5.*

EXPLORING

National Steinbeck Center. The center's exhibits document the life of Pulitzer- and Nobel-prize winner John Steinbeck and the history of the nearby communities that inspired novels such as *East of Eden*. Highlights include reproductions of the green pickup-camper from *Travels with Charley* and of the bunkroom from *Of Mice and Men*. **Steinbeck House,** the author's Victorian birthplace, at 132 Central Avenue, is two blocks from the center in a so-so neighborhood. Now a decent lunch spot, it displays memorabilia. ⊠ *1 Main St., at Central Ave., Salinas* ☎ *831/775–4721* ⊕ *www.steinbeck.org* ✉ *$15* ⊙ *Daily 10–5.*

FAMILY **Pinnacles National Park.** California's newest national park has many unusual attractions, including talus caves, 30 miles of hiking trails, and hundreds of rock climbing routes. A mosaic of diverse habitats supports an amazing number of wildlife species: 149 birds, 49 mammals, 69 butterflies, and nearly 400 bees. The park is also home to 32 of the world's remaining 405 condors in captivity and release areas. Fourteen of California's 34 bat species live in caves in the park. President Theodore Roosevelt declared this remarkable 26,000-acre geologic and wildlife preserve a national monument in 1908. President Barack Obama officially designated it a national park in January 2013. It's believed to have been created when two of the Earth's major tectonic plates heaved and lurched at their meeting points, spawning extensive volcanic activity in what's now called the Gabilan Mountains, southeast of Salinas and Monterey. The volcano eventually dried up and began to erode, leaving a rugged landscape with rocky spires and crags, or pinnacles, at the plates' intersection. Boulders fell into canyons and valleys, creating talus caves and a paradise for modern-day rock climbers. Spring is the most popular time to visit, when colorful wildflowers blanket the meadows; summer heat can be brutal. The park has two entrances— east and west—but they are not connected (there's no way to build a road over the spires). The Pinnacles Visitor Center, Bear Gulch Nature Center, Park Headquarters, the Pinnacles Campground, and the Bear Gulch Cave and Reservoir are on the east side. The Chaparral Ranger Station is on the west side, where you can feast on fantastic views of the Pinnacles High Peaks from the parking area. Dogs are not allowed on hiking trails. The east entrance is 32 miles southeast of Hollister via Highway 25. The west entrance is about 12 miles east of Soledad via Highway 146. ⊠ *5000 Hwy. 146, Paicines* ☎ *831/389–4485, 831/389–4427 Westside* ⊕ *www.nps.gov/pinn* ✉ *$5 per vehicle day use, $3 per visitor if biking or walking* ⊙ *West entrance, daily 7:30 am–8 pm; West Pinnacles Visitor Center, daily 9–5. East entrance, daily 24 hrs; Pinnacles Visitor Center, daily 9:30–5.*

FAMILY **Monterey Zoo.** More than a hundred exotic animals—many of them retired from film, television, and live-production work, or rescued from less-than-ideal environments—find sanctuary at the Monterey Zoo (formerly called Wild Things) at Vision Quest Ranch. Visit tigers, lions, bears, elephants, and primates on guided hourlong walking tours with professional trainers and handlers. For an in-depth experience, stay in a safari bungalow at Vision Quest Safari B&B where, in the morning, breakfast from a basket is delivered by a resident elephant. ⊠ *400 River Rd., off Hwy. 68, Salinas* ☎ *831/455–1901, 800/228–7382* ⊕ *www. montereyzoo.com* ✉ *Tours $10, optional post-tour elephant feeding $5* ⊙ *Tours daily at 1 pm; a second tour at 3 pm Jun.–Aug.*

MOSS LANDING

17 miles north of Monterey on Hwy. 1; 12 miles north of Salinas on Highway 183.

Moss Landing is not much more than a couple of blocks of cafés and restaurants, art galleries, and studios, plus a busy fishing port, but therein lies its charm. It's a fine place to overnight or stop for a meal and get a dose of nature.

GETTING HERE AND AROUND

From Highway 1 north or south, exit at Moss Landing Road on the ocean side. MST buses serve Moss Landing via Watsonville.

ESSENTIALS

Tour Contacts Elkhorn Slough Safari Nature Boat Tours. This outfit's naturalists lead two-hour tours of Elkhorn Sough aboard a 27-foot pontoon boat. Reservations are required. ⊠ *Moss Landing Harbor* ☏ *831/633–5555* ⊕ *www.elkhornslough.com* ⊠ *$35.*

Visitor Information Moss Landing Chamber of Commerce ☏ *831/633–4501* ⊕ *www.mosslandingchamber.com.*

EXPLORING

Elkhorn Slough National Estuarine Research Reserve. In the Elkhorn Slough National Estuarine Research Reserve, 1,400 acres of tidal flats and salt marshes form a complex environment that supports some 300 species of birds. A walk along the meandering waterways and wetlands can reveal hawks, white-tailed kites, owls, herons, and egrets. Also living or visiting here are sea otters, sharks, rays, and many other animals. On weekends, guided walks from the visitor center to the heron rookery begin at 10 and 1. ⊠ *1700 Elkhorn Rd., Watsonville* ☏ *831/728–2822* ⊕ *www.elkhornslough.org* ⊠ *$4 day use fee* ☉ *Wed.–Sun. 9–5.*

WHERE TO EAT AND STAY

For expanded hotel reviews, visit Fodors.com.

$$ ✕ **Phil's Fish Market & Eatery.** Exquisitely fresh, simply prepared seafood
SEAFOOD (try the cioppino) is on the menu at this warehouse-like restaurant on the harbor; all kinds of glistening fish are for sale at the market in the front. ■ TIP➔ Phil's Snack Shack, a tiny sandwich-and-smoothie joint, serves quicker meals at the north end of town. ⑤ *Average main: $17* ⊠ *7600 Sandholdt Rd.* ☏ *831/633–2152* ⊕ *www.philsfishmarket.com.*

$$ ⊞ **Captain's Inn.** Commune with nature and pamper yourself with
B&B/INN upscale creature comforts at this green-certified getaway in the heart of town. **Pros:** walk to restaurants and shops; tranquil natural setting; homey atmosphere. **Cons:** rooms in historic building don't have water views; far from urban amenities; not appropriate for young children. ⑤ *Rooms from: $165* ⊠ *8122 Moss Landing Rd.* ☏ *831/633–5550* ⊕ *www.captainsinn.com* ⊅ *10 rooms* ⦵ *Breakfast.*

SPORTS AND THE OUTDOORS

Monterey Bay Kayaks. Rent a kayak to paddle out into Elkhorn Slough for up-close wildlife encounters. ⊠ *2390 Hwy. 1, at North Harbor* ☏ *831/373–5357, 800/649–5357 toll free* ⊕ *www.montereybaykayaks.com.*

WATSONVILLE

7 miles north of Moss Landing on Hwy. 1.

If ever a city was built on berries, Watsonville is it. Produce has long driven the economy here, and this is where the Santa Cruz County Fair takes place each September.

GETTING HERE AND AROUND

From Santa Cruz or Monterey, follow Highway 1 to Watsonville. From U.S. 101, take Highway 152 West from Gilroy (a curving but scenic road over the mountains) or Highway 129 West from just north of San Juan Bautista. MST and Santa Cruz METRO buses connect at the Watsonville Transit Center, at Rodriguez Street and West Lake Avenue.

EXPLORING

FAMILY **Agricultural History Project.** One feature of the Santa Cruz County Fairgrounds is this project, which preserves the history of farming in the Pajaro Valley. In the Codiga Center and Museum, you can examine antique tractors and milking machines, peruse an exhibit on the era when Watsonville was the "frozen food capital of the West," and watch experts restore farm implements and vehicles. ⊠ *2601 E. Lake Ave., Hwy. 152, at Carlton Rd.* ☎ *831/724–5898* ⊕ *www.aghistoryproject. org* ☜ *$2 suggested donation* ⊘ *Thurs.–Sun. noon–4.*

FAMILY **Watsonville Fly-in & Air Show.** Every Labor Day weekend, aerial performers execute elaborate aerobatics at this air show. More than 300 classic, experimental, and military aircraft are on display; concerts and other events fill three days. ⊠ *Watsonville Municipal Airport, 100 Aviation Way* ☎ *831/763–5600* ⊕ *www.watsonvilleairshow.org* ☜ *$15 plus $5 parking.*

APTOS

7 miles north of Watsonville on Hwy. 1.

Backed by a redwood forest and facing the sea, downtown Aptos—known as Aptos Village—is a place of wooden walkways and false-fronted shops. Antiques dealers cluster along Trout Gulch Road, off Soquel Drive east of Highway 1.

GETTING HERE AND AROUND

Use Highway 1 to reach Aptos from Santa Cruz or Monterey. Exit at State Park Drive to reach the main shopping hub and Aptos Village. You can also exit at Freedom Boulevard or Rio del Mar. Soquel Drive is the main artery through town.

ESSENTIALS

Visitor Information Aptos Chamber of Commerce ⊠ *7605-A Old Dominion Ct.* ☎ *831/688–1467* ⊕ *www.aptoschamber.com.*

BEACHES

Seacliff State Beach. Sandstone bluffs tower above popular Seacliff State Beach. You can fish off the pier, which leads out to a sunken World War I tanker ship built of concrete. Leashed dogs are allowed on the beach. **Amenities:** food and drink; lifeguards; parking (fee); showers; toilets. **Best for:** sunset; swimming; walking. ⊠ *201 State Park Dr., off Hwy. 1* ☎ *831/685–6442* ⊕ *www.parks.ca.gov* ☜ *$10 per vehicle.*

SAN JUAN BAUTISTA

About as close to early-19th-century California as you can get, San Juan Bautista (15 miles east of Watsonville on Highway 156) has been protected from development since 1933, when much of it became a state park. Small antiques shops and restaurants occupy the Old West and art deco buildings that line 3rd Street.

The wide green plaza of San Juan Bautista State Historic Park is ringed by 18th- and 19th-century buildings, many of them open to the public.

The cemetery of the long, low, colonnaded mission church contains the unmarked graves of more than 4,300 Native American converts. Nearby is an adobe home furnished with Spanish-colonial antiques, a hotel frozen in the 1860s, a blacksmith shop, a stable, a pioneer cabin, and a jailhouse.

The first Saturday of each month, costumed volunteers engage in quilting bees, tortilla making, and other frontier activities. ⊕ *www.san-juan-bautista.ca.us.*

WHERE TO EAT AND STAY

For expanded hotel reviews, visit Fodors.com.

$$$
MEDITERRANEAN
✕ **Bittersweet Bistro.** A large old tavern with cathedral ceilings houses this popular bistro, where chef-owner Thomas Vinolus draws culinary inspiration from the Mediterranean. The menu changes seasonally, but regular highlights include paella, seafood puttanesca, and maple-soy marinated skirt steak. The decadent chocolate desserts are not to be missed. Breakfast and lunch are available in the casual Bittersweet Café. Pets are welcome on the outdoor patio. $ *Average main: $25* ⊠ *787 Rio Del Mar Blvd., off Hwy. 1* ☎ *831/662–9799* ⊕ *www.bittersweetbistro.com.*

$$$
HOTEL
FAMILY
🏨 **Best Western Seacliff Inn.** Families and business travelers like this 6-acre property near Seacliff State Beach that's more resort than hotel. **Pros:** walking distance to the beach; family-friendly; hot breakfast buffet. **Cons:** close to freeway; occasional nighttime bar noise. $ *Rooms from: $180* ⊠ *7500 Old Dominion Ct.* ☎ *831/688–7300, 800/367–2003* ⊕ *www.seacliffinn.com* ⤢ *139 rooms, 10 suites* ❍| *Breakfast.*

$$$
B&B/INN
🏨 **Flora Vista.** Multicolor fields of flowers, strawberries, and veggies unfold in every direction at this luxury neo-Georgian inn set on two serene acres just south of Aptos, where innkeepers Deanna and Ed Boos transformed an 1867 home, a replica of Abe Lincoln's Springfield farmhouse, adding modern conveniences like Wi-Fi and spa tubs while retaining the house's original redwood floors and country charm. **Pros:** superprivate; near Sand Dollar Beach; flowers everywhere. **Cons:** no restaurants or nightlife within walking distance; not a good place for kids. $ *Rooms from: $195* ⊠ *1258 San Andreas Rd., La Selva Beach* ☎ *831/724–8663, 877/753–5672* ⊕ *www.floravistainn.com* ⤢ *5 rooms* ❍| *Breakfast.*

$$$$
RESORT
FAMILY
🏨 **Seascape Beach Resort.** On a bluff overlooking Monterey Bay, Seascape is a full-fledged resort that makes it easy to unwind. **Pros:** time-share-style apartments; access to miles of beachfront; superb views. **Cons:** far from city life; most bathrooms are small. $ *Rooms from: $300* ⊠ *1 Seascape Resort Dr.* ☎ *831/688–6800, 800/929–7727* ⊕ *www.seascaperesort.com* ⤢ *285 suites.*

CAPITOLA AND SOQUEL

4 miles northwest of Aptos on Hwy. 1.

On the National Register of Historic places as California's first sea-side resort town, the village of Capitola has been in a holiday mood since the late 1800s. Casual eateries, surf shops, and ice-cream parlors pack its walkable downtown. Inland, across Highway 1, antiques shops line Soquel Drive in the town of Soquel. Wineries dot the Santa Cruz Mountains beyond.

GETTING HERE AND AROUND

From Santa Cruz or Monterey, follow Highway 1 to the Capitola/Soquel (Bay Avenue) exit about 7 miles south of Santa Cruz and head west to reach Capitola and east to access Soquel Village. On summer weekends, park for free in the lot behind the Crossroads Center, a block west of the freeway, and hop aboard the free Capitola Shuttle to the village.

ESSENTIALS

Visitor Information Capitola-Soquel Chamber of Commerce ⊠ *716-G Capitola Ave.* ☎ *831/475–6522* ⊕ *www.capitolachamber.com.*

BEACHES

New Brighton State Beach. New Brighton State Beach, once the site of a Chinese fishing village, is now a popular surfing and camping spot. Its Pacific Migrations Visitor Center traces the history of the Chinese and other peoples who settled around Monterey Bay, as well as the migratory patterns of the area's wildlife, such as monarch butterflies and gray whales. Leashed dogs are allowed in the park. ■TIP➜ New Brighton Beach connects with Seacliff Beach, and at low tide you can walk or run along this scenic stretch of sand for nearly 16 miles south (you might have to wade through a few creeks). The 1½-mile stroll from New Brighton to Seacliff's cement ship is a local favorite. **Amenities:** parking (fee); showers; toilets. **Best for:** sunset; swimming; walking. ⊠ *1500 State Park Dr., off Hwy. 1* ☎ *831/464–6330* ⊕ *www.parks. ca.gov* ⊠ *$10 per vehicle.*

WHERE TO EAT

$

SEAFOOD

FAMILY

╳ **Carpo's.** Locals love this casual counter. Seafood predominates, but Carpo's also serves burgers, salads, and steaks. Favorites include the baskets of fresh battered snapper, calamari and prawns, seafood kebabs, and homemade olallieberry pie. Many items cost less than $10. Go early to beat the crowds. ⑤ *Average main: $10* ⊠ *2400 Porter St., at Hwy. 1* ☎ *831/476–6260* ⊕ *www.carposrestaurant.com/default1.html.*

$

CAFÉ

FAMILY

╳ **Gayle's Bakery & Rosticceria.** Whether you're in the mood for an orange-olallieberry muffin, a wild rice and chicken salad, or tri-tip on garlic toast, this bakery-cum-deli's varied menu is likely to satisfy. Munch your chocolate macaroon on the shady patio or dig into the daily blue-plate dinner amid the whirl of activity inside. ⑤ *Average main: $12* ⊠ *504 Bay Ave., at Capitola Ave.* ☎ *831/462–1200* ⊕ *www. gaylesbakery.com.*

$$

AMERICAN

╳ **Michael's on Main.** Creative variations on classic comfort food draw lively crowds to this upscale-but-casual creek-side eatery. Chef Michael

Clark's menu changes seasonally, but you can always count on finding such home-style dishes as pork osso bucco in red-wine tomato-citrus sauce, as well as unusual entrées like pistachio-crusted salmon with mint vinaigrette. For a quiet conversation spot, ask for a table on the romantic patio overlooking the creek. The busy bar area hosts live music Tuesday through Saturday. $ *Average main: $22* ✉ *2591 Main St., at Porter St.* ☎ *831/479–9777* ⊕ *www.michaelsonmain.net* ⊘ *Closed Mon.*

$$$$ ✕ **Shadowbrook.** To get to this
EUROPEAN romantic spot overlooking Soquel Creek, you can take a cable car or walk the stairs down a steep, fern-lined bank beside a running waterfall. Dining room options include the rooftop Redwood Room, the wood-paneled Wine Cellar, and the airy, glass-enclosed Garden Room. Prime rib and grilled seafood are the stars of the simple menu. A cheaper menu of light entrées is available in the lounge. $ *Average main: $32* ✉ *1750 Wharf Rd., at Lincoln Ave.* ☎ *831/475–1511, 888/475–1222 toll free* ⊕ *www.shadowbrook-capitola.com* ⊘ *No lunch.*

> ## CALIFORNIA'S OLDEST RESORT TOWN
>
> As far as anyone knows for certain, Capitola is the oldest seaside resort town on the Pacific Coast. In 1856 a pioneer acquired Soquel Landing, the picturesque lagoon and beach where Soquel Creek empties into the bay, and built a wharf. Another man opened a campground along the shore, and his daughter named it Capitola after a heroine in a novel series. After the train came to town in the 1870s, thousands of vacationers began arriving to bask in the sun on the glorious beach.

WHERE TO STAY

For expanded hotel reviews, visit Fodors.com.

$$$$ 🏨 **Inn at Depot Hill.** This inventively designed B&B in a former rail depot
B&B/INN sees itself as a link to the era of luxury train travel. **Pros:** short walk to beach and village; historic charm; excellent service. **Cons:** fills quickly; hot tub conversation on the patio may irk second-floor guests. $ *Rooms from: $259* ✉ *250 Monterey Ave.* ☎ *831/462–3376, 800/572–2632* ⊕ *www.innatdepothill.com* ⮒ *12 rooms* ⦿ *Breakfast.*

SANTA CRUZ

5 miles west of Capitola on Hwy. 1; 48 miles north of Monterey on Hwy. 1.

The big city on this stretch of the California coast, Santa Cruz (pop. 57,500) is less manicured than Carmel or Monterey. Long known for its surfing and its amusement-filled beach boardwalk, the town is a mix of grand Victorian-era homes and rinky-dink motels. The opening of the University of California campus in the 1960s swung the town sharply to the left politically, and the counterculture more or less lives on here. At the same time, the revitalized downtown and an insane real-estate market reflect the city's proximity to Silicon Valley and to a growing wine country in the surrounding mountains.

GETTING HERE AND AROUND

From the San Francisco Bay Area, take Highway 17 south over the mountains to Santa Cruz, where it merges with Highway 1. Use Highway 1 to get around the area. The Santa Cruz Transit Center is at 920 Pacific Avenue, at Front Street, a short walk from the Wharf and Boardwalk, with connections to public transit throughout the Monterey Bay and San Francisco Bay areas. You can purchase Santa Cruz METRO bus day passes here.

ESSENTIALS

Transportation Information Santa Cruz METRO ☎ *831/425–8600* ⊕ *www.scmtd.com.*

Visitor Information Santa Cruz County Conference and Visitors Council ✉ *303 Water St., #100* ☎ *831/425–1234, 800/833–3494* ⊕ *www.santacruz.org.*

EXPLORING

TOP ATTRACTIONS

Pacific Avenue. When you've had your fill of the city's beaches and waters, take a stroll in downtown Santa Cruz, especially on Pacific Avenue between Laurel and Water streets. Vintage boutiques and mountain sports stores, sushi bars and Mexican restaurants, day spas, and nightclubs keep the main drag and the surrounding streets hopping midmorning until late evening.

FAMILY **Santa Cruz Beach Boardwalk.** Santa Cruz has been a seaside resort since the mid-19th century. Along one end of the broad, south-facing beach, the boardwalk has entertained holidaymakers for more than a century. Its Looff carousel and classic wooden Giant Dipper roller coaster, both dating from the early 1900s, are surrounded by high-tech thrill rides and easygoing kiddie rides with ocean views. Video and arcade games, a mini-golf course, and a laser-tag arena pack one gigantic building, which is open daily even if the rides aren't running. You have to pay to play, but you can wander the entire boardwalk for free while sampling delicacies such as corn dogs and garlic fries. ✉ *Along Beach St.* ☎ *831/423–5590 info line* ⊕ *www.beachboardwalk.com* 🎫 *$32 day pass for unlimited rides, or pay per ride* ☉ *Apr.–early Sept., daily; early Sept.–late May, weekends, weather permitting; call for hrs.*

FAMILY **Santa Cruz Municipal Wharf.** Jutting half a mile into the ocean near one end of the boardwalk, the century-old Municipal Wharf is lined with seafood restaurants, a wine bar, souvenir shops, and outfitters offering bay cruises, fishing trips, and boat rentals. A salty soundtrack drifts up from under the wharf, where barking sea lions lounge in heaps on crossbeams. Docents from the Seymour Marine Discovery Center lead free, guided 30-minute tours Saturday and Sunday at 1 and 3; meet at the stage on the west side of the wharf between Olita's restaurant and Marini's candies. ✉ *Beach St., at Pacific Ave.* ☎ *831/420–6025 wharf administration, 831/459–3800 tour information* ⊕ *www.santacruzwharf.com.*

Santa Cruz Surfing Museum. This museum inside the Mark Abbott Memorial Lighthouse chronicles local surfing history. Photographs show old-time surfers, and a display of boards includes rarities such as a heavy redwood plank predating the fiberglass era and the remains of a modern board chomped by a great white shark. On-site surfer-docents talk about the good old days. ⊠ *Lighthouse Point Park, 701 W. Cliff Dr., near Pelton Ave.* ☎ *831/420–6289* ⊕ *www.santacruzsurfingmuseum. org* ⊠ *$2 suggested donation* ⊙ *Sept.–June, Thurs.–Mon. noon–4; July– Aug., Wed.–Mon. 10–5.*

West Cliff Drive. The road that winds along an oceanfront bluff from the municipal wharf to Natural Bridges State Beach makes for a spectacular drive, but it's even more fun to walk, blade, or bike the paved path that parallels the road. Surfers bob and swoosh in Monterey Bay at several points near the foot of the bluff, especially at a break known as Steamer Lane. Named for a surfer who died here in 1965, the nearby Mark Abbott Memorial Lighthouse stands at Point Santa Cruz, the cliff's major promontory. From here you can watch pinnipeds hang out, sunbathe, and frolic on Seal Rock.

WORTH NOTING

FAMILY **Monterey Bay National Marine Sanctuary Exploration Center.** Learn all about the treasures in the nation's largest marine sanctuary via interactive and multimedia exhibits in this fascinating interpretive center. The two-story building, right across the street from the main beach and municipal wharf, was completed in summer 2012. Exhibits educate about watersheds, underwater canyons, kelp forests, and intertidal zones. In the mini-theater, follow migratory species (whales, dolphins, sea turtles) as they travel through the open ocean. Head out to the second-floor deck for stellar ocean views, and to get real-time weather, surf, and buoy reports at an interactive station. The center also provides extensive information on the sanctuary's many activities. ⊠ *35 Pacific Ave.* ☎ *831/421–9993* ⊕ *montereybay.noaa.gov/vc/sec* ⊠ *Free* ⊙ *Wed.–Sun. 10–5.*

Mystery Spot. Hokey tourist trap or genuine scientific enigma? Since 1940, curious throngs baffled by the Mystery Spot have made it one of the most visited attractions in Santa Cruz. The laws of gravity and physics don't appear to apply in this tiny patch of redwood forest, where balls roll uphill and people stand on a slant. Advance online tickets ($6) are recommended for weekend and holiday visits. ⊠ *465 Mystery Spot Rd., off Branciforte Dr. (north off Hwy. 1)* ☎ *831/423– 8897* ⊕ *www.mysteryspot.com* ⊠ *$5 on-site, $6 in advance, parking $5* ⊙ *Late May–early Sept., daily 10–7; early Sept.–late May, weekdays 10–4, weekends 10–5.*

Santa Cruz Mission State Historic Park. On the northern fringes of downtown is the site of California's 12th Spanish mission, built in the 1790s and destroyed by an earthquake in 1857. A museum in a restored 1791 adobe and a half-scale replica of the mission church are part of the complex. ⊠ *144 School St., at Adobe St.* ☎ *831/425–5849* ⊕ *www.parks. ca.gov/?page_id=548* ⊠ *Free* ⊙ *Thurs.–Sat. 10–4 (call park to confirm).*

University of California at Santa Cruz. The 2,000-acre UC Santa Cruz campus nestles in the forested hills above town. Its sylvan setting, sweeping ocean vistas, and redwood architecture make the university worth a visit. Wander about on your own (maps available at the office of admissions) or on a guided tour (reservations required). Either way, the free campus shuttles can help you get around. ⊠ *Main entrance at Bay and High Sts.* ☎ *831/459–0111* ⊕ *www.ucsc.edu/visit.*

Surf City Vintners. A dozen limited-production winery tasting rooms cluster in renovated warehouse spaces in Swift Street Courtyard, on the westside near UC Santa Cruz. Other green-minded businesses here include Santa Cruz Mountain Brewing Company, a bakery/deli, and a popular shop with homemade organic sausages. ⊠ *334 Ingalls St. at Swift St., off Hwy. 1 (Mission St.)* ⊕ *www.surfcityvintners.com.*

Vinocruz. A slick, contemporary tasting room in downtown's Abbott Square, Vinocruz pours vintages from more than 60 wineries in the Santa Cruz Mountains AVA, including small operations that don't have their own tasting rooms. It's part of a historic building that was once part of an old jail. ⊠ *725 Front St., enter in Abbott Square off Cooper St.* ☎ *831/426–8466* ⊕ *www.vinocruz.com* ⊙ *Tues.–Thurs. noon–7, Fri. and Sat. noon–8, Sun. 1–6.*

OFF THE BEATEN PATH

Santa Cruz Mountains wineries. Highway 9 heads northeast from Santa Cruz into hills densely timbered with massive coastal redwoods. The road winds through the lush San Lorenzo Valley, past hamlets consisting of a few cafés, antiques shops, and old-style tourist cabins. Residents of the hunting-and-fishing persuasion coexist with hardcore flower-power survivors and wannabes, and a new generation has joined the pioneers who opened wineries decades ago. Mountain grapes produce some superb Chardonnays, Pinot Noirs, and Cabernet Sauvignons, among other wines. To sample some, you can start a **winery tour** in downtown Santa Cruz at Storrs Winery, at 303 Potrero Street—a block off River Street, which, heading north from here becomes Highway 9. Drive north to Felton to visit Hallcrest Vineyards and Organic Wine Works, just west of Highway 9 on Felton Empire Road downtown. Continue north on Highway 9 and east on Bear Creek Road to the classy Byington and David Bruce wineries, both in Los Gatos. ■**TIP**➜ **The Santa Cruz Mountains Winegrowers Association (**⊕ **www.scmwa.com) distributes a wine-touring map at member wineries and many lodgings and attractions around Santa Cruz.**

BEACHES

FAMILY **Natural Bridges State Beach.** At the end of West Cliff Drive lies Natural Bridges State Beach, a stretch of soft sand edged with tide pools and sea-sculpted rock bridges. ■**TIP**➜ **From October to early March a colony of monarch butterflies roosts in a eucalyptus grove.** **Amenities:** lifeguards; parking (fee); toilets. **Best for:** sunrise; sunset; surfing; swimming. ⊠ *2531 W. Cliff Dr.* ☎ *831/423–4609* ⊕ *www.parks.ca.gov* ⊠ *Beach free, parking $10* ⊙ *Beach: daily 8 am–sunset. Visitor center: Oct.–Feb., daily 10–4; Mar.–Sept., weekends 10–4.*

Twin Lakes State Beach. Stretching a half mile along the coast on both sides of the small-craft harbor jetties, Twin Lakes is one of the sunniest beaches on the bay. It encompasses Seabright State Beach (with access in a residential neighborhood on the upcoast side) and Black's Beach on the downcoast side. Families often come here to sunbathe, picnic, and hike the nature trail around adjacent Schwann Lake. Limited parking is available next to the main access down from the harbor—arrive early in the day to nab a space (free during the week, permits required on weekends from April through September). You can also park in the pay lot in the harbor. Leashed dogs are allowed. **Amenities:** food and drink; lifeguards (seasonal); parking; showers; toilets; water sports (seasonal). **Best for:** sunset; surfing; swimming; walking. ⊠ *7th Ave., at East Cliff Dr.* ☎ *831/427–4868* ⊕ *www.parks.ca.gov/?page_id=547.*

WHERE TO EAT

$$
SEAFOOD
✕ **Crow's Nest.** This classic California beachside eatery sits right on the water in Santa Cruz Harbor. Vintage surfboards and local surf photography line the walls in the main dining room; nearly every table overlooks the sand and surf. Seafood and steaks, served with local veggies, dominate the menu; favorite appetizers include the chilled shrimp-stuffed artichoke and crispy tempura prawns, served with rice pilaf. No need to pile high on your first trip to the endless salad bar—you can return as often as you like. For sweeping ocean views and more casual fare (think fish tacos and burgers), head upstairs to the Breakwater Bar & Grill. Live entertainment several days a week makes for a dynamic atmosphere year-round. $ *Average main: $20* ⊠ *2218 E. Cliff Dr., west of 7th Ave.* ☎ *831/476–4560* ⊕ *www.crowsnest-santacruz.com.*

$$
ITALIAN
✕ **Gabriella Café.** The work of local artists hangs on the walls of this petite, romantic café in a tile-roof cottage. Featuring organic produce from area farms, the seasonal Italian menu has included wild-mushroom risotto; bouillabaisse; marinated chicken with apricots, currants, and olives; and roasted beet salad with arugula, goat cheese, and pistachios. $ *Average main: $22* ⊠ *910 Cedar St., at Church St.* ☎ *831/457–1677* ⊕ *www.gabriellacafe.com.*

$$
AFGHAN
✕ **Laili Restaurant.** Exotic Mediterranean flavors with an Afghan twist take center stage in this artsy, stylish space with soaring ceilings across from Cooper Square. The chef uses authentic herbs and spices and fresh, healthy ingredients sourced from local purveyors. Traditional dishes range from Moroccan beet salad and grilled chicken flatbread to pomegranate eggplant and *maush-awa* soup with lentils, beans, and lamb, topped with yogurt. The menus also include housemade pastas and numerous vegetarian options; fresh *naan* and delectable chutneys and dips accompany every meal. Evenings are especially lively, when locals come to relax over wine and soft jazz at the blue-concrete bar, the heated patio with twinkly lights, or at a communal table near the stainless-steel open kitchen. $ *Average main: $18* ⊠ *101–B Cooper St.* ☎ *831/423–4545* ⊕ *www.lailirestaurant.com.*

$$
ITALIAN
✕ **La Posta.** Authentic Italian fare made with fresh local produce lures diners into cozy, modern-rustic La Posta. Nearly everything is housemade, from the pizzas and breads baked in the brick oven to the pasta and the vanilla-bean gelato. The seasonal menu includes flavorful dishes such as fried artichokes, ravioli filled with crab, chicken with Brussels sprouts, or sautéed fish from local waters. $ *Average main: $22* ⊠ *538 Seabright Ave., at Logan St.* ☎ *831/457–2782* ⊕ *www.lapostarestaurant.com* ☽ *Closed Mon. No lunch.*

$$$
EUROPEAN

✗**Oswald.** Sophisticated yet unpretentious European-inspired California cooking is the order of the day at this intimate and stylish bistro. The menu changes seasonally but might include such items as perfectly prepared seafood stew or roasted rack of lamb. Sit at the slick marble bar and order a creative concoction like whiskey mixed with apple and lemon juices and bitters, or tequila with celery juice and lime. $ *Average main: $25* ✉ *121 Soquel Ave., at Front St.* ☎ *831/423-7427* ⊕ *www. oswaldrestaurant.com* ☾ *Closed Mon. Lunch Fri. only.*

$
AMERICAN

✗**Seabright Brewery.** Great burgers, big salads, and stellar microbrews make this a favorite hangout in the youthful Seabright neighborhood east of downtown. Sit outside on the patio or inside at a comfortable, spacious booth; both are popular with families. $ *Average main: $13* ✉ *519 Seabright Ave., at Murray St.* ☎ *831/426-2739* ⊕ *www. seabrightbrewery.com.*

$$
MEDITERRANEAN

✗**Soif.** Wine reigns at this sleek bistro and wine shop that takes its name from the French word for thirst. The lengthy list includes selections from near and far, many of which you can order by the taste or glass. Infused with the tastes of the Mediterranean, small plates and mains are served at the copper-top bar, the big communal table, and private tables. A jazz combo or solo pianist plays some evenings. $ *Average main: $22* ✉ *105 Walnut Ave., at Pacific Ave.* ☎ *831/423-2020* ⊕ *www. soifwine.com* ☾ *No lunch.*

$
AMERICAN

✗**Zachary's.** This noisy café filled with students and families defines the funky essence of Santa Cruz. It also dishes up great breakfasts: stay simple with sourdough pancakes, or go for Mike's Mess—eggs scrambled with bacon, mushrooms, and home fries, then topped with sour cream, melted cheese, and fresh tomatoes. ■TIP➔ If you arrive after 9 am, expect a long wait for a table; lunch is a shade calmer (closing time is 2:30 pm). $ *Average main: $12* ✉ *819 Pacific Ave.* ☎ *831/427-0646* ⌂ *Reservations not accepted* ☾ *Closed Mon. No dinner.*

WHERE TO STAY

For expanded hotel reviews, visit Fodors.com.

$$$
B&B/INN

⌂ **Babbling Brook Inn.** Though it's smack in the middle of Santa Cruz, this B&B has lush gardens, a running stream, and tall trees that make you feel as if you're in a secluded wood. **Pros:** close to UCSC; within walking distance of downtown shops; woodsy feel. **Cons:** near a high school; some rooms close to a busy street. $ *Rooms from: $185* ✉ *1025 Laurel St.* ☎ *831/427-2437, 800/866-1131* ⊕ *www.babblingbrookinn. com* ⇱ *13 rooms* ❧ *Breakfast.*

$$$
RESORT

⌂ **Chaminade Resort & Spa.** A full-on renovation of the entire property, completed in 2009, sharpened this hilltop resort's look, enhanced its amenities, and qualified it for regional green certification. **Pros:** far from city life; spectacular property; ideal spot for romance and rejuvenation. **Cons:** must drive to attractions and sights; near major hospital. $ *Rooms from: $249* ✉ *1 Chaminade La.* ☎ *800/283-6569 reservations, 831/475-5600* ⊕ *www.chaminade.com* ⇱ *112 rooms, 44 suites.*

$
B&B/INN

⌂ **Harbor Inn.** Family-run, friendly, and funky, this basic but sparkling-clean lodge offers exceptional value just a few blocks from Santa Cruz

Harbor and Twin Lakes Beach. **Pros:** affordable; free Wi-Fi; park your car and walk to the beach. **Cons:** not fancy; not near downtown. $ *Rooms from: $89* ✉ *645 7th Ave.* ☎ *831/479–9731* ⊕ *www. harborinnsantacruz.com* ⤳ *17 rooms, 2 suites.*

$$$ 🏨 **Hotel Paradox.** Less than two miles from the wharf and boardwalk

HOTEL and a short walk to Pacific Avenue, this new stylish, forest-themed complex is among the few full-service hotels in town. **Pros:** close to downtown and main beach; good alternative to beach-oriented lodgings; new property. **Cons:** pool area can get crowded on warm-weather days; some rooms on the small side. $ *Rooms from: $215* ✉ *611 Ocean St.* ☎ *831/425–7100, 855/425–7200* ⊕ *www.thehotelparadox.com* ⤳ *164 rooms, 6 suites* ⦿ *No meals.*

$$$ 🏨 **Pacific Blue Inn.** Green themes reign in this three-story, eco-friendly

B&B/INN B&B, built from scratch in 2009 on a sliver of prime property downtown. **Pros:** free bicycles; five-minute walk to boardwalk and wharf; right in downtown. **Cons:** tiny property; not suitable for children. $ *Rooms from: $189* ✉ *636 Pacific Ave.* ☎ *831/600–8880* ⊕ *www. pacificblueinn.com* ⤳ *9 rooms* ⦿ *Breakfast.*

$$$$ 🏨 **Santa Cruz Dream Inn.** Just a short stroll from the boardwalk and

HOTEL wharf, this full-service luxury hotel is the only lodging in Santa Cruz directly on the beach. **Pros:** directly on the beach; easy parking; walk to boardwalk and downtown. **Cons:** expensive; area gets congested on busy weekends. $ *Rooms from: $309* ✉ *175 W. Cliff Dr.* ☎ *831/426–4330, 866/774–7735 reservations* 📠 *831/427–2025* ⊕ *www.dreaminnsantacruz.com* ⤳ *149 rooms, 16 suites.*

$$$ 🏨 **West Cliff Inn.** Perched on the bluffs across from Cowell Beach, this

B&B/INN posh nautical-theme inn commands sweeping views of the boardwalk and Monterey Bay. **Pros:** killer views; walking distance of the beach; close to downtown. **Cons:** boardwalk noise; street traffic. $ *Rooms from: $185* ✉ *174 West Cliff Dr.* ☎ *800/979–0910 toll free, 831/457–2200* ⊕ *www. westcliffinn.com* ⤳ *7 rooms, 2 suites, 1 cottage* ⦿ *Breakfast.*

NIGHTLIFE AND THE ARTS

NIGHTLIFE

Catalyst. Dance with the crowds at this huge, grimy club that regularly features bands ranging from punk groups like Dropkick Murphys to death-metal bands like Decapitated. ✉ *1011 Pacific Ave.* ☎ *831/423–1338* ⊕ *www.catalystclub.com.*

Kuumbwa Jazz Center. The renowned center draws top performers such as the Brubeck Brothers Quartet, Ladysmith Black Mambazo, and Chick Corea; the café serves meals an hour before most shows. ✉ *320–2 Cedar St.* ☎ *831/427–2227* ⊕ *www.kuumbwajazz.org.*

Moe's Alley. Blues, salsa, reggae, funk: Moe's has it all (and more), six nights a week. ✉ *1535 Commercial Way* ☎ *831/479–1854* ⊕ *www. moesalley.com.*

THE ARTS

Cabrillo Festival of Contemporary Music. Each August, this music festival brings some of the world's finest artists to the Santa Cruz Civic Auditorium to play groundbreaking symphonic music, including major world premieres. ☎ *831/426–6966, 831/420–5260 box office* ⊕ *www. cabrillomusic.org.*

Santa Cruz Baroque Festival. Using period and reproduction instruments, the festival presents classical music at various venues. As the name suggests, the focus is on 17th- and 18th-century composers such as Bach and Handel. ☎ *831/457–9693* ⊕ *www.scbaroque.org.*

Shakespeare Santa Cruz. This six-week festival in July and August occasionally includes a modern dramatic performance. Most performances are outdoors under the redwoods. A holiday program takes place in December. ✉ *SSC/UCSC Theater Arts Center, 1156 High St.* ☎ *831/459–2121 administration, 831/459–2159 tickets* ⊕ *www. shakespearesantacruz.org.*

Tannery Arts Center. The grounds of a former leather tannery were transformed into a major arts complex, with a performing arts center, galleries, workshops, retail stores, and cafés opening in stages in 2013–14. ✉ *1050 River St., at intersection of Hwys. 1 and 9* ☎ *831/621–6226* ⊕ *www.tanneryartscenter.org.*

SPORTS AND THE OUTDOORS

ADVENTURE TOURS

Mount Hermon Adventures. Zipline through the redwoods, climb a giant live oak tree, and hunt for edibles in the Santa Cruz Mountains at this adventure center near Felton, 9 miles north of downtown Santa Cruz. On the two-hour Redwood Canopy Tour, follow a guide along a series of six ziplines and two suspension bridges in the redwood canopy. You can also join an ECO tour, where you harness up and ascend a live oak tree using a double-rope system, then go on an ecology walk to forage for sustainable edibles or learn about sand hill habitat restoration (four hours total). On select summer weekends, you can sign up for an aerial adventure course with a set of obstacles and challenges in the redwoods. You must be at least 10 years old and weigh between 75 and 250 pounds to join a tour. Reservations are essential. ✉ *17 Conference Drive, Mount Hermon* ☎ *831/430–4357* ⊕ *www. mounthermonadventures.com* ✍ *Redwood canopy tours $80, tree climbing tours $50* ⊙ *Redwood Canopy Tour: Apr.–Oct., daily 8–6. Nov.–Mar., Thurs.–Mon., 11–4. ECO Tours: weekdays at 9 and 1:30.*

BICYCLING

Another Bike Shop. Mountain bikers should head here for tips on the best area trails and to browse cutting-edge gear made and tested locally. ✉ *2361 Mission St., at King St.* ☎ *831/427–2232* ⊕ *www. anotherbikeshop.com.*

BOATS AND CHARTERS

Chardonnay Sailing Charters. The 70-foot *Chardonnay II* departs year-round from Santa Cruz yacht harbor on whale-watching, sunset, and other cruises around Monterey Bay. Most regularly scheduled excursions cost $50; food and drink are served on many of them. Reservations are essential. ☎ *831/423–1213* ⊕ *www.chardonnay.com.*

Stagnaro Sport Fishing, Charters, & Whale Watching Cruises. Stagnaro operates salmon, albacore, and rock-cod fishing expeditions; the fees ($55 to $80) include bait. The company also runs whale-watching, dolphin, and sea-life cruises ($46) year-round. ⊠ *June–Aug., Santa Cruz Municipal Wharf; Sept.–May, Santa Cruz West Harbor* ☎ *831/427–2334, 800/979–3370 tickets, 212/209–3370 international tickets* ⊕ *www. stagnaros.com.*

GOLF

Pasatiempo Golf Club. Designed by famed golf architect Dr. Alister MacKenzie in 1929, this semiprivate course, set amid undulating hills just above the city, is among the nation's top championship courses. Golfers rave about the spectacular views and challenging terrain. ⊠ *20 Clubhouse Rd.* ☎ *831/459–9155* ⊕ *www.pasatiempo.com* ⚑ *18 holes. 6,125 yds. Par 72. Greens fees: $220/$250* ⚲ *Driving range, putting green, pitching area, golf carts, pull carts, caddies, rental clubs, pro shop, golf lessons, restaurant, bar.*

KAYAKING

Kayak Connection. In March, April, and May, participants on this outfit's tours mingle with gray whales and their calves on their northward journey to Alaska. Throughout the year, the company rents kayaks and paddle boards and conducts tours of Natural Bridges State Beach, Capitola, and Elkhorn Slough. Most regularly scheduled tours cost $55. ⊠ *Santa Cruz Harbor, 413 Lake Ave. #3* ☎ *831/479–1121* ⊕ *www. kayakconnection.com.*

Venture Quest Kayaking. Explore hidden coves and kelp forests on guided nature tours that depart from Santa Cruz Wharf or Harbor, depending on the season. A two-hour kayak nature tour and introductory lesson costs $58. A three-hour kayak rental is $30 and includes wet suit and gear. Venture Quest also arranges tours at other Monterey Bay destinations, including Capitola and Elkhorn Slough. ⊠ *#2 Santa Cruz Wharf* ☎ *831/427–2267 kayak hotline, 831/425–8445 rental office* ⊕ *www. kayaksantacruz.com.*

SURFING

Pleasure Point. Surfers gather for the spectacular waves and sunsets here. ⊠ *E. Cliff and Pleasure Point Drs.*

Steamer Lane. This area near the lighthouse on West Cliff Drive has a decent break. Steamer Lane hosts several competitions in summer.

EQUIPMENT AND LESSONS

Club-Ed Surf School and Camps. Find out what all the fun is about at Club-Ed. Your first private or group lesson ($85 and up) includes all equipment. ⊠ *Cowell Beach, at Santa Cruz Dream Inn* ☎ *831/464–0177* ⊕ *www.club-ed.com.*

Cowell's Beach Surf Shop. This shop sells gear, clothing, and swimwear; rents surfboards, standup paddle boards, and wet suits; and offers lessons. ⊠ *30 Front St.* ☎ *831/427–2355* ⊕ *www.cowellssurfshop.com.*

SHOPPING

Annieglass. The works of famed Santa Cruz glass artist Annie Morhauser are on display at the Smithsonian and New York's MOMA—but at the gallery in Cooper Square you can collect your own luxury Annieglass tableware, decorative accessories, and jewelry, all designed and hand-made in Santa Cruz County. The store also sells discounted studio seconds with barely perceptible flaws and gift items made by other artists. ⊠ *110 Cooper St.* ☎ *800/347–6133* ⊕ *www.annieglass.com.*

Bookshop Santa Cruz. The town's best and most beloved independent bookstore has been sating readers' thirst for new, used, and discount books since 1966. The children's section is especially comprehensive, and the shop's special events calendar is packed with readings, social mixers, booksignings, and discussions. ⊠ *1520 Pacific Ave.* ☎ *831/423–0900* ⊕ *www.bookshopsantacruz.com.*

O'Neill Surf Shop. O'Neill operates two flagship stores, this one in downtown Santa Cruz and one at 1115 41st Avenue, Capitola, close to Jack O'Neill's home on Pleasure Point. There's also a smaller outlet on the Santa Cruz Wharf at 400 Beach Street. Sporting stores all over town also carry the line (it's everywhere). ⊠ *110 Cooper St.* ☎ *831/469–4377* ⊕ *www.oneill.com.*

The True Olive Connection. Taste your way through boutique extra-virgin olive oils and balsamic vinegars from around the world at this family-run shop just off Pacific Avenue. You can also pick up gourmet food products and olive-oil-based gift items. ⊠ *106 Lincoln St.* ☎ *831/458–6457* ⊕ *www.trueoliveconnection.com.*

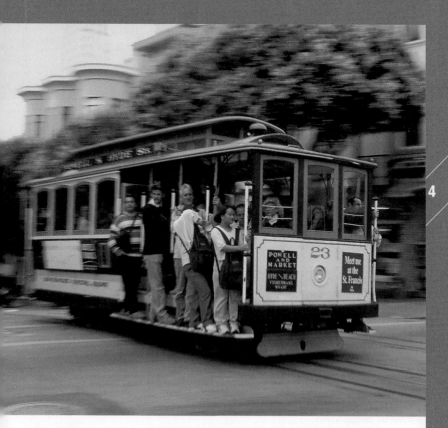

SAN FRANCISCO

WELCOME TO SAN FRANCISCO

TOP REASONS TO GO

★ **The bay:** It's hard not to gasp as you catch sight of sunlight dancing on the water when you crest a hill, or watch the Golden Gate Bridge vanish and reemerge in the summer fog.

★ **The food:** San Franciscans are serious about what they eat, and with good reason. Home to some of the nation's best chefs, top restaurants, and finest local produce, it's hard not to eat well here.

★ **The shopping:** Shopaholics visiting the city will not be disappointed: San Francisco is packed with browsing destinations, everything from quirky boutiques to massive malls.

★ **The good life:** A laid-back atmosphere, beautiful surroundings, and oodles of cultural, culinary, and aesthetic pleasures . . . if you spend too much time here, you might not leave!

★ **The great outdoors:** From Golden Gate Park to sidewalk cafés in North Beach, San Franciscans relish their outdoor spaces.

1 Union Square and Chinatown. Union Square has hotels, public transportation, and shopping; walking through Chinatown is like visiting another country.

2 SoMa and Civic Center. SoMa is anchored by SFMOMA and Yerba Buena Gardens; the city's performing arts venues are in Civic Center.

3 Nob Hill and Russian Hill. Nob Hill is old money San Francisco; Russian Hill's steep streets have excellent eateries and shopping.

4 North Beach. This small Italian neighborhood is a great place to enjoy an espresso.

5 On the Waterfront. Head here to visit the exquisitely restored Ferry Building, Fisherman's Wharf, Pier 39, and Ghirardelli Square.

6 The Marina and the Presidio. The Marina has trendy boutiques, restaurants, and cafés; the wooded Presidio offers great views of the Golden Gate Bridge.

5 WATERFRONT
Fisherman's Wharf ◆
◆ Pier 39
4

Marina Green

Ghirardelli Square ◆
Bay St.
NORTH BEACH

6 MARINA

RUSSIAN HILL
◆ Coit Tower

Palace of Fine Arts
Lombard St.
101

101
Hyde St.
Larkin St.
Columbus Ave.
TELEGRAPH HILL

Broadway
3 (tunnel)
CHINATOWN

NOB HILL

PACIFIC HEIGHTS
Washington St.
The Embarcadero
Ferry Building

Sacramento St.
California St.
Grant Ave.
Powell St.
1
FINANCIAL DISTRICT

10
Polk St.
Van Ness Ave.
Franklin St.
Gough St.
Laguna St.
Post St.
Geary St.
UNION SQUARE
1st St.

Pine St.
Bush St.

Presidio Ave.
Arguello Ave.
Divisadero St.
Steiner St.

Geary Blvd.
JAPANTOWN
Turk St.

Turk St.
Golden Gate Ave.
Fulton St.
CIVIC CENTER
Hayes St.
2
SOMA
Mission St.
2nd St.
3rd St.
4th St.
5th St.
6th St.
Bryant St.
Brannan St.
Townsend St.
Berry St.

Fell St.
Market St.
7th St.
8th St.
9th St.
10th St.
Folsom St.
Harrison St.

HAIGHT
Haight St.

Stanyan St.
Clayton St.
Buena Vista Park
Duboce

CASTRO
Castro Theater
8
Market St.
Castro St.
9
17th St.
Dolores St.
Guerrero St.
Mission St.
Van Ness Ave.
Harrison St.
Potrero Ave.
Mariposa St.
Pennsylvania Ave.
3rd St.
Indiana St.

Clarenden Ave.
Twin Peaks
MISSION
20th St.
24th St.
25th St.
Cesar Chavez St.

101

280
80
San Francisco Bay
San Francisco-Oakland Bay Bridge

4

Central Basin

Islais Cr. Channel

---

7 **Golden Gate Park and the Western Shoreline.** San Francisco's 1,000-acre backyard has sports fields, windmills, museums, and gardens; the windswept Western Shoreline stretches for miles.

8 **The Haight, the Castro, and Noe Valley.** After you've seen the blockbuster sights, come to these neighborhoods to see where the city's heart beats.

9 **The Mission.** This Latino neighborhood has destination restaurants, bargain ethnic eateries, and a hip bar scene.

10 **Pacific Heights and Japantown.** Pacific Heights has some of the city's most opulent real estate; Japantown is packed with authentic Japanese shops and restaurants.

GETTING ORIENTED

San Francisco is a compact city; just 46.7 square miles. Essentially a tightly packed cluster of extremely diverse neighborhoods, the city dearly rewards walking. The areas that most visitors cover are easy (and safe) to reach on foot, but many have steep— make that *steep*—hills.

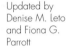

Updated by Denise M. Leto and Fiona G. Parrott

"You could live in San Francisco a month and ask no greater entertainment than walking through it," wrote Inez Hayes Irwin, author of *The Californiacs*, an effusive 1921 homage to the Golden State and the City by the Bay. Follow in her footsteps, and you'll find that her claim still rings true today: simply wandering around this beautiful metropolis on foot is the best way to experience all of its diverse wonders.

Snuggling on a 46½-square-mile strip of land between San Francisco Bay and the Pacific Ocean, San Francisco is a relatively small city of about 750,000 residents. San Franciscans cherish their city for the same reasons visitors do: the proximity to the bay and its pleasures, rows of Victorian homes clinging precariously to the hillsides, the sun setting behind the Golden Gate Bridge. But the city's attraction goes much deeper, from the diversity of its neighborhoods to the progressive free spirit here. Take all these things together, and you'll begin to understand why many San Franciscans can't imagine calling anyplace else home— despite the dizzying cost of living.

San Francisco's charms are great and small. You won't want to miss Golden Gate Park, the Palace of Fine Arts, the Golden Gate Bridge, or a cable car ride over Nob Hill. But a walk down the Filbert Street Steps or through Macondray Lane or an hour gazing at murals in the Mission or the thundering Pacific from the cliffs of Lincoln Park can be equally inspiring.

PLANNING

WHEN TO GO

You can visit San Francisco comfortably any time of year. Possibly the best time is September and October, when the city's summer-like weather brings outdoor concerts and festivals. The climate here always feels Mediterranean and moderate—with a foggy, sometimes chilly bite. The temperature rarely drops below 40°F, and anything warmer than 80°F is considered a heat wave. Be prepared for rain in winter, especially

December and January. Winds off the ocean can add to the chill factor. That old joke about summer in San Francisco feeling like winter is true at heart, but once you move inland, it gets warmer. (And some locals swear that the thermostat has inched up in recent years.)

GETTING HERE AND AROUND
AIR TRAVEL

The major gateway to San Francisco is San Francisco International Airport (SFO), 15 miles south of the city. It's off U.S. 101 near Millbrae and San Bruno. Oakland International Airport (OAK) is across the bay, not much farther away from downtown San Francisco (via I–80 east and I–880 south), but rush-hour traffic on the Bay Bridge may lengthen travel times considerably. San Jose International Airport (SJC) is about 40 miles south of San Francisco; travel time depends largely on traffic flow, but plan on an hour and a half with moderate traffic.

Airports San Francisco International Airport (*SFO*). ☏ 800/435–9736, 650/821–8211 ⊕ www.flysfo.com. **Oakland International Airport** (*OAK*). ☏ 510/563–3300 ⊕ www.flyoakland.com.

Airport Transfers American Airporter ☏ 415/202–0733 ⊕ www.americanairporter.com. **BayPorter Express** ☏ 415/467–1800 ⊕ www.bayporter.com. **Caltrain** ☏ 800/660–4287 ⊕ www.caltrain.com. **East Bay Express Airporter** ☏ 877/526–0304 ⊕ www.eastbaytransportation. com. **GO Lorrie's Airport Shuttle** ☏ 415/334–9000 ⊕ www.gosfovan.com. **Marin Airporter** ☏ 415/461–4222 ⊕ www.marinairporter.com. **Marin Door to Door** ☏ 415/457–2717 ⊕ www.marindoortodoor.com. **SamTrans** ☏ 800/660–4287 ⊕ www.samtrans.com. **South and East Bay Airport Shuttle** ☏ 800/548–4664 ⊕ www.southandeastbayairportshuttle.com. **SuperShuttle** ☏ 800/258–3826 ⊕ www.supershuttle.com. **VIP Airport Shuttle** ☏ 408/986–6000, 800/235–8847 ⊕ www.viptransportgroup.com.

BART TRAVEL

BART (Bay Area Rapid Transit) trains, which run until midnight, travel under the bay via tunnel to connect San Francisco with Oakland, Berkeley, and other cities and towns beyond. Within San Francisco, stations are limited to downtown, the Mission, and a couple of outlying neighborhoods.

Trains travel frequently from early morning until evening on weekdays. After 8 pm weekdays and on weekends there's often a 20-minute wait between trains on the same line. Trains also travel south from San Francisco as far as Millbrae. BART trains connect downtown San Francisco to San Francisco International Airport; the ride costs $8.25.

Intracity San Francisco fares are $1.75; intercity fares are $3.15 to $8.50. BART bases its ticket prices on miles traveled and does not offer price breaks by zone. The easy-to-read maps posted in BART stations list fares based on destination, radiating out from your starting point of the current station.

Contact Bay Area Rapid Transit (*BART*). ☏ 415/989–2278 ⊕ www.bart.gov.

BOAT AND FERRY TRAVEL

Several ferry lines run out of San Francisco. Blue & Gold Fleet operates a number of routes, including service to Sausalito ($11 one-way) and Tiburon ($11 one-way). Tickets are sold at Pier 41 (between Fisherman's Wharf and Pier 39), where the boats depart. Alcatraz Cruises, owned by Hornblower Yachts, operates the ferries to Alcatraz Island ($28 including audio tour and National Park Service ranger-led programs) from Pier 33, about a half-mile east of Fisherman's Wharf ($3 shuttle buses serve several area hotels and other locations). Boats leave 10 times a day (14 times a day in summer), and the journey itself takes 30 minutes. Allow roughly 2½ hours for a round-trip jaunt. Golden Gate Ferry runs daily to and from Sausalito and Larkspur ($9.75 and $9 one-way), leaving from Pier 1, behind the San Francisco Ferry Building. The Alameda/Oakland Ferry operates daily between Alameda's Main Street Ferry Building, Oakland's Jack London Square, and San Francisco's Pier 41 and the Ferry Building ($6.25 one-way); some ferries go only to Pier 41 or the Ferry Building, so ask when you board. Purchase tickets on board.

Ferry Lines Alameda/Oakland Ferry ☎ 510/522–3300 ⊕ www.eastbayferry.com. **Alcatraz Cruises** ☎ 415/981–7625 ⊕ www.alcatrazcruises.com. **Blue & Gold Fleet** ☎ 415/705–8200 ⊕ www.blueandgoldfleet.com. **Golden Gate Ferry** ☎ 415/455–2000 ⊕ www.goldengateferry.org. **San Francisco Ferry Building** ✉ 1 Ferry Bldg., at foot of Market St. on Embarcadero ☎ 415/983–8030 ⊕ www.ferrybuildingmarketplace.com.

CABLE CAR TRAVEL

The fare (for one direction) is $6 (Muni Passport holders only pay a $1 supplement). You can buy tickets on board (exact change isn't necessary) or at the kiosks at the cable-car turnarounds at Hyde and Beach streets and at Powell and Market streets.

The heavily traveled Powell–Mason and Powell–Hyde lines begin at Powell and Market streets near Union Square and terminate at Fisherman's Wharf; lines for these routes can be long, especially in summer. The California Street line runs east and west from Market and California streets to Van Ness Avenue; there is often no wait to board this route.

CAR TRAVEL

Driving in San Francisco can be a challenge because of the one-way streets, snarly traffic, and steep hills. The first two elements can be frustrating enough, but those hills are tough for unfamiliar drivers. ■TIP→ **Remember to curb your wheels when parking on hills—turn wheels away from the curb when facing uphill, toward the curb when facing downhill. You can get a ticket if you don't do this.**

MUNI TRAVEL

The San Francisco Municipal Railway, or Muni, operates light-rail vehicles, the historic F-line streetcars along Fisherman's Wharf and Market Street, trolley buses, and the world-famous cable cars. Light rail travels along Market Street to the Mission District and Noe Valley (J line), the Ingleside District (K line), and the Sunset District (L, M, and N lines); during peak hours (Monday through Friday, 6 am–9 am and 3 pm–7 pm) the J line continues around the Embarcadero to the Caltrain station at 4th and King streets. The T-line light rail runs from the Castro, down Market Street, around the Embarcadero, and south past Hunters Point and Monster Park to Sunnydale Avenue and Bayshore Boulevard. Muni provides 24-hour service on select lines to all areas of the city.

On buses and streetcars the fare is $2. Exact change is required, and dollar bills are accepted in the fare boxes. For all Muni vehicles other than cable cars, 90-minute transfers are issued free upon request at the time the fare is paid. These are valid for two additional transfers in any direction. Cable cars cost $6 and include no transfers (⇨ *see Cable-Car Travel, above*).

One-day ($14), three-day ($22), and seven-day ($28) Passports valid on the entire Muni system can be purchased at several outlets, including the cable-car ticket booth at Powell and Market streets and the visitor information center downstairs in Hallidie Plaza. A monthly ticket, called a Fast Pass, is available for $74, and can be used on all Muni lines (including cable cars) and on BART within city limits. The San Francisco CityPass, a discount ticket booklet to several major city attractions, also covers all Muni travel for seven consecutive days.

The San Francisco Municipal Transit and Street Map ($3) is a useful guide to the extensive transportation system. You can buy the map at most bookstores and at the San Francisco Visitor Information Center, on the lower level of Hallidie Plaza at Powell and Market streets.

Outside the city, AC Transit serves the East Bay, and Golden Gate Transit serves Marin County and a few cities in southern Sonoma County.

Bus Lines AC Transit ☎ *510/891–4777* ⊕ *www.actransit.org.* **Golden Gate Transit** ☎ *511, 415/455–2000* ⊕ *www.goldengate.org.* **San Francisco Municipal Railway System** (*Muni*). ☎ *311, 415/701–3000* ⊕ *www.sfmta.com.*

TAXI TRAVEL

Taxi service is notoriously bad in San Francisco, and hailing a cab can be frustratingly difficult in some parts of the city, especially on weekends. Popular nightspots such as the Mission, SoMa, North Beach, the Haight, and the Castro have a lot of cabs but a lot of people looking for taxis, too. Midweek, and during the day, you shouldn't have much of a problem—unless it's raining. In a pinch, hotel taxi stands are an option, as is calling for a pick-up. But be forewarned: taxi companies frequently don't answer the phone in peak periods. The absolute worst time to find a taxi is Friday afternoon and evening; plan well ahead, and if you're going to the airport, make a reservation or book a shuttle instead. Most taxi companies take reservations for airport and out-of-town runs but not in-town rides.

Taxis in San Francisco charge $3.50 for the first 1/5 mile (one of the highest base rates in the United States), 55¢ for each additional 1/5 mile, and 55¢ per minute in stalled traffic; a $2 surcharge is added for trips to the airport. There is no charge for additional passengers; there is no surcharge for luggage. For trips outside city limits, multiply the metered rate by 1.5; tolls and tip are extra.

Taxi Companies **DeSoto Cab** ☎ *415/970–1300* ⊕ *www.desotosf.com.*
Luxor Cab ☎ *415/282–4141* ⊕ *www.luxorcab.com.* **Veteran's Taxicab**
☎ *415/648–1313.* **Yellow Cab** ☎ *415/626–2345* ⊕ *yellowcabsf.com.*

Complaints **San Francisco Police Department Taxi Complaints**
☎ *415/553–1447.*

TRAIN TRAVEL

Amtrak trains travel to the Bay Area from some cities in California and the United States. The *Coast Starlight* travels north from Los Angeles to Seattle, passing the Bay Area along the way, but contrary to its name, the train runs inland through the Central Valley for much of its route through Northern California; the most scenic stretch is in Southern California, between San Luis Obispo and Los Angeles. Amtrak also has several routes between San Jose, Oakland, and Sacramento. The *California Zephyr* travels from Chicago to the Bay Area, and has spectacular alpine vistas as it crosses the Sierra Nevada range. San Francisco doesn't have an Amtrak train station but does have an Amtrak bus station, at the Ferry Building, from which shuttle buses transport passengers to trains in Emeryville, just over the Bay Bridge. Shuttle buses also connect the Emeryville train station with downtown Oakland, the Caltrain station, and other points in downtown San Francisco. You can buy a California Rail Pass, which gives you 7 days of travel in a 21-day period for $159.

Caltrain connects San Francisco to Palo Alto, San Jose, Santa Clara, and many smaller cities en route. In San Francisco, trains leave from the main depot, at 4th and Townsend streets, and a rail-side stop at 22nd and Pennsylvania streets. One-way fares are $3 to $13, depending on the number of zones through which you travel; tickets are valid for four hours after purchase time. A ticket is $7 from San Francisco to Palo Alto, at least $9 to San Jose. You can also buy a day pass ($6–$26) for unlimited travel in a 24-hour period. It's worth waiting for an express train for trips that last from 1 to 1¾ hours. On weekdays, trains depart three or four times per hour during the morning and evening, twice per hour during daytime non-commute hours, and as little as once per hour in the evening. Weekend trains run once per hour. The system shuts down at midnight. There are no onboard ticket sales. You must buy tickets before boarding the train or risk paying a $250 fine for fare evasion.

Train Contacts **Amtrak** ☎ *800/872–7245* ⊕ *www.amtrak.com.*
Caltrain ☎ *800/660–4287* ⊕ *www.caltrain.com.* **San Francisco Caltrain Station** ✉ *700 4th St., at King St.* ☎ *800/660–4287.*

VISITOR INFORMATION

The San Francisco Convention and Visitors Bureau can mail you brochures, maps, and festivals and events listings. Once you're in town, you can stop by the bureau's info center near Union Square. Information about the Wine Country, redwood groves, and northwestern California is available at the California Welcome Center on Pier 39.

Contacts **San Francisco Visitor Information Center** ✉ *Hallidie Plaza, lower level, 900 Market St., at Powell St., Union Sq.* ☎ *415/391–2000 TDD* ⊕ *www.onlyinsanfrancisco.com.*

EXPLORING SAN FRANCISCO

UNION SQUARE AND CHINATOWN

The Union Square area bristles with big-city bravado, while just a stone's throw away is a place that feels like a city unto itself, Chinatown. The two areas share a strong commercial streak, although manifested very differently. In Union Square the crowds zigzag among international brands, trailing glossy shopping bags. A few blocks north, people dash between small neighborhood stores, their arms draped with plastic totes filled with groceries or souvenirs.

EXPLORING IN UNION SQUARE

Maiden Lane. Known as Morton Street in the raffish Barbary Coast era, this former red-light district reported at least one murder a week during the late 19th century. Things cooled down after the 1906 fire destroyed the brothels, and these days Maiden Lane is a chic, boutique-lined pedestrian mall stretching two blocks, between Stockton and Kearny streets. Wrought-iron gates close the street to traffic most days between 11 am and 5 pm, when the lane becomes a patchwork of umbrella-shaded tables.

At **140 Maiden Lane** you can see the only Frank Lloyd Wright building in San Francisco. Walking through the brick archway and recessed entry feels a bit like entering a glowing cave. The interior's graceful, curving ramp and skylights are said to have been his model for the Guggenheim Museum in New York. Xanadu Gallery, which showcases expensive Baltic, Latin American, and African folk art, occupies the space and welcomes Lloyd Wright fans. ⊠ *Between Stockton and Kearny Sts.*

San Francisco Visitor Information Center. Head downstairs from the cable-car terminus to the visitor center, where multilingual staffers answer questions and provide maps and pamphlets. Muni Passports are sold here, and you can pick up discount coupons—the savings can be significant, especially for families. If you're planning to hit the big-ticket stops like the California Academy of Sciences and the Exploratorium and ride the cable cars, consider purchasing a CityPass (⊕ *www.citypass.com/ san-francisco*) here. ∎TIP➜ **The CityPass ($84, $59 ages 5–11), good for nine days, including seven days of transit, will save you more than 40%.** The pass is also available at the attractions it covers, though if you choose the pass that includes Alcatraz—an excellent deal—you'll have to buy it directly from Alcatraz Cruises (➪ *see On the Waterfront section*). ⊠ *Hallidie Plaza, lower level, 900 Market St., at Market and Powell Sts.* ☎ *415/391–2000* ⊕ *www.sanfrancisco.travel* ⊙ *Weekdays 9–5, Sat. 9–3; also Sun. 9–3 May–Oct.*

Union Square. Ground zero for big-name shopping in the city and within walking distance of many hotels, Union Square is home base for many visitors. The Westin St. Francis Hotel and Macy's line two of the square's sides, and Saks, Neiman-Marcus, and Tiffany & Co. edge the other two. Four globular lamp sculptures by the artist R. M. Fischer preside over the landscaped, 2½-acre park, which has a café with out-door seating, an open-air stage, and a visitor-information booth—along with a familiar kaleidoscope of characters: office workers sunning and brown-bagging, street musicians, shoppers taking a rest, kids chasing pigeons, and a fair number of homeless people. The constant clang of cable cars traveling up and down Powell Street helps maintain a festive mood.

The heart of San Francisco's downtown since 1850, the square takes its name from the violent pro-Union demonstrations staged here before the Civil War. At center stage, Robert Ingersoll Aitken's *Victory Monument* commemorates Commodore George Dewey's victory over the Spanish fleet at Manila in 1898. The 97-foot Corinthian column, topped by a bronze figure symbolizing naval conquest, was dedicated by Theodore Roosevelt in 1903 and withstood the 1906 earthquake. After the earthquake and fire of 1906, the square was dubbed "Little St. Francis" because of the temporary shelter erected for residents of the St. Francis Hotel. Actor John Barrymore (grandfather of actress Drew Barrymore and a notorious carouser) was among the guests pressed into volunteering to stack bricks in the square. His uncle, thespian John Drew, remarked, "It took an act of God to get John out of bed and the United States Army to get him to work."

The square sits atop a handy four-level garage, allegedly the world's first underground parking structure. Aboveground the convenient **TIX Bay Area** (*415/433–7827* ⊕ *www.tixbayarea.com*) provides half-price, day-of-performance tickets to performing-arts events, as well as regular full-price box-office services. ✉ *Bordered by Powell, Stockton, Post, and Geary Sts.*

Westin St. Francis Hotel. The second-oldest hotel in the city, established in 1904, was conceived by railroad baron and financier Charles Crocker and his associates as a hostelry for their millionaire friends. Swift service and sumptuous surroundings have always been hallmarks of the property. After the hotel was ravaged by the 1906 fire, a larger, more luxurious Italian Renaissance–style residence was opened in 1907 to attract loyal clients from among the world's rich and powerful. The hotel's checkered past includes the ill-fated 1921 bash in the suite of the silent-film superstar Fatty Arbuckle, at which a woman became ill and later died. Arbuckle endured three sensational trials for rape and murder before being acquitted, by which time his career was kaput. In 1975 Sara Jane Moore, standing among a crowd outside the hotel, attempted to shoot then-president Gerald Ford. As might be imagined, no plaques in the lobby commemorate these events. ■TIP→ One of the best views in the city is from the glass elevators here—and best of all, a ride is free. Zip up to the 32nd floor for a bird's-eye view; the

CABLE CAR TERMINUS

Two of the three cable-car lines begin and end their runs at Powell and Market streets, a couple of blocks south of Union Square. These two lines are the most scenic, and both pass near Fisherman's Wharf, so they're usually clogged with first-time sightseers. The wait to board a cable car at this intersection is longer than at any other stop in the system. If you'd rather avoid the mob, board the less-touristy California line at the bottom of Market Street, at Drumm Street.

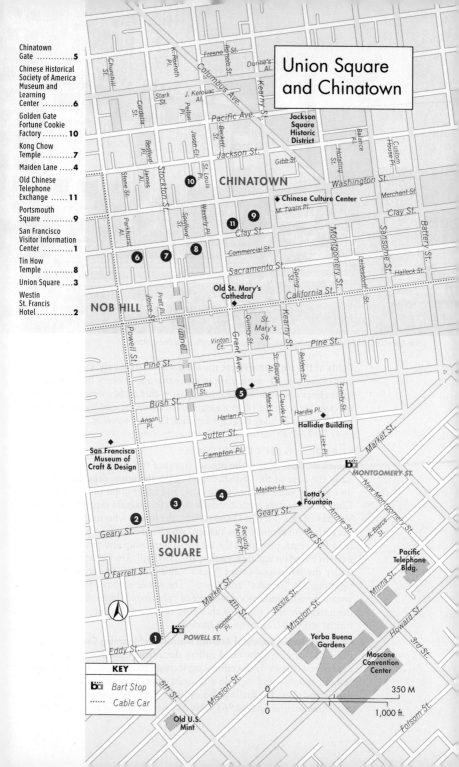

Union Square and Chinatown

CHINATOWN

NOB HILL

UNION SQUARE

Jackson Square Historic District

Chinese Culture Center

Old St. Mary's Cathedral

St. Mary's Sq.

San Francisco Museum of Craft & Design

Hallidie Building

Lotta's Fountain

Pacific Telephone Bldg.

Yerba Buena Gardens

Moscone Convention Center

Old U.S. Mint

KEY

🅱 *Bart Stop*

.... *Cable Car*

0   350 M
0   1,000 ft.

The Epicenter of high-end shopping, Union Square is lined with department stores.

lights of the nighttime cityscape are particularly lovely. Don't be shy if you're not a guest: some visitors make this a stop every time they're in town. Every November the hotel's pastry chef adds a new touch to his spectacular, rotating 12-foot gingerbread castle, on display in the grand lobby—a fun holiday treat for families. ⊠ *335 Powell St., at Geary St.* ☏ *415/397–7000* ⊕ *www.westinstfrancis.com*

EXPLORING IN CHINATOWN

Chinatown Gate. This is the official entrance to Chinatown. Stone lions flank the base of the pagoda-topped gate; the lions, dragons, and fish up top symbolize wealth, prosperity, and other good things. The four Chinese characters immediately beneath the pagoda represent the philosophy of Sun Yat-sen (1866–1925), the leader who unified China in the early 20th century. Sun Yat-sen, who lived in exile in San Francisco for a few years, promoted the notion of friendship and peace among all nations based on equality, justice, and goodwill. The vertical characters under the left pagoda read "peace" and "trust," the ones under the right pagoda "respect" and "love." The whole shebang telegraphs the internationally understood message of "photo op." Immediately beyond the gate, dive into souvenir shopping on Grant Avenue, Chinatown's tourist strip. ⊠ *Grant Ave. at Bush St.*

Chinese Historical Society of America Museum and Learning Center. The displays at this airy, light-filled gallery document the Chinese-American experience—from 19th-century agriculture to 21st-century food and fashion trends—and include a thought-provoking collection of racist games and toys. The facility also exhibits works by contemporary Chinese-American artists. ⊠ *965 Clay St., between Stockton and Powell*

CHINATOWN'S HISTORY

Sam Brannan's 1848 cry of "Gold!" didn't take long to reach across the world to China. Struggling with famine, drought, and political upheaval at home, thousands of Chinese jumped at the chance to try their luck in California. Most came from the Pearl River Delta region, in the Guangdong province, and spoke Cantonese dialects. From the start, Chinese businesses circled around Portsmouth Square, which was conveniently central. Bachelor rooming houses sprang up, since the vast majority of new arrivals were men. By 1853, the area was called Chinatown.

COLD WELCOME

The Chinese faced discrimination from the get-go. Harrassment became outright hostility as first the gold rush, then the work on the Transcontinental Railroad petered out. Special taxes were imposed to shoulder aside competing "coolie labor." Laws forbidding the Chinese from moving outside Chinatown kept the residents packed in like sardines,

The Street of Gamblers (Ross Alley), 1898 (top). The first Chinese telephone operator in Chinatown (bottom).

with nowhere to go but up and down—thus the many basement establishments in the neighborhood. State and federal laws passed in the 1870s deterred Chinese women from immigrating, deeming them prostitutes. In the late 1870s, looting and arson attacks on Chinatown businesses soared.

The coup de grace, though, was the Chinese Exclusion Act, passed by the U.S.

Sts. ☎ 415/391–1188 ⊕ *www.chsa.org* ✉ *$5, free 1st Thurs. of month* ⊙ *Tues.–Fri. noon–5, Sat. 11–4.*

FAMILY **Golden Gate Fortune Cookie Factory.** Follow your nose down Ross Alley to this tiny but fragrant cookie factory. Workers sit at circular motorized griddles and wait for dollops of batter to drop onto a tiny metal plate, which rotates into an oven. A few moments later out comes a cookie that's pliable and ready for folding. It's easy to peek in for a moment, and hard to leave without a few free samples. A bagful of cookies—with mildly racy "adult" fortunes or more benign ones—costs under $5. You can also purchase the cookies "fortuneless" in their wafer-like unfolded state, which makes snacking that much more efficient. ■TIP➔ **Photographing the cookie makers at work will set you back 50¢.** ⊠ *56 Ross Alley, off Washington or Jackson St. west of Grant Ave.* ☎ *415/781–3956* ✉ *Free* ⊙ *Daily 9–8.*

Kong Chow Temple. This ornate temple sets a somber, spiritual tone right away with a sign warning visitors not to touch *anything*. The god to whom the members of this temple pray represents honesty and trust. Chinese stores and restaurants often display his image because he's thought to bring good luck in business. Chinese immigrants established the temple in 1851; its congregation moved to this building in 1977. Take the elevator up to the fourth floor, where incense fills the air. You can show respect by placing a dollar or two in the donation box and by leaving your camera in its case. Amid the statuary, flowers, and richly colored altars (red wards off evil spirits and signifies virility, green symbolizes longevity, and gold connotes majesty), a couple of plaques announce that "Mrs. Harry S. Truman came to this temple in June 1948 for a prediction on the outcome of the election … this fortune came true." ■TIP➔ **The temple's balcony has a good view of Chinatown.** ⊠ *855 Stockton St.* ✉ *Free* ⊙ *Mon.–Sat. 9–4.*

Old Chinese Telephone Exchange. After the 1906 earthquake, many Chinatown buildings were rebuilt in Western style with pagoda roof and fancy balconies slapped on. This building—today EastWest Bank—is the exception, an example of top-to-bottom Chinese architecture. The intricate three-tier pagoda was built in 1909. To the Chinese, it's considered rude to refer to a person as a number, so the operators were required to memorize each subscriber's name. As the San Francisco Chamber of Commerce boasted in 1914: "These girls respond all day with hardly a mistake to calls that are given (in English or one of five Chinese dialects) by the name of the subscriber instead of by his number—a mental feat that would be practically impossible for most high-schooled American misses." ⊠ *EastWest Bank, 743 Washington St.*

Portsmouth Square. Chinatown's living room buzzes with activity. The square, with its pagoda-shaped structures, is a favorite spot for morning tai chi; by noon dozens of men huddle around Chinese chess tables, engaged in not-always-legal competition. Kids scamper about the square's two grungy playgrounds (warning: the bathrooms are sketchy). Back in the late 19th century this land was near the waterfront. The square is named for the U.S.S. *Portsmouth*, the ship helmed by Captain John Montgomery, who in 1846 raised the American flag here

4

and claimed the then-Mexican land for the United States. A couple of years later, Sam Brannan kicked off the gold rush at the square when he waved his loot and proclaimed, "Gold from the American River!" Robert Louis Stevenson, the author of *Treasure Island*, often dropped by, chatting up the sailors who hung out here. Some of the information he gleaned about life at sea found its way into his fiction. A bronze galleon sculpture, a tribute to Stevenson, anchors the square's northwest corner. A plaque marks the site of California's first public school, built in 1847. ⊠ *Bordered by Walter Lum Pl. and Kearny, Washington, and Clay Sts.*

Fodor's Choice
★

Tin How Temple. Duck into the inconspicuous doorway, climb three flights of stairs, and be assaulted by the aroma of incense in this tiny, altar-filled room. In 1852, Day Ju, one of the first three Chinese to arrive in San Francisco, dedicated this temple to the Queen of the Heavens and the Goddess of the Seven Seas, and the temple looks largely the same today as it did more than a century ago. In the entryway, elderly ladies can often be seen preparing "money" to be burned as offerings to various Buddhist gods or as funds for ancestors to use in the afterlife. Hundreds of red-and-gold lanterns cover the ceiling; the larger the lamp, the larger its donor's contribution to the temple. Gifts of oranges, dim sum, and money left by the faithful, who kneel mumbling prayers, rest on altars to different gods. Tin How presides over the middle back of the temple, flanked by one red and one green lesser god. Take a good look around, since taking photographs is not allowed. ⊠ *125 Waverly Pl., between Clay and Washington Sts.* ☞ *Free, donations accepted* ⊙ *Daily 9–4.*

SOMA AND CIVIC CENTER

To a newcomer, SoMa (short for "south of Market") and the Civic Center may look like cheek-by-jowl neighbors—they're divided by Market Street. To locals, though, these areas are separate entities, especially since Market Street itself is considered such a strong demarcation line. Both neighborhoods have a core of cultural sights but more than their share of sketchy blocks. North of the Civic Center lie the western sections of the frisky Tenderloin neighborhood, while to the east is hip Hayes Valley.

EXPLORING SOMA

California Historical Society. If you're not a history buff, the CHS might seem like an obvious skip—who wants to look at fading old photographs and musty artifacts?—but these airy galleries are worth a stop. The shows here draw from the society's vast repository of Californiana—hundreds of thousands of photographs, publications, paintings, and gold-rush paraphernalia. Special exhibits have included *A Wild Flight of the Imagination: The Story of the Golden Gate Bridge* and *Hobos to Street People: Artists' Responses to Homelessness from the New Deal to the Present.* ■ **TIP➔ From out front, take a look across the street: this is the best view of the Museum of the African Diaspora's three-story photo mosaic.** ⊠ *678 Mission St.* ☎ *415/357–1848* ⊕ *www. californiahistoricalsociety.org* ☞ *$5* ⊙ *Tues.–Sun. noon–5; galleries close between exhibitions.*

Continued on page 169

CHINATOWN

Chinatown's streets flood the senses. Incense and cigarette smoke mingle with the scents of briny fish and sweet vanilla. Rooflines flare outward, pagoda-style. Loud Cantonese bargaining and honking car horns rise above the sharp clack of mah-jongg tiles and the eternally humming cables beneath the street.

Most Chinatown visitors march down Grant Avenue, buy a few trinkets, and call it a day. Do yourself a favor and dig deeper. This is one of the largest Chinese communities outside Asia, and there is far more to it than buying a back-scratcher near Chinatown Gate. To get a real feel for the neighborhood, wander off the main drag. Step into a temple or an herb shop and wander down a flag-draped alley. And don't be shy: residents welcome guests warmly, though rarely in English.

Whatever you do, don't leave without eating something. Noodle houses, bakeries, tea houses, and dim sum shops seem to occupy every other storefront. There's a feast for your eyes as well: in the market windows on Stockton and Grant, you'll see hanging whole roast ducks, fish, and shellfish swimming in tanks, and strips of shiny, pink-glazed Chinese-style barbecued pork.

Chinatown's Grant Avenue.

Women and children flooded into the neighborhood after the Great Quake.

Congress in 1882, which slammed the doors to America for "Asiatics." This was the country's first significant restriction on immigration. The law also prevented the existing Chinese residents, including American-born children, from becoming naturalized citizens. With a society of mostly men (forbidden, of course, from marrying white women), San Francisco hoped that Chinatown would simply die out.

OUT OF THE ASHES

When the devastating 1906 earthquake and fire hit, city fathers thought they'd seize the opportunity to kick the Chinese out of Chinatown and get their hands on that desirable piece of downtown real estate. Then Chinatown businessman Look Tin Eli had a brainstorm of Disneyesque proportions.

He proposed that Chinatown be rebuilt, but in a tourist-friendly, stylized, "Oriental" way. Anglo-American architects would design new buildings with pagoda roofs and dragon-covered columns. Chinatown would attract more tourists— the curious had been visiting on the sly

for decades—and add more tax money to the city's coffers. Ka-ching: the sales pitch worked.

PAPER SONS

For the Chinese, the 1906 earthquake turned the virtual "no entry" sign into a flashing neon "welcome!" All the city's immigration records went up in smoke, and the Chinese quickly began to apply for passports as U.S. citizens, claiming their old ones were lost in the fire. Not only did thousands of Chinese become legal overnight, but so did their sons in China, or "sons," if they weren't really related. Whole families in Chinatown had passports in names that weren't their own; these "paper sons" were not only a windfall but also an uncomfortable neighborhood conspiracy. The city caught on eventually and set up an immigration center on Angel Island in 1910. Immigrants spent weeks or months being inspected and interrogated while their papers were checked. Roughly 250,000 people made it through. With this influx, including women and children, Chinatown finally became a more complete community.

A GREAT WALK THROUGH CHINATOWN

■ Start at the Chinatown Gate and walk ahead on Grant Avenue, entering the souvenir gauntlet. (You'll also pass Old St. Mary's Cathedral.)

■ Make a right on Clay Street and walk to Portsmouth Square. Sometimes it feels like the whole neighborhood's here, playing chess and exercising.

■ Head up Washington Street to the Old Chinese Telephone Exchange building, now the EastWest Bank. Across Grant, look left for Waverly Place. Here Free Republic of China (Taiwanese) flags flap over some of the neighborhood's most striking buildings, including Tin How Temple.

■ At the Sacramento Street end of Waverly Place stands the First Chinese Baptist Church of 1908. Just across the way, the Clarion Music Center is full of unusual instruments, as well as exquisite lion-dance sets.

■ Head back to Washington Street and check out the herb shops, like the Superior Trading Company (No. 839) and the Great China Herb Co. (No. 857).

■ Follow the scent of vanilla down Ross Alley (entrance across from Superior Trading Company) to the Golden Gate Fortune Cookie Factory. Then

head across the alley to Sam Bo Trading Co., where religious items are stacked in the narrow space. Tell the owners your troubles and they'll prepare a package of joss papers, joss sticks, and candles, and tell you how and when to offer them up.

■ Turn left on Jackson Street; ahead is the real Chinatown's

main artery, Stockton Street, where most residents do their grocery shopping. Vegetarians will want to avoid Luen Fat Market (No. 1135), with tanks of live frogs, turtles, and lobster as well as chickens and ducks. Look toward the back of stores for Buddhist altars with offerings of oranges and grapefruit. From here you can loop one block east back to Grant.

ALL THE TEA IN CHINATOWN

Preparing a perfect brew at Red Blossom Tea.

San Francisco's close ties to Asia have always made it more tea-conscious than other American burgs, but these days the city is in the throes of a tea renaissance, with new tasting rooms popping up in every neighborhood. Below are our favorite spots for every tea under the sun.

Blest Tea. Chinatown's smallest tea shop is a calm, modern space with a thoughtful selection of teas by the pound. The Taiwane owners sell teas from many Asian countries, but their offerings emphasize Taiwan. Regulars rave about the service. ⊠ *752 Grant Ave.* ☎ *415/951–8516.*

Red Blossom Tea. A light and modern shop—the staff really know their stuff. It's a favorite among younger tea enthusiasts, who swear by its excellent bang-for-the-buck value. While Red Blossom doesn't do formal tastings or sell tea by the cup, they'll gladly brew up perfect samples of the teas you're interested in. ⊠ *831 Grant Ave.* ☎ *415/395–0868.*

Vital Tea Leaf. Tastings here work like those for wine—one of the gregarious, knowledgeable servers chooses the teas and describes them as you sample. It's a great spot for tea newbies to get their feet wet without a hard sell, but local connoisseurs grumble about the high prices and the self-promotion. ⊠ *1044 Grant Ave.* ☎ *415/981–2388.*

Imperial Tea Court. If you want to visit the most respected of traditional tea purveyors, you'll need to venture outside of Chinatown. Imperial Tea Court may have left Chinatown, but you'll find the same great selection and expertise at their fancy digs in the Ferry Building. ☎ *415/544–9830.*

WAITING FOR CUSTARD

As you're strolling down Grant Avenue, past the plastic Buddhas and yin/yang balls, be sure to stop at the Golden Gate Bakery (No. 1029) for some delicious eggy *dan tat* (custard tarts). These flaky-crusted treats are heaven for just a buck. There's often a line, but it's worth the wait.

DON'T-MISS SHOPS

Locals snap up flowers from an outdoor vendor.

If you're in the market for a pair of chirping metal crickets (oh you'll hear them, trust us), you can duck into any of the obvious souvenir-stuffed storefronts. But if you're looking for something special, head for these tempting sources.
■ **TIP➜** Fierce neighborhood competition keeps prices within reason, but for popular wares like jade, it pays to shop around before making a serious investment. Many stores accept cash only.

Chinatown Kite Shop. Family-run shop selling bright, fun-shaped kites—dragons, butterflies, sharks—since the 1960s. ✉ *717 Grant Ave.* ☎ *415/989–5182.*

Dragon House. A veritable museum: the store sells authentic, centuries-old antiques like ivory carvings. ✉ *455 Grant Ave.* ☎ *415/421–3693.*

Old Shanghai. One of the largest selections of hand-painted robes, formal dresses, and jackets in Chinatown, plus chic Asian-inspired pieces. ✉ *645 Grant Ave.* ☎ *415/986–1222.*

CHINATOWN WITH KIDS

It can be tough for the little ones to keep their hands to themselves, especially when all sorts of curios spill out onto the sidewalk at just the right height. To burn off some steam (in them) and relieve some stress (in you), take them to the small but spruce playground in the park in St. Mary's Square, across California from Old St. Mary's. If that setting's too tranquil, head to the more boisterous Willie Wong Playground, on Sacramento Street at Waverly Place.

Cartoon Art Museum. Krazy Kat, Zippy the Pinhead, Batman, and other colorful cartoon icons greet you at the Cartoon Art Museum, established with an endowment from cartoonist-icon Charles M. Schulz. The museum's strength is its changing exhibits, which explore such topics as America from the perspective of international political cartoons, and the output of women and African-American car-

LOOK UP!

When wandering around Chinatown, don't forget to look up! Above the chintziest souvenir shop might loom an ornate balcony or a curly pagoda roof. The best examples are on the 900 block of Grant Avenue (at Washington Street) and at Waverly Place.

toonists. Serious fans of cartoons—especially those on the quirky underground side—will likely enjoy the exhibits; those with a casual interest may be bored. The store here carries cool titles to add to your collection. ⊠ *655 Mission St.* ☎ *415/227–8666* ⊕ *www.cartoonart.org* ✉ *$7, pay what you wish 1st Tues. of month* ◷ *Tues.–Sun. 11–5.*

Contemporary Jewish Museum. Daniel Liebeskind designed the postmodern CJM, whose impossible-to-ignore diagonal blue cube juts out of a painstakingly restored power substation. A physical manifestation of the Hebrew phrase *l'chaim* (to life), the cube may have obscure philosophical origins, but Liebeskind created a unique, light-filled space that merits a stroll through the lobby even if current exhibits don't entice you into the galleries. Be sure to check out the seam where old building meets new. ■**TIP→** **At the museum's StoryCorps StoryBooth, a project of the NPR oral-history series, you can listen to past interviews—or slip into the recording studio and preserve a loved one's memories right on the spot.** ⊠ *736 Mission St., between 3rd and 4th Sts.* ☎ *415/655–7800* ⊕ *www.thecjm.org* ✉ *$12, $5 Thurs. after 5 pm, free 1st Tues. of the month* ◷ *Thurs. 1–8, Fri.–Tues. 11–5.*

Museum of the African Diaspora (MoAD). Dedicated to the influence that people of African descent have had all over the world, MoAD provokes discussion from the get-go with the question, "When did you discover you are African?" painted on the wall at the entrance. With no permanent collection, the museum is light on displays and heavy on interactive exhibits. For instance, you can sit in a darkened theater and listen to the moving life stories of slaves; hear snippets of music that helped create genres from gospel to hip-hop; and see videos about the Civil Rights movement or the Haitian Revolution. Some grumble that sweeping generalities replace specific information, but almost everyone can appreciate the museum's most striking exhibit in the front window. The three-story mosaic, made from thousands of photographs, forms the image of a little girl's face. Walk up the stairs inside the museum and view the photographs up close—Malcolm X is there, Muhammad Ali, too, along with everyday folks—but the best view is from across the street. ⊠ *685 Mission St.* ☎ *415/358–7200* ⊕ *www.moadsf.org* ✉ *$10* ◷ *Wed.–Sat. 11–6, Sun. noon–5.*

San Francisco Jazz Center. Opened in 2013 to much fanfare, the center is devoted entirely to jazz. The debut week alone saw performances by McCoy Tyner, Joshua Redman, Regina Carter, Chick Corea, and Savion Glover, among others. Walk by and the street-level glass walls will make you feel as if you're inside; head indoors and the acoustics will knock your socks off. ■TIP→ You can grab a quick bite—or breakfast, lunch, or dinner—at the on-site South at SFJAZZ, a New Orleans–style restaurant developed by Charles Phan, the celebrated chef of the Slanted Door. ✉ *201 Franklin St., at Fell St., Hayes Valley* ☎ *866/920–5299* ⊕ *www.sfjazz.org.*

San Francisco Museum of Modern Art. SFMOMA closed for a massive expansion project in 2013 and is scheduled to reopen in 2016. Until then, the museum will draw from its collection to create joint exhibitions with the Asian Art Museum,

HAYES VALLEY

An offbeat neighborhood due west of Civic Center, Hayes Valley has terrific eateries, cool watering holes, and great browsing in its funky clothing, home-decor, and design boutiques. Locals love this quarter, but without any big-name draws it remains off the radar for many visitors, though that may change with the opening of the SF Jazz Center on Franklin Street. Swing down main drag Hayes Street between Franklin and Laguna streets and you can hit the neighborhood's highlights, including two very popular restaurants, Absinthe and Suppenküche.

the Yerba Buena Center for the Arts, and other institutions. SFMOMA's store—known for its fun gadgets, artsy doodads, and superb art and kids' books—is relocating temporarily to 51 Yerba Buena Lane, off Mission and Market Streets near 4th Street. ✉ *151 3rd St.* ☎ *415/357–4000* ⊕ *www.sfmoma.org.*

Yerba Buena Center for the Arts. You never know what's going to be on display at this facility in Yerba Buena Gardens, but whether it's an exhibit of Mexican street art (graffiti to laypeople), innovative modern dance, or baffling video installations, it's likely to be memorable. The productions here tend to draw a young, energetic crowd, and lean toward the cutting edge. ■TIP→ Present any library card to receive a $2 discount. ✉ *701 Mission St.* ☎ *415/978–2787* ⊕ *www.ybca.org* 🎟 *Galleries $10, free 1st Tues. of month* ⊙ *Thurs.–Sat. noon–8, Sun. noon–6, 1st Tues. of the month noon–8.*

Fodor's Choice
★
FAMILY

Yerba Buena Gardens. There's not much south of Market Street that encourages lingering outdoors—or indeed walking at all—with this notable exception. These two blocks encompass the Center for the Arts, the Metreon, Moscone Convention Center, and the convention center's rooftop Children's Creativity Museum, but the gardens themselves are the everyday draw. Office workers escape to the green swath of the East Garden, the focal point of which is the memorial to Martin Luther King Jr. Powerful streams of water surge over large, jagged stone columns, mirroring the enduring force of King's words that are carved on the stone walls and on glass blocks behind the waterfall. Moscone North is behind the memorial, and an overhead walkway leads to Moscone South and its rooftop attractions. ■TIP→ The gardens are liveliest during the week and especially during the Yerba Buena Gardens Festival from May through October (⊕ www.ybgf.org), with free performances of everything from Latin music to Balinese dance.

SoMa and Civic Center

San Francisco Craft and Folk Art Museum ◆

Palace Hotel ◆

Transbay Terminal

Old U.S. Mint

St. Mary's Cathedral

Veterans Building ◆
War Memorial Opera House ◆
Louise M. Davies Symphony Hall ◆

San Francisco Public Library

KEY

🅱 Bart Stop

Asian Art Museum **10**
California Historical Society **7**
Cartoon Art Museum **6**
City Hall **11**

Contemporary Jewish Museum **1**
Museum of African Diaspora **4**
San Francisco Jazz Center **8**

San Francisco Museum of Modern Art **5**
United Nations Plaza **9**
Yerba Buena Center for the Arts **3**
Yerba Buena Gardens **2**

Atop the Moscone Convention Center perch a few lures for kids. The historic Looff carousel (✉ *$3 for two rides*) twirls daily 11 to 6. South of the carousel is the Children's Creativity Museum (☎ 415/820–3320 ⊕ *creativity.org*), a high-tech, interactive arts-and-technology center (✉ *$11*) geared to children ages 3 to 12. Kids can make Claymation videos, work in a computer lab, check out new games and apps, and perform and record music videos. The museum is open year-round between 10 and 4 from Wednesday through Sunday, and also on Tuesdays during the summer. Just outside, kids adore the excellent slides, including a 25-foot tube slide, at the play circle. Also part of the rooftop complex are gardens, an ice-skating rink, and a bowling alley. ⊠ *Bordered by 3rd, 4th, Mission, and Folsom Sts.* ⊕ *www.yerbabuenagardens.com* ✉ *Free* ⊙ *Daily sunrise–10 pm.*

EXPLORING CIVIC CENTER

Fodor's Choice
★

Asian Art Museum. You don't have to be a connoisseur of Asian art to appreciate a visit to this splendid museum, whose monumental exterior conceals a light, open, and welcoming space. The fraction of the museum's items on display (about 2,500 pieces from a 15,000-plus-piece collection) is laid out thematically and by region, making it easy to follow developments.

Begin on the third floor, where highlights of Buddhist art in Southeast Asia and early China include a large, jewel-encrusted, exquisitely painted 19th-century Burmese Buddha and clothed rod puppets from Java. On the second floor you can find later Chinese works, as well as pieces from Korea and Japan. Look for a cobalt tiger jauntily smoking a pipe on a whimsical Korean jar and delicate Japanese tea implements. The ground floor displays temporary exhibits, including traveling shows. ■TIP➔ **For much of the year the museum stays open late on Thursdays and hosts Matcha, an evening of cocktails, music, and activities related to current exhibitions.** ⊠ *200 Larkin St., between McAllister and Fulton Sts.* ☎ *415/581–3500* ⊕ *www. asianart.org* ✉ *$12, free 1st Sun. of month; $10 Thurs. 5–9; tea ceremony $27, includes museum admission* ⊙ *Tues.–Sun. 10–5; Feb.–Oct., Thurs. until 9.*

City Hall. This imposing 1915 structure with its massive gold-leaf dome—higher than the U.S. Capitol's—is about as close to a palace as you're going to get in San Francisco. (Alas, the metal detectors detract from the grandeur.) The classic granite-and-marble behemoth was modeled after St. Peter's Basilica in Rome. Architect Arthur Brown Jr., who also designed Coit Tower and the War Memorial Opera House, designed an interior with grand columns and a sweeping central staircase. San Franciscans were thrilled, and probably a bit surprised, when his firm built City Hall in just a few years. The 1899 structure it replaced had taken 27 years to erect, as corrupt builders and politicians lined their pockets with funds earmarked for it. That building collapsed in about 27 seconds during the 1906 earthquake, revealing trash and newspapers mixed into the construction materials.

City Hall was spruced up and seismically retrofitted in the late 1990s, but the sense of history remains palpable. Some noteworthy events that have taken place here include the marriage of Marilyn Monroe and Joe DiMaggio (1954); the hosing—down the central staircase— of civil-rights and freedom-of-speech protesters (1960); the murders of Mayor George Moscone and openly gay supervisor Harvey Milk (1978); the torching of the lobby by angry members of the gay community in response to the light sentence given to the former supervisor who killed both men (1979); and the registrations of scores of gay couples in celebration of the passage of San Francisco's Domestic Partners Act (1991). February 2004 has come to be known as the Winter of Love: thousands of gay and lesbian couples responded to Mayor Gavin Newsom's decision to issue marriage licenses to same-sex partners, turning City Hall into the site of raucous celebration and joyful nuptials for a month before the state Supreme Court ordered the practice stopped. That celebratory scene replayed during 2008, when scores of couples were wed between the court's June ruling that everyone enjoys the civil right to marry and the November passage of California's ballot proposition banning same-sex marriage. (By 2013, the issue had reached the U.S. Supreme Court.) Free tours are offered weekdays at 10, noon, and 2.

On display in the South Light Court are artifacts from the collection of the **Museum of the City of San Francisco** (⊕ *www.sfmuseum.org*), including maps, documents, and photographs. That enormous, 700-pound iron head once crowned the *Goddess of Progress* statue, which topped the old City Hall building until it crumbled during the 1906 earthquake. City Hall's centennial in 2013 kicked off three years of exhibits—the same amount of time it took to raise the building.

Across Polk Street from City Hall is **Civic Center Plaza,** with lawns, walkways, seasonal flower beds, a playground, and an underground parking garage. This sprawling space is generally clean but somewhat grim. A large part of the city's homeless population hangs out here, so the plaza can feel dodgy. ⊠ *Bordered by Van Ness Ave. and Polk, Grove, and McAllister Sts.* ☎ *415/554–6023* ⊕ *www.sfgov.org/site/ cityhall* 🔁 *Free* ⊘ *Weekdays 8–8.*

United Nations Plaza. Locals know this plaza for two things: the farmers' market held on Wednesdays and Sundays—cheap and earthy to the Ferry Building's pricey and beautiful—and the many homeless people, a consistent presence despite numerous efforts by the city to shunt them aside. Brick pillars listing various nations and the dates of their admittance into the United Nations line the plaza, and its floor is inscribed with the goals and philosophy of the United Nations Charter, which was signed at the War Memorial Opera House in 1945. The food-truck gathering Off the Grid (⊕ *offthegridsf.com*) livens up lunchtime on Tuesdays and Thursdays, with several vendors selling gourmet foods. ⊠ *Fulton St. between Hyde and Market Sts.*

NOB HILL AND RUSSIAN HILL

In place of the quirky charm and cultural diversity that mark other San Francisco neighborhoods, Nob Hill exudes history and good breeding. Topped with some of the city's most elegant hotels, Gothic Grace

Cathedral, and private blue-blood clubs, it's the pinnacle of privilege. One hill over, across Pacific Avenue, is another old-family bastion, Russian Hill. It may not be quite as wealthy as Nob Hill, but it's no slouch—and it's got jaw-dropping views.

EXPLORING NOB HILL

FAMILY **Cable Car Museum.** One of the city's best free offerings, this museum is an absolute must for kids. You can even ride a cable car here—all three lines stop between Russian Hill and Nob Hill. The facility, which is inside the city's last cable-car barn, takes the top off the system to let you see how it all works. Eternally humming and squealing, the massive powerhouse cable wheels steal the show. You can also climb aboard a vintage car and take the grip, let the kids ring a cable-car bell (briefly), and check out vintage gear dating from 1873.

The gift shop sells cable-car paraphernalia, including an authentic gripman's bell for $600 (it'll sound like Powell Street in your house every day). For significantly less, you can pick up a key chain made from a piece of worn-out cable. ⊠ *1201 Mason St., at Washington St.* ☏ *415/474–1887* ⊕ *www.cablecarmuseum.org* ⊠ *Free* ⊗ *Oct.–Mar., daily 10–5; Apr.–Sept., daily 10–6.*

Grace Cathedral. Not many churches can boast an altarpiece by Keith Haring and not one but two labyrinths. The seat of the Episcopal Church in San Francisco, this soaring Gothic-style structure, erected on the site of Charles Crocker's mansion, took 53 years to build, wrapping up in 1964. The gilded bronze doors at the east entrance were taken from casts of Lorenzo Ghiberti's incredible Gates of Paradise, which are on the Baptistery in Florence, Italy. A black-and-bronze stone sculpture of St. Francis by Beniamino Bufano greets you as you enter.

The 35-foot-wide limestone labyrinth is a replica of the 13th-century stone maze on the floor of Chartres Cathedral. All are encouraged to walk the ¼-mile-long labyrinth, a ritual based on the tradition of meditative walking. There's also a terrazzo outdoor labyrinth on the church's north side. The AIDS Interfaith Chapel, to the right as you enter Grace, contains a metal triptych by the late artist Keith Haring and panels from the AIDS Memorial Quilt. ■TIP→ Especially dramatic times to view the cathedral are during Thursday-night evensong (5:15 pm) and during special holiday programs. ⊠ *1100 California St., at Taylor St.* ☏ *415/749–6300* ⊕ *www.gracecathedral.org* ⊠ *Free* ⊗ *Weekdays 7–6, Sat. 8–6, Sun. 8–7; tours weekdays at 1, Sat. at 11:30, and Sun. at 12:40.*

EXPLORING RUSSIAN HILL

Fodor's Choice
★
Ina Coolbrith Park. If you make it all the way up here, you may have the place all to yourself, or at least feel that you do. The park's terraces are carved from a hill so steep that it's difficult to see if anyone else is there or not. Locals love this park because it feels like a secret no one else knows about—one of the city's magic hidden gardens, with a meditative setting and spectacular views of the bay peeking out from among the trees. A poet, Oakland librarian, and niece of Mormon prophet Joseph Smith, Ina Coolbrith (1842–1928) introduced Jack London and Isadora Duncan to the world of books. For years she

Nob Hill and
Russian Hill

entertained literary greats in her Macondray Lane home near the park. In 1915 she was named poet laureate of California. ✉ *Vallejo St. between Mason and Taylor Sts.*

Lombard Street. The block-long "Crookedest Street in the World" makes eight switchbacks down the east face of Russian Hill between Hyde and Leavenworth streets. Residents bemoan the traffic jam outside their front doors, but the throngs continue. Join the line of cars waiting to drive down the steep hill, or avoid the whole mess and walk down the steps on either side of Lombard. You take in super views of North Beach and Coit Tower whether you walk or drive—though if you're the one behind the wheel, you'd better keep your eye on the road lest you become yet another of the many folks who ram the garden barriers. ■TIP→ **Can't stand the traffic? Thrill seekers of a different stripe may want to head two blocks south of Lombard to Filbert Street. At a gradient of 31.5%, the hair-raising descent between Hyde and Leavenworth streets is the city's steepest. Go slowly!** ✉ *Lombard St. between Hyde and Leavenworth Sts.*

Fodor's Choice ★ **Macondray Lane.** San Francisco has no shortage of impressive, grand homes, but it's the tiny fairy-tale lanes that make most folks want to move here, and Macondray Lane is the quintessential hidden garden. Enter under a lovely wooden trellis and proceed down a quiet, cobbled pedestrian lane lined with Edwardian cottages and flowering plants and trees. Watch your step—the cobblestones are quite uneven in spots. A flight of steep wooden stairs at the end of the lane leads to Taylor Street—on the way down you can't miss the bay views. If you've read any of Armistead Maupin's *Tales of the City* books, you may find the lane vaguely familiar. It's the thinly disguised setting for part of the series' action. ⊠ *Between Jones and Taylor Sts., and Union and Green Sts.*

San Francisco Art Institute. A Moorish-tile fountain in a tree-shaded courtyard draws the eye as soon as you enter the institute. The number-one reason for a visit is Mexican master Diego Rivera's *The Making of a Fresco Showing the Building of a City* (1931), in the student gallery to your immediate left inside the entrance. Rivera himself is in the fresco—his broad behind is to the viewer—and he's surrounded by his assistants. They in turn are surrounded by a construction scene, laborers, and city notables such as sculptor Robert Stackpole and architect Timothy Pfleuger. *Making* is one of three San Francisco murals painted by Rivera. The number-two reason to come here is the café, or more precisely the eye-popping, panoramic view from the café, which serves surprisingly decent food for a song.

The older portions of the Art Institute, including the lovely Mission-style bell tower, were erected in 1926. To this day, otherwise pragmatic people claim that ghostly footsteps can be heard in the tower at night. Ansel Adams created the school's fine-arts photography department in 1946, and school directors established the country's first fine-arts film program. Notable faculty and alumni have included painter Richard Diebenkorn and photographers Dorothea Lange, Edward Weston, and Annie Leibovitz.

The **Walter & McBean Galleries** (☎ *415/749–4563* ⊙ *Open Tues. 11–7, Wed.–Sat. 11–6*) exhibit the often provocative works of established artists. ⊠ *800 Chestnut St.* ☎ *415/771–7020* ⊕ *www.sfai.edu* 🖼 *Galleries free* ⊙ *Hrs vary but building generally open Mon.–Sat. 9–7.*

NORTH BEACH

Italian bakeries appear frozen in time, homages to Jack Kerouac and Allen Ginsberg pop up everywhere, and strip joints, the modern equivalent of the Barbary Coast's "houses of ill repute," do business on Broadway. With its outdoor café tables, throngs of tourists, and holiday vibe, this is probably the part of town Europeans are thinking of when they say San Francisco is the most European city in America.

EXPLORING NORTH BEACH

Beat Museum. This two-level museum is likely to see an uptick in visitors in response to the 2012 film version of *On the Road*, whose director donated the 1949 Hudson from the movie. Check out exhibits such as the "Beat pad," a mock-up of one of the cheap, tiny North Beach apartments the writers and artists populated in the 1950s, complete with bongos and bottle-as-candleholder. Memorabilia include the shirt Neal Cassady wore while driving Ken Kesey's Merry Prankster bus, "Further." An early photo of the legendary bus is juxtaposed with a

Continued on page 181

CABLE CARS

The moment it dawns on you that you severely underestimated the steepness of the San Francisco hills will likely be the same moment you look down and realize those tracks aren't just for show—or just for tourists.

POWELL AND MARKET

BAY & TAYLOR FISHERMANS WHARF

12

"Meet me at the St. Francis"

Sure, locals rarely use the cable cars for commuting these days. (That's partially due to the $6 fare—hear that, Muni?) So you'll likely be packed in with plenty of fellow sightseers. You may even be approaching cable-car fatigue after seeing its image on so many souvenirs. But if you fear the magic is gone, simply climb on board, and those jaded thoughts will dissolve. Grab the pole and gawk at the view as the car clanks down an insanely steep grade toward the bay. Listen to the humming cable, the clang of the bell, and the occasional quip from the gripman. It's an experience you shouldn't pass up, whether on your first trip or your fiftieth.

HOW CABLE CARS WORK

The mechanics are pretty simple: cable cars grab a moving subterranean cable with a "grip" to go. To stop, they release the grip and apply one or more types of brakes. Four cables, totaling 9 miles, power the city's three lines. If the gripman doesn't adjust the grip just right when going up a steep hill, the cable will start to slip and the car will have to back down the hill and try again. This is an extremely rare occurrence—imagine the ribbing the gripman gets back at the cable car barn!

Gripman: Stands in front and operates the grip, brakes, and bell. Favorite joke, especially at the peak of a steep hill: "This is my first day on the job folks..."

Conductor: Moves around the car, deals with tickets, alerts the grip about what's coming up, and operates the rear wheel brakes.

① Cable: Steel wrapped around flexible sisal core; 2 inches thick; runs at a constant 9½ mph.

② Bells: Used for crew communication; alerts other drivers and pedestrians.

③ Grip: Vice-like lever extends through the center slot in the track to grab or release the cable.

④ Grip Lever: Left-hand lever; operates grip.

⑤ Car: Entire car weighs 8 tons.

⑥ Wheel Brake: Steel brake pads on each wheel.

⑦ Wheel Brake Lever: Foot pedal; operates wheel brakes.

⑧ Rear Wheel Brake Lever: Applied for extra traction on hills.

⑨ Track Brake: 2-foot-long sections of Monterey pine push down against the track to help stop the car.

⑩ Track Brake Lever: Middle lever; operates track brakes.

⑪ Emergency Brake: 18-inch steel wedge, jams into street slot to bring car to an immediate stop.

⑫ Emergency Brake Lever: Right-hand lever, red; operates emergency brake.

ROUTES

Cars run at least every 15 minutes, from around 6 AM to about 1 AM.

Powell–Hyde line: Most scenic, with classic Bay views. Begins at Powell and Market streets, then crosses Nob Hill and Russian Hill before a white-knuckle descent down Hyde Street, ending near the Hyde Street Pier.

Powell–Mason line: Also begins at Powell and Market streets, but winds through North Beach to Bay and Taylor streets, a few blocks from Fisherman's Wharf.

California line: Runs from the foot of Market Street, at Drumm Street, up Nob Hill and back. Great views (and aromas and sounds) of Chinatown on the way up. Sit in back to catch glimpses of the Bay. ■TIP→ Take the California line if it's just the cable-car experience you're after—the lines are shorter, and the grips and conductors say it's friendlier and has a slower pace.

RULES OF THE RIDE

Tickets. A whopping $6 each way. There are ticket booths at all three turnarounds, or you can pay the conductor after you board (they can make change). Try not to grumble about the price—they're embarrassed enough as it is.

■TIP→ If you're planning to use public transit a few times, or if you'd like to ride back and forth on the cable car without worrying about the price, consider a one-day Muni passport ($14). You can get passports online, at the Powell Street turnaround, the TIX booth on Union Square, or the Fisherman's Wharf cable-car ticket booth at Beach and Hyde streets.

All Aboard. You can board on either side of the cable car. It's legal to stand on the running boards and hang on to the pole, but keep your ears open for the gripman's warnings. ■TIP→ Grab a seat on the outside bench for the best views.

Most people wait (and wait) in line at one of the cable car turnarounds, but you can also hop on along the route. Board wherever you see a white sign showing a figure climbing aboard a brown cable car; wave to the approaching driver, and wait until the car stops.

Riding on the running boards can be part of the thrill.

CABLE CAR HISTORY

HALLIDIE FREES THE HORSES

In the 1850s and '60s, San Francisco's streetcars were drawn by horses. Legend has it that the horrible sight of a car dragging a team of horses downhill to their deaths roused Andrew Smith Hallidie to action. The English immigrant had invented the "Hallidie Ropeway," essentially a cable car for mined ore, and he was convinced that his invention could also move people. In 1873, Hallidie and his intrepid crew prepared to test the first cable car high on Russian Hill. The anxious engineer peered down into the foggy darkness, failed to see the bottom of the hill, and promptly turned the controls over to Hallidie. Needless to say, the thing worked . . . but rides were free for the first two days because people were afraid to get on.

SEE IT FOR YOURSELF

The **Cable Car Museum** is one of the city's best free offerings and an absolute must for kids. (You can even ride a cable car there, since all three lines stop between Russian Hill and Nob Hill.) The museum, which is inside the city's last cable-car barn, takes the top off the system to let you see how it all works.

Eternally humming and squealing, the massive powerhouse cable wheels steal the show. You can also climb aboard a vintage car and take the grip, let the kids ring a cable-car bell (briefly, please!), and check out vintage gear dating from 1873.

✉ *1201 Mason St., at Washington St., Nob Hill* ☎ *415/474–1887* ⊕ *www. cablecarmuseum.com* ✉ *Free* ◷ *Oct.– Mar., daily 10–5; Apr.–Sept., daily 10–6*

■ **TIP➔** The gift shop sells cable car paraphernalia, including an authentic gripman's bell for $600 (it'll sound like Powell Street in your house every day). For significantly less, you can pick up a key chain made from a piece of worn-out cable.

CHAMPION OF THE CABLE CAR BELL

Each September the city's best and brightest come together to crown a bell-ringing champion at Union Square. The crowd cheers gripmen and conductors as they stomp, shake, and riff with the rope. But it's not a popularity contest; the ringers are judged by former bell-ringing champions who take each ping and gong very seriously.

more current picture showing it covered with moss and overgrowth, labeled "Nothing lasts." Indeed. There are also manuscripts, letters, and early editions by Jack Kerouac, Allen Ginsberg, and Lawrence Ferlinghetti. The gift store has a good selection of Beat philosophy, though it's nothing you won't find across the street at City Lights. ✉ *540 Broadway* ☎ *414/399–9626* ⊕ *www.thebeatmuseum.org* 🔲 *$8* ⊙ *Daily 10–7.*

Fodor's Choice **City Lights Bookstore.** Take a look at the exterior of the store: the replica
★ of a revolutionary mural destroyed in Chiapas, Mexico, by military forces; the art banners hanging above the windows; and the sign that says "Turn your sell [sic] phone off. Be here now." This place isn't just doling out best sellers. Designated a city landmark, the hangout of Beat-era writers—Allen Ginsberg and store founder Lawrence Ferlinghetti among them—and independent publisher remains a vital part of San Francisco's literary scene. Browse the three levels of sometimes haphazardly arranged poetry, philosophy, politics, fiction, history, and local zines, to the tune of creaking wood floors. ■TIP→ Be sure to check the calendar of literary events.

Back in the day, the basement was a kind of literary living room, where writers like Ginsberg and Jack Kerouac would read and even receive mail. Ferlinghetti cemented City Lights' place in history by publishing Ginsberg's *Howl and Other Poems* in 1956. The small volume was ignored in the mainstream . . . until Ferlinghetti and the bookstore manager were arrested for obscenity and corruption of youth. In the landmark First Amendment trial that followed, the judge exonerated both men, declaring that a work that has "redeeming social significance" can't be obscene. *Howl* went on to become a classic.

Stroll Kerouac Alley, branching off Columbus Avenue next to City Lights, to read the quotes from Ferlinghetti, Maya Angelou, Confucius, John Steinbeck, and the street's namesake embedded in the pavement. ✉ *261 Columbus Ave.* ☎ *415/362–8193* ⊕ *www.citylights.com* ⊙ *Daily 10 am–midnight.*

Coit Tower. Whether or not you agree that it resembles a fire-hose nozzle, this 210-foot tower is among San Francisco's most distinctive skyline sights. Although the monument wasn't intended as a tribute to firemen, it's often considered as such because of the donor's special attachment to the local fire company. As the story goes, a young gold rush–era girl, Lillie Hitchcock Coit (known as Miss Lil), was a fervent admirer of her local fire company—so much so that she once deserted a wedding party and chased down the street after her favorite engine, Knickerbocker No. 5, while clad in her bridesmaid finery. She became the Knickerbocker Company's mascot and always signed her name "Lillie Coit 5." When Lillie died in 1929 she left the city $125,000 to "expend in an appropriate manner . . . to the beauty of San Francisco."

You can ride the elevator to the top of the tower—the only thing you have to pay for here—to enjoy the view of the Bay Bridge and the Golden Gate Bridge; due north is Alcatraz Island. Most visitors saunter right past the 19 fabulous Depression-era murals inside the tower that depict California's economic and political life, but take the time to appreciate the first New Deal art project supported by taxpayer money. The federal government commissioned the paintings from 25 local artists, and ended up funding a controversy. The radical Mexican painter Diego Rivera inspired the murals' socialist-realist style, with its biting cultural commentary, particularly about the exploitation of workers. At the time the murals were painted, clashes between management and labor along the waterfront and elsewhere in San Francisco were widespread. The elements, the thousands of visitors that pass by them every year, and the lack of climate control in the tower have taken their toll on the murals, but restoration work done on the tower in 2013 should help protect them. ■TIP➜ The views from the tower's base are also expansive—and free. Parking at Coit Tower is limited; in fact, you may have to wait (and wait) for a space. Spare yourself the frustration and hike up, if you're in good shape, or take the 39 bus. ⊠ *Telegraph Hill Blvd. at Greenwich St. or Lombard St.* ☎ *415/362–0808* ☜ *Free; elevator to top $7* ☉ *Mar.–Sept., daily 10–5:30; Oct.–Feb., daily 9–4:30.*

Grant Avenue. Originally called Calle de la Fundación, Grant Avenue is the oldest street in the city, but it's got plenty of young blood. Here dusty bars such as the Saloon and perennial favorites like the Savoy Tivoli mix with hotshot boutiques, odd curio shops like the antique jumble that is Aria, atmospheric cafés such as the boho haven Caffè Trieste, and authentic Italian delis. While the street runs from Union Square through Chinatown, North Beach, and beyond, the fun stuff in this neighborhood is crowded into the four blocks between Columbus Avenue and Filbert Street.

Levi Strauss headquarters. The carefully landscaped complex appears so collegiate that it's affectionately known as LSU—short for Levi Strauss University. Lawns complement the redbrick buildings, and gurgling fountains drown out the sounds of traffic, providing a perfect environment for brown-bag and picnic lunches. The Vault, the lobby exhibition space, has displays focusing on the history of the company, including jeans that saw the gold rush, videos about Levi's marketing and textile restoration, and temporary displays such as decades' worth of vintage Levi's shirts on a rotating dry-cleaner's rack. ■TIP➜ Get Levi's and Dockers straight from the source at the cozy lobby boutique here, open daily. The wonderful Filbert Steps to Coit Tower are across the street. ⊠ *Levi's Plaza, 1155 Battery St.* ☎ *415/501-6000* ⊕ *www.levistrauss. com* ☉ *Weekdays 9–6, weekends noon–5.*

Fodor'sChoice
★

Telegraph Hill. Residents here have some of the city's best views, as well as the most difficult ascents to their aeries. The hill rises from the east end of Lombard Street to a height of 284 feet and is capped by Coit Tower (see above). Imagine lugging your groceries up that! If you brave the slope, though, you can be rewarded with a "secret treasure" San Francisco moment. Filbert Street starts up the hill, then becomes the Filbert Steps when the going gets too steep. You can cut between the Filbert Steps and another flight, the Greenwich Steps, on up to the hill-top. As you climb, you can pass some of the city's oldest houses and be surrounded by beautiful, flowering private gardens. In some places the trees grow over the stairs so it feels like you're walking through a

CLOSE UP

The Birds

While on Telegraph Hill, you might be startled by a chorus of piercing squawks and a rushing sound of wings. No, you're not about to have a Hitchcock bird-attack moment. These small, vivid green parrots with cherry red heads number in the hundreds; they're descendants of former pets that escaped or were released by their owners. (The birds dislike cages, and they bite if bothered ... must've been some disillusioned owners along the way.)

The parrots like to roost high in the aging cypress trees on the hill, chattering and fluttering, sometimes taking wing en masse. They're not popular with some residents, but they did find a champion in local bohemian Mark Bittner, a former street musician. Bittner began chronicling their habits, publishing a book and battling the homeowners who wanted to cut down the cypresses. A documentary, *The Wild Parrots of Telegraph Hill*, made the issue a cause célèbre. In 2007 City Hall, which recognizes a golden goose when it sees one, stepped in and brokered a solution to keep the celebrity birds in town. The city would cover the homeowners' insurance worries and plant new trees for the next generation of wild parrots.

–Denise M. Leto

green tunnel; elsewhere, you'll have wide-open views of the bay. And the telegraphic name? It comes from the hill's status as the first Morse code signal station back in 1853. ⊠ *Bordered by Lombard, Filbert, Kearny, and Sansome Sts.*

Washington Square. Once the daytime social heart of Little Italy, this grassy patch has changed character numerous times over the years. The Beats hung out in the 1950s, hippies camped out in the 1960s and early '70s, and nowadays you're more likely to see kids of Southeast Asian descent tossing a Frisbee than Italian men or women chatting about their children and the old country. In the morning, elderly Asians perform the motions of tai chi, and any time of day the park may attract homeless people, who stretch out to rest on the benches and grass, and young locals sunbathing or running their dogs. Lillie Hitchcock Coit, in yet another show of affection for San Francisco's firefighters, donated the statue of two firemen with a child they rescued. ■TIP→ The North Beach Festival, the city's oldest street fair, celebrates the area's Italian culture here each June; 2014 marks the event's 60th year. ⊠ *Bordered by Columbus Ave. and Stockton, Filbert, and Union Sts.*

ON THE WATERFRONT

San Francisco's waterfront neighborhoods have fabulous views and utterly different personalities. Kitschy, overpriced Fisherman's Wharf struggles to maintain the last shreds of its existence as a working wharf, while Pier 39 is a full-fledged consumer circus. The Ferry Building draws well-heeled locals with its culinary pleasures, firmly reconnecting the Embarcadero to downtown. Between the Ferry Building and Pier 39 a former maritime no-man's-land is filling in with the recently relocated

Exploratorium, a new $90 million cruise-ship terminal, Alcatraz Landing, fashionable waterfront restaurants, and restored, pedestrian-friendly piers.

EXPLORING THE WATERFRONT

Alcatraz. Thousands of visitors come every day to walk in the footsteps of Alcatraz's notorious criminals. The stories of life and death on "the Rock" may sometimes be exaggerated, but it's almost impossible to resist the chance to wander the cellblock that tamed the country's toughest gangsters and saw daring escape attempts of tremendous desperation. Fewer than 2,000 inmates ever did time on the Rock, and though they weren't the worst criminals, they were definitely the worst prisoners, include Al "Scarface" Capone, Robert "The Birdman" Stroud, and George "Machine Gun" Kelly.

Some tips for escaping to Alcatraz: 1) Buy your ticket in advance. Visit the website for Alcatraz Cruises (⊕ *www.alcatrazcruises.com*) to scout out available departure times for the ferry. Prepay by credit card and keep a receipt record; the ticket price covers the boat ride and the audio tour. Pick up your ticket at the "will call" window at Pier 33 up to an hour before sailing. 2) Dress smart. Bring a jacket to ward off the chill from the boat ride and wear comfortable shoes. 3) Go for the evening tour. You'll get even more out of your Alcatraz experience at night. The evening tour has programs not offered during the day, the bridge-to-bridge view of the city twinkles at night, and your "prison experience" will be amplified as darkness falls. 4) Be mindful of scheduled and limited-capacity talks. Some programs are only given once a day (the schedule is posted in the cell house) and have limited seating, so keep an eye out for a cell-house staffer handing out passes shortly before the start time.

The boat ride to the island is brief (15 minutes), but affords beautiful views of the city, Marin County, and the East Bay. The audio tour, highly recommended, includes observations by guards and prisoners about life in one of America's most notorious penal colonies. Plan your schedule to allow at least three hours for the visit and boat rides combined. ⊠ *Pier 33, Embarcadero* ☎ *415/981–7625* ⊕ *www.nps.gov/ alca* ᴥ *$28, including audio tour; $35 evening tour, including audio* ⊙ *Ferry departs every 30–45 mins Sept.–late May, daily 9:30–2:15, 4:20 for evening tour Thurs.–Mon. only; late May–Aug., daily 9:30– 4:15, 6:30 and 7:30 for evening tour.*

Fodor's Choice ★ FAMILY **Exploratorium.** Walking into this fascinating "museum of science, art, and human perception" is like visiting a mad-scientist's laboratory. Most of the exhibits are supersize, and you can play with everything. After moving into larger digs on the Embarcadero in April 2013,

WORD OF MOUTH

"The part I was really looking forward to was walking down [Telegraph Hill] and looking for parrots. I'd seen the movie *The Wild Parrots of Telegraph Hill,* and the neighborhood was one of the things that meant 'San Francisco' to me. The neighborhood itself was beautiful, and we did indeed see parrots."

—sunny16

4

Thousands of visitors take ferries to Alcatraz each day to walk in the footsteps of the notorious criminals who were held on "The Rock."

the Exploratorium has even more space for its signature experiential exhibits, including a brand-new Tinkering Studio and a glass Bay Observatory building, where the exhibits inside help visitors better understand what they see outside.

Quintessential exhibits remain: Get an *Alice in Wonderland* feeling in the distortion room, where you seem to shrink and grow as you walk across the slanted, checkered floor. In the shadow room, a powerful flash freezes an image of your shadow on the wall; jumping is a favorite pose. "Pushover" demonstrates cow-tipping, but for people: stand on one foot and try to keep your balance while a friend swings a striped panel in front of you (trust us, you're going to fall).

More than 650 other exhibits focus on sea and insect life, computers, electricity, patterns and light, language, the weather, and more. "Explainers"—usually high-school students on their days off—demonstrate cool scientific tools and procedures, like DNA sample-collection and cow-eye dissection. One surefire hit is the pitch-black, touchy-feely Tactile Dome (extra fee; reservations required), newly built in the Embarcadero space. In this geodesic dome strewn with textured objects, you crawl through a course of ladders, slides, and tunnels, relying solely on your sense of touch. Lovey-dovey couples sometimes linger in the "grope dome," but be forewarned: the staff will turn on the lights if necessary. ■ TIP→ **Patrons must be at least seven years old to enter the Tactile Dome, and the space is not for the claustrophobic. Check the Exploratorium's website for ticket prices.** ⊠ *Piers 15–17, Embarcadero* ☎ *415/561–0360 general information, 415/561–0362 Tactile Dome res-*

ervations ⊕ *www.exploratorium.edu* ✉ *$25* ⊙ *Tues. and Thurs.–Sun. 10–5, Wed. 10–10; Thurs. 6 pm–10 pm ages 18 and over only.*

Fodor's Choice **Ferry Building.** The jewel of the Embarcadero, erected in 1896, is topped
★ by a 230-foot clock tower modeled after the campanile of the cathedral in Seville, Spain. On the morning of April 18, 1906, the tower's four clock faces, powered by the swinging of a 14-foot pendulum, stopped at 5:17—the moment the great earthquake struck—and stayed still for 12 months.

Today San Franciscans flock to the street-level marketplace, stocking up on supplies from local favorites such as Acme Bread, Scharffen Berger Chocolate, Cowgirl Creamery, and Blue Bottle Coffee. Lucky diners claim a coveted table at Slanted Door, the city's beloved high-end Vietnamese restaurant. The seafood bars at Hog Island Oyster Company and Ferry Plaza Seafood have fantastic city panoramas— or you can take your purchases around to the building's bay side, where benches face views of the Bay Bridge. On Saturday mornings the plazas outside the building buzz with an upscale farmers' market where you can buy exotic sandwiches and other munchables. Extending from the piers on the north side of the building south to the Bay Bridge, the waterfront promenade is a favorite among joggers and picnickers, with a front-row view of the sailboats slipping by. The Ferry Building also serves actual ferries: from behind the building they sail to Sausalito, Larkspur, Tiburon, and the East Bay. ⊠ *Embarcadero at foot of Market St., Embarcadero* ☎ *415/983–8030* ⊕ *www. ferrybuildingmarketplace.com.*

QUICK BITES

Buena Vista Café. At the end of the Hyde Street cable-car line, the Buena Vista packs 'em in for its famous Irish coffee—which, according to owners, was the first served stateside (in 1952). The place oozes nostalgia, drawing devoted locals as well as out-of-towners relaxing after a day of sightseeing. It's narrow and can get crowded, but this spot is a welcome respite from the overpriced generic tourist joints nearby. ⊠ **2765 Hyde St., at Beach St., Fisherman's Wharf** ☎ **415/474–5044** ⊕ **www.thebuenavista.com.**

FAMILY **Fisherman's Wharf.** It may be one of the city's best-known attractions, but the Wharf is a no-go zone for most locals, who shy away from the tourist crowds, overpriced food, and cheesy shops at third-rate shopping centers like the Cannery at Del Monte Square. If you can't resist a visit here, come early to avoid the crowds and get a sense of the Wharf's functional role—it's not just an amusement park replica. ⊠ *Jefferson St. between Leavenworth St. and Pier 39, Fisherman's Wharf* ⊕ *www.fishermanswharf.org.*

Ghirardelli Square. Most of the redbrick buildings in this early-20th-century complex were once part of the Ghirardelli factory. Now tourists come here to pick up the famous chocolate, though you can purchase it all over town and save yourself a trip to what is essentially a mall. But this is the only place to watch the cool chocolate manufactory in action. There are no fewer than three Ghirardelli stores here, as well as gift shops and a couple of restaurants—including Ana Mandara—that even locals love. Fairmont has an upscale urban time-share directly on the square. Placards throughout the square describe the factory's history. ⊠ *900 N. Point St., Fisherman's Wharf* 🖷 *415/775–5500* ⊕ *www. ghirardellisq.com.*

Fodor's Choice
★
FAMILY

Hyde Street Pier. Cotton candy and souvenirs are all well and good, but if you want to get to the heart of the Wharf—boats—there's no better place to do it than at this pier, one of the Wharf area's best bargains. Depending on the time of day, you might see boatbuilders at work or children pretending to man an early-1900s ship.

Don't pass up the centerpiece collection of historic vessels, part of the **San Francisco Maritime National Historic Park,** almost all of which can be boarded. The *Balclutha,* an 1886 full-rigged three-masted sailing vessel that's more than 250 feet long, sailed around Cape Horn 17 times. Kids especially love the *Eureka,* a side-wheel passenger and car ferry, for her onboard collection of vintage cars. The *Hercules* is a steam-powered tugboat. The *C.A. Thayer,* a three-masted schooner, recently underwent a painstaking restoration.

Across the street from the pier and almost a museum in itself is the maritime park's **Visitor Center** (⊠ *499 Jefferson St.* 🖷 *415/447–5000* ☉ *Open June–Aug., daily 9:30–5:30; Sept.–May, daily 9:30–5*), whose fun, large-scale exhibits, such as a huge First Order Fresnel lighthouse lens and a shipwrecked boat, make it an engaging quick stop. ⊠ *Hyde and Jefferson Sts., Fisherman's Wharf* 🖷 *415/561–7100* ⊕ *www.nps. gov/safr* 🖷 *Ships $5 (ticket good for five days)* ☉ *June–Aug., daily 9:30–5:30; Sept.–May, daily 9:30–5.*

Jackson Square Historic District. This was the heart of the Barbary Coast of the Gay Nineties (the 1890s, that is). Although most of the red-light district was destroyed in the fire that followed the 1906 earthquake, the remaining old redbrick buildings, many of them now occupied by advertising agencies, law offices, and antiques firms, retain hints of the romance and rowdiness of San Francisco's early days.

With its gentrified gold rush–era buildings, the 700 block of **Montgomery Street** just barely evokes the Barbary Coast days, but this was a colorful block in 19th century and on into the 20th. Writers Mark Twain and Bret Harte were among the contributors to the spunky *Golden Era* newspaper, which occupied No. 732 (now part of the building at No. 744). From 1959 to 1996 the late ambulance-chaser extraordinaire, lawyer Melvin Belli, had his headquarters at Nos. 722 and 728–730. There was never a dull moment in Belli's world; he represented clients from the actress Mae West to Gloria Sykes (who in 1964 claimed that a cable-car accident turned her into a nymphomaniac) to the disgraced televangelists Jim and Tammy Faye Bakker. Whenever he won a case, he fired a cannon and raised the Jolly Roger. Belli was also known for receiving a letter from the never-caught Zodiac killer.

Restored 19th-century brick buildings line Hotaling Place, which connects Washington and Jackson streets. The lane is named for the head of the **A.P. Hotaling Company whiskey distillery** (⊠ *451 Jackson St., at Hotaling Pl.*), the largest liquor repository on the West Coast in its day. (Anchor Distillery still makes an occasional Hotaling whiskey in the city, by the way; look for this single malt for a sip of truly local flavor.) ■TIP➔ The exceptional City Guides (☎415/557-4266 ⊕ www.sfcity-guides.org) Gold Rush City walking tour covers this area and brings its history to life. ⊠ *Bordered by Columbus Ave., Broadway and Pacific Ave., Washington St., and Sansome St., Jackson Square.*

FAMILY **Pier 39.** The city's most popular waterfront attraction draws millions of visitors each year who come to browse through its shops and concessions hawking every conceivable form of souvenir. The pier can be quite crowded, and the numerous street performers may leave you feeling more harassed than entertained. Arriving early in the morning ensures you a front-row view of the sea lions that bask here, but if you're here to shop—and make no mistake about it, Pier 39 wants your money—be aware that most stores don't open until 9:30 or 10 (later in winter).

F-LINE TROLLEYS

F-line. The city's system of vintage electric trolleys, the F-line, gives the cable cars a run for their money as San Francisco's best-loved mode of transportation. These beautifully restored streetcars—some dating from the 19th century—run from the Castro District down Market Street to the Embarcadero, then north to Fisherman's Wharf. Each car is unique, restored to the colors of its city of origin, from New Orleans and Philadelphia to Moscow and Milan. Purchase tickets on board; exact change is required. ⊕ www.streetcar.org ⊠ $2.

Brilliant colors enliven the double-decker **San Francisco Carousel** (⊠ $3 *per ride*), decorated with images of such city landmarks as the Golden Gate Bridge and Lombard Street.

Follow the sound of barking to the northwest side of the pier to view the **sea lions** that flop about the floating docks. During the summer, orange-clad naturalists answer questions and offer fascinating facts about the playful pinnipeds—for example, that all the animals here are males.

At the **Aquarium of the Bay** (☎415/623-5300 or 888/732-3483 ⊕ *www.aquariumofthebay.org $18, June–Sept., daily 9–8; Mar.–May and Sept.–Oct., Mon.–Thurs. 10–7, Fri.–Sun. 10–8; Nov.–Feb., Mon.–Thurs. 10–6, Fri.–Sun. 10–7*) moving walkways transport you through a space surrounded on three sides by water filled with indigenous San Francisco Bay marine life, from fish and plankton to sharks. Many find the aquarium overpriced; if you can, take advantage of the family rate ($50 for two adults and two kids under 12).

The **California Welcome Center** (☎415/981-1280 ⊕ *www.visitcwc. com Daily 9–7*), on Pier 39's second level, can help you reserve tours and plan your time in the city.

Parking is across the street at the **Pier 39 Garage** (with validation from a Pier 39 restaurant, one hour free before 6 pm, two hours after 6 pm), off Powell Street at the Embarcadero. ⊠ *Beach St. at Embarcadero, Fisherman's Wharf* ⊕ *www.pier39.com.*

FAMILY **San Francisco Railway Museum.** A labor of love brought to you by the same vintage-transit enthusiasts responsible for the F-line's revival, this one-room museum and store celebrates the city's storied streetcars and cable cars with photographs, models, and artifacts. The permanent exhibit includes the replicated end of a streetcar with a working cab—complete with controls and a bell—for kids to explore; the cool, antique Wiley birdcage traffic signal; and models and display cases to view. Right on the F-line track, just across from the Ferry Building, this is a great quick stop. ⊠ *77 Steuart St., Embarcadero* ☏ *415/974–1948* ⊕ *www.streetcar. org* ✉ *Free* ☉ *Tues.–Sun. 10–6.*

Transamerica Pyramid. It's neither owned by Transamerica nor is it a pyramid, but this 853-foot-tall obelisk *is* the most photographed of the city's high-rises. Excoriated in the design stages as "the world's largest architectural folly," the icon was quickly hailed as a masterpiece when it opened in 1972. Today it's probably the city's most recognized structure after the Golden Gate Bridge. Visit the small, street-level visitor center to see the virtual view from the top, watch videos about the building's history, and perhaps pick up a T-shirt. ■ TIP→ A fragrant redwood grove along the east side of the building, replete with benches and a cheerful fountain, is a placid patch in which to unwind. ⊠ *600 Montgomery St., Financial District* ⊕ *www.thepyramidcenter.com.*

THE MARINA AND THE PRESIDIO

Yachts bob at their moorings, satisfied-looking folks jog along the Marina Green, and multimillion-dollar homes overlook the bay in the picturesque, if somewhat sterile, Marina neighborhood. Does it all seem a bit too perfect? Well, it got this way after the hard knock of Loma Prieta—the current pretty face was put on after hundreds of homes collapsed in the 1989 earthquake. Just west of this waterfront area is a more natural beauty: the Presidio. Once a military base, this beautiful, sprawling park is mostly green space, with hills, woods, and the marshlands of Crissy Field.

EXPLORING THE MARINA

Fodor's Choice ★ **Palace of Fine Arts.** At first glance this stunning, rosy rococo palace seems to be from another world, and indeed, it's the sole survivor of the many tinted-plaster structures (a temporary classical city of sorts) built for the 1915 Panama-Pacific International Exposition, the world's fair that celebrated San Francisco's recovery from the 1906 earthquake and fire. The expo buildings originally extended about a mile along the shore. Bernard Maybeck designed this faux–Roman classic beauty, which was reconstructed in concrete and reopened in 1967. A victim of the elements, the Palace required a piece-by-piece renovation that was completed in 2008.

The pseudo-Latin language adorning the Palace's exterior urns continues to stump scholars. The massive columns (each topped with four "weeping maidens"), great rotunda, and swan-filled lagoon have been used in countless fashion layouts, films, and wedding photo shoots. After admiring the lagoon, look across the street to the house at 3460 Baker Street. If the maidens out front look familiar, they should—they're original casts of the lovely "garland ladies" you can see in the Palace's colonnade. ⊠ *3301 Lyon St., at Beach St* ☏ *415/561–0364 Palace history tours* ⊕ *www.palaceoffinearts.org* ✉ *Free* ☉ *Daily 24 hrs.*

EXPLORING THE PRESIDIO

FAMILY **Fort Point.** Dwarfed today by the Golden Gate Bridge, this brick fortress constructed between 1853 and 1861 was designed to protect San Francisco from a Civil War sea attack that never materialized. It was also used as a coastal-defense fortification post during World War II, when soldiers stood watch here. this national historic site is now a sprawling museum of military memorabilia. The building, which surrounds a lonely, windswept courtyard, has a gloomy air and is suitably atmospheric. It's usually chilly, too, so bring a jacket. The top floor affords a unique angle on the bay. ■TIP➔ Take care when walking along the front side of the building, as it's slippery, and the waves have a dizzying effect.

On the days when Fort Point is staffed (Fridays and weekends), guided group tours and cannon drills take place. The popular, guided candlelight tours, available only in winter, sell out in advance, so book ahead. Living-history days take place throughout the year, when Union soldiers perform drills, a drum-and-fife band plays, and a Civil War–era doctor shows his instruments and describes his surgical technique (gulp). ✉ *Marine Dr. off Lincoln Blvd.* ☎ *415/556–1693* ⊕ *www.nps.gov/fopo* 🎟 *Free* ☉ *Fri.–Sun. 10–5.*

Fodor's Choice ★ **Golden Gate Bridge.** With its simple but powerful art deco design, the 1.7-mile suspension span that connects San Francisco and Marin County was built to withstand winds of more than 100 mph. It's also not a bad place to be in an earthquake: designed to sway almost 28 feet, the Golden Gate Bridge (unlike the Bay Bridge) was undamaged by the 1989 Loma Prieta quake. If you're on the bridge when it's windy, stand still and you can feel it swaying a bit.

Crossing the Golden Gate Bridge under your own power is exhilarating— a little scary, and definitely chilly. From the bridge's eastern-side walkway, the only side pedestrians are allowed on, you can take in the San Francisco skyline and the bay islands; look west for the wild hills of the Marin Headlands, the curving coast south to Lands End, and the Pacific Ocean. On sunny days, sailboats dot the water, and brave windsurfers test the often-treacherous tides beneath the bridge. A vista point on the Marin County side provides a spectacular city panorama.

A structural engineer, dreamer, and poet named Joseph Strauss worked tirelessly for 20 years to make the bridge a reality, first promoting the idea of it and then overseeing design and construction. Though the final structure bore little resemblance to his original plan, Strauss guarded his legacy jealously, refusing to recognize the seminal contributions of engineer Charles A. Ellis. In 2007, the Golden Gate Bridge district finally recognized Ellis's role, though Strauss, who died less than a year after opening day in 1937, would doubtless be pleased with the inscription on his statue, which stands sentry in the southern parking lot: "The Man Who Built the Bridge."

You won't see it on a T-shirt, but the bridge is perhaps the world's most publicized suicide platform, with one jumper about every 10 days. Signs on the bridge refer the disconsolate to special telephones, and officers patrol the walkway and watch by security camera to spot potential jumpers. A public campaign to install a suicide barrier is underway. The unobtrusive net supported by most locals—not unlike the one that during construction saved 19 workers—completed the design phase in 2013.

While at the bridge you can grab a healthy snack at the art deco–style Bridge Café. The recently erected Bridge Pavilion sells attractive, high-quality souvenirs and has a small display of historical artifacts. At the outdoor exhibits, you can see the bridge rise before your eyes on holo-gram panels, learn about the features that make it art deco, and read about the personalities behind its design and construction. Head up to the Round House to join a 45-minute bridge tour, or have a photo taken ($20) of your family walking up the main cable—courtesy of a background screen, of course. ⊠ *Lincoln Blvd. near Doyle Dr. and Fort Point, Presidio* ☎ *415/921–5858* ⊕ *www.goldengatebridge.org* ☜ *Bridge free, tour $12.95* ☉ *Pedestrians Mar.–Oct., daily 5 am–9 pm; Nov.–Feb., daily 5 am–6 pm; hrs change with daylight saving time. Bicyclists daily 24 hrs. Tour on the half hour, 10:30–3:30.*

Fodor's Choice   **Presidio.** When San Franciscans want to spend a day in the woods, they
★   head here. The Presidio has 1,400 acres of hills and majestic woods, two small beaches, and stunning views of the bay, the Golden Gate Bridge, and Marin County. Famed environmental artist Andy Goldsworthy's sculpture greets visitors at the Arguello Gate entrance. The 100-plus-foot *Spire,* made of 37 cypress logs reclaimed from the Presidio, looks like a rough, natural version of a church spire. ■**TIP**→ **The Presidio's best lookout points lie along Washington Boulevard, which meanders through the park.**

Part of the **Golden Gate National Recreation Area,** the Presidio was a military post for more than 200 years. Don Juan Bautista de Anza and a band of Spanish settlers first claimed the area in 1776. It became a Mexican garrison in 1822, when Mexico gained its independence from Spain; U.S. troops forcibly occupied the Presidio in 1846. The U.S. Sixth Army was stationed here until October 1994.

The area has been transformed into a self-sustaining national park with a combination of public, commercial, and residential projects. In 2005 Bay Area filmmaker George Lucas opened the **Letterman Digital Arts Center,** his 23-acre digital studio "campus," along the eastern edge of the land. Seventeen of those acres are exquisitely landscaped and open to the public. If you have kids in tow or are a *Star Wars* fan yourself, sidle over to the **Yoda Fountain** (⊠ *Letterman Drive and Dewitt Road*), between two of the arts-center buildings.

The battle over the fate of the rest of the Presidio is ongoing. Many older buildings have been reconstructed; the issue now is how to fill them. The Presidio's overseeing trust was tasked with making the park financially self-sufficient, which means generating enough revenue to keep afloat without the federal government's monthly $20 million checks, leading many to fear that money will trump culture. Since then the Asian-theme SenSpa, the Walt Disney museum, and a fabu-lous lodge at the Main Post have opened. With old military housing now repurposed as apartments and homes with rents up to $10,000 a

The Marina and the Presidio

San Francisco Bay

Golden Gate National Recreation Area

Golden Gate

Fort Point

Baker Beach

Lincoln Blvd.

Washington Blvd.

Park Presido Blvd.

Doyle Dr.

Golden Gate Promenade

Mason St.

The Presidio

Presidio Golf Course

West Pacific Ave.

Presidio Blvd.

Lincoln Blvd.

Funston Ave.

Sheridan Ave.

Montgomery St.

Moraga Ave.

Arguello Blvd.

Yacht Rd.

Marina Park

Wave Organ

Marina Blvd.

Cervantes Blvd.

Beach St.

North Point St.

Richardson Ave.

Scott St.

Francisco St.

Bay St.

North Point St.

Baker St.

Lyon St.

MARINA

Fort Mason

Aquatic Park

Beach St.

North Point

Buchanan

North Point St.

Steiner St.

Divisadero St.

Broadway

Fillmore St.

Alta Plaza Park

PACIFIC HEIGHTS

Lombard St.

Greenwich St.

Filbert St.

Union St.

Green St.

Vallejo St.

Chestnut St.

Francisco St.

Bay St.

Van Ness Ave.

Gough St.

Laguna St.

Lafayette Park

Washington St.

Sacramento St.

California St.

Polk St.

Hyde St.

Leavenworth St.

Jefferson St.

Beach St.

North Point St.

Powell-Hyde Cable Car

NOB HILL

101

101

1

KEY

········· Cable Car

0 ____ 1/4 mile

0 ____ 400 meters

month, there's some concern that the Presidio will become an incoherent mix of pricey real estate. Still, the $6 million that Lucas shells out annually for rent does plant a lot of saplings.

The Presidio also has two beaches, a golf course, a visitor center, and picnic sites; the views from the many overlooks are sublime.

Especially popular is **Crissy Field**, a stretch of restored marshland along the sand of the bay. Kids on bikes, folks walking dogs, and joggers share the paved path along the shore, often winding up at the Warming Hut, a combination café and fun gift store at the end of the path, for a hot chocolate in the shadow of the Golden Gate Bridge. Midway along the Golden Gate Promenade that winds along the shore is the Gulf of the Farallones National Marine Sanctuary Visitor Center, where kids can get a close-up view of small sea creatures and learn about the rich ecosystem offshore. Temporarily relocated to East Beach, just across from the Palace of Fine Arts, Crissy Field Center offers great children's programs and has cool science displays; grab lunch at the Beach Hut Café next door. West of the Golden Gate Bridge is sandy **Baker Beach,** beloved for its spectacular views and laid-back vibe (read: you'll see naked people here). This is one of those places that inspires local pride. ⊠ *Between Marina and Lincoln Park* ⊕ *www.nps.gov/prsf and www.presidio.gov.*

Walt Disney Family Museum. This beautifully refurbished, brick, barracks house is a tribute to the man behind Mickey Mouse, the Disney Studios, and Disneyland. The smartly organized displays include hundreds of family photos, and well-chosen videos play throughout. Disney's legendary attention to detail becomes particularly evident in the cels and footage of *Fantasia, Sleeping Beauty,* and other animation classics. "The Toughest Period in My Whole Life" exhibit sheds light on lesser-known bits of history: the animators' strike at Disney Studios, the films Walt Disney made for the U.S. military during World War II, and his testimony before the House Un-American Activities Committee during its investigation of Communist influence in Hollywood. The glass-walled gallery showcasing Disney's wildlife films takes full advantage of the museum's location, with a lovely view of Presidio trees and the Golden Gate Bridge in the background. The liveliest exhibit and the largest gallery documents the creation of Disneyland with a fun, detailed model of what Disney imagined the park would be. Teacups spin, the Matterhorn looms, and that world-famous castle leads the way to Fantasyland. You won't be the first to leave humming "It's a Small World." In the final gallery, titled simply "December 16, 1966," a series of sweet cartoons chronicles the world's reaction to Disney's sudden death. The one-way flow of the galleries deposits you near the attractive gift shop, which carries cool Disney-related stuff, and a café serving sandwiches, salads, and drinks. The downstairs theater shows Disney films (free with admission, $7 without) twice daily. ⊠ *Main Post, 104 Montgomery St., off Lincoln Blvd.* ☎ *415/345–6800* ⊕ *www.waltdisney.org* 🖃 *$20* ☺ *Wed.–Mon. 10–6.*

GOLDEN GATE PARK AND THE WESTERN SHORELINE

More than 1,000 acres, stretching from the Haight all the way to the windy Pacific coast, Golden Gate Park is a vast patchwork of woods, trails, lakes, lush gardens, sports facilities, museums—even a herd of buffalo. There's more natural beauty beyond the park's borders, along San Francisco's wild Western Shoreline.

EXPLORING GOLDEN GATE PARK

California Academy of Sciences. With its native plant–covered living roof, retractable ceiling, three-story rain forest, gigantic planetarium, living coral reef, and frolicking penguins, the Cal Academy is one of the city's most spectacular treasures. Dramatically designed by Renzo Piano, it's an eco-friendly, energy-efficient adventure in biodiversity and green architecture. The roof's large mounds and hills mirror the local topography, and Piano's audacious design completes the dramatic transformation of the park's Music Concourse. Moving away from a restrictive role as a backward-looking museum that catalogued natural history, the new academy is all about sustainability and the future, but you'll still find those beloved dioramas in African Hall.

By the time you arrive, hopefully you've decided which shows and programs to attend, looked at the academy's floorplan, and designed a plan to cover it all in the time you have. And if not, here's the quick version: Head left from the entrance to the wooden walkway over otherworldly rays in the Philippine Coral Reef, then continue to the Swamp to see Claude, the famous albino alligator. Swing through African Hall and gander at the penguins, take the elevator up to the living roof, then return to the main floor and get in line to explore the Rainforests of the World, ducking free-flying butterflies and watching for other live surprises. You'll end up below ground in the Amazonian Flooded Rainforest, where you can explore the academy's other aquarium exhibits. Phew. ■TIP➔ **During peak periods the museum adds a $5 surcharge to tickets purchased at the door, so buy yours online ahead of time.** ⊠ *55 Music Concourse Dr.* ☎ *415/379–8000* ⊕ *www.calacademy.org* ✑ *$29.95, free one Sun. per quarter* ☺ *Mon.– Sat. 9:30–5, Sun. 11–5.*

Conservatory of Flowers. Whatever you do, be sure to at least drive by the Conservatory of Flowers—it's too darn pretty to miss. The gorgeous, white-framed 1878 glass structure is topped with a 14-ton glass dome. Stepping inside the giant greenhouse is like taking a quick trip to the rain forest, with its earthy smell and humid warmth. The undeniable highlight is the Aquatic Plants section, where lily pads float and carnivorous plants dine on bugs to the sounds of rushing water. On the east side of the conservatory (to the right as you face the building), cypress, pine, and redwood trees surround the Dahlia Garden, which blooms in summer and fall. To the west is the Rhododendron Dell, which contains 850 varieties, more than any other garden in the country. It's a favorite local Mother's Day picnic spot. ⊠ *John F. Kennedy Dr. at Conservatory Dr.* ☎ *415/666–7001* ⊕ *www.conservatoryofflowers.org* ✑ *$7, free 1st Tues. of month* ☺ *Tues.–Sun. 10–4:30.*

de Young Museum. It seems that everyone in town has a strong opinion about the de Young Museum: Some adore its striking copper facade, while others just hope that the green patina of age will mellow the effect. Most maligned is the 144-foot tower, but the view from its ninth-story observation room, ringed by floor-to-ceiling windows and free to the public, is worth a trip here by itself. The building almost overshadows the de Young's respected collection of American, African, and Oceanic art. The museum also plays host to major international exhibits, such as postimpressionist works on loan from the Musée d'Orsay and 100 works from Paris's Musée National Picasso. ⊠ *50 Hagiwara Tea Garden Dr.* 🕾 *415/750–3600* ⊕ *deyoung.famsf.org* ✍ *$10, free 1st Tues. of month* ☉ *Tues.–Sun. 9:30–5:15; mid-Jan.–Nov., Fri. until 8:45.*

San Francisco Japanese Tea Garden. As you amble through the manicured landscape, past Japanese sculptures and perfect miniature pagodas, and over ponds of carp, you may feel transported to a more peaceful plane. Or maybe the shrieks of kids clambering over the almost vertical "humpback" bridges will keep you firmly in the here and now. Either way, this garden is one of those tourist spots that's truly worth a stop (a half hour will do). And at 5 acres, it's large enough that you'll always be able to find a bit of serenity, even when the tour buses drop by. The garden is especially lovely in April, when the cherry blossoms are in bloom. ⊠ *Hagiwara Tea Garden Dr., off John F. Kennedy Dr.* 🕾 *415/752–4227* ⊕ *www.japaneseteagardensf.com* ✍ *$7, free Mon., Wed., and Fri. if you enter by 10 am* ☉ *Mar.–Oct., daily 9–6; Nov.– Feb., daily 9–4:45.*

San Francisco Botanical Garden at Strybing Arboretum. One of the best picnic spots in a very picnic-friendly park, the 55-acre arboretum specializes in plants from areas with climates similar to that of the Bay Area. Walk the Eastern Australian garden to see tough, pokey shrubs and plants with cartoon-like names, such as the hilly-pilly tree. Kids gravitate toward the large shallow fountain and the pond with ducks, turtles, and egrets. Alas, the city began charging admission to the gardens in 2010, so it's a slightly less alluring picnic spot compared to the free stretches in front of the Conservatory of Flowers and on the Music Concourse between the de Young and the Cal Academy. ⊠ *Lincoln Way and 9th Ave. entrance* 🕾 *415/661–1316* ⊕ *www.sfbotanicalgarden.org* ✍ *$7, free 2nd Tues. of month* ☉ *Apr.–Oct., daily 9–6; Nov.–Mar., daily 9–5.*

EXPLORING THE WESTERN SHORELINE

Cliff House. A meal at the Cliff House isn't about the food—the spectacular ocean view is what brings folks here. The vistas, which include offshore Seal Rock (the barking marine mammals who reside there are actually sea lions), can be 30 miles or more on a clear day—or less than a mile on foggy days. ■TIP→ Come for drinks just before sunset; then head back into town for dinner.

Three buildings have occupied this site since 1863. The current building dates from 1909; a 2004 renovation has left a strikingly attractive restaurant and a squat concrete viewing platform out back. The complex, owned by the National Park Service, includes a gift shop.

Armed with only helmets, safety harnesses, and painting equipment, a full-time crew of 38 painters keeps the Golden Gate Bridge clad in International Orange.

Sitting on the observation deck is the **Giant Camera,** a camera obscura with its lens pointing skyward housed in a cute yellow-painted wooden shack. Built in the 1940s and threatened many times with demolition, it's now on the National Register of Historic Places. Step into the dark, tiny room inside (for a $3 fee); a fascinating 360-degree image of the surrounding area—which rotates as the "lens" on the roof rotates—is projected on a large, circular table. ■**TIP→ In winter and spring you may also glimpse migrating gray whales from the observation deck.**

To the north of the Cliff House lie the ruins of the once-grand glass-roof **Sutro Baths,** which you can explore on your own (they look a bit like water-storage receptacles). Adolf Sutro, eccentric onetime San Francisco mayor and Cliff House owner, built the bath complex, including a train out to the site, in 1896, so that everyday folks could enjoy the benefits of swimming. Six enormous baths (some freshwater and some seawater), more than 500 dressing rooms, and several restaurants covered 3 acres north of the Cliff House and accommodated 25,000 bathers. Likened to Roman baths in a European glass palace, the baths were for decades the favorite destination of San Franciscans in search of entertainment. The complex fell into disuse after World War II, was closed in 1952, and burned down (under officially questionable circumstances, wink wink) during demolition in 1966. ⊠ *1090 Point Lobos Ave., Richmond* ☎ *415/386–3330* ⊕ *www.cliffhouse.com* ✉ *Free* ☉ *Weekdays 9 am–9:30 pm, weekends 9 am–10 pm.*

Fodor's Choice
★ **Legion of Honor.** The old adage of real estate—location, location, location—is at full force here. You can't beat the site of this museum of European art atop cliffs overlooking the ocean, the Golden Gate Bridge, and

the Marin Headlands. A pyramidal glass skylight in the entrance court illuminates the lower-level galleries, which exhibit prints and drawings, English and European porcelain, and ancient Assyrian, Greek, Roman, and Egyptian art. The 20-plus galleries on the upper level display the permanent collection of European art (paintings, sculpture, decorative arts, and tapestries) from the 14th century to the present day.

The noteworthy Auguste Rodin collection includes two galleries devoted to the master and a third with works by Rodin and other 19th-century sculptors. An original cast of Rodin's *The Thinker* welcomes you as you walk through the courtyard. As fine as the museum is, the setting and view outshine the collection and also make a trip here worthwhile.

The **Legion Café,** on the lower level, serves tasty light meals (soup, sandwiches, grilled chicken) inside and on a garden terrace. (Unfortunately, there's no view.) Just north of the museum's parking lot is George Segal's *The Holocaust,* a stark white installation that evokes life in concentration camps during World War II. It's haunting at night, when backlighted by lights in the Legion's parking lot. ■**TIP**➔ Admission to the Legion is also good for same-day admission to the de Young Museum in Golden Gate Park. ✉ *34th Ave. at Clement St., Richmond* ☎ *415/750–3600* ⊕ *legionofhonor.famsf.org* ✉ *$10, $2 off with Muni transfer, free 1st Tues. of month* ◷ *Tues.–Sun. 9:30–5:15.*

Fodor's Choice **Lincoln Park.** Although many of the city's green spaces are gentle and
★ welcoming, Lincoln Park is a wild, 275-acre park in the Outer Richmond with windswept cliffs and panoramic views. The newly renovated Coastal Trail, the park's most dramatic one, leads out to **Lands End;** pick it up west of the Legion of Honor (at the end of El Camino del Mar) or from the parking lot at Point Lobos and El Camino del Mar. Time your hike to hit Mile Rock at low tide, and you might catch a glimpse of two wrecked ships peeking up from their watery graves. ⚠ Be careful if you hike here; landslides are frequent, and people have fallen into the sea by standing too close to the edge of a crumbling bluff top.

On the tamer side, large Monterey cypresses line the fairways at Lincoln Park's 18-hole golf course, near the Legion of Honor. At one time this land was the Golden Gate Cemetery, where the dead were segregated by nationality; most were indigent and interred without ceremony in the potter's field. In 1900 the Board of Supervisors voted to ban burials within city limits, and all but two city cemeteries (at Mission Dolores and the Presidio) were moved to Colma, a small town just south of San Francisco. When digging has to be done in the park, bones occasionally surface again. ✉ *Entrance at, 34th Ave. at Clement St., Richmond.*

Ocean Beach. Stretching 3 miles along the western side of the city from the Richmond to the Sunset, this sandy swath of the Pacific coast is good for jogging or walking the dog—but not for swimming. The water is so cold that surfers wear wet suits year-round, and riptides are strong. As for sunbathing, it's rarely warm enough here; think meditative walking instead of sun worshipping.

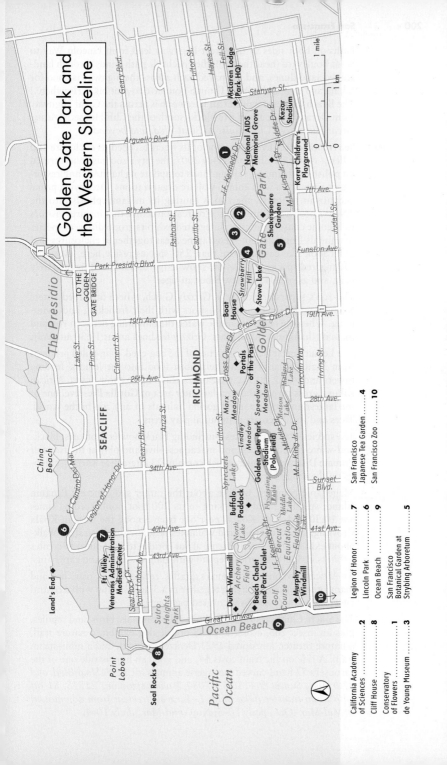

Golden Gate Park and the Western Shoreline

Geary Blvd.
Hayes St.
Fell St.
Fulton St.
McLaren Lodge (Park HQ)
Stanyan St.
Arguello Blvd.
J.F. Kennedy Dr.
National AIDS Memorial Grove
Kezar Stadium
M.L. King Jr. Dr.
Koret Children's Playground
7th Ave.
Shakespeare Garden
8th Ave.
Balboa St.
Cabrillo St.
Golden Gate Park
Funston Ave.
Judah St.
Strawberry Hill
Stowe Lake
Boat House
Park Presidio Blvd.
TO THE GOLDEN GATE BRIDGE
The Presidio
Lake St.
Pine St.
Clement St.
Cross Over Dr.
Portals of the Past
19th Ave.
19th Ave.
25th Ave.
Marx Meadow
Speedway Meadow
Lindley Meadow
Metson Lake
Mallard Lake
Lincoln Way
Irving St.
China Beach
SEACLIFF
RICHMOND
El Camino Del Mar
Geary Blvd.
Anza St.
Fulton St.
Middle Dr.
M.L. King Jr. Dr.
28th Ave.
34th Ave.
Spreckels Lake
Golden Gate Park Stadium (Polo Field)
Fly Casting Pools
Sunset Blvd.
Legion of Honor Dr.
Fort Miley Veterans Administration Medical Center
40th Ave.
43rd Ave.
North Lake
Buffalo Paddock
Middle Lake
Bercut Equitation Field
Golf Course
J.F. Kennedy Dr.
41st Ave.
Land's End
Seal Rock Dr.
Point Lobos Ave.
Archery Field
Beach Chalet and Park Chalet
Dutch Windmill
Murphy Windmill
South Lake
Point Lobos
Sutro Heights Park
Great Highway
Seal Rocks
Ocean Beach
Pacific Ocean

1
2
3
4
5
6
7
8
9
10
11

1 km
1 mile

Paths on both sides of the Great Highway lead from Lincoln Way to Sloat Boulevard (near the zoo); the beachside path winds through landscaped sand dunes, and the paved path across the highway is good for biking and in-line skating. (Though you have to rent bikes elsewhere.) The **Beach Chalet** restaurant and brewpub is across the Great Highway from Ocean Beach, about five blocks south of the Cliff House. ⊠ *Along Great Hwy. from Cliff House to Sloat Blvd. and beyond.*

FAMILY **San Francisco Zoo.** Ever since one of its tigers escaped its enclosure and killed a visitor on Christmas Day 2007, the city's zoo has concentrated on polishing its image, raising funds to update its habitats, and restoring its reputation with animal welfare organizations. Occupying prime oceanfront property, the zoo is touting its metamorphosis into the "New Zoo," a wildlife-focused recreation center that inspires visitors to become conservationists. Integrated exhibits group different species of animals from the same geographic areas together in enclosures that don't look like cages. More than 250 species reside here, including endangered species such as the snow leopard, Sumatran tiger, grizzly bear, and as of 2011, a new Siberian tiger.

The zoo's superstar exhibit is **Grizzly Gulch,** where orphaned sisters Kachina and Kiona enchant visitors with their frolicking and swimming. When the bears are in the water, the only thing between you and them is (thankfully thick) glass. Grizzly feedings are at 11:30 am daily.

The **Lemur Forest** has five varieties of the bug-eyed, long-tailed primates from Madagascar. You can help hoist food into the lemurs' feeding towers and watch the fuzzy creatures climb up to chow down. African Kikuyu grass carpets the circular outer area of **Gorilla Preserve,** one of the largest and most natural gorilla habitats of any zoo in the world. Trees and shrubs create communal play areas.

Ten species of rare primates—including black howler monkeys, black-and-white ruffed lemurs, and macaques—live and play at the two-tier **Primate Discovery Center,** which contains 23 interactive learning exhibits on the ground level.

Magellanic penguins waddle about the rather sad concrete **Penguin Island,** splashing and frolicking in its 200-foot pool. Feeding times are 10:30 and 3:30. Koalas peer out from among the trees in **Koala Crossing,** and kangaroos and wallabies headline the **Australian Walkabout** exhibit. The 7-acre **Puente al Sur** (Bridge to the South) re-creates habitats in South America, replete with giant anteaters and capybaras.

An **African Savanna** exhibit mixes giraffes, zebras, kudus, ostriches, and many other species, all living together in a 3-acre section with a central viewing spot accessed by a covered passageway.

The 6-acre **Children's Zoo** has about 300 mammals, birds, and reptiles, plus an insect zoo, a meerkat and prairie-dog exhibit, a nature trail, a nature theater, a restored 1921 Dentzel carousel, and a mini–steam train. A ride on the train costs $4, and you can hop astride one of the carousel's 52 hand-carved menagerie animals for $2. ⊠ *Sloat Blvd. and 47th Ave., Sunset* ☎ *415/753–7080* ⊕ *www.sfzoo.org* ✆*$15, $1 off with Muni transfer (take Muni L–Taraval streetcar from downtown)* ☉ *Mid-Mar.–Oct., daily 10–5; Nov.–mid-Mar., daily 10–4.*

THE HAIGHT, THE CASTRO, AND NOE VALLEY

These distinct neighborhoods are where the city's soul resides. They wear their personalities large and proud, and all are perfect for just strolling around. Like a slide show of San Franciscan history, you can move from the Haight's residue of 1960s counterculture to the Castro's connection to 1970s and '80s gay life to 1990s gentrification in Noe Valley. Although historic events thrust the Haight and the Castro onto the international stage, both are anything but stagnant—they're still dynamic areas well worth exploring.

EXPLORING THE HAIGHT

Haight-Ashbury Intersection. On October 6, 1967, hippies took over the intersection of Haight and Ashbury streets to proclaim the "Death of Hip." If they thought hip was dead then, they'd find absolute confirmation of it today, what with the only tie-dye in sight on the famed corner being Ben & Jerry's storefront.

Everyone knows the Summer of Love had something to do with free love and LSD, but the drugs and other excesses of that period have tended to obscure the residents' serious attempts to create an America that was more spiritually oriented, more environmentally aware, and less caught up in commercialism. The Diggers, a radical group of actors and populist agitators, for example, operated a free shop a few blocks off Haight Street. Everything really was free at the free shop; people brought in things they didn't need and took things they did.

Among the folks who hung out in or near the Haight during the late 1960s were writers Richard Brautigan, Allen Ginsberg, Ken Kesey, and Gary Snyder; anarchist Abbie Hoffman; rock performers Marty Balin, Jerry Garcia, Janis Joplin, and Grace Slick; LSD champion Timothy Leary; and filmmaker Kenneth Anger. If you're keen to feel something resembling the hippie spirit these days, there's always Hippie Hill, just inside the Haight Street entrance of Golden Gate Park. Think drum circles, guitar players, and whiffs of pot smoke.

EXPLORING THE CASTRO

Fodor'sChoice **Castro Theatre.** Here's a classic way to join in the Castro community:
★ grab some popcorn and catch a flick at this gorgeous, 1,500-seat art deco theater; opened in 1922, it's the grandest of San Francisco's few remaining movie palaces. The neon marquee, which stands at the top of the Castro strip, is the neighborhood's great landmark. The Castro was the fitting host of 2008's red-carpet preview of Gus Van Sant's film *Milk*, starring Sean Penn as openly gay San Francisco supervisor Harvey Milk. The theater's elaborate Spanish baroque interior is fairly well preserved. Before many shows the theater's pipe organ rises from the orchestra pit and an organist plays pop and movie tunes, usually ending with the Jeanette McDonald standard "San Francisco" (go ahead, sing along). The crowd can be enthusiastic and vocal, talking back to the screen as loudly as it talks to them. Classics such as *Who's Afraid of Virginia Woolf?* take on a whole new life, with the assembled beating the actors to the punch and fashioning even snappier comebacks for Elizabeth Taylor. Head here to catch classics, a Fellini film retrospective, or the latest take on same-sex love. ⊠ *429 Castro St.* ☎ *415/621–6120* ⊕ *www.castrotheatre.com.*

Harvey Milk Plaza. An 18-foot-long rainbow flag, the symbol of gay pride, flies above this plaza named for the man who electrified the city in 1977 by being elected to its Board of Supervisors as an openly gay candidate. In the early 1970s Milk had opened a camera store on the block of Castro Street between 18th and 19th streets. The store became the center for his campaign to open San Francisco's social and political life to gays and lesbians.

The liberal Milk hadn't served a full year of his term before he and Mayor George Moscone, also a liberal, were shot in November 1978 at City Hall. The murderer was a conservative ex-supervisor named Dan White, who had recently resigned his post and then became enraged when Moscone wouldn't reinstate him. Milk and White had often been at odds on the board, and White thought Milk had been part of a cabal to keep him from returning to his post. Milk's assassination shocked the gay community, which became infuriated when the infamous "Twinkie defense"—that junk food had led to diminished mental capacity—resulted in a manslaughter verdict for White. During the so-called White Night Riot of May 21, 1979, gays and their allies stormed City Hall, torching its lobby and several police cars.

Milk, who had feared assassination, left behind a tape recording in which he urged the community to continue the work he had begun. His legacy is the high visibility of gay people throughout city government; a bust of him was unveiled at City Hall on his birthday in 2008, and the 2008 film *Milk* gives insight into his life. A plaque at the base of the flagpole lists the names of past and present openly gay and lesbian state and local officials. ⊠ *Southwest corner of Castro and Market Sts..*

EXPLORING NOE VALLEY

Golden fire hydrant. When all the other fire hydrants went dry during the fire that followed the 1906 earthquake, this one kept pumping. Noe Valley and the Mission District were thus spared the devastation wrought elsewhere in the city, which explains the large number of pre-quake homes here. Every year on April 18rh (the anniversary of the quake) folks gather here to share stories about the earthquake, and the famous hydrant gets a fresh coat of gold paint. ⊠ *Church and 20th Sts., southeast corner, across from Dolores Park.*

CASTRO AND NOE WALK

The Castro and Noe Valley are both neighborhoods that beg to be walked—or ambled through, really, without time pressure or an absolute destination. Hit the Castro first, beginning at **Harvey Milk Plaza** under the gigantic rainbow flag. If you're going on to Noe Valley, first head east down **Market Street** for the cafés, bistros, and shops, then go back to **Castro Street** and head south, past the glorious art-deco Castro Theatre, checking out boutiques and cafés along the way (Cliff's Variety, at 479 Castro Street, is a must). To tour Noe Valley, go east down **18th Street** to **Church** (at Dolores Park), and then either strap on your hiking boots and head south over the hill or hop the **J–Church** to **24th Street**, the center of this rambling neighborhood.

A colorful mosaic mural in the Castro

MISSION DISTRICT

The Mission has a number of distinct personalities: it's the Latino neighborhood, where working-class folks raise their families and where gangs occasionally clash; it's the hipster hood, where tattooed and pierced twenty- and thirtysomethings hold court in the coolest cafés and bars in town; it's a culinary epicenter, with the strongest concentration of destination restaurants and affordable ethnic cuisine; and it's the artists' quarter, where murals adorn literally blocks of walls. It's also the city's equivalent of the Sunshine State—this neighborhood's always the last to succumb to fog.

EXPLORING THE MISSION DISTRICT

Balmy Alley murals. Mission District artists have transformed the walls of their neighborhood with paintings, and Balmy Alley is one of the best-executed examples. Murals fill the one-block alley, with newer ones continually filling in the blank spaces. Local children working with adults started the project in 1971. Since then dozens of artists have steadily added to it, with the aim of promoting peace in Central America, as well as community spirit and AIDS awareness. ■TIP→ Be alert here: the 25th Street end of the alley adjoins a somewhat dangerous area. ⊠ *24th St. between and parallel to Harrison and Treat Sts., alley runs south to 25th St.*

Galería de la Raza. San Francisco's premier showcase for contemporary Latino art, the gallery exhibits the works of mostly local artists. Events include readings and spoken word by local poets and writers, screenings of Latin American and Spanish films, and theater works by local minority theater troupes. Just across the street, amazing art festoons the

24th Street/York Street Minipark, a tiny urban playground. A mosaic-covered Quetzalcoatl serpent plunges into the ground and rises, creating hills for little ones to clamber over, and mural-covered walls surround the space. ✉ *2857 24th St., at Bryant St.* ☎ *415/826–8009* ⊕ *www. galeriadelaraza.org* ⊙ *Gallery Tues.–Sat. noon–6.*

Mission Dolores. Two churches stand side by side at this mission, including the small adobe **Mission San Francisco de Asís,** the oldest standing structure in San Francisco. Completed in 1791, it's the sixth of the 21 California missions founded by Franciscan friars in the 18th and early 19th centuries. Its ceiling depicts original Ohlone Indian basket designs, executed in vegetable dyes. The tiny chapel includes frescoes and a hand-painted wooden altar.

There's a hidden treasure here, too. In 2004 an archaeologist and an artist crawling along the ceiling's rafters opened a trap door behind the altar and rediscovered the mission's original mural, painted with natural dyes by Native Americans in 1791. The centuries have taken their toll, so the team photographed the 20-by-22-foot mural and began digitally restoring the photographic version. Among the images is a dagger-pierced Sacred Heart of Jesus.

The small museum here covers the mission's founding and history, and the pretty little cemetery—which appears in Alfred Hitchcock's film *Vertigo*—contains the graves of mid-19th-century European immigrants. (The remains of an estimated 5,000 Native Americans lie in unmarked graves.) Services are held in both the old mission and next door in the handsome multidome basilica. ✉ *Dolores and 16th Sts.* ☎ *415/621–8203* ⊕ *www.missiondolores.org* ✏ *$5, audio tour $7* ⊙ *Nov.–Apr., daily 9–4; May–Oct., daily 9–4:30.*

Precita Eyes Mural Arts and Visitors Center. The muralists of this nonprofit arts organization design and create murals and lead guided walks of area murals. The Classic Mission Mural Walk ($20) starts with a 45-minute slide presentation before participants head outside to view murals on Balmy Alley and 24th Street. The Mission Trail Mural Walk ($15) includes some of the same murals and impressive ones at Cesar Chavez Elementary School. You can pick up a map of 24th Street's murals at the center and buy art supplies, T-shirts, postcards, and other mural-related items. ✉ *2981 24th St.* ☎ *415/285–2287* ⊕ *www. precitaeyes.org* ✏ *Center free, tours $15–$20* ⊙ *Center weekdays 10–5, Sat. 10–4, Sun. noon–4; walks weekends at 11 (Mission Trail) and 1:30 (Classic).*

PACIFIC HEIGHTS AND JAPANTOWN

Pacific Heights and Japantown are something of an odd couple: privileged, old-school San Francisco and the workaday commercial center of Japanese American life in the city, stacked virtually on top of each other. The sprawling, extravagant mansions of Pacific Heights gradually give way to the more modest Victorians and unassuming housing tracts of Japantown. The most interesting spots in Japantown huddle in the Japan Center, the neighborhood's two-block centerpiece, and along Post Street. You can find plenty of authentic Japanese treats in

The Haight, the Castro, Noe Valley and the Mission District

Balmy Alley murals **7**
Castro Theatre **2**
Galeria de la Raza **8**
Golden fire hydrant **4**
Haight-Ashbury
intersection **3**
Harvey Milk Plaza **1**
Mission Dolores **5**
Precita Eyes Mural Arts
and Visitors Center **6**

350 M
1,000 ft

the shops and restaurants. ■TIP→ Japantown is a relatively safe area, but the Western Addition, south of Geary Boulevard, can be dangerous even during the daytime. Also avoid going too far west of Fillmore Street on either side of Geary.

EXPLORING PACIFIC HEIGHTS

FAMILY **Alta Plaza Park.** Golden Gate Park's longtime superintendent, John McLaren, designed Alta Plaza in 1910, modeling its terracing on that of the Grand Casino in Monte Carlo, Monaco. From the top you can see Marin to the north, downtown to the east, Twin Peaks to the south, and Golden Gate Park to the west. Kids love the many play structures at the large, enclosed playground at the top; everywhere else is dog territory. ⊠ *Bordered by Clay, Steiner, Jackson, and Scott Sts.*

Atherton House. The mildly daffy design of this Victorian-era house incorporates Queen Anne, Stick-Eastlake, and other architectural elements. Many claim the house—now apartments—is haunted by the ghosts of its 19th-century residents, who regularly whisper, glow, and generally cause a mild fuss. ⊠ *1990 California St..*

Franklin Street buildings. What at first looks like a stone facade on the **Golden Gate Church** (⊠ *1901 Franklin St.*) is actually redwood painted white. A Georgian-style residence built in the early 1900s for a coffee merchant sits at 1735 Franklin. On the northeast corner of Franklin and California streets is a **Christian Science church**; built in the Tuscan revival style, it's noteworthy for its terra-cotta detailing. **The Coleman House** (⊠ *1701 Franklin St.*) is an impressive twin-turret Queen Anne mansion that was built for a gold-rush mining and lumber baron. Don't miss the large, brilliant-purple stained-glass window on the house's north side. ⊠ *Franklin St. between Washington and California Sts.*

Haas-Lilienthal House. A small display of photographs on the bottom floor of this elaborate, gray 1886 Queen Anne house makes clear that despite its lofty stature and striking, round third-story tower, the house was modest compared with some of the giants that fell victim to the 1906 earthquake and fire. The Foundation for San Francisco's Architectural Heritage operates the home, whose carefully kept rooms provide a glimpse into late-19th-century life through period furniture, authentic details (antique dishes in the kitchen built-in), and photos of the family that occupied the house until 1972. ■TIP→ You can admire hundreds of gorgeous San Francisco Victorians from the outside, but this is the only one that's open to the public, and it's worth a visit. Volunteers conduct one-hour house tours three days a week, and informative two-hour walking tours of Pacific Heights on Sunday afternoons (call or check website for schedule). ⊠ *2007 Franklin St., between Washington and Jackson Sts.* ☎ *415/441–3004* ⊕ *www.sfheritage.org* 🖾 *Tours $8* ☽ *1-hr tour Wed. and Sat. noon–3, Sun. 11–4; 2-hr tour Sun. at 12:30.*

Octagon House. This eight-sided home sits across the street from its original site on Gough Street; it's one of two remaining octagonal houses in the city (the other is on Russian Hill), and the only one open to the public. White quoins accent each of the eight corners of the pretty blue-gray

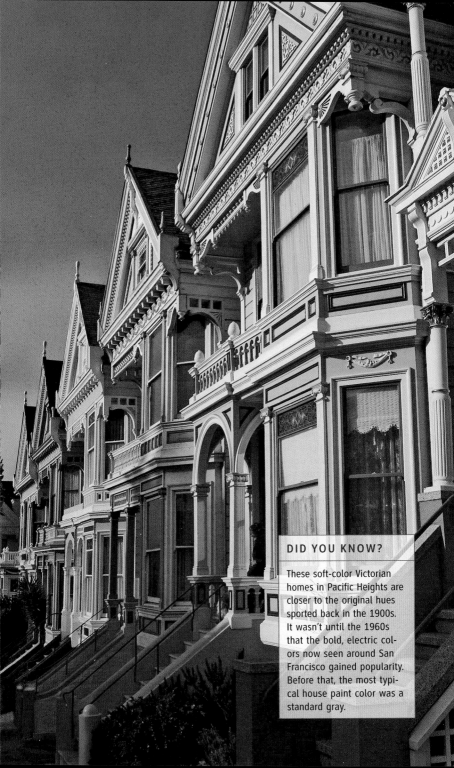

DID YOU KNOW?

These soft-color Victorian homes in Pacific Heights are closer to the original hues sported back in the 1900s. It wasn't until the 1960s that the bold, electric colors now seen around San Francisco gained popularity. Before that, the most typical house paint color was a standard gray.

Pacific Heights and Japantown

exterior, and a colonial-style garden completes the picture. The house is full of antique American furniture, decorative arts (paintings, silver, rugs), and documents from the 18th and 19th centuries. A deck of Revolutionary-era hand-painted playing cards takes an antimonarchist position: in place of kings, queens, and jacks, the American upstarts substituted American statesmen, Roman goddesses, and Indian chiefs. ✉ *2645 Gough St. near Union St., Cow Hollow* ☎ *415/441–7512* 🌐 *Free, donations encouraged* 🕙 *Feb.–Dec., 2nd Sun. and 2nd and 4th Thurs. of month noon–3; group tours weekdays by appointment.*

Spreckels Mansion. Shrouded behind tall juniper hedges at the corner of lovely winding, brick Octavia Street, overlooking Lafayette Park, the estate was built for sugar heir Adolph Spreckels and his wife Alma. Mrs. Spreckels was so pleased with her house that she commissioned George Applegarth to design another building in a similar vein: the Legion of Honor. One of the city's great iconoclasts, Alma Spreckels was the model for the bronze figure atop the *Victory* monument in Union Square. Today this house belongs to prolific romance novelist Danielle Steel. ✉ *2080 Washington St., at Octavia St.*

Whittier Mansion. With a Spanish-tile roof and scrolled bay windows on all four sides, this is one of the most elegant 19th-century houses in the state. Unlike other grand mansions lost in the 1906 quake, the Whittier

Mansion was built so solidly that only a chimney toppled over during the disaster. Built by William Franklin Whittier, the founder of (what became) PG&E, the house served as the German consulate during the Nazi period. Legend has it that the house is haunted. ⊠ *2090 Jackson St.*

EXPLORING JAPANTOWN

Japan Center. Cool and curious trinkets, noodle houses and sushi joints, a destination bookstore, and a peek at Japanese culture high and low await at this 5-acre complex designed in 1968 by noted American architect Minoru Yamasaki. The Japan Center includes the shop- and restaurant-filled Kintetsu and Kinokuniya buildings; the excellent Kabuki Springs & Spa; the Hotel Kabuki; and the Sundance Kabuki, Robert Redford's fancy, reserved-seating cinema/restaurant complex. Unfortunately, the development hasn't aged well, and its Peace Plaza, where seasonal festivals are held, is an unwelcoming sea of cement.

The Kinokuniya Bookstores, in the Kinokuniya Building, have an extensive selection of Japanese-language books, *manga* (graphic novels), books on design, and English-language translations and books on Japanese topics. Just outside, follow the Japanese teenagers to Pika Pika, where you and your friends can step into a photo booth and then use special effects and stickers to decorate your creation. On the bridge connecting the center's two buildings, check out Shige Antiques for *yukata* (lightweight cotton kimonos) for kids and lovely silk kimonos, and Asakichi and its tiny incense shop for tinkling wind chimes and display-worthy teakettles. Continue into the Kintetsu Building for a selection of Japanese restaurants.

Between the Miyako Mall and Kintetsu Building are the five-tier, 100-foot-tall **Peace Pagoda** and the Peace Plaza. The pagoda, which draws on the 1,200-year-old tradition of miniature round pagodas dedicated to eternal peace, was designed in the late 1960s by Yoshiro Taniguchi to convey the "friendship and goodwill" of the Japanese people to the people of the United States. The plaza itself is a shadeless, unwelcoming stretch of cement with little seating. Continue into the Miyako Mall to Ichiban Kan, a Japanese dollar store where you can pick up fun Japanese kitchenware, tote bags decorated with hedgehogs, and erasers shaped like food. ⊠ *Bordered by Geary Blvd. and Fillmore, Post, and Laguna Sts.*

Buchanan Mall. The buildings lining this open-air mall are of the shoji school of architecture. The shops are geared more toward locals—travel agencies, electronics shops—but there are some fun Japanese-goods stores. Arrive early in the day and you may score some fabulous *mochi* (a soft, sweet Japanese rice treat) at **Benkyodo Company** (⊠ *1747 Buchanan St. 415/922–1244* ⊕ *www.benkyodocompany. com*). It's easy to spend hours among the fabulous origami and craft papers at **Paper Tree** (⊠ *1743 Buchanan St. 415/921–7100* ⊕ *paper-tree.com*). You can have a seat on local artist Ruth Asawa's twin origami-style fountains, which sit in the middle of the mall; they're squat circular structures made of fieldstone, with three levels for sitting and a brick floor. ⊠ *Buchanan St. between Post and Sutter Sts.*

Fodor's Choice
★

Kabuki Springs & Spa. This serene spa is one Japantown destination that draws locals from all over town, from hipster to grandma, Japanese-

American or not. Balinese urns decorate the communal bath area of this house of tranquillity.

The massage menu has also expanded well beyond traditional shiatsu technique. The experience is no less relaxing, however, and the treatment regimen includes facials, salt scrubs, and mud and seaweed wraps. You can take your massage in a private room with a bath or in a curtained-off area.

The communal baths ($22 weekdays, $25 weekends) contain hot and cold tubs, a large Japanese-style bath, a sauna, a steam room, and showers. Bang the gong for quiet if your fellow bathers are speaking too loudly. The clothing-optional baths are open for men only on Mondays, Thursdays, and Saturdays; women bathe on Wednesdays, Fridays, and Sundays. Bathing suits are required on Tuesdays, when the baths are coed.

Men and women can reserve private rooms daily. An 80-minute massage-and-private-bath package costs $155 weekdays, $170 weekends; a package that includes a 50-minute massage and the use of the communal baths costs $100 weekdays, $109 weekends. ✉ *1750 Geary Blvd.* ☎ *415/922–6000* ⊕ *www.kabukisprings.com* ☽ *Daily 10–10.*

New People. The kids' counterpart to the Japan Center, this fresh shopping center combines a cinema, a café, shops, and a gallery with a successful synergy. The basement cinema shows classic and cutting-edge Asian (largely Japanese) films and is home to the San Francisco Film Society. Grab some *onigiri* (rice balls) and a cup of Blue Bottle coffee at the café, then head upstairs and peruse Japanese pop-culture items and anime-inspired fashion. The cuteness radiating from the Rilakkuma store may overwhelm you. The tiny Superfrog Gallery upstairs exhibits cutting-edge contemporary art. ✉ *1746 Post St.* ☎ *415/525–8630 store, 415/525–8600 cinema* ⊕ *www.newpeopleworld.com* ☽ *Mon.–Sat. noon–7, Sun. noon–6.*

WHERE TO EAT

Updated
by Christine
Ciarmello

Make no mistake, San Francisco is one of America's top food cities. Some of the biggest landmarks are restaurants; and Alice Waters is probably just as big a draw as Alcatraz. On a Saturday, the Ferry Building may attract more visitors than the Golden Gate Bridge. This temple to local eating sells cheeses, breads, "salty pig parts," homemade delicacies, and sensory-perfect vegetables and fruits that attract a rabidly dedicated group. You see, San Franciscans are a little loco about their edibles. If you ask them what their favorite season is, don't be surprised if they respond, "tomato season."

Some renowned restaurants are booked weeks or even months in advance. But you can get lucky at the last minute if you're flexible—and friendly. Most restaurants keep a few tables open for walk-ins and VIPs. Show up for dinner early (5:30 pm) or late (after 9 pm) and politely inquire about any last-minute vacancies or cancellations. *Prices in the reviews are the average cost of a main course or equivalent combination of smaller plates at dinner.*

Use the coordinate (✛ A1) at the end of each listing to locate a site on the corresponding map.

BEST BETS FOR SAN FRANCISCO DINING

With thousands of restaurants to choose from, how will you decide where to eat? Fodor's writers and editors have selected their favorite restaurants by price, cuisine, and experience in the Best Bets lists below. In the first column, Fodor's Choice designations represent the "best of the best" in every price category. You can also search by neighborhood for excellent eats—just peruse the following pages.

Fodor's Choice★

Acquerello, $$$$, p. 217
Benu, $$$$, p. 212
Boulevard, $$$$, p. 221
Central Kitchen, $$$, p. 225
Coi, $$$$, p. 220
Delfina, $$$, p. 225
Dosa on Fillmore, $$, p. 229
Dosa on Valencia, $$, p. 226
Gary Danko, $$$$, p. 220
Nopalito, $$, p. 224
Rich Table, $$$, p. 212
Swan Oyster Depot, $$, p. 217
Zuni Café, $$$, p. 213

By Price

$

Burma Superstar, p. 230
SanJalisco, p. 227

$$

Dosa on Fillmore, p. 229
Flour + Water, p. 226
Nojo, p. 213
Nopalito, p. 224
Tony's Pizza Napoletana, p. 220
Zarzuela, p. 217

$$$

Bar Tartine, p. 225
Canteen, p. 212
Central Kitchen, p. 225
Delfina, p. 225
Local's Corner, p. 227
Locanda, p. 227
Rich Table, p. 212
St. Vincent, p. 227
Wexler's, p. 216

$$$$

Acquerello, p. 217
Benu, $$$$, p. 212
Boulevard, p. 221
Coi, p. 220
Gary Danko, p. 220

By Cuisine

AMERICAN

Canteen, $$$, p. 212
Central Kitchen, $$$, p. 225
Nopa, $$$, p. 224
Rich Table, $$$, p. 212
Wexler's, $$$, p. 216

CHINESE

Yank Sing, $$, p. 216

INDIAN

Dosa on Fillmore, $$, p. 229
Dosa on Valencia, $$, p. 226
Indian Oven, $$, p. 223

ITALIAN

A16, $$$, p. 223
Delfina, $$$, p. 225
Locanda, $$$, p. 227

JAPANESE

Nojo, $$, p. 213

MEDITERRANEAN

Zarzuela, $$, p. 217
Zuni Café, $$$, p. 213

MEXICAN

Nopalito, $$, p. 224
SanJalisco, $, p. 227

SEAFOOD

Hog Island Oyster Company, $$, p. 222
Local's Corner, $$$, p. 227
Swan Oyster Depot, $$, p. 217

By Experience

BAY VIEWS

Slanted Door, $$$, p. 222

BRUNCH

Bar Tartine, $$$, p. 225
Local's Corner, $$$, p. 227
Rose's Café, $$, p. 223

CHILD-FRIENDLY

Mifune, $, p. 229
Yank Sing, $$, p. 216

SPECIAL OCCASION

Boulevard, $$$$, p. 221
Central Kitchen, $$$, p. 225
Gary Danko, $$$$, p. 220

UNION SQUARE

$$$

AMERICAN

✕ **Canteen.** Blink, and you'll miss this place. Chef-owner Dennis Leary has transformed a narrow coffee shop into a popular spot where locals and visiting gourmands rub elbows. The intimate dining room has just 20 seats (seven at a counter and a quartet of booths). But that's all Leary, with a modest open kitchen and a single assistant, can handle. The inspired dinner menu, which changes often, offers only four first courses, four mains, and three or four desserts. A typical meal might start with chestnut soup and rabbit confit, followed by a gratin of chanterelles and tomatoes, or pork tenderloin with braised cranberry beans and fig-olive jus, and then a stellar vanilla soufflé. Because this is a one-man band, a three-course prix-fixe menu is in force, and there are two set times to dine: 6 pm and 8 pm nightly. ⑤ *Average main: $26* ✉ *817 Sutter St., Tenderloin* ☎ *415/928–8870* ⊕ *www.sfcanteen.com* ⌕ *Reservations essential* ⊘ *Closed Mon. No lunch.* ✛ *D4.*

SOMA

$$$$

MODERN
AMERICAN

Fodor's Choice
★

✕ **Benu.** One of the most high-profile restaurants to open in the city, chef-owner Corey Lee launched his contemporary American restaurant much to the delight of food-obsessed locals and travelers alike. His pedigree spans 15 years in fine dining (including a position as chef de cuisine at the French Laundry), but Benu is decidedly more relaxed—no jacket required. The dining room is very minimalist, with bare-wood tables and high-backed banquettes along the walls. While some guests come early in the week to dine on the à la carte menu, the tasting menu, which has anywhere from 14 to 18 courses and is mandatory on Friday and Saturday nights, is the way to go if your pocketbook can handle it ($180). Each dish is a marvel, from the meticulous presentation (Lee has had pieces specifically designed for the restaurant and each course) to the sophisticated flavors and textures. Fans of Asian cuisine will be particularly thrilled to see his elegant handling of ingredients like *xiao long bao* dumplings and sea cucumber. He utilizes many modern techniques, but never in an alienating way. You may find dishes like Hokkaido sea cucumber stuffed with lobster, pork belly, eggplant, fermented pepper or eel, *feuille de brik* (flaky pastry), crème fraiche, lime. An extremely professional staff is behind the quick pacing and on-point wine pairings. Couples expecting an ultraromantic environment may be a bit disappointed by the stark atmosphere, but culinary adventurers will be thrilled. ⑤ *Average main: $160* ✉ *22 Hawthorne St.* ☎ *415/685–4860* ⊕ *www.benusf.com* ⌕ *Reservations essential* ⊘ *Closed Sun. and Mon. No lunch* ✛ *G5.*

HAYES VALLEY

$$$

MODERN
AMERICAN

Fodor's Choice
★

✕ **Rich Table.** A new addition to Hayes Valley, this restaurant is a brilliant example of fine-dining minus preciousness or formality. It starts with bar bites, which take simple ingredients like Castelvetrano olives and make them exquisite by marinating them in a wasabi, seaweed, and lime juice. A casual concept like doughnuts becomes masterful at the hands of co-chefs Evan and Sarah Rich whose dried-porcini ones are served with a raclette béchamel sauce for dipping. To this point, it's all finger food. But forks and knives are put to use for the half-dozen pastas and an equal amount of appetizer and mains created by the Riches, alumni of NYC's Bouley and Mas (farmhouse), and Quince, Michael Mina, and Coi. Vased branches decorate the dining room that has weathered-wood wallboards repurposed from a Northern California sawmill. Ten bar seats are available for walk-ins. There's a nice selection of wines by the glass, artisanal cocktails, and even original dessert cocktails like the One Up (for Mario Bros. fans), with porcini-infused gin, sherry, egg, and cream. $ *Average main: $30* ✉ *199 Gough St., at Oak* 🕿 *415/355–9085* ⊕ *www.richtablesf.com* ⌒ *Reservations essential* ✆ *Closed Tues. No lunch* ✛ *C6.*

$$ ✕ **Nojo.** For a little bonhomie before the symphony, this buzzy yakitori
JAPANESE and izakaya spot serves stellar Japanese pub food, made from Bay Area ingredients, and it encourages sharing. The menu is divided into items "on a stick" and "not on a stick." For the stick items, much of it is *yakitori* (grilled chicken), like chicken skin with matcha sea salt, neck with *tare* (a thick grilled sauce), or *tsukune* (a chicken meatball) with egg yolk sauce—all the different notes in the varied sauces are part of the taste adventure. The savory, rich custard, *chawan mushi*, has chunks of Dungeness crabmeat and shiitake mushrooms. Seating is at bamboo tables in a mod-Japanese-slash-San Franciscan setting with large windows overlooking Hayes Valley's main thoroughfare of Franklin. There are 20 sakes by the glass. Warning, they require a credit card number to hold a reservation. $ *Average main: $20* ✉ *231 Franklin St.* 🕿 *415/896–4587* ⊕ *www.nojosf.com* ✆ *Closed Tues. No lunch Mon.* ✛ *C6.*

$$$ ✕ **Zuni Café.** After one bite of chef Judy Rodgers' succulent brick-oven-
MEDITERRANEAN roasted whole chicken with Tuscan bread salad, you'll understand
Fodor's Choice why she's a national star (and why it's the most-well-known chicken
★ dish in town). Food is served here on two floors; the rabbit warren of rooms on the second level includes a balcony overlooking the main dining room. Mingle among a disparate mix that reflects the makeup of the city—casual and dressy, young and old, hip and staid—at the long copper bar where trays of briny, fresh oysters on the half shell are dispensed along with cocktails and wine. The southern French–Italian menu changes daily, though the signature chicken, prepared for two, is a fixture (and, alas, its cost reflects its popularity). Rotating dishes are simple but made with excellent ingredients, like house-cured anchovies with Parmigiano-Reggiano, deep-fried squid and lemons, ricotta gnocchi with seasonal vegetables, and brick-oven squab with polenta. Nearly as famous as the chicken is the chocolatey flourless *gâteau Victoire*, served here since the '80s. The most cheerful spot to sit is at the tip of the "pyramid window" near the bar, easier to score if you plan a late lunch—the restaurant serves straight through. $ *Average main: $28* ✉ *1658 Market St.* 🕿 *415/552–2522* ⊕ *www. zunicafe.com* ✆ *Closed Mon.* ✛ *C6.*

NORCAL'S LOCAVORE FOOD MOVEMENT

Organic, *local*, and *sustainable* are buzzwords in Northern California, home to hundreds of small family farmers, sustainable ranchers, and artisan producers leading the country's back-to-the-earth food movement.

When Alice Waters opened Chez Panisse in Berkeley in 1971, she sparked a culinary revolution that continues today. Initially called California cuisine, the cooking style showcased local, seasonal ingredients in fresh preparations. It also marked a new willingness by American chefs to experiment with international influences. As the movement spread, it became known as New American cooking. This "eat local, think global" ethos has led to a resurgence of artisanal producers across the country.

The *locavore* (focused on sustainable, local foods) movement's epicenter is still Northern California. At the Ferry Plaza Farmers' Market in San Francisco alone, farmers bring over 1,200 varieties of fruits and vegetables to market every year. Chefs proudly call out their purveyors on menus and websites, elevating humble vegetable growers to starring culinary roles.

FARMERS' MARKETS

One of the best ways to taste Northern California's bounty is by stopping by the Ferry Plaza Farmers' Market, held outside the Ferry Building on the Embarcadero, at Market Street on Tuesday, Thursday, and Saturday mornings. The market offers produce, meats, fish, and flowers from small regional farmers and ranchers, many of whom are certified organic.

It is also a great place to pick up items for a picnic. Prepared foods like tamales and pasta are available, as are specialties like jams, breads, and cheeses from local artisan producers.

Check ⊕ *www.cuesa.org* for hours.

FRUIT

Northern California's diverse climate makes it an ideal place to grow all types of fruit, from berries to stone fruit. Farmers' markets and restaurants abound with a staggering selection of produce: Blossom Bluff Orchards, south of San Francisco, offers more than 150 varieties of stone fruits, like apricots, nectarines, and peaches. North of the city, the Apple Farm grows 80 varieties of apples, pears, persimmons, quince, and French plums. The Bay Area is also one of the best places in the country to find rare fruit varieties like aprium, cherimoya, cactus pear, jujube, and loquat; California's famous Meyer lemons—sweeter and less acidic than common lemons—are celebrated in restaurant desserts.

VEGETABLES

Some chefs give top billing to their produce purveyors, like a recently observed menu touting a salad of Star Route Farm field greens with Picholine olives, sweet herbs, and goat cheese. Along with these tantalizing items, be on the lookout for locally grown artichokes, Asian vegetables, multihued beets and carrots, and heirloom varieties of tomatoes, squash, and beans.

MEAT

Family-owned ranches and farms are prominent in the region, with many raising organic or "humane certified"

beef, pork, lamb, and poultry. Upscale Bay Area restaurants are fervent about recognizing their high-quality protein producers. From recent menus at two well-known San Francisco restaurants: Wolfe Ranch quail and foie gras crostini with Murcott mandarins, smoked bacon and bok choy, and vanilla gastrique; and Prather Ranch lamb with fava greens, cranberry beans, crispy artichokes, and salsa verde.

FISH

Diners and shoppers will find myriad seafood from local waters, from farm-raised scallops to line-caught California salmon. On menus, look for Hog Island Oysters, a local producer that raises more than 3 million oysters a year in Tomales Bay. Sardines netted in Monterey Bay are popular in preparations like mesquite-grilled sardines with fava beans, French radish and fennel salad, and preserved Meyer lemon.

CHEESE

Restaurant cheese plates, often served before—or in lieu of—dessert, are a great way to experience the region's excellent local cheeses. Look for selections from Cypress Grove Chevre, popular for its artisan goat cheeses, and Cowgirl Creamery, a renowned local producer of fresh and aged cow's milk cheeses. Additionally, some shops and bakeries offer fresh local butter and cheeses.

FINANCIAL DISTRICT

$$$ ✗**Bocadillos.** The name means "sandwiches," but that's only half the
SPANISH   story here. You'll find 13 bocadillos at lunchtime: plump rolls filled
with everything from serrano ham to Catalan sausage with arugula to
a memorable lamb burger (pick two for $10). But at night chef-owner
Gerald Hirigoyen, who also owns the high-profile Piperade, focuses on
tapas, offering some two dozen choices, including a roasted Monterey
Bay squid, an equally superb pig's trotters with chopped egg salad, and
patatas bravas (potatoes) with *romesco* sauce (a thick combination of
red pepper, tomato, almonds, and garlic). His wine list is well matched
to the dishes. A youngish crowd typically piles into the dining space,
decorated with redbrick walls, wire chairs, and small square light fix-
tures. Be prepared to wait for a seat. The large communal table is a good
perch for singles. If you're in the neighborhood at breakfast time, there
is plenty here to keep you happy, including a scrambled-eggs-and-cheese
bocadillo or house-made chorizo and eggs. ⑤ *Average main: $25* ✉ *710
Montgomery St.* ☎ *415/982–2622* ⊕ *www.bocasf.com* ◅ *Reservations
not accepted* ⊘ *Closed Sun. No lunch Sat.* ✛ *F3.*

$$$ ✗**Wexler's.** Four words: Bourbon banana cream pie. Of course, there's a
BARBECUE   whole slew of tempting barbecue items that threaten whether you'll have
room at the end of the meal. This upscale comfort-food joint neighbors
Wayfare Tavern; but for our food money, Wexler's is first choice. The
interior is chic, almost minimalist, with one mighty interesting ceiling
sculpture and a couple of red chandeliers to liven up the place. Barbecue
traditionalists should come with an open mind. The crispy Scotch eggs,
fork-tender short ribs, and smoked wings (with Point Reyes blue cheese
dressing) take their cues from barbecue but wander into more creative
territory (chef Charlie Kleinman earned accolades while at Fifth Floor).
Purists might do better with Wexler's new food truck parked out back,
serving pulled pork, chicken, and brisket with traditional sides like hush
puppies, on weekdays. A secret? The cocktails are fantastic. ⑤ *Average
main: $24* ✉ *568 Sacramento St.* ☎ *415/983–0102* ⊕ *www.wexlerssf.com*
⊘ *Closed Sun. No dinner Mon. No lunch weekends.* ✛ *F3.*

$$ ✗**Yank Sing.** The granddaddy of SF dim sum teahouses, Yank Sing
CHINESE   opened in a plain-Jane storefront in Chinatown in 1959, but left its Can-
FAMILY   tonese neighbors behind for the high-rises of downtown by the 1970s.
This brightly decorated location on quiet Stevenson Street (there's also
a big, brassy branch in the Rincon Center) serves some of San Fran-
cisco's best dim sum to office workers on weekdays and to big, boister-
ous families on weekends. The kitchen cooks up some 100 varieties of
dim sum on a rotating basis, offering 60 different types daily. These
include both the classic (steamed pork buns, shrimp dumplings, egg
custard tartlets) and the creative (scallion-skewered prawns tied with
bacon, lobster and *tobiko* roe dumplings, basil seafood dumplings).
The Shanghai soup dumplings are a classic—and some of the best in the
city. The carts will keep whirring up to your table, and the tab can rise
quickly, so diners should pace themselves. A take-out counter makes a
meal on the run a satisfying and penny-wise compromise when office
duties—or touring—won't wait. ⑤ *Average main: $16* ✉ *49 Stevenson
St.* ☎ *415/541–4949* ⊕ *www.yanksing.com* ⊘ *No dinner* ✛ *F4.*

RUSSIAN HILL

$$ ✕**Zarzuela.** Full-blooded Spaniards swear by the paella at this tiny
TAPAS old-world-style bistro with matador art on the wall not far from the
crookedest street in the world (Lombard). Also not to be missed is the
homemade Sangria, the goat cheese baked in tomato sauce, and poached
octopus prepared by chef Lucas Gasco who grew up in Madrid. Opened
in 1994, Zarzuela may well have been one of the first tapas restaurants
in the Bay Area, and today offers about 30 small plates, as well as a
selection of heartier dishes, like a Catalan seafood stew. Arched win-
dows overlook Hyde Street and the cable cars rolling by. Riding the
Powell–Hyde line to and from dinner adds to the romance of the eve-
ning (plus parking is a nightmare). ⑤ *Average main: $21* ⊠ *2000 Hyde
St.* ☎ *415/346–0800* ⌣ *Reservations not accepted* ⊘ *Closed Sun. and
Mon. No lunch* ✛ *D2.*

VAN NESS/POLK

$$$$ ✕**Acquerello.** For years, devotees of chef-owner Suzette Gresham-
ITALIAN Tognetti's high-end but soulful Italian cooking have been swooning
Fodor's Choice over her incomparable Parmesan *budino* (pudding) as well as the ridged
★ pasta with foie gras and truffles. The latter dish, even with the recent
California ban on foie gras, is still a favorite—Tognetti's chef de cuisine
Mark Pensa has created a faux foie that is a dead ringer. Classics pep-
per the menu but there are also some cutting-edge touches, techniques,
and flavors. Dinners are prix-fixe, with three ($75), four ($90), or five
($105) courses and at least six choices within each course. Tognetti also
tempts with a seasonal eight-course tasting menu ($135). The cheese
course is not to be missed, with rare cheeses from Piemonte, and other
regions, rolled tableside. Co-owner Giancarlo Paterlini (and his son,
Gianpaolo) oversee the service and the roughly 1,900-bottle list of Ital-
ian wines. The room, in a former chapel, with gorgeous wooden vaulted
ceiling and terra-cotta and pale-ocher palette, is refined but never
stuffy—and neither is the service. Every member of the dining staff is
honest and welcoming, knowing that many people here are celebrating
special occasions. They will make it a night to be remembered. This is
a true San Francisco dining gem that is worth every penny. ⑤ *Average
main: $75* ⊠ *1722 Sacramento St., Van Ness/Polk* ☎ *415/567–5432*
⊕ *www.acquerello.com* ⌣ *Reservations essential* ⊘ *Closed Sun. and
Mon. No lunch* ✛ *C3.*

$$ ✕**Swan Oyster Depot.** Half fish market and half diner, this small, slim,
SEAFOOD family-run seafood operation, open since 1912, has no tables, just a
Fodor's Choice narrow marble counter with about a dozen-and-a-half stools. Most
★ people come in to buy perfectly fresh salmon, halibut, crabs, and other
seafood to take home. Everyone else hops onto one of the rickety stools
to enjoy a bowl of clam chowder—the only hot food served—a dozen
oysters, half a cracked crab, a slice of crusty sourdough, a big shrimp
salad, or a smaller shrimp cocktail. And it's all served up with a side of
big personality from the jovial folks behind the counter who make you
feel like a regular. Come early or late to avoid a long wait. And since
this place is notoriously cash only (and seafood is not exactly cheap!), be

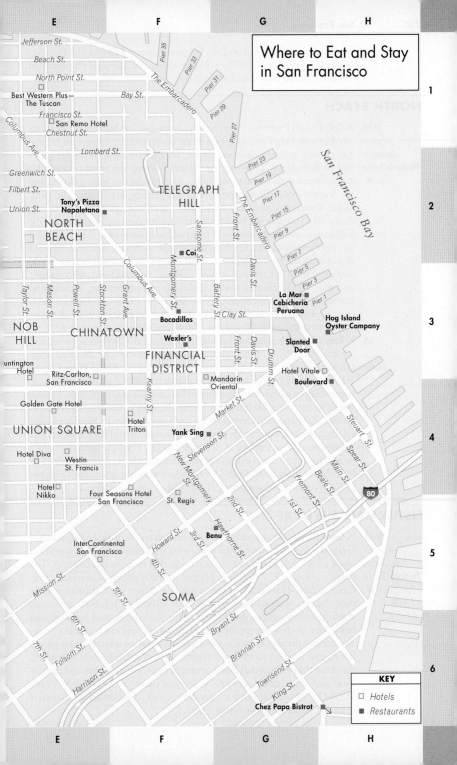

Where to Eat and Stay in San Francisco

E   F   G   H

Jefferson St.
Beach St.
North Point St.
Best Western Plus—
The Tuscan
Francisco St.
San Remo Hotel
Chestnut St.
Lombard St.
Greenwich St.
Filbert St.
Union St.
Tony's Pizza
Napoletana
NORTH
BEACH
Columbus Ave.
Bay St.
The Embarcadero
Pier 35
Pier 33
Pier 31
Pier 29
Pier 27

TELEGRAPH
HILL
Sansome St.
Coi
Montgomery St.

Pier 23
Pier 19
Pier 17
Pier 15
Pier 9
Pier 7
Pier 5
Pier 3
Pier 1

San Francisco Bay

The Embarcadero
Front St.
Davis St.

Taylor St.
Mason St.
Powell St.
Stockton St.
Grant Ave.
Columbus Ave.

NOB
HILL
CHINATOWN
Bocadillos
Wexler's
FINANCIAL
DISTRICT
Battery St.
Clay St.
Front St.
Davis St.
Drumm St.

La Mar
Cebicheria
Peruana
Pier 1
Hog Island
Oyster Company
Slanted
Door
Hotel Vitale
Boulevard

Huntington
Hotel
Ritz-Carlton,
San Francisco
Golden Gate Hotel
UNION SQUARE
Hotel Diva
Westin
St. Francis
Hotel
Nikko
Four Seasons Hotel
San Francisco
St. Regis
Kearny St.
Hotel
Triton
Yank Sing
New Montgomery St.
Stevenson St.
Market St.
2nd St.
Hawthorne St.
Howard St.
3rd St.
Benu
InterContinental
San Francisco
SOMA
4th St.
5th St.
6th St.
7th St.
Folsom St.
Harrison St.
Mission St.
Bryant St.
Brannan St.
Townsend St.
King St.
Chez Papa Bistrot

Steuart St.
Spear St.
Main St.
Beale St.
Fremont St.
1st St.
80

1
2
3
4
5
6

KEY
□ Hotels
■ Restaurants

E   F   G   H

sure to come with a full wallet. $\boxed{\$}$ *Average main: $18* ✉ *1517 Polk St., Nob Hill* ☎ *415/673–1101* 🍴 *Reservations not accepted* 🚫 *No credit cards* 🕐 *Closed Sun. No dinner* ✛ *D3.*

NORTH BEACH

$$$$
MODERN
AMERICAN
Fodor'sChoice
★

✗**Coi.** Daniel Patterson, who has made a name for himself internationally both as a chef and as a pundit on contemporary restaurant trends, has created a destination restaurant, an enchanting spot on the gritty end of Broadway. There are two dining rooms: the front room, a bit more casual with rustic wood tables and banquettes with pillows, and the 30-seat formal dining room, with soft lighting, luxe linens, and gold-taupe banquettes along the two walls. On offer is an 11-course tasting menu ($165), full of the bounty of Bay Area produce and ingredients. The highly seasonal and obsessively sourced food (some of it is even foraged by chef Patterson) matches the space in sophistication, with such inspired dishes as Dungeness crab raviolo with sheep sorrel and butter crab broth; and aged duck breast with stuffed cabbage, roasted beets, horseradish, and dill. The kitchen is always tinkering and innovating, brining and curing, so the menu feels like a new and often exciting culinary experience. $\boxed{\$}$ *Average main: $165* ✉ *373 Broadway* ☎ *415/393–9000* 🌐 *www.coirestaurant.com* 🕐 *Closed Sun., Mon. and Tues. No lunch* ✛ *F2.*

$$
PIZZA
FAMILY

✗**Tony's Pizza Napoletana.** Locals hotly debate the city's best pizza, and for many this North Beach pizzeria occupies the top spot. Pizzaioli Tony Gemignani won World Champion Pizza Maker at World Pizza Cup in Naples, beating out the Italians. The dough is flavorful and fired just right, with multiple wood-burning ovens in his casual, modern pizzeria turning out different styles, like the famed Neapolitan-style Margherita as well as Sicilian, Romana, and Detroit styles, and even coal-fired. Other items, like salads, antipasti, homemade pastas, and calzone, round out the menu. His counter next door lets you grab a slice quickly. Try a pie here, and you'll be able to stake a claim in the ongoing pizza dispute. $\boxed{\$}$ *Average main: $15* ✉ *1570 Stockton St.* ☎ *415/835-9888* 🌐 *www.tonyspizzanapoletana.com* 🍴 *Reservations not accepted* 🕐 *Closed Mon. and Tues.* ✛ *E2.*

FISHERMAN'S WHARF

$$$$
MODERN
AMERICAN
Fodor'sChoice
★

✗**Gary Danko.** Be prepared to wait your turn for a table behind chef Gary Danko's legion of loyal fans, who typically keep the reservation book chock-full here (plan on reserving two months in advance). The cost of a meal ($73–$107) is pegged to the number of courses, from three to five. The decadent menu spans a classic yet Californian style that changes seasonally; it may include risotto with lobster and rock shrimp, lemon pepper duck breast with duck hash, and herb-crusted lamb loin. A diet-destroying chocolate soufflé with two sauces is usually among the desserts. The wine list is the size of a small-town phone book, and the banquette-lined rooms, with beautiful wood floors and stunning (but restrained) floral arrangements, are as memorable as the food and impeccable service. $\boxed{\$}$ *Average main: $73* ✉ *800 N. Point St.* ☎ *415/749-2060* 🌐 *www.garydanko.com* 🍴 *Reservations essential* 👔 *Jacket required* 🕐 *No lunch* ✛ *D1.*

Eating with Kids

Kids can be fussy eaters, and parents can be, too. Fortunately, there are plenty of excellent options in the city that will satisfy both.

✕ **City View Restaurant.** Nearby in Chinatown, City View Restaurant serves a varied selection of dim sum, with tasty pork buns for kids and more-exotic fare for adults. $ *Average main: $1* ⊠ *662 Commercial St., near Kearny St.* ☎ *415/398–2838.*

The Ferry Building on the Embarcadero has plenty of kid-friendly options, from **Mijita Cocina Mexicana,** which has its own kids' menu, to **Gott's Roadside,** for burgers, shakes, and more. (And the outdoor access can help keep the little ones entertained.)

✕ **La Corneta.** The Mission has dozens of no-frills taco-and-burrito parlors; especially worthy is bustling La Corneta, which has a baby burrito

and well-made quesadillas. $ *Average main: $1* ⊠ *2731 Mission St., between 23rd and 24th Sts.* ☎ *415/643–7001.*

Rosamunde Sausage Grill. In Lower Haight, the small Rosamunde Sausage Grill serves just that—a slew of different sausages, from Polish to duck to *Weisswurst* (Bavarian veal). You get your choice of two toppings, like grilled onions, sauerkraut, and chili, and since there are only six stools, plan on take-out. ■ **TIP→** Head to nearby Duboce Park, with its cute playground. ⊠ *545 Haight St., between Steiner and Fillmore Sts.* ☎ *415/437–6851.*

Park Chalet. Finally, both kids and adults love to be by the ocean, and the Park Chalet, hidden behind the two-story Beach Chalet, offers pizza, mac and cheese, sticky ribs, and a big banana split. ⊠ *1000 Great Hwy., at Fulton St.* ☎ *415/386–8439.*

4

EMBARCADERO

$$$$
AMERICAN
Fodor's Choice
★

✕ **Boulevard.** Two of San Francisco's top restaurant celebrities—chef Nancy Oakes and designer Pat Kuleto—are responsible for this high-profile, high-priced eatery in the magnificent 1889 Audiffred Building, a Parisian look-alike and one of the few downtown structures to survive the 1906 earthquake. Kuleto's Belle-Époque interior and Oakes's sophisticated-American-food-with-a-French-accent attract well-dressed locals and flush out-of-towners. The menu changes seasonally, but count on standout appetizers and generous portions of dishes like Maine lobster ravioli, grilled king salmon with wild rice and vegetables that include chanterelle mushrooms, and a wood-grilled pork prime rib chop with Kabocha squash gnocchi (all the entrées come with delicious side dishes). Save room (and calories) for one of the dynamite desserts, such as dark chocolate brioche custard. There's counter seating for folks too hungry to wait for a table, and an American Wagyu beef burger with Cowgirl Creamery cheese at lunchtime that lets you eat with the swells without raiding your piggy bank. The well-chosen wine list and excellent service are also hallmarks here. $ *Average main: $36* ⊠ *1 Mission St.* ☎ *415/543–6084* ⊕ *www.boulevardrestaurant.com* ⊰ *Reservations essential* ☾ *No lunch weekends* ✛ *H4.*

$$ ╳ **Hog Island Oyster Company.** Hog Island, a thriving oyster farm in Tomales
SEAFOOD Bay, north of San Francisco, serves up its harvest at this attractive raw bar
and retail shop in the busy Ferry Building. The U-shape counter and a
handful of tables seat no more than three dozen diners, who come here for
impeccably fresh oysters (from Hog Island and elsewhere) or clams (from
Hog Island) on the half shell. Other mollusk-centered options include a
first-rate oyster stew, baked oysters, clam chowder, and "steamer" clams
with Israeli couscous. The bar also turns out what is arguably one of the
city's best grilled-cheese sandwiches (with three artisanal cheeses on arti-
sanal bread) this side of Wisconsin. You need to eat early, however, as the
bar closes at 8 on weekdays and 6 on weekends. Happy hour, 5 to 7 on
Monday and Thursday, is an oyster lover's dream and jam-packed: chef's
choice of half-priced oysters and a pint of beer for $4. ⑤ *Average main:
$20 ⊠ Ferry Bldg., Embarcadero at Market St.* ☎ *415/391–7117* ⊕ *www.
hogislandoysters.com* ⌲ *Reservations not accepted* ⊹ *H3.*

$$$ ╳ **La Mar Cebicheria Peruana.** Set right on the water's edge, this casually
PERUVIAN chic restaurant is divided into three areas: a lounge with a long ceviche
bar where diners watch chefs put together their plates; the savvy Pisco
Bar facing the Embarcadero, where bartenders make a dozen different
cocktails based on Peru's famed Pisco brandy; and a bright blue and
whitewashed dining room overlooking an outdoor patio and the bay.
Your waiter will start you out with a pile of potato and plantain chips
with three dipping sauces, but then you're on your own, choosing from
a long list of ceviches, can't-miss *causas* (whipped potatoes topped
with a choice of fish, shellfish, or vegetable salads), and everything
from crisp, lightly deep-fried fish and shellfish to soups and stews and
rice dishes, many spiked with Peruvian chilis. The original La Mar is
in Lima, Peru. San Francisco was the first stop in its campaign to open
a string of cebicherias across the United States and Latin America. The
view of the water is especially enjoyable during lunch or a warm evening. ⑤ *Average main: $25 ⊠ Pier 1½ between Washington and Jackson
Sts.* ☎ *415/397–8880* ⊕ *www.lamarcebicheria.com* ⊹ *G3.*

$$$ ╳ **Slanted Door.** If you're looking for homey Vietnamese food served in
VIETNAMESE a down-to-earth dining room at a decent price, *don't* stop here. Cel-
ebrated chef-owner Charles Phan has mastered the upmarket, Western-
accented Vietnamese menu. To showcase his cuisine, he built a big space
with sleek wooden tables and chairs, white marble floors, a cocktail
lounge, a bar, and an enviable bay view. Among his popular cult dishes
are green-papaya salad, daikon rice cakes, cellophane crab noodles,
chicken clay pot, and shaking beef (tender beef cubes with garlic and
onion)—and they don't come cheap, although the dishes are made with
quality ingredients. The restaurant has also become a regular stop for
those who appreciate finely made cocktails, many of them created by
star bartender Erik Adkins. To avoid the midday and evening crowds
(and to save some bucks), stop in for the afternoon-tea menu, dine at the
bar, or visit Out the Door, Phan's take-out counter around the corner.
Phan also has another more-reasonably priced Vietnamese restaurant
in the city: Heaven's Dog in the Civic Center neighborhood. ⑤ *Average
main: $29 ⊠ Ferry Bldg., Embarcadero at Market St.* ☎ *415/861–8032*
⊕ *www.slanteddoor.com* ⌲ *Reservations essential* ⊹ *H3.*

MARINA

$$$
ITALIAN

✕A16. Marina residents—and, judging from the crowds, everybody else—gravitate to this lively trattoria, named for the autostrada that winds through Italy's sunny south. The kitchen serves the food of Naples and surrounding Campania, with a twist of seasonal California ingredients. Cult classics on the menu include creamy burrata with olive oil and crostini and crisp-crust pizzas, including a classic Neapolitan Margherita (mozzarella, tomato, and basil). Among the regularly changing pastas are rustic favorites like *maccaronara* with *ragu napoletana* and house-made ricotta salata, and dishes like petrale sole with Monterey squid, sunchokes, and grilled lemon with *salmoriglio* (a southern Italian sauce with garlic and herbs). An expertly chosen wine list of primarily southern Italian with some California wines suits the fare perfectly, along with a newly expanded beer list. The long dining room includes an animated bar scene near the door; ask for a table in the quieter alcove at the far end or try for the patio. Reservations are easier to snag midweek. ⑤ *Average main: $24* ⊠ *2355 Chestnut St.* ☎ *415/771–2216* ⊕ *www.a16sf.com* ⩔ *Reservations essential* ⊗ *No lunch Sat.–Tues.* ⊹ *A1.*

COW HOLLOW

$$
ITALIAN
FAMILY

✕Rose's Café. Sleepy-headed locals turn up at Rose's for the breakfast pizza of smoked ham, eggs, and fontina; house-baked pastries and breads; poached eggs with Yukon Gold potato and mushroom hash; or soft polenta with mascarpone and jam. Midday is time for a roasted chicken and fontina sandwich; pizza with wild nettles; or linguine with clams. Evening hours find customers eating their way through more pizza and pasta if they are on a budget, and skirt steak and roasted chicken if they aren't. The ingredients are top-notch, the service is friendly, and the seating is in comfortable booths, at tables, and at a counter. At the outside tables, overhead heaters keep you toasty when the temperature dips. Expect long lines for Sunday brunch. ⑤ *Average main: $22* ⊠ *2298 Union St.* ☎ *415/775–2200* ⊕ *www.rosescafesf.com* ⊹ *A2.*

THE HAIGHT

$$
INDIAN

✕Indian Oven. This white-tablecloth northern Indian restaurant draws diners from all over the city who come for the tandoori specialties—chicken, lamb, breads. Classics like *saag paneer* (spinach with Indian cheese), *aloo gobhi* (potato, cauliflower, and spices), and *bengan bartha* (roasted eggplant with onions and spices) are also excellent. The chef wants to keep his clientele around for the long haul, too, and puts a little "heart healthy" icon next to some of the menu items. On Friday and Saturday nights famished patrons overflow onto the sidewalk as they wait for open tables. If you try to linger over a mango *lassi* or an order of the excellent *kheer* (rice pudding) on one of these nights, you'll probably be hurried along by a waiter. For better service, come on a slower weeknight or for lunch. ⑤ *Average main: $16* ⊠ *233 Fillmore St., Lower Haight* ☎ *415/626–1628* ⊹ *A6.*

$$$
AMERICAN

✕ **Nopa.** In the mid-2000s North of the Panhandle became the city's newest talked-about neighborhood in part because of the big, bustling Nopa, which was cleverly named after it. This casual space, with its high ceilings, concrete floor, long bar, and sea of tables, suits the high-energy crowd of young professionals mixed with stylish neighborhood residents that fill it every night (and since the kitchen doesn't close until 1 am, plenty of restaurant-industry types come in and pack the bar late into the night). Diners come primarily for the rustic fare, like an always winning flat bread topped with fennel sausage and caramelized onions; the vegetable tagine with lemon yogurt; smoky, crisp-skinned rotisserie chicken; a juicy grass-fed hamburger with thick-cut fries; one of the city's best pork chops; and for dessert, the donut-like sopapillas. But they also love the lively spirit of the place. Unfortunately, that buzz sometimes means that raised voices are the only way to communicate with fellow diners. A big communal table and the friendly bar ease the way for anyone dining out on his or her own. Wine lovers are happily satisfied here with the excellent list, and weekend brunch is one of the city's best (and most popular—arrive a few minutes before they open at 11 am to score a table). $ *Average main: $24* ✉ *560 Divisadero St., Western Addition* ☎ *415/864–8643* ⊕ *www.nopasf.com* ☽ *No lunch weekdays* ✛ *A6.*

$$
MEXICAN
Fodor's Choice
★
FAMILY

✕ **Nopalito.** This place is one of the more unusual (and delicious) Mexican restaurants in the city—the two chefs here were originally cooks in the kitchen at Nopa around the corner, and their staff/family meals were so delicious that the Nopa owners were inspired to create this restaurant around their cooking. The menu features authentic recipes prepared skillfully with excellent ingredients, from seasonal salads and a spicy beef empanada to the succulent pork carnitas and a fulfilling posole. All the tortillas are made from an organic house-ground masa (also used in the delicious tortilla chips layering the *chilaquiles* during weekend brunch). And dishes expertly feature so many of Mexico's flavorful peppers like the guajillo, chile de arbol, and pasilla. It's a casual space with a variety of tables, communal seating, and a counter, and quite popular with families yet equally pleasing for adult groups perusing its well-selected tequila list. Expect a substantial wait in the evening—you'll have to leave your name on a list, but you can call before heading over to get your name on the waiting list in advance. There's also a take-out window if you're feeling impatient. Or try a late weekday lunch, like at 2 when it's cleared out. $ *Average main: $15* ✉ *306 Broderick St., Western Addition* ☎ *415/437–0303* ⊕ *www. nopalitosf.com* ✛ *A6.*

THE CASTRO

$$$
FRENCH

✕ **Frances.** One of the hottest tickets in town, Frances is located, ironically, on a sleepy residential street in the Castro. Chef-owner Melissa Perello's menu of California and French cuisine is well executed, balanced, and notably affordable for the high quality. Bacon beignets, tender gnocchi, and a savory bavette steak are becoming favorites on the seasonally driven menu, while new entries like baked clams with bacon cream and a duck confit and kale salad are angling to become stand-bys as well. An apple galette for dessert hits all the right notes. The small space is simply designed and casual, with a limited number of tables (hence the difficulty in landing a reservation). Service here is both very professional and warm, and there's a small bar area for desperate diners who want to try their luck for a walk-in spot at the counter. $ *Average main: $27* ✉ *3870 17th St.* ☎ *415/621-3870* ⊕ *www.frances-sf.com* ⚓ *Reservations essential* ⊘ *Closed Mon. No lunch* ✢ *A6.*

THE MISSION

$$$ ✗ **Bar Tartine.** An offshoot of the cult-like Tartine Bakery, this restaurant
MODERN provides one way you can get a taste of their famed (and always sold-out)
AMERICAN country loaf. It's a definite neighborhood restaurant, drawing an energetic crowd to the artsy space. Chef Nicolaus Balla's flavor-packed menu is all about an Eastern European sensibility with California seasonality and some Japanese influences. It includes an array of house-pickled items, the indulgent *langos* (fried potato bread), seasonal salads like one with persimmons, pressed cheese, chicories, walnuts, and orange honey, pickled housemade sausage, and larger (and homey) dishes like chicken *paprikas* and a fisherman's stew. The extensive wine-and-beer list makes this a fun place to swing by for a glass—if you can find a seat. Weekend brunch is one of the more distinct offerings in the city, with an array of *smørrebrød* (toppings like trumpet mushrooms, mizuna, and cultured butter on sprouted rye) and buckwheat blintzes, and a beef-brisket hash with celery root, parsnip, Yukon Gold potatoes, and fried eggs. The restaurant also operates a sandwich shop Wednesday, Thursday, and Friday afternoons, serving up sandwiches, *smørrebrød*, and light snacks. $ *Average main: $25* ✉ *561 Valencia St.* ☎ *415/487-1600* ⊕ *www.bartartine.com* ⊘ *Closed Mon. No lunch Tues* ✢ *B6.*

$$$ ✗ **Central Kitchen.** It's nearly impossible to score seats at chef Thomas
MODERN McNaughton's highly lauded Flour + Water. That's why many had plum
AMERICAN visions of eating his food again when the Gary Danko alumnus opened
Fodor's Choice his latest spot in a former sausage factory. Central Kitchen is the center-
★ piece in a modern open space, with tea lights strung along the ceiling; also in the building is Salumeria (a deli and larder, which sells Flour + Water pastas) and Trick Dog, an energetic cocktail bar. The menu is original, with playful combos and surprising flavors: Parker House rolls baked with coffee and caraway; raw Hamachi topped with fennel (from the rooftop garden) roasted till it's ash, for a strong smokiness that combines with citruses into a vinaigrette; an inky cioppino, with burnt peppers as its base, making the broth luscious. There are about four main-dish items nightly (plus starters). For the ultimate food journey, the seven-course tasting menu is the way to go ($89). $ *Average main: $25* ✉ *3000 20th St.* ☎ *415/826-7004* ⊕ *www.centralkitchensf. com* ⊘ *No lunch Mon.–Sat* ✢ *D6.*

$$$ ✗ **Delfina.** "Irresistible." That's how countless die-hard fans describe
ITALIAN Craig and Anne Stoll's Delfina. Such wild enthusiasm has made patience
Fodor's Choice the critical virtue for anyone wanting a reservation here (although walk-
★ ins can find some success at a counter and in the bar area). The urban interior is comfortable, with hardwood floors, aluminum-top tables, and a tile bar. Although the menu changes daily, among the usual

offerings are grilled squid with warm white-bean salad and excellent tripe. As boring as spaghetti with tomato sauce may sound, it's been dialed to perfection here, and there would be a neighborhood revolt if it ever disappeared. If Piemontese fresh white truffles have made their way to San Francisco, you are likely to find hand-cut tagliarini dressed with butter, cream, and the pricey aromatic fungus on the menu alongside dishes built on more-prosaic ingredients. The panna cotta is the best in its class. The storefront next door is home to pint-size Pizzeria Delfina. And for folks who can't get to the Mission, the Stolls have opened a second pizzeria on California Street in lively Lower Pacific Heights. ⑤ *Average main: $25 ⊠ 3621 18th St. ☎ 415/552–4055 ⊕ www.delfinasf. com ⚐ Reservations essential ⊘ No lunch ✛ B6.*

$$
INDIAN
Fodor's Choice
★

✕ **Dosa on Valencia.** Like Indian food but crave more than chicken tikka masala and naan? Dosa is your answer. This temple of South Indian cuisine, done in cheerful tones of tangerine and turmeric, serves not only the large, thin savory pancake for which it is named, but also curries, *uttapam* (open-face pancakes), and various starters, breads, rice dishes, and chutneys. You can select from about 10 different dosa fillings, ranging from traditional potatoes, onions, and cashews to spinach and fennel stems. Each comes with tomato and fresh coconut chutneys and *sambar* (lentil curry) for dipping. Tamil lamb curry with fennel and tomatoes and poppy seed prawns are popular, as are starters like Chennai chicken (chicken marinated in yogurt and spices and lightly fried), and the new Indian street-food additions, like *vada pav* (a vegetarian slider). The wine and beer lists are top drawer, and both include some Indian labels; the cocktail list is also very food friendly. Weekend brunch offers a nice change from the usual brunch suspects (the flavorful *pani puri* are a must). Queues for this Mission District spot convinced the owners to open a second, splashier branch on the corner of Fillmore and Post in Japantown. ⑤ *Average main: $18 ⊠ 995 Valencia St., at 21st St. ☎ 415/642–3672 ⊕ www.dosasf.com ⊘ No lunch weekdays ✛ B6.*

$$
ITALIAN

✕ **Flour + Water.** It used to be that people flooded the gates of this hot spot for the blistery thin-crust Neapolitan pizza, but these days it's the pasta that holds court, merging beautifully with chef Thomas McNaughton's whole animal sensibilities. A grand experience is the 7-course pasta-tasting menu at $65 per person (plus $45 for wine pairings). The homemade mustard tagliatelle with smoked lamb's tongue is surprisingly zippy with lemon zest lifting and extracting flavors. The perfectly chewy rigatoni comes with a braised-pork-laced tomato sauce. Pizzas are still being pulled from the 900-degree wood burning oven, but they aren't what they used to be. The dining room was designed by whimsical Paxton Gate, with their touches felt throughout, like table-top beakers for candle holders, a moth-wing wall mural, and a cabinet of taxidermy in the bathroom. Expect a noisy, boisterous scene. Tables are jockeyed over here and getting a reservation is one of the longest-running jokes in town. (Walk-ins are ecstatic to nab a seat at the reclaimed wood bar, made from wine-barrel staves). Best bet is to come when the doors open. ⑤ *Average main: $20 ⊠ 2401 Harrison St. ☎ 415/826-7000 ⊕ www.flourandwater.com ⊘ No lunch ✛ D6.*

$$$ ✕ **Local's Corner.** Hang on, because chef Jake Des Voignes is about take
MODERN you on a seafood joyride. With no industrial ovens or high-powered
AMERICAN burners, this 30-seat place is really about the delicate, natural flavors
of California's seasonal bounty, from the fish to the fennel, Japanese
yams, and sunchokes. In typical San Francisco style, the menu reads
like a jumble of ingredients, making it difficult to imagine how they
might taste together, but each dish works beautifully, like creamy uni
with crunchy English peas and preserved Meyer lemon, or a cured
halibut with diced, sweet pluots. To get acquainted with Des Voignes'
skill, reserve at the chef's counter for the seven-course tasting ($65).
The three-course brunches are as well-crafted as dinner, featuring
waffles with chicory syrup or chicken sausage and polenta. Although
the food is solid, service is too casual. $ *Average main: $25* ✉ *2500
Bryant St.* ☎ *415/800–7945* ⊕ *www.localscornersf.com* ⊗ *Closed
Mon.* ✛ *C6.*

$$$ ✕ **Locanda.** The owners of Delfina, Annie and Craig Stoll, have given
ITALIAN the city another culinary gift. This time her name is Locanda; and
the menu is Roman-inspired. A dangerously addictive starter is *pizza
bianca*: chewy, hot bread that holds mini puddles of olive oil and is
sprinkled with sea salt. It's hard to decide on a pasta with so many
represented on the menu. One of the signature pastas, *tonnarelli cacio
e pepe*, is a creamy, peppery smack of flavor. But the best route is
doubling down on pastas and antipasti, then sharing a main, like
the lamb *scottadito*, seasoned with anchovies and coriander. Finely
made cocktails (Negroni flights even) arrive at dark-wood tables on
a candlelit tray, and white Heath wall tiles pump up the sophisticated
interior. It's a busy place with bar stools occupied steadily, and the
communal table filling quickly to get a taste of this Italian-accented
cuisine. $ *Average main: $28* ✉ *557 Valencia St.* ☎ *415/863–6800*
⊕ *www.locandasf.com* ⊗ *No lunch* ✛ *B6.*

$ ✕ **SanJalisco.** This old-time, sun-filled, colorful, family-run restaurant
MEXICAN is a neighborhood gem (and that's not just because it serves breakfast
FAMILY all day). Try the hearty *chilaquiles,* made from day-old tortillas cut
into strips and cooked with cheese, eggs, chilis, and sauce. Or order
eggs scrambled with cactus or with *chicharrones* (crisp pork skins) and
served with freshly made tortillas. Soup offerings change daily, with
Tuesday's *albondigas* (meatballs) comfort food at its best. On weekends,
adventurous eaters may opt for *birria,* a spicy goat stew, or *menudo,* a
tongue-searing soup made from tripe, calf's foot, and hominy. The latter
is a time-honored hangover cure—but don't come expecting margaritas
here (although you will find beer and sangria). Bring plenty of change
for the jukebox loaded with Latin hits. $ *Average main: $11* ✉ *901 S.
Van Ness Ave.* ☎ *415/648–8383* ✛ *C6.*

$$$ ✕ **St. Vincent.** Sommelier David Lynch is the man behind this modern-
MODERN day American tavern with a Bay Area spin. Previously at Babbo in
AMERICAN New York and Quince in San Francisco, Lynch has put together a wine
list that is mostly European selections, with an innovative half-bottle
program, while chef Bill Niles (formerly of Bar Tartine) creates rustic
upscale food as its companion. On the snacky side of things, we chal-
lenge you to eat just *one* curried, pickled egg. They are outrageously

good, as is the hand-rolled pretzel; the dry-aged sirloin for two comes with some of the best gratin potatoes known to man. This is lick-your-plate-clean food in a welcoming, somewhat noisy atmosphere (wood surfaces, soaring ceilings) where Lynch himself will suggest a wine, or cicerone Sayre Piotrkowski will pair a beer with dinner or dessert. Winning seats are at the zinc-topped bar, where you can bend the ear of both men. They also do a wine retail business. ⑤ *Average main: $27* ⊠ *1270 Valencia St.* ☎ *415/285–1200* ⊕ *www.stvincentsf.com* ⊗ *Closed Sun. No lunch* ✛ *B6.*

POTRERO HILL

$$$ ✕ **Chez Papa Bistrot.** France arrived on Potrero Hill with this restaurant,
FRENCH which delivers food, waiters, and charm that would be right at home in Provence. The modest corner restaurant, with a Mediterranean blue awning, big windows overlooking the street, and a small heated patio, caters to a lively crowd that can make conversation difficult. Small plates include bistro classics like mussels in pastis, beef tartare, and a leek and tomato tart. Big plates range from duck confit, to grilled flat-iron steak and frites, to homey lamb daube. The lavender crème brûlée or chocolate fondant provides a sweet ending. The $34.95 prix-fixe (Sun.–Thurs.) is also a good deal for the penny-wise. To accommodate the overflow of Hill residents who have packed this place since day one, the owners opened the tiny (and more casual) Chez Maman (crepes, burgers, salads) a few doors down the block. ⑤ *Average main: $24* ⊠ *1401 18th St.* ☎ *415/824–8205* ⊕ *www.chezpapasf.com* ⊗ *No lunch Sun.* ✛ *H6.*

PACIFIC HEIGHTS

$$$$ ✕ **Spruce.** One of the hottest reservations in town from the day it opened,
MODERN Spruce caters to the city's social set, with the older crowd sliding into
AMERICAN oversized faux ostrich leather chairs in the early hours and the younger set taking their places after 8 (there's also quite the lunch club during the week). The large space, a former 1930s auto barn, shelters a high-style dining room and a more casual bar and library lounge. Charcuterie, bavette steak with bordelaise sauce and duck-fat potatoes, and sweetbreads reflect the French slant of the modern American menu. The wine list is a star here (especially a delight for Riesling fans). If you can't wrangle a table, stop in at the take-out café next door, which carries not only sandwiches, salads, and pastries (like the exquisite palmiers), but also anything from the dining room menu to go. And if you are watching your pocketbook, you can graze off the bar menu (which includes their excellent burger and *boudin blanc*) and watch the swells come and go over a well-crafted cocktail. ⑤ *Average main: $34* ⊠ *3640 Sacramento St.* ☎ *415/931–5100* ⊕ *www.sprucesf.com* ⌕ *Reservations essential* ⊗ *No lunch weekends* ✛ *A3.*

JAPANTOWN

$$
INDIAN
Fodor's Choice
★

X **Dosa on Fillmore.** As soon as the large door swings open to this happening two-level space, diners are greeted with a sexy atmosphere with bright colors, vivid artwork, upbeat music, a lively bar scene, and the smell of spices in the air. This is the second location of the popular Dosa on Valencia, but it's definitely the glamorous younger sister, with a full bar, an expanded menu, and much more room. The menu entices with savory fish dishes, fall-off-the-bone pepper chicken, and papery dosas stuffed with a variety of fillings. The restaurant handles group dining often, and has a special menu you can customize. Return for lunch and indulge in the Indian street-food selections, and the famed *pani puri* (little crisp puffs you fill with mint and tamarind water and pop all at once into your mouth). $ *Average main: $17* ⊠ *1700 Fillmore St.* ☎ *415/441–3672* ⊕ *www.dosasf.com* ⊘ *No lunch Mon. and Tues.* ✛ *A4.*

$
JAPANESE
FAMILY

X **Mifune.** Thin brown soba and thick white udon are the stars at this long-popular North American outpost of an Osaka-based noodle empire. A line regularly snakes out the door, but the house-made noodles, served both hot and cold and with a score of toppings, are worth the wait (and the line moves quickly). Seating is at wooden tables, where diners of every age can be heard slurping down big bowls of such traditional Japanese combinations as *nabeyaki udon,* wheat noodles topped with tempura, chicken, and fish cake; and *tenzaru,* cold noodles and hot tempura with gingery dipping sauce served on lacquered trays. The noodle-phobic can choose from a few rice dishes and sushi. $ *Average main: $12* ⊠ *Japan Center, Kintetsu Bldg., 1737 Post St.* ☎ *415/922–0337* ⊕ *www.mifune.com* ✛ *B4.*

$$$
MODERN
AMERICAN

X **State Bird Provisions.** Eating at this tiny 14-table spot can be described as a festive parade of hors d'oeuvre, with bite-sized "provisions" rolled around on carts and diners picking what they want. Prices for provisions, ranging from $3 to $8, are displayed on placards and tallied up as the dinner unfolds. Those who eat with their eyes, and not their stomachs, should be cautious. This is dim-sum format, only rather than dumplings, it's half-dollar sized thick savory pancakes stuffed with sauerkraut; giant nori chips topped with Hamachi, radishes, and avocados; or kimchee yuba noodles with housemade egg bottarga. Each night roughly a dozen provisions are offered, along with commandables (larger dishes, including the state bird, quail, batter-dipped), and desserts. The colorful, airy dining room with pegboard walls has a high school art-room vibe, decorated as it is with string art and folksy wooden cutouts shaped like food. The staff is superfriendly. Because it's currently the most-sought-after reservation in the city, the wait can be onerous (but the host will take your number, recommend a nearby wine bar, and call when a table is ready). $ *Average main: $30* ⊠ *1529 Fillmore St., Western Addition* ☎ *415/795–1272* ⊕ *www.statebirdsf. com* ⊘ *Closed Sun. No lunch.* ✛ *A4.*

4

RICHMOND

$ ✕ **Burma Superstar.** Locals make the trek to the "Avenues" for the
ASIAN   extraordinary tea-leaf salad, a combo of spicy, salty, crunchy, and sour
that is mixed table-side, with fermented tea leaves from Burma, fried
garlic, and peanuts. Another hit is the hearty vegetarian *samusa* soup.
Forget having to decide between Thai, Indian, or Chinese. Burmese
fuses flavors and techniques from all these (mostly) bordering countries.
The modestly decorated, no-reservations restaurant is small so lines
can be long during peak times. Leave your number and wait for the
call, or walk a couple blocks east to B-Star, owned by the same people
but lesser known and often less crowded. $ *Average main: $14* ✉ *309
Clement St.* ☎ *415/387–2147* ⊕ *www.burmasuperstar.com* ⌕ *Reservations not accepted* ✛ *A4.*

WHERE TO STAY

Updated by   Hotels here are more than hotels: they are a part of the cityscape,
Michele Bigley   some as old as the city itself, beloved by visitors and locals alike. Like
its neighborhoods, San Francisco's accommodations are diverse, from
cozy inns and kitschy motels, to chic boutiques and true grande dames.

*Prices in the reviews are the lowest cost of a standard double room in
high season.*

*Use the coordinate (✛ A1) at the end of each listing to locate a site on
the corresponding map.*

UNION SQUARE

For expanded hotel reviews, visit Fodors.com.

$ ⊞ **Golden Gate Hotel.** Budget seekers looking for accommodations in
B&B/INN   the Union Square area will delight in this homey, family-run B&B.
Fodor's Choice   **Pros:** friendly staff; free Wi-Fi; spotless rooms; comfortable bedding;
★   good location if you're a walker. **Cons:** only some of the rooms have
FAMILY   private baths. $ *Rooms from: $115* ✉ *775 Bush St.* ☎ *415/392–3702,
800/835–1118* ⊕ *www.goldengatehotel.com* ⇌ *25 rooms, 14 with bath*
†⊙| *Breakfast* ✛ *E4.*

$$$ ⊞ **Hotel Diva.** Entering this hotel requires stepping over footprints,
HOTEL   handprints, and autographs embedded in the sidewalk by visiting
Fodor's Choice   stars; with two major theaters, the Curran and the American Conser-
★   vatory Theater, just across the street, this hotel has long been a magnet
FAMILY   for actors, musicians, writers, and artists. **Pros:** punchy design; in the
heart of the theater district; accommodating service. **Cons:** no frills;
tiny bathrooms. $ *Rooms from: $249* ✉ *440 Geary St.* ☎ *415/885–
0200, 800/553–1900* ⊕ *www.hoteldiva.com* ⇌ *115 rooms, 3 suites*
†⊙| *No meals* ✛ *E4.*

$$$$ ⊞ **Hotel Nikko, San Francisco.** The vast surfaces of gray-flecked white
HOTEL   marble that dominate the neoclassical lobby of this hotel have the
Fodor's Choice   starkness of an airport; however, the crisply designed rooms in muted
★   tones, with flat-screen TVs, modern (and newly renovated) bathrooms
FAMILY   with sinks that sit on top of granite bases, plus separate showers

and tubs, please the business-traveler clientele. **Pros:** friendly multi-lingual staff; tastefully designed rooms; large indoor pool; very clean. **Cons:** antiseptic lobby lacks color; some may find the atmosphere cold; expensive parking. ⑤ *Rooms from: $375* ✉ *222 Mason St.* ☎ *415/394–1111, 800/248–3308* ⊕ *www.hotelnikkosf.com* ⚓ *510 rooms, 22 suites* ◎ *No meals* ✛ *E4.*

$$ ⚏ **Hotel Triton.** A spirit of fun has taken up full-time residence in this
HOTEL Kimpton property, which has a youngish, superfriendly staff; pink-
Fodor'sChoice and-blue-neon elevators; and a colorful psychedelic lobby mural
★ depicting the San Francisco art and music scene—think flower power mixed with Andy Warhol. **Pros:** attentive service; refreshingly funky atmosphere; hip arty environs; good location. **Cons:** rooms and baths are on the small side. ⑤ *Rooms from: $189* ✉ *342 Grant Ave.* ☎ *415/394–0500, 800-800-1299* ⊕ *www.hoteltriton.com* ⚓ *133 rooms, 7 suites* ◎ *No meals* ✛ *F4.*

$$$$ ⚏ **Westin St. Francis.** If you love Hollywood lore, Westin St. Francis is
HOTEL the site of many sensational, headline-making scandals (This is where Sara Jane Moore tried to assassinate President Gerald Ford and where singer Al Jolson died playing poker—not to mention the tempest that erupted after a party hosted by Jazz Age comedian Fatty Arbuckle that ended in the death of an aspiring actress); Hollywood fan or not, everyone can appreciate the panache of this grand dame property. **Pros:** fantastic beds; prime location; spacious rooms, some with great views. **Cons:** some guests comment on the long wait at check-in; rooms in original building can be small; glass elevators are not for the faint of heart. ⑤ *Rooms from: $299* ✉ *335 Powell St.* ☎ *415/397–7000, 800/917–7458* ⊕ *www.westinstfrancis.com* ⚓ *1,157 rooms, 38 suites* ◎ *No meals* ✛ *E4.*

SOMA

$$$$ ⚏ **Four Seasons Hotel San Francisco.** Occupying floors 5 through 17 of a
HOTEL skyscraper, this exclusive, award-winning hotel is sandwiched between
Fodor'sChoice multimillion-dollar condos, elite shops, and a premier sports-and-fit-
★ ness complex. **Pros:** near museums, galleries, restaurants, shopping, and clubs; terrific fitness facilities; luxurious rooms and amenities. **Cons:** pricey; staff can be uppity. ⑤ *Rooms from: $395* ✉ *757 Market St.* ☎ *415/633–3000, 800/332–3442, 800/819–5053* ⊕ *www.fourseasons. com/sanfrancisco* ⚓ *231 rooms, 46 suites* ◎ *No meals* ✛ *F4.*

$$$$ ⚏ **InterContinental San Francisco.** The arctic-blue glass exterior and sub-
HOTEL dued, Zen-like lobby of this sparkling hotel may be as bland as an airport concourse, but they're merely a prelude to the spectacularly light, expansive, thoughtfully laid-out guest rooms, which have all the ultramodern conveniences. **Pros:** a stone's throw from the Moscone Center; well-equipped gym; near hip clubs and edgy eateries. **Cons:** conservative decor is a bit short on character; borders a rough neighborhood; a few blocks off from many major points of interest for tourists. ⑤ *Rooms from: $289* ✉ *888 Howard St.* ☎ *415/616–6500, 866/781–2364* ⊕ *www.intercontinentalsanfrancisco.com* ⚓ *536 rooms, 14 suites* ◎ *No meals* ✛ *E5.*

$$$$ 🖭 **The St. Regis San Francisco.** Though this may be the most luxuri-
HOTEL ous hotel in the city, guests often remark that it's hipper and more
Fodor'sChoice modern than other hotels in the St. Regis chain. **Pros:** tasteful, yet
★ current; lap pool; good location; luxe spa; views. **Cons:** expensive;
some guests report inconsistent service; hallway noise; long waits for
room service and valet parking. $⑤ Rooms from: $585 ⊠ 125 3rd St.
☎ 415/284–4000 ⊕ www.stregis.com/sanfrancisco ⤴ 214 rooms, 46
suites ⦿ No meals ✛ F4._

THE TENDERLOIN

$$$ 🖭 **Phoenix Hotel.** A magnet for the hip at heart and ultracool—Little
HOTEL Richard, Elijah Wood, Sean Lennon, and members of R.E.M. and Pearl
Jam have stayed here—the Phoenix isn't the best choice for those seek-
ing peace and quiet (or anyone put off by the hotel's location, on the
fringes of the sketchy Tenderloin District). **Pros:** boho atmosphere;
cheeky design; popular with musicians; hip new restaurant/bar; free
parking. **Cons:** somewhat seedy location; no elevators; can be loud in
the evenings. $⑤ Rooms from: $249 ⊠ 601 Eddy St. ☎ 415/776–1380,
800/248–9466 ⊕ www.thephoenixhotel.com ⤴ 41 rooms, 3 suites
⦿ Breakfast ✛ D5._

FINANCIAL DISTRICT

$$$$ 🖭 **Mandarin Oriental, San Francisco.** Two towers connected by glass-
HOTEL enclosed sky bridges compose the top 11 floors of one of San Francisco's
tallest buildings, offering spectacular panoramas from every room; the
windows open so you can hear that trademark San Francisco sound:
the "ding ding" of the cable cars some 40 floors below (and rooms even
include binoculars). **Pros:** spectacular "bridge-to-bridge" views; atten-
tive service; in the running for the most comfy beds in the city. **Cons:**
located in a business area that's quiet on weekends; extremely pricey.
$⑤ Rooms from: $395 ⊠ 222 Sansome St. ☎ 415/276–9600, 800/622–
0404 ⊕ www.mandarinoriental.com/sanfrancisco ⤴ 151 rooms, 7
suites ⦿ No meals ✛ F3._

NOB HILL

$$$$ 🖭 **The Huntington Hotel.** Stars from Bogart and Bacall to Picasso and Pava-
HOTEL rotti have stayed in this venerable ivy-covered hotel famed for its gracious
Fodor'sChoice personal service and spacious rooms and suites—apartments in a former
★ life—most with great views of Grace Cathedral, the bay, or the city sky-
line. **Pros:** personal service; spacious rooms; an aura of old San Francisco;
guests have access to the primo spa with city views; cable car passes by
right out front. **Cons:** up a steep hill from downtown. $⑤ Rooms from:
$439 ⊠ 1075 California St. ☎ 415/474–5400, 800/227–4683 ⊕ www.
huntingtonhotel.com ⤴ 96 rooms, 40 suites ⦿ No meals ✛ E3._

$$$$ 🖭 **Ritz-Carlton, San Francisco.** A preferred destination for travel-industry
HOTEL honchos, movie stars, and visitors alike, this hotel—a stunning tribute
Fodor'sChoice to beauty and attentive, professional service—completed a $12.5-mil-
★ lion renovation to offer a modern twist to that classic Ritz style. **Pros:**

terrific service; all-day food available on Club Level; beautiful surroundings; fantastic new restaurant and lobby lounge; renovated fitness center. **Cons:** expensive; hilly location; no pool. $ *Rooms from: $375* ⊠ *600 Stockton St., at California St.* ☎ *415/296–7465* ⊕ *www.ritzcarlton.com* ⊷ *276 rooms, 60 suites* ⊠ *No meals* ✢ *E3.*

NORTH BEACH

$ ⚑ **San Remo Hotel.** A few blocks from Fisherman's Wharf, this three-
HOTEL story 1906 Italianate Victorian—once home to longshoremen and Beat
Fodor'sChoice poets—has a narrow stairway from the street leading to the front desk
★ and labyrinthine hallways; rooms are small but charming, with lace
curtains, forest-green-painted wood floors, and brass beds and other
antique furnishings. **Pros:** inexpensive; historic; cozy. **Cons:** some rooms
are dark; only the penthouse suite has a private bath; spartan amenities.
$ *Rooms from: $109* ⊠ *2237 Mason St.* ☎ *415/776–8688, 800/352–
7366* ⊕ *www.sanremohotel.com* ⊷ *64 rooms with shared baths, 1 suite*
⊠ *No meals* ✢ *E1.*

FISHERMAN'S WHARF

$$$$ ⚑ **Argonaut Hotel.** When the four-story Haslett Warehouse was a fruit-
HOTEL and-vegetable canning complex in 1907, boats docked right up against
Fodor'sChoice the building; today it's a hotel with a nautical decor—think anchors,
★ ropes, compasses, and a row of cruise-ship deck chairs in the lobby—
FAMILY that makes perfect sense given the fact that the Argonaut is part of
the San Francisco Maritime National Historical Park (whose visitors
center occupies the ground floor). **Pros:** bay views; near Hyde Street
cable car; sofa beds; toys for the kids. **Cons:** nautical theme isn't for
everyone; cramped public areas; service can be hit or miss; location is
a bit of a trek from other parts of town. $ *Rooms from: $449* ⊠ *495
Jefferson St., at Hyde St.* ☎ *415/563–0800, 866/415–0704* ⊕ *www.
argonauthotel.com* ⊷ *239 rooms, 13 suites* ⊠ *No meals* ✢ *D1.*

$$$$ ⚑ **Best Western Plus–The Tuscan.** Described by some Fodors.com users as a
HOTEL "hidden treasure," this hotel's redbrick facade barely hints at the Tuscan
country villa that lies within. **Pros:** wine and beer hour; cozy feeling;
great location near Fisherman's Wharf. **Cons:** congested touristy area;
small rooms. $ *Rooms from: $269* ⊠ *425 N. Point St., at Mason St.*
☎ *415/561–1100, 800/648–4626* ⊕ *www.tuscaninn.com* ⊷ *212 rooms,
12 suites* ⊠ *No meals* ✢ *E1.*

$$$$ ⚑ **Fairmont Heritage Place, Ghirardelli Square.** Housed in the former Ghi-
RENTAL rardelli chocolate factory, these one-to-three-bedroom serviced apart-
Fodor'sChoice ments might possibly be the most luxurious accommodations in San
★ Francisco. **Pros:** luxury at its finest; gigantic apartments with heaps of
FAMILY amenities; bay views from most apartments; free hotel car to deliver
you within a 2-mile radius. **Cons:** a bit of a trek from downtown; quite
expensive. $ *Rooms from: $899* ⊠ *950 North Point St.* ☎ *415/268–
9900* ⊕ *www.fairmont.com/ghirardelli* ⊠ *Breakfast* ✢ *C1.*

4

Fairmont Heritage Place, Ghirardelli Square

The Huntington Hotel

Argonaut Hotel

Hotel Vitale

Ritz-Carlton, San Francisco.

Hotel Drisco

Hotel Tomo

Union Street Inn

BEST BETS FOR SAN FRANCISCO LODGING

Fodor's offers a selective listing of quality lodging experiences at every price range, from the city's best budget motel to its most sophisticated luxury hotel. Here we've compiled our top recommendations by price and experience. The very best properties—in other words, those that provide a particularly remarkable experience in their price range—are designated in the listings with the Fodor's Choice logo.

Fodor'sChoice★

Argonaut Hotel, $$$$, p. 233
Cow Hollow Motor Inn and Suites, $, p. 238
Fairmont Heritage Place, Ghirardelli Square, $$$$, p. 233
Four Seasons Hotel San Francisco, $$$$, p. 231
Golden Gate Hotel, $, p. 230
Hotel Diva, $$$, p. 230
Hotel Drisco, $$$$, p. 238
Hotel Nikko, San Francisco, $$$$, p. 230
Hotel Tomo, $, p. 237
Hotel Triton, $$, p. 231

Hotel Vitale, $$$$, p. 237
Huntington Hotel, $$$$, p. 232
Inn at the Presidio, $$, p. 237
Ritz-Carlton, San Francisco $$$$, p. 232
San Remo Hotel, $, p. 233
The St. Regis San Francisco, $$$$, p. 232
Union Street Inn, $$$, p. 238

By Price

$
Cow Hollow Motor Inn and Suites, p. 238
Golden Gate Hotel, P. 230
Hotel Tomo, p. 237
San Remo Hotel, p. 233

$$
Hotel Triton, p. 231
Inn at the Presidio, p. 237

$$$
Hotel Diva, p. 230
Union Street Inn, p. 238

$$$$
Argonaut Hotel, p. 233
Fairmont Heritage Place, Ghirardelli Square, p. 233
Four Seasons Hotel San Francisco, p. 231
Hotel Drisco, p. 238
Hotel Nikko, San Francisco, p. 230
Hotel Vitale, p. 237
Huntington Hotel, p. 232
Ritz-Carlton, San Francisco, p. 232
The St. Regis San Francisco, p. 232

By Experience

BUSINESS TRAVELERS
Four Seasons Hotel San Francisco, $$$$, p. 231

Hotel Nikko, San Francisco, $$$$, p. 230

GREAT CONCIERGE
Ritz-Carlton, San Francisco $$$$, p. 232

HISTORICAL FLAVOR
Inn at the Presidio, $$, p. 237
Westin St. Francis, $$$$, p. 231

MOST KID-FRIENDLY
Argonaut Hotel, $$$$, p. 233
Four Seasons Hotel San Francisco, $$$$, p. 231
Hotel del Sol, $$$, p. 237
Hotel Tomo, $, p. 237

MOST ROMANTIC
Hotel Drisco, $$$$, p. 238
Huntington Hotel, $$$$, p. 232
Inn at the Presidio, $$, p. 237
Union Street Inn, $$$, p. 238

TOP B&BS
Hotel Drisco, $$$$, p. 238

TOP SPAS
Huntington Hotel, $$$$, p. 232
Mandarin Oriental San Francisco, $$$$, p. 232
The St. Regis San Francisco, $$$$, p. 232

EMBARCADERO

$$$$
HOTEL
Fodor'sChoice
★
FAMILY

🏨 **Hotel Vitale.** "Luxury, naturally," the theme of this eight-story terraced bay-front hotel, is apparent in every thoughtful detail: little vases of aromatic herbs mounted outside each room; the penthouse day spa with soaking tubs set in a rooftop bamboo forest; and the aromatherapy garden off the patio of the restaurant Americano, whose outdoor terrace is packed with hip jet-setters. **Pros:** family-friendly studios; great views; fanciful spa; luxurious amenities throughout. **Cons:** some rooms can feel cramped or be noisy; some guests report inconsistent service from staff; rates are expensive. $ *Rooms from: $599* ⊠ *8 Mission St.* ☎ *415/278–3700, 888/890–8688* ⊕ *www.hotelvitale.com* ⇨ *190 rooms, 9 suites* ◯ *No meals* ✛ *H3.*

THE MARINA AND THE PRESIDIO

$$$
HOTEL
FAMILY

🏨 **Hotel Del Sol.** This beach-themed, three-story 1950s motor lodge's proximity to Funston Playground, the Walt Disney Family Museum, the Presidio, Crissy Field, and Chestnut Street's munchkin-favored shops already make this place kid-friendly, but that plus free toys, the outdoor saltwater heated pool with plenty of inflatable playthings, games, DVDs, and afternoon cookies and milk make it a virtual haven for little ones. **Pros:** kid-friendly; plenty of nearby places to eat and shop; renovated in 2013. **Cons:** far from downtown and the landmark attractions around Fisherman's Wharf; faces a busy thoroughfare. $ *Rooms from: $209* ⊠ *3100 Webster St., Marina* ☎ *415/921–5520, 877/433–5765* ⊕ *www.thehoteldelsol.com* ⇨ *42 rooms, 15 suites* ◯ *Breakfast* ✛ *B2.*

$$
B&B/INN
Fodor'sChoice
★

🏨 **The Inn at the Presidio.** A brick facade, porches with rocking chairs, and an outdoor fire pit set the backdrop for this idyllic hotel at the base of numerous hiking and biking trails in the Presidio, a National Land Trust. **Pros:** playful design; outdoor fire pit; only hotel in the Presidio; spacious rooms; views of Golden Gate Bridge. **Cons:** no on-site restaurant; no elevator; challenging to get a taxi; very far from downtown attractions. $ *Rooms from: $195* ⊠ *42 Moraga Ave., Presidio* ☎ *415/800–7356* ⊕ *www.innatthepresidio.com* ⇨ *9 rooms, 17 suites* ◯ *Breakfast* ✛ *A2.*

JAPANTOWN

$
HOTEL
Fodor'sChoice
★
FAMILY

🏨 **Hotel Tomo.** Inspired by the comic phenomena manga and anime, the Tomo draws hipsters and Japanophiles eager to surround themselves with Japanese pop culture, or J-Pop as it is known across the pond. **Pros:** Cool J-Pop style; anime playing on the lobby TV and manga in your room; great price in a fun neighborhood. **Cons:** tight quarters; a trek from downtown. $ *Rooms from: $149* ⊠ *1800 Sutter St.* ☎ *415/921–4000* ⊕ *www.hoteltomo.com* ⇨ *125 rooms, 1 suite* ◯ *No meals* ✛ *B4.*

PACIFIC HEIGHTS/COW HOLLOW

$
HOTEL
Fodor's Choice
★

🛏 **Cow Hollow Motor Inn and Suites.** Newly refreshed suites at this large, family-owned, modern motel are more spacious than average, featuring one or two bedrooms, hardwood floors, sitting and dining areas, Oriental rugs, marble wood-burning fireplaces, big living rooms, and fully equipped kitchens. **Pros:** suites are the size of apartments; good for families; covered parking in building. **Cons:** congested neighborhood has a college-rush-week feel; standard rooms are on a loud street. ⑤ *Rooms from: $118* ✉ *2190 Lombard St., Marina* ☎ *415/921–5800* ⊕ *www.cowhollowmotorinn.com* ⤴ *117 rooms, 12 suites* ⦿| *No meals* ✛ *A1.*

$$$$
HOTEL
Fodor's Choice
★

🛏 **Hotel Drisco.** Pretend you're a resident of one of the wealthiest residential neighborhoods in San Francisco at this understated, elegant 1903 Edwardian hotel. **Pros:** great service; comfortable rooms; quiet residential retreat. **Cons:** far from downtown. ⑤ *Rooms from: $425* ✉ *2901 Pacific Ave.* ☎ *415/346–2880, 800/634–7277* ⊕ *www.hoteldrisco.com* ⤴ *29 rooms, 19 suites* ⦿| *Breakfast* ✛ *A3.*

$$$
B&B/INN
Fodor's Choice
★

🛏 **Union Street Inn.** Precious family antiques and unique artwork helped British innkeepers Jane Bertorelli and David Coyle (former chef for the Duke and Duchess of Bedford) transform this green-and-cream 1902 Edwardian into a delightful B&B. **Pros:** personal service; Jane's excellent full breakfast; romantic setting. **Cons:** parking in the neighborhood is tricky; no air-conditioning; no elevator. ⑤ *Rooms from: $229* ✉ *2229 Union St., Cow Hollow* ☎ *415/346–0424* ⊕ *www.unionstreetinn.com* ⤴ *6 rooms* ⦿| *Breakfast* ✛ *A2.*

NIGHTLIFE

Updated by
Jerry James
Stone

After hours, business folk and the working class give way to costume-clad partygoers, hippies and hipsters, downtown divas, frat boys, and those who prefer something a little more clothing-optional.

THE 4-1-1

Entertainment information is printed in the pink Sunday "Datebook" section (⊕ *www.sfgate.com/datebook*) and the more calendar-based Thursday "96 Hours" section (⊕ *www.sfgate.com/96hours*) in the *San Francisco Chronicle.* Also consult any of the free alternative weeklies, notably the *SF Weekly* (⊕ *www.sfweekly.com*), which blurbs nightclubs and music, and the *San Francisco Bay Guardian* (⊕ *www.sfbg.com*), which lists neighborhood, avant-garde, and budget events. SF Station (⊕ *www.sfstation.com*; online only) has an up-to-date calendar of entertainment goings-on.

UNION SQUARE

BARS

Cantina. Let the skull and crossbones over the entryway of this intimate little Latin bar be fair warning, because the magic the bartenders perform here is pure voodoo. The drinks are completely handcrafted with fresh ingredients, homemade bitters, and even homegrown citrus fruits, so service can be slow during busy times; fortunately, many cocktails are served in pitchers. ■ TIP→ **The most popular (and interesting) cocktail is the laughing buddha, a vibrant mix of lime, ginger, and serrano chilies.** Arrive early and grab a seat in the lounge toward the back. ✉ *580 Sutter St., at Mason St.* ☎ *415/398–0195* ⊕ *www.cantinasf.com.*

Redwood Room. Opened in 1933 and updated by designer Philippe Starck in 2001, the Redwood Room at the Clift Hotel is a San Francisco icon. The entire room, floor to ceiling, is paneled with the wood from a single redwood tree, giving the place a rich, monochromatic look. The gorgeous original art deco sconces and chandeliers still hang, but bizarre video installations on plasma screens also adorn the walls. It's packed on weekend evenings after 10, when young scenesters swarm in; for maximum glamour, visit on a weeknight. ✉ *Clift Hotel, 495 Geary St., at Taylor St.* ☎ *415/929–2372 for table reservations, 415/775–4700 for hotel* ⊕ *www.clifthotel.com.*

SOMA

BARS

City Beer Store. Called CBS by locals, this friendly tasting room cum liquor mart has a wine-bar's sensibility. Perfect for beer connoisseurs and the merely beer-curious alike, CBS stocks more than 300 different beers, more than a dozen on tap. The staff allows the indecisive to mix and match six-packs to go. Come early: The small space, which fills up quickly on event nights, closes at 10 pm except Sunday (6 pm). ✉ *1168 Folsom St., at 8th St.* ☎ *415/503-1033* ⊕ *www.citybeerstore.com* ⊗ *Closed Mon.*

GAY NIGHTLIFE

The Stud. Glam trannies, gay bears, tight-teed pretty boys, ladies and their ladies, and a handful of straight onlookers congregate here to dance to live DJ sounds and watch world-class drag performers on the small stage. The entertainment is often campy, pee-your-pants funny, and downright fantastic. Each night's music is different—from funk, soul, and hip-hop to '80s tunes and disco favorites. ■ TIP→ **At Frolic, the Stud's most outrageous party (second Saturday of the month), clubgoers dance the night away dressed as bunnies, kittens, and even stranger creatures.** ✉ *1284 Harrison St., at 9th St.* ☎ *415/863–6623* ⊕ *www.studsf.com* ⊗ *Closed Mon.*

THE TENDERLOIN

BARS

Bourbon & Branch. The address and phone are unlisted, the black outer door unmarked, and when you make your reservation (required), you get a password for entry. In short, Bourbon & Branch reeks of Prohibition-era speakeasy cool. It's not exclusive, though: everyone is granted a password. The place has sex appeal, with tin ceilings, bordello-red silk wallpaper, intimate booths, and low lighting; loud conversations and cell phones are not allowed. The menu of expertly mixed cocktails and quality bourbon and whiskey is substantial, but the servers aren't always authorities. ■TIP→ **This place is small, so couples or groups of four or fewer are ideal.** Your reservation dictates your exit time, which is strictly enforced. ⊠ *501 Jones St., at O'Farrell St.* ⊕ *www.bourbonandbranch.com.*

ROCK, POP, HIP-HOP, FOLK, AND BLUES CLUBS

Fodor's Choice **Great American Music Hall.** You can find top-drawer entertainment at
★ this eclectic nightclub. Acts range from the best in blues, folk, and jazz to up-and-coming college-radio and American-roots artists to of-the-moment indie rock stars (OK Go, Mates of State) and the establishment (Cowboy Junkies). The colorful marble-pillared emporium (built in 1907 as a bordello) also accommodates dancing at some shows. Pub grub is available most nights. ⊠ *859 O'Farrell St., between Polk and Larkin Sts.* ☎ *415/885–0750* ⊕ *www.slimspresents.com.*

HAYES VALLEY

BARS

Hôtel Biron Wine Bar and Art Gallery. Sharing an alley-like block with the backs of Market Street restaurants, this tiny, cave-like (in a good way) spot displays artworks of the Mission School aesthetic on its brick walls. The well-behaved twenty- to thirtysomething clientele enjoys the off-the-beaten-path quarters, the wines from around the world, the soft lighting, and the hip music. ⊠ *45 Rose St., off Market St. near Gough St.* ☎ *415/703–0403* ⊕ *www.hotelbiron.com.*

Smuggler's Cove. With the decor of a pirate ship and a slew of rum-based cocktails, you half expect Captain Jack Sparrow to sidle up next to you at this offbeat, Disney-esque hangout. But don't let the kitschy surroundings fool you. The folks at Smuggler's Cove take rum so seriously that they even make their own, which you can sample along with more than 200 other offerings, some of them vintage and very hard to find. A punchcard is provided so you can try all 70 cocktails and remember where you left off without getting shipwrecked. The small space has won numerous awards and fills up quickly, so arrive early. ⊠ *650 Gough St., at McAllister St.* ☎ *415/869–1900* ⊕ *www.smugglerscovesf.com.*

NORTH BEACH

BARS

Vesuvio Cafe. If you're only hitting one bar in North Beach, it should be this one. The low-ceiling second floor of this raucous boho hangout, little altered since its 1960s heyday (when Jack Kerouac frequented the place), is a fine vantage point for watching the colorful Broadway and Columbus Avenue intersection. Another part of Vesuvio's appeal is its diverse clientele (twenties to sixties), from neighborhood regulars and young couples to Bacchanalian posses of friends. ⊠ *255 Columbus Ave., at Broadway* ☎ *415/362–3370* ⊕ *www.vesuvio.com.*

ROCK, POP, HIP-HOP, FOLK, AND BLUES CLUBS

Bimbo's 365 Club. The plush main room and adjacent lounge of this club, here since 1951, retain a retro vibe perfect for the "Cocktail Nation" programming that keeps the crowds entertained. For a taste of the old-school San Francisco nightclub scene, you can't beat this place. Indie low-fi and pop bands like Stephen Malkmus and the Jicks and Camera Obscura fill the bill. ⊠ *1025 Columbus Ave., at Chestnut St.* ☎ *415/474–0365* ⊕ *www.bimbos365club.com.*

THE WESTERN SHORELINE

BARS

Cliff House. Classier than the nearby Beach Chalet, with a more impressive view of Ocean Beach, the Cliff House is our pick if you must choose just one oceanfront restaurant/bar. Sure, it's the site of many high-school prom dates, and you could argue that the food and drinks are overpriced, and some say the sleek facade looks like a mausoleum—but the views are terrific. The best window seats are reserved for diners, but there's a small upstairs lounge where you can watch gulls sail high above the vast blue Pacific. Come before sunset. ⊠ *1090 Point Lobos, at Great Hwy., Lincoln Park* ☎ *415/386–3330* ⊕ *www.cliffhouse.com.*

THE MISSION

GAY NIGHTLIFE

Lexington Club. According to its slogan, "every night is ladies' night" at this all-girl club geared to urban alterna-dykes in their twenties and thirties (think piercings and tattoos, not lipstick). ■ **TIP→ The women's room has awesome graffiti.** ⊠ *3464 19th St., at Valencia* ☎ *415/863–2052* ⊕ *www.lexingtonclub.com.*

Martuni's. A mixed crowd enjoys cocktails in the semirefined environment of this bar at the intersection of the Castro, the Mission, and Hayes Valley; variations on the martini are a specialty. ■ **TIP→ The Godiva Chocolate Martini is a crowd favorite.** In the intimate back room a pianist plays nightly, and patrons take turns boisterously singing show tunes. It's a favorite post-theater spot—especially after the symphony or opera, which are within walking distance. ⊠ *4 Valencia St., at Market St.* ☎ *415/241–0205.*

POTRERO HILL

ROCK, POP, HIP-HOP, FOLK, AND BLUES CLUBS

Bottom of the Hill. This is a great live-music dive—in the best sense of the word—and truly the epicenter for Bay Area indie rock. The club has hosted some great acts over the years, including the Strokes and the Throwing Muses. Rap and hip-hop acts occasionally make it to the stage. ⊠ *1233 17th St., at Texas St.* ☎ *415/621–4455* ⊕ *www.bottomofthehill.com.*

Built as a bordello in 1907, the Great American Music Hall now pulls in top-tier performers.

WESTERN ADDITION

JAZZ CLUBS

Yoshi's. The legendary Oakland jazz venue's San Francisco location has terrific acoustics, a 9-foot Steinway grand piano (broken in by Chick Corea), and seating for 411; it's been hailed as "simply the best jazz club in the city." Yoshi's serves Japanese food in an adjoining restaurant set in a soaring two-story space, decorated with blond wood and hanging paper lanterns (you can also order food at café tables in the club). And yes, the coupling of sushi and jazz *is* as elegant as it sounds. Sightlines are good from just about any vantage point, including the back balcony. Yoshi's is in the old Fillmore District, which was known as the "Harlem of the West" in its 1940s and '50s heyday. The club is on a tough block in the even tougher Western Addition neighborhood, so take advantage of the valet parking. ⊠ *1330 Fillmore St., at Eddy St.* ☎ *415/655–5600* ⊕ *www.yoshis.com.*

ROCK, POP, HIP-HOP, FOLK, AND BLUES CLUBS

The Fillmore. This is *the* club that all the big names, from Coldplay to Clapton, want to play. San Francisco's most famous rock-music hall presents national and local acts: rock, reggae, grunge, jazz, folk, acid house, and more. Most tickets cost $20–$30, and some shows are open to all ages. ■ TIP→ Avoid steep service charges by purchasing tickets at the Fillmore box office on Sundays from 10 to 4. At the end of each show, apples are set near the door and free for the taking, and staffers hand out collectible posters that at the very least will sell well on eBay. ⊠ *1805 Geary Blvd., at Fillmore St.* ☎ *415/346–6000* ⊕ *www.thefillmore.com.*

THE ARTS

Updated by
Jerry James
Stone

Sophisticated, offbeat, and often ahead of the curve, San Francisco's performing arts scene supports world-class opera, ballet, and theater productions, along with alternative-dance events, avant-garde plays, groundbreaking documentaries, and a slew of spoken-word and other literary happenings.

TICKETS

City Box Office. This charge-by-phone service, sells tickets for many performances and lectures. You can also buy tickets in person at its downtown location weekdays 9:30–5:30 or online. ⊠ *180 Redwood St., Suite 100, off Van Ness Ave. between Golden Gate Ave. and McAllister St., Civic Center* ☎ *415/392–4400* ⊕ *www.cityboxoffice.com.*

San Francisco Performances. SFP brings an eclectic array of top-flight global music and dance talents to various venues—mostly the Yerba Buena Center for the Arts, Davies Symphony Hall, and Herbst Theatre. Artists have included Yo-Yo Ma, Edgar Meyer, the Paul Taylor Dance Company, and Midori. Tickets can be purchased in person, online, or by phone. ⊠ *500 Sutter St., Suite 710* ☎ *415/392-2545* ⊕ *www.performances.org.*

TIX Bay Area. Half-price, same-day tickets for many local and touring shows go on sale (cash only) at the TIX Booth located in Union Square, which is open daily from 10-6. Discount purchases can also be made online at their website. ⊠ *Powell St. between Geary and Post Sts., Union Sq.* ☎ *415/433–7827* ⊕ *www.tixbayarea.com.*

THE 4-1-1

The best guide to the arts is the Sunday "Datebook" section (⊕ *www. sfgate.com/datebook*) of the *San Francisco Chronicle.* The four-day entertainment supplement "96 Hours" (⊕ *www.sfgate.com/96hours*) is in the Thursday *Chronicle.* Also check out the city's free alternative weeklies, including *SF Weekly* (⊕ *www.sfweekly.com*) and the *San Francisco Bay Guardian* (⊕ *www.sfbg.com*).

Online, SF Station (⊕ *www.sfstation.com*) has a frequently updated arts and nightlife calendar. San Francisco Arts Monthly (⊕ *www.sfarts. org*), which is published at the end of the month, has arts features and events listings, plus a helpful "Visiting San Francisco?" section. For offbeat, emerging-artist performances, consult CounterPULSE (⊕ *www. counterpulse.org*).

DANCE

Fodor's Choice ★ **San Francisco Ballet.** For ballet lovers, this company is reason alone to visit the Bay Area. It's the nation's oldest professional ballet company. Under artistic director Helgi Tomasson, the San Francisco Ballet's pieces—both classical and contemporary—have won critical raves. The primary season runs from February through May. The repertoire includes full-length ballets such as *Don Quixote* and *Sleeping Beauty*; the December presentation of *The Nutcracker* is truly spectacular. The company also performs bold new dances from star choreographers such as William Forsythe and Mark Morris, alongside modern classics by George Balanchine and Jerome Robbins. Tickets and information are available at the **War Memorial Opera House.** ⊠ *War Memorial Opera House, 301 Van Ness Ave., at Grove St., Civic Center* ☎ *415/865–2000* ⊕ *www.sfballet.org* ☉ *Weekdays 10–4.*

FILM

Fodor's Choice **Castro Theatre.** An art deco showstopper, the theater's exterior is marked ★ by a large neon sign that is the neighborhood's crown jewel. The interior, along with the Mighty Wurlitzer preshow, transports you back to 1922 when the theater first opened. Foreign films, revivals, and local film festivals are just a few of the events you will find at this local treasure. ■ TIP→ Its sing-along movie musicals are most popular, drawing diverse crowds from across the city and creating lines that wrap around the block. Parking is limited in the Castro District, so taking public transportation is advised. ⊠ *429 Castro St., near Market St., Castro* ☎ *415/621–6120* ⊕ *www.castrotheatre.com.*

MUSIC

Fodor's Choice **San Francisco Symphony.** One of America's top orchestras, the symphony ★ performs from September through May, with additional summer performances of light classical music and show tunes; visiting artists perform here the rest of the year. The orchestra and its charismatic music director, Michael Tilson Thomas, who is known for his daring programming of 20th-century American works (most notably his Grammy Award–winning Mahler cycle), often perform with soloists of the caliber of Andre Watts, Gil Shaham, and Renée Fleming. The adventuresome side of the organization is amply illustrated by this symphony's collaboration with the heavy-metal group Metallica. David Byrne has performed here, as well. Tickets run from $15 to $100. ⊠ *Davies Symphony Hall, 201 Van Ness Ave., at Grove St., Civic Center* ☎ *415/864–6000* ⊕ *www.sfsymphony.org.*

Summer in the City. Many members of the San Francisco Symphony perform in this concert series, held in the 2,400-seat Davies Symphony Hall. The schedule includes light classics and Broadway, country, and movie music. ☎ *415/864–6000* ⊕ *www.sfsymphony.org*

MUSIC FESTIVALS

Stern Grove Festival. The nation's oldest continual free summer music festival hosts Sunday-afternoon performances of symphony, opera, jazz, pop music, and dance. The amphitheater is in a beautiful eucalyptus grove below street level, perfect for picnicking before the show. (Dress for cool weather.) ⊠ *Sloat Blvd. at 19th Ave., Sunset* ☎ *415/252–6252* ⊕ *www.sterngrove.org.*

OPERA

Fodor's Choice **San Francisco Opera.** Founded in 1923, this world-renowned company ★ has resided at the Civic Center's War Memorial Opera House since the building's completion in 1932. Over its split season—September through January and June through July—the opera presents about 70 performances of 10 to 12 operas. Translations are projected above the stage during almost all non-English operas. Long considered a major international company, the opera frequently embarks on productions with European opera companies and adopts unconventional projects, some edgy and designed to attract younger audiences. Ticket prices can range from $25 to $195. The full-time box office (Monday 10–5, Tuesday through Friday 10–6) is at 199 Grove Street, at Van Ness Avenue. ⊠ *War Memorial Opera House, 301 Van Ness Ave., at Grove St., Civic Center* ☎ *415/864–3330 tickets* ⊕ *www.sfopera.com.*

THEATER

American Conservatory Theater. Not long after its founding in the mid-1960s, the city's major nonprofit theater company became one of the nation's leading regional theaters. During its season, which runs from early fall to late spring, ACT presents approximately eight plays, from classics to contemporary works, often in rotating repertory. In December ACT stages a much-loved version of Charles Dickens's *A Christmas Carol.* ⊠ *415 Geary St., Union Sq.* ☎ *415/749-2228* ⊕ *www.act-sf.org.*

ACT ticket office. The **ACT ticket office** is next door to the American Conservatory Theater. ⊠ *405 Geary St., Union Sq.* ☎ *415/749–2228*

Fodor's Choice ★ **Teatro ZinZanni.** Contortionists, chanteuses, jugglers, illusionists, and circus performers entertain the audiences who dine on a surprisingly good five-course dinner in a fabulous antique Belgian dance-hall tent. Dress up, be ready to laugh, and arrive early for a front-and-center table. Reservations are essential; tickets are $125 to $150. In 2013, the troupe was relocating to a permanent home on Broadway and the Embarcadero, and was slated to reopen later in the year. Call or check the website to confirm its current performance schedule. ⊠ *Broadway and the Embarcadero, Northern Waterfront* ☎ *415/438–2668* ⊕ *www.zinzanni.org.*

SPORTS AND THE OUTDOORS

BASEBALL

FAMILY Fodor's Choice ★ **San Francisco Giants.** The National League's New York Giants became the San Francisco Giants when they moved to California in 1958, the same year that the Brooklyn Dodgers moved to Los Angeles. Today the classic design of the Giants' AT&T Park and the team's 2010 and 2012 World Series titles have created new legions of fans. Buy your tickets in advance—nearly every game sells out. ⊠ *AT&T Park, 24 Willie Mays Plaza, between 2nd and 3rd Sts., SoMa* ☎ *415/972–2000, 800/734–4268* ⊕ *sanfrancisco.giants.mlb.com.*

Tickets.com. This service sells game tickets online and charges a per-ticket service charge that ranges from $1.50 to $7.50. ☎ *877/473–4849* ⊕ *www.tickets.com.*

Giants Dugout. The team sells tickets at the ballpark and numerous Dugout locations, among them Embarcadero Center and Union Square. A surcharge is added except at the ballpark. ⊠ *AT&T Park, 24 Willie Mays Plaza, at 3rd St., SoMa* ☎ *415/972–2000, 800/734–4268* ⊕ *sanfrancisco.giants.mlb.com/sf/ballpark/dugout_stores.jsp* ⊠ *4 Embarcadero Center, Embarcadero* ☎ *415/951–8888.*

BICYCLING

San Francisco Bicycle Coalition. The San Francisco Bicycle Coalition has extensive information about the policies and politics of riding and lists local events for cyclists on its website. You can download (but not print) a PDF version of the *San Francisco Bike Map and Walking Guide.* ☎ *415/431–2453* ⊕ *www.sfbike.org.*

WHERE TO RENT

Bike and Roll. You can rent bikes at this national outfit's locations for $8 per hour or $32 per day; discounted weekly rates are available, and complimentary maps are provided. ⊠ *899 Columbus Ave., at Lombard St., North Beach* ☎ *415/229–2000* ⊕ *www.bikethegoldengate.com* ⊠ *353 Jefferson St., between Jones and Leavenworth Sts., Fisherman's Wharf* ⊠ *2800 Leavenworth St., at Beach St., Fisherman's Wharf.*

Blazing Saddles. This outfitter rents bikes for $8 to $9 an hour ($32 to $105 a day), depending on the type of bike, and shares tips on sights to see along the paths. ⊠ *2715 Hyde St., at Beach St., Fisherman's Wharf* ☎ *415/202–8888* ⊕ *www.blazingsaddles.com* ⊠ *433 Mason St., at Post St., Union Sq.* ⊠ *Pier 41, Fisherman's Wharf* ⊠ *465 Jefferson St., at Hyde St., Fisherman's Wharf* ⊠ *2555 Powell St., at the Embarcadero, Fisherman's Wharf* ⊠ *1095 Columbus, at Francisco St., North Beach* ⊠ *721 Beach St., at Hyde St., North Beach.*

SHOPPING

UNION SQUARE

Fodor's Choice
★
Diptyque. The original Diptyque boutique in Paris has attracted a long line of celebrities. You can find the full array of scented candles and fragrances in this chic shop that would be at home on the boulevard St-Germain. Trademark black-and-white labels adorn the popular L'eau toilet water, scented with geranium and sandalwood. Candles come in traditional and esoteric scents, including lavender, basil, leather, and fig tree. Also available are French Mariage Frères teas. ⊠ *171 Maiden La., near Stockton St.* ☎ *415/402–0600* ⊕ *www.diptyqueparis.com.*

Gump's. It's a San Francisco institution, dating to the 19th century, and it's a strikingly luxurious one. The airy store exudes a museum-like vibe, with its large decorative vases, sumptuous housewares, and Tahitian-pearl display. It's a great place to pick up gifts, such as the Golden Gate Bridge note cards or silver-plated butter spreaders in a signature Gump's box. ⊠ *135 Post St., near Kearny St.* ☎ *415/982–1616* ⊕ *www.gumps.com.*

The beat movement of the 1950s was born in San Francisco's most famous bookstore, City Lights.

Fodor's Choice
★

Hang Art. A spirit of fun imbues this inviting gallery that showcases emerging artists. Prices range from a few hundred dollars to several thousand, making it an ideal place for novice collectors to get their feet wet. ⊠ *567 Sutter St., 2nd fl., near Mason St.* ☎ *415/434–4264* ⊕ *www.hangart.com.*

Fodor's Choice
★

Margaret O'Leary. If you can only buy one piece of clothing in San Francisco, make it a hand-loomed, locally made cashmere sweater by this Irish-born local legend. The perfect antidote to the city's wind and fog, the sweaters are so beloved by San Franciscans that some of them never wear anything else. Pick up an airplane wrap for your trip home and a media cozy to keep your iPod toasty, too. Another store is in Pacific Heights, at 2400 Fillmore Street. ⊠ *1 Claude La. at Sutter St.* ☎ *415/391–1010* ⊕ *www.margaretoleary.com.*

Nordstrom. Somehow Nordstrom manages to be all things to all people, and this location, with spiral escalators circling a four-story atrium, is no exception. Whether you're an elegant lady of a certain age shopping for a new mink coat or a teen on the hunt for a Roxy hoodie, the salespeople are known for being happy to help. Nordstrom carries the best selections in town of new designers like Tory Burch, but its own brands have loyal followings, too. ■ TIP→ The café upstairs is a superb choice for a ladies-who-lunch shopping break. ⊠ *San Francisco Shopping Centre, 865 Market St., at 5th St.* ☎ *415/243–8500* ⊕ *shop. nordstrom.com.*

CHINATOWN

Chinatown Kite Shop. The kites sold here range from basic diamond shapes to box- and animal-shaped configurations. Colorful dragon kites make great souvenirs. ⊠ *717 Grant Ave., near Sacramento St.* ☎ *415/989–5182* ⊕ *www.chinatownkite.com.*

SOMA

Chronicle Books. This local beacon of publishing produces inventively designed fiction, cookbooks, art books, and other titles, as well as diaries, planners, and address books—all of which you can purchase at three locations in town. The light and airy spaces are a far cry from the cramped, dusty bookshops of yore. In addition to this branch, there are stores at 680 2nd Street, near AT&T Park, and 1846 Union Street, in Cow Hollow. ⊠ *Metreon Westfield Shopping Center, 165 4th St., near Howard St.* ☎ *415/369–6271* ⊕ *www.chroniclebooks.com.*

K&L Wine Merchants. More than any other wine store, this one has an ardent cult following around town. The friendly staffers promise not to sell what they don't taste themselves, and weekly events—on Thursdays from 5 pm to 6:30 pm and Saturdays from noon to 3 pm—open the tastings to customers. The best-seller list for varietals and regions for both the under- and over-$30 categories appeals to the wine lover in everyone. ⊠ *638 4th St., between Brannan and Townsend Sts.* ☎ *415/896–1734* ⊕ *www.klwines.com.*

HAYES VALLEY

Miette Confiserie. There is truly nothing sweeter than a cellophane bag tied with blue-and-white twine and filled with malt balls or chocolate sardines from this European-style apothecary. The lovely pastel-color cake stands make even window-shopping a treat. ⊠ *449 Octavia Blvd., between Hayes and Fell Sts.* ☎ *415/626–6221* ⊕ *www.miette.com.*

NORTH BEACH

Fodor'sChoice
★

City Lights Bookstore. The city's most famous bookstore is where the Beat movement of the 1950s was born. Neal Cassady and Jack Kerouac hung out in the basement, and now regulars and tourists while hours away in this well-worn space. The upstairs room holds impressive poetry and Beat literature collections. Poet Lawrence Ferlinghetti, the owner, remains active in the workings of this three-story shop. City Lights Publishers, which issued the poet Allen Ginsberg's *Howl* in 1956, publishes a dozen new titles each year. ⊠ *261 Columbus Ave., at Broadway* ☎ *415/362–8193* ⊕ *www.citylights.com.*

Fodor'sChoice
★

Molinari Delicatessen. This store has been making its own salami, sausages, and cold cuts since 1896. Other homemade specialties include meat and cheese ravioli, tomato sauces, and fresh pastas. ■TIP➔ **Do like the locals: grab a made-to-order sandwich for lunch and eat it at one of the sidewalk tables.** ⊠ *373 Columbus Ave. at Vallejo St.* ☎ *415/421–2337.*

EMBARCADERO

Fodor's Choice ★ **Ferry Plaza Farmers' Market.** The party-like Saturday edition of the city's most upscale and expensive farmers' market places baked goods, gourmet cheeses, smoked fish, and fancy pots of jam alongside organic basil, specialty mushrooms, heirloom tomatoes, and juicy-ripe locally grown fruit. On Saturdays about 100 vendors pack along three sides of the building, and sandwiches and other prepared foods are for sale in addition to fruit, vegetable, and other samples free for the nibbling. Smaller markets take place on Tuesdays and Thursdays (the Thursday one doesn't operate from about late December through March.) ✉ *Ferry Plaza at Market St., Embarcadero* ☎ *415/291–3276* ⊕ *www. ferrybuildingmarketplace.com* ☉ *Tues. and Thurs. 10–2, Sat. 8–2.*

4

THE HAIGHT

Fodor's Choice ★ **Amoeba Music.** With more than 2.5 million new and used CDs, DVDs, and records, this warehouselike store (and the original Berkeley location) carries titles you can't find on Amazon at bargain prices. No niche is ignored—from electronica and hip-hop to jazz and classical—and the stock changes daily. Weekly in-store performances attract large crowds. ✉ *1855 Haight St., between Stanyan and Shrader Sts.* ☎ *415/831–1200* ⊕ *www.amoeba.com.*

THE MISSION

Fodor's Choice ★ **Paxton Gate.** Elevating gardening to an art, this serene shop offers beautiful earthenware pots, amaryllis and narcissus bulbs, decorative garden items, and coffee-table books such as *An Inordinate Fondness for Beetles.* The collection of taxidermy and preserved bugs provides more unusual gift ideas. ✉ *824 Valencia St., between 19th and 20th Sts.* ☎ *415/824–1872* ⊕ *www.paxtongate.com.*

PACIFIC HEIGHTS

BeneFit Cosmetics. You can find this locally based line of cosmetics and skin-care products at Macy's and Sephora, but it's much more fun to come to one of the eponymous boutiques. No-pressure salespeople dab you with whimsical makeup such as Ooh La Lift concealer and Tinted Love, a stain for lips and cheeks. ✉ *2117 Fillmore St., between California and Sacramento Sts.* ☎ *415/567–0242* ⊕ *www. benefitcosmetics.com.*

JAPANTOWN

Kinokuniya Bookstore. The selection of English-language books about Japanese culture—everything from medieval history to origami instructions—is one of the finest in the country. Kinokuniya is the city's biggest seller of Japanese-language books. Dozens of glossy Asian fashion magazines attract the young and trendy; the manga and anime books and magazines are wildly popular, too. ✉ *Kinokuniya Bldg., 1581 Webster St. at Geary Blvd.* ☎ *415/567–7625.*

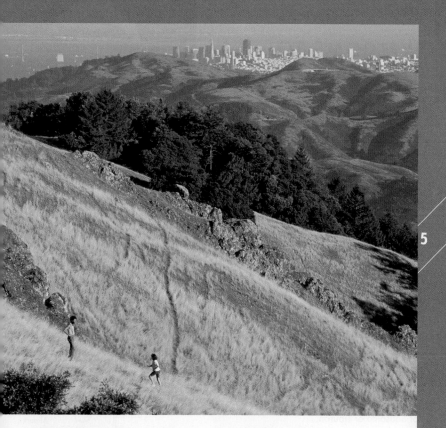

THE BAY AREA

WELCOME TO THE BAY AREA

TOP REASONS TO GO

★ **Bite into the "Gourmet Ghetto":** Eat your way through this area of North Berkeley, starting with a slice of perfect pizza from the Cheese Board (just look for the line).

★ **Find solitude at Point Reyes National Seashore:** Hike beautifully rugged—and often deserted—beaches at one of the most beautiful places on earth, period.

★ **Sit on a dock by the bay:** Admire the beauty of the Bay Area from the rocky, picturesque shores of Sausalito or Tiburon.

★ **Go bar-hopping in Oakland's hippest hood:** Spend an evening swinging through the watering holes of Uptown, Oakland's artsy-hip and fast-rising corner of downtown.

★ **Walk among giants:** Walking into Muir Woods, a mere 12 miles north of the Golden Gate Bridge, is like entering a cathedral built by God.

1 Berkeley. This college town has long been known for its liberal ethos, stimulating university community (and perhaps even more stimulating coffee shops), and activist streak. But these days, the lively restaurant and arts scenes are luring even those who wouldn't be caught dead in Birkenstocks.

2 Oakland. Life in this harbor-front city is strongly defined by a turbulent history. But the up-and-coming downtown scene and rejuvenated waterfront are signals of good things ahead.

3 Marin County. Marin is considered the prettiest of the Bay Area counties, primarily because of its wealth of open space. Anchored by water on three sides, the county is mostly parkland, including long stretches of undeveloped coastline. The picturesque small towns here—Sausalito, Tiburon, Mill Valley, and Bolinas among them—may sometimes look rustic, but they're mostly in a dizzyingly high tax bracket. There's a reason why people call BMWs "basic Marin wheels."

GETTING ORIENTED

Cross the Golden Gate Bridge and head north to reach Marin County's rolling hills and green expanses, where residents enjoy an haute-suburban lifestyle. Farther afield, the wild landscapes of the Marin Headlands, Muir Woods, Mt. Tamalpais, Stinson Beach, and Point Reyes National Seashore await.

East of the city, across the San Francisco Bay, are Berkeley and Oakland, which most Bay Area residents refer to as the East Bay. These two towns have distinct personalities, but life here feels more relaxed than in the city—though every bit as vibrant.

5

Updated by
Denise M. Leto It's rare for a metropolis to compete with its suburbs for visitors, but the view from any of San Francisco's hilltops shows that the Bay Area's temptations extend far beyond the city limits. East of town are two energetic urban centers, Berkeley and Oakland. Famously radical Berkeley is also comfortably sophisticated, while Oakland has an art and restaurant scene so hip that it pulls San Franciscans to this side of the bay. To the north is Marin County, the beauty queen, with dramatic coastal scenery of breathtaking beauty and chic, affluent villages like Tiburon and Mill Valley.

PLANNING

WHEN TO GO

As with San Francisco, you can visit the rest of the Bay Area comfortably at any time of year, and it's especially nice in late spring and fall. Unlike in San Francisco, though, the surrounding areas are reliably sunny in summer—it gets hotter as you head inland. Even the rainy season has its charms, as hills that are golden the rest of the year turn a rich green and wildflowers become plentiful. Precipitation is usually the heaviest between November and March. Berkeley is a university town, so the rhythm of the school year might affect your visit. It's easier to navigate the streets and find parking near the university between semesters, but there's also less buzz around town.

GETTING HERE AND AROUND
BART TRAVEL

Using public transportation to reach Berkeley or Oakland is ideal. The under- and aboveground BART (Bay Area Rapid Transit) trains make stops in both towns. Trips to either take about a half hour one-way from the center of San Francisco.

Contacts BART ☎ 510/465–2278 ⊕ www.bart.gov.

BOAT AND FERRY TRAVEL

For sheer romance, nothing beats the ferry; there's service from San Francisco to Sausalito and Tiburon in Marin County, and to Alameda and Oakland in the East Bay.

The Golden Gate Ferry crosses the bay to Sausalito from San Francisco's Ferry Building (⊠ *Market Street and the Embarcadero*). Blue & Gold Fleet ferries depart daily for Sausalito and Tiburon from Pier 41 at Fisherman's Wharf; weekday commuter ferries leave from the Ferry Building for Tiburon. The trip to Sausalito takes 25 minutes to an hour; to Tiburon, it takes 25 to 55 minutes.

The Angel Island–Tiburon Ferry sails to the island daily April through October and weekends the rest of the year.

The San Francisco Bay Ferry runs several times daily between San Francisco's Ferry Building or Pier 41, Alameda, and Jack London Square in Oakland; one-way tickets are $6.25. The trip lasts 20 to 45 minutes, depending on your departure point, and leads to Oakland's waterfront shopping and restaurant district. Purchase tickets on board.

Boat and Ferry Lines Angel Island–Tiburon Ferry ☎ 415/435–2131 ⊕ www.angelislandferry.com. **Blue & Gold Fleet** ☎ 415/705–8200 ⊕ www.blueandgoldfleet.com. **Golden Gate Ferry** ☎ 415/923–2000 ⊕ www.goldengateferry.org. **San Francisco Bay Ferry** ☎ 510/522–3300 ⊕ sanfranciscobayferry.com.

BUS TRAVEL

Golden Gate Transit buses travel to Sausalito, Tiburon, and Mill Valley from Folsom and 7th streets and from other points in San Francisco. For Mt. Tamalpais State Park and West Marin (e.g., Stinson Beach, Bolinas, and Point Reyes Station), take bus 10, 70, or 80 to Marin City; in Marin City transfer to the West Marin Stagecoach (schedules vary). San Francisco Muni bus 76 runs hourly from Sutter and Sansome streets to the Marin Headlands Visitor Center on weekends and major holidays only. The trip takes about 45 minutes.

Though much less convenient than BART, AC Transit buses run between San Francisco's Transbay Temporary Terminal (on the block bordered by Main, Folsom, Beale and Howard streets) and the East Bay. AC Transit's F and FS lines stop near the university and 4th Street shopping, respectively, in Berkeley. Lines C and P travel to Piedmont in Oakland. The O bus stops at the edge of Chinatown near downtown Oakland.

Bus Lines AC Transit ☎ 511 ⊕ www.actransit.org. **Golden Gate Transit** ☎ 415/455–2000, 511 hotline ⊕ www.goldengate.org.**SamTrans** ☎ 800/660–4287 ⊕ www.samtrans.com. **San Francisco Muni** ☎ 311 ⊕ www.sfmta.com. **West Marin Stagecoach** ☎ 415/526–3239 ⊕ www.marintransit.org/stage.html.

CAR TRAVEL

To reach the East Bay from San Francisco, take Interstate 80 East across the Bay Bridge. For most of Berkeley, take the University Avenue exit through downtown Berkeley to the campus or take the Ashby Avenue exit and turn left on Telegraph Avenue; there's a parking garage on Channing Way near the campus. For Oakland, take Interstate 580 off the Bay Bridge to the Grand Avenue exit for Lake Merritt. To reach downtown and the waterfront, take Interstate 980 from Interstate 580 and exit at 12th Street. Both trips take about 30 minutes unless it's rush hour or a weekend afternoon, when you should count on an hour.

Head north on U.S.101 and cross the Golden Gate Bridge to reach all points in Marin by car, which is essential to visit the outer reaches unless you want to spend all day on the bus. From San Francisco, the towns of Sausalito and Tiburon and the Marin Headlands and Point Reyes National Seashore are accessed off U.S. 101. The coastal route, Highway 1, also known as Shoreline Highway, can be accessed off U.S. 101 as well. Follow this road to Mill Valley, Muir Woods, Mt. Tamalpais State Park, Stinson Beach, and Bolinas. From Bolinas, you can continue north on Highway 1 to Point Reyes. Depending on traffic, it takes from 20 to 45 minutes to get to Sausalito, Tiburon, and the Marin Headlands; driving directly to Point Reyes from San Francisco takes about 90 minutes in moderate traffic if you drive north on U.S. 101 and west on Sir Francis Drake Boulevard. Trips to Muir Woods take from 35 minutes to an hour from San Francisco. Add another 30 minutes for the drive to Stinson Beach (the curving roads make the going slower), 10 more if you continue on to Bolinas. The drive from Bolinas to Point Reyes takes an additional half hour.

SIGHTSEEING GUIDES

Great Pacific Tour Co. runs 3½-hour morning and afternoon tours of Muir Woods and Sausalito for $55, with hotel pickup, in 14-passenger vans with excellent interpretation. Super Sightseeing offers a four-hour bus tour of Muir Woods. The tour, which stops in Sausalito en route, leaves at 9 am and 2 pm daily from North Point and Taylor Street at Fisherman's Wharf and costs $55.

By Bus and Van Great Pacific Tour Co. ☎ 415/626–4499
⊕ www.greatpacifictour.com. **Super Sightseeing** ☎ 415/353–5310
⊕ www.supersightseeing.com.

RESTAURANTS

The Bay Area is home to some of the most popular and innovative restaurants in the country, including Chez Panisse in Berkeley and Commis in Oakland—for which reservations must be made well in advance. Expect an emphasis on locally grown produce, hormone-free meats, and California wine. Keep in mind that many Marin cafés don't serve dinner, and that dinner service ends on the early side. (No 10 pm reservations in that neck of the woods.)

Prices in the reviews are the average cost of a main course at dinner or, if dinner isn't served, at lunch.

HOTELS

Hotels in Berkeley and Oakland tend to be standard-issue, but many Marin hotels package themselves as cozy retreats. Summer is often booked well in advance, despite weather that can be downright chilly. Check for special packages during this season.

Prices in the reviews are the lowest cost of a standard double room in high season.Hotel reviews have been condensed for this book. Please go to Fodors.com for expanded reviews of each property.

THE EAST BAY

When San Franciscans refer to it, the East Bay often means nothing more than what you can see across the bay from the city—mainly Oakland and Berkeley. There's far more here—industrial-chic Emeryville, the wooded ranchland of Walnut Creek, and sprawling, urban Richmond, to name a few other communities—but Berkeley, anchored by its world-class university, and Oakland, which struggles with violence but has booming arts, nightlife, and restaurant scenes, are the magnets that draw folks across the bay.

BERKELEY

2 miles northeast of Bay Bridge.

The birthplace of the Free Speech Movement, the radical hub of the 1960s, the home of arguably the nation's top public university, and the city whose government condemned the bombing of Afghanistan—Berkeley is all of those things. The city of 100,000 facing San Francisco across the bay is also culturally diverse, a breeding ground for social trends, a bastion of the counterculture, and an important center for Bay Area writers, artists, and musicians. Berkeley residents, students, and faculty spend hours nursing various coffee concoctions while they read, discuss, and debate at any of the dozens of cafés that surround the campus. It's the quintessential university town, and many who graduated years ago still bask in daily intellectual conversation, great weather, and good food. Residents will walk out of their way to go to the perfect bread shop or consult with their favorite wine merchant.

Oakland may have Berkeley beat when it comes to cutting-edge arts, and the city may have forfeited some of its renegade 1960s' spirit over the years, but unless a guy in a hot-pink satin body suit, skullcap, and cape rides a unicycle around *your* town, you'll likely find Berkeley offbeat indeed.

GETTING HERE AND AROUND

BART is the easiest way to get to Berkeley from San Francisco. Alight at the Downtown Berkeley (not North Berkeley) Station, and walk a block up Center Street to get to the western edge of campus. AC Transit buses F and FS lines stop near the university and 4th Street shopping. By car, take I–80 east across the Bay Bridge then take the University Avenue exit through downtown Berkeley to the campus or take the Ashby Avenue exit and turn left on Telegraph Avenue. Once you arrive, explore on foot. Berkeley is very pedestrian-friendly.

ESSENTIALS

Visitor Information Berkeley Convention and Visitors Bureau
✉ *2030 Addison St., #102* ☎ *510/549–7040* ⊕ *www.visitberkeley.com.*

EXPLORING

TOP ATTRACTIONS

4th Street. An industrial area on 4th Street north of University Avenue has been converted into a pleasant shopping stretch, with popular eateries, and shops selling pricey handcrafted and eco-conscious goods and fashion. About six blocks long, this compact area (the action has spilled onto neighboring streets) is busiest on bright weekend afternoons. Stained Glass Garden, Builders Booksource, and the Apple Store are among shoppers' favorites, along with a minislew of upscale boutiques and wonderful paper stores. ■**TIP**➜ A walk through the East Bay Vivarium (✉ 1827 5th St. ☎ 510/841–1400 ⊕ www.eastbayvivarium.com), where turtles swim, Amazonian snakes slither, and baby mice (dinner) cower, is better than a walk through the reptile house at the zoo—and it's free. ✉ *4th St., between University Ave. and Delaware Sts.* ⊕ *www.fourthstreet.com.*

QUICK BITES

Cheese Board Pizza. With a jazz combo playing in the storefront and a long line snaking down the block, Cheese Board Pizza taps into the pulse of the Gourmet Ghetto. The cooperatively owned takeout spot and restaurant draws devoted customers with the smell of just-baked garlic, fresh vegetables, and perfect sauces. There's one pizza a day, which is always vegetarian. For just a nibble, the Cheese Board bakery–cheese shop next door sells cookies, muffins, scones, bialys, and the best sourdough baguettes in town. ✉ *1504–1512 Shattuck Ave., at Vine St.* ☎ *510/549–3055* ⊙ *Tues.–Sat. 11:30–3 and 4:30–8.*

Fodor's Choice ★

Gourmet Ghetto. The success of Chez Panisse restaurant attracted other food-related enterprises to its stretch of Shattuck Avenue, and the area surrounding the intersection of Shattuck and Vine Street became known as the Gourmet Ghetto. If you love food at all, it's worth a couple of hours to poke around the food shops and grab a quick bite or a full meal at one of the neighborhood's eateries.

The line stretches down the block in front of **Cheese Board Pizza** (No. 1512), where live jazz bands sometimes serenade the diners that spill out onto the sidewalk and median. Next door is the **Cheese Board Collective**—worker owned since 1971—and its fabulous bakery and extensive cheese counter. Next door to Chez Panisse, **César** (No. 1515) wine bar and tapas house is a good place for an afternoon quaff or late-night drink.

The small food stands of **Epicurious Garden**, at 1509–1513 Shattuck, sell everything from sushi to gelato. Outside, you can find a terraced garden—the best place to sit—that winds up four levels and ends at the **Imperial Tea Court**. Around the corner on Vine Street is **Love at First Bite**, a cupcakery that sells scrumptious confections. Across the street, the **Vintage Berkeley** wine shop occupies the historic former pump house at No. 2113; the offerings here are shrewdly selected and reasonably priced. Coffee lovers of the **Peet's** persuasion may want to pay respects at No. 2124, at Walnut Street, where the famed roaster got its start; the small café includes a display chronicling Peet's history.

South of Cedar Street in the next block of Shattuck is the art-filled **Guerilla Cafe** (No. 1620), a breakfast and lunch spot beloved for its waffles (the Blue Bottle Coffee doesn't hurt). Also look for the **Local Butcher Shop** (No. 1600), with locally sourced meat and hearty made-to-order sandwiches. A former Ritz-Carlton chef brings white-linen quality to his to-go counter, **Grégoire**, around the corner on Cedar Street (No. 2109). In the block north of Vine Street on Shattuck is popular **Saul's** deli and restaurant and beautiful **Masse's Pastries**. On Thursdays, an organic farmers' market sets up shop here. The list goes on, but you get the idea. ✉ *Shattuck Ave. between Cedar and Rose Sts., North Berkeley* ⊕ *www.gourmetghetto.org*.

FAMILY **Tilden Regional Park.** The **Regional Parks Botanic Garden** is the star of this beautiful 2,000-acre park in the hills east of the UC Berkeley campus. Botanically speaking, a stroll through the garden, which focuses on native plants of California, provides a whirlwind tour of the entire state. At the garden's visitors center, you can pick up information about Tilden's other attractions, including its picnic spots, Lake Anza swimming site, golf course, and hiking trails (the paved **Nimitz Way**, at

The epicenter of Berkeley's energy and activism: the University of California.

Inspiration Point, is a popular hike with wonderful views, especially at sunset). Children love Tilden Park's miniature steam trains; Little Farm, where kids can feed the animals; and the vintage carousel with wooden animals. ⊠ *Regional Parks Botanic Garden, Wildcat Canyon Rd. and South Park Dr., Tilden Park* ☎ *510/544–2747* ⊕ *www.ebparks.org/parks/tilden* ⊠ *Free to park and botanic garden* ⊘ *Daily 8 am–10 pm.*

University of California. Known simply as "Cal," the founding campus of California's university system is one of the leading intellectual centers in the United States and a major site for scientific research. Chartered in 1868, the university sits on 178 oak-covered acres split by Strawberry Creek. Bounded by Bancroft Way to the south, Hearst Avenue to the north, Oxford Street to the west, and Gayley Road to the east, Cal has more than 30,000 students and a full-time faculty of 1,500.

Below are a few places of note on campus:

Berkeley Art Museum & Pacific Film Archive. The museum's collection spans five centuries and is strong on mid-20th-century art, particularly abstract expressionist works; admission to the downstairs galleries is free. The Pacific Film Archive, at 2575 Bancroft Way, is a major venue for foreign, independent, and avant-garde film. ⊠ *2626 Bancroft Way, at Bowditch St.* ☎ *510/642–1124* ⊕ *www.bampfa.berkeley.edu* ⊠ *$10, free 1st Thurs. of month* ⊘ *Wed.–Sun. 11–5, some Fri. 11–9.*

Berkeley Visitor Information Center. You can get your bearings here and find out about campus events. Free, 90-minute tours leave from here on weekdays. ⊠ *101 Sproul Hall, Bancroft Way and Telegraph Ave.* ☎ *510/642–5215* ⊘ *Weekdays 8:30–4:30, tours at 10 am.*

Sather Tower. Weekend campus tours leave from this landmark, popularly known as the Campanile, at 10 am on Saturdays and 1 pm on Sundays. The 307-foot structure, modeled on St. Mark's Tower in Venice, can be seen for miles. For a view of the campus and beyond, take the elevator up 175 feet, then walk another 38 steps to the observation deck. ⌨ *Elevator $2* ⊙ *Weekdays 10–4, Sat. 10–5, Sun. 10–1:30 and 3–5.*

Sproul Plaza. The site of free-speech and civil-rights protests in the 1960s, the plaza remains a platform for political and social activists, musicians, and students. Preachers orate atop milk crates, amateur entertainers bang on makeshift drum sets, and protesters distribute leaflets about everything from marijuana to the Middle East. Walk through at noon for the liveliest show of student spirit. ⊠ *Telegraph Ave. and Bancroft Way.*

University of California Botanical Garden. Thanks to Berkeley's temperate climate, about 13,500 species of plants from all over the world flourish in this 34-acre garden. Free tours are given on Thursdays and weekends at 1:30; the views are breathtaking. ⊠ *200 Centennial Dr.* *510/643–2755* ⊕ *botanicalgarden.berkeley.edu $10, free 1st Thurs. of month.* ⊙ *Daily 9–5. Closed 1st Tues. of month.* ⊕ *www.berkeley.edu.*

WORTH NOTING

Berkeley Marina. The marina has spectacular views of San Francisco and Angel Island from a ¾-mile-long wooden pier, and there are grassy expanses good for a picnic. On sunny days, the 92-acre **Cesar E. Chavez Park,** at the marina's northern tip, fills with kite flyers, dog walkers, and families grilling and riding bikes. The Berkeley Kite Festival happens here each July, and thousands watch San Francisco's Fourth of July fireworks from this spot—when they can be seen through the fog. ⊠ *University Ave., ½ mile west of I–80* ⊕ *www.ci.berkeley.ca.us/marina.*

Elmwood. Shops and cafés pack this pleasant neighborhood centered on College Avenue, just south of the U.C. campus. You'll know you're here when you see the logo for the beloved art-house cinema and performance space, the **Elmwood theater,** near College and Ashby avenues, though you're just as apt to see a line snaking outside nearby **Ici Ice Cream,** at 2948 College. All the treats here are made on the premises. While you're waiting, check out the architectural details of the nearby pre-World War II storefronts. Century-old shingled houses line the tree-shaded streets nearby. ⊠ *College Ave. between Dwight Way and Alcatraz Ave., Elmwood.*

Indian Rock. An outcropping of nature in a sea of North Berkeley homes, this is an unbeatable spot for a sunset picnic. You know you've reached the rock when you see amateur rock climbers clinging precariously to

---

A TASTING TOUR

For an unforgettable foodie experience, take Lisa Rogovin's **Culinary Walking Tour** (☎ *415/806–5970* ⊕ *www.edible-excursions.net*). You'll taste your way through the Gourmet Ghetto, learn some culinary history, and meet the chefs behind the food. Tours ($75) run on Thursdays from 11 to 2:15 and on Saturdays from 10 to 1.

5

its side. After-work walkers and cuddling couples, all watching the sun sinking beneath the Golden Gate Bridge, join you at the top. Come early to grab a spot on the rock while it's still light. ⊠ *Head east on Indian Rock Path at Solano Ave. and the Alameda.*

FAMILY **Lawrence Hall of Science.** At this dazzling hands-on science museum, kids can look at insects under microscopes, solve crimes using chemical forensics, and explore the physics of baseball. Out front they'll climb on Pheena, a life-size blue-whale model, and clamber over a giant strand of DNA. Out back, it's all about how earthquakes and water have shaped the bay, and from all vantage points sweeping views of the bay and beyond can be had. On weekends come special lectures, demonstrations, and planetarium shows. ⊠ *1 Centennial Dr., Berkeley* ☎ *510/642–5132* ⊕ *www.lawrencehallofscience.org* ☑ *$12, planetarium $4 extra* ⊘ *Daily 10–5.*

San Pablo Avenue. Berkeley's diversity is front and center along this evolving north–south artery in West Berkeley, where the old and new stand side by side: sari shops and a Mexican grocery do business near a hipster dive bar, a bait-and-tackle store, a typewriter store, and a dozen cool boutiques, all cheek by jowl in a six-block microhood that doesn't have a name . . . yet.

Start at University Avenue, where you can duck into **Mi Tierra Foods** (No. 2082) for piñatas and chorizo—notice the Mission-like mural—and **Middle Eastern Market** (No. 2054) for rose water and rockin' baklava. **Café V** (No. 2056) has fresh, reliably good, and reasonably priced Vietnamese food, and pretty much everyone loves the thin-crust pies at **Lanesplitter Pizza & Pub** (No. 2033). The coffee at **Local 123** (No. 2049) is strong, delicious, and beautiful, and the back patio is a lovely surprise.

Old-fashioned, family-run **Country Cheese** (No. 2101) has hundreds of cheeses, of course, but it also carries great bulk foods and makes a heck of a sandwich to order. Or grab a table at industrial-cute **Gaumenkitzel** (No. 2121) and tuck in to schnitzel and other traditional German fare. The pierced-and-tattooed set loves **Acme Bar & Company** (No. 2115) for its Bloody Marys and whiskey selection.

As you move south, you'll pass lots of home-decor shops. Peek into **Side** (No. 2363) to check out the beautifully restored antiques, and nearby witness the reupholstering genius on display at **Mignonne Décor** (No. 2447). One of the Bay Area's oldest salvage shops, **Ohmega Salvage** (Nos. 2400–2407) makes for fun browsing, though its claw-foot tubs and Victorian window frames are pricey.

At the corner of Dwight Way, stop for more caffeine at **Caffè Trieste** (No. 2500), Berkeley's homey branch of North Beach's bohemian coffee bar. Arousing browsing can be had at sex-positive, woman-friendly **Good Vibrations** (No. 2504). Find wonderful gifts at **Juniper Tree Supplies** (No. 2520), with everything for the soap and candle maker; **Kiss My Ring** (No. 2522), which stocks jewelry designed by the owner; and **Gorgeous and Green** (No. 2524), best known for its sustainable wedding floral arrangements but worth a stop for its well-curated selection of vintage gifts and letterpress cards. ⊠ *San Pablo Ave., between University Ave. and Parker St., Berkeley.*

Telegraph Avenue. Berkeley's student-oriented thoroughfare, Telegraph Avenue is the best place to get a dose of the city's famed counter-culture. On any given day, you might encounter a troop of chanting Hare Krishnas or a drumming band of Rastafarians. First and foremost, however, Telegraph is a place for socializing and shopping, the only uniquely Berkeley shopping experience in town and a definite don't-miss (though locals complain that Telegraph is heading downhill fast, with too many panhandlers, and businesses closing up shop). ■TIP➜ Take care at night, when things get edgier. The nearby People's Park, mostly harmless by day, is best avoided after sunset. Cafés, bookstores, poster shops, and street vendors line the avenue. T-shirt vendors and tarot-card readers come and go on a whim, but a few establishments—**Rasputin Music** (No. 2401), **Amoeba Music** (No. 2455), and **Moe's Books** (No. 2476)—are neighborhood landmarks. Allen Ginsberg wrote his acclaimed poem "Howl" at **Caffe Mediterraneum** (No. 2475), a relic of 1960s-era café culture that also lays claim to inventing the café latte.

WHERE TO EAT

Dining in Berkeley is a low-key affair; even in the finest restaurants, most folks dress casually. Late diners be forewarned: Berkeley is an "early to bed" kind of town.

$$
SOUTHERN

✗ **Angeline's Louisana Kitchen.** There's always a line winding out the door for the delicious food at Angeline's. The brick walls, maps of Louisana, ceiling fans, and New Orleans music create a festive atmosphere that's both welcoming and exciting. Specialties include Voo Doo shrimp with blue lake beans, crawfish étouffée, and buttermilk fried chicken. The Creole pecan pie is so good you'll be coming back for more. ⑤ *Average main: $14* ⊠ *2261 Shattuck Ave., near Kittredge St.* ☎ *510/548–6900* ⊕ *www.angelineskitchen.com.*

$
AMERICAN

✗ **Bette's Oceanview Diner.** Buttermilk pancakes are just one of the specialties at this 1930s-inspired diner complete with checkered floors and burgundy booths. Huevos rancheros and lox and eggs are other breakfast options; kosher franks, generous slices of pizza, and a slew of sandwiches are available for lunch. The wait for a seat can be quite long; thankfully, 4th Street was made for strolling. ■TIP➜ If you're starving, head to Bette's to Go, next door, for takeout. ⑤ *Average main: $10* ⊠ *1807 4th St., near Delaware St., 4th Street* ☎ *510/644-3230* ⊕ *www.bettesdiner.com* ⌕ *Reservations not accepted* ⊗ *No dinner.*

$$
MEDITERRANEAN

✗ **Café Rouge.** You can recover from 4th Street shopping in this spacious two-story bistro complete with zinc bar, skylights, and festive lanterns. The short, seasonal menu ranges from the sophisticated, such as duck confit and green-garlic risotto, to the homey, like spit-roasted chicken or pork loin, or cheddar-topped burgers. If you visit by day, take a peek at the meat market in the back. ⑤ *Average main: $21* ⊠ *1782 4th St., at Delaware St.* ☎ *510/525–1440* ⊕ *www.caferouge.net* ⊗ *No dinner Mon.*

$$
SPANISH

✗ **César.** In true Spanish style, dinners are served late at César, whose kitchen closes at 11:30 pm on Friday and Saturday and at 11 pm the rest of the week. Couples spill out from its street-level windows on warm nights, or rub shoulders at the polished bar or center communal table. Founded by a trio of former Chez Panisse chefs, César is like a first cousin to Chez Panisse, each restaurant recommending the other if there's a long wait ahead. For tapas and perfectly grilled *bocadillos* (small sandwiches), there's no better choice. The bar also makes a mean martini and has an impressive wine list. ■ **TIP→ Come early to get seated quickly and also to hear your tablemates; the room gets loud when the bar is in full swing.** ⑤ *Average main: $15* ✉ *1515 Shattuck Ave., at Vine St., North Berkeley* ☎ *510/883-0222* ⊕ *cesarberkeley.com* ⚇ *Reservations not accepted.*

$$$$

AMERICAN

Fodor's Choice

★

✕ **Chez Panisse Café & Restaurant.** At Chez Panisse even humble pizza is reincarnated, with innovative toppings of the freshest local ingredients. The downstairs portion of Alice Waters's legendary eatery is noted for its formality and personal service. The daily-changing multicourse dinners are prix-fixe ($$$$), with the cost slightly lower on weekdays. Upstairs, in the informal café, the crowd is livelier, the prices are lower ($$–$$$), and the ever-changing menu is à la carte. The food is simpler, too: penne with new potatoes, arugula, and sheep's-milk cheese; fresh figs with Parmigiano-Reggiano cheese and arugula; and grilled tuna with Savoy cabbage, for example. Legions of loyal fans insist that Chez Panisse lives up to its reputation and delivers a dining experience well worth the price. Visiting foodies won't want to miss a meal here; be sure to make reservations a few weeks ahead of time. ⑤ *Average main: $95* ✉ *1517 Shattuck Ave., at Vine St., North Berkeley* ☎ *510/548-5525 restaurant, 510/548-5049 café* ⊕ *www.chezpanisse.com* ⚇ *Reservations essential* ☾ *Closed Sun. No lunch in the restaurant.*

$$

TUSCAN

✕ **Corso Trattoria.** On the edge of Berkeley's Gourmet Ghetto, this lively spot serves up excellent Florentine cuisine in a spare but snazzy space. The open kitchen at the back dominates the room (which can get smoky at times), and the closely spaced tables add to the festivity of dining here. The seasonal menu might include grilled local swordfish with breadcrumb salsa verde or butter-roasted chicken breast. Side dishes are ordered separately; the baked polenta with mascarpone and Parmesan is a definite crowd pleaser. An extensive Italian wine list complements the menu; save room for the memorable panna cotta. ⑤ *Average main: $18* ✉ *1788 Shattuck Ave., at Delaware St., North Berkeley, Berkeley* ☎ *510/704-8004* ⊕ *www.trattoriacorso.com* ☾ *No lunch.*

$$

AMERICAN

✕ **Gather.** Here organic, sustainable, and all things Berkeley reside harmoniously beneath one tasty roof. This vibrant, well-lit eatery boasts funky lighting fixtures, a variety of shiny wood furnishings, and banquettes made of recycled leather belts. Everything feels contemporary and local, especially the food. The vegan "charcuterie," made of root vegetables, put the restaurant on the national map; the stinging nettles pizza is refreshing, and the grilled chicken is oh so juicy. This is a haven for vegetarian, vegan, and gluten-free eaters, but there's plenty for meat eaters to choose from, too. Desserts don't get much better than the chocolate semifreddo with Zinfandel-braised Mission figs and pine nuts. Yum, yum. ⑤ *Average main: $20* ✉ *2200 Oxford St., at Allston Way* ☎ *510/809-0400* ⊕ *www.gatherrestaurant.com.*

The pioneer restaurant Chez Panisse focuses on seasonal local ingredients.

$$ ✕ **Ippuku.** More Tokyo street chic than standard sushi house, this
JAPANESE   *izakaya*—the Japanese equivalent of a bar with appetizers—with
bamboo-screen booths serves up surprising fare, from chicken tartare
to wonderful *yakitori*, skewers such as bacon-wrapped mushrooms
and pork belly. (Anything skewered here is sure to please.) Dinner
beats lunch at Ippuku, and savvy diners make reservations and arrive
early for the best selection. The bar, which opens onto the street,
pours an impressive array of sakes and *shōchū* (liquor distilled from
sweet potatoes, rice, or barley). ⑤ *Average main: $15 ⊠ 2130 Center
St., Downtown ☎ 510/665–1969 ⊕ www.ippukuberkeley.com ⊗ No
lunch Sun.–Thurs.*

$$ ✕ **Lalime's.** Inside a charming, flower-covered house, this restaurant
MEDITERRANEAN   serves dishes that reflect the entire Mediterranean region. The menu,
Fodor's Choice   constantly changing and unfailingly great, depends on the availability
★   of fresh seasonal ingredients. Choices might include grilled ahi tuna
or creamy Italian risotto. Light colors used in the dining room, which
has two levels, help to create a cheerful mood. A star in its own right,
Lalime's is a good second choice if Chez Panisse is booked. ⑤ *Average
main: $24 ⊠ 1329 Gilman St., at Tevlin St., North Berkeley ☎ 510/527–
9838 ⊕ www.lalimes.com ⚖ Reservations essential ⊗ No lunch.*

$ ✕ **Picante.** A barnlike space full of cheerful Mexican tiles and folk-art
MEXICAN   masks, Picante is a find for anyone seeking good, Cal-Mex food for
FAMILY   a song. The masa is freshly ground for the tortillas and tamales (it's
fun to watch the tamale maker in action), the salsas are complex,
and the flavor combinations are inventive. Try tamales filled with
butternut squash and chilis or a simple taco of roasted poblanos and
sautéed onions; we challenge you to finish a plate of supernachos.

Picante is beloved of Berkeley families with raucous children, as they fit right in to the festival-like atmosphere and are happily distracted by the fountain on the back patio. $ *Average main: $11* ✉ *1328 6th St., near Camelia St.* ☎ *510/525–3121* ⊕ *www.picanteberkeley.com* ⌳ *Reservations not accepted.*

$ ✗ **Saul's.** Well known for its homemade sodas and enormous sand-
AMERICAN   wiches, the Saul's of today also uses sustainably sourced seafood, grass-
FAMILY   fed beef, and organic eggs. The restaurant is a Berkeley institution, and its loyal clientele swears by the pastrami sandwiches, stuffed-cabbage rolls, and tuna melts. For breakfast, the challah French toast is so thick it's almost too big to bite, and the deli omelets are served pancake style. The high ceilings and red-leather booths add to the friendly, retro atmosphere. Don't overlook the glass deli case, where you can order food to go. $ *Average main: $15* ✉ *1475 Shattuck Ave., near Vine St., North Berkeley* ☎ *510/848–3354* ⊕ *www.saulsdeli.com* ⌳ *Reservations not accepted* ⊘ *Closed Thanksgiving and Yom Kippur.*

WHERE TO STAY

For inexpensive lodging, investigate University Avenue, west of campus. The area can be noisy, congested, and somewhat dilapidated, but it does include a few decent motels and chain properties. All Berkeley lodgings, except for the swanky Claremont, are strictly midrange.

For expanded hotel reviews, visit Fodors.com.

$ ⛶ **The Bancroft Hotel.** Lovingly remodeled in 2012, this green boutique
HOTEL   hotel—across from the U.C. campus—is fresh, stylish, and completely eco-friendly. **Pros:** heating under the floorboards; great rooftop deck; closest hotel in Berkeley to campus. **Cons:** some rooms are small; bathrooms could be freshened up; no elevator. $ *Rooms from: $120* ✉ *2680 Bancroft Way* ☎ *510/549–1000* ⊕ *bancrofthotel.com* ⇱ *22 rooms* ⦿ *Breakfast.*

$$$$ ⛶ **Claremont Resort and Spa.** Straddling the Oakland–Berkeley border,
HOTEL   this amenities-rich resort beckons like a gleaming white castle in the
Fodor'sChoice   hills. **Pros:** amazing spa; supervised child care; solid business amenities;
★   great bay views from some rooms. **Cons:** parking is pricey; facilities charge for use of spa, tennis courts, pool, gym, et cetera; no Wi-Fi in rooms; additional fee for breakfast. $ *Rooms from: $260* ✉ *41 Tunnel Rd., at Ashby and Domingo Aves., Claremont* ☎ *510/843–3000, 800/551–7266* ⊕ *www.claremontresort.com* ⇱ *249 rooms, 30 suites* ⦿ *No meals.*

$ ⛶ **Holiday Inn Express.** Convenient to the freeway and 4th Street shop-
HOTEL   ping, this inviting, peach-and-beige hotel offers good bang for the buck. **Pros:** good breakfast; short walk to restaurant options on San Pablo and University. **Cons:** area can get noisy and congested with traffic during commute hours; neighborhood can feel a bit sketchy after dark. $ *Rooms from: $144* ✉ *1175 University Ave., at Curtis St.* ☎ *510/548–1700, 866/548–1700* ⊕ *www.hiexberkeley.com* ⇱ *69 rooms, 3 suites* ⦿ *Breakfast.*

$$ ⛶ **Hotel Durant.** Long a mainstay of parents visiting their children at
HOTEL   U.C. Berkeley, this boutique hotel is also a good option for those who want to be a short walk from Telegraph Avenue. **Pros:** convenient

location to Cal; blackout shades; organic bathrobes. **Cons:** downstairs bar can get noisy during Cal games; parking can be pricey; hotel shows its age. $ *Rooms from: $179* ✉ *2600 Durant Ave., at Bowditch St.* ☎ *510/845-8981* ⊕ *www.hoteldurant.com* ⇌ *139 rooms, 5 suites* ❖❖ *No meals.*

$$
HOTEL
Fodors Choice
★

🏨 **Hotel Shattuck Plaza.** This historic boutique hotel sits amid Berkeley's downtown arts district, just steps from the U.C. campus and a short walk from the Gourmet Ghetto. **Pros:** central location; modern facilities; good views; great restaurant. **Cons:** pricey parking; limited fitness center. $ *Rooms from: $185* ✉ *2086 Allston Way, at Shattuck Ave., Downtown* ☎ *510/845-7300* ⊕ *www.hotelshattuckplaza.com* ⇌ *199 rooms, 17 suites* ❖❖ *No meals.*

NIGHTLIFE AND THE ARTS

Berkeley Repertory Theatre. One of the region's highly respected resident professional companies, this theater group performs classic and contemporary plays from autumn to spring. Well-known pieces such as *Crime and Punishment* and *The Arabian Nights* mix with edgier fare like Green Day's *American Idiot* and Lemony Snicket's *The Composer Is Dead.* The theater's complex is in the heart of downtown Berkeley's arts district, near BART's Downtown Berkeley station. ✉ *2025 Addison St., near Shattuck Ave.* ☎ *510/647-2949* ⊕ *www.berkeleyrep.org.*

Berkeley Symphony Orchestra. The works of 20th-century composers are a focus of this prominent orchestra, but traditional pieces are also performed. BSO plays a handful of concerts each year, in Zellerbach Hall and other locations. ✉ *1942 University Ave., Suite 207* ☎ *510/841–2800* ⊕ *www.berkeleysymphony.org.*

Cal Performances. The series, running from September through May at Zellerbach Hall and various other U.C. Berkeley venues, offers the Bay Area's most varied bill of internationally acclaimed artists in all disciplines, from classical soloists to the latest jazz, world-music, theater, and dance ensembles. Look for frequent campus colloquiums or preshow talks featuring Berkeley's professors. ✉ *Zellerbach Hall, Telegraph Ave. and Bancroft Way* ☎ *510/642-9988* ⊕ *calperformances.org.*

Fodors Choice
★

Freight & Salvage Coffeehouse. Some of the most talented practitioners of folk, blues, Cajun, and bluegrass perform in this alcohol-free space, one of the finest folk houses in the country. Most tickets cost less than $25. ✉ *2020 Addison St., between Shattuck Ave. and Milvia St.* ☎ *510/644–2020* ⊕ *www.thefreight.org.*

SHOPPING

Fodors Choice
★

Amoeba Music. Heaven for audiophiles, this legendary Berkeley favorite is *the* place to head for new and used CDs, records, cassettes, and DVDs. The dazzling stock includes thousands of titles for all music tastes. The store even has its own record label. There are branches in San Francisco and Hollywood, but this is the original. ✉ *2455 Telegraph Ave., at Haste St.* ☎ *510/549-1125.*

Body Time. Founded in Berkeley in 1970, this local chain uses premium-quality ingredients to create its natural perfumes and skin-care and aromatherapy products. Sustainably harvested essential oils that you can combine and dilute to create your own personal fragrances are the specialty. The Citrus, Lavender-Mint, and China Rain scents are all popular. ⊠ *1942 Shattuck Ave., at Berkeley Way* ☎ *510/841–5818.*

Kermit Lynch Wine Merchant. Lynch's newsletters describing his finds are legendary, as is his friendship with Alice Waters of Chez Panisse. Credited with taking American appreciation of French wine to another level, this shop is a great place to peruse as you educate your palate. The friendly salespeople can direct you to the latest French bargains. ⊠ *1605 San Pablo Ave., at Dwight Way* ☎ *510/524–1524* ⊕ *kermitlynch.com.*

Moe's Books. The spirit of Moe—the cantankerous, cigar-smoking late proprietor—lives on in this four-story house of books. Students and professors come here to browse the large selection of used books, including literary and cultural criticism, art titles, and literature in foreign languages. ⊠ *2476 Telegraph Ave., near Haste St.* ☎ *510/849–2087* ⊕ *moesbooks.com.*

Rasputin Music. A huge selection of new music for every taste draws crowds. In any other town, Rasputin's stock of used CDs and vinyl would likely be unsurpassed. ⊠ *2403 Telegraph Ave., at Channing Way* ☎ *510/848–9004* ⊕ *www.rasputinmusic.com.*

OAKLAND

Directly east of Bay Bridge.

Often overshadowed by San Francisco's beauty and Berkeley's storied counterculture, Oakland's allure lies in its amazing diversity. Here you can find a Nigerian clothing store, a beautifully renovated Victorian home, a Buddhist meditation center, and a lively salsa club, all within the same block.

Oakland's multifaceted nature reflects its colorful and often tumultuous history. Once a cluster of Mediterranean-style homes and gardens that served as a bedroom community for San Francisco, the city became a hub of shipbuilding and industry almost overnight when the United States entered World War II. New jobs in the city's shipyards and factories attracted thousands of workers, including some of the first female welders, and the city's neighborhoods were imbued with a proud but gritty spirit. In the 1960s and '70s this intense community pride gave rise to such militant groups as the Black Panther Party and the Symbionese Liberation Army, but they were little match for the economic hardships and racial tensions that plagued Oakland. In many neighborhoods the reality was widespread poverty and gang violence—subjects that dominated the songs of such Oakland-bred rappers as the late Tupac Shakur. The highly publicized protests of the Occupy Oakland movement in 2011 and 2012 illustrated just how much Oakland remains a mosaic of its past.

The affluent reside in the city's hillside homes, wooded enclaves like Claremont and Montclair, which provide a warmer, more spacious, and more affordable alternative to San Francisco, while a constant flow of newcomers—many from Central America and Asia—ensures continued diversity, vitality, and growing pains. Many neighborhoods to the west and south of the city center remain run-down and unsafe, but a renovated downtown area—sparking a vibrant arts scene—and the waterfront around Jack London Square on the edge of finding its footing have injected new energy into the city. Even San Franciscans, often loathe to cross the Bay Bridge—why should they?—come to Uptown and Temescal for the crackling arts and restaurant scenes there.

Everyday life here revolves around the neighborhood, with a main business strip attracting both shoppers and strollers. In some areas, such as high-end Piedmont and Rockridge, you'd swear you were in Berkeley or San Francisco's Noe Valley or Cow Hollow. Along Telegraph Avenue just south of 51st Street, Temescal is pulsing with creative culinary and design energy. These are perfect places for browsing, eating, or just relaxing between sightseeing trips to Oakland's architectural gems, rejuvenated waterfront, and numerous green spaces.

GETTING HERE AND AROUND

Driving from San Francisco, take Interstate 80 East across the Bay Bridge, then take Interstate 580 to the Grand Avenue exit for Lake Merritt. To reach downtown and the waterfront, take Interstate 980 from Interstate 580 and exit at 12th Street; exit at 18th Street for Uptown. For Temescal, take Interstate 580 to Highway 24 and exit at 51st Street.

By BART, use the Lake Merritt Station for the Oakland Museum and southern Lake Merritt; the Oakland City Center–12th Street Station for downtown, Chinatown, and Old Oakland; and the 19th Street Station for Uptown, the Paramount Theatre, and the north side of Lake Merritt.

By bus, take the AC Transit's C and P lines to get to Piedmont in Oakland. The O bus stops at the edge of Chinatown near downtown Oakland.

Oakland's Jack London Square is an easy hop on the ferry from San Francisco. Those without cars can take advantage of the free Broadway Shuttle, which runs from the square down Broadway through Chinatown/Old Oakland, downtown, Uptown, and Lake Merritt, all the way to 27th Street. The shuttle runs late on Friday and Saturday nights; its website has full schedule information.

Once you arrive, be aware of how quickly neighborhoods can change. Walking is safe downtown and in the Piedmont and Rockridge areas, but avoid walking west and south of downtown.

ESSENTIALS

Shuttle Contact Broadway Shuttle ✉ *Oakland* ⊕ *www.meetdowntownoak.com.*

Visitor Information Oakland Convention and Visitors Bureau ✉ *463 11th St.* ☎ *510/839-9000* ⊕ *www.oaklandcvb.com.*

EXPLORING
TOP ATTRACTIONS

Fodor's Choice ★ FAMILY

Oakland Museum of California. One of Oakland's top attractions, the museum surveys the state's art, history, and natural wonders in three galleries of absorbing, detailed exhibits. You can travel through myriad ecosystems in the Gallery of California Natural Sciences, from the sand dunes of the Pacific to the coyotes and brush of the Nevada border. Kids love the lifelike wild-animal exhibits, especially the snarling wolverine, big-eyed harbor seal, and trove of hidden creatures. The rambling Gallery of California History includes everything from Spanish-era armor to a small but impressive collection of vintage vehicles, including a candy-apple-red "Mystery" car from the 1960s and a gleaming red, gold, and silver fire engine that battled the flames in San Francisco following the 1906 earthquake. The Gallery of California Art holds an eclectic collection of modern works and early landscapes. Of particular interest are paintings by Richard Diebenkorn, Joan Brown, Elmer Bischoff, and David Park, all members of the Bay Area figurative school, which flourished here after World War II. Fans of Dorothea Lange won't want to miss the gallery's comprehensive collection of her work. The museum also has a sculpture garden with a view of the Oakland and Berkeley hills in the distance. ⊠ *1000 Oak St., at 10th St., Downtown* ☎ *510/238–2200* ⊕ *www.museumca.org* ☜ *$12, free 1st Sun. of month* ☉ *Wed.–Sun. 11–5, Fri. until 9.*

Fodor's Choice **Paramount Theatre.** Perhaps the most glorious art deco specimen in the ★ city, if not the entire Bay Area, the Paramount operates as a venue for concerts and performances of all kinds, from the Oakland East Bay Symphony to Tom Waits and Elvis Costello. The popular monthly movie nights start off with a 30-minute Wurlitzer concert preceding classic films such as *Casablanca.* ■**TIP→ At 10 am on the first and third Saturday of each month, you can take a marvelous two-hour tour of the building.** ⊠ *2025 Broadway, at 20th St., Uptown* ☎ *510/465–6400* ⊕ *www.paramounttheatre.com* ☜ *Tour $5.*

Rockridge. The upscale neighborhood of Rockridge is one of Oakland's most desirable places to live. Explore the tree-lined streets that radiate out from **College Avenue** just north and south of the Rockridge BART station for a look at California bungalow architecture at its finest. By day College Avenue between Broadway and Alcatraz Avenue is crowded with shoppers buying fresh flowers, used books, and clothing; by night the same folks are back for dinner and locally brewed ales in the numerous restaurants and pubs. With its pricey specialty-food shops, **Market Hall,** an airy European-style marketplace at Shafter Avenue, is a hub of culinary activity. ⊕ *www.rockridgedistrict.com.*

Fodor's Choice **Temescal.** Centering on Telegraph Avenue between Piedmont and South
★ Berkeley, up-and-coming Temescal ("sweat house" in the language of the Aztec) is a low-pretension, moneyed-hipster hood with a lot of young families and—gasp—middle-aged folks thrown into the mix. A critical mass of excellent eateries, from veteran Doña Tomás and favorites Pizzaiola and Aunt Mary's to **Bakesale Betty** (✉ *5098 Telegraph Ave.*), where folks line up down the block for the fried-chicken sandwich on the one-item menu, and **Doughnut Dolly** (✉ *482B 49th St.*), who fills her fried treats to order, draws folks from around the Bay Area. Old-time dive bars and check-cashing places share space with newer arrivals like crafty, local children's clothing shop **Ruby's Garden** (✉ *5026 Telegraph Ave.*); **Article Pract** (✉ *5010 Telegraph Ave.*), purveyor of gorgeous yarn; and the wonderful **East Bay Depot for Creative Reuse** (✉ *4695 Telegraph Ave.*), where you might find a bucket of buttons or 1,000 muffin wrappers for $1 among bird cages, furniture, lunch boxes, and ribbon.

Around the corner, **Temescal Alley** (✉ *49th St.*), a tucked-away lane of tiny storefronts, crackles with the creative energy of the craftspeople who have set up shop there, among them fashion designer Ali Golden and jewelry designer Marisa Haskell. You can make some surprising finds at Crimson Horticultural Rarities and the fresh home-decor shops Lot 49 and Bounty and Feast.

This neighborhood is *the* place to go to put your finger on the pulse of Oakland right now. ✉ *Telegraph Ave., between 45th and 51st Sts., Oakland* ⊕ *www.temescaldistrict.org.*

Uptown. This is where nightlife and cutting-edge art happens in Oakland, along the formerly gritty, currently crazy-cool Telegraph Avenue/Broadway corridor north of downtown. Dozens of galleries cluster around Telegraph, showing everything from photography and video installations to glasswork and textile arts. On the first Friday of the month, thousands descend for the neighborhood's biggest happening, the gallery walk **Art Murmur** (⊕ *oaklandartmurmur.org*). In addition to galleries open late, Art Murmur has expanded into **First Friday,** a veritable festival featuring food trucks, street vendors, and live music along Telegraph Avenue. Less raucous and more intimate is the **Saturday Stroll,** with 17 galleries and eight mixed-use venues open on Saturdays from 1 to 5, often with special events.

Lively restaurants with a distinctly urban vibe make the neighborhood a dining destination; favorites include friendly **Luka's Taproom and Lounge** (✉ *2221 Broadway*); beautiful art deco **Flora** (✉ *1900*

Telegraph Ave.), one of the best brunch places in town; trendy, graffiti-walled **Hawker Fare** (⊠ *2300 Webster St.*), serving Asian street food; elegant **Picán** (⊠ *2295 Broadway*), for upscale Southern comfort food; and the sophisticated **Plum** (⊠ *2214 Broadway*) and its attached bar, just to name a few.

Toss in the bevy of bars, and there's plenty within walking distance to keep you busy for an entire evening: **Cafe Van Kleef** (⊠ *1621 Telegraph Ave.*), the friendly jumble that started it all Uptown; **Bar Three Fifty-Five** (⊠ *355 19th St.*), a house of great cocktails; strikingly beautiful but low-key **Dogwood** (⊠ *1644 Telegraph Ave.*), which has tasty nibbles; and **Somar** (⊠ *1727 Telegraph Ave.*), a bar, music lounge, and gallery in one. Uptown's shopping element hasn't yet gelled, making this more of an evening destination. The Paramount Theatre, the Fox Theater, and other late-art deco architectural gems distinguish this neighborhood. ⊠ *Telegraph Ave. and Broadway from 16th to 26th Sts., Oakland.*

WORTH NOTING

Chinatown. Across Broadway from Old Oakland but worlds apart, Chinatown is a densely packed, bustling neighborhood. Unlike its San Francisco counterpart, Oakland's Chinatown makes no concessions to tourists; you won't find baskets of trinkets lining the sidewalk and souvenir displays in the shop windows. But supermarkets such as **Yuen Hop Noodle Company and Asian Food Products** (⊠ *824 Webster St.*), open since 1931, overflow with goodies. And the line for sweets, breads, and towering cakes snakes out the door of **Napoleon Super Bakery** (⊠ *810 Franklin St.*). ⊠ *Between Broadway and Lakeside Dr. and between 6th and 12th Sts.*

Fox Theater. An art deco movie palace built in 1928, the Fox sat decaying and mostly unused for decades until the last of several redevelopment schemes culminated in a stunning renovation. The Mediterranean Moorish–style theater and its attached buildings contain the main theater, these days used for music concerts; the Oakland School for the Arts; and the Den, a gorgeous lounge. The theater's restoration helped revive what's now known as the Uptown neighborhood. ⊠ *1807 Telegraph Ave., at 18th St., Uptown* ⊕ *www.thefoxoakland.com.*

Jack London Square. A few shops, some minor historic sites, and a growing number of noteworthy restaurants (along with the well-established Yoshi's Jazz Club) line Jack London Square, which is named after the author of *The Call of the Wild, The Sea Wolf,* and other books. London, who was born in San Francisco, also lived in Oakland, where he spent many a day boozing and brawling in the waterfront area, most notably at the tiny, wonderful **Heinold's First and Last Chance Saloon** (⊠ *48 Webster St., at Embarcadero W.*). The saloon has been serving since 1883, although it's a little worse for the wear since the 1906 earthquake. Next door is the Klondike cabin in which London spent a summer in the late 1890s. The cabin was moved from Alaska and reassembled here in 1970.

During the week, the square can feel desolate, albeit with great views. Weekends are much livelier, with diners filling the many outdoor patios,

A fun place to wet your whistle, Heinold's First and Last Chance Saloon

and shoppers perusing Sunday's farmers' market, which takes place from 9 am to 2 pm. ■TIP→ The square is an obvious spot for tourists to visit, and it's worth a peek if you've arrived on the ferry that docks here; but to get a real feel for Oakland, you'll do better to check out downtown, Temescal, or at least Rockridge. ✉ *Embarcadero W. at Broadway* ☎ *866/295–9853* ⊕ *www.jacklondonsquare.com.*

Lake Merritt. Joggers and power walkers charge along the 3-mile path that encircles this 155-acre natural saltwater lake in downtown Oakland. Crew teams often glide across the water, and boatmen guide snuggling couples in authentic Venetian gondolas (☎ *510/663–6603* ⊕ *gondolaservizio.com* ✏ *Fares start at $40 per couple for 30 min.*). **Lakeside Park,** which surrounds the north side of Lake Merritt, has several outdoor attractions, including a small children's park and a waterfowl refuge. The lake is less an attraction than a pleasant backdrop to Oaklanders' everyday life. ✉ *Lakeside Park, Bellevue and Grand Aves.*

Old Oakland. In the shadow of the convention center and towering downtown hotels, Old Oakland was once a booming business district. Today the restored Victorian storefronts lining four historic blocks house restaurants, cafés, shops, galleries, and a lively three-block farmers' market, which takes place on Friday mornings. Architectural consistency distinguishes the area from surrounding streets and lends it a distinct neighborhood feel. The Italian grocery **Ratto's International Market** (✉ *827 Washington St.*) has been in business for more than a century. Stop in for a deli sandwich there, or head over to the genial **Pacific Coast Brewing Company** (✉ *902 Washington St.*) for a microbrew on the patio. One of the best beer bars in California, the **Trappist**

(⌂ *460 8th St.*) wins loyalty for its exhaustive selection of Belgian ales. Various pop-up boutiques throughout the neighborhood are reinvigorating the storefront scene. ⌂ *Bordered by 7th, 10th, Clay, and Washington Sts.* ⊕ *www.old-oakland.com.*

Redwood Regional Park. *Sequoia sempervirens,* or coastal redwoods, grow to 150 feet tall in Redwood Regional Park, one of the few spots in the Bay Area that escaped timber-hungry loggers in the 19th century. The 1,836-acre park has forested picnic spots and dozens of hiking trails, including part of the 31-mile **Skyline National Trail,** which links Redwood to four other parks in the Berkeley–Oakland hills. From downtown Oakland take Interstate 580 east toward Hayward, exit at 35th Avenue/MacArthur Boulevard, and then take 35th Avenue east (which becomes Redwood Road). Watch for a park entrance on the left, 3 to 4 miles down the road. ⌂ *7867 Redwood Rd.* ☎ *888/327–2757* ⊕ *www.ebparks.org/parks/redwood* ▭ *Free; $5 per vehicle at some major entrances, $4 per trailered vehicle* ☉ *Daily 8 am–9 pm.*

WHERE TO EAT

$$
MEDITERRANEAN

✕ **À Côté.** This place for Mediterranean food is all about small plates, cozy tables, family-style eating—and truly excellent food. The butternut-squash ravioli, rabbit *boudin blanc* (white sausage), and duck confit flatbread with apples and cantelet cheese are all fine choices, and you won't find a better plate of *pommes frites* (french fries) anywhere. The restaurant pours more than 40 wines by the glass. Among the tempting desserts here are the lemon pudding cake with lemon cream, huckleberries, and candied pistachios, and the tangy pomegranate sorbet. The heavy wooden tables, cool tiles, and natural light make this a destination for students, families, couples, and the after-work crowd; the heated back patio is warm and welcoming in any weather. $ *Average main: $18* ⌂ *5478 College Ave., at Taft Ave., Rockridge* ☎ *510/655–6469* ⊕ *www.acoterestaurant.com* ☉ *No lunch.*

$
AMERICAN

✕ **Brown Sugar Kitchen.** Chef and owner Tanya Holland—named chef of 2012 by the California Travel Association—uses local, organic, and seasonal products to craft meals influenced by her African-American heritage and her culinary education in France. Holland blends sweet and savory flavors like no one else, and pairs her dishes with well-chosen wines. The dining room is fresh and bright, with a long, sleek counter, red-leather stools, and spacious booths and tables. This is *the* place to come for chicken and waffles. $ *Average main: $13* ⌂ *2534 Mandela Pkwy., at 26th St., West Oakland* ☎ *510/839–7685* ⊕ *www. brownsugarkitchen.com* ☉ *Closed Mon. No dinner.*

$$$
AMERICAN

✕ **Camino.** The first solo venture of chef-owner Russell Moore (a Chez Panisse alum of 21 years) and co-owner Allison Hopelain focuses on simple, seasonal, and straightforward dishes cooked in the enormous, crackling *camino* (Italian for "fireplace"). Everything is made with top-notch ingredients, including local sardines; grilled lamb and sausage with shell beans; and Dungeness crab grilled in the fireplace with rutabagas. The menu changes nightly and includes vegetarian options such as eggplant gratin. The restaurant is decorated in a Craftsman-meets-refectory style, with brick walls, and two long redwood communal tables. Seasonally inspired cocktails from the small bar are not to be missed; the gin-based drink with house-made cherry and hibiscus bitters is notably delicious. $ *Average main: $24* ✉ *3917 Grand Ave., at Boulevard Way, Lake Merritt* ☎ *510/547–5035* ⊕ *www.caminorestaurant. com* ⊗ *Closed Tues. No lunch (weekend brunch 10–2).*

$$ ✕**Chop Bar.** The walls and tables are made of reclaimed wood at this
MODERN   small, stylish space whose knowing, tattooed bartenders serve potent
AMERICAN cocktails to a crowd of hipsters and area residents and workers. A great neighborhood joint for every meal of the day (and brunch on weekends), Chop Bar serves upmarket gastro–pub grub, including favorites such as oxtail poutine, pork confit with polenta and kale, and burgers that rank among the Bay Area's best. On sunny days when the glass garage door is raised, extending the outdoor seating area out front, you'll feel like an insider who's stumbled upon an industrial neighborhood's cool secret. $ *Average main: $17* ✉ *247 4th St., at Alice St., Jack London Square, Oakland* ☎ *510/834–2467* ⊕ *www.oaklandchopbar.com.*

$$$$ ✕**Commis.** Blink and you'll miss the only East Bay restaurant with a
MODERN   Michelin star. No sign announces Commis, a slender, unassuming store-
AMERICAN front in Oakland's Piedmont neighborhood, and the room is simple and polished: nothing distracts from the artistry of the food served here. Chef James Syhabout creates a fixed, multicourse menu ($75, wine pairing $45 additional) based on the season and his distinctive vision. Dishes might include poached egg yolk with smoked dates and alliums (members of the onion/garlic family) in malt vinegar, or duck roasted on the bone over charcoal with renderings, walnut, and persimmon. Diners don't see the menu until after the meal, the chef's way of ensuring that everyone comes to the table with an open mind. This isn't a place to grab a quick bite: meals last about three hours. The service is excellent. $ *Average main: $75* ✉ *3859 Piedmont Ave., at Rio Vista Ave., Piedmont, Oakland* ☎ *510/653–3902* ⊕ *www.commisrestaurant.com* ⌕ *Reservations essential* ⊗ *Closed Mon.–Tues. No lunch.*

$$ ✕**Doña Tomás.** A neighborhood favorite, this spot in Oakland's up-
MEXICAN   and-coming Temescal District serves seasonal Mexican fare to a hip but low-key crowd. Mexican textiles and art adorn walls in two long rooms; there's also a vine-covered patio. Banish all images of taqueria grub and tuck into starters such as quesadillas filled with butternut squash and goat cheese and entrées such as *albondigas en sopa de zanahoria* (pork-and-beef meatballs in carrot purée). Some mighty fine tequilas complement the offerings. Brunch is served on weekends. $ *Average main: $18* ✉ *5004 Telegraph Ave., near 51st St., Temescal* ☎ *510/450–0522* ⊕ *www.donatomas.com* ⊗ *Closed Mon. No lunch weekdays. No dinner Sun.*

$$$ ✕**Haven.** Daniel Patterson of San Francisco's revered Coi opened this
MODERN   waterfront space in 2011, focusing on vegetables, whole-animal prepa-
AMERICAN rations, dishes to share, and great cocktails. Floor-to-ceiling windows overlook the yachts of Jack London Square, and warm lighting casts a glow over the wood-and-brick dining room. Look for anything smoked or with marrow on executive chef Kim Alter's menu and you can't miss; smoked black rice with citrus and *uni* (sea urchin) is striking and flavorful, and the shepherd's pie—pig belly, rutabaga, and potato purée—is earthy and delicious. The market menu ($60), served family-style and

based on what's fresh at the market, is a fun way to experience this restaurant's inventive approach. Sunday brunch is served from 10:30 am to 2:30 pm. $ *Average main: $24* ⌧ *44 Webster St., at 1st St. and Embarcadero W., Jack London Square, Oakland* ☎ *510/663–4440* ⊕ *www. havenoakland.com* ⊘ *Closed Mon.–Tues. No lunch.*

$ ✕ **Le Cheval Restaurant.** This cavernous restaurant, a lunchtime favorite,

VIETNAMESE is a good place to sample *pho*, Hanoi-style beef noodle soup fragrant with star anise. Other entrées include lemon chicken, cubed beefsteak, clay-pot snapper, and shark in coconut milk. It's hard to spend more than $20 for an entire meal unless you order the special crab (about $30). The complimentary minibowls of soup that are placed on the table as soon as you sit down are a great balm to hungry diners, though the service is lightning-quick anyway. $ *Average main: $12* ⌧ *1019 Clay St., at 11th St., Old Oakland* ☎ *510/763–8495* ⊕ *www.lecheval.com* ⊘ *No lunch Sun.*

$$ ✕ **Luka's Taproom & Lounge.** Luka's is a real taste of downtown Oakland:

BELGIAN hip and urban, with an unpretentious vibe. Diners nibble on *frites* (fries) any Belgian would embrace and entrées like the *bourride* (seafood stew with cod, prawns, mussels, clams, artichokes, leeks, and potatoes). The brews draw them in, too—a nice selection of Trappist ales complements plentiful beers on tap and international bottles—and the DJs in the adjacent lounge keep the scene going late. $ *Average main: $22* ⌧ *2221 Broadway, at West Grand Ave., Uptown* ☎ *510/451–4677* ⊕ *www. lukasoakland.com* ⊘ *No lunch Sat.*

$$ ✕ **Pizzaiolo.** Apparently no length of a wait can discourage locals who

PIZZA persevere to enjoy the legendary thin-crust, wood-fired pizza served up by Chez Panisse alum Charlie Hallowell in this rustic-chic dining room. Diners—mostly neighborhood hipsters but also young families and foodies of all ages—perch in wooden chairs with red-leather backs; weathered wood floors and brick walls peeking through the plaster create an always-been-here feel. Seasonal pizza options might include wild nettles and pecorino, or rapini and house-made sausage; don't overlook non-pizza dishes such as wild steelhead salmon with fava greens, English peas, and Meyer-lemon butter. Except on Sundays, early risers get to skip the crowds and enjoy Blue Bottle Coffee and pastries from 8 until noon. $ *Average main: $17* ⌧ *5008 Telegraph Ave., at 51st St., Temescal, Oakland* ☎ *510/652–4888* ⊕ *www.pizzaiolooakland.com* ⊘ *Closed Sun. No lunch.*

WHERE TO STAY

For expanded hotel reviews, visit Fodors.com.

$$ ⊡ **Best Western Plus Bayside Hotel.** Sandwiched between the serene and

HOTEL scenic Oakland Estuary on one side and train tracks and a 10-lane freeway on the other, this all-suites property has handsome accommodations with balconies or patios, many overlooking the water. **Pros:** attractive, budget-conscious choice; free parking; recently renovated; water views make city bustle seem far away. **Cons:** not near anything of interest; city-side rooms can be loud. $ *Rooms from: $179* ⌧ *1717 Embarcadero, off I–880, at 16th St. exit, Oakland* ☎ *510/356–2450* ⊕ *www.bestwestern.com* ⇥ *81 suites* ⍾⊙ *Breakfast.*

$$ 🖼 **Waterfront Hotel.** The only waterfront hotel in town, this thoroughly
HOTEL   modern, pleasantly appointed Joie de Vivre property sits among the
appealing restaurants (including the hotel's own) of Jack London
Square. **Pros:** great location; lovely views; dog-friendly. **Cons:** passing
trains can be noisy; parking is pricey; hotel is beginning to show its
age. *⑤ Rooms from: $159 ⊠ 10 Washington St., Jack London Square*
☎ *510/836–3800, 800/729–3638 ⊕ www.waterfrontplaza.com ⇆ 143
rooms* ⫟⊙⫟ *No meals.*

NIGHTLIFE AND THE ARTS

Artists have found cheap rent and loft spaces in Oakland, giving rise to
an underground cultural scene—visual arts, indie music, spoken word,
film—that's definitely buzzing, especially in Uptown (which is pretty
much downtown). Trendy bars and clubs seem to pop up by the week—
everything from artisan breweries to all-out retro dives. The nightlife
scene here is less crowded and more intimate than what you'll find in
San Francisco. Music is just about everywhere, though the most popular
venues are downtown.

Fodor's Choice   **Café Van Kleef.** Dutch artist Peter Van Kleef's candle-strewn, funky café-
★   bar crackles with creative energy. Van Kleef has a lot to do with the
convivial atmosphere; the garrulous owner loves sharing tales about
his quirky, floor-to-ceiling collection of mementos, including what he
claims are Cassius Clay's boxing gloves and Dorothy's ruby slippers
from *The Wizard of Oz*. The café also has a consistently solid calendar
of live music, heavy on the jazz side. The drinks are among the stiffest
in town. ⊠ *1621 Telegraph Ave., between 16th and 17th Sts., Uptown*
☎ *510/763–7711 ⊕ www.cafevankleef.com.*

Fox Theater. Willie Nelson, Counting Crows, Rebelution, and B.B.
King have all played at this renovated art deco stunner that has good
sight lines, a state-of-the-art sound system and acoustics, and bars and
other amenities aplenty. ⊠ *1807 Telegraph Ave., at 18th St., Uptown*
☎ *510/548–3010 ⊕ www.thefoxoakland.com.*

The Layover Music Bar and Lounge. Bright, bold, and very hip, this hangout
filled with recycled furniture is constantly evolving because everything is
for sale, from the artwork to the pillows, rugs, and lamps. The busy bar
serves up organic cocktails, and depending on the night, the entertain-
ment might include comedy or live or DJ music. ⊠ *1517 Franklin St.,
near 15th St., Uptown* ☎ *510/834–1517 ⊕ www.oaklandlayover.com.*

Mua. Cuisine, cocktails, and culture—Mua puts it all together in a bright
and airy former garage. The chefs serve up beautifully crafted meals like
soft-shell crab and duck confit; the bartenders shake up elegant cock-
tails; and the rich cultural offerings include poetry readings, art shows,
DJ music, and more. ⊠ *2442a Webster St., between 16th and 17th Sts.,
Uptown* ☎ *510/238–1100 ⊕ www.muaoakland.com.*

Paramount Theatre. The art deco movie palace is home to the Oakland
East Bay Symphony and also presents ballet, comedy (Cedric, Sinbad,
Bill Cosby), well-known rock and other musical acts, and monthly
classic films. ⊠ *2025 Broadway, at 20th St., Uptown* ☎ *510/465–6400
⊕ www.paramounttheatre.com.*

The Trappist. Grand pillars, brick walls, soft lighting, and the buzz of conversation set a warm and mellow tone inside this Victorian space that's been renovated to resemble a traditional Belgian pub. The setting is definitely a draw, but the real stars are the artisan beers: more than a hundred Belgian, Dutch, and North American ones. The light fare includes panini made with organic ingredients. ✉ *460 8th St., at Broadway, Old Oakland* ☎ *510/238–8900* ⊕ *www.thetrappist.com.*

Fodor's Choice **Yoshi's.** Omar Sosa and Charlie Hunter are among the musicians who
★ play at Yoshi's, one of the area's best jazz venues. Shows start at 8 pm and 10 pm except on Sundays, when they're usually at 6 and 8. The cover runs from $16 to $50. ✉ *510 Embarcadero St., between Washington and Clay Sts., Jack London Square* ☎ *510/238–9200* ⊕ *www. yoshis.com.*

SPORTS AND THE OUTDOORS

BASKETBALL **Golden State Warriors.** The NBA team plays basketball at **Oracle Arena** from November through April. BART trains serve the arena; get off at the Coliseum/Oakland Airport Station. Purchase tickets through Ticketmaster (☎ *800/653–8000* ⊕ *www.ticketmaster.com*). ✉ *Oracle Arena, 7000 Coliseum Way, off I–880, north of Hegenberger Rd.* ☎ *510/986– 2200, 888/479–4667* ⊕ *www.nba.com/warriors.*

BASEBALL **Oakland A's.** Billy Beane of *Moneyball* fame is the general manager of the American League baseball team. Same-day tickets can usually be purchased at the **O.co Coliseum** box office (Gate D). To get to the game, take a BART train to the Coliseum/Oakland Airport Station. ✉ *O.co Coliseum, 7000 Coliseum Way, off I–880, north of Hegenberger Rd.* ☎ *510/638–4900* ⊕ *oakland.athletics.mlb.com.*

FOOTBALL **Oakland Raiders.** The National Football League's brawling Oakland Raiders play at **O.co Coliseum.** Tickets are available through Ticketmaster. ✉ *O.co Coliseum, 7000 Coliseum Way, off I–880, north of Hegenberger Rd.* ☎ *510/864–5000* ⊕ *www.raiders.com.*

SHOPPING

College Avenue is great for upscale strolling, shopping, and people-watching. The more casual streets around Lake Merritt and Grand Lake have smaller, less fancy boutiques.

Diesel. Wandering bibliophiles collect armfuls of the latest fiction and nonfiction here. The loftlike space, with its high ceilings and spare design, encourages contemplation, and on chilly days a fire burns in the hearth. Past participants in the excellent authors' events have included Jeannette Winterson, Annie Leibovitz, Kareem Abdul-Jabbar, and Michael Moore. ✉ *5433 College Ave., at Kales Ave., Rockridge* ☎ *510/653–9965* ⊕ *www.dieselbookstore.com.*

Maison d'Etre. Close to the Rockridge BART station, this store epitomizes the Rockridge neighborhood's funky-chic shopping scene. Look for impulse buys like whimsical watches, imported fruit-tea blends, and a basket of funky slippers near the back. ✉ *5640 College Ave., at Keith Ave., Rockridge* ☎ *510/658–2801* ⊕ *maisondetre.com.*

MARIN COUNTY

Marin is quite simply a knockout—some go so far as to call it spectacular and wild. This isn't an extravagant claim, since more than 40% of the county (180,000 acres), including the majority of the coastline, is parkland. The territory ranges from chaparral, grassland, and coastal scrub to broadleaf and evergreen forest, redwood, salt marsh, and rocky shoreline. It's well worth the drive over the Golden Gate Bridge to explore the Headlands and the stunning beauty of sprawling Point Reyes National Seashore, with over 80 miles of shoreline.

Regardless of its natural beauty, what gave the county its reputation was Cyra McFadden's 1977 book *The Serial,* a literary soap opera that depicted the county as a bastion of hot-tubbing and "open" marriages. Indeed old-time bohemian, but also increasingly jet-set, Marinites still spend a lot of time outdoors, and surfing, cycling, and hiking are common after-work and weekend activities. Adrenaline junkies mountain bike down Mt. Tamalpais, and those who want solitude take a walk on one of Point Reyes's many empty beaches. The hot tub remains a popular destination, but things have changed since the boho days. Artists and musicians who arrived in the 1960s have set the tone for mellow country towns, but Marin is now undeniably chic, with BMWs supplanting VW buses as the cars of choice.

After exploring Marin's natural beauty, consider a stop in one of its lovely villages. Most cosmopolitan is Sausalito, the town just over the Golden Gate Bridge from San Francisco. Across the inlet from Sausalito, Tiburon and Belvedere are lined with grand homes that regularly appear on fund-raising circuits, and to the north, landlocked Mill Valley is a hub of wining and dining and tony boutiques. Book Passage, a noted bookseller in the next town, Corte Madera, hosts regular readings by top-notch authors, and Larkspur, San Anselmo, and Fairfax beyond have walkable downtown areas, each a bit folksier than the next but all with good restaurants and shops and a distinct sense of place.

In general, the farther you get from the Golden Gate Bridge the more country things become, and West Marin is about as far as you can get from the big city, both physically and ideologically. Separated from the inland county by the slopes and ridges of giant Mt. Tamalpais, this territory beckons to mavericks, artists, ocean lovers, and other free spirits. Stinson Beach has tempered its isolationist attitude to accommodate out-of-towners, as have Inverness and Point Reyes Station. Bolinas, on the other hand, would prefer you not know its location.

VISITOR INFORMATION

Contact Marin Convention & Visitors Bureau ✉ *1 Mitchell Blvd., Suite B, San Rafael* ☎ *415/925–2060* ⊕ *www.visitmarin.org.*

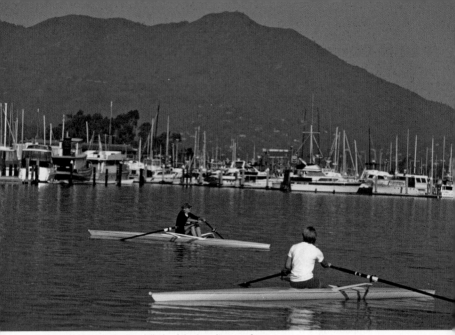

The crowded piers and rolling hillside of the Sausalito waterfront

SAUSALITO

2 miles north of Golden Gate Bridge.

Bougainvillea-covered hillsides and an expansive yacht harbor give Sausalito the feel of an Adriatic resort. The town sits on the northwestern edge of San Francisco Bay, where it's sheltered from the ocean by the Marin Headlands; the mostly mild weather here is perfect for strolling and outdoor dining. Nevertheless, morning fog and afternoon winds can roll over the hills without warning, funneling through the central part of Sausalito once known as Hurricane Gulch.

South on Bridgeway (toward San Francisco), which snakes between the bay and the hills, a waterside esplanade is lined with restaurants on piers that lure diners with good seafood and even better views. Stairs along the west side of Bridgeway climb the hill to wooded neighborhoods filled with both rustic and opulent homes. As you amble along Bridgeway past shops and galleries, you'll notice the absence of basic services. If you need an aspirin or some groceries (or if you want to see the locals), you'll have to head to Caledonia Street, which runs parallel to Bridgeway, north of the ferry terminus and inland a couple of blocks. The streets closest to the ferry landing flaunt their fair share of shops selling T-shirts and kitschy souvenirs. Venture into some of the side streets or narrow alleyways to catch a bit more of the town's taste for eccentric jewelry and handmade crafts.

■ TIP → The ferry is the best way to get to Sausalito from San Francisco; you get more romance (and less traffic) and disembark in the heart of downtown.

Sausalito had a raffish reputation before it went upscale. Discovered in 1775 by Spanish explorers and named Sausalito (Little Willow) for the trees growing around its springs, the town served as a port for whaling ships during the 19th century. By the mid-1800s wealthy San Franciscans were making Sausalito their getaway across the bay. They built lavish Victorian summer homes in the hills, many of which still stand. In 1875 the railroad from the north connected with ferryboats to San Francisco, bringing the merchant and working classes with it. This influx of hardworking, fun-loving folk polarized the town into "wharf rats" and "hill snobs," and the waterfront area grew thick with saloons, gambling dens, and bordellos. Bootleggers flourished during Prohibition, and shipyard workers swelled the town's population in the 1940s.

Sausalito developed its bohemian flair in the 1950s and '60s, when creative types, led by a charismatic Greek portraitist named Varda, established an artists' colony and a houseboat community here. Today more than 450 houseboats are docked in Sausalito, which has since also become a major yachting center. Some of these floating homes are ragged, others deluxe, but all are quirky (one, a miniature replica of a Persian castle, even has an elevator inside). For a close-up view of the community, head north on Bridgeway—Sausalito's main thoroughfare—from downtown, turn right on Gate Six Road, park where it dead-ends at the public shore, and enter through the unlocked gates. Keep a respectful distance; these are homes, after all, and the residents become a bit prickly from too much ogling.

GETTING HERE AND AROUND

From San Francisco by car or bike, follow U.S. 101 north across the Golden Gate Bridge and take the first exit, Alexander Avenue, just past Vista Point; continue down the winding hill to the water to where the road becomes Bridgeway. Golden Gate Transit buses 10 and 2 will drop you off in downtown Sausalito, and the ferries dock downtown as well. The center of town is flat, with plenty of sidewalks and bay views. It's a pleasure and a must to explore on foot.

ESSENTIALS

Visitor Information Sausalito Chamber of Commerce ⊠ *780 Bridgeway* ☏ *415/332–0505* ⊕ *www.sausalito.org.*

EXPLORING

FAMILY **Bay Area Discovery Museum.** Sitting at the base of the Golden Gate Bridge, this indoor-outdoor museum offers entertaining and enlightening hands-on exhibits for children under eight. Kids can fish from a boat at the indoor wharf, imagine themselves as marine biologists in the Wave Workshop, and play outdoors at Lookout Cove (made up of scaled-down sea caves, tidal pools, and even a re-created shipwreck). At Tot Spot, toddlers and preschoolers dress up in animal costumes and crawl through miniature tunnels. From San Francisco, take U.S. 101's Alexander Avenue exit and follow signs to East Fort Baker. ⊠ *557 McReynolds Rd., at East Rd. off Alexander Ave.* ☏ *415/339–3900* ⊕ *www.baykidsmuseum.org* ▨ *$11, free 1st Wed. of the month* ☉ *Tues.–Sun. 9–5.*

FAMILY **Bay Model.** An anonymous-looking World War II shipyard building holds a great treasure: the sprawling (more than 1½ acres) Bay Model of the entire San Francisco Bay and the San Joaquin–Sacramento River delta, complete with flowing water. The U.S. Army Corps of Engineers uses the model to reproduce the rise and fall of tides, the flow of currents, and the other physical forces at work on the bay. ⊠ *2100 Bridgeway, at Marinship Way* ☎ *415/332–3870 recorded information, 415/332–3871 operator assistance* ⊕ *www.spn.usace.army.mil/bmvc* ⎙ *Free* ☉ *Late May–early Sept., Tues.–Fri. 9–4, weekends 10–5; early Sept.–late May, Tues.–Sat. 9–4.*

Drinking Fountain. On the waterfront between the Hotel Sausalito and the Sausalito Yacht Club is an unusual historic landmark—a drinking fountain. It's inscribed with "Have a drink on Sally" in remembrance of Sally Stanford, the former San Francisco madam who later became the town's mayor in the 1970s. Sassy Sally, as they called her, would have appreciated the fountain's eccentric custom attachment: a knee-level basin that reads "Have a drink on Leland," in memory of her beloved dog.

QUICK
BITES

Hamburgers. Patrons queue up daily for a sandwich made from the juicy, hand-formed beef patties sizzling on the grill here. Brave the line (it moves fast), get your food to go, and head to the esplanade to enjoy the sweeping views. ⊠ *737 Bridgeway, at Humboldt Ave.* ☎ *415/332–9471* ☉ *Daily 11–5.*

Plaza Viña del Mar. The landmark Plaza Viña del Mar, named for Sausalito's sister city in Chile, marks the center of town. Flanked by two 14-foot-tall elephant statues (created in 1915 for the Panama-Pacific International Exposition), the fountain is a great setting for snapshots and people-watching. ⊠ *Bridgeway and Park St.*

Sausalito Visitors Center and Historical Exhibit. The local historical society operates the center, where you can get your bearings, learn some history, and find out what's happening in town. ⊠ *780 Bridgeway, at Bay St.* ☎ *415/332–0505* ⊕ *www.sausalitohistoricalsociety.com* ☉ *Closed Mon.*

WHERE TO EAT

$$
SEAFOOD
Fodor'sChoice
★
FAMILY

✕**Fish.** When locals want fresh seafood, they head to this gleaming dockside fish house a mile north of downtown. Order at the counter and then grab a seat by the floor-to-ceiling windows or at a picnic table on the pier, overlooking the yachts and fishing boats. Most of the sustainably caught fish are hauled in from the owner's boats, docked right outside. Try the ceviche, crab Louis, cioppino, barbecue oysters, or anything fresh that's being grilled over the oak-wood fire. Outside, kids can doodle with sidewalk chalk on the pier. 🖇 *Average main: $22* ⊠ *350 Harbor Dr., off Bridgeway* ☎ *415/331–3474* ⊕ *www.331fish. com* ⚄ *Reservations not accepted* ▭ *No credit cards.*

$$$
BISTRO

✕**Le Garage.** Brittany-born Olivier Souvestre serves traditional French bistro fare in a relaxed, sidewalk café–style bayside setting. The menu is small, but the dishes are substantial in flavor and presentation. Standouts include frisé salad with poached egg, bacon, croutons, and pancetta vinaigrette; steak frites with a shallot confit and crispy fries; and a chef's selection of cheese or charcuterie with soup and mixed greens. The restaurant only seats 35 inside and 15 outside, so to avoid a long

Marin County

```
0        5 mi
0        5 km
```

wait for lunch, arrive before 11:30 or after 1:30. ⑤ *Average main: $23* ✉ *85 Liberty Ship Way, off Marinship Way* ☎ *415/332–5625* ⊕ *www. legaragebistrosausalito.com* ⚠ *Reservations essential* ⊘ *No dinner Sun.*

$
SCANDINAVIAN

✗ **Lighthouse Cafe.** A cozy spot with a long coffee bar and dose of Scandinavian flair, this local establishment has been a favorite brunch destination for nearly two decades. The hearty Norwegian salmon omelet with spinach and cream cheese or fruit pancakes, as well as the grilled burgers, sandwiches, and Danish specials like meatballs with potato salad always hit the spot, especially on chilly days. Expect a wait. ⑤ *Average main: $12* ✉ *1311 Bridgeway, near Turney St.* ☎ *415/331–3034* ⊕ *www.lighthouse-restaurants.com* ⚠ *Reservations not accepted* ⊘ *No dinner.*

$$
TUSCAN

✗ **Poggio.** One of the few restaurants in Sausalito to attract both food-savvy locals and tourists, Poggio serves modern Tuscan cuisine in a handsome, open-wall space that spills onto the street. Expect dishes such as grilled chicken with roasted beets and sunchokes, braised artichokes with polenta, featherlight gnocchi, and pizzas from the open kitchen's wood-fired oven. ⑤ *Average main: $22* ✉ *777 Bridgeway, at Bay St.* ☎ *415/332–7771* ⊕ *www.poggiotrattoria.com* ⚠ *Reservations essential.*

$$
SUSHI
Fodor'sChoice
★

✕ **Sushi Ran.** Sushi aficionados swear that this is the Bay Area's best option for raw fish, but don't overlook the excellent Pacific Rim fusions, a melding of Japanese ingredients and French cooking techniques, served up in unusual presentations. Because Sushi Ran is so highly ranked among area foodies, book two to seven days in advance for dinner. Otherwise, expect a long wait, which you can soften by sipping one of the 45 by-the-glass sakes from the outstanding wine-and-sake bar. ■**TIP➔** If you arrive without a reservation and can't get a table, you can sometimes dine in the noisy bar. $ *Average main: $18* ✉ *107 Caledonia St., at Pine St.* ☎ *415/332–3620* ⊕ *www.sushiran.com* ⌒ *Reservations essential* ⊘ *No lunch weekends.*

$
WINE BAR

✕ **Wellingtons Wine Bar.** British memorabilia decorates the walls of this establishment that celebrates English and Californian liquid culture. The space is bright, warm, and welcoming, and when the weather is nice, you can sit on the boat dock and drink your pint of lager or sip a glass of wine while scooping up hummus with garlic pita chips. The menu is as big as a book. Wellingtons opens at 3 pm on Fridays and weekends, and at 4 the rest of the week. $ *Average main: $12* ✉ *300 Turney St., at Bridgeway* ☎ *415/331–9463* ⊕ *www.wellingtonswinebar. com* ⌒ *Reservations not accepted* ⊘ *No lunch.*

WHERE TO STAY
For expanded hotel reviews, visit Fodors.com.

$$$$
HOTEL

⌹ **Cavallo Point.** Set in the Golden Gate National Recreation Area, this luxury hotel and resort's location is truly one of a kind, featuring turn-of-the-20th-century buildings converted into well-appointed yet eco-friendly rooms. **Pros:** stunning views and numerous activities: a cooking school, yoga classes, and nature walks; spa with a tea bar; art gallery. **Cons:** landscaping feels incomplete; isolated from urban amenities. $ *Rooms from: $375* ✉ *601 Murray Circle, Fort Baker* ☎ *415/339– 4700* ⊕ *www.cavallopoint.com* ⤺ *68 historic and 74 contemporary guest rooms* ⦿ *No meals.*

$$
B&B/INN

⌹ **Hotel Sausalito.** Handmade furniture and tasteful original art and reproductions give this well-run inn the feel of a small European hotel. **Pros:** great staff; excellent central location; feels like home away from home. **Cons:** no room service; some rooms feel cramped. $ *Rooms from: $170* ✉ *16 El Portal* ☎ *415/332–0700, 888/442–0700* ⊕ *www. hotelsausalito.com* ⤺ *14 rooms, 2 suites* ⦿ *No meals.*

$$$$
B&B/INN

⌹ **The Inn Above Tide.** This is the only hotel in the Bay Area with balconies literally hanging over the water, and each of its rooms has a perfect-10 view that takes in wild Angel Island as well as the city lights across the bay. **Pros:** great complimentary breakfast; minutes from restaurants/attractions; free in-room binoculars let you indulge in the incredible views. **Cons:** costly parking; some rooms are on the small side. $ *Rooms from: $360* ✉ *30 El Portal* ☎ *415/332–9535, 800/893– 8433* ⊕ *www.innabovetide.com* ⤺ *29 rooms, 3 suites* ⦿ *Breakfast.*

SPORTS AND THE OUTDOORS
Sea Trek Ocean Kayaking and SUP Center. The center offers guided half-day sea-kayaking trips underneath the Golden Gate Bridge and full- and half-day trips to Angel Island, both for beginners. Starlight and

full-moon paddles are particularly popular. Trips for experienced kayakers, classes, and rentals are also available. Prices start at $20 per hour for rentals; $65 for a three-hour guided trip. ⊠ *Schoonmaker Point Marina, off Libertyship Way* ☎ *415/332–8494* ⊕ *www.seatrek.com.*

SF Bay Adventures. This outfit's expert skippers conduct sunset and full-moon sails around the bay, as well as fascinating eco and whale-watching tours with the possibility of viewing great white sharks. If you're interested, they can arrange for you to barbecue on Angel Island or even spend the night in a lighthouse. ⊠ *60 Liberty Ship Way, Suite 4* ☎ *415/331–0444* ⊕ *www.sfbayadventures.com.*

THE ARTS

Sausalito Art Festival. The annual festival ($25), held over Labor Day weekend, attracts more than 30,000 people to the northern waterfront; Blue & Gold Fleet ferries from San Francisco dock at the pier adjacent to the festival. ☎ *415/332–3555* ⊕ *www.sausalitoartfestival.org.*

SHOPPING

FAMILY **Sausalito Ferry Co.** Eccentric and fun, this shop is a great place to buy trendy T-shirts, wallets, and clocks—not to mention solar-powered bobbleheads, outrageous cocktail napkins, and one-of-a-kind key chains. ⊠ *688 Bridgeway, near Princess St.* ☎ *415/332–9590* ⊕ *www. sausalitoferry.com.*

Something/Anything Gallery. Where Bridgeway ends and curves toward the dock, this gallery with a friendly staff carries jewelry and gifts, from unique watches to humorous pendants. It's a good spot to pick up your Sausalito memento. ⊠ *20 Princess St., at Broadway* ☎ *415/339–8831* ⊕ *www.somethinganythinggallery.com.*

THE MARIN HEADLANDS

Due west of the Golden Gate Bridge's northern end.

★ The term *Golden Gate* may now be synonymous with the world-famous bridge, but it originally referred to the grassy, poppy-strewn hills flanking the passageway into San Francisco Bay. To the north of the gate lie the Marin Headlands, part of the Golden Gate National Recreation Area (GGNRA) and among the most dramatic scenery in these parts. Windswept hills plunge down to the ocean, and creek-fed thickets shelter swaying wildflowers.

GETTING HERE AND AROUND

Driving from San Francisco, head north on U.S. 101. Just after you cross the Golden Gate Bridge, take the Alexander Avenue exit. From there take the first left (signs read "San Francisco/U.S. 101 South"), go through the tunnel under the freeway, and turn right up the hill where the sign reads "Forts Barry and Cronkhite." Muni bus 76X runs hourly from Sutter and Sansome streets to the Marin Headlands Visitor Center on weekends and major holidays only. Once here, you can explore this beautiful countryside on foot.

EXPLORING

TOP ATTRACTIONS

Fodor's Choice
★
FAMILY

Marin Headlands. The headlands stretch from the Golden Gate Bridge to Muir Beach. Photographers perch on the southern headlands for shots of the city, with the bridge in the foreground and the skyline on the horizon. Equally remarkable are the views north along the coast and out to sea, where the Farallon Islands are visible on clear days. ■ TIP➔ Nearly all the roads, all of them very windy, offer great coastal views.

The headlands' strategic position at the mouth of San Francisco Bay made them a logical site for World War II military installations. Today you can explore the crumbling concrete batteries where naval guns protected the approaches from the sea. The headlands' main attractions are centered on Forts Barry and Cronkhite, which lie just across Rodeo Lagoon from each other. Fronting the lagoon is Rodeo Beach, a dark stretch of sand that attracts sand-castle builders and dog owners. ■ TIP➔ The beaches at the Marin Headlands are not safe for swimming. The giant cliffs are steep and unstable, so hiking down them can be dangerous. Stay on trails.

When the visitor center is open—reliably on weekends and Mondays from April through October between 9:30 and 4:30; staffing at other times varies—it's a worthwhile stop for its exhibits on the area's history and ecology. Kids enjoy the "please touch" educational sites and small play area inside. You can pick up guides to historic sites and wildlife at the center, as well as the park's newspaper, which has a schedule of guided walks. ⊠ *Visitor Center, Fort Barry Chapel, Fort Barry, Building 948, Sausalito* 🖀 *415/331–1540* ⊕ *www.nps.gov/goga/marin-headlands.htm.*

FAMILY **Point Bonita Lighthouse.** At the end of Conzelman Road, in the southern headlands, is the Point Bonita Lighthouse, a restored beauty that still guides ships to safety with its original 1855 refractory lens. Half the fun of a visit is the steep ½-mile walk from the parking area down to the lighthouse, which takes you through a rock tunnel and across a suspension bridge. Signposts along the way detail the bravado of surfmen, as the early lifeguards were called, and the tenacity of the "wickies," the first keepers of the light. ⊠ *End of Conzelman Rd.* ⊕ *www.nps.gov/ goga/pobo.htm* 🖾 *Free* ☉ *Sat.–Mon. 12:30–3:30.*

WORTH NOTING

Green Gulch Farm Zen Center. Giant eucalyptus trees frame the long and winding road that leads to this tranquil retreat. Meditation programs, workshops, and various events take place here, and there's an extensive organic garden. Visitors are welcome to roam the acres of gardens that reach down toward Muir Beach. ■ TIP➔ Follow the main dirt road to a peaceful path (birds, trees, ocean breezes) that meanders to the beach. ⊠ *1601 Shoreline Hwy., at Green Gulch Rd., Muir Beach* 🖀 *415/383–3134* ⊕ *www.sfzc.org* 🖾 *Free* ☉ *Tues.–Sat. 9–noon and 2–4, Sun. 9–10 am.*

Headlands Center for the Arts. The center's main building, formerly the army barracks, exhibits contemporary art in a rustic natural setting; the downstairs "archive room" contains objects found and created by residents, such as natural rocks, interesting glass bottles filled with

Shutterbugs rejoice in catching a scenic Muir Beach sunset.

collected items, and unusual masks. Stop by the industrial gallery space, two flights up, to see what the resident visual artists are up to—most of the work is quite contemporary. ⊠ *Fort Barry, 944 Simmonds Rd., Sausalito* ☎ *415/331–2787* ⊕ *www.headlands.org* ☉ *Sun.–Thurs. noon–5.*

FAMILY **Marine Mammal Center.** If you're curious about the rehabilitation of sea mammals from the Pacific—and the human practices that endanger them—stop by this amazing facility for rescued seals, sea lions, dolphins, and otters. An observation area overlooks the pools where the animals convalesce, and nearby plaques describe what you're seeing. ■TIP➔ You'll learn even more on a docent-led tour. ⊠ *Fort Cronkhite, 2000 Bunker Rd., off U.S. 101's Alexander Ave. exit, Sausalito* ☎ *415/289–7325* ⊕ *www.marinemammalcenter.org* ⊠ *Center free, tour $7* ☉ *Daily 10–5.*

BEACHES

FAMILY **Muir Beach.** Small but scenic, this beach—a rocky patch of shoreline off Highway 1 in the northern headlands—is a good place to stretch your legs and gaze out at the Pacific. Locals often walk their dogs here; families and cuddling couples come for picnicking and sunbathing. At one end of the sand is a cluster of waterfront homes (and where nude sunbathers lay their towels), and at the other are the bluffs of Golden Gate National Recreation Area. The beach itself has an interesting history. Janis Joplin's ashes were scattered here among the sands, and this is where author Ken Kesey hosted the second of his famed Acid Tests. **Amenities:** parking (free); toilets. **Best for:** nudists; solitude; walking. ⊠ *190 Pacific Way, off Shoreline Highway, Muir Beach* ⊕ *www.nps. gov/goga/planyourvisit/muirbeach.htm.*

WHERE TO STAY

For expanded hotel reviews, visit Fodors.com.

$$$
B&B/INN
☷ **Pelican Inn.** From its slate roof to its whitewashed plaster walls, this inn looks so Tudor that it's hard to believe it was built in the 1970s, but the Pelican is English to the core, with its smallish guestrooms upstairs (no elevator), high half-tester beds draped in heavy fabrics, and bangers and grilled tomatoes for breakfast. **Pros:** five-minute walk to beach; great bar and restaurant; peaceful setting. **Cons:** 20-minute drive to nearby attractions; some rooms are quite small. ⑤ *Rooms from: $220* ✉ *10 Pacific Way, off Hwy. 1, Muir Beach* ☎ *415/383–6000* ⊕ *www. pelicaninn.com* ⤳ *7 rooms* ⦿ *Breakfast.*

MUIR WOODS NATIONAL MONUMENT

12 miles northwest of the Golden Gate Bridge.

GETTING HERE AND AROUND

Driving to Muir Woods, especially in summer and early fall, causes epic traffic jams around the tiny parking areas and miles-long walks to reach the entrance. Do yourself (and everyone else) a favor and take a shuttle instead, if you can. On weekends and holidays, Memorial Day through Labor Day, Marin Transit's Route 66 shuttle (☷ *$3 round-trip* ⊕ *www. marintransit.org*) is timed to meet boats at Sausalito's ferry landing four times daily en route to Muir Woods. The shuttle also runs every half hour from the Manzanita Park-and-Ride three miles north of the ferry. To get there, take the Highway 1 exit off U.S. 101 (look for the lot under the elevated freeway), or take connecting bus service from San Francisco with Golden Gate Transit. To drive directly from San Francisco by car, take U.S. 101 north across the Golden Gate Bridge to the Mill Valley/ Stinson Beach exit, then follow signs to Highway 1 north. Once here, you can wander by foot through this pristine patch of nature.

EXPLORING

FodorsChoice
★
Muir Woods National Monument. Walking among some of the last old-growth redwoods on the planet, trees hundreds of feet tall and a millennium or more old, is magical, an experience like few others to clearly illustrate our tiny place in a bigger world. Ancestors of redwood and sequoia trees grew throughout what is now the United States 150,000,000 years ago. Today the *Sequoia sempervirens* can be found only in a narrow, cool coastal belt from Monterey to Oregon. The 550 acres of Muir Woods National Monument contain some of the most majestic redwoods in the world—some nearly 250 feet tall. The stand was saved from destruction in 1905, when it was purchased by a couple who donated it to the federal government. Three years later it was named after naturalist John Muir, whose environmental campaigns helped to establish the national park system. His response: "Saving these woods from the ax and saw is in many ways the most notable service to God and man I have heard of since my forest wandering began."

Muir Woods, part of the Golden Gate National Recreation Area, is a pedestrian's park. Old paved trails have been replaced by wooden walkways, and the trails vary in difficulty and length. Beginning from the park headquarters, an easy 2-mile, wheelchair-accessible **loop trail**

crosses streams and passes ferns and azaleas, as well as magnificent redwood groves. Among the most famous are **Bohemian Grove** and the circular formation called **Cathedral Grove.** On summer weekends visitors oohing and aahing in a dozen languages line the trail. If you prefer a little serenity, consider the challenging **Dipsea Trail,** which climbs west from the forest floor to soothing views of the ocean and the Golden Gate Bridge. For a complete list of trails, check with rangers, who can also help you pick the best one for your ability level.

■TIP→ The weather in Muir Woods is usually cool and often wet, so wear warm clothes and shoes appropriate for damp trails. Picnicking and camping aren't allowed, and pets aren't permitted. Crowds can be large, especially from May through October, so try to come early in the morning or late in the afternoon. The newly renovated **Muir Woods Visitor Center** has books and exhibits about redwood trees and the woods' history; the café here serves locally sourced, organic food, and the gift shop has plenty of souvenirs. ⊠ *1 Muir Woods Trail, off Panoramic Hwy., Mill Valley* ☎ *415/388–2595 park information, 415/526–3239 shuttle information* ⊕ *www.nps.gov/muwo* ⊠ *$7* ☉ *Daily 8 am–sunset.*

MT. TAMALPAIS STATE PARK

16 miles northwest of Golden Gate Bridge.

GETTING HERE AND AROUND

By car, take the Highway 1–Stinson Beach exit off U.S. 101 and follow the road west and then north. From San Francisco, the trip can take from 30 minutes up to an hour, depending on traffic. By bus, take the 10, 70 or 80 to Marin City; in Marin City transfer to the West Marin Stagecoach (☎ *415/226–0855* ⊕ *www.marintransit.org/stage.html*). Once here, the only way to explore is on foot or by bike.

EXPLORING

Mt. Tamalpais State Park. Although the summit of Mt. Tamalpais is only 2,571 feet high, the mountain rises practically from sea level, dominating the topography of Marin County. Adjacent to Muir Woods National Monument, Mt. Tamalpais State Park affords views of the entire Bay Area and the Pacific Ocean to the west. The mountain was sacred to Native Americans, who saw in its profile—as you can see today—the silhouette of a sleeping Indian maiden. Locals fondly refer to it as the "Sleeping Lady." For years the 6,300-acre park has been a favorite destination for hikers. There are more than 200 miles of trails, some rugged but many developed for easy walking through meadows, grasslands, and forests and along creeks. Mt. Tam, as it's called by locals, is also the birthplace (in the 1970s) of mountain biking, and today many spandex-clad bikers whiz down the park's winding roads.

The park's major thoroughfare, the Panoramic Highway, snakes its way up from U.S. 101 to the **Pantoll Ranger Station.** The office is staffed sporadically, depending on funding. From the ranger station, the Panoramic Highway drops down to the town of Stinson Beach. Pantoll Road branches off the highway at the station, connecting up with Ridgecrest Boulevard. Along these roads are numerous parking areas, picnic spots, scenic overlooks, and trailheads. Parking is free along the roadside, but there's a fee at the ranger station and at some of the other parking lots ($8).

The **Mountain Theater,** also known as the Cushing Memorial Amphitheatre, is a natural amphitheater with terraced stone seats (for nearly 4,000 people) constructed in its current form by the Civilian Conservation Corps in the 1930s. The theater celebrated its 100th year of performances in 2013.

The **Rock Spring Trail** starts at the Mountain Theater and gently climbs about 1¾ miles to the **West Point Inn,** once a stop on the Mt. Tam railroad route. Relax at a picnic table and stock up on water before forging ahead, via Old Railroad Grade Fire Road and the Miller Trail, to Mt. Tam's Middle Peak, about 2 miles uphill.

Starting from the Pan Toll Ranger Station, the precipitous **Steep Ravine Trail** brings you past stands of coastal redwoods and, in the springtime, numerous small waterfalls. Take the connecting **Dipsea Trail** to reach the town of Stinson Beach and its swath of golden sand. If you're too weary to make the 3½-mile trek back up, Marin Transit Bus 61 (four times on weekdays and one to three times on weekends, depending on the season) takes you from Stinson Beach back to the ranger station. ⊠ *Pantoll Ranger Station, 3801 Panoramic Hwy., at Pantoll Rd.* ☎ *415/388–2070* ⊕ *www.parks.ca.gov.*

NIGHTLIFE AND THE ARTS

FAMILY **Mountain Play.** Every May and June, locals tote overstuffed picnic baskets to the Mountain Theater to see the Mountain Play, popular musicals such as *The Music Man* and *My Fair Lady.* Depending on the play, this can be a great family activity. Summer 2013 marked the 100th anniversary of this Bay Area tradition. ⊠ *Mt. Tamalpais, Richardson Blvd. off Panoramic Hwy.* ☎ *415/383–1100* ⊕ *www.mountainplay.org* 🎫 *$40.*

POINT REYES NATIONAL SEASHORE

Bear Valley Visitor Center is 12 miles north of Bolinas.

GETTING HERE AND AROUND

From San Francisco, take U.S. 101 north, head west at Sir Francis Drake Boulevard (Exit 450B), and follow the road just under 20 miles to Bear Valley Road. From Stinson Beach or Bolinas, drive north on Highway 1 and turn left on Bear Valley Road. If you're going by bus, take the 10, 70, or 80 to Marin City; in Marin City transfer to the West Marin Stagecoach (you'll switch buses in Olema). Once at the visitor center, the best way to get around is on foot.

EXPLORING

FAMILY **Bear Valley Visitor Center.** A mildly menacing orca model hovers over the center's engaging exhibits about the wildlife and history of the Point Reyes National Seashore. The rangers at the barnlike facility are fonts of information about beaches, whale-watching, hiking trails, and camping. Winter hours may be shorter; call or check the website for details. ⊠ *Bear Valley Visitor Center Access Rd., west of Hwy. 1* ☎ *415/464–5100* ⊕ *www.nps.gov/pore/planyourvisit* ☉ *Weekdays 9–5, weekends 8–5.*

FAMILY **Duxbury Reef.** Excellent tide pooling can be had along mile-long Duxbury Reef, the largest shale intertidal reef in North America. Look for starfish, barnacles, sea anemones, purple urchins, limpets, sea mussels, and the occasional abalone. But check a tide table (⊕ *www.wrh. noaa.gov/mtr/marine.php*) or the local papers if you plan to explore the reef—it's accessible only at low tide. The reef is a 30-minute drive from the Bear Valley Visitor Center. Take Highway 1 south from the center, turn right at Olema-Bolinas Road (keep an eye peeled; the road is easy to miss), left on Horsehoe Hill Road, right on Mesa Road, left on Overlook Drive, and then right on Elm Road, which dead-ends at the Agate Beach County Park parking lot.

FAMILY **Point Reyes Bird Observatory.** Birders adore the observatory, which lies in the southernmost part of Point Reyes National Seashore and is accessed through Bolinas. (Those not interested in birds might find it ho-hum.) The unstaffed visitor center, open daily from sunrise to sunset, has excellent interpretive exhibits, including a comparative display of real birds' talons. The surrounding woods harbor more than 200 bird species. As you hike the quiet trails through forest and along ocean cliffs, you're likely to see biologists banding birds to aid in the study of their life cycles. Visit the observatory's website to find out when banding will occur; it's a fun time to visit. ⊠ *Mesa Rd., Bolinas* ☎ *415/868–0655* ⊕ *www.prbo.org* ⊠ *Free* ⊙ *Daily 9–5.*

FAMILY **Point Reyes Lighthouse.** In operation since December 1, 1870, this light-
Fodor'sChoice house is one of the premier attractions of the Point Reyes National
★ Seashore. It occupies the tip of Point Reyes, 22 miles from the Bear Valley Visitor Center, a scenic 45-minute drive over hills scattered with longtime cattle ranches. The lighthouse originally cast a rotating beam lighted by four wicks that burned lard oil. Keeping the wicks lighted and the 6,000-pound Fresnel lens soot-free in Point Reyes's perpetually foggy climate was a constant struggle that reputedly drove the early attendants to alcoholism and insanity. ∎TIP→ **The lighthouse is one of the best spots on the coast for watching gray whales: on both legs of their annual migration, the magnificent animals pass close enough to see with the naked eye.** Southern migration peaks in mid-January, and the whales head back north in March; see the slower mothers and calves in late April and early May.

On busy whale-watching weekends (from late December through mid-April), parking at the lighthouse may be restricted. On these days, buses shuttle visitors from the Drakes Beach parking lot to the top of the stairs leading down to the lighthouse (*Bus $5, admission free*). However you've arrived, consider whether you have it in you to walk down—and up—the 308 steps to the lighthouse. The view from the bottom is worth the effort, but the whales are visible from the cliffs above the lighthouse. ⊠ *Visitor Center, Western end of Sir Francis Drake Blvd., Inverness* ☎ *415/669–1534* ⊙ *Thurs.–Mon. 10–4:30; weather lens room 2:30–4, except during very windy weather.*

Point Reyes National Seashore. One of the Bay Area's most spectacular treasures and the only national seashore on the West Coast, the 66,500-acre Point Reyes National Seashore encompasses hiking trails, secluded beaches, and rugged grasslands as well as Point Reyes itself, a triangular peninsula that juts into the Pacific. The town of **Point Reyes Station** is a quaint, one-main-drag affair, with a charming bakery, some good gift shops with locally made and imported goods, and a few places to eat. It's nothing fancy, but that's part of its relaxed charm.

When explorer Sir Francis Drake sailed along the California coast in 1579, he missed the Golden Gate and San Francisco Bay, but he did land at what he described as a convenient harbor. In 2012 the federal government finally officially recognized Drake's Bay, which flanks the point on the east, as that harbor, designating the spot a National Historic Landmark and silencing competing claims in the 433-year-old controversy. Today Point Reyes's hills and dramatic cliffs attract other kinds of explorers: hikers, whale-watchers, and solitude seekers.

The infamous San Andreas Fault runs along the eastern edge of the park and up the center of Tomales Bay; take the short **Earthquake Trail** from the visitor center to see the impact near the epicenter of the 1906 earthquake that devastated San Francisco. A ½-mile path from the visitor center leads to **Kule Loklo**, a brilliantly reconstructed Miwok village that sheds light on the daily lives of the region's first inhabitants. From here, trails also lead to the park's free campgrounds (camping permits are required).

■TIP→ In late winter and spring, take the short walk at Chimney Rock, just before the lighthouse, to the Elephant Seal Overlook. Even from the cliff, the male seals look enormous as they spar, growling and bloodied, for resident females.

You can experience the diversity of Point Reyes's ecosystems on the scenic **Coast Trail**, which starts at the Palomarin Trailhead, just outside Bolinas. From here, it's a 3-mile trek through eucalyptus groves and pine forests and along seaside cliffs to beautiful and tiny Bass Lake. To reach the Palomarin Trailhead, take Olema–Bolinas Road toward Bolinas, follow signs to the Point Reyes Bird Observatory, and then continue until the road dead-ends.

The 4.7-mile-long (one-way) **Tomales Point Trail** follows the spine of the park's northernmost finger of land through a Tule Elk Preserve, providing spectacular ocean views from the high bluffs. Expect to see elk, but keep your distance from the animals. To reach the fairly easy hiking trail, look for the Pierce Point Road turnoff on the right, just north of the town of Inverness; park at the end of the road by the old ranch buildings. ✉ *Bear Valley Visitor Center, Bear Valley Visitor Center Access Rd., off Hwy. 1, Point Reyes Station* ☎ *415/464–5100* ⊕ *www.nps.gov/pore.*

WHERE TO EAT

$ ✕ **Pine Cone Diner.** A block off the main drag, this oh-so-cute diner
AMERICAN serves great traditional breakfasts as well as Mexican specialties such
FAMILY as huevos rancheros. At lunch expect hearty homemade soups, fresh salads, and thick sandwiches, all made with local, organic ingredients. ■TIP→ Kids love the outdoor picnic tables. $ *Average main: $11* ✉ *60 4th St., at B St., Point Reyes Station* ☎ *415/663–1536* ◷ *No dinner.*

DID YOU KNOW?

The majestic Point Reyes National Seashore offers many attractions for nature lovers: hiking, bird-watching, camping, or whale-watching, depending on the season. But flower picking isn't an approved activity; the wild flowers here are protected.

$$ ✕ **Station House Cafe.** In good weather, hikers fresh from the park fill
AMERICAN the Station House's garden to enjoy alfresco dining, and on weekends
there's not a spare seat on the banquettes in the dining room. The focus
is on local, seasonal, and sustainable food: oyster shooters, Niman
Ranch braised lamb, Californian white sea bass, and sweet bread pud-
ding are the standbys. The place is also open for breakfast, and there's
a full bar. $ *Average main: $22* ✉ *11180 Hwy. 1, Point Reyes Station*
☎ *415/663–1515* ⊕ *www.stationhousecafe.com* ✆ *Closed Wed.*

$$$ ✕ **Tomales Bay Foods.** A renovated hay barn off the main drag houses
AMERICAN this collection of food shops, a favorite stopover among Bay Area food-
FAMILY ies. Watch workers making Cowgirl Creamery cheese; then buy some at
a counter that sells exquisite artisanal cheeses from around the world.
Tomales Bay Foods showcases local organic fruits and vegetables and premium packaged foods, and the kitchen turns the best ingredients into creative sandwiches, salads, and soups. You can eat at a small café table or
on the lawn. $ *Average main: $23* ✉ *80 4th St., at B. St., Point Reyes Station* ☎ *415/663–9335 cheese shop* ✆ *Closed Mon. and Tues. No dinner.*

WHERE TO STAY
For expanded hotel reviews, visit Fodors.com.

$$ ⊞ **Inverness Valley Inn.** Amid a 15-acre valley on the north end of
B&B/INN town, this secluded getaway offers spacious private cabins with patios
FAMILY that are perfect for sunset barbecues and leisurely breakfasts. **Pros:**
spacious accommodations; great place to bring kids. **Cons:** 3-plus
miles from downtown Inverness; small pool. $ *Rooms from: $160*
✉ *13275 Sir Francis Drake Blvd., Inverness* ☎ *415/669–7250* ⊕ *www.
invernessvalleyinn.com* ⤳ *20 cabins* ❒ *No meals.*

$$$$ ⊞ **Manka's Inverness Lodge.** Chef-owner Margaret Grade takes rustic
B&B/INN fantasy to extravagant heights in her 1917 hunting lodge and cabins,
where mica-shaded lamps cast an amber glow, and bearskin rugs warm
wide-planked floors. **Pros:** extremely romantic, remote and quiet. **Cons:**
no on-site restaurant; sounds from neighboring rooms are easily heard;
some question the value for the price. $ *Rooms from: $450* ✉ *30 Call-
endar Way, at Argyle Way, Inverness* ☎ *415/669–1034* ⊕ *www.mankas.
com* ⤳ *8 rooms, 1 boathouse, 4 cabins.*

$$$$ ⊞ **Olema Druids Hall.** Set on a quiet hill beneath towering eucalyptus
B&B/INN trees, the inn, built in 1885 as a meeting hall for the Ancient Order of
Fodor's Choice Druids, now holds gorgeously appointed rooms, each of which seems
★ like a designer showcase. **Pros:** heated hardwood floors; wood-burning
fireplaces. **Cons:** not much to do at night; some traffic noise. $ *Rooms
from: $325* ✉ *9870 Shoreline Hwy., Box 96, Olema* ☎ *415/663–8727,
866/554–4255* ⊕ *www.olemadruidshall.com* ⤳ *2 rooms, 1 suite, 1 cot-
tage* ❒ *Breakfast.*

$$ ⊞ **Ten Inverness Way.** This is the kind of down-to-earth place where
B&B/INN you sit around after breakfast and share tips for hiking Point Reyes
or linger around the living room with its stone fireplace and library.
Pros: great base for exploring nearby wilderness; peaceful garden and
friendly staff. **Cons:** overly folksy decor; some rooms are on the small
side; poor cell-phone reception. $ *Rooms from: $165* ✉ *10 Inverness
Way, Inverness* ☎ *415/669–1648* ⊕ *www.teninvernessway.com* ⤳ *5
rooms* ❒ *Breakfast.*

5

SPORTS AND THE OUTDOORS

Blue Waters Kayaking. This outfit rents kayaks, stand-up paddleboards, and electric bikes and offers tours and lessons. ✉ *12944 Sir Francis Drake Blvd., Inverness* ☎ *415/669–2600* ⊕ *www.bwkayak.com.*

Five Brooks Stable. Tour guides here lead private and group horse rides lasting from one to six hours ($40–$240); trails from the stable wind through Point Reyes National Seashore and along the beaches. ✉ *8001 Hwy. 1, north of town, Olema* ☎ *415/663–1570* ⊕ *www.fivebrooks.com.*

STINSON BEACH

20 miles northwest of Golden Gate Bridge.

GETTING HERE AND AROUND

If you're driving, take the Highway 1–Stinson Beach exit off U.S. 101 and follow the road west and then north. The journey from San Francisco can take from 35 minutes to more than an hour, depending on traffic. By bus, take the 10, 70, or 80 to Marin City; in Marin City transfer to the West Marin Stagecoach. The intimate town is perfect for casual walking.

BEACHES

FAMILY   **Stinson Beach.** When the fog hasn't rolled in, this expansive stretch of sand is about as close as you can get in Marin to the stereotypical feel of a Southern California beach. There are several clothing-optional areas, among them a section called Red Rock Beach. ⚠ **Swimming at Stinson Beach is recommended only from early May through September, when lifeguards are on duty, because the undertow can be strong and shark sightings, although infrequent, aren't unheard of.** On any hot summer weekend, every road to Stinson is jam-packed, so factor this into your plans. The down-to-earth town itself—population 600, give or take—has a surfer vibe, with a few good eating options and pleasant hippie-craftsy browsing. **Amenities:** food and drink; lifeguards; parking (free); showers; toilets. **Best for:** nudists; sunset; surfing; swimming; walking. ✉ *Hwy. 1* ⊕ *www.pointreyes.org.*

WHERE TO EAT AND STAY

For expanded hotel reviews, visit Fodors.com.

$$ ✕ **Parkside Cafe.** The Parkside is popular for its beachfront snack bar
AMERICAN   (cash only), but inside is Stinson's best restaurant, with classic Cal-cuisine offerings such as the day-boat-scallop and ceviche appetizers, and mains like the lamb with goat-cheese-stuffed red peppers. Breakfast is served until 2 pm. Creeping vines on the sunny patio shelter diners from the wind; for a cozier ambience eat by the fire in the dining room. Ⓢ *Average main: $20* ✉ *43 Arenal Ave., off Shoreline Hwy. 1* ☎ *415/868–1272.*

$ ✕ **Sand Dollar.** The town's oldest restaurant still attracts all the old salts
AMERICAN   from Muir Beach to Bolinas, but these days they sip whiskey over an up-to-date bar or beneath market umbrellas on the spiffy deck. The food is good—try the panfried sand dabs (small flatfish) and pear salad with blue cheese—but the big draw is the lively atmosphere. Musicians play on Sundays in summer, and on sunny afternoons the deck gets so packed

that people sit on the fence rails sipping beer. $ *Average main: $13* ✉ *3458 Shoreline Hwy.* ☎ *415/868–0434* ☉ *No lunch Tues. Nov.–Mar.*

$$
B&B/INN
FAMILY
🏨 **The Sandpiper.** Recharge, rest, and enjoy the local scenery at this ultra-popular lodging that books up months, even years, in advance. **Pros:** bright rooms; lush gardens; minutes from the beach. **Cons:** not exactly on the beach; walls are thin. $ *Rooms from: $165* ✉ *1 Marine Way, at Arenal Ave.* ☎ *415/868–1632* ⊕ *www.sandpiperstinsonbeach.com* 🍴 *6 rooms, 4 cabins* ⦶ *No meals.*

$$
B&B/INN
🏨 **Stinson Beach Motel.** Built in the 1930s, this motel surrounds three courtyards that burst with flowering greenery, and rooms are immaculate, simple, and summery, with freshly painted walls, new carpets, new mattresses, and some kitchenettes. **Pros:** minutes from the beach; cozy, unpretentious rooms. **Cons:** smaller rooms feel cramped; some linens need replacing. $ *Rooms from: $150* ✉ *3416 Shoreline Hwy. 1* ☎ *415/868–1712* ⊕ *www.stinsonbeachmotel.com* 🍴 *8 rooms* ⦶ *No meals.*

BOLINAS

7 miles north of Stinson Beach.

The tiny town of Bolinas wears its 1960s idealism on its sleeve, attracting potters, poets, and peace lovers to its quiet streets. With a funky gallery, a general store selling organic produce, a café, and an offbeat saloon, the main thoroughfare, Wharf Road, looks like a hippie-fied version of Main Street, USA.

GETTING HERE AND AROUND

Bolinas isn't difficult to find, though locals notoriously remove the street sign for their town from the highway: heading north from Stinson Beach, follow Highway 1 west and then north. Make a left at the first road just past the Bolinas Lagoon (✉ *Olema–Bolinas Road*), and then turn left at the stop sign. The road dead-ends smack-dab in the middle of town. By bus, take the 10, 70, or 80 to Marin City; in Marin City, transfer to the West Marin Stagecoach. Walking is the only way to see this small town.

WHERE TO EAT

$$
AMERICAN
✗ **Coast Cafe.** Decked out in a nautical theme with surfboards and buoys, the dining room at the Coast serves dependably good American fare, including specials such as shepherd's pie, pot roast, local fresh fish, grass-fed steaks, and gorgeous salads. Live music accompanies dinner on Thursdays and Sundays. On weekends, the café is open for brunch. $ *Average main: $18* ✉ *46 Wharf Rd., off Olema–Bolinas Rd.* ☎ *415/868–2298* ⊕ *www.bolinascoastcafe.com.*

TIBURON

2 miles north of Sausalito, 7 miles north of Golden Gate Bridge.

On a peninsula that was called Punta de Tiburon (Shark Point) by the Spanish explorers, this beautiful Marin County community retains the feel of a village—it's more low-key than Sausalito—despite the encroachment of commercial establishments from the downtown area. The harbor faces Angel Island across Raccoon Strait, and San Francisco is directly south across the bay—which makes the views from the decks of harbor restaurants a major attraction. Since its incarnation, in 1884, when ferries from San Francisco connected the point with a railroad to San Rafael, the town has centered on the waterfront. ■TIP→ The ferry is the most relaxing (and fastest) way to get here, particularly in summer, allowing you to skip traffic and parking problems. If visiting midweek, keep in mind that many shops close either Tuesday or Wednesday, or both.

ESSENTIALS

Visitor Information Tiburon Peninsula Chamber of Commerce ⊠ *96-B Main St.* ☎ *415/435–5633* ⊕ *www.tiburonchamber.org.*

GETTING HERE AND AROUND

By car, head north from San Francisco on U.S. 101 and get off at CA 131/Tiburon Boulevard/East Blithedale Avenue (Exit 447). Turn right onto Tiburon Boulevard and drive just over 4 miles to downtown. Golden Gate Transit bus 8 serves downtown Tiburon from San Francisco, as does the Blue & Gold Fleet Ferry service. Tiburon's Main Street is made for wandering, as are the footpaths that frame the water's edge.

EXPLORING

Ark Row. Past the pink-brick bank building, Main Street is known as Ark Row, and has a tree-shaded walk lined with antiques and specialty stores. Some of the buildings are actually old houseboats that floated in Belvedere Cove before being beached and transformed into stores. If you're curious about architectural history, the Tiburon Heritage & Arts Commission prints a self-guided walking-tour map, available online and at local businesses. ⊠ *Ark Row, parallel to Main St.* ⊕ *www.landmarks-society.org.*

Old St. Hilary's Landmark and Wildflower Preserve. The architectural centerpiece of the Old St. Hilary's Landmark and Wildflower Preserve is a stark-white 1886 Carpenter Gothic church that overlooks the town and the bay from its hillside perch. Surrounding the church, which was barged over from Strawberry Point in 1957, is a wildflower preserve that's spectacular in May and June, when the rare black jewelflower blooms. Expect a steep walk uphill to reach the preserve. ■TIP→ The hiking trails behind the landmark wind up to a peak that has 360-degree views of the entire Bay Area (and great photo ops). ⊠ *201 Esperanza St., off Mar West St. or Beach Rd.* ☎ *415/435–1853* ⊕ *www.landmarks-society.org* ⊡ *$3 suggested donation* ⊙ *Apr.–Oct., Sun. 1–4 and by appointment.*

WHERE TO EAT

$$$

AMERICAN

✗ **The Caprice.** For more than 50 years this Tiburon landmark that overlooks the bay has been the place to come to mark special occasions. The views are spectacular, and soft-yellow walls and starched white tablecloths help to make the space bright and light. Elegant comfort food is the premise, with choices like seared day-boat scallops or pan-roasted filet mignon. Polishing off the warm chocolate cake with almond ice cream while gazing out at the sunset and porpoises bobbing in the waves below is a near perfect end to the evening. ⑤ *Average main: $27* ⊠ *2000 Paradise Dr.* ☎ *415/435–3400* ⊕ *www.thecaprice.com* ⊙ *No lunch.*

$ ✕ **New Morning Cafe.** Omelets and scrambles are served all day long at
AMERICAN   this homey café. If you're past morning treats, choose from the many
soups, salads, and sandwiches. The café is open from 6:30 until 2:30 on
weekdays, until 4 on weekends. ⑤ *Average main: $11* ✉ *1696 Tiburon
Blvd., near Main St.* ☎ *415/435–4315* ⊘ *No dinner.*

$$$ ✕ **Sam's Anchor Cafe.** Open since 1921, this casual dockside restaurant
AMERICAN   with mahogany wainscoting is the town's most famous eatery. Today
most people flock here for the deck, where out-of-towners and old
salts sit shoulder to shoulder for bay views, beer, seafood, and Ramos
fizzes. The lunch menu has the usual suspects—burgers, sandwiches,
salads, fried fish with tartar sauce—and you'll sit on plastic chairs at
tables covered with blue-and-white-checked oilcloths. At night you can
find standard seafood dishes with vegetarian and meat options. Mind
the seagulls; they know no restraint. ■TIP➔ Expect a wait for outside
tables on sunny summer days or weekends; there are no reservations
for deck seating or weekend lunch. ⑤ *Average main: $23* ✉ *27 Main
St.* ☎ *415/435–4527.*

WHERE TO STAY

For expanded hotel reviews, visit Fodors.com.

$$ ▦ **The Lodge at Tiburon.** A block from Main Street and framed by stone
HOTEL   pillars and sloped rooftops, the Lodge at Tiburon has the feel of a
winter ski chalet, though the outdoor pool and its cabanas provide
a summery counterpoint. **Pros:** free parking; spacious work desks in
each room; plush bathrobes; room service from the Tiburon Tavern.
Cons: breakfast for a fee; some rooms have a few too many mirrors;
no bay views. ⑤ *Rooms from: $170* ✉ *1651 Tiburon Blvd., at Beach
St.* ☎ *415/435–3133* ⊕ *lodgeattiburon.com* ⇨ *102 rooms* ⦿ *No meals.*

$$$ ▦ **Waters Edge Hotel.** Checking into this elegant hotel feels like tucking
B&B/INN   away into an inviting retreat by the water—the views are stunning and
the lighting is perfect. **Pros:** complimentary wine and cheese for guests
every evening; restaurants/sights are minutes away; free bike rentals
for guests. **Cons:** downstairs rooms lack privacy and views; except for
breakfast delivery, no room service; fitness center is off-site; not a great
place to bring small children. ⑤ *Rooms from: $250* ✉ *25 Main St., off
Tiburon Blvd.* ☎ *415/789–5999, 877/789–5999* ⊕ *www.marinhotels.
com* ⇨ *23 rooms* ⦿ *Breakfast.*

MILL VALLEY

2 miles north of Sausalito, 4 miles north of Golden Gate Bridge.

Chic and woodsy Mill Valley has a dual personality. Here, as elsewhere
in the county, the foundation is a superb natural setting. Virtually sur-
rounded by parkland, the town lies at the base of Mt. Tamalpais and
contains dense redwood groves traversed by countless creeks. But this is
no lumber camp. Smart restaurants and chichi boutiques line the streets,
and more rock stars than one might suspect live here.

The rustic village flavor isn't a modern conceit but a holdover from
the town's early days as a logging camp. In 1896 the Mill Valley and
Mt. Tamalpais Scenic Railroad—called "the crookedest railroad in the
world" because of its curvy tracks—began transporting visitors from

Mill Valley to the top of Mt. Tam and down to Muir Woods, and the town soon became a vacation retreat for city slickers. The trains stopped running in the 1940s, but the old railway depot still serves as the center of town: the 1924 building has been transformed into the popular Depot Bookstore & Cafe, at 87 Throckmorton Avenue.

The small downtown area has the constant bustle of a leisure community; even at noon on a Tuesday, people are out shopping for fancy cookware and lacy pajamas.

ESSENTIALS

Visitor Information Mill Valley Chamber of Commerce ⊠ 85 Throckmorton Ave. ☎ 415/388–9700 ⊕ www.millvalley.org.

GETTING HERE AND AROUND

By car from San Francisco, head north on U.S. 101 and get off at CA 131/Tiburon Boulevard/East Blithedale Avenue (Exit 447). Turn left onto East Blithedale and continue west to Throckmorton Avenue; turn left to reach Lytton Square, then park. Golden Gate Transit bus 4 leaves for Mill Valley from 8th and Folsom streets in San Francisco every 30 minutes during commute hours. Once here, explore the town on foot; it's great for strolling.

EXPLORING

FAMILY **Lytton Square.** Mill Valley locals congregate on weekends to socialize in the many coffeehouses near the town's central square (which is unmarked), but it bustles most any time of day. Shops, restaurants, and cultural venues line the nearby streets. ⊠ Miller and Throckmorton Aves.

OFF THE BEATEN PATH **Marin County Civic Center.** This wonder of arches, circles, and skylights was Frank Lloyd Wright's last major architectural undertaking. Docent-led tours ($5) leave from the gift shop, on the second floor, on Wednesday mornings at 10:30. You can also wander about on your own; pick up a self-guided tour map at the gift shop (50¢) or access one on the center's website. ■TIP→ Don't miss the photographs on the first floor, which show Marin County homes designed by Wright. ⊠ 3501 Civic Center Dr., off N. San Pedro Rd., San Rafael ☎ 415/499–7009 ⊕ www.marincounty.org ☒ Free ☉ Weekdays 8–5.

FAMILY **Old Mill Park.** To see one of the numerous outdoor oases that make Mill Valley so appealing, follow Throckmorton Avenue a quarter of a mile west from Lytton Square to Old Mill Park, a shady patch of redwoods that shelters a playground and reconstructed sawmill and hosts September's Mill Valley Arts Festival. From the park, Cascade Way winds its way past creek-side homes to the trailheads of several forest paths. ⊠ Throckmorton Ave. and Cascade Dr.

WHERE TO EAT

$$$ AMERICAN ✕ **Buckeye Roadhouse.** This is Mill Valley's secret den of decadence, where house-smoked meats and fish, grilled steaks, and old-fashioned dishes such as brisket bring the locals coming back for more. The restaurant also serves beautiful organic, locally grown salads and desserts so heavenly—like the rich but light crème brûlée—you'll just about melt into the floor. The look of the 1937 roadhouse is decidedly hunting-lodge chic, with trophy heads and a river-rock fireplace dominating one wall.

Marin County's Jaguar-driving bon vivants pack the place every night. The busy but cozy bar with elegant mahogany paneling and soft lighting is a good place to quench your thirst for a Marin martini or Californian Merlot. $ *Average main: $23* ⊠ *15 Shoreline Hwy., off U.S. 101* ☎ *415/331–2600* ⊕ *buckeyeroadhouse.com* ⚑ *Reservations essential.*

$$$
CONTEMPORARY
Fodor's Choice
★

✕ **El Paseo House of Chops.** Chef Tyler Florence and rocker Sammy Hagar teamed up to restore El Paseo, which was established in 1947 and remains *the* place for a romantic and culinary night out. You'll feel as if you're on one of Spain's tiny cobbled lanes as you enter the secluded brick walkway that wraps around a candlelit dining room. If you reserve well in advance you can sit in the bougainvillea-framed courtyard, but the dining room casts its own atmospheric charms, with soft leather chairs, white tablecloths, and dark wooden walls. And then there's Tyler Florence's famous seasonal Californian cuisine. The spinach-and-artichoke dip is rich and full of fresh flavors, as is the grass-fed veal chop with porcini butter and sage. Don't overlook the decadent desserts. $ *Average main: $27* ⊠ *17 Throckmorton Ave., at E. Blithedale Ave.* ☎ *415/388–0741* ⊕ *www.elpaseomillvalley.com* ⚑ *Reservations essential* ⊘ *No lunch.*

$
BURGER
FAMILY

✕ **Pearl's Phat Burgers.** Families, couples, and teenagers flock to Pearl's for juicy, grass-fed organic burgers stacked high with tomatoes, lettuce, bacon, and cheese; sweet-potato fries that are not too crispy and not too soft; and thick, creamy milkshakes. The food here is among the freshest, biggest, and fastest in town. No wonder there's always a line out the door. $ *Average main: $9* ⊠ *8 E. Blithedale Ave., at Sunnyside Ave.* ☎ *415/381–6010* ⊕ *www.pearlsdeluxe.com.*

WHERE TO STAY
For expanded hotel reviews, visit Fodors.com.

$$$
B&B/INN

🛏 **Mill Valley Inn.** The only hotel in downtown Mill Valley has smart-looking rooms done up in Tuscan colors of ocher and olive, with handcrafted beds, armoires, and lamps by local artisans. **Pros:** minutes from local shops and restaurants; great complimentary Continental breakfast; free parking. **Cons:** some rooms are noisy; dark in winter because of surrounding trees; some rooms aren't accessible via elevator; no in-room coffee makers. $ *Rooms from: $239* ⊠ *165 Throckmorton Ave., near Miller Ave.* ☎ *415/389–6608, 800/595–2100* ⊕ *www.marinhotels. com* ⇨ *25 rooms, 1 suite, 2 cottages* ❑ *Breakfast.*

$$$$
B&B/INN
Fodor's Choice
★

🛏 **Mountain Home Inn.** Abutting 40,000 acres of state and national parks, the inn sits on the skirt of Mt. Tamalpais, where you can follow hiking trails all the way to Stinson Beach. **Pros:** amazing deck and views; peaceful, remote setting. **Cons:** nearest town is a 20-minute drive away; restaurant can get crowded on sunny weekend days; too rustic for some. $ *Rooms from: $279* ⊠ *810 Panoramic Hwy., at Edgewood Ave.* ☎ *415/381–9000* ⊕ *www.mtnhomeinn.com* ⇨ *10 rooms* ❑ *Breakfast.*

NIGHTLIFE AND THE ARTS
142 Throckmorton Theatre. This ultra-quirky venue presents plays, musical acts, and comedy shows, along with visual and related arts. Top events include the DjangoFest Mill Valley, celebrating the gypsy-jazz artist Django Reinhardt; a film series hosted by comedian Mort Sahl; and the

annual Writers with Attitude festival of short-play readings. Stunning murals cover the theater's ceiling, and the foyer has an old-fashioned popcorn maker. ✉ *142 Throckmorton Ave., at Madrona St., Mill Valley* ☎ *415/383–9600 tickets* ⊕ *www.142throckmortontheatre.com.*

Mill Valley Beerworks. A place to rest your feet after shopping or hiking, Beerworks serves more than 100 local, national, and international beers, from ale to port to lager. For food, you'll find cheese plates, olives, homemade pretzels, and sandwiches. ✉ *173 Throckmorton Ave., at Madrona St.* ☎ *415/888–8218* ⊕ *millvalleybeerworks.com.*

Sweetwater Music Hall. With the help of part-owner Bob Weir of the Grateful Dead, this renowned club reopened in an old Masonic Hall. The location may be new, but the Sweetwater's reputation as the best music club and bar in Marin remains. In its former life, it hosted the likes of John Lee Hooker and Jerry Garcia. Today, famous as well as up-and-coming bands play nightly, and local stars such as Bonnie Raitt and Huey Lewis have been known to stop in for a pickup session. ✉ *19 Corte Madera Ave., between Throckmorton and Lovell Aves.* ☎ *415/388–3850* ⊕ *www.sweetwatermusichall.com.*

THE WINE COUNTRY

6

WELCOME TO WINE COUNTRY

TOP REASONS TO GO

★ **Biking:** Cycling is one of the best ways to see the Wine Country—the Russian River and Dry Creek valleys, in Sonoma County, are particularly beautiful.

★ **Browsing the farmers' markets:** Many towns in Napa and Sonoma have seasonal farmers' markets, each rounding up an amazing variety of local produce.

★ **Wandering di Rosa:** Though this art and nature preserve is just off the busy Carneros Highway, it's a relatively unknown treasure. The galleries and gardens are filled with hundreds of pieces of art.

★ **Canoeing on the Russian River:** Trade in your car keys for a paddle and glide down the Russian River in Sonoma County. From May through October is the best time to be on the water.

★ **Touring Wineries:** Let's face it: this is the reason you're here, and the range of excellent sips to sample would make any oenophile (or novice drinker, for that matter) giddy.

1 Napa Valley.
You'll find big names all around, from high-profile wineries to world-renowned chefs. Napa, the valley's oldest town, sweet-life St. Helena, and down-to-earth Calistoga all make good home bases here. (Calistoga has the extra draw of local thermal springs.) Yountville has become a culinary boomtown, while the tiny communities of Oakville and Rutherford are home to major wineries such as Robert Mondavi and Beaulieu. Rutherford in particular is the source for outstanding Cabernet Sauvignon.

2 Sonoma Valley.
Historic attractions and an unpretentious attitude prevail here. The town of Sonoma, with its picture-perfect central plaza, is rich with 19th-century buildings. Glen Ellen, meanwhile, has a special connection with author Jack London.

| 0 | | 5 miles |
| 0 | | 5 km |

GETTING ORIENTED

The Napa and Sonoma valleys run roughly parallel, northwest to southeast, and are separated by the Mayacamas Mountains. Northwest of the Sonoma Valley are several more important viticultural areas in Sonoma County, including the Dry Creek, Alexander, and Russian River valleys. The Carneros region, which spans southern Sonoma and Napa counties, is just north of San Pablo Bay.

6

3 Elsewhere in Sonoma.
The winding, rural roads here feel a world away from Napa's main drag. The lovely Russian River, Dry Creek, and Alexander valleys are all excellent places to seek out Pinot Noir, Zinfandel, and Sauvignon Blanc. The small town of Healdsburg gets lots of attention, thanks to its terrific restaurants, bed-and-breakfasts, and chic boutiques.

Updated by
Daniel Mangin

Life is lived well in the California Wine Country. Eating and drinking are cultivated as high arts. If you've been daydreaming about driving through vineyards, stopping for a wine tasting or a picnic, well, that fantasy is just everyday life here.

It's little wonder that so many visitors to San Francisco take a day or two—or five or six—to unwind in the Napa and Sonoma valleys. They join the locals in the tasting rooms, from serious wine collectors making their annual pilgrimages to wine newbies who don't know the difference between a Merlot and Mourvèdre but are eager to learn.

The state's wine industry is booming, and the Napa and Sonoma valleys have long led the field. For instance, in 1975 Napa Valley had no more than 20 wineries; today there are more than 400. A recent up-and-comer is the Carneros region, which overlaps Napa and Sonoma counties at the head of the San Francisco Bay. Another exciting area: Coombsville, in southeastern Napa, which in 2011 received an official AVA (American Viticultural Area) designation recognizing its unique characteristics.

Great dining and wine go hand in hand, and the local viticulture has naturally encouraged a robust passion for food. Several outstanding chefs have taken root here, sealing the area's reputation as one of the best restaurant destinations in the country. The lust for fine food doesn't stop at the doors of the bistros, either. Whether you visit an artisanal olive-oil producer, nibble locally made cheese, or browse the fresh vegetables in the farmers' markets, you'll soon see why Napa and Sonoma are a food-lover's paradise.

Napa and Sonoma counties are also rich in history. In the town of Sonoma, for example, you can explore buildings from California's Spanish and Mexican past. Some wineries, such as Napa Valley's Beringer, have cellars or tasting rooms dating to the late 1800s. The town of Calistoga is a flurry of Steamboat Gothic architecture, gussied up with the fretwork favored by late-19th-century spa goers. Modern architecture is the exception rather than the rule, but one standout example is sleek Artesa, built gracefully into a hillside west of downtown Napa.

Binding all these temptations together is the sheer scenic beauty of the place. Much of Napa Valley's landscape unspools in orderly, densely planted rows of vines. Sonoma's vistas are broken by rolling hills or stands of ancient oak and madrone trees. Even the climate cooperates, as the warm summer days and refreshingly cool evenings that make the area one of the world's best grape-growing regions make perfect weather for traveling, too. If you're inspired to dig further into the Wine Country, grab a copy of *Fodor's InFocus Napa & Sonoma* or the in-depth *Compass American Guide: California Wine Country*.

PLANNING

WHEN TO GO

"Crush," the term used to indicate the season when grapes are picked and crushed, usually takes place in September or October, depending on the weather. From September until November the entire Wine Country celebrates its bounty with street fairs and festivals. The Sonoma County Harvest Fair, with its famous grape stomp, is held the first weekend in October. Golf tournaments, wine auctions, and art and food fairs occur from spring through fall.

In season (April through November), Napa Valley draws crowds of tourists, and traffic along Highway 29 from St. Helena to Calistoga is often backed up on weekends. The Sonoma Valley, Santa Rosa, and Healdsburg are less crowded (though even that's changing). In season and over holiday weekends, it's best to book lodging, restaurant, and winery reservations at least a month in advance. Many wineries give tours at specified times and require appointments.

To avoid crowds, visit the Wine Country during the week and get an early start (most wineries open around 10). Because many wineries close as early as 4 or 4:30—and few are open past 5—you'll need to get a reasonably early start if you want to fit in more than one or two, especially if you're going to enjoy the leisurely lunch customary in the Wine Country. Summer is usually hot and dry, and autumn can be even hotter, so dress appropriately if you go during these times.

GETTING HERE AND AROUND

AIR TRAVEL

If you'd like to bypass San Francisco or Oakland, you can fly directly to the small Charles M. Schulz Sonoma County Airport (STS) in Santa Rosa on Alaska Airlines, which has direct flights from San Diego, Los Angeles, Portland, and Seattle. Rental cars are available from Avis, Budget, Enterprise, Hertz, and National at the airport.

BUS TRAVEL

Bus travel is an inconvenient way to explore the Wine Country. Service is infrequent and buses from San Francisco can only get you to downtown Santa Rosa, hardly in the thick of the vineyard action. Sonoma County Transit offers daily bus service to points all over the county. VINE (Valley Intracity Neighborhood Express) provides bus service within the city of Napa and between other Napa Valley towns.

6

Bus Lines Greyhound ☎ *800/231–2222* ⊕ *www.greyhound.com.*
Sonoma County Transit ☎ *707/576–7433, 800/345–7433*
⊕ *www.sctransit.com.* **VINE** ☎ *707/251–2800, 800/696–6443*
⊕ *www.nctpa.net/routes-schedules/vine.html.*

CAR TRAVEL

Driving your own car is by far the best way to explore the Wine Country. Well-maintained roads zip through the centers of the Napa and Sonoma valleys, while scenic routes thread through the backcountry. Distances between towns are fairly short, and you can often drive from one end of the Napa or Sonoma valley to the other in less than an hour—if there's no significant traffic. This may be a relatively rural area, but the usual rush hours still apply, and high-season weekend traffic can be excruciatingly slow, especially on Highway 29.

Five major roads cut through the Napa and Sonoma valleys. U.S. 101 and Highways 12 and 121 travel through Sonoma County. Highway 29 heads north from Napa. The 25-mile Silverado Trail, which runs parallel to Highway 29 north from Napa to Calistoga, is Napa Valley's more scenic, less-crowded alternative to Highway 29.

■ **TIP→** If you're wine tasting, either select a designated driver or be careful of your wine intake. (When you're taking just a sip or two of any given wine, it can be hard to keep track of how much you're drinking.) Also, keep in mind that you'll likely be sharing the road with cyclists and joggers; keep a close eye on the shoulder.

When calculating the time it will take you to drive between the Napa and Sonoma valleys, remember that the Mayacamas Mountains are between the two. If it's not too far out of your way, you might want to travel between the two valleys along Highway 12/121 to the south, or along Highway 128 to the north, to avoid the slow, winding drive on the Oakville Grade, which connects Oakville, in Napa, and Glen Ellen, in Sonoma.

From San Francisco to Napa: Cross the Golden Gate Bridge, then go north on U.S. 101. Next go east on Highway 37 toward Vallejo, then north on Highway 121, also called the Carneros Highway. Turn left (north) when Highway 121 runs into Highway 29. This should take about 1½ hours when traffic is light.

From San Francisco to Sonoma: Cross the Golden Gate Bridge, then go north on U.S. 101, east on Highway 37 toward Vallejo, and north on Highway 121, aka the Carneros Highway. When you reach Highway 12, take it north. If you're going to any of the Sonoma County destinations north of the valley, take U.S. 101 all the way north through Santa Rosa to Healdsburg. This should take about an hour, not counting substantial traffic.

From Berkeley and other East Bay towns: Take Interstate 80 north to Highway 37 west, then on to Highway 29 north. To head up the Napa Valley, continue on Highway 29; to reach Sonoma County, turn off Highway 29 onto Highway 121 heading north. Getting from Berkeley to Napa will take at least 45 minutes, from Berkeley to Sonoma at least an hour.

RESTAURANTS

Star chefs from around the world have come into the Wine Country's orbit, drawn by the area's phenomenal produce, artisanal foods, and wines. These days, many visitors come to Napa and Sonoma as much for the restaurants' tasting menus as for the wineries' tasting rooms.

Although excellent meals can be found virtually everywhere in the region, the small town of Yountville has become a culinary crossroads under the influence of chef Thomas Keller. If a table at Keller's famed French Laundry is out of reach, keep in mind that he's also behind three more modest operations in town. In St. Helena the elegant Restaurant at Meadowood has achieved almost as much critical acclaim as the French Laundry, yet is considerably easier to get into. And the buzzed-about restaurants in Sonoma County, including the Farmhouse Inn, offer plenty of mouthwatering options.

Inexpensive eateries include high-end delis that serve superb picnic fare, and brunch is a cost-effective strategy at pricey restaurants, as is sitting at the bar and ordering a few appetizers instead of sitting down to a full-blown meal.

With few exceptions (*which are noted in individual restaurant listings*), dress is informal. Where reservations are indicated as essential, you may need to make them a week or more ahead. In summer and early fall you may need to book several weeks ahead.

Prices in the reviews are the average cost of a main course at dinner or, if dinner isn't served, at lunch.

HOTELS

Napa and Sonoma know the tourism ropes well; their inns and hotels range from low-key to utterly luxurious, and generally maintain high standards. Most of the bed-and-breakfasts are in historic Victorian and Spanish buildings, and the breakfast part of the equation often involves fresh local produce. The newer hotels tend to have a more modern, streamlined aesthetic and elaborate, spa-like bathrooms. Many hotels and B&Bs have excellent restaurants on their grounds, and those that don't are still just a short drive away from gastronomic bliss.

However, all of this comes with a hefty price tag. As the cost of vineyards and grapes has risen, so have lodging rates. Santa Rosa, the largest population center in the area, has the widest selection of moderately priced rooms. Try there if you've failed to reserve in advance or have a limited budget. In general, all accommodations in the area often have lower rates on weeknights, and prices are about 20% lower in winter.

On weekends, two- or even three-night minimum stays are commonly required, especially at smaller inns and B&Bs. If you'd prefer to stay a single night, though, innkeepers are usually more flexible in winter. Many B&Bs book up long in advance of the summer and fall seasons. Many B&Bs and small inns also discourage the presence of children though fall short of actually prohibiting them. If you're traveling with children, be sure to ask about them when booking to make sure they will receive a warm welcome.

6

Prices in the re views are the lowest cost of a standard double room in high season.Hotel reviews have been condensed for this book. Please go to Fodors.com for expanded reviews of each property.

BED-AND-BREAKFAST ASSOCIATIONS

Bed & Breakfast Association of Sonoma Valley ☎ 800/969–4667
⊕ *www.sonomabb.com.*

The Wine Country Inns of Sonoma County ☎ 800/946–3268
⊕ *www.winecountryinns.com.*

TOURS

Whether you want to tour the Wine Country in a full-size bus with dozens of other passengers or spring for your own private limo to take you to your favorite wineries, there are plenty of operators who can accommodate you. Tours generally last from five to seven hours and stop at four or five wineries. Rates vary—from $80 to $100 per person to $250 or more, depending on the vehicle and whether the tour includes other guests. Some include lunch, tasting fees, or both, but not all do, so ask. On most tours, at least one of the day's stops includes a behind-the-scenes look at wine-production facilities and the chance to meet winemakers or others involved in the wine-making process. Most tour operators will pick you up at Wine Country hotels or a specified meeting place.

California Wine Tours takes in large and small wineries. Perata Luxury Tours & Car Services creates customized tours. Platypus Wine Tours specializes in "fun" experiences at off-the-beaten-path wineries. The personable, well-informed owner of Woody's Wine Tours favors small wineries.

The tour operators below are based in the Wine Country. For information about day trips from San Francisco, see the Day Tours and Guides section of this book's Travel Smart chapter.

Tour Operators California Wine Tours ☎ 800/294–6386
⊕ *www.californiawinetours.com.* **Perata Luxury Tours & Car Services**
☎ 707/227–8271 ⊕ *www.perataluxurycarservices.com.* **Platypus Wine Tours**
☎ 707/253–2723 ⊕ *www.platypustours.com.* **Woody's Wine Tours** ☎ 707/396–
8235 ⊕ *www.woodyswinetours.com.* **Wine Country Bikes.** This family-owned
Healdsburg outfitter rents bikes by the day and organizes one-day and multi-day
trips throughout Sonoma County. ✉ *61 Front St., Healdsburg* ☎ *707/473–0610,
866/922–4537* ⊕ *www.winecountrybikes.com.*

VISITOR INFORMATION

Pre-Trip Planning Visit Napa Valley ☎ 707/251–5895
⊕ *www.visitnapavalley.com.* **Visit Sonoma** ☎ 707/522–5800, 800/576–6662
⊕ *www.sonomacounty.com.*

Visitor Centers California Welcome Center ✉ *9 4th St., at Wilson St., Santa
Rosa* ☎ *800/404–7673* ⊕ *www.visitcalifornia.com/california-welcome-centers/
santa-rosa.* **Napa Valley Welcome Center** ✉ *600 Main St., at 5th St., Napa*
☎ *707/251–5895* ⊕ *www.visitnapavalley.com/welcome_centers.htm.* **Sonoma
Valley Visitors Center** ✉ *453 1st St. E, in Sonoma Plaza, Sonoma* ☎ *707/996–
1090, 866/996–1090* ⊕ *www.sonomacounty.com/sonoma-listings/visitor-centers.*

Napa Valley

THE NAPA VALLEY

When it comes to wine production in the United States, Napa Valley rules the roost, with more than 400 wineries and many of the biggest brands in the business. Vastly diverse soils and microclimates give Napa winemakers the chance to make a tremendous variety of wines. But what's the area like beyond the glossy advertising and boldface names?

The small towns strung along Highway 29 are where wine-industry workers live, and they're also where most of the area lodging is. Napa—the valley's largest town—lures with its growing cultural attractions and accommodations that are (relatively) reasonably priced. A few miles farther north, compact Yountville is a culinary boomtown, densely packed with top-notch restaurants and hotels, including a few luxury properties. Continuing north, St. Helena teems with elegant boutiques and restaurants; mellow Calistoga, known for spas and hot springs, feels a bit like an Old West frontier town, and has a more casual attitude.

NAPA

46 miles northeast of San Francisco

The town of Napa is the valley's largest, and visitors who get a glimpse of the strip malls and big-box stores from Highway 29 often speed right past on the way to smaller and more seductive Yountville or St. Helena. But Napa is changing. After many years as a blue-collar town that more or less turned its back on the Wine Country scene, Napa has spent the last few years attempting to increase its appeal to visitors. A walkway that follows the river through town, completed in 2008, makes the city more pedestrian-friendly, and each year high-profile new restaurants pop up. Of course there's also the Oxbow Public Market, a klatch of high-end food purveyors. At night, catch a show at either the circa-1880 Napa Valley Opera House or the renovated Uptown Theatre, or sip in style at the chic 1313 Main wine bar.

Many visitors choose to stay in Napa after experiencing hotel sticker shock; prices in Napa are marginally more reasonable than elsewhere. If you set up your home base here, you'll undoubtedly want to spend some time getting out of town and into the beautiful countryside, but don't neglect taking a stroll to see what the valley's least pretentious town has to offer, or checking out the ever-changing culinary landscape.

GETTING HERE AND AROUND

To get to downtown Napa from Highway 29, take the 1st Street exit and follow the signs for Central Napa less than a mile through town until you reach the corner of 2nd Street and Main Street. Most of the town's sights and many of its restaurants are clustered in an easily walkable area near this intersection.

EXPLORING
TOP ATTRACTIONS

Fodor'sChoice
★

Artesa Vineyards & Winery. With its modern, minimalist architecture blending harmoniously into a Carneros hilltop, Artesa is a far cry from the region's many faux-French châteaus and Italian-style villas. It's surrounded by elegant outdoor sculptures and fountains. The winemaker, Mark Beringer—a great-great-grandson of the 19th-century Napa wine-making pioneer Jacob Beringer—focuses on Chardonnay and Pinot Noir, but also produces Cabernet Sauvignon and other limited-release wines such as Albariño and Tempranillo. Call ahead to reserve a spot on a wine-and-cheese pairing ($60), a wine-and-chocolate pairing ($45), and a tapas-and-wine tasting ($60). ⊠ *1345 Henry Rd., off Old Sonoma Rd. and Dealy La.* ☎ *707/224–1668* ⊕ *www. artesawinery.com* ☒ *Tastings $10–$15, tour $20* ☉ *Daily 10–5, tour daily at 11 and 2.*

Fodor'sChoice
★

di Rosa. It's not unusual for Wine Country moguls to collect art and display it in their wineries, but the late Rene di Rosa took the practice one grand step further: in 1986 he sold his winery and used the proceeds to finance this 217-acre art preserve. Thousands of 20th-century artworks by Northern California artists crop up everywhere—in galleries, in the former di Rosa residence, on every lawn, in every courtyard, and even on the lake. Some of the works were commissioned especially for the preserve, such as Paul Kos's meditative *Chartres Bleu*, a video installation in a chapel-like setting that replicates a stained-glass window from the cathedral in Chartres, France. If you stop by without a reservation, you'll gain access only to the Gatehouse Gallery, where there's a small collection of riotously colorful figurative and abstract sculptures and paintings, as well as rotating modern-art exhibits. ■**TIP**➔ **To see the rest of the property, sign up for one of the various tours of the grounds.** ⊠ *5200 Sonoma Hwy./Hwy. 121* ☎ *707/226–5991* ⊕ *www.dirosaart. org* ☒ *Gatehouse Gallery $5, tours $12–$15* ☉ *May–Oct., Wed.–Sat. 10–6; Nov.–Apr., Wed.–Sat. 10–4.*

Fodor'sChoice
★

Domaine Carneros. A visit to this majestic château is an opulent way to enjoy the Carneros District—especially in fine weather, when the vineyard views are spectacular. The château was modeled after the Château de la Marquetterie, an 18th-century mansion owned by the Taittinger family near Epernay, France. Carved into the hillside beneath the winery, the cellars produce delicate sparkling wines reminiscent of those made by Taittinger, using only Los Carneros AVA grapes. The winery sells full glasses, flights, and bottles of its wines, which also include such still wines as Pinot Noir, Merlot, and Chardonnay. Enjoy them all with cheese and charcuterie plates, caviar, or smoked salmon. Seating is in the Louis XV–inspired salon or on the terrace overlooking the vines. The tour at Domaine Carneros covers traditional methods of making sparkling wines, from the vineyard to the bottle. ⊠ *1240 Duhig Rd., at Hwy. 121* ☎ *707/257–0101, 800/716–2788* ⊕ *www.domainecarneros.com* ☒ *Tastings $7.50–$85, tour $30* ☉ *Daily 10–6; tour daily at 11, 1, and 3.*

Continued on page 322

6

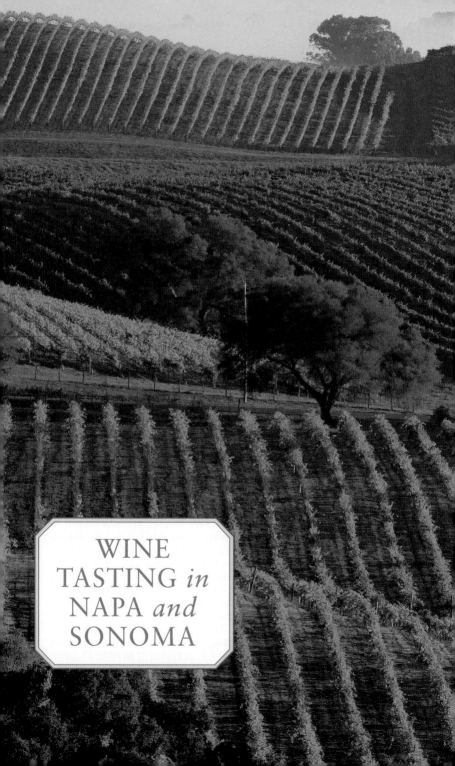

WINE
TASTING *in*
NAPA *and*
SONOMA

VISITING WINERIES

Napa and Sonoma are outstanding destinations for both wine newcomers and serious wine buffs. Tasting rooms range from modest to swanky, offering everything from a casual conversation over a few sips of wine to in-depth tours of winemaking facilities and vineyards. And there's a tremendous variety of wines to taste. The one constant is a deep, shared pleasure in the experience of wine tasting.

Wineries in Napa and Sonoma range from faux châteaux with vast gift shops to rustic converted barns where you might have to step over the vintner's dog in the doorway. Many are regularly open to the public, usually daily from around 10 am to 5 pm. Others require advance reservations to visit, and still others are closed to the public entirely. When in doubt, call ahead.

There are many, many more wineries in Napa and Sonoma than we could possibly include here. Free maps pinpointing most of them are widely available, though; ask the staff at the tasting rooms you visit or look for the ubiquitous free tourist magazines.

Pick a designated driver before setting out for the day. Although wineries rarely advertise it, many will provide a free non-alcoholic drink for the designated driver; it never hurts to ask.

Fees. In the past few years, tasting fees have skyrocketed. Most Napa wineries charge $10 to $25 to taste four or so wines, though $30, $40 or even $50 fees aren't unheard of. Sonoma wineries are often a bit cheaper, in the $5 to $15 range, and you'll still find the occasional freebie.

Some winery tours are free, in which case you're usually required to pay a separate fee if you want to taste the wine. If you've paid a fee for the tour—often $15 to $35—your wine tasting is usually included in that price.

The tantalizing pop of a cork. Roads unspooling through hypnotically even rows of vines. Sun glinting through a glass of sparkling wine or ruby colored cabernet. If these are your daydreams, you won't be disappointed when you get to Napa and Sonoma. The vineyard-blanketed hills, shady town squares, and ivy-draped wineries—not to mention the luxurious restaurants, hotels, and spas—really *are* that captivating.

(opposite page) Carneros vineyards in autumn, Napa Valley. (top) Pinot Gris grapes (bottom) Bottles from Far Niente winery.

MAKING THE MOST OF YOUR TIME

■ Call ahead. Some wineries require reservations to visit or tour and others are closed to the public entirely. It's wise to check before visiting.

■ Come on weekdays, especially if you're visiting during high season (May to November), to avoid traffic-clogged roads and crowded tasting rooms. For more info on the best times of year to visit, see this chapter's Planner.

■ Get an early start. Tasting rooms are often deserted before 11 am or so, when most visitors are still lingering over a second cup of coffee. If you come early, you'll have the staff's undivided attention. You'll usually encounter the largest crowds between 3 and 5 pm.

■ Consider skipping Napa. If you've got less than two days to spend in the Wine Country, dip into the Carneros area or the Sonoma Valley rather than Napa Valley or northern Sonoma County. Though you might find fewer big-name wineries and critically acclaimed

(top) Sipping and swirling in the De Loach tasting room. (bottom) Learning about barrel aging at Robert Mondavi Winery.

restaurants, these regions are only about an hour and half away from the city . . . if you don't hit traffic.

■ Divide your attention. If you're lucky enough to have three nights or more here, split your overnights between Napa and Sonoma to easily see the best that both counties have to offer.

Domaine Carneros.

AT THE BAR

In most tasting rooms, you'll be handed a list of the wines available that day. The wines will be listed in a suggested tasting order, starting with the lightest-bodied whites, progressing to the most intense reds, and ending with dessert wines. If you can't decide which wines to choose, tell the server what types of wines you usually like and ask for a recommendation.

The server will pour you an ounce or so of each wine you select. As you taste it, feel free to take notes or ask questions. Don't be shy—the staff are there to educate you about the wine. If you don't like a wine, or you've simply tasted enough, feel free to pour the rest into one of the dump buckets on the bar.

TOURS

Tours tend to be the most exciting (and the most crowded) in September and October, when the harvest and crush-

ing are underway. Tours typically last from 30 minutes to an hour and give you a brief overview of the winemaking process. At some of the older wineries, the tour guide might focus on the history of the property.

■ TIP→ If you plan to take any tours, wear comfortable shoes, since you might be walking on wet floors or dirt or gravel pathways or stepping over hoses or other equipment.

MONEY-SAVING TIPS

■ Many hotels and B&Bs distribute coupons for free or discounted tastings to their guests—don't forget to ask.

■ If you and your travel partner don't mind sharing a glass, servers are happy to let you split a tasting.

■ Some wineries will refund all or part of the tasting fee if you buy a bottle. Usually one fee is waived per bottle purchased, though sometimes you must buy two or three.

■ Almost all wineries will also waive the fee if you join their wine club program. However, this typically commits you to buying a certain number of bottles on a regular basis, so be sure you really like the wines before signing up.

Preston Vineyards bottles only estate-grown grapes.

TOP 2-DAY ITINERARIES

First-Timer's Napa Tour

Start: Oxbow Public market, Napa. Get underway by browsing the shops selling wines, spices, locally grown produce, and other fine foods, for a taste of what the Wine Country has to offer.

Inglenook, Rutherford. The tour here is a particularly fun way to learn about the history

of Napa winemaking—and you can see the old, atmospheric, ivy-covered château.

Frog's Leap, Rutherford. Friendly, unpretentious, and knowledgeable staff makes this place great for wine newbies. (Make sure you get that reservation lined up.)

Dinner and Overnight: St. Helena. Splurge at Meadowood Napa Valley and you won't need to leave the property for

Domaine Carneros

di Rosa Preserve

Old Sonoma Rd.

121

12

Oxbow Public Market
Napa
29

NAPA COUNTY

Robert Mondavi

Far Niente

Yountville

Oakville

KEY
First-Timer's Napa Tour
Wine Buff's Tour

Silverado Trail

Stag's Leap Wine Cellars

Wine Buff's Tour

Start: Stag's Leap Wine Cellars, Yountville. Famed for its cabernet sauvignon and Bordeaux blends.

Beaulieu Vineyard, Rutherford. Pony up the extra fee to visit the reserve tasting room to try the flagship Cabernet Sauvignon.

Mumm Napa, Rutherford. Come for the bubbly—which is available in a variety of tastings—stay for the photography exhibits.

Dinner and Overnight: Yountville. Have dinner at one of the Thomas Keller restaurants. Splurge at Bardessono; save at

Maison Fleurie.

Next Day: Robert Mondavi, Oakville. Spring for the reserve room tasting so you can sip the top-of-the-line wines, especially the stellar Cabernet Sauvignon. Head across Highway 29 to the Oakville Grocery to pick up a picnic lunch.

an extravagant dinner at its restaurant. Save at El Bonita Motel with dinner at Gott's.

Next Day: Poke around St. Helena's shops, then drive to Yountville for lunch.

di Rosa, Napa. Call ahead to book a one- or two-hour tour of the acres of gardens and galleries, which

are chock-full of thousands of works of art.

Domaine Carneros, Napa. Toast your trip with a glass of outstanding bubbly.

Sonoma Backroads

Start: Iron Horse Vineyards, Russian River Valley.
Soak up a view of vine-covered hills and Mount St. Helena while sipping a sparkling wine or Pinot Noir at this beautifully rustic spot.

Hartford Family Winery, Russian River Valley.
A terrific source for Pinot Noir and Chardonnay, the stars of this valley.

Dinner and Overnight: Forestville. Go all out with a stay at the Farmhouse Inn, whose award-winning restaurant is one of the best in all of Sonoma.

Next Day: Westside Road, Russian River Valley.
This scenic route, which follows the river, is crowded with worthwhile wineries like Gary Farrell and Rochioli—but it's not crowded with visitors. Pinot fans will find a lot to love. Picnic at Rochioli and enjoy the lovely view.

Matanzas Creek Winery, near Santa Rosa. End on an especially relaxed note with a walk through the lavender fields (best in June).

Far Niente, Oakville. You have to make a reservation and the fee for the tasting and tour is steep, but the

payoff is an especially intimate winery experience. You'll taste excellent Cabernet and Chardonnay, then end your trip on a sweet note with a dessert wine.

WINE TASTING 101

TAKE A GOOD LOOK.
Hold your glass by the stem, raise it to the light, and take a close look at the wine. Check for clarity and color. (This is easiest to do if you can hold the glass in front of a white background.) Any tinge of brown usually means that the wine is over the hill or has gone bad.

BREATHE DEEP.
1. Sniff the wine once or twice to see if you can identify any smells.

2. Swirl the wine gently in the glass. Aerating the wine this way releases more of its aromas. (It's called "volatilizing the esters," if you're trying to impress someone.)

3. Take another long sniff. You might notice that experienced wine tasters spend more time sniffing the wine than drinking it. This is because this step is where the magic happens. The number of scents you might detect is almost endless, from berries, apricots, honey, and wildflowers to leather, cedar, or even tar. Does the wine smell good to you? Do you detect any "off" flavors, like wet dog or sulfur?

Sniff

AT LAST! TAKE A SIP.
1. Swirl the wine around your mouth so that it makes contact with all your taste buds and releases more of its aromas. Think about the way the wine feels in your mouth. Is it watery or rich? Is it crisp or silky? Does it have a bold flavor, or is it subtle? The weight and intensity of a wine are called its body.

2. Hold the wine in your mouth for a few seconds and see if you can identify any developing flavors. More complex wines will reveal many different flavors as you drink them.

SPIT OR SWALLOW.
The pros typically spit, since they want to preserve their palate (and sobriety!) for the wines to come, but you'll find that swallowers far outnumber the spitters in the winery tasting rooms. Whether you spit or swallow, notice the flavor that remains after the wine is gone (the finish).

Sip

DODGE THE CROWDS

To avoid bumping elbows in the tasting rooms, look for wineries off the main drags of Highway 29 in Napa and Highway 12 in Sonoma. The back roads of the Russian River, Dry Creek, and Alexander valleys, all in Sonoma, are excellent places to explore. In Napa, try the northern end. Also look for wineries that are open by appointment only; they tend to schedule visitors carefully to avoid a big crush at any one time.

HOW WINE IS MADE

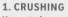

1. CRUSHING
Harvested grapes go into a stemmer-crusher, which separates stems from fruit and crushes the grapes to release "free-run" juice.

2. PRESSING
Remaining juice is gently extracted from grapes. Usually done by pressing grapes against the walls of a tank with an inflatable bladder.

3. FERMENTING
Extracted juice (and also grape skins and pulp, when making red wine) goes into stainless-steel tanks or oak barrels to ferment. During fermentation, sugars convert to alcohol.

4. AGING
Wine is stored in stainless-steel or oak casks or barrels to develop flavors.

5. RACKING
Wine is transferred to clean barrels; sediment is removed. Wine may be filtered and fined (clarified) to improve its clarity, color, and sometimes flavor.

6. BOTTLING
Wine is bottled either at the winery or at a special facility, then stored again for bottle-aging.

WHAT'S AN APPELLATION?

A specific region with a particular set of grape-growing conditions, such as soil type, climate, and elevation, is called an appellation. What makes things a little confusing is that appellations, which are defined by the Alcohol and Tobacco Tax and Trade Bureau, often overlap. California is an appellation, for example, but so is the Napa Valley. Napa and Sonoma counties are each county appellations, but they, too, are divided into even smaller regions, usually called subappellations or AVAs (American Viticultural Areas). You'll hear a lot about these AVAs from the staff in the tasting rooms; they might explain, for example, why the Russian River Valley AVA is such an excellent place to grow Pinot Noir grapes.

By law, if the label on a bottle of wine lists the name of an appellation, then at least 85% of the grapes in that wine must come from that appellation.

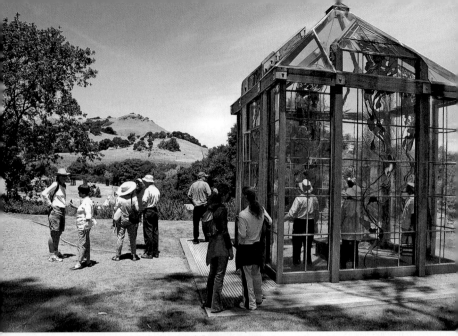
Wine and contemporary art find a home at di Rosa.

Fodor'sChoice ★ **The Hess Collection.** About 9 miles northwest of Napa, up a winding road ascending Mt. Veeder, this winery is a delightful discovery. The simple limestone structure, rustic from the outside but modern and airy within, contains Swiss owner Donald Hess's personal art collection, including mostly large-scale works by contemporary artists such as Robert Motherwell, Anselm Kiefer, Robert Rauschenberg, and Francis Bacon. Cabernet Sauvignon is a major strength, and the Mount Veeder 19 Block Mountain Cuvée—available only at the winery and through the Hess wine club—shows off the Malbec and other estate varietals. ■TIP➔ Several food and wine pairings are available, including one with chocolates that go ever so well with the robust Mount Veeder Cabernet. ✉ *4411 Redwood Rd., west off Hwy. 29 at Trancas St./Redwood Rd. exit* ☎ *707/255–1144* ⊕ *www.hesscollection.com* ✉ *Art gallery free, tasting $10–$75* ⊙ *Daily 10–5:30; guided tours daily 10:30–3:30.*

Fodor'sChoice ★ **Oxbow Public Market.** This market's two-dozen shops, wine bars, and artisanal food producers provide an introduction to Napa Valley's wealth of foods and wines. Swoon over decadent charcuterie at the Fatted Calf, slurp down bivalves at Hog Island Oyster Company, chow down on tacos with homemade tortillas at C Casa, or get a whiff of hard-to-find seasonings at Whole Spice Company before sitting down to a glass of wine at the Oxbow Wine Merchant & Wine Bar. The retro fast-food joint Gott's Roadside tempts those who prefer hamburgers (or egg-and-cheese breakfast sandwiches) to duck-liver mousse. ■TIP➔ Locals line up at Model Bakery at around 3 pm for hot-from-the-oven "late bake" bread. ✉ *610 and 644 1st St., at McKinstry St.* ⊕ *www.oxbowpublicmarket.com* ✉ *Free* ⊙ *Weekdays 9–9, weekends 10–9; hrs of some merchants vary.*

WORTH NOTING

Bouchaine Vineyards. Tranquil Bouchaine lies just north of the tidal sloughs of San Pablo Bay—to appreciate the setting, have your tasting on the back patio and scan the skies for hawks and golden eagles soaring above the vineyards. Patio tastings ($35) include cheeses, almonds, and olives. The alternately breezy and foggy weather in this part of the Carneros works well for the Burgundian varietals Pinot Noir and Chardonnay. These account for most of Bouchaine's excellent wines, but also look for Pinot Gris, Riesling, and Syrah. Tastings may end with the silky-sweet late-harvest Chardonnay called Bouche d'Or. ■TIP➔ Pick up a brochure if you're interested in taking a self-guided ¾-mile walking tour through the vineyards. ✉ 1075 Buchli Station Rd., off Duhig Rd., south of Hwy. 121 ☎ 707/252-9065 ⊕ www.bouchaine.com ☜ Tastings $20–$35 ⊙ Mid-Mar.–Oct., daily 10:30–5:30; Nov.–mid-Mar., daily 10:30–4:30.

Etude Wines. The well-conceived wine and food seminars are a big draw, but perhaps the most seductive part of a visit to Etude is tasting the suave Pinot Noirs. Though the handsome, modern winery is in Napa County, its flagship Carneros Estate Pinot Noir comes from grapes grown in the Sonoma County portion of Los Carneros, as does the rarer Heirloom Carneros Pinot Noir. Both are gentle, sophisticated wines whose smooth tannins linger on the palate. Pinot Noir accounts for much of Etude's production, but the winery also makes Pinot Gris, Chardonnay, Cabernet Sauvignon, and a few other wines. Some of them are paired with small bites of food at informative tasting seminars ($35). ■TIP➔ Don't leave without stopping to survey the landscape. You're apt to see (or hear) geese, hawks, egrets, and other wildlife. ✉ 1250 Cuttings Wharf Rd., 1 mile south of Hwy. 121 ☎ 877/586-9361 ⊕ www.etudewines.com ☜ Tastings $15–$35 ⊙ Daily 10–4:30.

Napa Valley Wine Train. Leave driving to someone else—a train engineer. The Napa Valley Wine Train runs a scenic route between Napa and St. Helena with several restored 1915–1917 Pullman railroad cars. The ride often includes a meal, such as brunch or dinner. Although it's no bargain and can feel a bit hokey, the train gives you a chance to enjoy the vineyard views without any driving worries. ✉ 1275 McKinstry St., off 1st St. ☎ 707/253-2111, 800/427-4124 ⊕ www.winetrain.com ☜ Lunch and dinner $114 ⊙ Lunch: Mar.–Nov., daily 11:30; Dec.–Feb., Fri.–Sun. 11:30. Dinner: Jan.–Mar., Sat. 6:30; Apr. and Nov.–Dec., Fri. and Sat. 6:30; May, Fri.–Sun. 6:30; June–Sept., Thurs. and Fri. 6:30; Oct., Thurs.–Sun. 6:30.

WHERE TO EAT

$$
MODERN
AMERICAN
Fodor's Choice
★

✕ **Boon Fly Café.** Part of the Carneros Inn west of downtown Napa, this small spot melds rural charm with industrial chic. Outside, swings occupy the porch of a modern red barn; inside, things get sleek with high ceilings and galvanized-steel tabletops. The menu of three squares a day updates American classics, with such dishes as Dungeness crab cakes with a citrus salad, roasted pork chop with sweet potatoes, and chicken and waffles. The flatbread topped with bacon, Point Reyes blue cheese, and portobello mushrooms is a local

Climbing ivy and lily pads decorate the Hess Collection's rustic exterior.

favorite. If there's a wait for a table, never fear: belly up to the bar, where you'll find a good selection of wines by the glass. Reservations are a good idea at dinner. ■TIP→ One of the rare Wine Country restaurants open all day, Boon Fly makes a convenient morning or midday stop. ⑤ *Average main: $18* ⊠ *4048 Sonoma Hwy.* ☎ *707/299–4870* ⊕ *www.theboonflycafe.com.*

$$$
AMERICAN
Fodor's Choice
★
✕ **Bounty Hunter.** A triple threat, Bounty Hunter is a wine store, wine bar, and restaurant in one. You can stop by for just a glass—about 40 choices are available in both 2- and 5-ounce pours—or a bottle, but it's best to come with an appetite. A minuscule kitchen means the menu is also small, but every dish is a standout, including the pulled-pork and beef brisket sandwiches served with three types of barbecue sauce, the signature beer-can chicken, and meltingly tender St. Louis–style ribs. The space is whimsically rustic, with stuffed game trophies mounted on the wall and leather saddles standing in for seats at a couple of tables. ■TIP→ The restaurant remains open until midnight on Friday and Saturday, making it popular for late-night bites. ⑤ *Average main: $24* ⊠ *975 1st St., at Main St.* ☎ *707/226–3976* ⊕ *www.bountyhunterwinebar.com* ⌲ *Reservations not accepted.*

$$$$
JAPANESE
✕ **Morimoto Napa.** *Iron Chef* star Masuharu Morimoto, owner of eponymous restaurants around the world, is the big name behind this hot spot in downtown Napa. Organic materials like twisting grapevines above the bar and rough-hewn wooden tables seem simultaneously earthy and modern, which seems a fitting setting for the gorgeously plated Japanese fare, from super-fresh sashimi served with grated fresh wasabi to elaborate concoctions like sea-urchin carbonara, made with udon noodles. For the full experience, consider leaving the choice up to the chef with

the *omakase* menu ($120 and up). If no tables are available, you can order many dishes in the lounge, where a young and lively crowd drinks specialty cocktails along with quirky fare like the pork skins, peanut butter, and wasabi-powder appetizer. $ *Average main: $44* ✉ *610 Main St., at 5th St.* ☎ *707/252–1600* ⊕ *www.morimotonapa.com.*

$$
MEDITERRANEAN
Fodor's Choice
★

✕**Tarla Mediterranean Grill.** Celebrating his Greek roots, hip chef Michael Benjamin Powell challenges the Napa Valley's notoriously Italo-centric diners to venture deeper into the Mediterranean. You might be tempted to build a meal by combining such traditional mezes (tapas) as stuffed grape leaves with fresh *tzatziki* (a thick yogurt sauce with cucumber, dill, and mint) and spanakopita (phyllo dough stuffed with spinach and feta cheese) with contemporary ones like the roasted bone marrow paired with a lemon-zesty gremolata sauce and served on grilled ciabatta bread. With his entrées, Powell proves himself equally comfortable updating moussaka and other Greek and Turkish standbys or going fancifully modern, as he does with beef short ribs, braising them with a pomegranate-wine sauce and accompanying them with pumpkin-sage risotto, pickled sweet peppers, and fried shallot petals. Locals have really bonded with this place. $ *Average main: $17* ✉ *1480 1st St., at School St.* ☎ *707/255–5599* ⊕ *www.tarlagrill.com* ☖ *Reservations essential.*

$$$
SPANISH
Fodor's Choice
★

✕**ZuZu.** A recent seismic retrofitting changed the look of ZuZu but not the festive vibe or the sharp focus on Spanish favorites like tapas and paella. Diners down *cava* (Spanish sparkling wine) or sangria with such dishes as white anchovies with boiled egg and remoulade on grilled bread. Locals revere the paella, made with Spanish Bomba rice. Latin jazz on the stereo helps make this place a popular spot for get-togethers. ■TIP→ Reservations aren't accepted, so expect a wait on weekends, when local young adults flood the zone. $ *Average main: $29* ✉ *829 Main St., near 3rd St.* ☎ *707/224–8555* ⊕ *www.zuzunapa.com* ☖ *Reservations not accepted* ⊘ *No lunch weekends.*

WHERE TO STAY

For expanded hotel reviews, visit Fodors.com.

$
HOTEL
Fodor's Choice
★

⌂**Andaz Napa.** Hands down, this boutique hotel is the hippest place to stay in Napa; the rooms, most of them suites, are modern, but welcomingly so. **Pros:** proximity to downtown restaurants, theaters, and tasting rooms; modern fitness center. **Cons:** parking can be a challenge on weekends; though generally good, service can be inconsistent. $ *Rooms from: $169* ✉ *1450 1st St.* ☎ *707/224–3900* ⊕ *www.napa.andaz.hyatt.com* ⇆ *50 rooms, 91 suites.*

$$$$
RESORT
Fodor's Choice
★

⌂**Carneros Inn.** Freestanding board-and-batten cottages with rocking chairs on each porch are simultaneously rustic and chic at this luxurious property. **Pros:** cottages have lots of privacy; beautiful views from the hilltop pool and hot tub; heaters on each private patio encourage lounging outside in the evening. **Cons:** a long drive from destinations up-valley; smallish rooms with limited seating options. $ *Rooms from: $600* ✉ *4048 Sonoma Hwy./Hwy. 121* ☎ *707/299–4900, 888/400–9000* ⊕ *www.thecarnerosinn.com* ⇆ *76 cottages, 10 suites.*

$$$
B&B/INN

⌂**Milliken Creek Inn.** Wine-and-cheese receptions at sunset set a romantic mood in this hotel's intimate lobby, with its terrace overlooking a lush lawn and the Napa River. **Pros:** soft-as-clouds beds; serene spa;

Where to Eat and Stay in Napa Valley

KEY

1 Restaurants

1 Hotels

Restaurants ▼

Ad Hoc **6**
Angèle **1**
Barolo **20**
Bistro Don Giovanni **5**
Bottega **7**
Bouchon **9**
Bounty Hunter **2**
Calistoga Inn Restaurant
and Brewery **18**
Étoile **10**
Farmstead Restaurant **15**

French Laundry **8**
Gott's Roadside Market **13**
Jole **19**
Market **14**
Morimoto Napa **4**
Mustards Grill **11**
Norman Rose Tavern **3**
Terra **16**
The Restaurant at
Meadowood **12**
Wine Spectator
Greystone Restaurant **17**

Hotels ▼

Auberge du Soleil **12**
Avia Napa **2**
Bardessono **6**
Brannan Cottage Inn **17**
Calistoga Ranch **16**
Carneros Inn **1**
Cottage Grove Inn **18**
El Bonita Motel **14**
Hotel Luca **10**
Indian Springs **21**
Maison Fleurie **7**

Meadowlark Country
House **20**
Meadowood Resort **13**
Milliken Creek Inn **5**
Mount View Hotel & Spa ...**19**
Napa River Inn **3**
Napa Valley Railway Inn ...**11**
Solage **22**
Villagio Inn & Spa **8**
Vintage Inn **9**
Westin Verasa **4**
Wine Country Inn **15**

breakfast delivered to your room (or wherever you'd like to eat on the grounds). **Cons:** expensive; road noise can be heard from the admittedly beautiful outdoor areas. $\boxed{\$}$ *Rooms from: $379* ✉ *1815 Silverado Trail* ☎ *707/255–1197, 800/835–6112* ⊕ *www.millikencreekinn.com* ⤢ *12 rooms.*

$$
$$ | **Napa River Inn.** Almost everything's close here: this waterfront inn is part of a complex of restaurants, shops, a nightclub, and a spa, all
B&B/INN within easy walking distance of downtown Napa. **Pros:** a pedestrian walkway connects the hotel to downtown Napa; unusual pet-friendly policy; wide range of room sizes and prices. **Cons:** river views could be more scenic; some rooms get noise from nearby restaurants. $\boxed{\$}$ *Rooms from: $248* ✉ *500 Main St.* ☎ *707/251–8500, 877/251–8500* ⊕ *www.napariverinn.com* ⤢ *65 rooms, 1 suite.*

$$$ | **Westin Verasa Napa.** Across the street from the Napa Valley Wine
HOTEL Train depot and adjacent to the Oxbow Public Market, this spacious resort is sophisticated and soothing, with pristine white bedding, and furniture in warm earth tones. **Pros:** pool is heated year-round; most rooms have well-equipped kitchenettes; spacious double-headed showers. **Cons:** "amenities fee" added to room rate. $\boxed{\$}$ *Rooms from: $350* ✉ *1314 McKinstry St.* ☎ *707/257–1800, 800/937–8461* ⊕ *www.westinnapa.com* ⤢ *160 suites, 20 rooms.*

NIGHTLIFE AND THE ARTS

Fodor's Choice **1313 Main.** This sexy lounge increased Napa's cool exponentially,
★ at least among the youngish set that has flocked here since day one. They drink in the hip vibe along with flights of fancy, well-selected sparkling and still wines. The bar menu includes cheeses, charcuterie, breads, and sweets. ✉ *1313 Main St., at Clinton St.* ☎ *707/258–1313* ⊕ *www.1313main.com.*

Napa Valley Opera House. The interior of the Italianate Victorian Napa Valley Opera House, which opened its doors in 1880, isn't quite as majestic as the facade, but the intimate 500-seat venue is still an excellent place to see all sorts of performances, from comedian Paul Reiser to the Vienna Boys Choir to the Napa Valley Film Festival. There's even the occasional opera. ✉ *1030 Main St., at 1st St.* ☎ *707/226–7372* ⊕ *www.nvoh.org.*

Uptown Theatre. Dating from 1937, this Napa icon opened as a movie house and now serves as a top-notch live-music venue that attracts performers like Bootsy Collins, Clint Black, and Los Lobos. ✉ *1350 3rd St., at Franklin St.* ☎ *707/259–0123* ⊕ *www.uptowntheatrenapa.com.*

YOUNTVILLE

9 miles north of the town of Napa.

These days Yountville is something like Disneyland for food lovers. It all started with Thomas Keller's French Laundry, simply one of the best restaurants in the United States. Now Keller is also behind two more-casual restaurants a few blocks from his mother ship—and that's only the tip of the iceberg. You could stay here for a week and not exhaust all the options in this tiny town with a big culinary reputation.

Yountville is full of small inns and high-end hotels that cater to those who prefer to walk (not drive) after an extravagant meal. It's also well located for excursions to many big-name Napa wineries, especially those in the Stags Leap District, from which big, bold Cabernet Sauvignons helped put the Napa Valley on the wine-making map.

GETTING HERE AND AROUND
To get to Yountville from Highway 29 traveling north, take the Yountville exit and then take the first left, onto Washington Street. Almost all of Yountville's businesses and restaurants are clustered along Washington Street in the first half-mile. Yountville Cross Road connects tiny downtown Yountville to the Silverado Trail, along which many of the area's best wineries are located.

EXPLORING

TOP ATTRACTIONS

Domaine Chandon. On a knoll shaded by ancient oak trees, this French-owned winery west of downtown claims one of Yountville's prime pieces of real estate. Basic tours of the sleek, modern facilities ($15) don't include a tasting, but other tours ($36–$42) focusing on topics ranging from food-and-wine pairing to sparkling-wine production end with a seated tasting. The top-quality sparklers are made using the laborious *méthode champenoise.* For the complete experience, order hors d'oeuvres to accompany the wines in the tasting room. Although Chandon is best known for its bubblies, the Cabernet Sauvignon, Chardonnay, Pinot Noir, and Pinot Meunier still wines are also worth a try. The tasting lounge is restricted to those 21 years or older, but guests with children are welcome on the outdoor terrace. ✉ *1 California Dr., at Solano Ave., west of Hwy. 29* ☎ *707/204–7530, 888/242–6366* ⊕ *www.chandon.com* ☉ *Tastings $18–$25* ☉ *Daily 10–5; tours daily at 10:30, 1, and 3.*

Fodor's Choice ★   **Ma(i)sonry Napa Valley.** An art-and-design gallery that also pours the wines of 19 limited-production wineries, Ma(i)sonry occupies an atmospheric stone manor house constructed in 1904. Tasting flights can be sampled in fair weather in the beautiful garden, in a private nook, or at the communal redwood table, and in any weather indoors among the contemporary artworks and some well-chosen *objets*—which might include 17th-century furnishings, industrial lamps, or slabs of petrified wood. ■TIP➔ **Walk-ins are welcome if space permits, but during summer, at harvesttime, and on weekends and holidays it's best to book in advance.** ✉ *6711 Washington St., at Pedroni St.* ☎ *707/944–0889* ⊕ *www.maisonry.com* ☉ *Tasting $10–$35* ☉ *Mid-Nov.–May, daily 10–7; June–mid-Nov., Sun.–Thurs. 10–7 and Fri. and Sat. 10–9.*

Stag's Leap Wine Cellars. The 1973 Cabernet Sauvignon produced here put the winery—and the Napa Valley—on the map by placing first in the famous Paris tasting of 1976. Today, a visit to the winery is a no-frills affair. Visitors in the tasting room are clearly serious about tasting wine, and aren't interested in distractions like a gift shop. It costs $30 to taste the top-of-the-line wines, including the limited-production estate-grown Cabernets, a few of which sell for well over $100. If you're interested in more-modestly priced wines, try the $15 tasting, which usually includes a Sauvignon Blanc, Chardonnay, Merlot, and Cabernet.

(Note: Don't confuse this winery with Stags' Leap Winery; that's a different operation entirely.) ⊠ *5766 Silverado Trail, at Wappo Hill Rd., Napa* ☎ *707/944–2020, 866/422–7523* ⊕ *www.cask23.com* ⊠ *Tasting $15–$30, tour $40* ⊘ *Daily 10–4:30; tours by appointment.*

WORTH NOTING

Fodor's Choice
★

Robert Sinskey Vineyards. Although the winery produces a well-regarded Stags Leap Cabernet Sauvignon, two supple red blends called Marcien and POV, and white wines, it's best known for intense, brambly Pinot Noirs grown in the cooler Carneros District. All the grapes are grown in organic, certified biodynamic vineyards. The influence of Robert's wife, Maria Helm Sinskey—a chef and cookbook author and the winery's culinary director—is evident during the tastings, accompanied by a few bites of food with each wine. Reserve a spot on the culinary tour ($75), which takes you through the winery's gardens and ends with a seated pairing of food and wine. ⊠ *6320 Silverado Trail, at Yountville Cross Rd.,* ☎ *707/944–9090* ⊕ *www.robertsinskey.com* ⊠ *Tasting $25, tour $75* ⊘ *Daily 10–4:30; tours daily at 11 by appointment.*

V Marketplace. This vine-covered market, which once housed a winery, a livery stable, and a brandy distillery, contains a smattering of clothing boutiques, art galleries, and gift stores. NapaStyle, a large deli and wine bar, sells cookbooks, luxury food items, and kitchenware, as well as an assortment of prepared foods perfect for picnics. The complex's signature restaurant, Bottega, features the food of celebrity chef Michael Chiarello. ⊠ *6525 Washington St., near Mulberry St.* ☎ *707/944–2451* ⊕ *www.vmarketplace.com.*

WHERE TO EAT

$$$$
MODERN
AMERICAN
Fodor's Choice
★

✕ **Ad Hoc.** When superstar chef Thomas Keller first opened this relatively casual spot, he meant to run it for six months until he launched a burger joint in the same space, but locals were so charmed by the homey food that they clamored for the stopgap to stay. Now a single, seasonal, fixed-price menu ($52) is offered nightly, with a small menu of decadent brunch items served on Sunday. The selection might include a juicy pork loin and buttery polenta, served family style, or a delicate panna cotta with a citrus glaze. The dining room is warmly low-key, with zinc-top tables, wine served in tumblers, and rock and jazz on the stereo. If you can't wait to know what's going be served before you visit, call a day in advance for the menu. ⑤ *Average main: $52* ⊠ *6476 Washington St., at Oak Circle* ☎ *707/944–2487* ⊕ *www.adhocrestaurant.com* ⊘ *No lunch Mon.–Sat. No dinner Tues. and Wed.*

$$$$
ITALIAN

✕ **Bottega.** The food at this lively trattoria is simultaneously soulful and inventive, transforming local ingredients into regional Italian dishes with a twist. The antipasti shine: you can order olives grown on chef Michael Chiarello's own property in St. Helena, house-made charcuterie, or incredibly fresh fish. Potato gnocchi might be served with pumpkin *fonduta* (Italian-style fondue) and roasted root vegetables, and hearty main courses like twice-cooked pork chops with peck seasoning might be accompanied by cinnamon-stewed plums and crispy black kale. The vibe is more festive than formal, with exposed-brick walls, an open kitchen, and paper-topped tables, but service is spot-on, and the reasonably priced wine list offers lots of interesting choices from both Italy and California. $ *Average main: $35* ✉ *6525 Washington St., near Mulberry St.* ☎ *707/945–1050* ⊕ *www.botteganapavalley.com* ⊘ *No lunch Mon.*

$$$
FRENCH
✕ **Bouchon.** The team that brought French Laundry to its current pinnacle is also behind this place, where everything—the lively and crowded zinc-topped bar, the elbow-to-elbow seating, the traditional French onion soup—could have come straight from a Parisian bistro. Roast chicken with mustard greens and fingerling potatoes and steamed mussels served with crispy, addictive *frites* (french fries) are among the hearty dishes served in the high-ceilinged room. ■**TIP**➜ **A limited menu is served until midnight—a rarity in the Wine Country, where it's often difficult to find a place that's open after 10.** $ *Average main: $27* ✉ *6534 Washington St., near Humboldt St.* ☎ *707/944–8037* ⊕ *www. bouchonbistro.com.*

$$$$
AMERICAN
Fodor'sChoice
★
✕ **Étoile.** Domaine Chandon's quietly elegant restaurant seems built for romance, with delicate orchids on each table and views of the wooded grounds from the large windows. Chef Perry Hoffman has racked up numerous awards for his sophisticated California cuisine. Such starters as terrine of duck and artichokes or oxtail aspic and sweet white corn play with a variety of textures, and succulent black mission figs might accompany main courses like Liberty Farms duck with Padrón peppers. Four- and six-course tasting menus can be ordered with or without wine pairings. The wine list features Domaine Chandon sparklers, but it's strong in wines from throughout California as well. $ *Average main: $34* ✉ *1 California Dr., at Solano Ave., west of Hwy. 29* ☎ *888/242–6366* ⊕ *www.chandon.com/etoile-restaurant* ⊘ *Closed Tues. and Wed.*

$$$$
AMERICAN
Fodor'sChoice
★
✕ **French Laundry.** An old stone building laced with ivy houses the most acclaimed restaurant in Napa Valley—and, indeed, one of the most highly regarded in the country. The restaurant's two nine-course prix-fixe menus (both $270), one of which highlights vegetables, vary, but "oysters and pearls," a silky dish of pearl tapioca with oysters and white sturgeon caviar, is a signature starter. Some courses rely on luxe ingredients like *calotte* (cap of the rib eye), while others take humble foods like fava beans and elevate them to art. Many courses also offer the option of "supplements," such as sea urchin or black truffles. Reservations at French Laundry are hard-won, and not accepted more than two months in advance. ■**TIP**➜ **Call two months ahead to the day at 10 am, on the dot. Didn't get a reservation? Call on the day you'd like to dine here to be considered if there's a cancellation.** $ *Average main: $270* ✉ *6640 Washington St., at Creek St.* ☎ *707/944–2380* ⊕ *www. frenchlaundry.com* ⚶ *Reservations essential* 🏛 *Jacket required* ⊘ *No lunch Mon.–Thurs.*

$$$
AMERICAN
✕ **Mustards Grill.** There's not an ounce of pretension at Cindy Pawlcyn's longtime Napa favorite, despite the fact that it's filled nearly every day and night with fans of her hearty cuisine. The menu mixes updated renditions of traditional American dishes (what the restaurant likes to call "deluxe truck stop classics"), such as barbecued baby back pork ribs and a lemon-lime tart piled high with browned meringue, with a handful of more innovative choices such as sweet corn tamales with

tomatillo-avocado salsa and wild mushrooms. A black-and-white marble tile floor and upbeat artwork set a scene that one Fodors.com reader describes as "pure fun, if not fancy." $ *Average main: $27* ✉ *7399 St. Helena Hwy./Hwy. 29, 1 mile north of Yountville* ☎ *707/944–2424* ⊕ *www.mustardsgrill.com.*

$$$
MODERN
AMERICAN
Fodor's Choice
★

✕ **Redd.** The minimalist dining room seems a fitting setting for chef Richard Reddington's up-to-date menu. The culinary influences include California, Mexico, Europe, and Asia, but the food always feels modern and never fussy. The glazed pork belly with apple purée, set amid a pool of soy caramel, is a prime example of the East-meets-West style. The seafood preparations—among them petrale sole, mussels, and chorizo poached in a saffron-curry broth—are deft variations on the original dishes. Desserts like the butterscotch "sundae"—a scoop of vanilla-rum ice cream served with an airy butterscotch cream and salted butter shortbread—put a novel twist on the classics. For the full experience, consider the five-course tasting menu ($80 per person, $125 with wine pairing). ■**TIP**➔ **For a quick bite, order small plates and a cocktail and sit at the bar.** $ *Average main: $29* ✉ *6480 Washington St., at Oak Circle* ☎ *707/944–2222* ⊕ *www.reddnapavalley. com* ⌕ *Reservations essential.*

$$
ITALIAN

✕ **Redd Wood.** Not to be confused with his ultrachic Redd, chef Richard Reddington's more casual restaurant specializes in thin-crust wood-fired pizzas and contemporary variations on rustic Italian classics. The cool nonchalance of the industrial decor mirrors the service (which at its best provides an antidote to the fussiness found elsewhere) and the cuisine itself. The glazed beef short ribs, for instance, seem like yet another fancy take on a down-home favorite until you realize how cleverly the sweetness of the glaze plays off the creamy polenta and the piquant splash of salsa verde. Redd Wood does for Italian comfort food what nearby Mustards Grill does for the American version: it spruces it up but retains its innate pleasures. $ *Average main: $22* ✉ *North Block Hotel, 6755 Washington St., at Madison St.* ☎ *707/299–5030* ⊕ *www.redd-wood.com.*

WHERE TO STAY

For expanded hotel reviews, visit Fodors.com.

$$$$
RESORT
Fodor's Choice
★

🏨 **Bardessono.** Although Bardessono bills itself as the "greenest luxury hotel in America," there's nothing spartan about its accommodations. **Pros:** large rooftop lap pool; exciting restaurant; polished service. **Cons:** expensive; the view from many rooms is uninspiring. $ *Rooms from: $500* ✉ *6526 Yount St.* ☎ *707/204–6000* ⊕ *www.bardessono.com* ⌕ *50 rooms, 12 suites* ⦿*No meals.*

$
B&B/INN

🏨 **Maison Fleurie.** If you'd like to be within easy walking distance of Yountville's fine restaurants, and possibly score a great bargain, look into this casual, comfortable inn. **Pros:** smallest rooms are some of the most affordable in town; free bike rental; refrigerator stocked with free bottled water and soda. **Cons:** breakfast room can be crowded at peak times; bedding could be nicer. $ *Rooms from: $175* ✉ *6529 Yount St.* ☎ *707/944–2056, 800/788–0369* ⊕ *www.maisonfleurienapa.com* ⌕ *13 rooms* ⦿*Breakfast.*

6

$$$$
HOTEL
☷ **North Block Hotel.** With a rustic-chic Tuscan style, this 20-room hotel has dark-wood furniture and soothing decor in brown and sage. **Pros:** extremely comfortable beds; attentive service; breakfast, included in rates, can be delivered to your room. **Cons:** outdoor areas get some traffic noise. ⑤ *Rooms from: $425* ✉ *6757 Washington St.* ☎ *707/944–8080* ⊕ *northblockhotel.com* ⇋ *20 rooms* ❂❘ *Breakfast.*

$$$
RESORT
Fodor's Choice
★
☷ **Villagio Inn & Spa.** Quiet, refined luxury is the hallmark of this relaxing haven built to resemble a Tuscan village. **Pros:** amazing buffet breakfast; no extra charge for the spa facilities; steps away from many dining options. **Cons:** can be bustling with large groups; you can hear highway noise from many balconies or patios. ⑤ *Rooms from: $375* ✉ *6481 Washington St.* ☎ *707/944–8877, 800/351–1133* ⊕ *www.villagio.com* ⇋ *86 rooms, 26 suites* ❂❘ *Breakfast.*

SPAS

Spa Villagio. With a Mediterranean style, this 13,000-square-foot spa has all the latest gadgets, including men's and women's outdoor hot tubs and showers with an extravagant number of showerheads. Huge spa suites—complete with flat-panel TV screens and wet bars—are perfect for couples and groups. The pièce de résistance, perhaps for the entire Napa Valley, is the Suite Sensations experience ($575), which combines treatments drawn from Asian, Mediterranean, and Middle-Eastern traditions and includes wine-and-food pairings matched to these cultural influences. The spa also provides the full array of services, including massages, body peels, facials, and manicures. ✉ *6481 Washington St., at Oak Circle* ☎ *707/948–5050, 800/351–1133* ⊕ *www.villagio.com/spavillagio* ✑ *Treatments $75–$575.*

SPORTS AND THE OUTDOORS

BALLOONING
Napa Valley Aloft. The friendly Kimball family, longtime operators in the Napa Valley, take between 8 and 12 passengers for rides in balloons that launch from downtown Yountville's V Marketplace. Preflight refreshments and a huge breakfast are included in the rates. ✉ *V Marketplace, 6525 Washington St., near Mulberry St.* ☎ *707/944–4400, 855/944–4408* ⊕ *www.nvaloft.com* ✑ *$195–$220.*

Napa Valley Balloons. Departing from Domaine Chandon, the valley's oldest balloon company offers trips that are elegant from start to finish. Satisfied customers include Chelsea Clinton and *Today* show host Matt Lauer. ✉ *Domaine Chandon, 1 California Dr., at Solano Ave., west of Hwy. 29* ☎ *707/944–0228, 800/253–2224* ⊕ *www.napavalleyballoons.com* ✑ *$215 per person.*

BICYCLING
Fodor's Choice
★
Napa Valley Bike Tours. Napa Valley Bike Tours will deliver bikes, which rent for $39 to $78 a day, to many hotels in the Napa Valley if you're renting at least two bikes for a full day. In addition to hourly rentals, guided and self-guided winery and other tours are available. ✉ *6795 Washington St., at Madison St.* ☎ *707/944–2953* ⊕ *www.napavalleybiketours.com.*

OAKVILLE

2 miles northwest of Yountville.

There are three reasons to visit the town of Oakville: its gourmet grocery store; its scenic mountain road; and its highly exclusive wineries.

GETTING HERE AND AROUND

Those driving along Highway 29 will know they've reached Oakville when they see the Oakville Grocery on the east side of the road. Here the Oakville Cross Road provides access to the Silverado Trail, which runs parallel to Highway 29. Oakville wineries are scattered along Highway 29, Oakville Cross Road, and the Silverado Trail in roughly equal measure.

You can reach Oakville from the town of Glen Ellen in Sonoma County by heading east on Trinity Road from Highway 12. The twisting route, along the mountain range that divides Napa and Sonoma, eventually becomes the Oakville Grade. The views of both valleys on this drive are breathtaking, though the continual curves make it unsuitable for those who suffer from motion sickness.

EXPLORING

TOP ATTRACTIONS

Fodor'sChoice
★
Far Niente. Though the fee for the combined tour and tasting is at the high end, Far Niente is especially worth visiting if you're tired of elbowing your way through crowded tasting rooms and are looking for a more personal experience. Here you're welcomed by name and treated to a glimpse of one of the most beautiful Napa properties. Small groups are shepherded through the historic 1885 stone winery, including some of the 40,000 square feet of caves, for a lesson on the labor-intensive method for making Far Niente's two wines, a Cabernet blend and a Chardonnay. (The latter is made without undergoing malolactic fermentation, so it doesn't have that buttery taste that's characteristic of many California Chardonnays.) The next stop is the Carriage House, which holds a gleaming collection of classic cars. The tour concludes with a seated tasting of wines and cheeses. ✉ *1350 Acacia Dr., off Oakville Grade Rd.* ☎ *707/944–2861* ⊕ *www. farniente.com* ✎ *Tasting and tour $50* ☉ *By appointment.*

Opus One. The combined venture of the late California winemaker Robert Mondavi and the late French Baron Philippe de Rothschild, Opus One produces only one wine: a big, inky Bordeaux blend that was the first of Napa's ultrapremium wines, fetching unheard-of prices before it was overtaken by cult wines like Screaming Eagle. The winery's futuristic limestone-clad structure, built into the hillside, seems to be pushing itself out of the earth. Although the tours, which focus on why it costs so much to produce this exceptional wine, can come off as "stuffy" (in the words of one Fodors.com reader), the facilities are undoubtedly impressive, with gilded mirrors, exotic orchids, and a large semicircular cellar modeled on the Château Mouton Rothschild winery in France. You can also taste the current vintage without the tour ($40), as long as you've called ahead for a reservation. ■TIP➜ Take your glass up to the rooftop terrace if you want to appreciate the views out over the vineyards. ✉ *7900 St. Helena Hwy., / Hwy. 29* ☎ *707/944–9442, 800/292–6787* ⊕ *www.opusonewinery.*

6

Far Niente's wine cellars have a touch of ballroom elegance.

com ✉ *Tasting $40, tours $60–$85* ⊙ *Daily 10–4; tasting and tour by appointment.*

PlumpJack. If Opus One is the Rolls-Royce of the Oakville District—expensive, refined, and a little snooty—then PlumpJack is the Mini Cooper: fun, casual, and sporty. With its metal chandelier and wall hangings, the tasting room looks like it could be the stage set for a modern Shakespeare production. (The name "PlumpJack" is a nod to Shakespeare's Falstaff.) The reserve Chardonnay has a good balance of baked fruit and fresh citrus flavors, and a Merlot is blended with Cabernet Franc, Petit Verdot, and Cabernet Sauvignon, giving the wine sufficient tannins to ensure it can age another five years or more. ■**TIP→** If the tasting room is crowded, take a breather under the shady arbor on the back patio. ✉ *620 Oakville Cross Rd., off Hwy. 29* ☎ *707/945–1220* ⊕ *www.plumpjack.com* ✉ *Tasting $15* ⊙ *Daily 10–4.*

WORTH NOTING

Oakville Grocery. Built in 1881 as a general store, this popular spot carries unusual and high-end groceries and prepared foods. The place shines after a 2012 renovation, and the notoriously narrow aisles are now wider—helpful on busy summer weekends, when the grocery is often packed with customers stocking up on picnic provisions (meats, cheeses, breads, and hearty sandwiches). This is a fine place to sit on a bench and sip an espresso between winery visits. ✉ *7856 St. Helena Hwy./Hwy. 29, at Oakville Rd.* ☎ *707/944–8802* ⊕ *www.oakvillegrocery.com.*

Robert Mondavi. The arch at the center of the sprawling Mission-style building perfectly frames the lawn and the vineyard behind, inviting a stroll under the lovely arcades. You can head straight for one of the two tasting rooms, but if you've never taken a winery tour before, the comprehensive Signature Tour and Tasting ($25), which concludes with a seated tasting, is a good way to learn about enology, as well as the late Robert Mondavi's role in California wine making. Those new to tasting and mystified by all that swirling and sniffing should consider the 45-minute Wine Tasting Basics experience ($20). Serious wine lovers should opt for the one-hour $55 Exclusive Cellar tasting, where a well-informed server pours and explains limited-production, reserve, and older-vintage wines. Concerts, mostly jazz and R&B, take place in summer on the lawn; call ahead for tickets. ⊠ *7801 St. Helena Hwy./ Hwy. 29* ☎ *888/766–6328* ⊕ *www.robertmondaviwinery.com* ⊠ *Tastings and tours $15–$55* ⊗ *Daily 10–5; tour times vary.*

RUTHERFORD

2 miles northwest of Oakville.

With its singular microclimate and soil, Rutherford is an important viticultural center, with more big-name wineries than you can shake a corkscrew at. Cabernet Sauvignon is king here. The well-drained, loamy soil is ideal for those vines, and since this part of the valley gets plenty of sun, the grapes develop exceptionally intense flavors.

6

GETTING HERE AND AROUND
Wineries around Rutherford are dotted along Highway 29 and the parallel Silverado Trail just north and south of Rutherford Road/Conn Creek Road, which connect these two major thoroughfares.

EXPLORING
TOP ATTRACTIONS
Beaulieu Vineyard. The Cabernet Sauvignon produced at the ivy-covered Beaulieu Vineyard is a benchmark of the Napa Valley. André Tchelistcheff, who helped define the California style of wine making, worked his magic here from 1938 until his death in 1973. This helps explain why Beaulieu's flagship, the Georges de Latour Private Reserve Cabernet Sauvignon, still garners high marks from major wine publications. The wines being poured in the main tasting room, which might include anything from a spry Pinot Gris to a lush Syrah, are always competent and sometimes surprise. Still, it's worth the $35 to $50 fee to taste that special Cabernet in the less-crowded reserve tasting room. The tour, an excellent overview of the wine-making process, includes a barrel tasting. ⊠ *1960 St. Helena Hwy./Hwy. 29* ☎ *707/967–5200, 800/373–5896* ⊕ *www.bvwines.com* ⊠ *Tasting $15–$50, tours $20* ⊗ *Daily 10–5.*

FAMILY
Fodor's Choice
★
Frog's Leap. John Williams, owner of Frog's Leap, maintains a goofy sense of humor about wine that translates into an entertaining yet informative experience—if you're a novice, this is the perfect place to begin your education. You'll also taste some fine Zinfandel, Cabernet Sauvignon, Merlot, Chardonnay, Sauvignon Blanc, Rosé, and Frögenbeerenauslese, a variation on the German dessert wine Trockenbeerenauslese. The winery includes a red barn built in 1884, 5 acres of organic gardens, an eco-friendly visitor center, and, naturally, a frog pond topped with lily pads. The fun tour ($20; call ahead) is highly recommended, but you can also just sample wines while seated on a porch overlooking

Frog's Leap's picturesque country charm extends all the way to the white picket fence.

the garden. ⊠ *8815 Conn Creek Rd.* ☎ *707/963–4704, 800/959–4704* ⊕ *www.frogsleap.com* ▨ *Tasting $20, tour $20* ⊘ *Tasting daily 10–4 by appointment only; tours weekdays at 10:30 and 2:30.*

Inglenook. It's the house *The Godfather* built. Literally. Filmmaker Francis Ford Coppola began his wine-making career in 1975, when he bought part of the historic Inglenook estate. He eventually reunited the original Inglenook land and purchased the ivy-covered 19th-century château to boot. In 2006 he renamed the property Rubicon Estate, intending to focus on his premium wines, including the namesake Cabernet Sauvignon–based blend. Then, in 2011, he renamed the place Inglenook. Various tours cover the estate's history, the local climate and geology, and the sensory evaluation of wine. Two distinctly different tastings are held in an opulent, high-ceilinged tasting room. The Bistro, an on-site eatery, has seating in a picturesque courtyard. ⊠ *1991 St. Helena Hwy./Hwy. 29* ☎ *707/968–1100, 800/782–4266* ⊕ *www.inglenook.com* ▨ *Tastings $25–$50, tours $45–$95* ⊘ *Daily 10–5; call for tour times.*

Mumm Napa. Although this is one of California's best-known sparkling-wine producers, enjoying the bubbly from the light-filled tasting room—available in either single flutes or by the flight—isn't the only reason to visit Mumm. An excellent gallery displays 30 Ansel Adams prints and presents temporary exhibits by local photographers. You can even take that glass of crisp Brut Rosé with you as you wander. For a leisurely tasting of library wines while seated on the Oak Terrace ($40), reserve in advance. ■TIP➔ **A two-for-one tasting coupon for the Salon or Patio is available on the winery's website.** ⊠ *8445*

Silverado Trail ☎ *707/967–7700, 800/686–6272* ⊕ *www.mummnapa. com* ☕ *Tastings $8–$40, tours free–$25* ⊙ *Daily 10–4:45; tours daily at 10, 11, 1, and 3.*

Fodor's Choice
★

Round Pond Estate. Sophisticated wines come from Round Pond, but the estate also produces premium olive oils, most from olives grown and crushed on the property. Informative olive-related seminars begin with a look at some trees and a tour of the high-tech mill, followed by tastings of the aromatic oils, both alone and with house-made red-wine vinegars. You'll also sip wines, but for a full tasting, head across the street to the winery. The basic tasting includes a suave Sauvignon Blanc and Round Pond's supple, well-rounded reds. The flagship Estate Cabernet Sauvignon has the structure and heft of the classic 1970s Rutherford Cabs, but gracefully acknowledges 21st-century palates with smoother, if still sturdy, tannins. The Estate Tasting ($45) pairs small morsels with the wines. ✉ *875 Rutherford Rd., off Conn Creek Rd.* ☎ *707/302–2575, 888/302–2575* ⊕ *www.roundpond.com* ☕ *Wine tasting $20, tour and tasting $55; olive mill tour and tasting $35* ⊙ *All tastings and tours by appointment 24–48 hrs in advance.*

Rutherford Hill Winery. This place is a Merlot lover's paradise in a Cabernet Sauvignon world. When the winery's founders were deciding what grapes to plant, they discovered that the climate and soil conditions resembled those of Pomerol, a region of Bordeaux where Merlot is king. Now owned by the Terlato family, the winery has some of the most extensive wine caves in California—nearly a mile of tunnels and passageways. You can get a glimpse of the tunnels and the 8,000 barrels inside on the tours, then cap your visit with a picnic amid oak or olive groves. ■TIP→ With views over the valley from a perch high on a hill, the picnic grounds are more charming than many others in Napa. ✉ *200 Rutherford Hill Rd., east of Silverado Trail* ☎ *707/963–1871* ⊕ *www.rutherfordhill.com* ☕ *Tastings $15–$30; call for tour prices* ⊙ *Daily 10–5; tours daily at 11:30, 1:30, and 3:30.*

WORTH NOTING

Cakebread Cellars. Jack and Dolores Cakebread snapped up the property at Cakebread Cellars in 1973, after Jack fell in love with the area while visiting on a photography assignment. Since then, they've been making luscious Chardonnays, as well as Merlot, a great Sauvignon Blanc, and a beautifully complex Cabernet Sauvignon. You must make an appointment for a tasting, for which there are several different options. The most basic usually involves a stroll through the winery's barrel room and crush pad and past Dolores's kitchen garden before ending in a taste of six current releases. Other options focus on red wines, reserve wines, or the pairing of wine and food, and might take place in the winery's modern wing, where an elevator is crafted out of a stainless-steel fermentation tank and the ceiling is lined with thousands of corks. ✉ *8300 St. Helena Hwy./Hwy. 29* ☎ *707/963–5222, 800/588–0298* ⊕ *www.cakebread.com* ☕ *Tastings $15–$45, tour $25* ⊙ *Daily 10–4; tasting and tour by appointment.*

6

WHERE TO EAT

$$$$

MODERN
AMERICAN

Fodor's Choice
★

X**Restaurant at Auberge du Soleil.** Possibly the most romantic roost for a dinner in all the Wine Country is a terrace seat at the Auberge du Soleil's illustrious restaurant, and the Mediterranean-inflected cuisine of chef Robert Curry more than matches the dramatic views over the vineyards. The menu, which relies largely on local produce, changes with the seasons but might include veal sweetbreads with chanterelles, apples, horseradish, and watercress, or northern halibut served with string and shell beans, bacon, and a basil broth. Service is as polished as you would expect for a restaurant of this stature, and the wine list is one of the most extensive around. ■TIP➔ **The more casual Auberge Bistro & Bar serves lighter, less expensive fare nightly until 11.** ⑤ *Average main: $98* ⊠ *Auberge du Soleil, 180 Rutherford Hill Rd., off Silverado Trail* ☎ *707/963–1211, 800/348–5406* ⊕ *www.aubergedusoleil. com* ⚑ *Reservations essential.*

WHERE TO STAY

For expanded hotel reviews, visit Fodors.com.

$$$$

RESORT

Fodor's Choice
★

🛏 **Auberge du Soleil.** Taking a cue from the olive-tree-studded landscape, this hotel with a renowned restaurant and spa cultivates a luxurious Mediterranean look—earth-tone tile floors, heavy wood furniture, and terra-cotta colors—and backs it up with such lavish amenities as flat-screen TVs (in both the rooms and bathrooms), private terraces, jetted soaking tubs, and extra-large showers. **Pros:** stunning views over the valley; spectacular pool and spa areas; the most expensive suites are fit for a superstar. **Cons:** stratospheric prices; least expensive rooms get some noise from the bar and restaurant. ⑤ *Rooms from: $650* ⊠ *180 Rutherford Hill Rd., off Silverado Trail north of Hwy. 128* ☎ *707/963–1211, 800/348–5406* ⊕ *www.aubergedusoleil.com* ⚑ *31 rooms, 21 suites* ⦿❘ *Breakfast.*

ST. HELENA

2 miles northwest of Oakville.

Downtown St. Helena is a symbol of how well life can be lived in the Wine Country. Sycamore trees arch over Main Street (Highway 29), a funnel of outstanding restaurants and tempting boutiques. At the north end of town looms the hulking stone building of the Culinary Institute of America. Weathered stone and brick buildings from the late 1800s give off that gratifying whiff of history.

By the time pioneering winemaker Charles Krug planted grapes in St. Helena around 1860, vineyards already existed in the area. Today the town is hemmed in by wineries, and you could easily spend days visiting vintners within a few miles.

GETTING HERE AND AROUND

Downtown St. Helena stretches along Highway 29, which is called Main Street here. Many of the shops and restaurants are clustered on two pedestrian-friendly blocks of Main Street, between Pope Street and Adams Street. Wineries in the area are found both north and south of downtown along both Highway 29 and the Silverado Trail, but some of the less touristed and more scenic spots are on the slopes of Spring Mountain, which rises southwest of town.

EXPLORING

TOP ATTRACTIONS

Beringer Vineyards. Arguably the Napa Valley's most beautiful winery, the 1876 Beringer Vineyards is also the oldest continuously operating property. In 1884 Frederick and Jacob Beringer built the Rhine House Mansion to serve as Frederick's family home. Today it serves as the reserve tasting room, where you can sample wines surrounded by Belgian art-nouveau hand-carved oak and walnut furniture and stained-glass windows. The assortment includes a limited-release Chardonnay, a few big Cabernets, and a luscious white dessert wine named Nightingale. A less expensive tasting takes place in the original stone winery. ■ TIP→ First-time visitors to the valley will learn a lot about the region's wine-making history on the introductory tour. Longer tours, which might pass through a demonstration vineyard or end with a seated tasting in the Rhine House, are also offered. ⊠ *2000 Main St./ Hwy. 29, near Pratt Ave.* ☎ *707/967–4412, 866/708–9463* ⊕ *www. beringer.com* ☗ *Tastings $20–$40, tours $25–$40* ☉ *June–Oct. daily 10–6; Nov.–May daily 10–5; many tours daily, call for times.*

6

Fodor's Choice
★
Culinary Institute of America. The West Coast headquarters of the Culinary Institute of America, the country's leading school for chefs, are in the **Greystone Winery,** an imposing building that was the largest stone winery in the world when it was built in 1889. On the ground floor you can check out the quirky Corkscrew Museum and shop at a well-stocked store that tempts aspiring chefs with gleaming gadgets and an impressive selection of cookbooks. The adjacent Flavor Bar lets you sample certain types of ingredients (for example, chocolate or olive oil). Upstairs, if no special events are taking place, you can browse the Vintners Hall of Fame, where plaques fastened to 2,200-gallon redwood wine barrels commemorate winemakers past and present. Beguiling one-hour cooking demonstrations (reservations required) take place on weekends. ⊠ *2555 Main St./Hwy. 29* ☎ *707/967–1100* ⊕ *www.ciachef. edu* ☗ *Museum and store free, cooking demonstrations $20, tastings $10–$15, tour $10* ☉ *Museum and store daily 10:30–6; tour 11:45, 2:45, 5; restaurant Sun.–Thurs. 11:30–9, Fri. and Sat. 11:30–10.*

Hall. The award-winning Cabs, Merlots, and an impeccable Syrah produced here are works of art—and of up-to-the-minute organic-farming science and high technology. When a glass-wall tasting center opens here in late 2013, you'll see in action some of the technology winemaker Steve Leveque employs to craft wines that also include a Cabernet Franc and late-harvest Sauvignon Blanc dessert wine. The Production Tour and Barrel Tasting provides an even more in-depth look. ■ TIP→ For an understatedly elegant experience, book an Artisan Tasting at Hall's Rutherford winery, where the hilltop vistas enthrall and even the stainless-steel aging tanks are dazzling. Tastings take place deep inside a dramatic brick-lined cave. ⊠ *401 St. Helena Hwy./Hwy. 29, near White La.* ☎ *707/967–2626, 800/688–4255* ⊕ *www.hallwines. com* ☗ *Tastings $25–$50; tours with tastings start at $40* ☉ *St. Helena daily 10–5:30; Rutherford by appointment only.*

Fodor's Choice
★
Joseph Phelps Vineyards. Although an appointment is required for tastings at the winery started by the legendary Joseph Phelps—his son Bill now runs the operation—it's well worth the effort. In fair weather, the casual, self-paced wine tastings are held on the terrace of a modern barnlike building with stunning views down the slopes over oak trees and orderly vines. Phelps makes fine whites, but the blockbuster wines are reds, particularly the Cabernet Sauvignon and the flagship Bordeaux-style blend called Insignia. The luscious-yet-subtle Insignia sells for more than $200 a bottle. Luckily, all tastings include the current vintage. The 90-minute seminars include one on wine-and-cheese pairing and another focusing on blending (both $75). In the latter you mix the various varietals that go into the Insignia blend. ⊠ *200 Taplin Rd., off Silverado Trail* ☎ *707/963–2745, 800/707–5789* ⊕ *www. josephphelps.com* ⊠ *Tastings $35–$75, seminars $75–$150* ⊙ *Weekdays 9–5, weekends 10–4; tastings by appointment.*

WORTH NOTING

St. Clement Vineyards. A boutique winery steeped in history, St. Clement Vineyards is blessed with such splendid views that you might drift into reverie even before tasting the signature Bordeaux-style blend, Oroppas. (That's Sapporo spelled backward, because the famous Japanese brewery owned this place for a time.) The restored Rosenbaum House, built by a wealthy merchant in 1878, has an intimate tasting room. You can also sip wine at café tables on the front porch while taking in views of nearby vineyards and the more distant Howell Mountain. Tours of the property reveal details about its colorful past, as well as the workings of the winery. Only a portion of the fruit for the wines is grown on the estate; instead, the winemakers purchase grapes from various vineyards to produce their Sauvignon Blanc, Chardonnay, Merlot, and Cabernet Sauvignon wines. ⊠ *2867 St. Helena Hwy. N/Hwy. 29* ☎ *707/963–7221, 866/877–5939* ⊕ *www.stclement.com* ⊠ *Tastings $20–$30, tour $20* ⊙ *Wed.–Mon. 11–5, tour daily at 10:30 and 2:30 by appointment.*

WHERE TO EAT

$$
MODERN
AMERICAN
Fodor's Choice
★
✕**Cindy's Backstreet Kitchen.** At her upscale-casual St. Helena outpost, Cindy Pawlcyn serves variations on the comfort food her iconic Mustards Grill made popular, but spices things up with dishes influenced by Mexican, Central American, and occasionally Asian cuisines. Along with mainstays like herb-marinated hanger steak, meat loaf with garlic mashed potatoes, and beef and duck burgers served with flawless fries, the menu might include a rabbit tostada or duck legs and thighs cooked in a wood oven to succulent perfection. Two dessert favorites are the high-style yet homey warm pineapple upside-down cake and the nearly ethereal parfait. ■TIP➔ If you can't snag a table, try Pawlcyn's Wood Grill and Wine Bar; half a mile away, it also serves comfort food and many wines by the glass. ⑤ *Average main: $21* ⊠ *1327 Railroad Ave., at Hunt St., 1 block east of Main St.* ☎ *707/963–1200* ⊕ *www. cindysbackstreetkitchen.com.*

$$$$
MODERN
AMERICAN
✕**Farmstead at Long Meadow Ranch.** Housed in a former barn, Farmstead revolves around an open kitchen where chef Stephen Barber cooks with as many local and organic ingredients as possible. Many of them—including grass-fed beef, fruits and vegetables, eggs, extra-virgin olive

oil, wine, and honey—come from the property of parent company Long Meadow Ranch. Others are sourced from within a 30-mile radius. On Tuesday, three-course meals ($35) include such comfort food as chicken-fried grass-fed steak, slow-cooked ribs, or fried chicken and dessert. In warm weather, you can dine on an open-air patio among apple trees. Instead of charging a corkage fee, Farmstead collects $2 per bottle to donate to a local nonprofit organization. ⑤ *Average main: $35* ✉ *738 Main St., at Charter Oak Ave.* ☎ *707/963–4555, 877/627–2645* ⊕ *www.longmeadowranch.com/Farmstead-Restaurant.*

$$$ ✕ **Goose & Gander.** At the clubby Goose & Gander, the pairing of food
MODERN and drink is as likely to involve cocktails as it is wine. Main courses
AMERICAN like Scottish salmon with wild-dandelion spaetzle work well with such
Fodor's Choice starters as an heirloom chicory salad and a rich yet rustic cream of
★ mushroom soup made from both wild and cultivated varieties. You might enjoy your meal with a top-notch Chardonnay or Pinot Noir—or a Manhattan made with three kinds of bitters and poured over a hand-carved block of ice. On cold days a fireplace warms the main dining room, and in good weather the outdoor patio is a splendid spot for dining alfresco. ■ TIP➜ **Year-round the basement bar is a great place for a drink, whether you're dining here or not.** ⑤ *Average main: $24* ✉ *1245 Spring St., at Oak St.* ☎ *707/967–8779* ⊕ *www.goosegander.com.*

$ ✕ **Gott's Roadside.** A slick 1950s-style outdoor hamburger stand goes
AMERICAN upscale at this hugely popular spot whose customers brave long lines to order breakfast sandwiches, juicy burgers, root-beer floats, and garlic fries. You'll also find plenty of choices not available a half century ago, such as the ahi tuna burger and the chili spice–marinated chicken breast served with Mexican slaw. Try to arrive early or late for lunch, or all the shaded picnic tables on the lawn might be filled. ⑤ *Average main: $12* ✉ *933 Main St./Hwy. 29* ☎ *707/963–3486* ⊕ *www.gotts.com.*

$$$$ ✕ **Press.** Few taste sensations surpass the combination of a sizzling steak
MODERN and a Napa Valley red, a union that the chef and sommeliers here cel-
AMERICAN ebrate with a reverence bordering on obsession. Beef from carefully
Fodor's Choice selected local and international purveyors is the star—especially the rib
★ eye for two—but chef Stephen Rogers also prepares pork chops and free-range chicken and veal on his cherry-and-almond-wood-fired grill and rotisserie. The cellar holds thousands of wines; if you recall having a great steak with a 1985 Mayacamas Mt. Veeder Cab, you'll be able to re-create, and perhaps exceed, the original event. The kitchen's attention to detail is matched by the efforts at the bar, whose tenders know their way around both rad and trad cocktails. ⑤ *Average main: $36* ✉ *587 St. Helena Hwy./Hwy. 29, at White La.* ☎ *707/967–0550* ⊕ *www.pressthelena. com* ⚑ *Reservations essential* ⊘ *Closed Tues. No lunch.*

$$$$ ✕ **The Restaurant at Meadowood.** Chef Christopher Kostow has garnered
MODERN rave reviews for creating a unique dining experience that starts when
AMERICAN you make your reservation. You and your guests will be interviewed
Fodor's Choice about food likes and dislikes, allergies and aversions, and desired level
★ of culinary adventure. Based on notes from these conversations, Kostow crafts a specific menu for your table, transforming seasonal local ingredients, some grown on or near the property, into elaborate, elegant Modern American fare. There are two options, a Chef's Tasting Menu

($225, $450 with wine pairings), composed of eight or nine courses, and a Chef's Counter Menu ($500, $850 with wine pairings). For the latter, you and up to three guests sit inside the kitchen and watch Kostow's team prepare your meal. The warm lighting and beautiful finishes in the dining room, renovated in 2012, make this a top choice for a romantic tête-à-tête. [$] *Average main: $225* ✉ *900 Meadowood La., off Silverado Trail N* ☎ *707/967–1205, 800/458–8080* ⊕ *www. meadowood.com* ⊗ *Closed Sun. No lunch.*

$$$$ ✕ **Terra.** For old-school romance and service, many diners return year
MEDITERRANEAN after year to this quiet favorite in an 1884 fieldstone building. Since
Fodor's Choice 1988, chef Hiro Sone has been giving an unexpected twist to Italian
★ and southern French cuisine in such dishes as mussel soup with caramelized onions and garlic croutons, heavily perfumed with saffron. A few standouts, like the signature sake-marinated black cod in a shiso broth, draw on Sone's Japanese background. Homey yet elegant desserts, courtesy of Sone's wife, Lissa Doumani, might include a chocolate caramel tart topped with *fleur de sel* (a kind of sea salt). Next door, the livelier Bar Terra serves inventive cocktails, local wines, and a menu of smaller, lighter dishes, among them succulent fried rock shrimp with a chive-and-mustard sauce. [$] *Average main: $36* ✉ *1345 Railroad Ave., off Hunt Ave.* ☎ *707/963–8931* ⊕ *www.terrarestaurant.com* ⊗ *Closed Tues. No lunch.*

$$$ ✕ **Wine Spectator Greystone Restaurant.** The Culinary Institute of Amer-
MEDITERRANEAN ica runs this place in the Greystone Winery, which once served as the Christian Brothers Winery. Century-old stone walls encase a spacious restaurant that bustles at both lunch and dinner, with several cooking stations in full view. On busy nights you may find the hard-at-work chefs more entertaining than your dining companions. The tables on the terrace, shaded by red umbrellas, are away from the action, but on fair days they're even more appealing, providing a panoramic view down the hillside. The menu has a Mediterranean spirit and emphasizes locally grown produce. Typical main courses include seared breast of Sonoma duck with a celery-root purée and house-made pasta with trumpet mushrooms and a sherry cream sauce. [$] *Average main: $26* ✉ *2555 Main St./Hwy. 29* ☎ *707/967–1010* ⊕ *www.ciachef.edu.*

WHERE TO STAY

For expanded hotel reviews, visit Fodors.com.

$ 🏨 **El Bonita Motel.** Only in St. Helena would basic accommodations in
HOTEL a roadside motel cost around $150 a night in high season, but for budget-minded travelers the tidy rooms here are pleasant enough, and the landscaped grounds and picnic tables elevate this property over similar places. **Pros:** cheerful rooms; hot tub; microwaves and minirefrigerators. **Cons:** road noise is a problem in some rooms. [$] *Rooms from: $149* ✉ *195 Main St./Hwy. 29* ☎ *707/963–3216, 800/541–3284* ⊕ *www.elbonita.com* ⤳ *38 rooms, 4 suites* ⦿ *Breakfast.*

$$$ 🏨 **Harvest Inn.** Although this inn sits just off Highway 29, its patrons
HOTEL remain mostly above the fray, strolling 8 acres of landscaped gardens with views of adjoining vineyards, partaking in spa services, and drifting off to sleep in beds adorned with fancy linens and down pillows. **Pros:** garden setting; very spacious rooms; professional staff; plush

furnishings. **Cons:** some lower-priced rooms lack elegance; high week-end rates; complimentary breakfast is serviceable, not memorable. ⑤ *Rooms from: $319* ⊠ *1 Main St.* ☎ *707/963–9463, 800/950–8466* ⊕ *www.harvestinn.com* ↩ *54 rooms, 20 suites* ⦿⦁ *Breakfast.*

$$$$
RESORT
Fodor's Choice
★

⌗ **Meadowood Napa Valley.** A rambling lodge and several gray clapboard bungalows are scattered across this sprawling property, giving it an exclusive New England feel. **Pros:** site of one of Napa's best restaurants; lovely hiking trails on the property; the most gracious service in Napa. **Cons:** very expensive; far from downtown St. Helena. ⑤ *Rooms from: $525* ⊠ *900 Meadowood La.* ☎ *707/963–3646, 800/458–8080* ⊕ *www. meadowood.com* ↩ *85 rooms, suites, and cottages.*

SHOPPING

St. Helena's coolest stores are clustered in the 1200 and 1300 blocks of bucolic Main Street, where 19th-century redbrick buildings recall the town's past and make it a particularly pleasant place to while away an afternoon window-shopping.

CALISTOGA

6

3 miles northwest of St. Helena.

With false-fronted, Old West–style shops, 19th-century hotels, and unpretentious cafés lining Lincoln Avenue, the town's main drag, Calistoga has a slightly rough-and-tumble feel that's unique in the Napa Valley. It comes across as more down-to-earth than some of the polished towns to the south. And it's easier to find a bargain here, making it a handy home base for exploring the surrounding vineyards and back roads.

Ironically, Calistoga was developed as a swell, tourist-oriented getaway. In 1859 maverick entrepreneur Sam Brannan snapped up 2,000 acres of prime property and laid out a resort, intending to use the area's natural hot springs as the main attraction. Brannan's gamble didn't pay off as he'd hoped, but the hotels and bathhouses won a local following. Many of them are still going, and you can come for an old-school experience of a mud bath or a dip in a warm spring-fed pool.

GETTING HERE AND AROUND

To get to downtown Calistoga from anywhere farther south in the valley, take Highway 29 north and then turn right on Lincoln Avenue. Most of the town's sights are found along a five-block stretch of Lincoln Avenue, or just off one of the side streets that intersect it. After about a mile, Lincoln Avenue (whose name changes to Lake County Highway) intersects with the Silverado Trail.

EXPLORING
TOP ATTRACTIONS

Castello di Amorosa. Possibly the most astounding sight in Napa Valley is the Castello di Amorosa, built to resemble a medieval castle, complete with drawbridge and moat, chapel, stables, and secret passageways. Some of the 107 rooms contain replicas of 13th-century frescoes and the dungeon has an actual iron maiden from Nuremberg, Germany. You must pay for the tour ($33 or $49, depending on the wine you taste) to see the most of Dario Sattui's extensive eight-level property,

Floor-to-ceiling stacked bottles are no exaggeration in Schramsberg's cellars.

though basic tastings ($18 or $28) include access to a small portion of the complex. All include a sample of several Italian-style wines, including a "super Tuscan," a blend of Sangiovese and Merlot with Cabernet Sauvignon that has more heft than your average Italian red. ✉ *4045 N. St. Helena Hwy./Hwy. 29* ☎ *707/967–6272* ⊕ *www.castellodiamorosa. com* ✉ *Tastings $18–$28, tours $33–$49* ☉ *Mar.–Oct., daily 9:30–6; Nov.–Feb., daily 9:30–5; tour by appointment.*

Chateau Montelena. Set amid a bucolic northern Calistoga landscape, this winery helped establish the Napa Valley's reputation for high-quality wine making. At the legendary Paris tasting of 1976, the Chateau Montelena Chardonnay took first place, beating out four white Burgundies from France and five other California Chards. The 2008 movie *Bottle Shock* immortalized the event, and the winery honors its four decades of classic wine making with a special Beyond Paris & Hollywood tasting of the winery's Chardonnays ($40). You can also opt for a standard tasting ($20) of current releases and a library tasting ($40) that includes some stellar Cabernet Sauvignons and a limited-release Riesling. ✉ *1429 Tubbs La., off Hwy. 29* ☎ *707/942–5105* ⊕ *www.montelena. com* ✉ *Tastings $20–$40, tours $30–$50* ☉ *Daily 9:30–4, tours vary.*

Fodor's Choice ★ **Schramsberg.** Founded in 1865, the venerable Schramsberg produces bubblies made using the traditional *méthode champenoise* (which means, among other things, that the wine undergoes a second fermentation in the bottle before being "riddled," or turned every few days, to nudge the sediment into the neck of the bottle). To taste, you first must tour, but what a tour: in addition to glimpsing the winery's historic architecture, you see the underground cellars dug in the late 19th century by Chinese laborers. A mind-boggling 2.7 million bottles are stacked in gravity-defying configurations. The tour ($45) includes generous pours of several very different sparkling wines, as well as tiny snacks to enhance the experience. To learn more about sparkling wines, consider the three-day **Camp Schramsberg.** In the fall sessions, you harvest grapes and explore riddling, food-and-wine pairing, and other topics. Spring camps focus on blending sparkling wines. ✉ *1400 Schramsberg Rd., off Hwy. 29* ☎ *707/942–4558, 800/877–3623* ⊕ *www. schramsberg.com* ✆ *Tasting and tour $45* ☉ *Tours at 10, 11:30, 12:30, 1:30, and 2:30 by appointment.*

WORTH NOTING

Clos Pegase. Designed by postmodern architect Michael Graves, the Clos Pegase winery is a one-of-a-kind "temple to wine and art" packed with unusual works from the art collection of owner and publishing entrepreneur Jan Shrem. After tasting the bright Sauvignon Blanc, fruity Chardonnays, and mellow Pinot Noirs, Merlots, and Cabernets—they're made in a soft, approachable style and meant to be drunk somewhat young—be sure to check out the surrealist paintings near the main tasting room, which include one by Jean Dubuffet that you may have seen on a Clos Pegase label. Better yet, bring a picnic and have lunch in the courtyard, where a curvaceous Henry Moore sculpture depicting Gaia (or Mother Earth) is one of about two dozen works of art. ✉ *1060 Dunaweal La., off Hwy. 29* ☎ *707/942–4981* ⊕ *www.clospegase.com* ✆ *Tastings $20–$35, tour $20* ☉ *Daily 10:30–5; tour daily at 11:30 and 2.*

Dutch Henry Winery. The tasting room at this winery is barely more than a nook in the barrel room between towering American and French oak barrels full of excellent Cabernet Sauvignon, Merlot, Pinot Noir, and Zinfandel wines. The Sauvignon Blanc and charming Rosé also have their adherents. Most of Dutch Henry's output is sold on-site or through its wine club, which explains the simple facilities, but the wines are truly top-notch. Tasting-room staffers can occasionally be crotchety, but the lack of crowds and casual style at the pet-friendly winery make it a welcome change of pace from some of its overly serious neighbors. If you're lucky, you'll get a tour of the wine caves, which are less than a decade old but don't seem so. ✉ *4310 Silverado Trail, near Dutch Henry Canyon Rd.* ☎ *707/942–5771, 888/224–5879* ⊕ *www.dutchhenry.com* ✆ *Tasting $20* ☉ *Daily 10–5.*

Robert Louis Stevenson State Park. Encompassing the summit of Mt. St. Helena, this mostly undeveloped park is where Stevenson and his bride, Fanny Osbourne, spent their honeymoon in an abandoned bunkhouse of the Silverado Mine. This stay in 1880 inspired the writer's travel memoir *The Silverado Squatters,* and Spyglass Hill in *Treasure Island* is thought to be a portrait of Mt. St. Helena. A marble memorial marks the site of the bunkhouse. The 10-mile trail is steep and lacks shade in spots, but the summit is often cool and breezy. ■ **TIP➔** Bring plenty of water and dress in layers. ✉ *Hwy. 29, 7 miles north of Calistoga* ☎ *707/942–4575* ⊕ *www.parks.ca.gov/?page_ id=472* ✆ *Free* ☉ *Daily sunrise–sunset.*

WHERE TO EAT

$$
AMERICAN
✕ **All Seasons Bistro.** At this cheerful, sun-filled space, tables topped with flowers stand on an old-fashioned black-and-white checkerboard floor. The California-style bistro's seasonal menu might include risotto with seared scallops and shiitake mushrooms, fettuccine puttanesca, or flavorful lasagna. Among the homey desserts are a perfectly executed vanilla-bean crème brûlée and a warm dark-chocolate torte. You can order reasonably priced wines from the extensive list, or buy a bottle at the attached shop and have it poured at your table. Attentive service contributes to the welcoming atmosphere. $ *Average main: $20* ✉ *1400 Lincoln Ave., at Washington St.* ☎ *707/942–9111* ⊕ *www. allseasonsnapavalley.net* ☾ *Closed Mon.*

$$$$
MODERN
AMERICAN
✕ **JoLe.** Local produce plays a starring role at this modern American restaurant inside the Mount View Hotel, not surprising as chef Matt Spector is one of the area's biggest proponents of farm-to-table dining. Depending on when you visit, you might enjoy Mendocino-caught squid with crab stuffing; Forni, Brown & Welsh mixed greens with fresh Asian pears; and chicken-fried quail with fig jam. The menu is available à la carte, and there are four-, five- and six-course prix-fixe options. No visit is complete without a slice of coconut cream pie. Pastry chef Sonjia Spector also makes scrumptious cupcakes for patrons to buy and take home. $ *Average main: $20* ✉ *1457 Lincoln Ave., near Fair Way* ☎ *707/942–9538* ⊕ *jolerestaurant.com* ☾ *No Lunch.*

$$$
MODERN
AMERICAN
Fodor's Choice
★
✕ **Solbar.** Chef Brandon Sharp is known around the region for his subtle and sophisticated take on Wine Country cooking. As befits a restaurant at a spa resort, the menu here is divided into "healthy, lighter" dishes and "hearty" fare. On the lighter side, grilled yellow-fin tuna comes with baby artichokes and a prosciutto-mustard vinaigrette, with toasted farro replacing rice or potatoes as the starch. On the heartier side you might find confit of Niman Ranch pork shoulder served with bacon-roasted brussels sprouts, or the popular flatiron steak with Yukon-gold potato gnocchi and king trumpet mushrooms. The service at Solbar is uniformly excellent, and in summer the patio is a festive spot for breakfast, lunch, or dinner. The Sunday brunch is lighter than most in the valley. $ *Average main: $29* ✉ *Solage Calistoga, 755 Silverado Trail, at Rosedale Rd.* ☎ *707/226–0850* ⊕ *www. solagecalistoga.com/solbar.*

WHERE TO STAY

For expanded hotel reviews, visit Fodors.com.

$
HOTEL
Fodor's Choice
★
▥ **Best Western Plus Stevenson Manor.** Budget travelers get what they pay for—and a little bit more—at this clean, well-run motel a few blocks from Calistoga's downtown. **Pros:** great price for region; friendly staff; nice pool area; complimentary full breakfast. **Cons:** decidedly lacking in glamour. $ *Rooms from: $159* ✉ *1830 Lincoln Ave.* ☎ *707/942–1112, 800/780–7234* ⊕ *www.bestwestern.com* ⇌ *34 rooms* ⏷ *Breakfast.*

$$$$
RESORT
Fodor's Choice
★
▥ **Calistoga Ranch.** Spacious cedar-shingle lodges throughout this posh, wooded property have outdoor living areas, and even the restaurant, spa, and reception space have outdoor seating and fireplaces. **Pros:** almost half the lodges have private hot tubs on the deck; lovely hiking trails on the property; guests have reciprocal privileges at Auberge du

All it needs is a fair maiden: Castello di Amorosa's re-created castle.

Soleil and Solage Calistoga. **Cons:** innovative indoor-outdoor organization works better in fair weather than in rain or cold. ⑤ *Rooms from: $750* ✉ *580 Lommel Rd.* ☎ *707/254–2800, 800/942–4220* ⊕ *www.calistogaranch.com* ⇨ *48 rooms* ⑪ *No meals.*

$$ 🏨 **Cottage Grove Inn.** A long driveway lined with freestanding cottages,
B&B/INN each shaded by elm trees and with rocking chairs on the porch, looks a bit like Main Street, USA, but inside the skylighted buildings are all the perks necessary for a romantic weekend getaway. **Pros:** loaner bicycles available; plenty of privacy; huge bathtubs. **Cons:** no pool; decor may seem too old-school for some. ⑤ *Rooms from: $300* ✉ *1711 Lincoln Ave.* ☎ *707/942–8400, 800/799–2284* ⊕ *www.cottagegrove.com* ⇨ *16 cottages* ⑪ *Breakfast.*

$$ 🏨 **Indian Springs Resort and Spa.** Stylish Indian Springs—operating as a
RESORT spa since 1862—ably splits the difference between laid-back style and ultrachic touches. **Pros:** lovely grounds with outdoor seating areas; stylish for the price; enormous mineral pool; free touring bikes. **Cons:** lodge rooms are small; service could be more polished. ⑤ *Rooms from: $262* ✉ *1712 Lincoln Ave.* ☎ *707/942–4913* ⊕ *www.indianspringscalistoga.com* ⇨ *24 rooms, 17 suites* ⑪ *No meals.*

$ 🏨 **Meadowlark Country House.** Two charming European gents run this
B&B/INN laid-back but sophisticated inn on 20 wooded acres just north of down-
Fodor's Choice town. **Pros:** charming innkeepers; tasty sit-down breakfasts; welcoming
★ vibe that attracts diverse guests. **Cons:** clothing-optional pool policy isn't for everyone. ⑤ *Rooms from: $210* ✉ *601 Petrified Forest Rd.* ☎ *707/942–5651, 800/942–5651* ⊕ *www.meadowlarkinn.com* ⇨ *5 rooms, 3 suites, 1 cottage, 1 guesthouse* ⑪ *Breakfast.*

$$$$ ⌜▦⌝ **Solage Calistoga.** The aesthetic at this 22-acre property is Napa Val-
RESORT ley barn meets San Francisco loft, so the rooms have high ceilings, polished concrete floors, recycled walnut furniture, and all-natural fabrics
in soothingly muted colors. **Pros:** great service; complimentary bikes;
separate pools for kids and adults. **Cons:** the vibe may not suit everyone.
⑤ *Rooms from: $425* ⊠ *755 Silverado Trail* ☎ *866/942–7442, 707/226-*
0800 ⊕ *www.solagecalistoga.com* ⇝ *83 rooms, 6 suites* ⍟ *No meals.*

SPAS

Fodor's Choice **Spa Solage.** This eco-conscious spa has reinvented the traditional Cal-
★ istoga mud and mineral water therapies. Case in point: the hour-long
"Mudslide," is a three-part treatment that includes a mud body mask
(in a heated lounge), a soak in a thermal bath, and a power nap in
a comfy sound/vibration chair. The mud here is a mix of clay, volcanic ash, and essential oils. Traditional spa services—combination
Shiatsu-Swedish and other massages, full-body exfoliations, facials,
and waxes—are available, as are fitness and yoga classes. ⊠ *755 Sil-*
verado Trail, at Rosedale Rd. ☎ *866/942–7442, 707/226–0825* ⊕ *www.*
solagecalistoga.com/spa ▭ *Treatments $25–$335* ⊙ *Daily 8–8.*

SPORTS AND THE OUTDOORS

Calistoga Bikeshop. You can rent regular and fancy bikes here, or you
can opt for the self-guided Calistoga Cool Wine Tour ($80), which
includes tastings at small wineries. If you've bought more wine than
will fit into your bike's handy bottle carrier, the shop will pick it up
for you. ⊠ *1318 Lincoln Ave., near Washington St.* ☎ *707/942–9687*
⊕ *www.calistogabikeshop.net.*

THE SONOMA VALLEY

Although the Sonoma Valley may not have the cachet of the neighboring
Napa Valley, wineries here entice with an unpretentious attitude and
smaller crowds. The Napa-style glitzy tasting rooms with enormous
gift shops and $25 tasting fees aren't as common. Sonoma's landscape
seduces, too, its roads gently climbing and descending on their way to
wineries hidden from the road by trees.

The scenic valley, bounded by the Mayacamas Mountains on the east
and Sonoma Mountain on the west, extends north from San Pablo Bay
nearly 20 miles to the eastern outskirts of Santa Rosa. The varied terrain, soils, and climate (cooler in the south because of the bay influence
and hotter toward the north) allow grape growers to raise cool-weather
varietals such as Chardonnay and Pinot Noir as well as Merlot, Cabernet Sauvignon, and other heat-seeking vines. The valley is home to
dozens of wineries, many of them on or near Highway 12, which runs
the length of the valley.

ESSENTIALS

Contacts Sonoma County Tourism Bureau ⊠ *3637 Westwind Blvd.,*
Santa Rosa ☎ *707/522–5800, 800/576–6662* ⊕ *www.sonomacounty.com.*
Sonoma Valley Visitors Bureau ⊠ *453 1st St., E, Sonoma* ☎ *866/996–1090*
⊕ *www.sonomavalley.com.*

SONOMA

14 miles west of Napa, 45 miles northeast of San Francisco.

Founded in the early 1800s, Sonoma is the oldest town in the Wine Country. The central Sonoma Plaza dates from the Mission era; surrounding it are 19th-century adobes, atmospheric hotels, and the swooping marquee of the 1930s Sebastiani Theatre. On summer days the plaza is a hive of activity, with children blowing off steam in the playground while their folks stock up on picnic supplies and browse the boutiques surrounding the square.

On your way into town from the south, you pass through the Carneros wine district, which straddles the southern sections of Sonoma and Napa counties.

GETTING HERE AND AROUND

To get to the town of Sonoma from San Francisco, cross the Golden Gate Bridge, then go north on U.S. 101, east on Highway 37 toward Vallejo, and north on Highway 121, aka the Carneros Highway. When you reach Highway 12, turn left and take it north. It turns into Broadway, which dead-ends at Sonoma's Central Plaza. If you park around here, a pleasant stroll around the plaza will take you by many of the town's restaurants and shops. Interesting wineries can be found a mile or so east of the plaza; signs on East Spain Street or East Napa Street will direct you to most of them.

EXPLORING

TOP ATTRACTIONS

Fodor's Choice ★ **Bartholomew Park Winery.** Although this certified-organic winery was founded in 1994, grapes were grown in some of its vineyards as early as the 1830s. The emphasis here is on handcrafted, single-varietal wines—Cabernet, Merlot, Zinfandel, Syrah, Chardonnay, and Sauvignon Blanc. The wines alone make this a worthwhile stop, but another reason to visit is the small museum, with vivid exhibits about the history of the winery and the Sonoma region. Yet another plus is the beautiful, slightly off-the-beaten-path location in a 375-acre private park about 2 miles from downtown Sonoma (head east on East Napa Street and follow the signs). Pack a lunch to enjoy on the woodsy grounds, one of the prettier picnic spots in Sonoma, or hike 3 miles on the property's marked trails. ⊠ *1000 Vineyard La., off Castle Rd.* ☏ *707/935–9511* ⊕ *www.bartpark.com* ⌧ *Tasting $10, tour $20* ☉ *June–Oct., daily 11–5:30; Nov.–May, daily 11–4:30; tour Fri. and Sat. at 11:30 and 2, Sun. at 2, by reservation.*

Fodor's Choice ★ **Gundlach Bundschu.** Wine Country visitors may mispronounce this winery's name (it's gund-lak bund-shoe), but still they flock here to sample ultrapremium wines served by some of the friendliest pourers in Sonoma County. Most of the winery's land has been in the Bundschu family since the 1850s. The Cabernet Sauvignon, Cabernet Franc, Merlot, Tempranillo, and Chardonnay wines are worth trying, and all are included in the standard $10 tasting. For a more comprehensive experience that also includes a tasting, consider the cave tour ($20) or the vineyard excursion ($40; available only between May

Sonoma Valley

and October). ■TIP➔ In summer you can taste at outdoor tables with splendid vineyard views. ✉ *2000 Denmark St., at Bundschu Rd., off 8th St. E* ☏ *707/938–5277* ⊕ *www.gunbun.com* 🍷 *Tastings $10–$15, tours $20–$40* ⊗ *June–mid.-Oct., daily 11–5:30; mid.-Oct.–May, daily 11–4:30.*

Fodor's Choice
★
Ram's Gate Winery. Stunning views, ultrachic architecture, and wines made from grapes grown by acclaimed producers make a visit to Ram's Gate an event. The welcoming interior spaces—think Restoration Hardware with an extra dash of high-style whimsy—give you a sense of the entire western Carneros, and on many days you'll experience (in comfort) the cooling breezes that sweep through the area. The attention to detail at this newcomer extends to the wines, mostly Pinot Noirs and Chardonnays, but also Sauvignon Blanc, Cabernet Sauvignon, Syrah, late-harvest Zinfandel, and even a sparkler. With grapes from the high-profile Sangiacomo and Lee Hudson vineyards and other noteworthy growing spots, the focus of winemaker Jeff Gaffner is on creating balanced vintages that express what occurred in nature that year. Jesse Fox, the affable assistant winemaker, conducts one-on-one tours on Thursday morning. ✉ *28700 Arnold Dr./Hwy. 121* ☏ *707/721–8700* ⊕ *www.ramsgatewinery.com* 🍷 *Tasting $15–$125; winemaker tour $85* ⊗ *Thurs.–Mon. 10–6; tour Thurs. at 10 by appointment.*

Sonoma Mission. The northernmost of the 21 missions established by Franciscan friars in California, Sonoma Mission was founded in 1823 as Mission San Francisco Solano. It serves as the centerpiece of **Sonoma State Historic Park,** which includes several other sites in Sonoma and nearby Petaluma. Some early structures were destroyed, but all or part of several remaining buildings date to the days of Mexican rule over California. These include the **Sonoma Barracks,** a block west of the mission at 20 East Spain Street, which housed troops under the command of General Mariano Guadalupe Vallejo, who controlled vast tracks of land in the region. The modest museum contains displays about the missions and information about the other historic sites. ✉ *114 E. Spain St., at 1st St. E* ☏ *707/938–9560* ⊕ *www.parks.ca.gov/?page_id=479* 🍷 *$3, includes same-day admission to other historic sites* ⊗ *Daily 10–5 (weekday hrs sometimes vary).*

Fodor's Choice
★
Walt Wines. You could spend a very full day sampling wines in the tasting rooms bordering Sonoma Plaza, but the one place not to miss is Walt Wines, which specializes in Pinot Noir. Fruit-forward yet subtle, these wines win over even the purists who pine for the genre's days of lighter, more perfumed vintages. Walt is a good place to compare the Pinots one winemaker crafts from local grapes with others from grapes grown in Mendocino County (just north of Sonoma County), California's Central Coast, and even Oregon's Willamette Valley. Critics routinely bestow high ratings on all these wines. ✉ *380 1st St. W, at W. Spain St.* ☏ *707/933–4440* ⊕ *www.waltwines.com* 🍷 *Tasting $10.*

WORTH NOTING
Buena Vista Winery. The ebullient Jean-Charles Boisset, whose family owns wineries in France and elsewhere, purchased Buena Vista in 2011 and quickly set about transforming the site where modern California wine

making got its start into an entertaining homage to the accomplishments of 19th-century wine pioneer Count Agoston Haraszthy. Tours, sometimes conducted by the count himself—as channeled by actor George Webber and others—pass through the original aging caves dug deep into the hillside by Chinese laborers. Tastings take place in the former press house (used for pressing grapes into wine), which was built in 1862 and stylishly renovated in 2012. The best wines here are the Chardonnays and Pinot Noirs from Los Carneros AVA. ■TIP→ **On the mezzanine above the tasting room you can view reproductions of period photographs and prints of the winery.** ⊠ *18000 Old Winery Rd., off Napa Rd.* ☎ *800/926–1266* ⊕ *www.buenavistawinery.com* 🍷 *Tasting $10; tours $10–$30* ☉ *Daily 10–5; tours by appointment 1–2 days in advance.*

WHERE TO EAT

$$
AMERICAN
Fodor's Choice
★
✕ **Cafe La Haye.** In a postage-stamp-size open kitchen, the skillful chef turns out main courses that star on a small but worthwhile seasonal menu emphasizing local ingredients. Chicken, beef, pasta, and fish get deluxe treatment without fuss or fanfare. The daily roasted chicken and the risotto specials are always good. Butterscotch pudding is a homey signature dessert. The dining room is compact, but the friendly owner, always there to greet diners, maintains a particularly welcoming vibe. ⑤ *Average main: $22* ⊠ *140 E. Napa St., at 1st. St. E* ☎ *707/935–5994* ⊕ *www.cafelahaye.com* ☉ *Closed Sun. and Mon. No lunch.*

$$$
MODERN
AMERICAN
Fodor's Choice
★
✕ **El Dorado Kitchen.** The visual delights at this winning restaurant include its clean lines and handsome decor, but the eye inevitably drifts westward to the open kitchen, where chef Armando Navarro and his diligent crew craft flavorful dishes full of subtle surprises. Pumpkin seeds and spiced marshmallows top the popular butternut squash soup, for instance, adding a crunchy-sweet piquancy that plays well off the dish's predominantly savory sentiments. Focusing on locally sourced ingredients, the menu might include Petaluma duck breast enlivened by the tangy flavors of parsnip purée, braised endive, roasted turnips, persimmons, and huckleberries. Even a simple dish like truffle-oil fries, liberally sprinkled with Parmesan cheese, charms with its combination of tastes and textures. The noteworthy desserts include an apple tart tatin, banana crisp with lime curd, and molten chocolate cake. ⑤ *Average main: $26* ⊠ *El Dorado Hotel, 405 1st St. W, at W. Spain St.* ☎ *707/996–3030* ⊕ *www.eldoradosonoma.com/restaurant.*

$$$
FRENCH
✕ **The Girl & the Fig.** Chef Sondra Bernstein has transformed the historic bar room of the Sonoma Hotel into a hot spot for inventive French cooking. You can always find a dish with the signature figs on the menu, whether it's a fig-and-arugula salad or an aperitif blending sparkling wine with fig liqueur. Also look for duck confit with sweet potato Lyonnaise, a burger with matchstick fries, or wild flounder meunière. The wine list is notable for its emphasis on Rhône varietals, and a counter in the bar area sells artisanal cheese platters for eating here as well as cheese by the pound to go. The indulgent Sunday brunch includes ribsticking chorizo and eggs, and potato pancakes with smoked salmon, dill crème fraiche, and caviar. On weekend nights the kitchen serves until 11. ⑤ *Average main: $24* ⊠ *Sonoma Hotel, 110 W. Spain St., at 1st St. W* ☎ *707/938–3634* ⊕ *www.thegirlandthefig.com.*

6

$$
AMERICAN
Fodor'sChoice
★

✕ **Harvest Moon Cafe.** It's easy to feel like one of the family at this little restaurant with an odd, zigzagging layout. Diners seated at one of the two tiny bars chat with the servers like old friends, but the husband-and-wife team in the kitchen is serious about the food, much of which relies on local produce. The ever-changing menu might include homey dishes like grilled pork loin with crispy polenta and artichokes, Niman Ranch rib-eye steak with a red-wine sauce, or shepherd's pie with rabbit ragout. Everything is so perfectly executed and the vibe is so genuinely warm that a visit here is deeply satisfying. A spacious back patio with tables arranged around a fountain more than doubles the seating; a heated tent keeps this area warm in winter. $ *Average main: $22* ⊠ *487 1st St. W, at W. Napa St.* ☎ *707/933–8160* ⊕ *www. harvestmooncafesonoma.com* ☉ *Closed Tues. No lunch Mon.–Sat.*

$$$
MODERN
AMERICAN
Fodor'sChoice
★

✕ **Hot Box Grill.** Comfort foods aren't often described as *nuanced,* but the term aptly describes the locally sourced preparations chef Norm Owens conjures up at his modest roadside restaurant. Take the fries (but not too many): long and not at all lean, they're cooked in duck fat and served with malt-vinegar aioli, lending them a richness that lingers pleasingly in your memory. There's lots of frying going on here—of chicken, of course, but even the Cornish game hen gets the treatment. The corn-bread pudding on the side is creamy good. Up against these dishes, the daily-changing pasta offerings almost seem light, and the appetizers—think spicy ahi tuna with a ponzu sauce and persimmon "carpaccio"—downright dainty. $ *Average main: $24* ⊠ *18350 Sonoma Hwy./Hwy. 12* ☎ *707/939–8383* ⊕ *www.hotboxgrill. com* ☉ *Closed Mon. and Tues. No lunch.*

$$$
PORTUGUESE

✕ **LaSalette.** Born in the Azores and raised in Sonoma, chef-owner Manuel Azevedo serves dishes inspired by his native Portugal in this warmly decorated spot. The best seats are on a patio along an alleyway off Sonoma Plaza. Such boldly flavored dishes as pork tenderloin *recheado,* stuffed with olives and almonds and topped with a port sauce, might be followed by a dish of rice pudding with Madeira-braised figs or a port from the varied list. The daily seafood specials are also well worth a try. $ *Average main: $24* ⊠ *452 E. 1st St., between E. Spain and E. Napa Sts.* ☎ *707/938–1927* ⊕ *www.lasalette-restaurant.com.*

$$$$
AMERICAN
Fodor'sChoice
★

✕ **Santé.** This elegant dining room has gained a reputation as a destination restaurant through its focus on seasonal and locally sourced ingredients. The room is understated, with drapes in rich earth tones and softly lighted chandeliers, but the food is anything but. Dishes such as truffled organic *poussin* (spring chicken)—poached breast, braised leg, stuffed thigh—served with brussels sprouts, butternut squash, and black-truffle bread, are complex without being fussy. Others, like the butter-poached Maine lobster pot-au-feu, served with Parisian gnocchi, black trumpet mushrooms, delicata squash, pickled pearl onions, and lobster bouillabaisse, are pure decadence. The restaurant offers a seasonal tasting menu ($125). $ *Average main: $75* ⊠ *Fairmont Sonoma Mission Inn & Spa, 100 Boyes Blvd./Hwy. 12, 2.5 miles north of Sonoma Plaza, Boyes Hot Springs* ☎ *707/938–9000* ⊕ *www.fairmont. com/sonoma* ☉ *No lunch.*

$
AMERICAN
✕ **Sunflower Caffé.** This casual eatery's menu, composed mostly of salads and sandwiches, is simple but satisfying. Highlights include the smoked duck breast sandwich, served on a baguette and slathered with caramelized onions. A meal of soup and local cheeses is a good option if you just want to nibble. Both the pretty patio, which is in the back, and the sidewalk seating area facing Sonoma Plaza are equipped with heating lamps and get plenty of shade, so they're comfortable in all but the most inclement weather. On dreary days, cheerful artworks brighten up the interior, where locals hunker over their computers and take advantage of the free Wi-Fi. Omelets and waffles are the stars at breakfast. ⑤ *Average main: $13* ✉ *421 1st St. W, at W. Spain St.* ☎ *707/996–6645* ⊕ *www.sonomasunflower.com* ✆ *No dinner.*

WHERE TO STAY

For expanded hotel reviews, visit Fodors.com.

$
B&B/INN
▦ **El Dorado Hotel.** Rooms in this remodeled 1843 building strike a spare, modern pose with their pristine white bedding, but the Mexican-tile floors hint at Sonoma's Mission-era past. **Pros:** stylish for the price; hip on-site restaurant; good café for breakfast; central location. **Cons:** rooms are small; lighting could be better; noisy. ⑤ *Rooms from: $200* ✉ *405 1st St. W* ☎ *707/996–3220* ⊕ *www.eldoradosonoma.com/hotel* ✆ *27 rooms* ⦿ *No meals.*

$$$$
RESORT
▦ **Fairmont Sonoma Mission Inn & Spa.** The real draw at this Mission-style resort is the extensive, swanky spa, easily the biggest in Sonoma, with a vast array of massages and treatments, some using locally sourced grape and lavender products. **Pros:** enormous spa; excellent restaurant; free shuttle to downtown. **Cons:** standard rooms on the smaller side; not as intimate as some similarly priced places. ⑤ *Rooms from: $439* ✉ *100 Boyes Blvd./Hwy. 12, 2 miles north of Sonoma, Boyes Hot Springs* ☎ *707/938–9000* ⊕ *www.fairmont.com/sonoma* ✆ *166 rooms, 60 suites* ⦿ *No meals.*

$
B&B/INN
FAMILY
▦ **Sonoma Creek Inn.** The small but cheerful rooms at this roadside inn with a sunny yellow exterior are individually decorated with painted wooden armoires, cozy quilts, and brightly colored contemporary artwork, elevating this bargain option well above your average motel. **Pros:** clean, well-lighted bathrooms; a lot of charm for the low price. **Cons:** office not staffed 24 hours a day; a 10-minute drive from Sonoma Plaza. ⑤ *Rooms from: $145* ✉ *239 Boyes Blvd., off Hwy. 12* ☎ *707/939–9463, 888/712–1289* ⊕ *www.sonomacreekinn.com* ✆ *16 rooms.*

NIGHTLIFE AND THE ARTS

The nightlife scene in Sonoma is pretty subdued. The bar inside the El Dorado Kitchen (⇨ *Where to Eat, above*) or the one at the adjoining El Dorado Corner Cafe are both good spots for a drink. The Epicurean Connection (⇨ *Shopping, below*) hosts live jazz from Thursday through Saturday—and sometimes on other nights—from about 7:30 to 10. To float back in time, head to the truly retro (because it hasn't changed much) Swiss Hotel on the plaza's north side for some Glariffee, a cold and potent cousin to Irish coffee.

6

Where to Eat and Stay in Sonoma Valley

SPAS

Willow Stream Spa at Fairmont Sonoma Mission Inn & Spa. With 40,000 square feet and 30 treatment rooms—making it by far the largest spa in the Wine Country—Willow Stream offers every amenity you could possibly want, including several pools and hot tubs fed by local thermal springs. Although the spa bustles with patrons in summer and on some weekends, the vibe here is always soothing. The signature bathing ritual includes an exfoliating shower, dips in two mineral-water soaking pools, an herbal steam, a dry sauna, and cool-down showers. Guests experience this ritual on their own or in conjunction with other treatments such as the warm ginger-oil float, which involves relaxation in a weightless environment, and the perennially popular caviar facial. The most requested room among couples is outfitted with a two-person copper bathtub. ✉ *100 Boyes Blvd./Hwy. 12, 2.5 miles north of Sonoma Plaza, Boyes Hot Springs* ☎ *707/938–9000* ⊕ *www.fairmont.com/sonoma* ✎ *Treatments $65–$485.*

SHOPPING

Fodor's Choice ★ **Chateau Sonoma.** The fancy furniture, lighting fixtures, and objets d'art at this upscale shop make it a dangerous place to enter: after just a few minutes you may find yourself reconsidering your entire home's aesthetic. The owner's keen eye for style and sense of whimsy make a visit here a delight. ✉ *153 W. Napa St., near 2nd St. W* ☎ *707/935–8553* ⊕ *www.chateausonoma.com.*

The Epicurean Connection. Food-lover alert: In addition to selling Delice de La Vallee, her award-winning artisanal cheese made from triple-cream cow and goat milk, owner Sheana Davis offers jams, sauces, tapenades, and other toppings from local producers. You can also buy sandwiches and sweets, and in the evening from Thursday through Saturday (and sometimes other days) you can hear good live jazz. ✉ *122 W. Napa St., at 1st St.* ☎ *707/935–7960* ⊕ *www.theepicureanconnection.com.*

GLEN ELLEN

7 miles north of Sonoma.

Unlike its flashier Napa Valley counterparts, craggy Glen Ellen eschews well-groomed sidewalks lined with upscale boutiques and restaurants, preferring instead its crooked streets, some with no sidewalks at all, shaded with stands of old oak trees. Jack London, who represents Glen Ellen's rugged spirit, lived in the area for many years; the town commemorates him with place names and nostalgic establishments. Hidden among sometimes-ramshackle buildings abutting Sonoma and Calabasas creeks are low-key shops and galleries worth poking through, and several fine dining establishments.

GETTING HERE AND AROUND

To get to Glen Ellen from Sonoma Plaza, drive west on West Spain Street. After about a mile, turn right onto Highway 12. Drive about 7 miles, then take the Arnold Drive exit and turn left. Many of Glen Ellen's restaurants and inns are along a half-mile stretch of Arnold Drive.

Horseback riding tours loop around Jack London State Historic Park.

EXPLORING

Fodor's Choice ★ **Benziger Family Winery.** One of the best-known Sonoma County wineries sits on a sprawling estate in a bowl with 360-degree sun exposure, the benefits of which are explored on popular tram tours that depart several times daily. Guides explain Benziger's biodynamic farming practices and give you a glimpse of the extensive cave system. The regular tram tour costs $20; another costing $40 concludes with a seated tasting. Benziger is noted for its Merlot, Pinot Noir, Cabernet Sauvignon, Chardonnay, and Sauvignon Blanc wines. Bring a picnic lunch, as the grounds are lovely. ■TIP→ Reserve a seat on the tram tour through the winery's website or arrive early in the day on busy summer weekends and during the harvest. ⊠ *1883 London Ranch Rd., off Arnold Dr.* ☎ *707/935–3000, 888/490–2739* ⊕ *www.benziger. com* ✉ *Tastings $10–$20, tours $20–$40* ⊙ *Daily 10–5; tours daily at 11:15, 12:45, and 2:15.*

Fodor's Choice ★ **Jack London State Historic Park.** The pleasures are both pastoral and intellectual at the beloved former ranch of the late author Jack London. You could easily spend the afternoon hiking along the edge of vineyards and through stands of oaks. Several manuscripts and a handful of personal effects are on view at the House of Happy Walls Museum, which provides a tantalizing overview of the author's life and literary passions. A short hike away lie the ruins of Wolf House, which mysteriously burned down just before the writer was to move in. Also open to the public are a few restored farm outbuildings and the Cottage, a wood-framed building where he penned many of his later works. London is buried on the property. ⊠ *2400 London Ranch Rd., off*

Hitching a ride on the Benziger Family Winery tram tour.

Arnold Dr. ☎ *707/938–5216* ⊕ *jacklondonpark.com* 🚗 *Parking $10, includes admission to museum; cottage $4* ⏱ *Thurs.–Mon. park 9:30–5, museum 10–5, cottage noon–4.*

WHERE TO EAT

$$
FRENCH
Fodor's Choice
★

✕ **The Fig Cafe.** Pale sage walls, a sloping ceiling, and casual but very warm service set a sunny mood in this little bistro run by the same team behind Sonoma's Girl & the Fig. The compact menu focuses on California and French comfort food—pot roast and duck confit, for instance, as well as thin-crust pizza. Steamed mussels are served with terrific crispy fries, which also accompany the sirloin burger. Weekend brunch brings out locals and tourists for French toast, pizza with applewood-smoked bacon and poached eggs, corned-beef hash, and other delights. ■TIP→ **The unusual no-corkage-fee policy makes this a great place to drink the wine you discovered down the road.** ⑤ *Average main: $19* ✉ *13690 Arnold Dr., at O'Donnell La.* ☎ *707/938–2130* ⊕ *www.thefigcafe.com* 🍴 *Reservations not accepted* ⏱ *No lunch weekdays.*

$$
ECLECTIC

✕ **Glen Ellen Inn Oyster Grill & Martini Bar.** Tucked inside a creek-side 1940s cottage, this cozy restaurant exudes romance, especially if you sit in the shady garden or on the patio strung with tiny lights. After taking the edge off your hunger with some oysters on the half shell and an ice-cold martini, order from a menu that plucks elements from California, French, and other cuisines. You might find ginger tempura calamari with grilled pineapple salsa, or dry-aged rib-eye steak with chimichurri sauce and a heaping side of country-style fries. Desserts tend toward the indulgent; witness the warm cinnamon-pecan bread pudding with a chocolate center that sits in a puddle of brandy sauce. $ *Average main: $20* ✉ *13670 Arnold Dr., at O'Donnell La.* ☎ *707/996–6409* ⊕ *www.glenelleninn.com* ⊗ *No lunch Wed.*

WHERE TO STAY

For expanded hotel reviews, visit Fodors.com.

$ 🏨 **Beltane Ranch.** On a slope of the Mayacamas range a few miles from
B&B/INN   Glen Ellen, this 1892 ranch house, shaded by magnificent oak trees,
Fodor'sChoice   contains charmingly old-fashioned rooms, each individually deco-
★   rated with antiques and original artwork by noted artists. **Pros:** casual, friendly atmosphere; reasonable prices; beautiful grounds with ancient oak trees. **Cons:** downstairs rooms get some noise from upstairs rooms; ceiling fans instead of air-conditioning. $ *Rooms from: $175* ✉ *11775 Sonoma Hwy./Hwy. 12* ☎ *707/996–6501* ⊕ *www.beltaneranch.com* ⤳ *3 rooms, 2 suites, 1 cottage* ⦿ *Breakfast.*

$$$ 🏨 **Gaige House.** Gorgeous Asian objets d'art and leather club chairs
B&B/INN   cozied up to the lobby fireplace are just a few of the graceful touches
Fodor'sChoice   in this luxurious but understated bed-and-breakfast. **Pros:** beautiful
★   lounge areas; lots of privacy; excellent service; full breakfasts, afternoon wine and appetizers. **Cons:** sound carries in the main house; the least expensive rooms are on the small side. $ *Rooms from: $345* ✉ *13540 Arnold Dr.* ☎ *707/935–0237, 800/935–0237* ⊕ *www.gaige.com* ⤳ *10 rooms, 13 suites* ⦿ *Breakfast.*

$$ 🏨 **Olea Hotel.** The husband-and-wife team of Ashish and Sia Patel
B&B/INN   gave an extreme makeover to a run-down former B&B, and after a
Fodor'sChoice   year's labor unveiled a boutique lodging that's at once sophisticated
★   and down-home country casual. **Pros:** beautiful style; welcoming staff; chef-prepared breakfasts; handsome grounds. **Cons:** fills up quickly on weekends; away from downtown Glen Ellen; minor road noise in some rooms. $ *Rooms from: $257* ✉ *5131 Warm Springs Rd., west off Arnold Dr.* ☎ *707/996–5131* ⊕ *www.oleahotel.com* ⤳ *10 rooms, 2 cottages* ⦿ *Breakfast.*

KENWOOD

3 miles north of Glen Ellen.

Tiny Kenwood consists of little more than a few restaurants and shops and a historic train depot. But hidden in this pretty landscape of meadows and woods at the north end of Sonoma Valley are several good wineries, most just off the Sonoma Highway.

GETTING HERE AND AROUND

To get to Kenwood from Glen Ellen, drive 3 miles north on Highway 12.

EXPLORING

Deerfield Ranch Winery. The focus at Deerfield is on producing "clean wines"—ones low in histamines and sulfites—the better to eliminate the headaches and allergic reactions some red-wine drinkers experience. Winemaker Robert Rex accomplishes this goal with no loss of flavor or complexity. Deerfield wines are bold, fruit-forward wines with a long finish. The lush DRX and Meritage Bordeaux-style blends invite contemplation about the vineyards, weather, and wine-making skills involved in their creation, whereas the pleasures of the Red Rex blend revolve chiefly around its friskiness. To taste these and other vintages (Rex also makes white wines), you walk deep into a 23,000-square-foot cave. Standard tastings ($15) include five wines; for an additional $5, you can sample more, including one from the reserve list. ✉ *10200 Sonoma Hwy./Hwy. 12* ☎ *707/833–5215* ⊕ *www.deerfieldranch.com* 🍷 *Tastings $15–$20* ⊗ *Daily 10:30–4:30.*

Kunde Estate Winery & Vineyards. On your way into Kunde you pass a terrace flanked with fountains, virtually coaxing you to stay for a picnic with views over the vineyard. The winery is perhaps best known for its toasty Chardonnays, although tastings might also include Sauvignon Blanc, Cabernet Sauvignon, Merlot, and Zinfandel. For insight into the winery's approach to sustainable wine making, take a few minutes to wander around the demonstration vineyard outside the tasting room. The free basic tour of the grounds includes the extensive caves, some of which stretch 175 feet below a vineyard. ■**TIP→ Reserve ahead for the Mountain Top Tasting, a tour that ends with a sampling of reserve wines ($40).** ✉ *9825 Sonoma Hwy./Hwy. 12* ☎ *707/833–5501* ⊕ *www. kunde.com* 🍷 *Tastings $10–$40, tours free–$50* ⊗ *Daily 10:30–5, tours daily at various times.*

St. Francis Winery. Nestled at the foot of Mt. Hood, this winery occupies one of the most scenic locations in Sonoma. With its red-tile roof and dramatic bell tower, the visitor center, a marvelous evocation of the California Mission style, completes the pastoral picture. The charm of the surroundings is matched by the wines, most of them red, including rich, earthy Zinfandels from both the Russian River and Sonoma valleys. Executive chef David Bush, formerly of the Girl & the Fig, creates five-to-seven-course food-and-wine pairings—cassoulet with Merlot, for example—that are an excellent value at $42. They're offered from Thursday through Monday (reservations recommended), but $25 cheese-and-charcuterie pairings are available daily. Tours costing $30 explore the winery and barrel room and end with reserve-wine tastings. ✉ *100 Pythian Rd., off Hwy. 12* ☎ *888/675–9463, 707/833–6146* ⊕ *www.stfranciswine.com* 🍷 *Tastings $10–$42, tour $30* ⊗ *Daily 10–5, tour by appointment.*

WHERE TO EAT AND STAY
For expanded hotel reviews, visit Fodors.com.

$ ✕ **Café Citti.** Classical music in the background and a friendly staff (as well
ITALIAN   as a roaring fire when the weather's cold) keep this no-frills roadside café from feeling too spartan. Order dishes such as roast chicken and slabs of tiramisu from the counter and they're delivered to your table, indoors or on an outdoor patio. The array of prepared salads and sandwiches means the café does a brisk business in takeout for picnic packers, but you can also choose pasta made to order. ⑤ *Average main: $13* ✉ *9049 Sonoma Hwy./Hwy. 12* ☎ *707/833–2690* ⊕ *www.cafecitti.com.*

$$$$ 🏨 **Kenwood Inn and Spa.** Buildings resembling graceful old haciendas and
B&B/INN   the mature fruit trees shading the courtyards make it seem like this inn
Fodor's Choice   has been here for more than a century (it was actually built in 1990).
★   **Pros:** large rooms; lavish furnishings; extremely romantic. **Cons:** Wi-Fi

can be spotty in some areas; expensive. $ *Rooms from: $450* ✉ *10400 Sonoma Hwy./Hwy. 12* ☎ *707/833–1293, 800/353–6966* ⊕ *www. kenwoodinn.com* ↪ *25 rooms, 4 suites* ❍ *Breakfast.*

SPAS

Spa at Kenwood Inn. A pretty setting, expert practitioners, and rejuvenating French therapies make a visit to the Spa at Kenwood Inn a marvelously ethereal experience. The wine-based Vinothérapie treatments and beauty products from the French line Caudalíe combine in the delicious-sounding Honey Wine Wrap, which involves a warming, full-body slathering of wine yeast and honey, the better to rehydrate your parched and neglected skin. The Crushed Cabernet Scrub, designed to stimulate and soften your skin, raises the sweetness ante by adding brown sugar to the honey, along with crushed grape seeds and grape-seed oil. The spa's other services include massages and facials using the products and treatments by iS Clinical and Intraceuticals. ✉ *10400 Sonoma Hwy./Hwy. 12* ☎ *707/833–1293, 800/353–6966* ⊕ *www. kenwoodinn.com* ✑ *Treatments $125–$390.*

ELSEWHERE IN SONOMA COUNTY

6

At nearly 1,598 square miles, there's more to Sonoma County than the day-tripper favorites of Sonoma, Glen Ellen, and Kenwood. To the north is Healdsburg, a small town with killer shopping. The national media have latched onto it for its swank hotels and remarkable restaurants, and many Fodors.com readers recommend it as an ideal home base for wine tasting in northern Sonoma County.

Within easy striking distance of Healdsburg are the scenic vineyards of the Alexander, Dry Creek, and Russian River valleys. These lookers produce some of the country's best Pinot Noir, Cabernet Sauvignon, Zinfandel, and Sauvignon Blanc. Though these regions are hardly unknown names, their quiet, narrow roads feel a world away from Highway 29 in Napa. The western stretches of Sonoma County are sparsely populated in comparison to the above destinations and have fewer wineries. River Road heading west from U.S. 101—the exit is about 4 miles north of Santa Rosa—intersects Westside Road, which passes through Pinot Noir paradise on its way to Healdsburg.

SANTA ROSA

8 miles northwest of Kenwood.

Santa Rosa, the Wine Country's largest city, isn't likely to charm you with its office buildings, department stores, and frequent snarls of traffic along U.S. 101. It is, however, home to a couple of interesting cultural offerings. Its moderately priced chain lodgings can be handy, especially since Santa Rosa is roughly equidistant from Sonoma, Healdsburg, and the Russian River Valley, three of the most popular wine-tasting destinations.

GETTING HERE AND AROUND

To get to Santa Rosa from San Francisco, drive north over the Golden Gate Bridge and continue north on U.S. 101 to the downtown Santa Rosa exit. To get to Santa Rosa from Sonoma Valley, take Highway 12 north. Santa Rosa's hotels, restaurants, and wineries are spread over a wide area; factor in extra time when driving around Santa Rosa, especially during morning and evening commute hours.

EXPLORING

TOP ATTRACTIONS

Fodor's Choice ★ **Matanzas Creek Winery.** The visitor center at Matanzas Creek sets itself apart with an understated Japanese aesthetic, extending to a tranquil fountain and a koi pond. Best of all, huge windows overlook a vast field of lavender where you can wander on your own or on a tour of the grounds ($10). The winery specializes in Sauvignon Blanc, Chardonnay, and Merlot, although it also produces Syrah, a rich Bordeaux blend called Journey, and a late-harvest Sauvignon Blanc dessert wine. A second tour concludes with a taste of limited-production and library wines paired with artisanal cheeses. ■TIP→ **The ideal time to visit is in May and June, when the lavender perfumes the air.** ⊠ *6097 Bennett Valley Rd., at Lafranconi Rd.* ☎ *707/528–6464, 800/590–6464* ⊕ *www.matanzascreek.com* ⌕ *Tastings $10–$20, tours $10–$35* ☉ *Daily 10–4:30; estate tour daily at 10:30, others by appointment.*

FAMILY **Safari West.** An unexpected bit of wilderness in the Wine Country, this African wildlife preserve covers 400 acres on the outskirts of Santa Rosa. A visit begins with a stroll around enclosures housing lemurs, cheetahs, giraffes, and many varieties of rare birds, like the brightly colored scarlet ibis. Next, climb onto open-air vehicles that spend about two hours combing the expansive property, where more than 80 species—including African Cape buffalo, gazelles, wildebeests, and zebras—make their homes on the hillsides. All the while you're accompanied by guides who inform you about the animals, their behavior, and the threats they face in the wild. If you'd like to extend your stay, lodging in well-equipped tent cabins is available. ⊠ *3115 Porter Creek Rd., off Mark West Springs Rd.* ☎ *707/579–2551, 800/616–2695* ⊕ *www. safariwest.com* ⌕ *$78–$80.*

WORTH NOTING

FAMILY **Charles M. Schulz Museum.** Fans of Snoopy and Charlie Brown will love the Charles M. Schulz Museum, dedicated to the cartoonist who lived in Santa Rosa for the last 30 years of his life, until his death in 2000. Permanent installations like a re-creation of the artist's studio share space with temporary exhibits that often focus on a particular theme in Schulz's work. Children and adults can take a stab at creating cartoons in the Education Room or wander through the labyrinth in the form of Snoopy's head. ⊠ *2301 Hardies La., at W. Steele La.* ☎ *707/579–4452* ⊕ *www.schulzmuseum.org* ⌕ *$10* ☉ *Labor Day–Memorial Day, Wed.– Fri. and Mon. 11–5, weekends 10–5; Memorial Day–Labor Day, weekdays 11–5, weekends 10–5.*

De Loach Vineyards. Just far enough off the beaten track to feel like a real find, this winery produces old-vine Zinfandels, Chardonnays, and a handful of other varietals, but it's best for known for its Pinot Noir, some of which is made using open-top wood fermentation vats that are uncommon in Sonoma but have been used in France for centuries. (Some think they intensify a wine's flavor.) Tours focus on the estate vineyards, where you can learn about the labor-intensive biodynamic and organic farming methods used, and take you through the culinary garden. Call a day or two in advance if you want to taste wines paired with regional cheeses ($25) or purchase a picnic basket ($30) to enjoy in their attractive picnic area. ⊠ *1791 Olivet Rd.* ☎ *707/526–9111, 800/441–9298* ⊕ *www.deloachvineyards.com* ☞ *Tasting $10–$25, tour $15* ☉ *Daily 10–5; tours daily at 11 (or by appointment).*

WHERE TO EAT

$$$

ECLECTIC

Fodor's Choice

★

✕ **Willi's Wine Bar.** Don't let the name fool you: instead of a sedate spot serving flights of bubbly with delicate nibbles, you'll find a cozy warren of rooms where boisterous crowds snap up small plates from the globe-trotting menu. Such dishes as pork-belly pot stickers with shiitake mushrooms represent Asia, and Moroccan-style lamb chops and roasted flatbread with caramelized onions and feta are some of the Mediterranean-inspired foods. The delectable "fish-and-chips" plate of Monterey Bay sardines with garlic potato chips is among the many using California-sourced ingredients. Wines are available in 2-ounce pours, making it easier to pair each of your little plates with a different glass. ■ TIP→ The din inside can be deafening on busy nights, so consider a table on the covered patio. $ *Average main: $28* ⊠ *4404 Old Redwood Hwy., at Ursuline Rd.* ☎ *707/526–3096* ⊕ *williswinebar.net* ☉ *No lunch Sun. and Mon.*

WHERE TO STAY

For expanded hotel reviews, visit Fodors.com.

$$

HOTEL

▦ **Vintners Inn.** The owners of Ferrari-Carano Vineyards operate this oasis set amid 80 acres of vineyards that's known for its comfortable lodgings. **Pros:** spacious rooms with comfortable beds; jogging path through the vineyards; online deals pop up year-round. **Cons:** occasional noise from adjacent events center; some decor seems dated. $ *Rooms from: $265* ⊠ *4350 Barnes Rd.* ☎ *707/575–7350, 800/421–2584* ⊕ *www.vintnersinn.com* ⇆ *38 rooms, 6 suites* ❗ *No meals.*

RUSSIAN RIVER VALLEY

10 miles northwest of Santa Rosa.

The Russian River flows from Mendocino to the Pacific Ocean, but in terms of wine making, the Russian River Valley is centered on a triangle with points at Healdsburg, Guerneville, and Sebastopol. Tall redwoods shade many of the two-lane roads that access this scenic area, where, thanks to the cooling marine influence, Pinot Noir and Chardonnay are the king and queen of grapes.

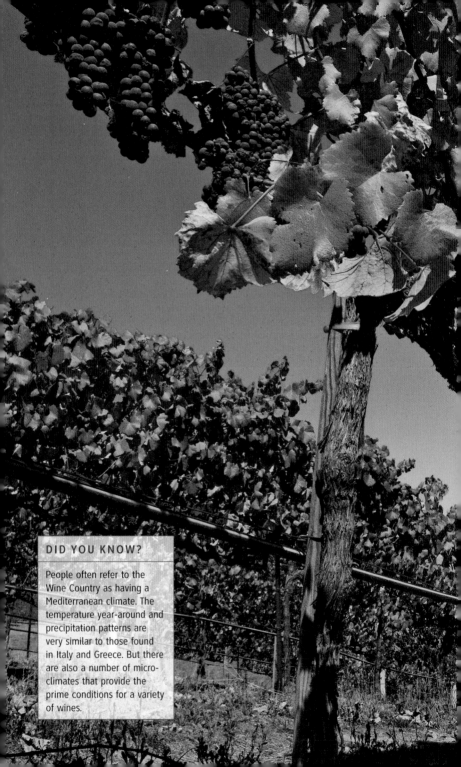

DID YOU KNOW?

People often refer to the Wine Country as having a Mediterranean climate. The temperature year-around and precipitation patterns are very similar to those found in Italy and Greece. But there are also a number of micro-climates that provide the prime conditions for a variety of wines.

ESSENTIALS

Contacts Russian River Wine Road ⊠ *498 Moore La., Healdsburg* ☎ *707/433–4335, 800/723–6336* ⊕ *www.wineroad.com.*

GETTING HERE AND AROUND

Many people visit the Russian River valley while based in nearby Healdsburg. To get to the wineries along Westside Road from Healdsburg's central plaza, head south on Center Street and turn right at Mill Street, which turns into Westside Road after it crosses U.S. 101. To reach the Forestville and Sebastopol areas, continue south and west along Westside Road until it runs into River Road and turn west. Turn south at Mirabel Road and follow it to Highway 116, where you'll turn west for Forestville and east for Sebastopol.

EXPLORING

TOP ATTRACTIONS

Fodor'sChoice
★ **Hartford Family Winery.** Pinot Noir lovers appreciate the subtle differences in the wines Hartford's Jeff Stewart crafts from grapes grown in Sonoma County's three top AVAs for the varietal—Los Carneros, Russian River Valley, and the Sonoma Coast—along with one from the Anderson Valley, just north in Mendocino County. The Pinot Noirs win consistent praise from major wine critics, and Stewart also makes highly rated Chardonnays and old-vine Zinfandels. A reserve tasting ($15) includes a flight of six wines; a tour of the winery is part of the seated private library tasting ($35). ■TIP→ **If the weather's good and you've made a reservation, your reserve tasting can take place on the patio outside the opulent main winery building.** ⊠ *8075 Martinelli Rd., off Hwy. 116 or River Rd., Forestville* ☎ *707/887–8011, 800/588–0234* ⊕ *www.hartfordwines.com* ⊠ *Tastings $15–$35* ☉ *Daily 10–4:30, tours by appointment.*

Fodor'sChoice
★ **Iron Horse Vineyards.** A meandering one-lane road leads to this winery known for its sparkling wines—from the bright and austere to the rich and toasty—as well as estate Chardonnays and Pinot Noirs. The sparklers have made history: Ronald Reagan served them at his summit meetings with Mikhail Gorbachev, George Herbert Walker Bush took some along to Moscow for treaty talks, and Barack Obama has included them at official state dinners. Despite the winery's frequent brushes with fame, a casual rusticity prevails at Iron Horse's outdoor tasting area (large heaters keep things comfortable on chilly days), which gazes out on acres of rolling, vine-covered hills. Tours, by appointment only, take place on weekdays at 10 am. Winemaker David Munksgard leads the Friday tour. ⊠ *9786 Ross Station Rd., off Hwy. 116, Sebastopol* ☎ *707/887–1507* ⊕ *www.ironhorsevineyards.com* ⊠ *Tasting $15, tour $20* ☉ *Daily 10–4:30, tour weekdays at 10 by appointment.*

Fodor'sChoice
★ **Merry Edwards Winery.** Winemaker Merry Edwards describes the Russian River Valley as "the epicenter of great Pinot Noir," and her namesake winery produces wines that express the unique characteristics of the soils, climates, and Pinot Noir clones from which they derive. (Edwards's research into Pinot Noir clones is so extensive that there's even one named after her.) The valley's advantage, says Edwards, are the warmer-than-average daytime temperatures that yield more intense

fruit; the famous evening fogs mitigate the potential negative effects of the extra heat. Group tastings of the well-composed single-vineyard and blended Pinots are offered several times a day—no waltzing up to the wine bar here. Edwards also makes a fine Sauvignon Blanc that's lightly aged in old oak. Tastings end, rather than begin, with this lively white wine so as not to distract guests' palates from the Pinot Noirs. ⊠ *2959 Gravenstein Hwy. N/Hwy. 16, near Oak Grove Ave., Sebastopol* ☎ *707/823–7466, 888/388–9050* ⊕ *www.merryedwards.com* ⊠ *Tasting free* ⊙ *Daily 9:30–4:30; call for appointment or drop in and join next available tasting.*

Fodor'sChoice ★ **Rochioli Vineyards and Winery.** Claiming one of the prettiest picnic sites in the area, with tables overlooking the vineyards, this winery also has an airy little tasting room hung with modern artwork. Production is small and fans on the winery's mailing list snap up most of the bottles, but the winery is still worth a stop. Because of the cool growing conditions in the Russian River Valley, the flavors of the Chardonnay and Sauvignon Blanc are intense and complex. It's the Pinot Noir, though, that is largely responsible for the winery's stellar reputation; it helped cement the Russian River's status as a Pinot powerhouse. ■TIP→ **Rochioli is one of the few wineries of its stature that still doesn't charge for tastings.** ⊠ *6192 Westside Rd., Healdsburg* ☎ *707/433–2305* ⊕ *www.rochioliwinery.com* ⊠ *Tasting free* ⊙ *Early Jan.–mid-Dec., Thurs.–Mon. 11–4, Tues. and Wed. by appointment.*

WORTH NOTING

Gary Farrell Winery. Pass through an impressive metal gate and wind your way up a steep hill to reach Gary Farrell, a spot with knock-out views over the rolling hills and vineyards below. The winery has changed hands a few times since Farrell sold it in 2004, but it's managed to continue producing well-regarded bottles, these days by winemaker Theresa Heredia. Though its Zinfandels and Chardonnays often excel, the winery has built its reputation on its Pinot Noirs. ⊠ *10701 Westside Rd., Healdsburg* ☎ *707/473–2909* ⊕ *www. garyfarrellwines.com* ⊠ *Tastings $15–$25, tour $35* ⊙ *Daily 10:30–4:30, tour by appointment.*

WHERE TO EAT

$$$$
FRENCH
Fodor'sChoice
★

✕**The Farmhouse Inn.** From the personable sommelier who assists you with wine choices to the servers who describe the provenance of the black truffles shaved over the intricate pasta dishes, the staff matches the quality of this restaurant's outstanding French-inspired cuisine. The signature dish called "Rabbit Rabbit Rabbit," a rich trio of confit of leg, rabbit loin wrapped in applewood-smoked bacon, and roasted rack of rabbit with a whole-grain mustard sauce, is typical of preparations that are both rustic and refined. ■TIP→ **The inn is a favorite of wine-industry foodies, so reserve well in advance; if it's full, you might be able to dine in the small lounge.** Ⓢ *Average main: $52* ⊠ *7871 River Rd., at Wohler Rd., Forestville* ☎ *707/887–3300, 800/464–6642* ⊕ *www.farmhouseinn.com* ⬟ *Reservations essential* ⊙ *Closed Tues. and Wed. No lunch.*

6

WHERE TO STAY

For expanded hotel reviews, visit Fodors.com.

$$$
B&B/INN
Fodor's Choice
★

The Farmhouse Inn. With a rustic-farmhouse-meets-modern-loft aesthetic, the spacious rooms in this pale yellow farmhouse dating from 1873 are filled with king-size four-poster beds, whirlpool tubs, and terraces overlooking the hillside. **Pros:** home of one of Sonoma's best restaurants; luxury bath products; full-service spa uses many local ingredients. **Cons:** rooms closest to the street get a bit of road noise. ⑤ *Rooms from: $350* ✉ *7871 River Rd., Forestville* ☎ *707/887–3300, 800/464–6642* ⊕ *www.farmhouseinn.com* ↪ *12 rooms, 6 suites* ⑩ *Breakfast.*

$
HOTEL
FAMILY

Sebastopol Inn. The simple but cheerful rooms at this reasonably priced inn, freshly painted a sunny yellow and hung with blue-and-white-striped curtains, have a spare California country style. **Pros:** friendly staff; just steps from a café, wine bar, and spa. **Cons:** nice, but no frills; some will find the beds too firm. ⑤ *Rooms from: $135* ✉ *6751 Sebastopol Ave., Sebastopol* ☎ *707/829–2500* ⊕ *www.sebastopolinn. com* ↪ *29 rooms, 2 suites.*

SPORTS AND THE OUTDOORS

Burke's Canoe Trips. You get a real feel for the Russian River's flora and fauna on a leisurely 10-mile paddle from Burke's downstream to Guerneville. A shuttle bus returns you to your car at the end of the journey, which is best taken from late May through mid-October. The cost is $60 per canoe. ✉ *8600 River Rd., at Mirabel Rd., Forestville* ☎ *707/887–1222* ⊕ *www.burkescanoetrips.com.*

HEALDSBURG

17 miles north of Santa Rosa.

Just when it seems that the buzz about Healdsburg couldn't get any more intense, there's another article published in a glossy food or wine magazine about the restaurant Spoonbar inside the fabulous h2hotel. The good news: you don't have to be a tycoon to stay here and enjoy the town. For every ritzy restaurant there's a great bakery or relatively modest B&B. A tin-roofed bandstand on Healdsburg's plaza hosts free summer concerts, where you might hear anything from bluegrass to Sousa marches. Add to that the fragrant magnolia trees shading the square and the bright flower beds, and the whole thing is as pretty as a Norman Rockwell painting.

The setting is no less idyllic in the nearby countryside, where stores straddling the relatively untrafficked roads sell just-plucked fruits and vine-ripened tomatoes. Winery buildings here are barely visible, since they're tucked behind groves of eucalyptus or hidden high on fog-shrouded hills.

GETTING HERE AND AROUND

To get to Healdsburg from San Francisco, cross the Golden Gate Bridge and continue north on U.S. 101. About 65 miles from San Francisco, take the Central Healdsburg exit and follow Healdsburg Avenue a few blocks to the town's central plaza. Many of the town's hotels and restaurants ring the scenic town square and the few blocks radiating out from here.

Annual barrel tasting along Russian River's wine road

WHERE TO EAT

$$$$
AMERICAN

✕**Barndiva.** This hip joint abandons the homey vibe of so many Wine Country spots for a younger, more urban feel. Electronic music plays quietly in the background while hipster servers ferry inventive seasonal cocktails. The food is as stylish as the well-dressed couples cozying up next to each other on the banquette seats. Make a light meal out of starters like "The Artisan," a bountiful plate of cheeses and charcuterie, or settle in for the evening with such dishes as pork tenderloin with potato purée or crispy young chicken served with roasted brussels sprouts, pancetta ricotta, and egg-yolk ravioli. During warm weather the open-air patio is the place to be. ⑤ *Average main: $31* ✉ *231 Center St., at Matheson St.* ☎ *707/431–0100* ⊕ *www.barndiva.com* ⊙ *Closed Mon. and Tues.*

$$$
FRENCH

✕**Bistro Ralph.** There was a time when Bistro Ralph was *the* good restaurant downtown, and long before the concept of "fresh, simple, local" became culinary gospel, that hallowed refrain coursed through the kitchen of this Healdsburg pioneer. The menu shifts seasonally. In spring, for example, you might find extraordinary grilled marinated asparagus; at other times look for grilled Columbia River sturgeon or Dungeness crab ravioli. Standbys include fried Szechuan-pepper calamari, chicken livers (locals love 'em), lamb burgers, and duck confit. This place does as spectacular a job with shoestring potatoes as it does with ahi tuna, and even the cocktails—martinis are a specialty—are executed with precision and flair. The wines are all from Healdsburg, but with dozens of wineries within city limits, the selection is more than sufficiently varied. ⑤ *Average main: $27* ✉ *109 Plaza St., near Healdsburg Ave.* ☎ *707/433–1380* ⊕ *www.bistroralph.com* ⊙ *No dinner Sun.*

$ ✕ **Costeaux.** This French-style bakery and café has won numerous
FRENCH   awards for its bread, and the croissants are among Sonoma County's
best. Breakfast, served all day, includes homemade quiche, the signature
omelet (sun-dried tomatoes, applewood-smoked bacon, and Brie), and
French toast made from thick slabs of cinnamon-walnut bread. Among
the lunch items are two au courant variations on classic sandwiches:
a French dip made from house-roasted rib eye and a Monte Cristo
(turkey, ham, and Jarlsberg cheese) on that addictive cinnamon-walnut
bread. ■**TIP→ Arrive early on weekends to grab a seat on the open-
air patio.** ⑤ *Average main: $13* ✉ *417 Healdsburg Ave., at North St.*
☎ *707/433–1913* ⊕ *www.costeaux.com* ☉ *No dinner.*

$ ✕ **Downtown Bakery & Creamery.** If you want to catch the Healdsburg
BAKERY   spirit, hit the plaza in the early morning to down a cup of coffee and a
Fodor's Choice   fragrant sticky bun or a too-darlin' *canelé*, a French-style pastry with
★   a soft custard center surrounded by a dense caramel crust. Until 2 pm
you can also go the full breakfast route: pancakes, granola, poached
farm eggs on polenta, or perhaps the dandy bacon-and-egg pizza. For
lunch there are sandwiches and focaccia. The bakery uses local fruit
and dairy products in its breads, pastries, and ice creams. ⑤ *Average
main: $8* ✉ *308A Center St., at North St.* ☎ *707/431–2719* ⊕ *www.
downtownbakery.net* ⌔ *Reservations not accepted* ☉ *No dinner.*

$$ ✕ **Scopa.** At this tiny eatery, chef Ari Rosen cooks up such rustic Italian
ITALIAN   specialties as house-made ravioli stuffed with ricotta cheese, braised
Fodor's Choice   chicken with greens and polenta, and *sugo Calabrese* (tomato-braised
★   beef and pork rib served with smoked mozzarella in a tomato sauce).
Simple thin-crust pizzas are worth ordering, too. Locals love the res-
taurant for its lack of pretension: wine is served in juice glasses, and the
friendly hostess makes the rounds to see that all are satisfied. You'll be
packed in elbow-to-elbow with your fellow diners, but for a convivial
evening over a bottle of Nebbiolo, there's no better choice. ⑤ *Average
main: $20* ✉ *109A Plaza St., near Healdsburg Ave.* ☎ *707/433–5282*
⊕ *www.scopahealdsburg.com* ☉ *No lunch.*

$$$ ✕ **Spoonbar.** Cantina doors that open onto Healdsburg Avenue make
MODERN   this trendy eatery especially appealing in summer, when warm breezes
AMERICAN   waft into the stylish space. Midcentury modern furnishings, concrete
Fodor's Choice   walls, and a long communal table fashioned from rough-hewn acacia
★   wood create an urbane setting for chef Louis Maldonado's contemporary American fare. Divided into five sections, the menu lets you mix
and match to create a memorable meal. The mains might include Cornish game hen roulade with artichokes or loin of beef in red wine jus,
served with quinoa and cider-braised root vegetables. The perpetually
packed bar, known for inventive seasonal and historic cocktails, is the
real draw for many locals. ⑤ *Average main: $23* ✉ *h2hotel, 219 Healds-
burg Ave., at Vine St.* ☎ *707/433–7222* ⊕ *www.h2hotel.com/spoonbar*
☉ *No lunch Mon.–Thurs. in winter.*

$$$ ✕ **Willi's Seafood & Raw Bar.** The perpetually packed Willi's draws a fes-
SEAFOOD   tive crowd that likes to enjoy specialty cocktails at the full bar before
Fodor's Choice   sitting down to a dinner of small, mostly seafood-oriented plates. A
★   few dishes, such as the warm Maine lobster roll with garlic butter
and fennel, conjure up a New England fish shack, and others, like the

top-notch ceviches and the scallops served with a cilantro-and-pumpkin-seed pesto, have a Latin American accent. The desserts transport diners to France (wildly flavorful crème brûlée) and beyond. ■ **TIP→ The same owners operate the Bravas Bar de Tapas at 420 Center Street, another good choice if this place is packed.** ⑤ *Average main: $25* ☒ *403 Healdsburg Ave., at North St.* ☎ *707/433–9191* ⊕ *www.willisseafood. net* ⌖ *Reservations not accepted.*

$$$ ✕ **Zin Restaurant and Wine Bar.** Concrete floors and large canvases on the
AMERICAN walls lend the restaurant a casual, industrial, and slightly artsy feel. The American cuisine—such as the roasted pork belly with pickled apples or the free-range chicken braised in red wine—is hearty and highly seasoned. Portions are large, so consider sharing if you hope to save room for such desserts as the brownie sundae with house-made ice cream. As you might have guessed from the name, Zinfandel is the drink of choice here, though Sonoma County's other major varietals show up on the 100-bottle wine list. From Sunday through Thursday, blue-plate specials featuring homey fare (like pot roast and chicken and dumplings) make this place a bargain. ⑤ *Average main: $25* ☒ *344 Center St., at North St.* ☎ *707/473–0946* ⊕ *zinrestaurant. com* ⊙ *No lunch weekends.*

WHERE TO STAY
For expanded hotel reviews, visit Fodors.com.

$$ ⌂ **h2hotel.** Eco-friendly touches abound at this hotel, from the undulat-
B&B/INN ing plant-covered "green roof" to wooden decks made from salvaged
Fodor's Choice lumber. **Pros:** stylish modern design; Healdsburg's most popular bar;
★ king beds can be converted to two twins. **Cons:** least expensive rooms lack bathtubs; no fitness facilities, but bike rentals are free. ⑤ *Rooms from: $200* ☒ *219 Healdsburg Ave.* ☎ *707/922–5251* ⊕ *www.h2hotel. com* ⟿ *34 rooms, 2 suites* �‖ *Breakfast.*

$$$ ⌂ **The Honor Mansion.** An 1883 Italianate Victorian houses this pho-
B&B/INN togenic hotel; rooms in the main house preserve a sense of the build-
Fodor's Choice ing's heritage, whereas the larger suites are comparatively understated.
★ **Pros:** homemade sweets available at all hours; spa pavilions by pool available for massages in fair weather. **Cons:** almost a mile from Healdsburg's plaza; walls can seem thin. ⑤ *Rooms from: $305* ☒ *891 Grove St.* ☎ *707/433–4277, 800/554–4667* ⊕ *www.honormansion. com* ⟿ *5 rooms, 7 suites, 1 cottage* ⊙ *Closed 2 wks around Christmas* �‖ *Breakfast.*

$$$ ⌂ **Hotel Healdsburg.** Across the street from the tidy town plaza, this
RESORT spare, sophisticated hotel caters to travelers with an urban sensibility. **Pros:** several rooms overlook the town plaza; comfortable lobby with a small attached bar; extremely comfortable beds. **Cons:** exterior rooms get some street noise; rooms could use better lighting. ⑤ *Rooms from: $375* ☒ *25 Matheson St.* ☎ *707/431–2800, 800/889–7188* ⊕ *www. hotelhealdsburg.com* ⟿ *49 rooms, 6 suites* �‖ *Breakfast.*

$$$$ ⌂ **Hôtel Les Mars.** This Relais & Châteaux property takes the prize for
HOTEL opulence with guest rooms spacious and elegant enough for French
Fodor's Choice nobility, 18th- and 19th-century antiques and reproductions, canopy
★ beds dressed in luxe linens, and gas-burning fireplaces. **Pros:** large rooms; just off Healdsburg's plaza; Bulgari bath products. **Cons:** very

expensive. ⑤ *Rooms from: $500* ✉ *27 North St.* ☎ *707/433–4211*
⊕ *www.hotellesmars.com* ➥ *16 rooms* ⊙| *Breakfast.*

SPAS

Fodor's Choice
★

Spa Dolce. Owner Ines von Majthenyi Scherrer has a good local rep,
having run a popular nearby spa before opening this stylish facility
just off Healdsburg Plaza. Spa Dolce specializes in skin and body care
for men and women, and makeup, waxing, and nail care for women.
Curved white walls and fresh-cut floral arrangements set a subdued
tone for such treatments as the exfoliating Hauschka body scrub, which
combines organic brown sugar with scented oil. There's a romantic
room for couples to enjoy massages for two. Many guests come just
for the facials, which range from a straightforward cleansing to an anti-
aging peel. ✉ *250 Center St., at Matheson St.* ☎ *707/433–0177* ⊕ *www.*
spadolce.com ⊠ *Treatments $20–$210* ⊙ *Tues.–Sun. 10–7.*

SPORTS AND THE OUTDOORS

Wine Country Bikes. This shop in downtown Healdsburg is perfectly
located for single or multiday treks into the Dry Creek and Russian
River valleys. Bikes, including tandems, rent for $35 to $125 a day.
One-day tours start at $139. ✉ *61 Front St., at Hudson St.* ☎ *707/473–*
0610, 866/922–4537 ⊕ *www.winecountrybikes.com.*

SHOPPING

Lime Stone. Owned by Dry Creek Kitchen chef Charlie Palmer and his
wife, Lisa, this shop carries wine-related items, kitchen accoutrements,
and household accessories. The hip and tasteful Lisa does all the buying. ✉ *Hotel Healdsburg, 318 Healdsburg Ave., near Matheson St.*
☎ *707/433–3080* ⊕ *www.limestonehealdsburg.com.*

Fodor's Choice
★

Saint Dizier Home. This shop is a reminder of why the universe provides us with decorators and designers—they really do know best. With
this selection of exquisitely crafted furniture and contemporary items
like hand-painted silk pillows, designer Jacques Saint Dizier and buyer
Cathy Hopkins prove the point. ✉ *259 Center St., at Matheson St.*
☎ *707/473–0980* ⊕ *www.saintdhome.com.*

DRY CREEK AND ALEXANDER VALLEYS

On the west side of U.S. 101, Dry Creek Valley remains one of the least-
developed appellations in Sonoma. Zinfandel grapes flourish on the
benchlands, whereas the gravelly, well-drained soil of the valley floor
is better known for Chardonnay and, in the north, Sauvignon Blanc.
The wineries in this region tend to be smaller, which makes them a good
bet on summer weekends, when larger spots and those along the main
thoroughfares fill up with tourists.

The Alexander Valley, which lies northeast of Healdsburg, is similarly
rustic. The largely family-owned wineries often produce Zinfandel and
Chardonnay, while the winding Highway 128 through Knights Valley
is a popular destination for cyclists and joggers alike.

GETTING HERE AND AROUND

The Dry Creek Valley sits west of downtown Healdsburg and U.S. 101. If you drive north on Healdsburg Avenue and turn left on Dry Creek Road you'll slip under the freeway and soon see signs pointing the way to wineries on that road and West Dry Creek Road, which runs roughly parallel about a mile to the west, accessible by the cross streets Lambert Bridge Road and Yoakim Bridge Road.

The Alexander Valley is just northeast of Healdsburg. To get here from the plaza, drive north on Healdsburg Avenue and veer right on Alexander Valley Road. Although there are a few wineries on Alexander Valley Road itself, most of them on are on Highway 128, which intersects after 3.3 miles.

EXPLORING
TOP ATTRACTIONS

Dry Creek Vineyard. Fumé Blanc is king at Dry Creek, where the refreshing white wine is made in the style of those in Sancerre, France. The winery also makes well-regarded Zinfandels, a zesty dry Chenin Blanc, a Pinot Noir, and a handful of Cabernet Sauvignon blends. Since many wines are priced below $30 a bottle (some less than $20), it's a popular stop for wine lovers looking to stock their cellars for a reasonable price. You can picnic on the lawn next to a flowering magnolia tree. Conveniently, a general store and deli is close by. ⊠ *3770 Lambert Bridge Rd., off Dry Creek Rd., Healdsburg* ☎ *707/433–1000, 800/864–9463* ⊕ *www.drycreekvineyard.com* ☜ *Tastings $5–$45, tour $15* ☉ *Daily 10:30–4:30, tour 11 and 1 by appointment.*

Fodor's Choice **Francis Ford Coppola Winery.** The famous film director's over-the-top fan-
★ tasyland is the sort of place the midlevel Mafiosi in his *The Godfather*
FAMILY saga might declare had "real class"; the "everyday wines" poured here are pretty much beside the point, but still, it's an entertaining scene. The fun is all in the excess, and you may find it hard to resist having your photo snapped standing next to Don Corleone's desk from *The Godfather,* at the re-created bandstand from its famous wedding scene, or beside memorabilia from other Coppola films, including some directed by his daughter, Sofia. The bandstand is the centerpiece of a large, popular pool area where you can rent a *cabine* (changing room), complete with shower, and spend the afternoon lounging under striped umbrellas, perhaps ordering food from the poolside café. The winery's more elaborate restaurant, Rustic, overlooks the vineyards. ⊠ *300 Via Archimedes, off U.S. 101, Geyserville* ☎ *707/857–1400* ⊕ *www.franciscoppolawinery.com* ☜ *Tastings free–$15, tours $20–$55, pool pass $20* ☉ *Tasting room daily 11–6, restaurant daily 11–9; pool hrs vary seasonally.*

Fodor's Choice **Locals Tasting Room.** Downtown Geyserville remains little more than a
★ crossroads with a few shops and a good restaurant, but this storefront is worth a stop for serious wine tasters. Area winemakers and visitors come to taste wines produced by about a dozen small wineries without tasting rooms of their own. There's no fee for tasting—rather a bargain for wines of this quality—and the extremely knowledgeable staff is happy to pour you a flight of several wines so you can compare, say,

different Cabernet Sauvignons. ⊠ *21023A Geyserville Ave., at Hwy. 128, Geyserville* ☎ *707/857–4900* ⊕ *www.tastelocalwines.com* ☜ *Tasting free* ⊙ *Daily 11–6.*

Fodor's Choice
★

Preston of Dry Creek. The long driveway at this winery, flanked by vineyards and punctuated by the occasional olive tree, winds down to some farmhouses encircling a shady yard with picnic tables. In summer a small selection of organic produce grown in the winery's gardens is sold at an impromptu stand on the front porch, and house-made bread and olive oil are available year-round. Owners Lou and Susan Preston are committed to organic growing techniques and use only estate-grown grapes in their wines, which include Sauvignon Blanc and such Rhône varietals as Syrah and Viognier. The family's down-home style is particularly in evidence on Sunday, the only day of the week that tasting-room staffers sell a 3-liter bottle of Guadagni Red, a primarily Zinfandel blend filled from the barrel right in front of you. ⊠ *9282 W. Dry Creek Rd., at Hartsock Rd. No. 1, Healdsburg* ☎ *707/433–3372* ⊕ *www. prestonvineyards.com* ☜ *Tasting $10* ⊙ *Daily 11–4:30.*

Fodor's Choice
★

Ridge Vineyards. Ridge stands tall among California wineries, and not merely because one of its 1971 Cabernet Sauvignons placed first in a 2006 re-creation of the 1976 Judgment of Paris tasting. The winery built its reputation on Cabernet Sauvignons, Zinfandels, and Chardonnays of unusual depth and complexity, but you'll also find blends of Rhône varietals. Although Ridge makes wines using grapes from several California locales—including Dry Creek Valley, Sonoma Valley, Napa Valley, and Paso Robles—the focus is on single-vineyard estate wines such as the exquisitely textured Lytton Springs Zinfandel blend from grapes grown near the tasting room. The $20 tasting option includes a pour of the top-of-the-line Monte Bello Cabernet Sauvignon blend from grapes grown in the Santa Cruz Mountains. ■ **TIP→** Before or after you taste, pause at the picnic tables outside to appreciate the rolling vineyard hills. ⊠ *650 Lytton Springs Rd., off U.S. 101, Healdsburg* ☎ *707/433–7721* ⊕ *www.ridgewine.com* ☜ *Tastings $5–$20, tour $30* ⊙ *Daily 11–4.*

WHERE TO EAT

$$
ITALIAN
Fodor's Choice
★

✕ **Diavola Pizzeria & Salumeria.** A cozy dining room with hardwood floors, a pressed-tin ceiling, and exposed-brick walls seems a fitting setting for the rustic cuisine at this Geyserville charmer. Chef Dino Bugica studied with several artisans in Italy before opening this spot, which specializes in pizzas pulled from a wood-burning oven and several types of house-cured meats. A small selection of salads and meaty main courses round out the menu. If you're impressed by the antipasto plate, stop by the deli case on your way out and pick up some smoked pork belly, pancetta, or spicy Calabrese sausage to take home. ⑤ *Average main: $19* ⊠ *21021 Geyserville Ave., at Hwy. 128, Geyserville* ☎ *707/814–0111* ⊕ *www.diavolapizzeria.com* ⌔ *Reservations not accepted.*

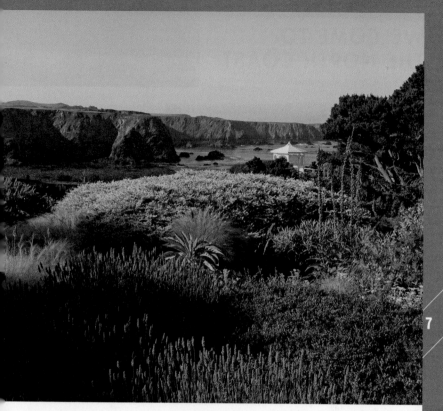

THE NORTH COAST

From the Sonoma Coast to
Redwood National Park

WELCOME TO THE NORTH COAST

TOP REASONS TO GO

★ **Scenic coastal drives:** There's hardly a road here that *isn't* scenic.

★ **Wild beaches:** This stretch of California is one of nature's masterpieces. Revel in the unbridled, rugged coastline, without a building in sight.

★ **Dinnertime:** When you're done hiking the beach, refuel with delectable food; you'll find everything from burritos to bouillabaisse.

★ **Romance:** Here you can end almost every day with a perfect sunset.

★ **Wildlife:** Sea lions and otters and deer, oh my!

1 The Sonoma Coast. As you enter Sonoma County from the south on Highway 1, you pass first through gently rolling pastureland. North of Bodega Bay dramatic shoreline scenery takes over. The road snakes up, down, and around sheer cliffs and steep inclines—some without guardrails—where cows seem to cling precariously. Stunning vistas (or cottony fog) and hairpin turns make for an exhilarating drive.

2 The Mendocino Coast. The timber industry gave birth to most of the small towns along this stretch of coastline. Although tourism now drives the economy, the region has retained much of its old-fashioned charm. The beauty of the landscape, of course, has not changed.

3 Redwood Country. There's a different state of mind in Humboldt County. Here, instead of spas, there are old-time hotels. Instead of wineries, there are breweries. The landscape is primarily thick redwood forest, which gets snow in winter and sizzles in summer while the coast sits covered in fog. Until as late as 1924, there was no road north of Willits; the coastal towns were reachable only by sea. That legacy is apparent in the communities of today: Eureka and Arcata, both former ports, are sizeable, but otherwise towns are tiny and nestled in the woods, and people have an independent spirit that recalls the original homesteaders. Coming from the south, Garberville is a good place to stop for picnic provisions and stretch your legs.

4 Redwood National and State Parks. For a pristine encounter with giant redwoods, make the trek to these coastal parks where even casual visitors have easy access to the trees. *(See Chapter 8, Redwood National Park.)*

GETTING ORIENTED

It's all but impossible to explore the Northern California coast without a car. Indeed, you wouldn't want to—driving here is half the fun. The main road is Highway 1, two lanes that twist and turn (sometimes 180 degrees) up cliffs and down through valleys. Towns appear every so often, but this is mostly a land of green pasture, dense forest, and natural, undeveloped coastline. ■TIP→ Pace yourself: Most drivers stop frequently to appreciate the views (and you can't drive faster than 20–40 mph on many portions of the highway), so don't plan to drive too far in one day.

7

Smith River
199
Point St. George
Crescent City
101
Klamath
96
Redwoods National & State Parks **4**
Orick

SISKIYOU MOUNTAINS

KLAMATH MOUNTAINS

Patrick's Point
Trinidad
McKinleyville
96
Willow Creek
Arcata Bay **3** Arcata
299
Humboldt Bay Eureka
Fortuna
Ferndale
Cape Mendocino
Rio Dell
36
Hayfork
Point Gorda
Humboldt Redwoods State Park

COAST RANGE

KING MTN RANGE

Garberville
Richardson Grove State Park
Leggett
Laytonville

101
Fort Bragg
20
Willits
Mendocino
Little River
Albion
128
2 Elk
Ukiah
20
Lucerne
Point Arena
Point Arena
Kelseyville
Clearlake
Lower Lake
Gualala
Cloverdale
Stewarts Point **1**
Healdsburg
Calistoga
Jenner
101
Saint Helena
Occidental
Santa Rosa
Sebastopol
Bodega Bay
29
Peraluma
Napa
Sonoma
Inverness
Novato
Vallejo
Point Reyes National Seashore
1
Richmond
80
Concord
Bolinas
Berkeley
Marin Headlands
San Francisco **Oakland**
Daly City

ANDERSON VALLEY
Pacific Coast Hwy

PACIFIC OCEAN

0   30 mi
0   30 km

Updated by Christine Vovakes

The spectacular coastline between Marin County and the Oregon border defies expectations. The landscape is defined by the Pacific Ocean, but instead of boardwalks and bikinis there are ragged cliffs and pounding waves — and the sunbathers are mostly sea lions.

Instead of strip malls and freeways, there are small towns that retire around sundown and a single-lane road that follows the fickle shoreline. And that's exactly why many Californians, especially those from the Bay Area, come here to escape the agitations of daily life.

This stretch of Highway 1 is made up of numerous little worlds, each different from the next. From Point Reyes toward Bodega Bay, the land spreads out into green, rolling pastures and sandy beaches. The road climbs higher and higher as it heads north through Sonoma County, and in Mendocino County the coastline follows the ins and outs of lush valleys where rivers pour down from the forests and into the ocean. At Humboldt County the highway heads inland to the redwoods, then returns to the shoreline at the tidal flats surrounding the ports of Eureka and Arcata. Heading north to the Oregon border, the coast is increasingly wild and lined with redwood trees.

Although the towns along the way vary from deluxe spa retreat to hippie hideaway, all are reliably sleepy. Most communities have fewer than 1,000 inhabitants, with main streets shuttered by 9 pm. Exceptions are Mendocino and Eureka, but even they are loved best by those who would rather cozy up in bed than paint the town.

PLANNING

WHEN TO GO

The North Coast is a year-round destination, though when you go determines what you will see. The migration of the Pacific gray whales is a wintertime phenomenon, which lasts roughly from mid-December to early April. Wildflowers follow the winter rain, as early as January in southern areas through June and July farther north. Summer is the high season for tourists, but spring, fall, and even winter are arguably better times to visit when the pace is slower, towns are quieter, and lodging is cheaper.

The coastal climate is similar to San Francisco's, although winter nights are colder than in the city. In July and August thick fog can drop temperatures to the high 50s, but fear not! You need only drive inland to find temperatures that are often 20 degrees higher.

GETTING HERE AND AROUND

AIR TRAVEL

The only North Coast airport with commercial air service, Arcata/Eureka Airport (ACV) receives United Express flights. The airport is in McKinleyville, which is 16 miles from Eureka. A taxi to Eureka costs about $50 and takes roughly 25 minutes. Door-to-door airport shuttles cost $20 to Arcata and Trinidad, $24 to Eureka, and $50 to Ferndale. All prices are for the first person, and go up $5 for each additional person.

Airport Contact Arcata/Eureka Airport ⊠ *3561 Boeing Ave., McKinleyville* ☎ *707/839-5401.*

Shuttle Contact Door to Door Airport Shuttle ☎ *888/338-5497, 707/839-4186* ⊕ *www.doortodoorairporter.com.*

BUS TRAVEL

Greyhound buses travel along U.S. 101 from San Francisco to Garberville, Eureka, and Arcata. Humboldt Transit Authority connects Eureka, Arcata, and Trinidad.

Bus Contacts Greyhound ☎ *800/231-2222* ⊕ *www.greyhound.com.*
Humboldt Transit Authority ☎ *707/443-0826* ⊕ *www.hta.org.*

CAR TRAVEL

Although there are excellent services along U.S. 101, long stretches separate towns along Highway 1, and services are even fewer and farther between on the smaller roads. ■TIP→ **If you're running low on fuel and see a gas station, stop for a refill.** Twisting Highway 1 is the scenic route to Mendocino from San Francisco, but the fastest one is U.S. 101 north to Highway 128 west (from Cloverdale) to Highway 1 north. The quickest route to the far North Coast is a straight shot up U.S. 101, which runs inland until Eureka. Weather sometimes forces closure of parts of Highway 1, but it's rare.

Road Conditions Caltrans ☎ *800/427-7623* ⊕ *www.dot.ca.gov.*

HEALTH AND SAFETY

In an emergency, dial 911. Bigger towns along the coast have hospitals, but for major medical emergencies you will need to go to Santa Rosa or San Francisco. Note that cell phone reception is poor along large swaths of the North Coast.

RESTAURANTS

A few restaurants with national reputations, plus several more of regional note, entice palates on the North Coast. Even workaday spots take advantage of the abundant fresh seafood and locally grown vegetables and herbs. Attire is usually informal, though at pricier establishments dressy casual is the norm. Most kitchens close at 8 or 8:30 and few places serve past 9:30. Many restaurants close for a winter break in January or early February. *Prices in the reviews are the average cost of a main course at dinner or, if dinner is not served, at lunch.*

HOTELS

Restored Victorians, rustic lodges, country inns, and vintage motels are among the accommodations available here. Few have air-conditioning (the ocean breezes make it unnecessary), and many have no phones or TVs in the rooms. Although several towns have only one or two places to spend the night, some of these lodgings are destinations in themselves. Budget accommodations are rare, but in winter you're likely to find reduced rates and nearly empty inns and B&Bs. In summer and on the weekends, though, make bed-and-breakfast reservations as far ahead as possible—rooms at the best inns often sell out months in advance. *Prices in the reviews are the lowest cost of a standard double room in high season. For expanded reviews, facilities, and current deals, visit Fodors.com.*

VISITOR INFORMATION

Contacts Humboldt County Convention and Visitors Bureau ✉ *1034 2nd St., Eureka* ☎ *707/443–5097, 800/346–3482* ⊕ *www.redwoods.info.* **Mendocino Coast Chamber of Commerce** ✉ *217 S. Main St., Fort Bragg* ☎ *707/961–6300* ⊕ *www.mendocinocoast.com.* **Redwood Coast Chamber: Sonoma to Mendocino** ☎ *707/884–1080, 800/778–5252* ⊕ *www.redwoodcoastchamber. com.* **Sonoma County Tourism** ☎ *707/522–5800, 800/576–6662* ⊕ *www. sonomacounty.com.* **Visit Mendocino County** ✉ *345 N. Franklin St., Ft. Bragg* ☎ *707/964–9010, 866/466–3636* ⊕ *www.visitmendocino.com.*

THE SONOMA COAST

BODEGA BAY

23 miles west of Santa Rosa.

From the busy harbor here, commercial boats pursue fish and Dungeness crab. There's nothing quaint about this working town without a center—it's just a string of businesses along several miles of Highway 1. But some tourists still come to see where Alfred Hitchcock shot *The Birds* in 1962. The Tides Wharf complex, an important location used for the movie, has been expanded and remodeled several times and is no longer recognizable. But a few miles inland, in Bodega, you can find Potter Schoolhouse, which is now a private residence.

GETTING HERE AND AROUND

To reach Bodega Bay, exit U.S. 101 at Santa Rosa and take Highway 12 west (it's called Bodega Highway west of Sebastopol) 23 miles to the coast. A scenic alternative is to take U.S. 101's East Washington Street/Central Petaluma exit and follow signs west to Bodega Bay; just after you merge onto Highway 1, you'll pass through down-home Valley Ford. Mendocino Transit Authority (⊕ *www.mendocinotransit.org*) Route 95 buses connect Bodega Bay with coastal towns and Santa Rosa.

BEACHES

Fodor's Choice
★
Sonoma Coast State Park. The park's gorgeous sandy coves stretch for 17 miles from Bodega Head to 4 miles north of Jenner. **Bodega Head** is an especially popular perch for whale watchers, though if you're lucky you'll catch sight of migrating whales from any of the beaches. **Rock Point, Duncan's Landing,** and **Wright's Beach,** clustered at about the halfway mark, have picnic areas, as do several other spots. Rogue waves have swept people off the rocks at Duncan's Landing, so don't stray past signs warning you away. Relatively calmer **Shell Beach,** about 2 miles north, is known for beachcombing, tidepooling, and fishing. About 2½ miles north of Shell Beach, near the mouth of the Russian River at Jenner, a long road leads from the highway to **Goat Rock.** Harbor seals lounge at the long beach here; pupping season is from March through June. Bring binoculars and walk north from the parking lot to view the seals. During summer lifeguards are on duty at Goat Rock and other beaches, but strong rip currents and heavy surf keep most would-be swimmers on shore. Wright's Beach and Bodega Dunes have developed campsites. **Amenities:** parking; toilets. **Best for:** solitude; sunset; walking. ⊠ *Park Headquarters/Salmon Creek Ranger Station, 3095 Hwy. 1, 2 miles north of Bodega Bay* ☎ *707/865–2391* ⊕ *www. parks.gov* ⊠ *$8 per vehicle* ⊙ *Daily 8 am–sunset (some beach hrs may be curtailed because of budget cuts).*

WHERE TO EAT AND STAY

For expanded reviews, facilities, and current deals, visit Fodors.com.

$$
SEAFOOD
✕ **Sandpiper Restaurant.** A local favorite for breakfast, this friendly café on the marina does a good job for a fair price. Peruse the board for the day's fresh catch or order a menu regular such as crab stew or steak and prawns; clam chowder is the house specialty. $ *Average main: $22* ⊠ *1400 N. Hwy. 1* ☎ *707/875–2278* ⊕ *www.sandpiperrestaurant.com.*

$$$$
HOTEL
🏨 **Bodega Bay Lodge.** Looking out to the ocean across a wetland, a group of shingle-and-river-rock buildings houses Bodega Bay's finest accommodations. **Pros:** pampering; ocean views. **Cons:** on the highway. $ *Rooms from: $309* ⊠ *103 Coast Hwy. 1* ☎ *707/875–3525, 888/875–2250* ⊕ *www.bodegabaylodge.com* ⬩ *78 rooms, 5 suites* ⦿ *No meals.*

$
HOTEL
🏨 **Bodega Harbor Inn.** As humble as can be, this is one of the few places on this stretch of the coast with rooms for less than $100 a night. **Pros:** budget choice; rooms for larger groups. **Cons:** uninspired decor; less-than-scenic setting. $ *Rooms from: $80* ⊠ *1345 Bodega Ave.* ☎ *707/875–3594* ⊕ *www.bodegaharborinn.com* ⬩ *14 rooms, 2 suites* ⦿ *No meals.*

SPORTS AND THE OUTDOORS

GOLF

The Links at Bodega Harbour. Robert Trent Jones II designed this Scottish-style, incredibly scenic, and fairly challenging 18-hole oceanfront course. Rates include a golf cart. ⊠ *21301 Heron Dr.* ☎ *707/875–3538, 866/905–4657* ⊕ *www.bodegaharbourgolf.com* ⬩ *18 holes. 6,290 yds. Par 70. Slope 129. Greens fees: $60/$90* ☞ *Facilities: Putting green, pitching area, golf carts, pull carts, rental clubs, pro shop, golf lessons, restaurant, bar.*

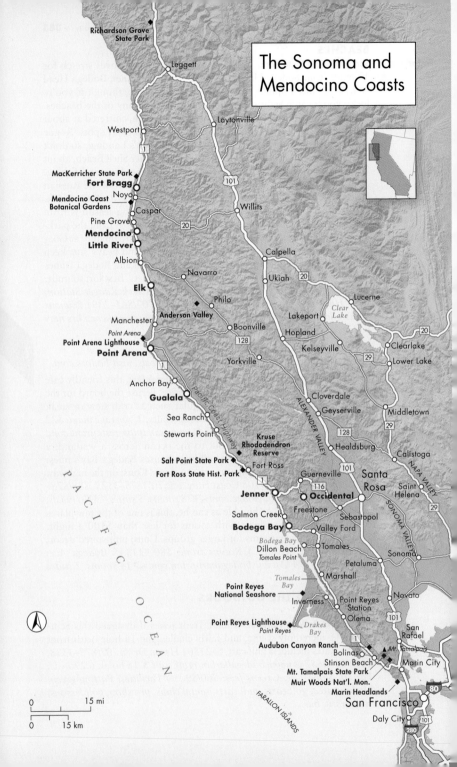

The Sonoma and Mendocino Coasts

Richardson Grove State Park
Leggett
Laytonville
Westport
MacKerricher State Park
Fort Bragg
Noyo
Mendocino Coast Botanical Gardens
Caspar
Pine Grove
Mendocino
Little River
Albion
Willits
101
20
Calpella
Ukiah
20
Elk
Navarro
Philo
Anderson Valley
Manchester
Point Arena
Point Arena Lighthouse
Point Arena
1
Boonville
128
Yorkville
Lucerne
Clear Lake
Lakeport
Hopland
Kelseyville
29
Clearlake
Lower Lake
20
Anchor Bay
Gualala
Sea Ranch
Stewarts Point
Pacific Coast Highway
Kruse Rhododendron Reserve
Salt Point State Park
Fort Ross State Hist. Park
Fort Ross
Jenner
Guerneville
116
Occidental
Freestone
Cloverdale
Geyserville
128
ALEXANDER VALLEY
Healdsburg
Middletown
29
Calistoga
Santa Rosa
Saint Helena
NAPA VALLEY
Salmon Creek
Bodega Bay
Valley Ford
Sebastopol
SONOMA VALLEY
29
Bodega Bay
Dillon Beach
Tomales Point
Tomales
Petaluma
Sonoma
Tomales Bay
Marshall
Point Reyes National Seashore
Inverness
Point Reyes Station
Novato
Point Reyes Lighthouse
Point Reyes
Olema
101
Drakes Bay
San Rafael
Audubon Canyon Ranch
Bolinas
Stinson Beach
Mt. Tamalpais State Park
Muir Woods Nat'l. Mon.
Marin Headlands
1
Mt. Tamalpais
Marin City
80
San Francisco
FARALLON ISLANDS
Daly City
280
101

PACIFIC OCEAN

0   15 mi
0   15 km

HORSEBACK RIDING

Horse N Around Trail Rides. Saddle up at this ranch for guided horseback trail rides, some along the beach. Reservations are required. ✉ *2660 N. Hwy. 1* ☎ *707/875–8849* ⊕ *www.horsenaroundtrailrides.com.*

WHALE-WATCHING

Bodega Bay Sportfishing. This outfitter charters ocean-fishing boats, rents equipment, and conducts whale-watching trips from midwinter through spring. ✉ *1410 B Bay Flat Rd.* ☎ *707/875–3344* ⊕ *www. bodegabaysportfishing.com.*

OCCIDENTAL

14 miles northeast of Bodega Bay.

A village surrounded by redwood forests, orchards, and vineyards, Occidental is a former logging hub with a bohemian vibe. The 19th-century downtown offers a top-notch B&B, good food, and a handful of art galleries and boutiques. The neighboring town of Freestone offers some of the same, but on a smaller scale.

GETTING HERE AND AROUND

To reach Occidental, take Highway 12 (Bodega Highway) east 5 miles from Highway 1. Take a left onto Bohemian Highway, where you'll find Freestone; after another 3½ miles you'll be in Occidental. From U.S. 101 north or south take Highway 12 west from Santa Rosa about 13 miles, then head north on Bohemian Highway about 3½ miles to the village.

EXPLORING

Fodor's Choice ★ **Joseph Phelps Vineyards.** Although an appointment is required for tastings at the winery started by the legendary Joseph Phelps—his son Bill now runs the operation—it's well worth the effort. In fair weather, the casual, self-paced wine tastings are held on the terrace of a modern barnlike building with stunning views down the slopes over oak trees and orderly vines. Phelps makes fine whites, but the blockbuster wines are reds, particularly the Cabernet Sauvignon and the flagship Bordeaux-style blend called Insignia. The luscious-yet-subtle Insignia sells for more than $200 a bottle. Luckily, all tastings include the current vintage. The 90-minute seminars include one on wine-and-cheese pairing and another focusing on blending (both $75). In the latter you mix the various varietals that go into the Insignia blend. ✉ *200 Taplin Rd., off Silverado Trail* ☎ *707/963–2745, 800/707–5789* ⊕ *www. josephphelps.com* ✍ *Tastings $35–$75, seminars $75–$150* ⊘ *Weekdays 9–5, weekends 10–4; tastings by appointment.*

Occidental Center for the Arts. The center hosts films, art shows, and classes, along with nine concerts presented by the Redwood Arts Council that feature world-class musicians. ✉ *3850 Doris Murphy Ct., off Bohemian Hwy.* ☎ *707/874–1124* ⊕ *www.redwoodarts.org.*

SPA

Osmosis Day Spa Sanctuary. The signature treatment at this locally popular spa is a traditional Japanese detoxifying bath. You'll slip into a deep redwood tub filled with damp cedar shavings and rice bran that are naturally heated to 140° F by the action of enzymes. Attendants bury you up to the neck and throughout the 20-minute session bring sips of water and place cool cloths on your forehead. After a shower, you can lie down and listen to brain-balancing music through headphones or have a massage, perhaps in one of the creek-side pagodas. Facials and other treatments are also available. Reservations are recommended. ⊠ *209 Bohemian Hwy., Freestone* ☎ *707/823–8231* ⊕ *www.osmosis. com* ✉ *Treatments $75–$200* ◷ *Daily 9–8.*

WHERE TO EAT AND STAY

For expanded reviews, facilities, and current deals, visit Fodors.com.

$
BAKERY

✕ **Wild Flour Bread.** The sticky buns at Wild Flour are legendary in western Sonoma, as are the mouthwatering rye bread and sock-it-to-me scones in flavors like double chocolate, espresso, and hazelnut. There's a long table inside, but most people enjoy their baked goods on the benches outside. ■ **TIP→ On weekends after 1 pm, the most popular items start running out.** ⑤ *Average main: $5* ⊠ *140 Bohemian Hwy., at El Camino Bodega, Freestone* ☎ *707/874–2938* ⊕ *www.wildflourbread. com* ⊟ *No credit cards* ◷ *Closed Tues.–Thurs. No dinner.*

$$$
B&B/INN

▦ **The Inn at Occidental.** Quilts, folk art, and original paintings and photographs fill this colorful and friendly inn. **Pros:** colorful; luxurious; friendly. **Cons:** not for those with minimalist tastes; not for kids. ⑤ *Rooms from: $239* ⊠ *3657 Church St.* ☎ *707/874–1047, 800/522–6324* ⊕ *www.innatoccidental.com* ⇄ *13 rooms, 3 suites, 1 cottage* ⏀ *Breakfast.*

FORT ROSS STATE HISTORIC PARK

22 miles north of Bodega Bay.

GETTING HERE AND AROUND

From Santa Rosa, head west on Highway 116 about 31 miles to Jenner, then north 12 miles on Highway 1 to the park entrance. The Mendocino Transit Authority (⊕ *www.mendocinotransit.org*) Route 95 bus provides service between Fort Ross and other coastal towns.

EXPLORING

FAMILY

Fort Ross State Historic Park. Established in 1812, Fort Ross became Russia's major outpost in California, meant to produce crops and other supplies for northerly fur-trading operations. The Russians brought Aleut sea-otter hunters down from Alaska. By 1841 the area was depleted of seals and otters, and the Russians sold their post to John Sutter, later of gold-rush fame. After a local Anglo rebellion against the Mexicans, the land fell under U.S. domain, becoming part of California in 1850. The state park service has reconstructed Fort Ross, including its Russian Orthodox chapel, a redwood stockade, the officers' barracks, and a blockhouse. The excellent museum here documents the history of the fort and this part of the North Coast. ⊠ *19005 Hwy. 1* ☎ *707/847–3286* ⊕ *www.parks.ca.gov* ✉ *$8 per vehicle* ◷ *Weekends 10–4:30* ⌇ *No dogs allowed past parking lot and picnic area.*

Surfers check out the waves near Bodega Bay on the Sonoma Coast.

SALT POINT STATE PARK

6 miles north of Fort Ross.

GETTING HERE AND AROUND

Exit U.S. 101 in Santa Rosa and travel west on Highway 116 about 31 miles to Jenner, then north 18 miles on Highway 1 to reach the park. Mendocino Transit Authority (⊕ *www.mendocinotransit.org*) Route 95 buses stop at Salt Point and connect with other North Coast towns.

EXPLORING

Salt Point State Park. For 5 miles, Highway 1 winds through this park, 6,000 acres of forest, meadows, and rocky shoreline. Heading north, the first park entrance (on the right) leads to forest hiking trails and several campgrounds. The next entrance—the park's main road—winds through meadows and along the wave-splashed coastline. This is also the route to the visitor center and Gerstle Cove, a favorite spot for abalone divers and sunbathing seals. Next along the highway is Stump Beach Cove, with picnic tables, toilets, and a ¼-mile walk to the sandy beach. The park's final entrance is at Fisk Mill Cove, where centuries of wind and rain erosion have carved unusual honeycomb patterns in the sandstone called "tafonis." A five-minute walk uphill from the parking lot leads to a dramatic view of Sentinel Rock, an excellent spot for sunsets.

Just up the highway, narrow, unpaved Kruse Ranch Road leads to the **Kruse Rhododendron State Reserve**, where each May thousands of rhododendrons bloom within a quiet forest of redwoods and tan oaks. ⊠ *25050 Hwy. 1* ☎ *707/847–3221, 707/865–2391* ⊕ *www.parks.ca.gov* ⊠ *$8 per vehicle* ☉ *Daily sunrise–sunset; some sections closed in winter, call to check.*

THE MENDOCINO COAST

GUALALA

16 miles north of Salt Point State Park.

This former lumber port on the Gualala River has become a headquarters for exploring the coast. The busiest town on Highway 1 between Bodega Bay and Mendocino, it has all the basic services plus some galleries and gift shops.

GETTING HERE AND AROUND

From San Francisco, take U.S. 101 to the East Washington Street/Central Petaluma exit and follow signs west through Valley Ford (you're on Highway 1 by this point) to Bodega Bay. From there, continue north on Highway 1. From Ukiah, exit U.S. 101 at Highway 253, driving southwest to Boonville/Highway 128. From Boonville, turn west on Mountain View Road, which winds 24 miles to Highway 1; from there, drive south 18½ miles. Mendocino Transit Authority (⊕ *www. mendocinotransit.org*) Routes 75 and 95 buses connect Gualala with coastal and inland towns.

EXPLORING

Gualala Point Regional Park. This park has a long, sandy beach and picnic areas, and is an excellent whale-watching spot from December through April. Along the river, shaded by redwoods, are two dozen campsites. ✉ *42401 Hwy. 1, 1 mile south of Gualala* ☎ *707/785–2377* ⊕ *www. sonoma-county.org/parks/pk_glala.htm* ▧ *$7 per vehicle (day use)* ⊙ *Daily 8 am–sunset.*

WHERE TO EAT AND STAY

For expanded reviews, facilities, and current deals, visit Fodors.com.

$$$$
AMERICAN
✕ **St. Orres.** Resembling a traditional Russian dacha with two onion-dome towers, this intriguing lodge stands on 42 acres of redwood forest and meadow. In one of the towers is a spectacular atrium dining room. Here, locally farmed and foraged ingredients appear in dishes such as garlic flan with black chanterelles and rack of venison medallions with wild huckleberries. The prix-fixe menu ($45) includes soup and salad but no appetizer or dessert (available à la carte). A fine brunch is served on weekends. ⑤ *Average main: $45* ✉ *36601 Hwy. 1, 3 miles north of Gualala* ☎ *707/884–3303* ⊕ *www.saintorres. com* ⌕ *Reservations essential* ⊙ *Closed Tues. and Wed Dec.–May. No lunch weekdays.*

$$$
HOTEL
▦ **Mar Vista Cottages.** The sparkling clean, refurbished 1930s cottages at Mar Vista are intentionally slim on modern gadgetry (no TV, phone, radio, or even a clock) but big on retro charm. **Pros:** charming, peaceful retreat. **Cons:** no other businesses in walking distance. ⑤ *Rooms from: $180* ✉ *35101 S. Hwy 1, 5 miles north of Gualala* ☎ *707/884–3522, 877/855–3522* ⊕ *www.marvistamendocino.com* ⌦ *8 1-bedroom cottages, 4 2-bedroom cottages* ⊙ *No meals.*

$$
HOTEL
▦ **Seacliff on the Bluff.** This motel hugs a bluff overlooking where the Gualala River joins the sea. **Pros:** budget choice; great views. **Cons:** less-than-scenic setting. ⑤ *Rooms from: $140* ✉ *39140 S. Hwy. 1*

☏ 707/884–1213, 800/400–5053 ⊕ *www.seacliffmotel.com* ⇆ *16 rooms* ⦿ *No meals.*

POINT ARENA

14 miles north of Gualala.

Occupied by an eclectic mix of long-time locals and long-haired surfers, this former timber town on Highway 1 is part New Age, part rowdy—and always laid-back. The one road going west out of downtown will lead you to the harbor, where fishing boats unload sea urchins and salmon and there's almost always someone riding the waves.

GETTING HERE AND AROUND

To reach Point Arena from Santa Rosa, drive north on U.S. 101, exit at Cloverdale, and follow Highway 128 northwest 28 miles to Boonville. From Boonville take winding Mountain View Road west 25 miles to Highway 1. Point Arena is 4 miles south. From points north, exit U.S. 101 at Ukiah, take Highway 253 southwest to Boonville and follow Mountain View Road west to Highway 1 south. Mendocino Transit Authority (⊕ *www.mendocinotransit.org*) Routes 75 and 95 buses stop in Point Arena.

EXPLORING

Point Arena Lighthouse. For an outstanding view of the ocean and, in winter, migrating whales, take the marked road off Highway 1 north of town to the 115-foot lighthouse. It's possible to stay out here, in one of four rental units ($$), all of which have full kitchens. (On weekends there's a two-night minimum.) ⊠ *45500 Lighthouse Rd., off Hwy. 1* ☏ *707/882–2809, 877/725–4448* ⊕ *www.pointarenalighthouse.com* ⛴ *Tour $7.50* ☉ *Late May–early Sept. daily 10–4:30, early Sept.–late May daily 10–3:30.*

BEACHES

Manchester State Park. Before slipping into the sea, the northernmost segment of the San Andreas Fault cuts through this park beloved by locals for its 5 miles of sandy, usually empty shoreline and trails that wind through dunes and wetlands. Hiking, bird-watching, and beach strolling are the popular activities here. There's steelhead fishing most of the year at Brush and Alder creeks, and beautiful coastal wildflowers bloom in early spring. Tundra swans overwinter in this area, and migrating whales are often spotted close to shore. Swimming and water sports are too dangerous because of the strong undertow. Dogs are not allowed on the beach. **Amenities:** parking. **Best for:** solitude; sunset; walking. ⊠ *Park entrance, 44500 Kinney La., off Hwy. 1, ½ mile north of Manchester, Manchester* ☏ *707/937–5804* ⊕ *www.parks.ca.gov* ☉ *Hrs vary, contact park for details.*

WHERE TO EAT

$ ✕ **Arena Market and Café.** The simple café at this all-organic grocery store
CAFÉ serves up hot soups and fine sandwiches and has an ample salad bar. The market, which specializes in food from local farms, sells cheese, bread, and other picnic items. ⑤ *Average main: $7* ⊠ *185 Main St.* ☏ *707/882–3663* ⊕ *www.arenaorganics.org* ☉ *No dinner.*

7

$
CAFÉ
✕ **Franny's Cup and Saucer.** Aided by her mother, Barbara, a former pastry chef at Chez Panisse, Franny turns out baked goods that are sophisticated and inventive. Take the coffee crunch cake: vanilla chiffon cake layered with coffee whipped cream, topped with chocolate ganache and puffs of coffee caramel "seafoam." More familiar options at this delightful spot include berry tarts and a strawberry-apricot crisp, plus a mouth-watering assortment of cookies, candy, jams, and jellies. $ *Average main: $5* ⊠ *213 Main St.* ☏ *707/882–2500* ⊕ *www.frannyscupandsaucer.com* ▭ *No credit cards* ◷ *Closed Sun.–Tues. No dinner.*

ELK

33 miles north of Gualala.

This quiet town is arranged on the cliff above Greenwood Cove, and just about every spot has a view of the rocky coastline and stunning Pacific sunsets. A few restaurants and inns do business here, but aside from strolling the beach there's little to occupy visitors. Families generally don't stay in Elk, perhaps because it's such a romantic place.

GETTING HERE AND AROUND

To reach Elk from the south, exit U.S. 101 in Cloverdale and follow Highway 128 northwest 29 miles to Highway 1, then drive south 6 miles. From Eureka and other points north, exit U.S. 101 at Leggett and follow Highway 1 south. Mendocino Transit Authority (⊕ *www.mendocinotransit. org*) Route 75 buses serve Elk from other coastal towns.

WHERE TO EAT AND STAY

For expanded reviews, facilities, and current deals, visit Fodors.com.

$
AMERICAN
✕ **Queenie's Roadhouse Cafe.** Locals usually occupy the chrome-and-patent-leather diner-style chairs here at this favorite spot for big breakfasts (served all day) and casual lunches (superb cheeseburgers). The wide windows provide a view of the Pacific to go with your coffee. If the day's sunny, grab one of the two picnic tables out front. $ *Average main: $12* ⊠ *6061 S. Hwy. 1* ☏ *707/877–3285* ⊕ *www.queeniesroadhousecafe. com* ◷ *Closed Tues. and Wed. Closed Jan. No dinner.*

$$
B&B/INN
🏨 **Elk Cove Inn & Spa.** Perched on a bluff above pounding surf and a driftwood-strewn beach, this property has stunning views from most rooms. **Pros:** steps to the beach; gorgeous views; great breakfast. **Cons:** rooms in main house are smallish and within earshot of common TV. $ *Rooms from: $135* ⊠ *6300 S. Hwy. 1* ☏ *707/877–3321, 800/275–2967* ⊕ *www.elkcoveinn.com* ↝ *7 rooms, 4 suites, 4 cottages* ⑩ *Breakfast.*

$$$$
B&B/INN
🏨 **Harbor House.** Constructed in 1916, this redwood Craftsman-style house is as elegant as its location is rugged. **Pros:** luxurious; romantic. **Cons:** not a place for kids. $ *Rooms from: $315* ⊠ *5600 S. Hwy. 1* ☏ *707/877–3203, 800/720–7474* ⊕ *www.theharborhouseinn.com* ↝ *6 rooms, 4 cottages* ⑩ *Some meals.*

ANDERSON VALLEY

28 miles east of Elk.

At the town of Albion, Highway 128 leads southeast into the Anderson Valley, where warm summer weather lures those weary of the persistent coastal fog. Most of the first 13 miles wind through redwood forest along the Navarro River, then the road opens up to reveal farms and vineyards. While the community here is anchored in ranching, in the past few decades a progressive, gourmet-minded counterculture has taken root and that is what defines most visitors' experiences. In the towns of Philo and Boonville you'll find B&Bs with classic Victorian style as well as small eateries.

Anderson Valley is best known to outsiders for its wineries. Tasting rooms here are more low-key than their counterparts in Napa; most are in farmhouses, and you're as likely to hear reggae as classical music as you sip. That said, Anderson Valley wineries produce world-class wines, particularly Pinot Noirs and Gewürztraminers, whose grapes thrive in the moderate coastal climate. Many wineries straddle Highway 128, mostly in Navarro and Philo with a few east of Boonville.

GETTING HERE AND AROUND

From the coast, pick up Highway 128 at Albion. From inland points south, take Highway 128 northwest from U.S. 101 at Cloverdale. From inland points north, exit U.S. 101 in Ukiah and take Highway 253 southwest 17 miles to Boonville. Mendocino Transit Authority (⊕ *www.mendocinotransit.org*) Route 75 buses serve the Anderson Valley between the coast and Ukiah.

EXPLORING
TOP ATTRACTIONS

Goldeneye Winery. The Napa Valley's well-respected Duckhorn Wine Company makes stellar Pinot Noirs here from local grapes, along with a Gewürztraminer, a Pinot Gris, and a blush Vin Gris of Pinot Noir. Leisurely tastings take place in either a restored farmhouse or on a patio with vineyard and redwood views. ⊠ *9200 Hwy. 128, Philo* ☎ *800/208–0438* ⊕ *www.goldeneyewinery.com* ⊑ *Tastings $10–$30* ⊙ *Daily 10:30–4:30.*

Handley Cellars. International folk art collected by winemaker Milla Handley adorns the tasting room at this Anderson Valley pioneer whose lightly oaked Chardonnays and Pinot Noirs earn high praise from wine critics. The winery, which has a picnic area, also makes Gewürztraminer, Pinot Gris, Riesling, and very good sparkling wines. ⊠ *3151 Hwy. 128, Philo* ☎ *707/895–3876* ⊕ *www.handleycellars.com* ⊑ *Tasting free* ⊙ *May–Oct., daily 10–6, Nov.–Apr., daily 10–5.*

Navarro River Redwoods State Park. Described by locals as the "11-mile-long redwood tunnel to the sea," this park that straddles Highway 128 is great for walks amid second-growth redwoods and for summer swimming in the gentle Navarro River. There's also fishing, canoeing, and kayaking in the late winter and spring, when the river is higher. The two campgrounds (one on the river "beach") are quiet and clean. ⊠ *Hwy. 128, 2 miles east of Hwy. 1, Navarro* ☎ *707/937–5804* ⊕ *www.parks.ca.gov.*

Navarro Vineyards. A visit to this family-run winery is a classic Anderson Valley experience. Make time if you can for a vineyard tour—the guides draw from years of hands-on experience to explain every aspect of production, from sustainable farming techniques to the choices made in aging and blending. Best known for Alsatian varietals such as Gewürztraminer and Riesling, Navarro also makes Chardonnay, Pinot Noir, and other wines. The tasting room sells cheese and charcuterie for picnickers. ⊠ *5601 Hwy. 128, Philo* ☎ *707/895–3686* ⊕ *www. navarrowine.com* 🍷 *Tasting free* ☉ *Apr.–Oct. daily 9–6; Nov.–Mar. daily 9–5; tour daily at 10:30 and 3 by appointment.*

Roederer Estate. The Anderson Valley is particularly hospitable to Pinot Noir and Chardonnay grapes, the two varietals used to create Roederer's well-regarded sparkling wines. The view from the patio here is splendid. ⊠ *4501 Hwy. 128, Philo* ☎ *707/895–2288* ⊕ *www.roedererestate.com* 🍷 *Tasting $6* ☉ *Tasting room daily 11–5.*

WORTH NOTING

Greenwood Ridge Vineyards. White Riesling is the specialty of this winery that also makes Pinot Noir, Syrah, and other wines. You can picnic here at tables on an island in the middle of a pond. ⊠ *5501 Hwy. 128, Philo* ☎ *707/895–2002* ⊕ *www.greenwoodridge.com* 🍷 *Tasting $5* ☉ *Daily 10–5.*

Husch Vineyards. Anderson Valley's oldest winery, known for white wines and its reasonably priced Pinot Noir, has a cozy tasting room next to sheep pastures and picnic tables under a grapevine-covered arbor. ⊠ *4400 Hwy. 128, Philo* ☎ *800/554–8724* ⊕ *www.huschvineyards.com* 🍷 *Tasting free* ☉ *Daily 10–5.*

WHERE TO EAT AND STAY

For expanded reviews, facilities, and current deals, visit Fodors.com.

$
CAFÉ ✕ **The Boonville General Store.** The café menu here is nothing surprising, but the exacting attention paid to ingredients elevates each dish above the ordinary. Sandwiches are served on fresh-baked bread, and the beet salad comes with roasted pecans and local blue cheese. Breakfast options include granola and pastries, made in-house. ⑤ *Average main: $10* ⊠ *14077A Hwy. 128, Boonville* ☎ *707/895–9477* ☉ *No dinner.*

$$$$
AMERICAN
Fodors Choice
★ ✕ **Table 128.** The restaurant at the Boonville Hotel takes small-town dining into the 21st century. Proprietor Johnny Schmitt and his kitchen staff prepare one prix-fixe meal per night ($40 for three courses, $50 for four) and serve it family-style, with platters of food brought to the table to be shared. Expect an expertly grilled or roasted meat (such as pork chops or flank steak), a sophisticated side dish (radicchio with polenta; heirloom-bean ragout with salsa verde), and don't forget dessert (linzer torte with Chantilly cream; panna cotta with fresh berries). This is essentially home cooking done at a high level, and despite the limited menu—posted a few days in advance on the restaurant's website—most diners will leave satisfied. ⑤ *Average main: $40* ⊠ *14050 Hwy. 128, Boonville* ☎ *707/895–2210* ⊕ *www.boonvillehotel.com* ☉ *No lunch; closed Mon.–Thurs. Nov.–Apr; closed Tues. and Wed. May–mid-June; closed Tues. mid-June–mid-Oct.*

You'll find excellent vintages and great places to taste wine in the Anderson Valley—but it's much more laid-back than Napa.

$$$ **Boonville Hotel.** From the street this looks like a standard small-town
HOTEL hotel, but once you cross the threshold you start picking up on the laid-back sophistication that makes the entire Anderson Valley so appealing. **Pros:** stylish but homey; building is the town's hub. **Cons:** friendly but straightforward service—don't expect to be pampered; two-night stay required most weekends. $ *Rooms from: $185* ⊠ *14050 Hwy. 128, Boonville* ☎ *707/895–2210* ⊕ *www.boonvillehotel.com* ⤳ *8 rooms, 7 suites* ❍| *Breakfast.*

$$$ **The Philo Apple Farm.** Set in an orchard of organic, heirloom apples,
HOTEL the three cottages and one guest room here are tasteful, spare, and inspired by the surrounding landscape. **Pros:** pretty; quiet; country feel. **Cons:** occasionally hot in summer. $ *Rooms from: $200* ⊠ *18501 Greenwood Rd., Philo* ☎ *707/895–2333* ⊕ *www.philoapplefarm.com* ⤳ *1 room, 3 cottages* ❍| *Breakfast.*

LITTLE RIVER

14 miles north of Elk.

The town of Little River is not much more than a post office and a convenience store; Albion, its neighbor to the south, is even smaller. Along this winding portion of Highway 1 though, you'll find numerous inns and restaurants, all of them quiet and situated to take advantage of the breathtaking ocean views.

GETTING HERE AND AROUND

From inland points south, exit U.S. 101 at Cloverdale and follow Highway 128 northwest about 56 miles to Highway 1, then head north 7 miles. From points north, exit U.S. 101 in Ukiah at Highway 253 and follow it west 17 miles to Boonville, where you'll pick up Highway 128 and drive northwest to Highway 1. Mendocino Transit Authority (⊕ *www.mendocinotransit.org*) Route 60 buses serve the area.

EXPLORING

Van Damme State Park. Best known for its beach, this park is a prime abalone diving spot. Upland trails lead through lush riparian habitat and the bizarre **Pygmy Forest,** where acidic soil and poor drainage have produced mature cypress and pine trees that are no taller than a person. The visitor center has displays on ocean life and the historical significance of the redwood lumber industry along the coast. ⊠ *Little River Park Rd., off Hwy. 1* ☎ *707/937–5804* ⊕ *www.parks.ca.gov.*

WHERE TO EAT AND STAY

For expanded reviews, facilities, and current deals, visit Fodors.com.

$$$
FRENCH
Fodor'sChoice
★

✕ **Ledford House.** The only thing separating this bluff-top wood-and-glass restaurant from the Pacific Ocean is a great view. Entrées evoke the flavors of southern France and include hearty bistro dishes—stews, cassoulets, and pastas—and large portions of grilled meats and freshly caught fish (though the restaurant also is vegetarian-friendly). The long bar, with its unobstructed water view, is a scenic spot for a sunset aperitif. ⑤ *Average main: $24* ⊠ *3000 N. Hwy. 1, Albion* ☎ *707/937–0282* ⊕ *www.ledfordhouse.com* ⊘ *Closed Mon. and Tues. No lunch.*

$$$
B&B/INN

🏨 **Albion River Inn.** Contemporary New England–style cottages at this inn overlook the dramatic bridge and seascape where the Albion River empties into the Pacific. **Pros:** great views; great bathtubs. **Cons:** newer buildings aren't as quaint as they could be. ⑤ *Rooms from: $195* ⊠ *3790 N. Hwy. 1, Albion* ☎ *707/937–1919, 800/479–7944* ⊕ *www.albionriverinn.com* ⮑ *18 rooms, 4 cottages* ⦿ *Breakfast.*

$$
B&B/INN
Fodor'sChoice
★

🏨 **Glendeven Inn.** If Mendocino is the New England village of the West Coast, then Glendeven is the local country manor with sea views. **Pros:** great ocean views; elegant; romantic. **Cons:** not within walking distance of town; on the main drag. ⑤ *Rooms from: $165* ⊠ *8205 N. Hwy. 1* ☎ *707/937–0083, 800/822–4536* ⊕ *www.glendeven.com* ⮑ *6 rooms, 4 suites* ⦿ *Breakfast.*

MENDOCINO

3 miles north of Little River.

Many of Mendocino's original settlers came from the Northeast and built houses in the New England style. Thanks to the logging boom, the town flourished for most of the second half of the 19th century. As the timber industry declined, many residents left, but the town's setting was too beautiful to be ignored. Artists and craftspeople began flocking here in the 1950s, and Elia Kazan chose Mendocino as the backdrop for his 1955 film adaptation of John Steinbeck's *East of Eden,* starring James Dean. As the arts community thrived, restaurants, cafés, and inns sprung up. Today, the small downtown area consists almost entirely of places to eat and shop.

GETTING HERE AND AROUND

From U.S. 101, exit at Cloverdale and follow Highway 128 northwest about 56 miles and Highway 1 north 10 miles. You can also exit at Willits and drive west on Highway 20 about 33 miles to Highway 1, then south 8 miles. Mendocino Transit Authority (⊕ *www.mendocinotransit. org*) Route 60 buses serve the area.

EXPLORING

Ford House. The restored Ford House, built in 1854, serves as the visitor center for Mendocino Headlands State Park and the town. The house has a scale model of Mendocino as it looked in 1890, when it had 34 water towers and a 12-seat public outhouse. From the museum, you can head out on a 3-mile trail across the spectacular seaside cliffs that border the town. ⊠ *735 Main St., west of Lansing St.* ☎ *707/937–5397* ⊕ *www.mendoparks.org* ⊡ *$2* ☉ *Daily 11–4.*

Kelley House Museum. An 1861 structure holds this museum, whose artifacts include Victorian-era furniture and historical photographs of Mendocino coast's logging days. ⊠ *45007 Albion St.* ☎ *707/937–5791* ⊕ *www.kelleyhousemuseum.org* ⊡ *$2* ☉ *June–Sept., Thurs.–Tues. 11–3; Oct.–May, Fri.–Mon. 11–3.*

Mendocino Art Center. The center has an extensive program of workshops, mounts exhibits in its galleries, and is the home of the Mendocino Theatre Company. ⊠ *45200 Little Lake St.* ☎ *707/937–5818, 800/653–3328* ⊕ *www.mendocinoartcenter.org.*

WHERE TO EAT AND STAY

For expanded reviews, facilities, and current deals, visit Fodors.com.

$$$
AMERICAN

✕ **Cafe Beaujolais.** The yellow Victorian cottage that houses this popular restaurant is surrounded by a garden of heirloom and exotic plantings. A commitment to the freshest possible organic and local ingredients guides the chef here. The menu is eclectic and ever-evolving, but often includes free-range fowl, line-caught fish, and Niman Ranch beef. The bakery turns out several delicious varieties of bread from a wood-fired oven. ⑤ *Average main: $29* ⊠ *961 Ukiah St.* ☎ *707/937–5614* ⊕ *www. cafebeaujolais.com* ☉ *No lunch Mon. and Tues.*

$$$$
B&B/INN
Fodor's Choice
★

🏠 **Brewery Gulch Inn.** The feel is modern yet tasteful at this smallish inn— furnishings are redwood and leather, beds are plush, and two rooms have whirlpool tubs with views. **Pros:** stylish; peaceful with ocean views; intimate. **Cons:** must drive to town. ⑤ *Rooms from: $295* ⊠ *9401 N. Hwy. 1, 1 mile south of Mendocino* ☎ *707/937–4752, 800/578–4454* ⊕ *www.brewerygulchinn.com* ⤳ *10 rooms, 1 suite* ⑧ *Breakfast.*

$$$
B&B/INN
🏠 **MacCallum House.** Set on two flower-filled acres in the middle of town, this inn is a perfect mix of Victorian charm and modern luxury. **Pros:** excellent breakfast; great central location. **Cons:** new luxury suites on a separate property are less charming. ⑤ *Rooms from: $199* ⊠ *45020 Albion St.* ☎ *707/937–0289, 800/609–0492* ⊕ *www.maccallumhouse. com* ⤳ *11 rooms, 13 suites, 7 cottages* ⑧ *Breakfast.*

7

NIGHTLIFE AND THE ARTS

Mendocino Theatre Company. The repertoire of this well-established company ranges all over the contemporary map, including works by David Mamet, Arthur Miller, Neil Simon, and local playwrights. ✉ *Mendocino Art Center, 45200 Little Lake St.* ☎ *707/937–4477* ⊕ *www.mendocinotheatre.org.*

SPORTS AND THE OUTDOORS

Catch-A-Canoe and Bicycles Too. Rent kayaks and regular and outrigger canoes here, as well as mountain and suspension bicycles. ✉ *Stanford Inn by the Sea, Comptche-Ukiah Rd., east of Hwy. 1* ☎ *707/937–0273* ⊕ *www.catchacanoe.com.*

FORT BRAGG

10 miles north of Mendocino.

Fort Bragg is a working-class town that many feel is the most authentic place on the coast; it's certainly less expensive than its neighbors to the south. The declining timber industry has been steadily replaced by booming tourism, but the city maintains a local feel since most people who work at the area hotels and restaurants also live here, as do many artists. A stroll down Franklin Street (one block east of Highway 1) takes you past numerous bookstores, antiques shops, and boutiques.

GETTING HERE AND AROUND

From U.S. 101 at Willits follow Highway 20 west about 33 miles to Highway 1 and drive north 2 miles. Mendocino Transit Authority (⊕ *www.mendocinotransit.org*) Route 60 buses serve the town and region.

EXPLORING

Fodor's Choice
★

Mendocino Coast Botanical Gardens. Something beautiful is always abloom in these marvelous gardens. Along 3½ miles of trails, including pathways with ocean views and observation points for whale-watching, lie a splendid profusion of flowers. The rhododendrons are at their peak from April through June; the dahlias begin their spectacular show in August and last until October. Even in winter, the heather and camellias add more than a splash of color. ✉ *18220 N. Hwy. 1, 2 miles south of Fort Bragg* ☎ *707/964–4352* ⊕ *www.gardenbythesea.org* 🏷 *$14* ☺ *Mar.–Oct., daily 9–5; Nov.–Feb., daily 9–4.*

Museum in the Triangle Tattoo Parlor. At the top of a steep staircase, this two-room museum pays homage to Fort Bragg's rough-and-tumble past with memorabilia that includes early 20th-century Burmese tattooing instruments, pictures of astonishing tattoos from around the world, and a small shrine to sword-swallowing sideshow king Captain Don Leslie. ✉ *356-B N. Main St.* ☎ *707/964–8814* ⊕ *www.triangletattoo.com* 🏷 *Free* ☺ *Daily noon–6.*

FAMILY **The Skunk Train.** In the 1920s, a fume-spewing gas-powered train car shuttled passengers along a rail line dating from the logging days of the 1880s. Nicknamed the Skunk Train, it traversed redwood forests inaccessible to automobiles. A reproduction train now travels the same route, making a 3½–4 hour round-trip trek between Fort Bragg and the town of Northspur, 21 miles inland. The schedule varies depending on

The North Coast is famous for its locally caught Dungeness crab; be sure to try some during your visit.

the season and in summer includes evening barbecue excursions and wine parties. ⊠ *Foot of Laurel St., west of Main St.* ☎ *707/964–6371, 866/457–5865* ⊕ *www.skunktrain.com* ✉ *$49–$70.*

BEACHES

Glass Beach. The ocean isn't visible from most of Fort Bragg, but a gravel path on Elm Street three blocks west of Main Street leads to wild coastline where you can walk for miles along the bluffs. The sandy coves nearest the road are called Glass Beach because here lies more sea glass than you've likely ever seen in one place (this area formerly served as the city dump, and the surf pulverized the trash into beautiful treasures). You can gaze at the dazzling colors, but don't take any glass with you; it's now against the law. No swimming at this beach either, for safety's sake. **Amenities:** parking; toilets. **Best for:** sunset; walking. ⊠ *Elm St. and Old Haul Rd.* ⊕ *www.parks.ca.gov.*

MacKerricher State Park. This park begins at Glass Beach and stretches north for 9 miles, beginning with rocky headlands that taper into dunes and sandy beaches. The headland is a good place for whale-watching from December to mid-April. Fishing at Lake Cleone (a freshwater lake stocked with trout), canoeing, hiking, tidepooling, jogging, bicycling, beachcombing, camping, and harbor seal watching at Laguna Point are among the popular activities, many of which are accessible to the mobility-impaired. Rangers, who lead nature hikes in summer, discourage swimming in the treacherous surf and remind those on shore to be vigilant for rogue waves and to never turn their backs on the sea. Dogs must be leashed. **Amenities:** parking; toilets. **Best for:** solitude; sunset; walking. ⊠ *Hwy. 1, 3 miles north of Fort Bragg* ☎ *707/937–5804* ⊕ *www.parks.ca.gov* ✉ *$8 per vehicle.*

WHERE TO EAT AND STAY

For expanded reviews, facilities, and current deals, visit Fodors.com.

$ ✕ **Piaci Pub and Pizzeria.** The seats are stools and your elbows might bang
ITALIAN a neighbor's, but nobody seems to mind at this cozy spot that's hands
down the area's most popular casual restaurant. The food is simple,
mostly pizza and calzones, but everything is carefully prepared and
comes out tasty. The well-chosen beers served here receive the same
respect the wines do: the list notes the origin, brewmaster, and alcohol
content. Dogs and their owners are welcome at the tables outside. Cash
only. ⑤ *Average main: $13* ⊠ *120 W. Redwood Ave.* ☎ *707/961–1133*
⊕ *www.piacipizza.com* ▭ *No credit cards* ⊙ *No lunch Sun.*

$$$ ⚏ **Weller House Inn.** It's hard to believe that this house was abandoned
B&B/INN and slated for demolition when it was purchased in 1994 and then
carefully restored into the loveliest Victorian in Fort Bragg. **Pros:** hand-
crafted details; radiant heat in the wood floors; friendly innkeepers.
Cons: some may find it too old-fashioned. ⑤ *Rooms from: $180* ⊠ *524
Stewart St.* ☎ *707/964–4415, 877/893–5537* ⊕ *www.wellerhouse.com*
⌷ *9 rooms* ⦿ *Breakfast.*

SPORTS AND THE OUTDOORS

HORSEBACK RIDING

Ricochet Ridge Ranch. Come here for private and group trail rides through
redwood forest and on the beach. ⊠ *24201 N. Hwy. 1* ☎ *707/964–
7669, 888/873–5777* ⊕ *www.horse-vacation.com.*

WHALE-WATCHING

All Aboard Adventures. Captain Tim of All Aboard operates fishing excur-
sions year-round and whale-watching trips from late December through
April. ⊠ *Noyo Harbor, 32410 N. Harbor Dr.* ☎ *707/964–1881* ⊕ *www.
allaboardadventures.com.*

REDWOOD COUNTRY

HUMBOLDT REDWOODS STATE PARK

20 miles north of Garberville, 43 miles south of Eureka.

Conservationists banded together a century ago as the Save the Red-
woods League and scored a key victory when a memorial grove was
dedicated in 1921. That grove is now part of Humboldt Redwoods
State Park, which these days has grown to nearly 53,000 acres, about
a third of which are filled with untouched old-growth coast redwoods.

GETTING HERE AND AROUND

Access the park right off U.S. 101. *(⇨ See Bus Travel, at the beginning of
this chapter, for Humboldt County public transportation information.)*

EXPLORING

Fodor's Choice **Avenue of the Giants.** Some of the tallest trees on Earth tower over this
★ magnficent 32-mile stretch of two-lane blacktop, also known as High-
FAMILY way 254, that follows the south fork of the Eel River through Hum-
boldt Redwoods State Park. The highway runs more or less parallel
to U.S. 101 from about 7 miles north of Garberville to the town of

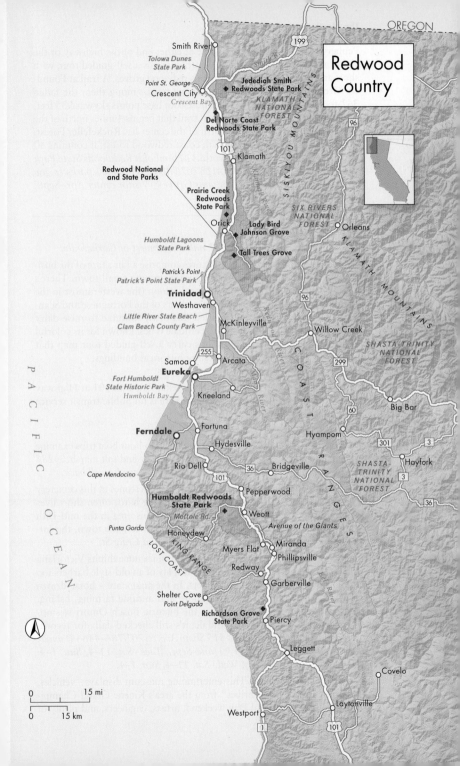

Pepperwood. A brochure available at either end of the highway or the **visitor center,** 2 miles south of Weott, contains a self-guided tour, with short and long hikes through various redwood groves. A trail at **Founders Grove** passes by several impressive trees, among them the fallen 362-foot-long Dyerville Giant, whose root base points skyward 35 feet. The tree can be reached via a short trail that begins 4 miles north of the visitor center. About 6 miles north of the center lies **Rockefeller Forest.** The largest remaining old-growth coast redwood forest, it contains 40 of the 100 tallest trees in the world. ⊠ *Humboldt Redwoods State Park Visitor Center, Hwy. 254, Weott* ☎ *707/946–2263* ⊕ *www.parks.ca.gov* 🖾 *Free; $8 day-use fee for Williams Grove* ☉ *Visitor center Apr.–Sept., daily 9–5; Oct.–Mar., daily 10–4.*

FERNDALE

35 miles northwest of Weott; 57 miles northwest of Garberville.

Though gift shops and ice-cream stores comprise a fair share of the businesses here, Ferndale remains a fully functioning small town. There's a butcher, a small grocery, and a local saloon (the westernmost in the contiguous United States), and descendants of the Portuguese and Scandinavian dairy farmers who settled this town continue to raise dairy cows in the surrounding pastures. Ferndale is best known for its colorful Victorian architecture; many shops carry a self-guided tour map that highlights the town's most interesting historical buildings.

GETTING HERE AND AROUND

Ferndale is about 19 miles south of Eureka. Exit U.S. 101 at Highway 211 and follow it southwest 5 miles. There is no public transit service to Ferndale.

EXPLORING

Eel River Delta Tours. Bruce Slocum's engaging two-hour boat trips examine the wildlife and history of the Eel River's estuary and salt marsh. ⊠ *285 Morgan Slough Rd.* ☎ *707/786–4902 leave message for call back.*

Ferndale Historic Cemetery. The worn, lovely gravestones at this cemetery on Ferndale's east side provide insight into the hard, often short lives of the European immigrants who cultivated this area in the mid-18th century. From the top of the hill here you can view the town, the surrounding farms, and the ocean. ⊠ *Bluff St. and Craig St.*

Ferndale Museum. The main building of this museum exhibits Victoriana and historical photographs and has a display of an old-style barbershop and another of Wiyot Indian baskets. In the annex are a horse-drawn buggy, a re-created blacksmith's shop, and antique farming, fishing, and dairy equipment. Don't miss the historic Bosch-Omori seismograph, installed in 1933 in Ferndale; it's still checked daily for recordings of earthquake activity. ⊠ *515 Shaw Ave.* ☎ *707/786–4466* ⊕ *www.ferndale-museum.org* 🖾 *$1* ☉ *June–Sept., Tues.–Sat. 11–4, Sun. 1–4; Oct.–Dec. and Feb.–May, Wed.–Sat. 11–4, Sun. 1–4.*

Ferndale Kinetic Museum. This entertaining museum displays "vehicles, costumes, awards, and bribes" from the area's Kinetic Grand Championship. Every Memorial Day weekend, artists, engineers, and plenty of hacks cobble together moving sculptures from used bicycle parts and other scraps and race them from Arcata to Ferndale. Contestants are judged as much on their creativity as on their ability to cross the finish line, and as a result sculptures have included the Albino Rhino and a 93-foot-long fish. ⊠ *Ferndale Art and Cultural Center, 580 Main St.* ☎ *Free* ⊘ *Daily 10–5.*

WHERE TO STAY

For expanded reviews, facilities, and current deals, visit Fodors.com.

$$
B&B/INN

Gingerbread Mansion. A dazzler that rivals San Francisco's "painted ladies," this Victorian mansion has detailed exterior spindle work, turrets, and gables. **Pros:** elegant; relaxing; friendly. **Cons:** some may find it gaudy. ⑤ *Rooms from: $150* ⊠ *400 Berding St.* ☎ *707/786–4000, 855/786–4001* ⊕ *www.thegingerbreadmansion.com* ↬ *7 rooms, 4 suites* ⑩ *Breakfast.*

EUREKA

19 miles north of Ferndale; 67 miles north of Garberville.

With a population of 27,191, Eureka is the North Coast's largest city. Over the past century, it has cycled through several periods of boom and bust—first with mining and later with timber and fishing—but these days tourism helps keep the local economy afloat. The town's nearly 100 Victorian buildings have inspired some to dub it "the Williamsburg of the West." Shops draw people to the renovated downtown, and a walking pier extends into the harbor.

GETTING HERE AND AROUND

U.S. 101 travels through Eureka. From Redding and Interstate 5, travel west along Highway 299 about 138 miles to U.S. 101; Eureka is 9 miles south. Eureka Transit (⊕ *www.eurekatransit.org*) buses serve the town and connect with regional transit.

EXPLORING

Blue Ox Millworks. This woodshop is among a handful in the country specializing in Victorian-era architecture, but what makes it truly unique is that its craftspeople use antique tools to do the work. The most modern tool here is a 1948 band saw. Lucky for curious craftspeople and history buffs, the shop doubles as a dusty historical park. Visitors can watch craftsmen use printing presses, lathes, and even a mill that pares down whole redwood logs into the ornate fixtures for Victorians like those around town. The museum is less interesting on Saturday, when most craftspeople take the day off. ⊠ *1 X St.* ☎ *707/444–3437, 800/248–4259* ⊕ *www.blueoxmill.com* ☎ *$7.50* ⊘ *Weekdays 9–5, Sat. 9–4.*

Clarke Historical Museum. The Native American Wing of this museum contains a beautiful collection of northwestern California basketry. Artifacts from Eureka's Victorian, logging, and maritime eras fill the rest of the space. ⊠ *240 E St.* ☎ *707/443–1947* ⊕ *www.clarkemuseum. org* ☎ *$3* ⊘ *Wed. and Thurs. 11–4; Fri. and Sat. 11–6.*

Eureka Chamber of Commerce Visitor Center. The center has maps of self-guided driving tours of Eureka's Victorian architecture, and you can learn about organized tours. ⊠ *2112 Broadway* ☎ *707/442–3738, 800/356–6381* ⊕ *www.eurekachamber.com* ⊘ *June–Aug., Mon.–Thurs. 8:30–5, Fri. 8:30–4, Sat. 10–3; Sept.–May, Mon.–Thurs. 8:30–5, Fri. 8:30–4.*

FAMILY **Fort Humboldt State Historic Park.** The structure that gives this park its name was built in response to conflicts between white settlers and Native Americans. It no longer stands, but on its grounds are some reconstructed buildings, fort and logging museums, and old logging locomotives. ⊠ *3431 Fort Ave.* ☎ *707/445–6547* ⊕ *www.parks.ca.gov* ☞ *Free* ⊙ *Daily 8–5.*

QUICK BITES

Lost Coast Brewery & Cafe. This bustling microbrewery is the best place in town to relax with a pint of ale or porter. Soups, salads, and light meals are served for lunch and dinner. ⊠ *617 4th St.* ☎ *707/445–4480* ⊕ *www.lostcoast.com.*

WHERE TO EAT AND STAY
For expanded reviews, facilities, and current deals, visit Fodors.com.

$$$ ✗**Restaurant 301.** Eureka's most elegant restaurant, situated in the
AMERICAN Carter House, uses ingredients selected from the farmers' market, local
Fodor's Choice cheese makers and ranchers, and the on-site gardens. Dishes are pre-
★ pared with a delicate hand and a sensuous imagination. There's always a fresh seafood offering, and you can dine à la carte or choose from two prix-fixe menus (five courses, $62; eight courses, $92). The restaurant has earned high praise for its comprehensive wine selection. ⑤ *Average main: $28* ⊠ *301 L St.* ☎ *707/444–8062, 800/404–1390* ⊕ *www. carterhouse.com* ⊙ *No lunch.*

$$ ✗**Samoa Cookhouse.** Waiters at this former cafeteria for local mill
AMERICAN workers deliver family-style bowls—whatever is being served at the
FAMILY meal you've arrived for—to long, communal tables. For breakfast that means eggs, sausage, biscuits and gravy, and the like. Lunch and dinner usually feature soup, potatoes, salad, and pie, plus daily-changing entrées such as pot roast and pork loin. A museum in the back pays homage to logging culture, but the entire place is a tribute to the rough-and-tumble life and hard work that tamed this wild land. Dieters and vegetarians should look elsewhere for sustenance. ⑤ *Average main: $16* ⊠ *908 Vance Ave., near Cookhouse Rd., Samoa* ☎ *707/442–1659* ⊕ *www.samoacookhouse.net.*

$ ⊞**Abigail's Elegant Victorian Mansion.** Innkeepers Doug and Lily Vieyra
HOTEL have devoted themselves to honoring this National Historic Landmark by decorating it with authentic, Victorian-era opulence. **Pros:** unique; lots of character; fun innkeepers. **Cons:** downtown is not within walking distance; bedrooms are a bit worn. ⑤ *Rooms from: $105* ⊠ *1406 C St.* ☎ *707/444–3144* ⊕ *www.eureka-california.com* ⊃*4 rooms, 2 with shared bath* ⊺⊙⊦ *No meals.*

$$$ ⊞**Carter House.** Owner Mark Carter says he trains his staff always to
HOTEL say yes; whether it's breakfast in bed or an in-room massage, some-
Fodor's Choice one here will get you what you want. **Pros:** elegant; every detail in
★ place; excellent dining at Restaurant 301; bar off lobby. **Cons:** kids are allowed, but it's best suited for grown-ups. ⑤ *Rooms from: $177* ⊠ *301 L St.* ☎ *707/444–8062, 800/404–1390* ⊕ *www.carterhouse.com* ⊃*22 rooms, 8 suites, 2 cottages* ⊺⊙⊦ *Breakfast.*

SHOPPING

Eureka has several art galleries and numerous antiques stores in the district running from C to I streets between 2nd and 3rd streets.

Eureka Books. Along with classics and bestsellers, this bibliophile's haven has an exceptional collection of used books on all topics. ☒ *426 2nd St.* ☏ *707/444–9593* ⊕ *www.eurekabooksellers.com.*

First Street Gallery. Run by Humboldt State University, this is the best spot for contemporary art by local and regional artists, with some national and international representation. ☒ *422 1st St.* ☏ *707/443–6363* ⊕ *www.humboldt.edu/first.*

SPORTS AND THE OUTDOORS

WHALE-WATCHING

Humboats Kayak Adventures. Kayak rentals and lessons are available here, along with group kayaking tours, including whale-watching trips ($75, December–June) that get you close enough for good photos of migrating gray whales and resident humpback whales. ☒ *Dock A, Woodley Island Marina* ☏ *707/443–5157* ⊕ *www.humboats.com.*

TRINIDAD

21 miles north of Eureka.

Trinidad got its name from the Spanish mariners who entered the bay on Trinity Sunday, June 9, 1775. The town became a principal trading post for the mining camps along the Klamath and Trinity rivers. Mining and whaling have faded from the scene, and now Trinidad is a quiet and genuinely charming community with ample sights and activities to entertain low-key visitors.

GETTING HERE AND AROUND

Trinidad sits right off U.S. 101. To reach the town from Interstate 5, head west from Redding on Highway 299 and turn north on U.S. 101 north of Arcata. Redwood Transit System (⊕ *www.redwoodtransit. org*) provides bus service between Trinidad, Eureka, and nearby towns.

EXPLORING

Patrick's Point State Park. On a forested plateau almost 200 feet above the surf, the park has stunning views of the Pacific, great whale- and sea lion–watching, picnic areas, bike paths, and hiking trails through old-growth spruce forest. There are also tidal pools at Agate Beach, a re-created Yurok Indian village, and a small museum with natural-history exhibits. Because the park is far from major tourist hubs, there are few visitors (most are local surfers)—it's sublimely quiet here. Three campgrounds amid spruce and alder trees have all amenities except RV hookups. Reservations are recommended in summer. Dogs are not allowed on trails or the beach. ☒ *U.S. 101, 5 miles north of Trinidad* ☏ *707/677–3570* ⊕ *www.parks.ca.gov* ☒ *$8 per vehicle.*

BEACHES

FAMILY **Clam Beach County Park and Little River State Beach.** Together these make a park that stretches from Trinidad to as far south as one can see. The sandy beach here is exceptionally wide, perfect for kids who need to get out of the car and burn off some energy. Beachcombing and clamming are favored activities, as well as savoring fabulous sunsets. The two parks share day use facilities. **Amenities:** parking; toilets. **Best for:** solitude; sunset; walking. ⊠ *Hwy. 1, 6½ miles south of Trinidad* ☎ *707/445–7651* ☺ *5 am–midnight.*

WHERE TO EAT AND STAY

For expanded reviews, facilities, and current deals, visit Fodors.com.

$

SEAFOOD

✕ **Katy's Smokehouse.** This tiny operation has been doing things the same way since the 1940s, curing day-boat, line-caught fish with its original smokers. Albacore jerky, smoked scallops, and salmon cured with brown sugar are popular. Buy bread and drinks in town and walk to the waterside for fine alfresco snacking. ⑤ *Average main: $10* ⊠ *740 Edwards St.* ☎ *707/677–0151* ⊕ *www.katyssmokehouse. com* ☺ *No dinner.*

$$$

AMERICAN

✕ **Larrupin' Cafe.** Locals consider this restaurant one of the best places to eat on the North Coast. Set in a two-story house on a quiet country road north of town, it's often thronged with people enjoying fresh seafood, Cornish game hen, or mesquite-grilled ribs. The garden setting and candlelight stir thoughts of romance. ⑤ *Average main: $29* ⊠ *1658 Patrick's Point Dr.* ☎ *707/677–0230* ⊕ *www.larrupin.com* ☺ *No lunch.*

$$$$

B&B/INN

▣ **Trinidad Bay Bed and Breakfast Inn.** Staying at this small Cape Cod–style inn perched above Trinidad Bay is like spending the weekend at a friend's vacation house. **Pros:** great location above bay; lots of light. **Cons:** if all rooms are full, the main house can feel a bit crowded. ⑤ *Rooms from: $260* ⊠ *560 Edwards St., Box 849* ☎ *707/677–0840* ⊕ *www.trinidadbaybnb.com* ⤳ *4 rooms* ⑩ *Breakfast.*

$$$$

B&B/INN

▣ **Turtle Rocks Oceanfront Inn.** This comfortable inn has the best view in Trinidad, and the builders have made the most of it. **Pros:** great ocean views; comfy king beds. **Cons:** no businesses within walking distance. ⑤ *Rooms from: $295* ⊠ *3392 Patrick's Point Dr., 4½ miles north of town* ☎ *707/677–3707* ⊕ *www.turtlerocksinn.com* ⤳ *5 rooms, 1 suite* ⑩ *Breakfast.*

REDWOOD
NATIONAL PARK

WELCOME TO REDWOOD NATIONAL PARK

TOP REASONS TO GO

★ **Giant trees:** These mature coastal redwoods are the tallest trees in the world.

★ **Hiking to the sea:** The park's trails wind through majestic redwood groves, and many connect to the Coastal Trail running along the western edge of the park.

★ **Rare wildlife:** Mighty Roosevelt elk favor the park's flat prairie and open lands; seldom-seen black bears roam the backcountry; trout and salmon leap through streams, and Pacific gray whales swim along the coast during their biannual migrations.

★ **Stepping back in time:** Hike Fern Canyon Trail and explore a prehistoric scene of lush vegetation and giant ferns.

★ **Cheeps, not beeps:** Amid the majestic redwoods you're out of range for cell-phone service—and in range for the soothing sounds of warblers and burbling creeks.

1 Del Norte Coast Redwoods State Park. The rugged terrain of this far northwest corner of California combines stretches of treacherous surf, steep cliffs, and forested ridges. On a clear day it's postcard-perfect; with fog, it's mysteriously mesmerizing.

2 Jedediah Smith Redwoods State Park. Gargantuan old-growth redwoods dominate the scenery here. The Smith River cuts through canyons and splits across boulders, carrying salmon to the inland creeks where they spawn.

3 Prairie Creek Redwoods State Park. The forests here give way to spacious, grassy plains where abundant wildlife thrives. Roosevelt elk are a common sight in the meadows and down to Gold Bluffs Beach.

4 Orick Area. The highlight of the southern portion of Redwood National Park is the Tall Trees Grove. It's difficult to reach and requires a special pass, but it's worth the hassle—this section has the tallest coast redwood trees, with a new record holder discovered in 2006.

CALIFORNIA

GETTING ORIENTED

U.S. 101 weaves through the southern portion of the park, skirts around the center, and then slips back through redwoods in the north and on to Crescent City. Kuchel Visitor Center, Prairie Creek Redwoods State Park and Visitor Center, Tall Trees Grove, Fern Canyon, and Lady Bird Johnson Grove are all in the park's southern section. The graveled Coastal Drive curves along ocean vistas and dips down to the Klamath River in the park's central section. To the north you'll find Mill Creek Trail, Enderts Beach, and Crescent Beach Overlook in Del Norte Coast Redwoods State Park as well as Jedediah Smith Redwoods State Park, Stout Grove, Little Bald Hills, and Simpson-Reed Grove.

8

Updated
by Christine
Vovakes

Soaring to more than 300 feet, the coastal redwoods that give this park its name are miracles of efficiency—some have survived hundreds of years (a few live for more than 2,000 years). These massive trees glean nutrients from the rich alluvial flats at their feet and from the moisture and nitrogen trapped in their uneven canopy. Their huge, thick-barked trunks can hold thousands of gallons of water, reservoirs that have helped them withstand centuries of firestorms.

REDWOOD PLANNER

WHEN TO GO

Campers and hikers flock to the park from mid-June to early September. Crowds disappear in winter, but you'll have to contend with frequent rains and nasty potholes on side roads. Temperatures fluctuate widely throughout the park: the foggy coastal lowland is much cooler than the higher-altitude interior.

The average annual rainfall here is 90 to 100 inches, and during dry summer months thick fog rolling in from the Pacific veils the forests, giving redwoods a large portion of their moisture intake.

GETTING HERE AND AROUND

CAR TRAVEL

U.S. 101 runs north–south along the park, and Highway 199 cuts east–west through its northern portion. Access routes off 101 include Bald Hills Road, Davison Road, Newton B. Drury Scenic Parkway, Coastal Drive, Requa Road, and Enderts Beach Road. From 199 take South Fork Road to Howland Hill Road. Many of the park's roads aren't paved, and winter rains can turn them into obstacle courses; sometimes they're closed completely. RVs and trailers aren't permitted on some routes.

PARK ESSENTIALS

PARK FEES AND PERMITS

Admission to Redwood National Park is free. There's an $8 day-use fee to enter one or all of Redwood's state parks; for camping at these state parks it's an additional $35. To visit Tall Trees Grove, you must get a free permit at the Kuchel Information Center in Orick. Permits also are needed to camp in Redwood Creek backcountry.

PARK HOURS

The park is open year-round, 24 hours a day.

VISITOR INFORMATION

PARK CONTACT INFORMATION

Redwood National and State Parks ⊠ *1111 2nd St., Crescent City* ☎ *707/465–7335* ⊕ *www.nps.gov/redw*.

VISITOR CENTERS

Crescent City Information Center. As the park's headquarters, this center is the main information stop if you're approaching the redwoods from the north. A gift shop and picnic area are here. ⊠ *Off U.S. 101 at 2nd and K Sts., 1111 Second St., near K St., Crescent City* ☎ *707/465–7335* ⊕ *www.nps.gov/redw* ⊙ *Mid-May–mid-Oct., daily 9–6; mid-Oct.–mid-May, daily 9–4.*

Hiouchi Information Center. Located in Jedediah Smith Redwoods State Park, 2 miles west of Hiouchi and 9 miles east of Crescent City off U.S. 199, this center has a bookstore, film, and exhibits about the flora and fauna in the park. It's also a starting point for seasonal ranger programs. ⊠ *Hiouchi Information Center, Hwy. 199* ☎ *707/458–3294, 707/465–7335* ⊕ *www.nps.gov/redw* ⊙ *Late May–early-Sept., daily 9–6.*

Jedediah Smith Visitor Center. Located off U.S. 199, this center has information about ranger-led walks and evening campfire programs in the summer in Jedediah Smith Redwoods State Park. Also here are nature and history exhibits, a gift shop, and a picnic area. ⊠ *Off U.S. 199* ☎ *707/458–3496, 707/465–7335* ⊕ *www.parks.ca.gov* ⊙ *Late May–early-Sept., daily 9–6; closed early Sept.–late-May.*

Fodor'sChoice ★ **Prairie Creek Visitor Center.** Housed in a redwood lodge, this center has wildlife displays and a massive stone fireplace that was built in 1933. Several trailheads begin here. Stretch your legs with an easy stroll along Revelation Trail, a short loop behind the lodge. Pick up information about summer programs in Prairie Creek Redwoods State Park. There's a nature museum, gift shop, picnic area, and exhibits on flora and fauna. A bonus sighting: Roosevelt elk often roam in the vast field adjacent to the center. ⊠ *Off southern end of Newton B. Drury Scenic Pkwy., Orick* ☎ *707/488–2039* ⊕ *www.parks.ca.gov* ⊙ *Mid-May–mid-Oct., daily 9–5; mid-Oct.–mid-May, daily 9-4.*

Thomas H. Kuchel Visitor Center. If you're approaching the park from the south end, stop here to get brochures, advice, and a free permit to drive up the access road to Tall Trees Grove. Whale-watchers find the deck of the visitor center an excellent observation point, and bird-watchers enjoy the nearby Freshwater Lagoon, a popular layover for migrating waterfowl. Many of the exhibits here are hands-on and kid-friendly. ⊠ *Off U.S. 101, Orick* ☎ *707/465–7765* ⊕ *www.nps.gov/redw* ⊙ *Mid-May–mid-Oct., daily 9–5; mid-Oct.–mid-May, daily 9-4.*

Plants and Wildlife in Redwood

Coast redwoods, the world's tallest trees (a new record holder, topping out at 379 feet, was found within the park in 2006) grow in the moist, temperate climate of California's North Coast. These ancient giants thrive in an environment that exists in only a few hundred coastal miles along the Pacific Ocean. They commonly live 600 years—though some have been around for 2,000 years.

A healthy redwood forest is diverse and includes Douglas firs, western hemlocks, tan oaks, and madrone trees. The complex soils of the forest floor support a verdant profusion of ferns, mosses, and fungi, along with numerous shrubs and berry bushes. In spring, California rhododendron bloom throughout the forest, providing a dazzling purple and pink contrast to the dense greenery.

Redwood National Park holds 45% of all California's old-growth redwood forests. Of the original 3,125 square miles (2 million acres) in the Redwoods Historic Range, only 4% remain following the logging that began in 1850; 1% is privately owned and managed, and 3% is on public land.

In the park's backcountry, you might spot mountain lions, black bears, black-tailed deer, river otters, beavers, and minks. Roosevelt elk roam the flatlands, and the rivers and streams teem with salmon and trout. Gray whales, seals, and sea lions cavort near the coastline. And thanks to the area's location along the Pacific Flyway, more than 400 species of birds have been recorded in the park.

EXPLORING

SCENIC DRIVES

Coastal Drive. This 9-mile, partially paved road is closed to trailers and RVs and takes about one hour to drive. The slow pace alongside stands of redwoods offers close-up views of the Klamath River and expansive panoramas of the Pacific. From here you'll find access to the Flint Ridge section of the Coastal Trail. Recurring landslides have closed sections of the original road; this loop is all that remains. ⊠ *1 mile south of Klamath on U.S. 101* ✢ *Take the Klamath Beach Rd. exit and follow signs to Coastal Drive.*

SCENIC STOPS

Crescent Beach Overlook. The scenery here includes ocean views and, in the distance, Crescent City and its working harbor; in balmy weather this is a great place for a picnic. From the overlook you can spot migrating gray whales going south November through December and returning north February through April. ⊠ *2 miles south of Crescent City, off Enderts Beach Rd.*

Fodor'sChoice **Fern Canyon.** Enter another world and be surrounded by 30-foot canyon ★ walls covered with sword, maidenhair, and five-finger ferns. Allow an hour to explore the ¼-mile-long vertical garden along a 0.7-mile loop.

From the north end of Gold Bluffs Beach it's an easy walk, although you'll have to wade across a small stream several times (in addition to driving across streams on the way to the parking area). But the lush surroundings are otherworldly, and worth a visit when creeks aren't running too high. Be aware that RVs longer than 24 feet and all trailers are not allowed here. ⊠ *10 miles northwest of Prairie Creek Visitor Center, via Davison Rd. off U.S. 101.*

Lady Bird Johnson Grove. This section of the park was dedicated by, and named for, the former first lady. A 1-mile nature loop follows an old logging road through a mature redwood forest. Allow 45 minutes to complete the trail. ⊠ *1 mile north of Orick on U.S. 101* ✛ *Turn onto Bald Hills Rd. for 2½ miles to trailhead.*

Tall Trees Grove. From the Kuchel Visitor Center, you can get a free permit to make the steep 14-mile drive (the last 6.5 miles, on Tall Trees Access Road, are unpaved) to the grove's trailhead (trailers and RVs not allowed). Access to the popular grove is first-come, first-served, and a maximum of 50 permits are handed out each day. ⊠ *1 mile north of Orick on U.S. 101* ✛ *Turn right at Bald Hills Rd. and follow signs about 6.5 miles to access road, then 6.5 miles, unpaved, to trailhead.*

SPORTS AND THE OUTDOORS

HIKING

MODERATE

Coastal Trail. Although this easy-to-difficult trail runs along most of the park's length, smaller sections—of varying degrees of difficulty—are accessible via frequent, well-marked trailheads. The moderate-to-difficult DeMartin section leads past 6 miles of old growth redwoods and through prairie. If you're up for a real workout, you'll be well rewarded with the brutally difficult but stunning Flint Ridge section, a 4.5-mile stretch of steep grades and numerous switchbacks that leads past redwoods and Marshall Pond. The moderate 5.5-mile-long Klamath section, which connects the Wilson Creek picnic area with Hidden Beach tidepools and up to the Klamath Overlook, provides coastal views and whale-watching opportunities. ⊠ *Flint Ridge trailhead: Douglas Bridge parking area, north end of Coastal Dr.*

KAYAKING

With many miles of often-shallow rivers and streams in the area, kayaking is a popular pastime in the park.

OUTFITTERS

Humboats Kayak Adventures. Kayak rental and lessons are available here, along with a variety of group kayak tours. ⊠ *Dock A, Woodley Island Marina, Eureka* ☎ *707/443-5157* ⊕ *www.humboats.com.*

8

Best Campgrounds in Redwood

CLOSE UP

Within a 30-minute drive of Redwood National and State parks there are nearly 60 public and private camping facilities. None of the four primitive areas in Redwood—DeMartin, Flint Ridge, Little Bald Hills, and Nickel Creek—is a drive-in site. Although you don't need a permit at these four hike-in sites, stop at a ranger station to inquire about availability. You will need to get a permit from a ranger station for camping along Redwood Creek in the backcountry. Bring your own water, since drinking water isn't available in any of these sites.

If you'd rather drive than hike in, Redwood has four developed campgrounds—Elk Prairie, Gold Bluffs Beach, Jedediah Smith, and Mill Creek—that are within the state-park boundaries. None has RV hookups, and some length restrictions apply. Fees are $35 in state park campgrounds. For details and reservations, call ☎ 800/444-7275 or check ⊕ www.reserveamerica.com. Neither Gold Bluffs Beach or Nickel Creek campgrounds accept reservations; it's first come, first served.

Elk Prairie Campground. Roosevelt elk frequent this popular campground adjacent to a prairie and old-growth redwoods. ⊠ 6 miles north of Orick on Newton B. Drury Scenic Pkwy. in Prairie Creek Redwoods State Park ☎ 800/444-7275.

Gold Bluffs Beach Campground. You can camp in tents or RVs right on the beach at this Prairie Creek Redwoods State Park campground near Fern Canyon. ⊠ At end of Davison Rd., which is 5 miles south of Redwood Information Center off U.S. 101 ☎ 707/488-2039.

Jedediah Smith Campground. This is one of the few places to camp—in tents or RVs—within groves of old-growth redwood forest. ⊠ 10 miles east of Crescent City on U.S. 199 ☎ 800/444-7275.

Mill Creek Campground. Mill Creek is the largest of the state-park campgrounds. ⊠ East of U.S. 101, 7 miles southeast of Crescent City ☎ 800/444-7275.

Nickel Creek Campground. An easy hike gets you to this primitive site, which is near tide pools and has great ocean views. You'll need to obtain a free backcountry camping permit from one of the visitor centers. ⊠ On Coastal Trail ½ mile from end of Enderts Beach Rd. ☎ 707/465-7335.

WHALE-WATCHING

Good vantage points for whale-watching include Crescent Beach Overlook, the Kuchel Visitor Center in Orick, points along the Coastal Drive, and the Klamath River Overlook. Late November through January are the best months to see their southward migrations; from February through April they return and generally pass closer to shore.

THE SOUTHERN SIERRA

Around Sequoia, Kings Canyon,
and Yosemite National Parks

WELCOME TO THE SOUTHERN SIERRA

TOP REASONS TO GO

★ **Strap 'em on:** Whether you walk the paved loops in the national parks (⇨ Chapter 10, Yosemite National Park, and Chapter 11, Sequoia and Kings Canyon National Parks) or head off the beaten path into the backcountry, a hike through groves and meadows or alongside streams and waterfalls will allow you to see, smell, and feel nature up close.

★ **Down you go:** Famous for its incredible snow-pack—some of the deepest in the North American continent—the Sierra Nevada has something for every winter-sports fan.

★ **Live it up:** Mammoth Lakes is eastern California's most exciting resort area.

★ **Pamper yourself:** Tucked in the hills south of Oakhurst, the elegant Château du Sureau will make you feel like you've stepped into a fairy tale.

★ **Go with the flow:** Three Rivers, the gateway to Sequoia National Park, is the launching pad for white-water trips down the Kaweah River.

1 South of Yosemite National Park. Several gateway towns to the south and west of Yosemite National Park (⇨ Chapter 10), most within an hour's drive of Yosemite Valley, have food, lodging, and other services.

2 Mammoth Lakes. A jewel in the vast Eastern Sierra Nevada, the Mammoth Lakes area lies just east of the Sierra crest, on the backside of Yosemite and the Ansel Adams Wilderness. It's a place of rugged beauty, where giant sawtooth mountains drop into the vast deserts of the Great Basin. In winter, 11,053-foot-high Mammoth Mountain offers the finest skiing and snowboarding in California—sometimes as late as June or even July. Once the snows melt, Mammoth transforms itself into a warm-weather play-ground, with fishing, mountain biking, golfing, hiking, and horseback riding. Nine deep-blue lakes are spread through the Mammoth Lakes Basin, and another 100 lakes dot the surrounding countryside.

3 East of Yosemite National Park. The area to the east of Yosemite National Park (⇨ Chapter 10) includes some ruggedly handsome, albeit desolate, terrain, most notably around Mono Lake. The area is best visited by car, as distances are great and public transportation is negligible. U.S. 395 is the main north–south road on the eastern side of the Sierra Nevada, at the western edge of the Great Basin. It's one of California's most beautiful highways; plan to snap pictures at roadside pullouts.

GETTING ORIENTED

The transition between the Central Valley and the rugged Southern Sierra may be the most dramatic in California sightseeing; as you head into the mountains, your temptation to stop the car and gawk will increase with every foot gained in elevation. Although you should spend most of your time here in the national parks (⇨ Chapter 10, Yosemite National Park, and Chapter 11, Sequoia and Kings Canyon National Parks), be sure to check out some of the mountain towns on the parks' fringes—in addition to being great places to stock up on supplies, they have worthy attractions, restaurants, and lodging options.

4 South of Sequoia and Kings Canyon: Three Rivers. Scenic Three Rivers is the main gateway for Sequoia and Kings Canyon National Parks (⇨ Chapter 11).

Updated by
Reed Parsell

Vast granite peaks and giant sequoias are among the Southern Sierra's mind-boggling natural wonders, many of which are protected in three national parks. Mother Nature goes so far over the top in this region that it might wow you even more than California's more famous urban attractions.

Outside the national parks (⇨ *Chapter 10, Yosemite National Park, and Chapter 11, Sequoia and Kings Canyon National Parks*), pristine lakes, superb skiing, rolling hills, and small towns complete the picture of the Southern Sierra. Heading up U.S. 395 on the Sierra's eastern side, you'll be rewarded with outstanding vistas of dramatic mountain peaks, including Mt. Whitney, the highest point in the contiguous United States, and Mono Lake, a vast expanse of deep blue—one of the most-photographed natural attractions in California—that is struggling to survive.

PLANNING

GETTING HERE AND AROUND

AIR TRAVEL
Fresno Yosemite International Airport (FYI) is the nearest airport to the national parks; Reno–Tahoe is the closest major airport to Mammoth Lakes.

Airports Fresno Yosemite International Airport ⊠ *5175 E. Clinton Ave., Fresno* ☎ *559/621–4500, 800/244–2359* ⊕ *www.flyfresno.org.* **Reno–Tahoe International Airport** ⊠ *U.S. 395, Exit 65B, Reno, Nevada* ☎ *775/328–6400* ⊕ *www.renoairport.com.*

CAR TRAVEL
From San Francisco, heading east on Interstate 80 to 580 to 205E is the most efficient connecting route to Interstate 5 and Highway 99, which straddle the western side of the Sierra Nevada. To best reach the eastern side from the Bay Area, take Interstate 80 to U.S. 395, then head south.

To get to Mammoth Lakes in summer and early fall (or whenever snows aren't blocking Tioga Road), you can travel via Highway 120 (to U.S. 395 south) through the Yosemite high country; the quickest route in winter is Interstate 80 to U.S. 50 to Highway 207 (also known as the Kingsbury Grade, just east of South Lake Tahoe) to U.S. 395 south; either route takes about seven hours. ■TIP→ Watch your gas gauge. Gas stations are few and far between in the Sierra, so fill your tank when you can. If you're traveling between October and May, heavy snow may cover mountain roads. Carry tire chains, know how to put them on (on Interstate 80 and U.S. 50 you can pay a chain installer $35 to do it for you, but on other routes you'll have to do it yourself), and always check road conditions before you leave.

Travel Reports Caltrans Current Highway Conditions ☎ 800/427-7623 ⊕ www.dot.ca.gov.

BUS TRAVEL

Greyhound serves Fresno, Madera, and other Central Valley towns west of the Sierra. Madera County Connection buses travel between Madera and Oakhurst (and Bass Lake). Eastern Sierra Transit Authority buses serve Mammoth Lakes, Bishop *(⇨ Chapter 16)*, and other eastern Sierra towns.

Bus Contacts Eastern Sierra Transit Authority ☎ 760/872-1901, 800/922-1930 ⊕ www.estransit.com. Greyhound ✉ Fresno ☎ 800/231-2222 ⊕ www.greyhound.com. Madera County Connection ✉ Madera ☎ 559/661-7433 ⊕ www.maderactc.com/pubtrans.html.

RESTAURANTS

Most small towns in the Sierra Nevada have at least one restaurant; with few exceptions, dress is casual. You'll most likely be spending a lot of time in the car while you're exploring the area, so pick up snacks and drinks to keep with you. With picnic supplies on hand, you'll be able to enjoy an impromptu meal under giant trees or in one of the eastern Sierra towns' municipal parks. *Prices in the reviews are the average cost of a main course at dinner or, if dinner is not served, at lunch.*

HOTELS

For visits to the Sierra Nevada's western side, book your hotel in advance—especially in summer—or you may wind up in the Central Valley, far from the action. Booking in advance is less crucial for travel to the Eastern Sierra. In either area, keep in mind that rural and rustic does not always mean inexpensive. *Prices in the reviews are the lowest cost of a standard double room in high season. For expanded hotel reviews, visit Fodors.com.*

Hotel Contacts Mammoth Lakes Visitors Bureau Lodging Referral ✉ Mammoth Lakes ☎ 760/934-2712, 888/466-2666 ⊕ www.visitmammoth.com. Mammoth Reservations ✉ Mammoth Lakes ☎ 800/223-3032 ⊕ www.mammothreservations.com.

SOUTH OF YOSEMITE NATIONAL PARK

People heading to Yosemite National Park, especially those interested in seeing the giant redwoods on the park's south side, pass through Oakhurst and Fish Camp on Highway 41.

OAKHURST

40 miles north of Fresno on Hwy. 41.

Motels, restaurants, gas stations, and small businesses line Highway 41 in Oakhurst, the last sizeable community before Yosemite (⇨ *Chapter 20*)—the south entrance is 23 miles north of town—and a good spot to find provisions. Continue north on Highway 41 to get to Yosemite. Three miles north of town on Highway 41, then 6 miles east, lies honky-tonk Bass Lake, a popular spot in summer with motorboaters, Jet Skiers, and families looking to cool off in the reservoir.

GETTING HERE AND AROUND

At the junction of highways 41 and 49, Oakhurst is a solid hour's drive north of Fresno. It's the southern gateway to Yosemite, so many people fly to Fresno and rent a car to get here and beyond. In town, there's no public transportation system of any consequence.

ESSENTIALS

Visitor Information Yosemite Sierra Visitors Bureau ☎ *559/683–4636* ⊕ *www.yosemitethisyear.com.*

WHERE TO EAT

$$$$
EUROPEAN
Fodor'sChoice
★

✕ **Erna's Elderberry House.** Erna Kubin-Clanin, the grande dame of Château du Sureau, created this culinary oasis, stunning for its understated elegance, gorgeous setting, and impeccable service. Red walls and wood beams accent the dining room's high ceilings, and arched windows reflect the glow of candles. The seasonal six-course prix-fixe dinner can be paired with superb wines, with every course delivered in perfect synchronicity by the elite waitstaff. A short bistro menu is served in the former wine cellar. $ *Average main: $95* ✉ *Château du Sureau, 48688 Victoria La., off Hwy. 41* ☎ *559/683–6800* ⊕ *www.elderberryhouse. com* ⟨ *Reservations essential* ⊙ *No lunch Mon.–Sat.*

WHERE TO STAY

For expanded hotel reviews, visit Fodors.com.

$$
HOTEL
FAMILY

🏨 **Best Western Yosemite Gateway Inn.** Oakhurst's best motel has carefully tended landscaping and rooms with attractive colonial–style furniture and slightly kitschy hand-painted wall murals of Yosemite. **Pros:** reasonably close to Yosemite; clean; two pools, one heated; comfortable. **Cons:** chain property; getting to Yosemite Valley from here is a haul. $ *Rooms from: $144* ✉ *40530 Hwy. 41, Oakhurst* ☎ *800/545–5462, 559/683–2378* ⊕ *www.yosemitegatewayinn.com* ⤢ *121 rooms, 16 suites.*

$$$$
RESORT
Fodor'sChoice
★

🏨 **Château du Sureau.** You'll feel pampered from the moment you drive through the wrought-iron gates of this fairy-tale castle. **Pros:** luxurious; great views. **Cons:** expensive; if you're not really into spas, it might not be worth your while. $ *Rooms from: $385* ✉ *48688 Victoria La.,*

Oakhurst ☎ *559/683–6860* ⊕ *www.chateausureau.com* 🛏 *10 rooms, 1 villa* 🍽 *Breakfast.*

$$
B&B/INN
🛏 **Homestead Cottages.** Set on 160 acres of rolling hills that once held a Miwok village, these cottages (the largest sleeps six) have gas fireplaces, fully equipped kitchens, and queen-size beds. **Pros:** remote location; quiet setting; friendly owners. **Cons:** might be a little *too* quiet for some. $ *Rooms from: $155* ✉ *41110 Rd. 600, 2½ miles off Hwy. 49, Ahwahnee* ☎ *559/683–0495, 800/483–0495* ⊕ *www.homesteadcottages.com* 🛏 *5 cottages, 1 loft.*

FISH CAMP

57 miles north of Fresno and 4 miles south of Yosemite National Park's south entrance.

As you climb in elevation along Highway 41 northbound, you see nothing but trees until you get to the small settlement of Fish Camp, where there's a post office and general store, but no gasoline (for gas, head 10 miles north to Wawona, in the park, or 17 miles south to Oakhurst).

GETTING HERE AND AROUND

Arrive here by car via Highway 41, from Yosemite National Park a few miles to the north, or from Oakhurst (and, farther down the road, Fresno) to the south. Unless you're on foot or a bicycle, a car is your only option.

EXPLORING

FAMILY
Yosemite Mountain Sugar Pine Railroad. Travel back to a time when powerful steam locomotives hauled massive log trains through the Sierra. This 4-mile, narrow-gauge railroad excursion takes you near Yosemite's south gate; there's also a moonlight special, with dinner and entertainment ($48). Take Highway 41 south from Yosemite about 8 miles to the departure point. ✉ *56001 Hwy. 41, Fish Camp* ☎ *559/683–7273* ⊕ *www.ymsprr.com* 🎫 *$19* ⊙ *Mar.–Oct., daily.*

WHERE TO STAY

For expanded hotel reviews, visit Fodors.com.

$$
B&B/INN
🛏 **Narrow Gauge Inn.** The well-tended rooms at this family-owned property have balconies with great views of the surrounding woods and mountains. **Pros:** close to Yosemite's south entrance; nicely appointed rooms; wonderful balconies. **Cons:** rooms can be a bit dark; dining options are limited, especially for vegetarians. $ *Rooms from: $145* ✉ *48571 Hwy. 41, Fish Camp* ☎ *559/683–7720, 888/644–9050* ⊕ *www.narrowgaugeinn.com* 🛏 *26 rooms, 1 suite* 🍽 *Breakfast.*

$$$$
HOTEL
🛏 **Tenaya Lodge.** One of the region's largest hotels, Tenaya Lodge is ideal for people who enjoy wilderness treks by day but prefer creature comforts at night. **Pros:** rustic setting with modern comforts; good off-season deals; very close to Yosemite National Park. **Cons:** so big it can seem impersonal; pricey during summer; few dining options. $ *Rooms from: $315* ✉ *1122 Hwy. 41* ☎ *559/683–6555, 888/514–2167* ⊕ *www.tenayalodge.com* 🛏 *244 rooms, 6 suites.*

9

EL PORTAL

14 miles west of Yosemite Valley on Hwy. 140.

The market in town is a good place to pick up provisions before you get to Yosemite (⇨ *Chapter 10)*. You'll find a post office and a gas station, but not much else.

GETTING HERE AND AROUND

The drive here on Highway 140 from Mariposa and, farther west, Merced, is the prettiest and gentlest (in terms of steep uphill and downhill portions) route to Yosemite National Park. Much of the road follows the Merced River in a rugged canyon. The Yosemite Area Regional Transportation System (YARTS ⊕ *www.yarts.com*) is a cheap and dependable way to go between Merced and Yosemite Valley; all buses stop in El Portal, where many park employees reside.

WHERE TO STAY

For expanded hotel reviews, visit Fodors.com.

$$$
RESORT
FAMILY

Evergreen Lodge at Yosemite. Near Hetch Hetchy on Yosemite National Park's northwest side, this sprawling property set in the woods is perfect for families: The 90-cabin complex includes a playground, an amphitheater, a movie room, a restaurant, a gift shop, and an activities desk. **Pros:** near the underrated Hetch Hetchy; family atmosphere; clean cabins. **Cons:** not cheap; about an hour's drive from Yosemite Valley. $ *Rooms from: $220* ✉ *33160 Evergreen Road* ☎ *209/379–2606, 888/935–6343* ⊕ *www.evergreenlodge.com* ⌁ *90 cabins.*

$$$
B&B/INN

Yosemite View Lodge. Just 2 miles outside the park's Arch Rock entrance, this modern property is the most convenient place to spend the night if you are unable to secure lodgings in the Valley. **Pros:** great location; good views; lots of on-site amenities. **Cons:** somewhat pricey; due to demand, it can be a challenge to get the dates you want. $ *Rooms from: $229* ✉ *11136 Hwy. 140, El Portal* ☎ *209/379–2681, 888/742–4371* ⊕ *www.yosemite-motels.com* ⌁ *279 rooms.*

MAMMOTH LAKES

30 miles south of eastern edge of Yosemite National Park on U.S. 395.

International real-estate developers joined forces with Mammoth Mountain Ski Area to transform the once sleepy town of Mammoth Lakes (elevation 7,800 feet) into an upscale ski destination. The Village at Mammoth is the epicenter of the recent development. Much of the architecture here is of the faux-alpine variety, but you'll find relatively sophisticated dining and lodging options. Winter is high season; in summer, room rates drop.

GETTING HERE AND AROUND

The best way to get to Mammoth Lakes is by car. The town is a couple of miles west of U.S. 395. The Yosemite Area Regional Transportation System (YARTS ⊕ *www.yarts.com*) provides once-a-day service between here and Yosemite Valley. The shuttle buses of Eastern Sierra Transit Authority (☎ *800/922–1930* ⊕ *www.estransit.com*) serve Mammoth Lakes, Bishop, and nearby tourist sites.

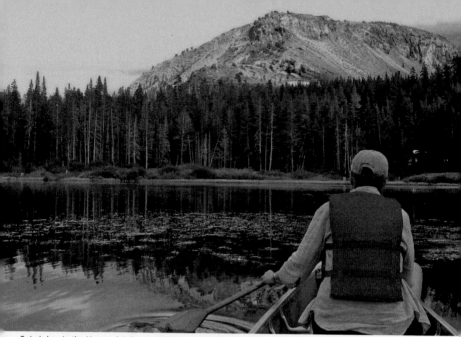

Twin Lakes, in the Mammoth Lakes region, is a great place to unwind.

Highway 203 heads west from U.S. 395, becoming Main Street as it passes through the town of Mammoth Lakes, and later Minaret Road (which makes a right turn) as it continues west to the Mammoth Mountain ski area and Devils Postpile National Monument.

ESSENTIALS

Visitor Information Mammoth Lakes Visitors Bureau ✉ *Welcome Center, 2510 Main St., near Sawmill Cutoff Rd.* ☎ *760/934–2712* ⊕ *www.visitmammoth.com.*

EXPLORING

Mammoth Lakes Basin. The lakes, reached by Lake Mary Road off Highway 203 southwest of town, are popular for fishing and boating in summer. First comes Twin Lakes, at the far end of which is Twin Falls, where water cascades 300 feet over a shelf of volcanic rock. Also popular are Lake Mary, the largest lake in the basin; Lake Mamie; and Lake George. Horseshoe Lake is the only lake in which you can swim.

Minaret Vista. The glacier-carved sawtooth spires of the Minarets, the remains of an ancient lava flow, are best viewed from the Minaret Vista, off Highway 203 west of Mammoth Lakes.

Fodor'sChoice
★
FAMILY
Panorama Gondola. Even if you don't ski, ride the gondola to see Mammoth Mountain, the aptly named dormant volcano that gives Mammoth Lakes its name. Gondolas serve skiers in winter and mountain bikers and sightseers in summer. The high-speed, eight-passenger gondolas whisk you from the chalet to the summit, where you can read about the area's volcanic history and take in top-of-the-world views.

Standing high above the tree line, you can look west 150 miles across the state to the Coastal Range; to the east are the highest peaks of Nevada and the Great Basin beyond. You won't find a better view of the Sierra High Country without climbing. Remember, though, that the air is thin at the 11,053-foot summit; carry water, and don't overexert yourself. The boarding area is at the Main Lodge. ⊠ *Off Hwy. 203* ☎ *760/934–2571 information, 3850 gondola station* ⌨ *$24* ⊘ *July 4– Oct., daily 9–4:30; Nov.–July 3, daily 8:30–4.*

Village at Mammoth. This huge complex of shops, restaurants, and luxury accommodations is the town's tourist center. Parking can be tricky, even seemingly impossible. There's a parking lot across the street on Minaret Road; cross your fingers and pay attention to time limits.

WHERE TO EAT

$$$
STEAKHOUSE
✗ **The Mogul.** This longtime favorite is the place to go when you want a straightforward steak and salad bar. The only catch is that the waiters cook your steak—and the result depends on the waiter's experience. But generally you can't go wrong. And kids love it. The knotty-pine walls lend a woodsy touch and suggest Mammoth Mountain before all the development. Ⓢ *Average main: $24* ⊠ *1528 Mammoth Tavern Rd., off Old Mammoth Rd.* ☎ *760/934–3039* ⊕ *www.themogul.com* ⊘ *No lunch.*

$$$
AMERICAN
✗ **Petra's Bistro & Wine Bar.** The ambience at Petra's—quiet, dark, and warm—complements the carefully prepared meat main dishes and seasonal sides, and the more than two dozen California wines from behind the bar. The service is top-notch. Downstairs, the Clocktower Cellar bar provides a late-night, rowdy alternative—or chaser. Ⓢ *Average main: $28* ⊠ *6080 Minaret Rd.* ☎ *760/934–3500* ⊕ *www.petrasbistro.com* ⚘ *Reservations essential* ⊘ *Closed Mon.; no lunch.*

$$$$
AMERICAN
✗ **Restaurant at Convict Lake.** Tucked in a tiny valley ringed by mile-high peaks, Convict Lake is one of the most spectacular spots in the eastern Sierra. Thank heaven the food lives up to the view. The chef's specialties include beef Wellington, rack of lamb, and pan-seared local trout, all beautifully prepared. The woodsy room has a vaulted knotty-pine ceiling and a copper-chimney fireplace that roars on cold nights. Natural light abounds in the daytime, but if it's summer, opt for a table outdoors under the white-barked aspens. Service is exceptional, as is the wine list, with reasonably priced European and California varietals. Ⓢ *Average main: $32* ⊠ *Convict Lake Rd. off U.S. 395, 4 miles south of Mammoth Lakes* ☎ *760/934–3803* ⊕ *www.convictlake.com* ⚘ *Reservations essential* ⊘ *No lunch early Sept.–July 4.*

$$
WINE BAR
✗ **Side Door Café.** Half wine bar, half café, this is a laid-back spot for an easy lunch or a long, lingering afternoon. The café serves grilled panini sandwiches, sweet and savory crepes, and espresso. At the wine bar, order cheese plates and charcuterie platters, designed to pair with the 25 wines (fewer in summertime) available by the glass. If you're lucky, a winemaker will show up and hold court at the bar. Ⓢ *Average main: $18* ⊠ *Village at Mammoth, 1111 Forest Trail, Unit 229* ☎ *760/934–5200* ⊕ *www.sidedoormammoth.com.*

$$ ✕**The Stove.** A longtime family favorite for down-to-earth, folksy cooking,
AMERICAN this is the kind of place you take the family to fill up before a long car ride.
The omelets, pancakes, huevos rancheros, and meat loaf won't win any
awards, but they're tasty. The room is cozy, with gingham curtains and
dark-wood booths, and service is friendly. Breakfast and lunch are the best
bets here. ⑤ *Average main: $16* ⊠ *644 Old Mammoth Rd.* ☏ *760/934–
2821* ⌑ *Reservations not accepted* ⊘ *No dinner Mon. and Tues.*

WHERE TO STAY

For expanded hotel reviews, visit Fodors.com.

$ ▦ **Alpenhof Lodge.** The owners of Alpenhof Lodge lucked out when
B&B/INN developers built the fancy-schmancy Village at Mammoth across the
street from their mom-and-pop motel, which remains a simple lodging
offering basic comforts and a few niceties like attractive pine furniture.
Pros: convenient for skiers; good price. **Cons:** could use an update;
rooms above the pub can be noisy. ⑤ *Rooms from: $124* ⊠ *6080 Mina-
ret Rd.* ☏ *760/934–6330, 800/828–0371* ⊕ *www.alpenhof-lodge.com*
↩ *54 rooms, 3 cabins.*

$$ ▦ **Cinnamon Bear Inn Bed and Breakfast.** In a business district off Main
B&B/INN Street, this bed-and-breakfast feels more like a small motel, with nicely
decorated rooms, many with four-poster beds. **Pros:** comparatively
quiet; affordable; friendly. **Cons:** a bit tricky to find; limited parking.
⑤ *Rooms from: $149* ⊠ *113 Center St.* ☏ *760/934–2873, 800/845–
2873* ⊕ *www.cinnamonbearinn.com* ↩ *22 rooms* ⑪ *Breakfast.*

$$$ ▦ **Double Eagle Resort and Spa.** You won't find a better spa retreat in the
RESORT eastern Sierra than the Double Eagle, which is in a spectacularly beautiful
spot under towering peaks and along a creek, near June Lake, 20 min-
utes north of Mammoth Lakes. **Pros:** pretty setting; generous breakfast;
spectacular indoor pool. **Cons:** expensive, remote. ⑤ *Rooms from: $229*
⊠ *5587 Hwy. 158* ☏ *760/648–7004, 877/648–7004* ⊕ *www.doubleeagle.
com* ↩ *16 2-bedroom cabins, 16 cabin suites, 1 3-bedroom cabin.*

$$ ▦ **Juniper Springs Lodge.** Tops for slope-side comfort, these condomin-
RESORT ium-style units have full kitchens and ski-in ski-out access to the moun-
tain. **Pros:** bargain during summer; direct access to the slopes; good
views. **Cons:** no nightlife within walking distance; no a/c. ⑤ *Rooms
from: $159* ⊠ *4000 Meridian Blvd.* ☏ *760/924–1102, 800/626–6684*
⊕ *www.mammothmountain.com* ↩ *10 studios, 99 1-bedrooms, 92
2-bedrooms, 3 3-bedrooms.*

$$ ▦ **Mammoth Mountain Inn.** If you want to be within walking distance
RESORT of the Mammoth Mountain Main Lodge, this is the place. **Pros:** great
location; big rooms; a traditional place to stay. **Cons:** can be crowded
in ski season; 9,000-feet elevation can affect sleep patterns. ⑤ *Rooms
from: $134* ⊠ *1 Minaret Rd.* ☏ *760/934–2581, 800/626–6684* ⊕ *www.
mammothmountain.com* ↩ *124 rooms, 91 condos.*

$$$ ▦ **Tamarack Lodge Resort & Lakefront Restaurant.** Tucked away on the
RESORT edge of the John Muir Wilderness Area, where cross-country ski trails
Fodor's Choice loop through the woods, this original 1924 lodge looks like some-
★ thing out of a snow globe, and the lake it borders is serenely beautiful.
Pros: rustic but not run-down; plenty of eco-sensitivity; tons of nearby

9

outdoor activities. **Cons:** pricey; some main lodge rooms have shared bathrooms. $ *Rooms from: $218* ✉ *Lake Mary Rd., off Hwy. 203* ☎ *760/934–2442, 800/626–6684* ⊕ *www.tamaracklodge.com* ⬏ *11 rooms, 35 cabins.*

$$$ ▥ **The Village Lodge.** At the epicenter of Mammoth's dining and night-
RESORT life scene, this cluster of four-story timber-and-stone condo buildings nods to Alpine style, with exposed timbers and peaked roofs. **Pros:** central location; clean; big rooms; lots of good restaurants nearby. **Cons:** comes with big price tag; can be noisy outside. $ *Rooms from: $239* ✉ *1111 Forest Trail* ☎ *760/934–1982, 800/626–6684* ⊕ *www. mammothmountain.com* ⬏ *277 units.*

SPORTS AND THE OUTDOORS

BICYCLING

Mammoth Mountain Bike Park. The park opens when the snow melts, usu-
ally by July, and has 70-plus miles of single-track trails—from mellow to super-challenging. Chairlifts and shuttles provide trail access, and rent-als are available. Various shops around town also rent bikes and provide trail maps, if you don't want to ascend the mountain. ✉ *Mammoth Mountain Ski Area* ☎ *760/934–0706* ⊕ *www.mammothmountain.com* ▱ *$45 day pass.*

FISHING

The fishing season runs from the last Saturday in April until the end of October. Crowley Lake is the top trout-fishing spot in the area; Con-vict Lake, June Lake, and the lakes of the Mammoth Basin are other prime spots. One of the best trout rivers is the San Joaquin, near Devils Postpile. Hot Creek, a designated Wild Trout Stream, is renowned for fly-fishing (catch-and-release only).

Kittredge Sports. This outfit rents rods and reels and also conducts guided trips. ✉ *3218 Main St., at Forest Trail* ☎ *760/934–7566* ⊕ *www. kittredgesports.com.*

Sierra Drifters Guide Service. To maximize your time on the water, get tips from local anglers, or better yet, book a guided fishing trip with this service. ☎ *760/935–4250* ⊕ *www.sierradrifters.com.*

HIKING

Hiking in Mammoth is stellar, especially along the trails that wind through the pristine alpine scenery around the Lakes Basin. Carry lots of water; and remember, the air is thin at 8,000 feet.

U.S. Forest Service Ranger Station and Welcome Center. Stop at the ranger station, just east of the town of Mammoth Lakes, for an area trail map and permits for backpacking in wilderness areas. ✉ *2510 Main St., Hwy. 203* ☎ *760/924–5500* ⊕ *www.fs.usda.gov/main/inyo.*

HORSEBACK RIDING

Stables around Mammoth are typically open from June through September.

Mammoth Lakes Pack Outfit. This company runs day and overnight horseback trips, or will shuttle you to the high country. ✉ *Lake Mary Rd., between Twin Lakes and Lake Mary* ☎ *888/475–8747* ⊕ *www. mammothpack.com.*

McGee Creek Pack Station. These folks customize pack trips or will shuttle you to camp alone. ☎ *760/935–4324 summer, 760/878–2207, 800/854–7407 ⊕ www.mcgeecreekpackstation.com.*

SKIING

In winter, check the On the Snow website or call the Snow Report for information about Mammoth weather conditions.

June Mountain Ski Area. In their rush to Mammoth Mountain, most people overlook June Mountain, a compact, low-key resort 20 miles north of Mammoth. Snowboarders especially dig it. Two freestyle terrain areas are for both skiers and boarders, including a huge 16-foot-wall super pipe. Best of all, there's rarely a line for the lifts—if you want to avoid the crowds but must ski on a weekend, this is the place. And in a storm, June is better protected from wind and blowing snow than Mammoth Mountain. (If it starts to storm, you can use your Mammoth ticket at June.) Expect all the usual services, including a rental-and-repair shop, ski school, and sports shop, but the food quality is better at Mammoth. Lift tickets cost $72, with discounts for multiple days. ✉ *3819 Hwy. 158, off June Lake Loop, June Lake* ☎ *760/648–7733, 888/586–3686 ⊕ www.junemountain.com ⛷ 35 trails on 500 acres, rated 35% beginner, 45% intermediate, 20% advanced. Longest run 2½ miles, base 7,510 feet, summit 10,174 feet. Lifts: 7.*

Fodor'sChoice
★ **Mammoth Mountain Ski Area.** One of the West's largest and best ski areas, Mammoth has more than 3,500 acres of skiable terrain and a 3,100-foot vertical drop. The views from the 11,053-foot summit are some of the most stunning in the Sierra. Below, you'll find a 6½-mile-wide swath of groomed boulevards and canyons, as well as pockets of tree-skiing and a dozen vast bowls. Snowboarders are everywhere on the slopes; there are three outstanding freestyle terrain parks of varying technical difficulty, with jumps, rails, tabletops, and giant super pipes (this is the location of several international snowboarding and, in summer months, mountain-bike competitions). Mammoth's season begins in November and often lingers into May. Lift tickets start at $79. Lessons and equipment are available, and there's a children's ski and snowboard school. Mammoth runs free shuttle-bus routes around town and to the ski area, and the Village Gondola runs from the Village complex to Canyon Lodge. However, only overnight guests are allowed to park at the Village for more than a few hours. ⚠ **The main lodge is dark and dated, unsuited in most every way for the crush of ski season. Within a decade, it's likely to be replaced.** ✉ *Minaret Rd., west of Mammoth Lakes* ☎ *760/934–2571, 800/626–6684, 760/934–0687 shuttle ⊕ www.mammothmountain.com ⛷ 150 trails on 3,500 acres, rated 30% beginner, 40% intermediate, 30% advanced. Longest run 3 miles, base 7,953 feet, summit 11,053 feet. Lifts: 27, including 9 high-speed and 2 gondolas.*

Tamarack Cross Country Ski Center. Trails at the center, adjacent to Tamarack Lodge, meander around several lakes. Rentals are available. The all-day inclusive rate is $55. ✉ *Lake Mary Rd., off Hwy. 203* ☎ *760/934–5293, 760/934–2442 ⊕ www.tamaracklodge.com.*

SKI RENTALS AND RESOURCES

Footloose. When the U.S. Ski Team visits Mammoth and needs boot adjustments, everyone heads to Footloose, the best place in town—and possibly all California—for ski-boot rentals and sales, as well as custom insoles. ⊠ *3043 Main St., at Mammoth Rd.* ☎ *760/934–2400* ⊕ *www. footloosesports.com.*

Kittredge Sports. Advanced skiers should consider this outfit, which has been around since the 1960s. ⊠ *3218 Main St.* ☎ *760/934–7566* ⊕ *www.kittredgesports.com.*

Mammoth Sporting Goods. This company rents good skis for intermediates and sells equipment, clothing, and accessories. ⊠ *1 Sierra Center Mall, Old Mammoth Rd.* ☎ *760/934–3239* ⊕ *www.mammothoutdoorsports.com.*

OntheSnow.com ⊕ *www.onthesnow.com/california/mammoth-mountain-ski-area/skireport.html.*

Snow Report. For information on winter conditions around Mammoth, call the Snow Report. ☎ *760/934–7669, 888/766–9778.*

EAST OF YOSEMITE NATIONAL PARK

Most people enter Yosemite National Park from the west, having driven out from the Bay Area or Los Angeles. The eastern entrance on Tioga Pass Road (Highway 120), however, provides stunning, sweeping views of the High Sierra. Gray rocks shine in the bright sun, with scattered, small vegetation sprinkled about the mountainside. To drive from Lee Vining to Tuolumne Meadows is an unforgettable experience, but keep in mind the road tends to be closed for at least seven months of the year.

LEE VINING

20 miles east of Tuolumne Meadows via Hwy. 120 to U.S. 395; 30 miles north of Mammoth Lakes on U.S. 395.

Tiny Lee Vining is known primarily as the eastern gateway to Yosemite National Park (summer only; ⇨ *Chapter 10*) and the location of vast and desolate Mono Lake. Pick up supplies at the general store year-round, or stop here for lunch or dinner before or after a drive through the high country. In winter the town is all but deserted, except for the ice climbers who come to scale frozen waterfalls. You can meet these hearty souls at Nicely's restaurant, where climbers congregate for breakfast around 8 on winter mornings. To try your hand at ice climbing, contact Doug Nidever (☎ *760/937–6922* ⊕ *www.themountainguide.com*), aka the Mountain Guide.

GETTING HERE AND AROUND

Lee Vining is on U.S. 395, just north of the road's intersection with Highway 120 and on the south side of Mono Lake. Yosemite Area Regional Transportation System (YARTS ⊕ *www.yarts.com*) can get you here from Yosemite Valley, but you'll need a car to explore the area.

ESSENTIALS

Visitor Information Lee Vining Chamber of Commerce ☎ *760/647–6629* ⊕ *www.leevining.com.* **Mono Lake** ☎ *760/647–6595* ⊕ *www.monolake.org.*

EXPLORING

Fodor's Choice **Mono Lake.** Since the 1940s Los Angeles has diverted water from this
★ lake, exposing striking towers of tufa, or calcium carbonate. Court vic-
tories by environmentalists have meant fewer diversions, and the lake is
rising again. Although to see the lake from U.S. 395 is stunning, make
time to walk about South Tufa, whose parking lot is 5 miles east of
U.S. 395 off Highway 120. There during the summer you can join the
naturalist-guided **South Tufa Walk,** which lasts about 1½ hours. The
sensational **Scenic Area Visitor Center,** on U.S. 395, is open daily from
June through September (Sunday to Thursday 8–5, Friday and Saturday
8–7); it's closed December through March and open weekends the rest of
the year. The center's hilltop and sweeping views of Mono Lake, along
with its interactive exhibits inside, make this one of California's best
visitor centers. Rangers and naturalists lead walking tours of the tufa
daily in summer and on weekends (sometimes on cross-country skis) in
winter. In town at U.S. 395 and 3rd Street, the **Mono Lake Committee
Information Center & Bookstore** has more information about this beautiful area. ⊠ *Hwy. 120, east of Lee Vining, Lee Vining* ☎ *760/647–3044.*

**EN
ROUTE**
June Lake Loop. Heading south from Lee Vining, U.S. 395 intersects the
June Lake Loop. This gorgeous 17-mile drive follows an old glacial
canyon past Grant, June, Gull, and other lakes before reconnecting
with U.S. 395 on its way to Mammoth Lakes. The loop is especially
colorful in fall. ⊠ *Hwy. 158 W.*

WHERE TO EAT AND STAY
For expanded hotel reviews, visit Fodors.com.

$ ✕ **Nicely's.** Artworks for sale decorate the walls of this vintage diner. The
AMERICAN country cooking isn't fancy—think blueberry pancakes for breakfast
and chicken-fried steak for dinner—but this is a good spot for families
with kids and unfussy eaters looking for a square meal. It's the kind of
place where the waitress walks up with a pot of coffee and asks, "Ya
want a warm-up, hon?" ⑤ *Average main: $15* ⊠ *U.S. 395 and 4th St.,
Lee Vining* ☎ *760/647–6477* ⊗ *Closed Tues. and Wed. in winter.*

$ ✕ **Tioga Gas Mart & Whoa Nelli Deli.** This might be the only gas station in
AMERICAN the United States that serves cocktails, but its appeal goes way beyond
novelty. The mahimahi tacos are succulent, the gourmet pizzas tasty,
and the herb-crusted pork loin with berry glaze elegant. Order at the
counter and grab a seat inside or out. ⑤ *Average main: $14* ⊠ *Hwy. 120
and U.S. 395, Lee Vining* ☎ *760/647–1088* ⊕ *www.whoanelliedeli.com*
⊗ *Closed mid-Nov.–mid-Apr.*

$ ▦ **Lake View Lodge.** Enormous rooms and lovely landscaping, which
B&B/INN includes several shaded sitting areas, set this motel apart from
its competitors in town. **Pros:** attractive; clean; friendly staff.
Cons: could use updating. ⑤ *Rooms from: $89* ⊠ *51285 U.S. 395*
☎ *760/647–6543, 800/990–6614* ⊕ *www.lakeviewlodgeyosemite.
com* ⊅ *76 rooms, 12 cottages.*

9

BODIE STATE HISTORIC PARK

23 miles northeast of Lee Vining via U.S. 395 to Hwy. 270.

The historic town of Bridgeport is the gateway to Bodie State Historic Park, and the only supply center for miles around. The scenery is spectacular, with craggy, snowcapped peaks looming over vast prairies. Tiny and for tourist purposes worth nothing more than a place to sleep and eat, Bridgeport's claim to fame is that most of the 1947 film-noir classic *Out of the Past* was filmed here. In winter, much of Bridgeport shuts down.

GETTING HERE AND AROUND

You need to get here by private car. About 15 miles north of Lee Vining (7 miles south of Bridgeport), look for signs pointing you east toward the ghost town, another 13 miles via Highway 270. The last 3 miles are unpaved, and possibly treacherous depending on erosion and the weather. A snowmobile might be necessary in winter.

EXPLORING

Fodor'sChoice ★ **Bodie Ghost Town.** The mining village of Rattlesnake Gulch, abandoned mine shafts, and the remains of a small Chinatown are among the sights at this fascinating ghost town. The town boomed from about 1878 to 1881, but by the late 1940s all its residents had departed. A state park was established here in 1962, with a mandate to preserve everything in a state of "arrested decay." Evidence of Bodie's wild past survives at an excellent museum, and you can tour an old stamp mill where ore was crushed into fine powder to extract gold and silver. The town is 23 miles from Lee Vining, north on U.S. 395, then east on Highway 270; the last 3 miles are unpaved. Snow may close Highway 270 from late fall through early spring. No food, drink, or lodging is available in Bodie. ⊠ *Main and Green Sts., Bodie* ☎ *760/647–6445* ⊕ *www.bodie. com* ⊠ *Park $5, museum free* ☺ *Park: late May–early Sept., daily 8–7; early Sept.–late May, daily 8–4. Museum: late May–early Sept., daily 9–6; early Sept.–late May, hrs vary.*

SOUTH OF SEQUOIA AND KINGS CANYON: THREE RIVERS

200 miles north of Los Angeles via I–5 to Hwy. 99 to Hwy. 198; 8 miles south of Ash Mountain/Foothills entrance to Sequoia National Park on Hwy. 198.

In the foothills of the Sierra along the Kaweah River, the serpentine hamlet of Three Rivers serves as the main gateway town to Sequoia and Kings Canyon national parks (⇨ *Chapter 11, Sequoia and Kings Canyon National Parks).* Its livelihood depends largely on tourism from the parks, courtesy of two markets, a few service stations, banks, a post office, and several lodgings, which are good spots to find a room when park accommodations are full (or if you dislike camping and would like to save money).

9

GETTING HERE AND AROUND

From Memorial Day through Labor Day, you can ride the city of Visalia's Sequoia Shuttle (☎ 877/404–6473 ⊕ *www.ci.visalia.ca.us*) to and from Three Rivers, up to and down from Sequoia National Park. You probably should count on driving here yourself, however, via Highway 198. The town is slender and long, and to walk from your hotel to a restaurant might wear you out before you set foot in the national park.

WHERE TO EAT AND STAY

For expanded hotel reviews, visit Fodors.com.

$ ✕ **We Three Bakery.** This friendly, popular spot packs lunches for trips
ECLECTIC into the nearby national parks; it's also open for breakfast. Baked goods for the curvy road ahead, anyone? ⑤ *Average main: $10* ⊠ *43688 Sierra Dr.* ☎ 559/561–4761.

$$ ⛺ **Buckeye Tree Lodge.** Every room at this two-story motel has a patio
B&B/INN facing a sun-dappled grassy lawn, right on the banks of the Kaweah River. **Pros:** near the park entrance; fantastic river views; friendly staff. **Cons:** can fill up quickly in the summer; could use a little updating. ⑤ *Rooms from: $123* ⊠ *46000 Sierra Dr., Hwy. 198, Three Rivers* ☎ *559/561–5900* ⊕ *www.buckeyetree.com* ⟲ *11 rooms, 1 cottage* ⦿I *Breakfast.*

$ ⛺ **Sequoia Motel.** An old-fashioned single-story mom-and-pop motel,
B&B/INN the Sequoia stands out with such extra touches as country-style quilts and mismatched Americana furnishings that lend a retro charm to the rooms. **Pros:** clean; friendly; comparatively affordable. **Cons:** not especially modern; fills up quickly in the summer. ⑤ *Rooms from: $109* ⊠ *43000 Sierra Dr., Hwy. 198, Three Rivers* ☎ *559/561–4453* ⊕ *www.sequoiamotel.com* ⟲ *11 rooms, 3 cottages.*

SPORTS AND THE OUTDOORS

TOUR OUTFITTERS

Sequoia Natural History Association. The association's highly regarded Sequoia Field Institute conducts single-day and mulitiday "edventure" tours that include backpacking hikes, natural-history walks, and kayaking excursions. ⊠ *47050 Generals Hwy. #10, Three Rivers* ☎ *559/565–3759* ⊕ *www.sequoiahistory.org.*

RAFTING

Kaweah White Water Adventures. From April through July, this outfit conducts two-hour and full-day rafting trips, with some Class III rapids. Longer trips may include some Class IV. ☎ *559/561–1000, 800/229–8658* ⊕ *www.kaweah-whitewater.com* ⊒ *$50 to $140 per person.*

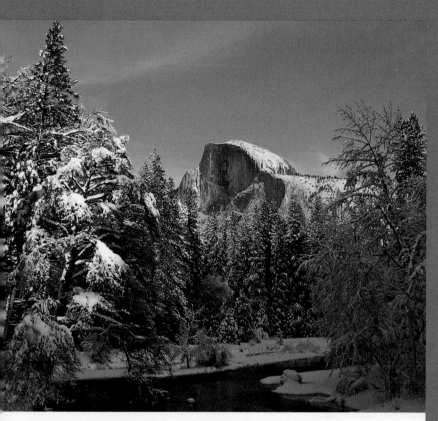

YOSEMITE
NATIONAL PARK

WELCOME TO YOSEMITE

TOP REASONS TO GO

★ **Wet and wild:** An easy stroll brings you to the base of Lower Yosemite Falls, where roaring springtime waters make for misty lens caps and lasting memories.

★ **Tunnel vision:** Approaching Yosemite Valley, Wawona Road passes through a mountainside and emerges before one of the park's most heart-stopping vistas.

★ **Inhale the beauty:** Pause to smell the light, pristine air as you travel about the High Sierra's Tiaga Pass and Tuolumne Meadows, where 10,000-foot granite peaks just might take your breath away.

★ **Walk away:** Leave the crowds behind—but do bring along a buddy—and take a hike somewhere along Yosemite's 800 miles of trails.

★ **Powder your nose:** Winter's hush floats into Yosemite on snowflakes. Lift your face to the sky and listen to the trees.

1 Yosemite Valley. At an elevation of 4,000 feet, in roughly the center of the park, beats Yosemite's heart. This is where you'll find the park's most famous sights and biggest crowds.

2 Wawona and Mariposa Grove. The park's southern tip holds Wawona, with its grand old hotel and pioneer history center, and the Mariposa Grove of Big Trees, filled with giant sequoias. These are closest to the South Entrance, 35 miles (a one-hour drive) south of Yosemite Village.

3 Tuolumne Meadows. The highlight of east-central Yosemite is this wildflower-strewn valley with hiking trails, nestled among sharp, rocky peaks. It's a two-hour drive northeast of Yosemite Valley along Tioga Road (closed mid-October to late May).

4 Hetch Hetchy. The most remote, least visited part of Yosemite accessible by automobile, this glacial valley is dominated by a reservoir and veined with wilderness trails. It's near the park's western boundary, about a half-hour drive north of the Big Oak Flat Entrance.

CALIFORNIA

GETTING ORIENTED

Yosemite is so large that you can think of it as five parks. Yosemite Valley, famous for waterfalls and cliffs, and Wawona, where the giant sequoias stand, are open all year. Hetch Hetchy, home of less-used backcountry trails, is most accessible from late spring through early fall. The subalpine high country, Tuolumne Meadows, is open for summer hiking and camping; in winter it's accessible via cross-country skis or snowshoes. Badger Pass Ski Area is open in winter only. Most visitors spend their time along the park's southwestern border, between Wawona and Big Oak Flat Entrance; a bit farther east in Yosemite Valley and Badger Pass Ski Area; and along the east–west corridor of Tioga Road, which spans the park north of Yosemite Valley and bisects Tuolumne Meadows.

10

Tilden Lake

Stubblefield Canyon

Matterhorn Canyon

Return Creek

Pettit Peak
10,788 ft.

Tuolumne River

TO MONO LAKE

Tioga Pass Entrance

Tuolumne Meadows 3

Visitor Center

120

Cathedral Peak

Cathedral Range

Lyell Fork

Yosemite Valley 1

Visitor Center

North Dome

Half Dome

Glacier Point

Merced River

Mount Lyell
13,114 ft.

Clark Range

Turner Ridge

Wawona

Mariposa Grove of Big Trees

41 South Entrance

Updated by
Reed Parsell

By merely standing in Yosemite Valley and turning in a circle, you can see more natural wonders in a minute than you could in a full day pretty much anywhere else. Half Dome, Yosemite Falls, El Capitan, Bridalveil Fall, Sentinel Dome, the Merced River, white-flowering dogwood trees, maybe even bears ripping into the bark of fallen trees or sticking their snouts into beehives—it's all in Yosemite Valley.

In the mid-1800s, when tourists were arriving to the area, the valley's special geologic qualities, and the giant sequoias of Mariposa Grove 30 miles to the south, so impressed a group of influential Californians that they persuaded President Abraham Lincoln to grant those two areas to the state for protection. On Oct. 1, 1890—thanks largely to lobbying efforts by naturalist John Muir and Robert Underwood Johnson, the editor of *Century Magazine*—Congress set aside 1,500 square miles for Yosemite National Park.

YOSEMITE PLANNER

WHEN TO GO

During extremely busy periods—such as the 4th of July—you will experience delays at the entrance gates. ■TIP➔ **For smaller crowds, visit midweek.** Or come mid-April through Memorial Day or mid-September through October, when the park is only a bit busy and the days usually are sunny and clear.

Summer rainfall is rare. In winter, heavy snows occasionally cause road closures, and tire chains or four-wheel drive may be required on the roads that remain open. The road to Glacier Point beyond the turnoff for Badger Pass is closed after the first major snowfall; Tioga Road is closed from late October through May or mid-June. Mariposa Grove Road is typically closed for a shorter period in winter.

GETTING HERE AND AROUND

BUS TRAVEL

Once you're in Yosemite you can take advantage of the free shuttle buses, which operate on low emissions, have 21 stops, and run every 10 minutes or so from 9 am to 6 pm year-round; a separate (but also free) summer-only shuttle runs out to El Capitan. Also during the summer, you can pay to take the morning "hikers' bus" from Yosemite Valley to Tuolumne or the bus up to Glacier Point. Bus service from Wawona is geared to people who are staying there and want to spend the day in Yosemite Valley. Free and frequent shuttles transport people between the Wawona Hotel and Mariposa Grove. During the snow season, buses run regularly between Yosemite Valley and Badger Pass Ski Area.

CAR TRAVEL

Roughly 200 miles from San Francisco, 300 miles from Los Angeles, and 500 miles from Las Vegas, Yosemite takes a while to reach—and its many sites and attractions merit much more time than what rangers say is the average visit: four hours. Most people arrive via automobile or tour bus, but public transportation (courtesy of Amtrak and the regional YARTS bus system) also can get you to the valley efficiently.

Of the park's four entrances, Arch Rock is the closest to Yosemite Valley. The road that goes through it, Route 140 from Merced and Mariposa, is a scenic western approach that snakes alongside the boulder-packed Merced River. Route 41, through Wawona, is the way to come from Los Angeles (or Fresno, if you've flown in and rented a car). Route 120, through Crane Flat, is the most direct route from San Francisco. The only way in from the east is Tioga Road, which may be the best route in terms of scenery—though due to snow accumulation it's open for a frustratingly short amount of time each year (typically early June through mid-October).

There are few gas stations within Yosemite (Crane Flat, Tuolumne Meadows, and Wawona; none in the valley), so fuel up before you reach the park. From late fall until early spring, the weather is especially unpredictable, and driving can be treacherous. You should carry chains.

PARK ESSENTIALS

PARK FEES AND PERMITS

The admission fee, valid for seven days, is $20 per vehicle or $10 per individual.

If you plan to camp in the backcountry or climb Half Dome, you must have a wilderness permit. Availability of permits, which are free, depends upon trailhead quotas. It's best to make a reservation, especially if you will be visiting May through September. You can reserve two days to 24 weeks in advance by phone (☎ 209/372–0740 or 209/372–0739); a $5-per-person processing fee is charged if and when your reservation is confirmed. Requests must include your name, address, daytime phone, the number of people in your party, trip date, alternative dates, starting and ending trailheads, and a brief itinerary. Without a reservation, you may still get a free permit on a first-come, first-served basis at wilderness permit offices at Big Oak Flat, Hetch Hetchy, Tuolumne, Wawona, the Wilderness Center in Yosemite Village, and Yosemite Valley in summer. From fall to spring, visit the Valley Visitor Center.

10

Plants and Wildlife in Yosemite

Dense stands of incense cedar and Douglas fir—as well as ponderosa, Jeffrey, lodgepole, and sugar pines—cover much of the park, but the stellar standout, quite literally, is the *Sequoia sempervirens*, the giant sequoia. Sequoias grow only along the west slope of the Sierra Nevada between 4,500 and 7,000 feet in elevation. Starting from a seed the size of a rolled-oat flake, each of these ancient monuments assumes remarkable proportions in adulthood; you can see them in the Mariposa Grove of Big Trees. In late May the valley's dogwood trees bloom with white, starlike flowers. Wildflowers, such as black-eyed Susan, bull thistle, cow parsnip, lupine, and meadow goldenrod, peak in June in the valley and in July at higher elevations.

The most visible animals in the park—aside from the omnipresent western gray squirrel—are the mule deer. Though sightings of bighorn sheep are infrequent in the park itself, you can sometimes see them on the eastern side of the Sierra Crest, just off Route 120 in Lee Vining Canyon. You may also see the American black bear, which often has a brown, cinnamon, or blond coat. The Sierra Nevada is home to thousands of bears, and you should take all necessary precautions to keep yourself—and the bears—safe. For one, do not feed the bears. Bears that acquire a taste for human food can become very aggressive and destructive and often must be destroyed by rangers.

Watch for the blue Steller's jay along trails, near public buildings, and in campgrounds, and look for golden eagles soaring over Tioga Road.

PARK HOURS

The park is open 24/7 year-round. All entrances are open at all hours, except for the Hetch Hetchy Entrance, which is open roughly dawn to dusk. Yosemite is in the Pacific time zone.

TOURS

Ansel Adams Photo Walks. Photography enthusiasts shouldn't miss these 90-minute guided camera walks offered four mornings (Mon., Tue., Thu., and Sat.) each week by professional photographers. All are free, but participation is limited to 15 people. Meeting points vary, and advance reservations are essential. ☎ *209/372–4413, 800/568–7398* ⊕ *www.anseladams.com* ☑ *Free.*

FAMILY **Wee Wild Ones.** Designed for kids under seven, this 45-minute program includes animal-theme games, songs, stories, and crafts. The event is held outdoors before the regular Yosemite Lodge or Curry Village evening programs in summer and fall; it moves to the Ahwahnee's big fireplace in winter and spring. All children must be accompanied by an adult. ☎ *209/372–1240* ☑ *Free.*

VISITOR INFORMATION

PARK CONTACT INFORMATION

Yosemite National Park ☎ *209/372–0200* ⊕ *www.nps.gov/yose.*

VISITOR CENTERS

Le Conte Memorial Lodge. This small but striking National Historic Landmark, with its granite walls and steeply pitched shingle roof, is Yosemite's first permanent public information center. Step inside to see the cathedral-like interior, which contains a library and environmental exhibits. To find out about evening programs, check the kiosk out front. ⊠ *Southside Dr., about ½ mile west of Curry Village* ☉ *Memorial Day–Labor Day, Wed.–Sun. 10–4.*

Valley Visitor Center. Learn about Yosemite Valley's geology, vegetation, and human inhabitants at this visitor center. Don't leave without watching *Spirit of Yosemite*, a 23-minute introductory film that runs every half-hour in the theater behind the visitor center. Strangely, the film shows no animals other than one deer. ⊠ *Yosemite Village* ☎ *209/372–0299* ☉ *Late May–early Sept., daily 9–7:30; early Sept.–late May, daily 9–5.*

EXPLORING

HISTORIC SITES

Ahwahneechee Village. This solemn smattering of structures, accessed by a short loop trail behind the Yosemite Valley Visitor Center, is a look at what Native American life might have been like in the 1870s. One interpretive sign points out that the Miwok people referred to the 19th-century newcomers as "Yohemite" or "Yohometuk," which have been translated as meaning "some of them are killers." ⊠ *Northside Dr., Yosemite Village* ☎ *Free* ☉ *Daily sunrise–sunset.*

Pioneer Yosemite History Center. Some of Yosemite's first structures—those not occupied by Native Americans, that is—were relocated here in the 1950s and 1960s. You can spend a pleasurable and informative half-hour walking about them and reading the signs, perhaps springing for a self-guided-tour pamphlet (50¢) to further enhance the history lesson. Weekends and some weekdays in the summer, costumed docents conduct free blacksmithing and "wet-plate" photography demonstrations, and for a small fee you can take a stagecoach ride. ⊠ *Rte. 41, Wawona* ☎ *209/375–9531, 209/379–2646* ☎ *Free* ☉ *Building interiors are open mid-June–Labor Day, Wed. 2–5, Thurs.–Sun. 10–1 and 2–5.*

10

SCENIC STOPS

El Capitan. Rising 3,593 feet—more than 350 stories—above the Valley, El Capitan is the largest exposed-granite monolith in the world. Since 1958, people have been climbing its entire face, including the famous "nose." You can spot adventurers with your binoculars by scanning the smooth and nearly vertical cliff for specks of color. ⊠ *Off Northside Dr., about 4 miles west of the Valley Visitor Center.*

Fodor's Choice **Glacier Point.** If you lack the time, desire, or stamina to hike more than
★ 3,200 feet up to Glacier Point from the Yosemite Valley floor, you can drive here—or take a bus from the Valley—for a bird's-eye view. You are likely to encounter a lot of day-trippers on the short, paved trail that leads

"This is us taking a break before conquering the top of Lembert Dome, while enjoying the beautiful view over Yosemite's high country." —photo by Rebalyn, Fodors.com member

from the parking lot to the main overlook. Take a moment to veer off a few yards to the Geology Hut, which succinctly explains and illustrates how the Valley looked like 10 million, 3 million, and 20,000 years ago. ⊠ *Glacier Point Rd., 16 miles northeast of Rte. 41* ☎ *209/372–1240.*

Half Dome. Visitors' eyes are continually drawn to this remarkable granite formation that tops out at more than 4,700 feet above the valley floor. Despite its name, the dome is actually about three-quarters intact. You can hike to the top of Half Dome on an 8.5-mile (one-way) trail whose last 400 feet must be ascended while holding onto a steel cable. Permits are required (and checked on the trail), and there's a 300-person limit each day. Back down in the valley, see Half Dome reflected in the Merced River by heading to Sentinel Bridge just before sundown. The brilliant orange light on Half Dome is a stunning sight.

Hetch Hetchy Reservoir. When Congress approved the O'Shaughnessy Dam in 1913, pragmatism triumphed over aestheticism. Some 2.5 million residents of the San Francisco Bay Area continue to get their water from this 117-billion-gallon reservoir. Although spirited efforts are being made to restore the Hetch Hetchy Valley to its former, pristine glory, three-quarters of San Francisco voters in 2012 ultimately opposed a measure to possibly drain the reservoir. Eight miles long, the reservoir is Yosemite's largest body of water, and one that can be seen up close from several trails. ⊠ *Hetch Hetchy Rd., about 15 miles north of the Big Oak Flat entrance station.*

Fodor's Choice ★ **Mariposa Grove of Big Trees.** Of Yosemite's three sequoia groves—the others being Merced and Tuolumne, both near Crane Flat well to the north—Mariposa is by far the largest and easiest to walk around.

Grizzly Giant, whose base measures 96 feet around, has been estimated to be one of the largest in the world. Perhaps more astoundingly, it's about 2,700 years old. Up the hill, you'll find many more sequoias, a small museum, and fewer people. Summer weekends are especially crowded here. Consider taking the free shuttle from Wawona. ⊠ *Rte. 41, 2 miles north of the South Entrance station.*

Tuolumne Meadows. The largest subalpine meadow in the Sierra (at 8,600 feet) is a popular way station for backpack trips along the Pacific Crest and John Muir trails. The setting is not as dramatic as Yosemite Valley, 56 miles away, but the almost perfectly flat basin, about 2½ miles long, is intriguing, and in July it's resplendent with wildflowers. The most popular day hike is up Lembert Dome, atop which you'll have breathtaking views of the basin below. Keep in mind that Tioga Road rarely opens before June and usually closes by mid-October. ⊠ *Tioga Rd. (Rte. 120), about 8 miles west of the Tioga Pass entrance station.*

WATERFALLS

Yosemite's waterfalls are at their most spectacular in May and June. When the snow starts to melt (usually peaking in May), streaming snowmelt spills down to meet the Merced River. By summer's end, some falls, including the mighty Yosemite Falls, trickle or dry up. Their flow increases in late fall, and in winter they may be hung dramatically with ice. Even in drier months, the waterfalls can be breathtaking. If you choose to hike any of the trails to or up the falls, be sure to wear shoes with no-slip soles; the rocks can be extremely slick. Stay on trails at all times.

■ TIP→ **Visit the park during a full moon and you can stroll in the valley without a flashlight and still make out the ribbons of falling water, as well as silhouettes of the giant granite monoliths.**

Bridalveil Fall. This 620-foot waterfall is often diverted dozens of feet one way or the other by the breeze. It is the first marvelous site you will see up-close when you drive into Yosemite Valley. ⊠ *Yosemite Valley, access from parking area off Wawona Rd.*

Nevada Fall. Climb Mist Trail from Happy Isles for an up-close view of this 594-foot cascading beauty. If you don't want to hike (the trail's final approach is quite taxing), you can see it—albeit distantly—from Glacier Point. Stay safely on the trail, as people sometimes die when they climb over the railing and onto the slippery rocks. ⊠ *Yosemite Valley, access via Mist Trail from Nature Center at Happy Isles.*

Ribbon Fall. At 1,612 feet, this is the highest single fall in North America. It's also the first waterfall to dry up in summer; the rainwater and melted snow that create the slender fall evaporate quickly at this height. Look just west of El Capitan for the best view of the fall from the base of Bridalveil Fall. ⊠ *Yosemite Valley, west of El Capitan Meadow.*

Vernal Fall. Fern-covered black rocks frame this 317-foot fall, and rainbows play in the spray at its base. You can get a distant view from Glacier Point, or hike to see it close up. You'll get wet, but the view is worth it. ⊠ *Yosemite Valley, access via Mist Trail from Nature Center at Happy Isles.*

10

Yosemite's
Valley Floor

GOOD READS

■ *The Photographer's Guide to Yosemite,* by Michael Frye, is an insider's guide to the park, with maps for shutterbugs looking to capture perfect images.

■ John Muir penned his observations of the park he long advocated for in *The Yosemite.*

■ *Yosemite and the High Sierra,* edited by Andrea G. Stillman and John Szarkowski, features beautiful reproductions of landmark photographs by Ansel Adams, accompanied by excerpts from the photographer's journals written when Adams traveled in Yosemite National Park in the early 20th century.

■ An insightful collection of essays accompanies the museum-quality artworks in *Yosemite: Art of an American Icon* by Amy Scott.

■ Perfect for beginning wildlife watchers, *Sierra Nevada Wildflowers,* by Karen Wiese, identifies more than 230 kinds of flora growing in the Sierra Nevada region.

Fodor's Choice
★
Yosemite Falls. Actually three falls, they together constitute the highest waterfall in North America and the fifth highest in the world. The water from the top descends a total of 2,425 feet, and when the falls run hard, you can hear them thunder across the valley. If they dry up—that sometimes happens in late summer—the valley seems naked without the wavering tower of spray. ■ TIP→ **If you hike the mile-long loop trail (partially paved) to the base of the Lower Falls in May, prepare to get wet.** You can get a good full-length view of the falls from the lawn of Yosemite Chapel, off Southside Drive. ⊠ *Yosemite Valley, access from Yosemite Lodge or trail parking area.*

EDUCATIONAL OFFERINGS

CLASSES AND SEMINARS

Art Classes. Professional artists conduct workshops in watercolor, etching, drawing, and other mediums. Bring your own materials or purchase the basics at the Art Activity Center, next to the Village Store. Children under 13 must be accompanied by an adult. ⊠ *Art Activity Center, Yosemite Village* ☎ 209/372–1442 ⊕ *www.yosemitepark.com* ☞ *Free* ⊙ *Early Apr.–early Oct., Mon.–Sat., 10 am–2 pm.*

Yosemite Outdoor Adventures. Naturalists, scientists, and park rangers lead multi-hour to multiday educational outings on topics from woodpeckers to fire management to pastel painting. Most sessions take place spring through fall, but a few focus on winter phenomena. ⊠ *Various locations* ☎ 209/379–2321 ⊕ *www.yosemitepark.com* ☞ *$82–$465.*

RANGER PROGRAMS

Junior Ranger Program. Children ages 3 to 13 can participate in the informal, self-guided Little Cub and Junior Ranger programs. A park activity handbook ($4) is available at the Valley Visitor Center or the Nature Center at Happy Isles. Once kids complete the book, rangers present them with a certificate and a badge. ⊠ *Valley Visitor Center or the Nature Center at Happy Isles* ☎ 209/372–0299.

10

Ranger-Led Programs. Rangers lead entertaining walks and give informative talks several times a day from spring to fall. The schedule is more limited in winter, but most days you can find a program somewhere in the park. In the evenings at Yosemite Lodge and Curry Village, lectures, slide shows, and documentary films present unique perspectives on Yosemite. On summer weekends, Camp Curry and Tuolumne Meadows Campground host sing-along campfire programs. Schedules and locations are posted on bulletin boards throughout the park. ⊕ *www. yosemitepark.com.*

SPORTS AND THE OUTDOORS

BICYCLING

One enjoyable way to see Yosemite Valley is to ride a bike beneath its lofty granite monoliths. The eastern valley has 12 miles of paved, flat bicycle paths across meadows and through woods, with bike racks at convenient stopping points. For a greater challenge but at no small risk, you can ride on 196 miles of paved park roads; bicycles are not allowed on hiking trails or in the backcountry. Kids under 18 must wear a helmet.

TOURS AND OUTFITTERS

Yosemite bike rentals. You can arrange for rentals from Yosemite Lodge and Curry Village bike stands. Bikes with child trailers, baby-jogger strollers, and wheelchairs are also available. The cost is about $11 per hour, or $32 a day. ⊠ *Yosemite Lodge or Curry Village* ☎ *209/372–1208* ⊕ *www.yosemitepark.com* ۞ *Apr.–Oct.*

BIRD-WATCHING

Nearly 250 bird species have been spotted in the park, including the sage sparrow, pygmy owl, blue grouse, and mountain bluebird. Park rangers lead free bird-watching walks in Yosemite Valley one day each week in summer; check at a visitor center or information station for times and locations. Binoculars sometimes are available for loan.

HIKING

TOURS AND OUTFITTERS

Wilderness Center. This facility provides free wilderness permits, which are required for overnight camping (advance reservations are available for $5 and are highly recommended for popular trailheads in summer and on weekends). The staff here also provides maps and advice to hikers heading into the backcountry. ☎ *209/372–0308.*

Yosemite Mountaineering School and Guide Service. From April to November, Yosemite Mountaineering School and Guide Service leads two-hour to full-day treks, as well as backpacking and overnight excursions. Reservations are recommended. ⊠ *Yosemite Mountain Shop, Curry Village* ☎ *209/372–8344* ⊕ *www.yosemitepark.com/ Activities_RockClimbing.aspx.*

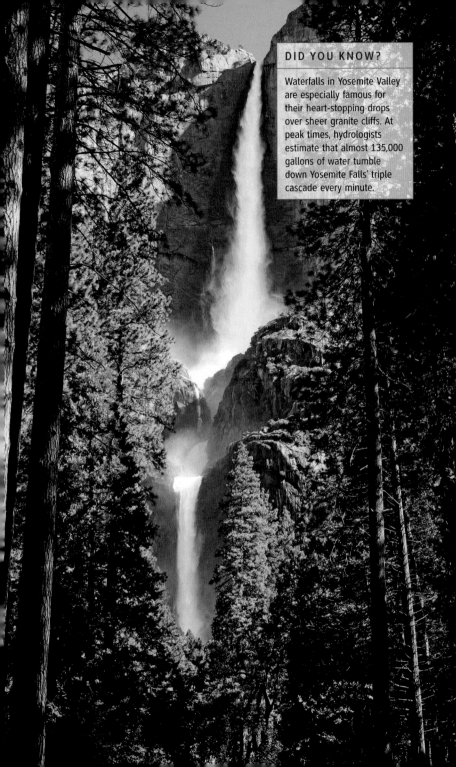

EASY

Yosemite Falls Trail. This is the highest waterfall in North America. The upper fall (1,430 feet), the middle cascades (675 feet), and the lower fall (320 feet) combine for a total of 2,425 feet and, when viewed from the valley, appear as a single waterfall. The ¼-mile trail leads from the parking lot to the base of the falls. Upper Yosemite Fall Trail, a strenuous 3½-mile climb rising 2,700 feet, takes you above the top of the falls. Lower trail: *Easy.* Upper trail: *Difficult.* ⊠ *Trailhead off Camp 4, north of Northside Dr.*

MODERATE

Mist Trail. Except for Lower Yosemite Falls, more visitors take this trail (or portions of it) than any other in the park. The trek up to and back from Vernal Fall is 3 miles. Add another 4 miles total by continuing up to 594-foot Nevada Fall; the trail becomes quite steep and slippery in its final stages. The elevation gain to Vernal Fall is 1,000 feet, and to Nevada Fall an additional 1,000 feet. Merced River tumbles down both falls on its way to a tranquil flow through the Valley. *Moderate.* ⊠ *Trailhead at Happy Isles.*

Panorama Trail. Few hikes come with the visual punch that this 8½-mile trail provides. The star attraction is Half Dome, visible from many intriguing angles, but you also see three waterfalls up close and walk through a manzanita grove. Before you begin, look down on Yosemite Valley from Glacier Point, a special experience in itself. ⚠ **If you start after taking the last bus from the valley floor to Glacier Point, you might run out of daylight before you finish.** *Moderate.* ⊠ *Trailhead at Glacier Point.*

DIFFICULT

Fodor'sChoice
★

John Muir Trail to Half Dome. Ardent and courageous trekkers continue on from Nevada Fall to the top of Half Dome. Some hikers attempt this entire 10- to 12-hour, 16¾-mile round-trip trek in one day; if you're planning to do this, remember that the 4,800-foot elevation gain and the 8,842-foot altitude will cause shortness of breath. Another option is to hike to a campground in Little Yosemite Valley near the top of Nevada Fall the first day, then climb to the top of Half Dome and hike out the next day. Get your wilderness permit (required for a one-day hike to Half Dome, too) at least a month in advance. Be sure to wear hiking boots and bring gloves. The last pitch up the back of Half Dome is very steep—the only way to climb this sheer rock face is to pull yourself up using the steel cable handrails, which are in place only from late spring to early fall. Those who brave the ascent will be rewarded with an unbeatable view of Yosemite Valley below and the high country beyond. *Difficult.* ⚠ **Only 300 hikers per day are allowed atop Half Dome, and they all must have permits.** ⊠ *Trailhead at Happy Isles.*

HORSEBACK RIDING

Reservations for guided trail rides must be made in advance at the hotel tour desks or by phone. For overnight saddle trips, which use mules, call ☎ *209/372–8348* on or after September 15 to request a lottery application for the following year. Scenic trail rides range from two hours to a full day; six-day High Sierra saddle trips are also available.

TOURS AND OUTFITTERS

Tuolumne Meadows Stables. Tuolumne Meadows Stables runs two-, four-, and eight-hour trips that start at $64, as well as four- to six-day camping treks on mules that begin at $625. Reservations are mandatory. ⊠ *Off Tioga Rd., 2 miles east of Tuolumne Meadows Visitor Center* ☎ *209/372–8427* ⊕ *www.yosemitepark.com.*

Wawona Stables. Wawona Stables has two- and five-hour rides starting at $64. Reservations are recommended. ⊠ *Rte. 41, Wawona* ☎ *209/375–6502.*

Yosemite Valley Stables. You can tour the valley and the start of the high country on two-hour, four-hour, and daylong rides at Yosemite Valley Stables. Reservations are strongly recommended for the trips, which start at $64. ⊠ *At entrance to North Pines Campground, 100 yards northeast of Curry Village* ☎ *209/372–8348* ⊕ *www.yosemitepark.com.*

RAFTING

Rafting is permitted only on designated areas of the Middle and South forks of the Merced River. Check with the Valley Visitor Center for closures and other restrictions.

OUTFITTERS

Curry Village raft stand. The per-person rental fee ($28.50 adults, $23.50 children) at Curry Village raft stand covers the four- to six-person raft, two paddles, and life jackets, plus a shuttle to the launch point on Sentinel Beach. ⊠ *South side of Southside Dr., Curry Village* ☎ *209/372–4386* ⊕ *www.yosemitepark.com* ⊠ *$28.50* ☉ *Late May–July.*

ROCK CLIMBING

Fodor's Choice
★ The granite canyon walls of Yosemite Valley are world renowned for rock climbing. El Capitan, with its 3,593-foot vertical face, is the most famous, but there are many other options here for all skill levels.

TOURS AND OUTFITTERS

Yosemite Mountaineering School and Guide Service. The one-day basic lesson at Yosemite Mountaineering School and Guide Service includes some bouldering and rappelling, and three or four 60-foot climbs. Climbers must be at least 10 years old and in reasonably good physical condition. Intermediate and advanced classes include instruction in first aid, anchor building, multi-pitch climbing, summer snow climbing, and big-wall climbing. There's a nordic program in the winter. ⊠ *Yosemite Mountain Shop, Curry Village* ☎ *209/372–8344* ⊕ *www.yosemitepark. com* ⊠ *Starting at $148* ☉ *Apr.–Nov.*

WINTER SPORTS

ICE-SKATING

Curry Village Ice Rink. Winter visitors have skated at this outdoor rink for decades, and there's no mystery why: it's a kick to glide across the ice while soaking up views of Half Dome and Glacier Point. ⊠ *South side of Southside Dr., Curry Village* ☎ *209/372–8319* ⊠ *$9.75 per session,*

10

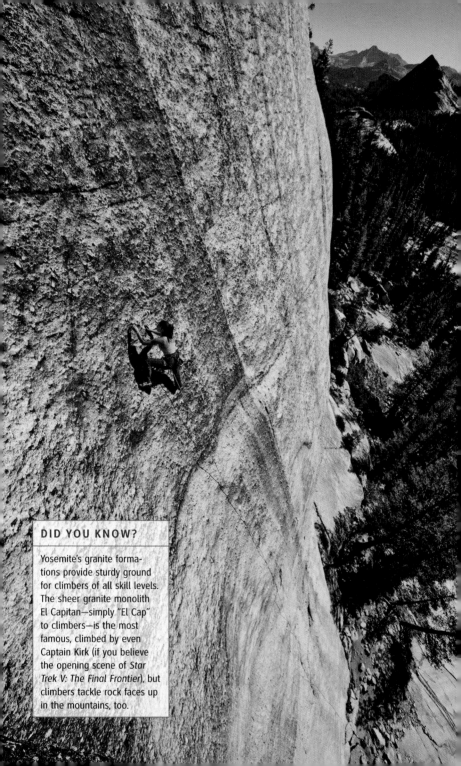

DID YOU KNOW?

Yosemite's granite formations provide sturdy ground for climbers of all skill levels. The sheer granite monolith El Capitan—simply "El Cap" to climbers—is the most famous, climbed by even Captain Kirk (if you believe the opening scene of *Star Trek V: The Final Frontier*), but climbers tackle rock faces up in the mountains, too.

$4 skate rental ⊙ Mid-Nov.–mid-Mar. afternoons and evenings daily, morning sessions weekends (hrs vary).

SKIING AND SNOWSHOEING

Badger Pass Ski Area. California's first ski resort has five lifts and 10 downhill runs, as well as 90 miles of groomed cross-country trails. Free shuttle buses from Yosemite Valley operate between December and early April, weather permitting. Lift tickets are $47, downhill equipment rents for $36, and snowboard rental with boots is $37.50. ⊠ *Badger Pass Rd., off Glacier Point Rd., 18 miles from Yosemite Valley* ☎ *209/372–8430.*

Yosemite Ski School. The gentle slopes of Badger Pass make Yosemite Ski School an ideal spot for children and beginners to learn downhill skiing or snowboarding for as little as $45.50 for a group lesson. ☎ *209/372–8430* ⊕ *www.yosemitepark.com.*

Yosemite Mountaineering School. Yosemite Mountaineering School conducts snowshoeing, cross-country skiing, telemarking, and skate-skiing classes starting at $35.50. ⊠ *Badger Pass Ski Area* ☎ *209/372–8344* ⊕ *www.yosemitepark.com.*

Yosemite Cross-Country Ski School. The highlight of Yosemite's cross-country skiing center is a 21-mile loop from Badger Pass to Glacier Point. You can rent cross-country skis for $25 per day at the Cross-Country Ski School, which also rents snowshoes ($24 per day) and telemarking equipment ($29.50). ☎ *209/372–8444* ⊕ *www.yosemitepark.com.*

WHERE TO EAT

In addition to the dining options listed here, you'll find fast-food grills and cafeterias, plus hamburger stands, pizza joints, and temporary snack bars near park roads in summer. Many dining facilities in the park are open summer only. *Prices in the reviews are the average cost of a main course at dinner or, if dinner is not served, at lunch.*

$$$$
EUROPEAN
Fodor's Choice
★

✕**Ahwahnee Hotel Dining Room.** Rave reviews about the dining room's appearance are fully justified—it features towering windows, a 34-foot-high ceiling with interlaced sugar-pine beams, and massive chandeliers. Although many continue to applaud the food, others have reported that they sense a dip in the quality both in the service and what is being served. Diners must spend a lot of money here, so perhaps that inflates the expectations and amplifies the disappointments. In any event, the $43 Sunday brunch is consistently praised. Reservations are always advised, and the attire is "resort casual." ⑤ *Average main: $40* ⊠ *Ahwahnee Hotel, Ahwahnee Rd., about ¾ mile east of Yosemite Valley Visitor Center, Yosemite Village* ☎ *209/372–1489* ⚐ *Reservations essential.*

$$$
AMERICAN

✕**Mountain Room.** Though good, the food becomes secondary when you see Yosemite Falls through this dining room's wall of windows—almost every table has a view. The chef makes a point of using locally sourced, organic ingredients, so you can be assured of fresh vegetables. Vegans are accommodated, too. The Mountain Room Lounge, a few steps away in the Yosemite Lodge complex, has a broad bar with about 10 beers on tap. ⑤ *Average main: $23* ⊠ *Yosemite Lodge, Northside Dr. about ¾ mile west of the visitor center, Yosemite Village* ☎ *209/372–1281* ⊙ *No lunch.*

10

$ **✕Tuolumne Meadows Grill.** Serving continuously throughout the day until
FAST FOOD 5 or 6 pm, this fast-food eatery cooks up breakfast, lunch, and snacks.
It's possible that ice cream tastes better at this altitude. Stop in for a
quick meal before exploring the Meadows. $ *Average main: $8 ⊠ Tioga
Rd. (Rte. 120), 1½ mile east of Tuolumne Meadows Visitor Center*
☎ *209/372–8426 ۞ Closed Oct.–Memorial Day.*

$$ **✕Tuolumne Meadows Lodge.** At the back of a small building that contains
AMERICAN the lodge's front desk and small gift shop, this restaurant serves hearty
American fare at breakfast and dinner. The decor is ultra-woodsy, with
dark-wood walls and red-and-white-checkered tablecloths. Meals are
mostly of the meat-and-potato variety, but vegetarians' requests are
honored. If you have any dietary restrictions, let the front desk know
in advance and the cooks will not let you down. Order box lunches
from here for before hikes. $ *Average main: $18 ⊠ Tioga Rd. (Rte. 120)*
☎ *209/372–8413 ⚐ Reservations essential ۞ Closed late Sept.–Memo-
rial Day. No lunch.*

$$$ **✕Wawona Hotel Dining Room.** Watch deer graze on the meadow while you
AMERICAN dine in the romantic, candlelit dining room of the whitewashed Wawona
Hotel, which dates from the late 1800s. The American-style cuisine
favors fresh ingredients and flavors; trout is a menu staple. There's also
a Sunday brunch Easter through Thanksgiving, and a barbeque on the
lawn Saturday evenings in summer. A jacket is required at dinner. $ *Av-
erage main: $27 ⊠ Wawona Hotel, Rte. 41, Wawona ☎ 801/559–4935*
⚐ *Reservations essential ۞ Closed Jan., Feb., and Mar.*

PICNIC AREAS

Considering how large the park is and how many visitors come here—
some 4 million people every year, most of them just for the day—it is
somewhat surprising that Yosemite has so few formal picnic areas,
though in many places you can find a smooth rock to sit on and enjoy
breathtaking views along with your lunch. The convenience stores all
sell picnic supplies, and prepackaged sandwiches and salads are widely
available. Those options can come in especially handy during the middle
of the day, when you might not want to spend precious daylight hours
in such a spectacular setting sitting in a restaurant for a formal meal.

WHERE TO STAY

*Prices in the reviews are the lowest cost of a standard double room in
high season. For expanded hotel reviews, visit Fodors.com.*

$$$$ **🏨 Ahwahnee Hotel.** A National Historic Landmark, the hotel is con-
HOTEL structed of sugar-pine logs and features Native American design
Fodor'sChoice motifs; public spaces are enlivened with art-deco flourishes, oriental
★ rugs, and elaborate iron- and woodwork. **Pros:** best lodge in Yosemite; helpful concierge. **Cons:** expensive rates; some reports that service
has slipped in recent years. $ *Rooms from: $471 ⊠ Ahwahnee Rd.,
about ¾ miles east of Yosemite Valley Visitor Center, Yosemite Village ☎ 801/559–4884 ⊕ www.yosemitepark.com ⤶ 99 lodge rooms,
4 suites, 24 cottage rooms.*

CLOSE UP

Best Campgrounds in Yosemite

If you are going to concentrate solely on valley sites and activities, you should endeavor to stay in one of the "Pines" campgrounds, which are clustered near Curry Village and within an easy stroll from that busy complex's many facilities. For a more primitive and quiet experience, and to be near many backcountry hikes, try one of the Tioga Road campgrounds.

National Park Service Reservations Office. Reservations are required at most of Yosemite's campgrounds, especially in summer; while you can book a site up to five months in advance, those made more than 21 days in advance require prepayment. ⑤ *Rooms from: $193* ☎ *800/436–7275* ⊕ *www.recreation. gov* ⊙ *Daily 7–7.*

Bridalveil Creek. This campground sits among lodgepole pines at 7,200 feet, above the valley on Glacier Point Road. From here, you can easily drive to Glacier Point's magnificent valley views. ⊠ *From Hwy. 41 in Wawona, go north to Glacier Point Rd. and turn right; entrance to campground is 25 miles ahead on right side.*

Camp 4. Formerly known as Sunnyside Walk-In, this is the only valley campground available on a first-come, first-served basis. ⊠ *Base of Yosemite Falls Trail, just west of Yosemite Lodge on Northside Dr., Yosemite Village.*

Crane Flat. This camp on Yosemite's western boundary, south of Hodgdon Meadow, is just 17 miles from the valley but far from its bustle. ⊠ *From Big Oak Flat entrance on Hwy. 120, drive 10 miles east to campground entrance on right.*

Housekeeping Camp. Composed of three walls (usually concrete) and covered with two layers of canvas, each unit has an open-ended fourth side that can be closed off with a heavy white canvas curtain. You rent "bedpacks," consisting of blankets, sheets, and other comforts. ⊠ *Southside Dr., ½ mile west of Curry Village.*

Lower Pines. This moderate-size campground sits directly along the Merced River; it's a short walk to the trailheads for the Mirror Lake and Mist trails. ⊠ *At east end of valley.*

Porcupine Flat. Sixteen miles west of Tuolumne Meadows, this campground sits at 8,100 feet. If you want to be in the high country, this is a good bet. ⊠ *16 miles west of Tuolumne Meadows on Hwy. 120.*

Tuolumne Meadow. In a wooded area at 8,600 feet, just south of its namesake meadow, this is one of the most spectacular and sought-after campgrounds in Yosemite. ⊠ *Hwy. 120, 46 miles east of Big Oak Flat entrance station.*

Upper Pines. This is the valley's largest campground and the closest one to the trailheads. Expect large crowds in the summer—and little privacy. ⊠ *At east end of valley, near Curry Village.*

Wawona. Near the Mariposa Grove, just downstream from a popular fishing spot, this year-round campground has larger, less densely packed sites than campgrounds in the valley. ⊠ *Hwy. 41, 1 mile north of Wawona.*

White Wolf. Set in the beautiful high country at 8,000 feet, this is a prime spot for hikers. ⊠ *From Big Oak Flat entrance, go 15 miles east on Tioga Rd.*

10

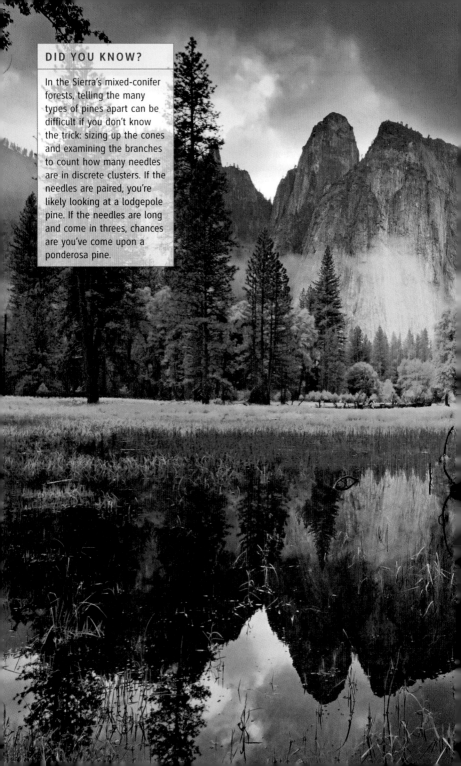

DID YOU KNOW?

In the Sierra's mixed-conifer forests, telling the many types of pines apart can be difficult if you don't know the trick: sizing up the cones and examining the branches to count how many needles are in discrete clusters. If the needles are paired, you're likely looking at a lodgepole pine. If the needles are long and come in threes, chances are you've come upon a ponderosa pine.

$$ 🏨 **Curry Village.** Opened in 1899 as
HOTEL   a place for budget-conscious travelers, Curry Village has plain accommodations: standard motel rooms, simple cabins, and tent cabins with private baths. **Pros:** close to many activities; family-friendly atmosphere. **Cons:** not that economical after a recent price surge; can be crowded; sometimes a bit noisy. $ *Rooms from: $124* ⊠ *South side of Southside Dr.* ☎ *801/559–4884* ⊕ *www.yosemitepark.com* ⇨ *18 rooms, 389 cabins* ⧖ *No meals.*

> **LODGING TIP**
>
> Reserve your room or cabin in Yosemite as far in advance as possible. You can make a reservation up to a year before your arrival (within minutes after the reservation office makes a date available, the Ahwahnee, Yosemite Lodge, and Wawona Hotel often sell out their weekends, holiday periods, and all days between May and September).

$$ 🏨 **Wawona Hotel.** This 1879
HOTEL   National Historic Landmark at Yosemite's southern end is an old-fashioned New England–style estate, with whitewashed buildings, wraparound verandas, and pleasant, no-frills rooms decorated with period pieces. **Pros:** lovely building; peaceful atmosphere. **Cons:** few modern amenities; an hour's drive from Yosemite Valley. $ *Rooms from: $160* ⊠ *Hwy. 41, Wawona* ☎ *801/559–4884* ⊕ *www.yosemitepark.com* ⇨ *104 rooms, 50 with bath* ⊗ *Closed Jan. and Feb.*

$ 🏨 **White Wolf Lodge.** Set in a subalpine meadow, the rustic accommo-
HOTEL   dations at White Wolf Lodge make it an excellent base camp for hiking the backcountry. **Pros:** quiet location; convenient for hikers; good restaurant. **Cons:** far from the Valley; not much to do here. $ *Rooms from: $115* ⊠ *Off Tioga Rd. (Rte. 120), 25 miles west of Tuolumne Meadows and 15 miles east of Crane Flat* ☎ *801/559–4884* ⇨ *24 tent cabins, 4 cabins* ⊗ *Closed mid-Sept.–mid-June.*

$$ 🏨 **Yosemite Lodge at the Falls.** This 1915 lodge near Yosemite Falls more
HOTEL   closely resembles a 1960s resort with its numerous two-story structures tucked beneath the trees. **Pros:** centrally located; dependably clean rooms; lots of tours leave from out front. **Cons:** can feel impersonal; appearance is little dated; prices recently skyrocketed. $ *Rooms from: $193* ⊠ *Northside Dr. about ¾ mile west of the visitor center, Yosemite Village* ☎ *801/559–4884* ⊕ *www.yosemitepark.com* ⇨ *245 rooms.*

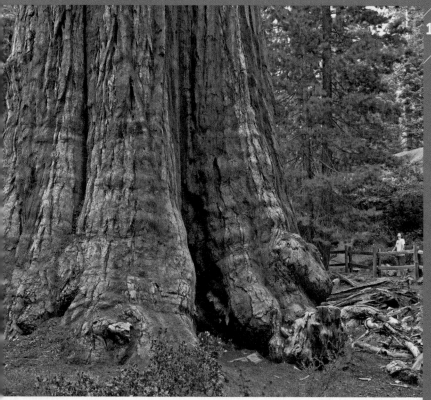

SEQUOIA AND KINGS CANYON NATIONAL PARKS

WELCOME TO SEQUOIA AND KINGS CANYON NATIONAL PARKS

TOP REASONS TO GO

★ **Gentle giants:** You'll feel small—in a good way—walking among some of the world's largest living things in Sequoia's Giant Forest and Kings Canyon's Grant Grove.

★ **Because it's there:** You can't even glimpse it from the main part of Sequoia, but the sight of majestic Mt. Whitney is worth the trek to the eastern face of the High Sierra.

★ **Underground exploration:** Far older even than the giant sequoias, the gleaming limestone formations in Crystal Cave will draw you along dark, marble passages.

★ **A grander-than-Grand Canyon:** Drive the twisting Kings Canyon Scenic Byway down into the jagged, granite Kings River Canyon, deeper in parts than the Grand Canyon.

★ **Regal solitude:** To spend a day or two hiking in a subalpine world of your own, pick one of the 11 trailheads at Mineral King.

1 **Giant Forest–Lodgepole Village.** The most heavily visited area of Sequoia lies at the base of the "thumb" portion of Kings Canyon National Park and contains major sights such as Giant Forest, General Sherman Tree, Crystal Cave, and Moro Rock.

2 **Grant Grove Village–Redwood Canyon.** The "thumb" of Kings Canyon National Park is its busiest section, where Grant Grove, General Grant Tree, Panoramic Point, and Big Stump are the main attractions.

3 **Cedar Grove.** Most visitors to the huge, high-country portion of Kings Canyon National Park don't go farther than Roads End, a few miles east of Cedar Grove on the canyon floor. Here, the river runs through Zumwalt Meadow, surrounded by magnificent granite formations.

4 **Mineral King.** In the southeast section of Sequoia, the highest road-accessible part of the park is a good place to hike, camp, and soak up the unspoiled grandeur of the Sierra Nevada.

5 **Mount Whitney.** The highest peak in the Lower 48 stands on the eastern edge of Sequoia; to get there from Giant Forest you must either backpack eight days through the mountains or drive nearly 300 miles around the park to its other side.

CALIFORNIA

GETTING ORIENTED

The two parks comprise 865,952 acres, mostly on the western flank of the Sierra. A map of the adjacent parks looks vaguely like a mitten, with the palm of Sequoia National Park south of the north-pointing, skinny thumb and long fingers of Kings Canyon National Park. Between the western thumb and eastern fingers, north of Sequoia, lies part of Sequoia National Forest, which includes Giant Sequoia National Monument.

LE CONTE DIVIDE

McClure Meadow

Le Conte Canyon

John Muir Trail

Bench Lake

MONARCH DIVIDE

Woods Creek Trail

Kings Canyon Scenic Byway

KINGS CANYON

Roads End Permit Station

Rae Lakes

Charlotte Lake

Roaring River

KINGS–KERN DIVIDE

Table Mountain 13,630 ft.

Tyndall Creek

Whitney Portal

Stony Creek Village

Wuksachi Village

Crystal Cave

Giant Forest Museum

General Sherman Tree

Bearpaw Meadow

Mount Whitney 14,491 ft.

Mount Kaweah 13,802 ft.

Crabtree

John Muir Trail

Moro Rock

Buckeye Flat

Potwisha

Mount Guyot 12,300 ft.

Rock Creek

Little Five Lakes

Ash Mountain Entrance

Mineral King

KERN CANYON

Lookout Point Entrance

Cold Springs

Hockett Meadows

South Fork

Kern Canyon

Sheep Mountain 10,050 ft.

Visitor Center

Highway

Updated by
Reed Parsell

Although *Sequoiadendron giganteum* is the formal name for the redwoods that grow here, everyone outside the classroom calls them sequoias, big trees, or Sierra redwoods. Their monstrously thick trunks and branches, remarkably shallow root systems, and neck-craning heights are almost impossible to believe, as is the fact they can live for more than 2,500 years. Many of these towering marvels are in the Giant Forest stretch of Generals Highway, which connects Sequoia and Kings Canyon national parks.

Next to or a few miles off the 43-mile road Generals Highway are most of Sequoia National Park's main attractions and Grant Grove Village, the orientation hub for Kings Canyon National Park. The two parks share a boundary that runs west–east, from the foothills of the Central Valley to the Sierra Nevada's dramatic eastern ridges. Kings Canyon has two portions: the smaller is shaped like a bent finger and encompasses Grant Grove Village and Redwood Mountain Grove (the two parks' largest concentration of sequoias), and the larger is home to stunning Kings River Canyon, whose vast, unspoiled peaks and valleys are a backpacker's dream. Sequoia is in one piece and includes Mt. Whitney, the highest point in the Lower 48 states (although it is impossible to see from the western part of the park and is a chore to ascend from either side).

SEQUOIA AND KINGS CANYON PLANNER

WHEN TO GO

The best times to visit are late spring and early fall, when temperatures are moderate and crowds thin. Summertime can draw hoards of tourists to see the giant sequoias, and the few, narrow roads mean congestion at peak holiday times. If you must visit in summer, go during the week. By contrast, in wintertime you may feel as though you have the parks all to yourself. But because of heavy snows, sections of the main park roads can be closed without warning, and low-hanging clouds can move in and obscure mountains and valleys for days. Check road and weather conditions before venturing out mid-November to late April.

GETTING HERE AND AROUND

CAR TRAVEL

Sequoia is 36 miles east of Visalia on Route 198; Kings Canyon is 53 miles east of Fresno on Route 180. There is no automobile entrance on the eastern side of the Sierra. Routes 180 and 198 are connected by Generals Highway, a paved two-lane road that sometimes sees delays at peak times due to ongoing improvements. The road is extremely narrow and steep from Route 198 to Giant Forest, so keep an eye on your engine temperature gauge, as the incline and congestion can cause vehicles to overheat; to avoid overheated brakes, use low gears on downgrades.

If you are traveling in an RV or with a trailer, study the restrictions on these vehicles. Do not travel beyond Potwisha Campground with an RV longer than 22 feet on Route 198; take straighter, easier Route 180 instead. Maximum vehicle length on Generals Highway is 40 feet, or 50 feet combined length for vehicles with trailers.

Generals Highway between Lodgepole and Grant Grove is sometimes closed by snow. The Mineral King Road from Route 198 into southern Sequoia National Park is closed 2 miles below Atwell Mill either on November 1 or after the first heavy snow. The Buckeye Flat–Middle Fork Trailhead Road is closed mid-October through mid-April when the Buckeye Flat Campground closes. The lower Crystal Cave Road is closed when the cave closes in November. Its upper 2 miles, as well as the Panoramic Point and Moro Rock–Crescent Meadow roads, are closed with the first heavy snow. Because of the danger of rockfall, the portion of Kings Canyon Scenic Byway east of Grant Grove closes in winter. For current conditions, call ☎ 559/565–3341 Ext. 4.

■TIP→ Snowstorms are common late October through April. Unless you have four-wheel drive with snow tires, you should carry chains and know how to apply them to the tires on the drive axle.

PARK ESSENTIALS

PARK FEES AND PERMITS

The admission fee is $20 per vehicle and $10 for those who enter by bus, on foot, bicycle, motorcycle, or horse; it is valid for seven days in both parks. U.S. residents over the age of 62 pay $10 for a lifetime pass, and permanently disabled U.S. residents are admitted free.

If you plan to camp in the backcountry, you need a permit, which costs $15 for hikers or $30 for stock users (e.g., horseback riders). One permit covers the group. Availability of permits depends upon trailhead quotas. Reservations are accepted by mail or fax for a $15 processing fee, beginning March 1 each year, and must be made at least 14 days in advance (☎ 559/565–3766). Without a reservation, you may still get a permit on a first-come, first-served basis starting at 1 pm the day before you plan to hike. For more information on backcountry camping or travel with pack animals (horses, mules, burros, or llamas), contact the Wilderness Permit Office (☎ 530/565–3761).

PARK HOURS

The parks are open 24/7 year-round. They are in the Pacific time zone.

VISITOR INFORMATION

PARK CONTACT INFORMATION

Sequoia and Kings Canyon National Parks ✉ *47050 Generals Hwy.(Rte. 198), Three Rivers* ☎ *559/565–3341, 559/565–3134* ⊕ *www.nps.gov/seki.*

SEQUOIA VISITOR CENTERS

Foothills Visitor Center. Exhibits focusing on the foothills and resource issues facing the parks are on display here. You can also pick up books, maps, and a list of ranger-led walks, and get wilderness permits. ✉ *Generals Hwy. (Rte. 198), 1 mile north of the Ash Mountain entrance* ☎ *559/565–4212* ⊙ *Oct.–mid-May, daily 8–4:30; mid-May–Sept., daily 8–5.*

Lodgepole Visitor Center. Along with exhibits on the area's geologic history, wildlife, and longtime American Indian inhabitants, this center screens an outstanding 22-minute film about bears. You can also buy books, maps, Wolverton barbecue, and cave tour tickets here. ✉ *Generals Hwy. (Rte. 198), 21 miles north of Ash Mountain entrance* ☎ *559/565–4436* ⊙ *June–Oct., daily 7–6; Nov.–May, weekends 7–6.*

KINGS CANYON VISITOR CENTERS

Cedar Grove Visitor Center. Off the main road and behind the Sentinel Campground, this small ranger station has books and maps, plus information about hikes and other things to do in the area. ✉ *Kings Canyon Scenic Byway, 30 miles east of park entrance* ☎ *559/565–3793* ⊙ *mid-May–late September, daily 9–5.*

Kings Canyon Visitor Center. Acquaint yourself with the varied charms of this two-section national park by watching a 15-minute film and perusing the center's exhibits on the canyon, sequoias, and human history. Books, maps, and free wilderness permits are available, as are updates on the parks' weather and air-quality conditions. ✉ *Generals Hwy. (Rte. 198), 3 miles northeast of Rte. 180, Big Stump entrance* ☎ *559/565–4307* ⊙ *Summer, daily 8–6; mid-May–late Sept., daily 9–4:30; winter, daily 9:30–4:30.*

SEQUOIA NATIONAL PARK

EXPLORING

SCENIC DRIVES

Generals Highway. One of the most scenic drives in a state replete with them is this 43-mile road, the main asphalt artery between Sequoia and Kings Canyon national parks. Named after the landmark Grant and Sherman trees that leave so many visitors awestruck, it runs from the Foothills Visitor Center north to Grant Grove Village. Along the way, it passes the turnoff to Crystal Cave, the Giant Forest Museum, Lodgepole Village, and Sequoia National Park's other most popular attractions. The lower portion, from Hospital Rock to the Giant Forest, is especially steep and windy. If your vehicle is 22 feet or longer, avoid that stretch by entering the parks via Route 180 (from Fresno) rather than Route 198

(from Visalia). And take your time on this road—there's a lot to see, and wildlife can scamper across at any time. ⚠ **Major roadwork between Foothills Visitor Center and Giant Forest Museum might not be completed by 2014, which could delay your drive up to an hour each way.**

SCENIC STOPS

Sequoia National Park is all about the trees, and to understand the scale of these giants you must walk among them. If you do nothing else, get out of the car for a short stroll through one of the groves. But there is much more to the park than the trees. Try to get up to one of the vista points that offer a panoramic view over the forested mountains. Whether you're driving south to north or north to south, Generals Highway (Route 198) will be your route to most of the park's sights. A few short spur roads lead off the highway to some sights, and Mineral King Road branches off Route 198 to enter the park at Lookout Point, winding east from there into the southernmost part of the park.

Crescent Meadow. John Muir called this the "gem of the Sierra." Walk around for an hour or two and you might decide that the Scotland-born naturalist was exaggerating a wee bit. Wildflowers bloom here throughout the summer. ⊠ *End of Moro Rock–Crescent Meadow Rd., 2.6 miles east off Generals Hwy.*

Crystal Cave. One of more than 200 caves in Sequoia and Kings Canyon national parks, Crystal Cave is unusual in that it's composed largely of marble, the result of limestone being hardened under heat and pressure. It contains several impressive formations that today are much easier to make out, thanks to an environmentally sensitive relighting project. Unfortunately, some of the cave's formations have been damaged or destroyed by early 20th-century dynamite blasting. The standard tour will give you 45 minutes inside the cave. ⊠ *Crystal Cave Rd., 6 miles west off Generals Hwy.* ☎ *559/565–3759* ⊕ *www.sequoiahistory.org* ⊠ *$15* ⊘ *Mid-May–mid-Oct., daily 10–4.*

Fodor's Choice ★   **General Sherman Tree.** Neither the world's tallest nor oldest sequoia, General Sherman is nevertheless tops in volume—and it is still putting on weight, adding the equivalent of a 60-foot-tall tree every year to its 2.7 million-pound mass. ⊠ *Generals Hwy. (Rte. 198), 2 miles south of Lodgepole Visitor Center.*

Mineral King. This subalpine valley sits at 7,800 feet at the end of a steep, winding road. The trip from the park's entrance can take up to two hours. This is the highest point to which you can drive in the park. ⊠ *End of Mineral King Rd., 25 miles east of Generals Hwy. (Rte. 198), east of Three Rivers.*

Fodor's Choice ★   **Moro Rock.** Sequoia National Park's best non-tree attraction offers panoramic views to those fit and determined enough to mount its 350-ish steps. In a case where the journey rivals the destination, Moro's stone stairway is so impressive in its twisty inventiveness that it's on the National Register of Historic Places. The rock's 6,725-foot summit overlooks the Middle Fork Canyon, sculpted by the Kaweah River and approaching the depth of Arizona's Grand Canyon, although smoggy, hazy air almost always compromises the view. ⊠ *Moro Rock–Crescent Meadow Rd., 2 miles east off Generals Hwy. (Rte. 198) to parking area.*

Tunnel Log. It's been almost 45 years since you could drive through a standing sequoia—and that was in Yosemite National Park's Mariposa Grove, not here. This 275-foot tree fell in 1937, and soon a 17-foot-wide, 8-foot-high hole was cut through it for vehicular passage that continues today. Large vehicles take the nearby bypass. ⊠ *Moro Rock–Crescent Meadow Rd., 2 miles east of Generals Hwy. (Rte. 198).*

EDUCATIONAL OFFERINGS

CLASSES AND SEMINARS

Evening Programs. In summer, the park shows documentary films and slide shows, and has evening lectures. Locations and times vary; pick up a schedule at any visitor center or check bulletin boards near ranger stations. ☎ *559/565–3341.*

Seminars. Expert naturalists lead seminars on a range of topics, including birds, wildflowers, geology, botany, photography, park history, backpacking, and pathfinding. Some courses offer transferable credits. Reserve in advance.

   Sequoia Natural History Association. For information and prices, pick up a course catalogue at any visitor center or contact the Sequoia Natural History Association. ☎ *559/565–3759* ⊕ *www.sequoiahistory.org.*

Sequoia Sightseeing Tours. The only licensed tour operator in either park offers daily interpretive sightseeing tours in a 10-passenger van with a friendly, knowledgeable guide. Reservations are essential. The company also offers private tours of Kings Canyon. ⊠ *Three Rivers* ☎ *559/561–4489* ⊕ *www.sequoiatours.com* ✉ *$65 half-day tour, $88 full-day tour.*

RANGER PROGRAMS

Free Nature Programs. Almost any summer day, half-hour to 1½-hour ranger talks and walks explore subjects such as the life of the sequoia, the geology of the park, and the habits of bears. Giant Forest, Lodgepole Visitor Center, Wuksachi Village, and Dorst Creek Campground are frequent starting points. Check bulletin boards throughout the park for the week's offerings.

SPORTS AND THE OUTDOORS

The best way to see Sequoia is to take a hike. Unless you do so, you'll miss out on the up-close grandeur of mist wafting among deeply scored, red-orange tree trunks bigger than you've ever seen. If it's winter, put on some snowshoes or cross-country skis and plunge into the snow-swaddled woodland. There are not too many other outdoor options: no off-road driving is allowed in the parks, and no special provisions have been made for bicycles. Boating, rafting, and snowmobiling also are prohibited.

BIRD-WATCHING

More than 200 species of birds inhabit Sequoia and Kings Canyon national parks. Not seen in most parts of the United States, the white-headed woodpecker and the pileated woodpecker are common in most mid-elevation areas here. There are also many hawks and owls, including the renowned spotted owl. Species are diverse in both parks due to the changes in elevation, and range from warblers, kingbirds, thrushes, and sparrows in the foothills to goshawk, blue grouse, red-breasted nuthatch, and brown creeper at the highest elevations. Ranger-led bird-watching tours are held on a sporadic basis. Call the park's main information number to find out more about these tours.

Sequoia Natural History Association. The association's highly regarded Sequoia Field Institute conducts single-day and multiday "edventure" tours that include backpacking hikes, natural-history walks, and kayaking excursions. ⊠ *47050 Generals Hwy. #10, Three Rivers* ☎ *559/565–3759* ⊕ *www.sequoiahistory.org.*

CROSS-COUNTRY SKIING

Wuksachi Lodge. Rent skis here. Depending on snowfall amounts, instruction may also be available. Reservations are recommended. Marked trails cut through Giant Forest, just 5 miles south of the lodge. ⊠ *Off Generals Hwy. (Rte. 198), 2 miles north of Lodgepole* ☎ *559/565–4070* 🖃 *$23–$30 ski rental* ☉ *Nov.–May (unless no snow), daily 9–4.*

HIKING

The best way to see the park is to hike it. The grandeur and majesty of the Sierra is best seen up close. Carry a hiking map—available at any visitor center—and plenty of water. Check with rangers for current trail conditions, and be aware of rapidly changing weather. As a rule of thumb, plan on trekking about a mile per hour.

EASY

Fodor's Choice ★ **Congress Trail.** This easy 2-mile trail, arguably the best hike in the parks in terms of natural beauty, is a paved loop that begins near General Sherman Tree and winds through the heart of the sequoia forest. You'll get close-up views of more big trees here than on any other Sequoia hike. Watch for the clusters known as the House and Senate. An easy offshoot leads to Crescent Meadow, where in summer you can catch free shuttles back to the Sherman parking lot. ■TIP→ Be sure to stop and gawk at the President Tree, which supplanted the General Grant Tree in 2012 as the world's second largest in volume (behind the General Sherman Tree). ⊠ *Trail begins off Generals Hwy. (Rte. 198), 2 miles north of Giant Forest.*

Crescent Meadow Trails. John Muir reportedly called Crescent Meadow the "gem of the Sierra." Brilliant wildflowers bloom here by midsummer, and a 1.8-mile trail loops around the meadow. A 1.6-mile trail begins at Crescent Meadow and leads to Tharp's Log, a cabin built from a fire-hollowed sequoia. ⊠ *Trail begins at the end of Moro Rock–Crescent Meadow Rd., 2.6 miles east off Generals Hwy. (Rte. 198).*

MODERATE

Tokopah Falls Trail. This moderate trail follows the Marble Fork of the Kaweah River for 1.75 miles one way and dead-ends below the impressive granite cliffs and cascading waterfall of Tokopah Canyon. It takes 2½ to 4 hours to make the 3.5-mile round-trip journey. The trail passes through a mixed-conifer forest. ⊠ *Trail begins off Generals Hwy. (Rte. 198), ¼ mile north of Lodgepole Campground.*

Plants and Wildlife in Sequoia and Kings Canyon

The parks can be divided into three distinct zones. In the west (1,500–5,000 feet) are the rolling, lower elevation foothills, covered with shrubby chaparral vegetation or golden grasslands dotted with oaks. Chamise, red-barked manzanita, and the occasional yucca plant grow here. Fields of white popcorn flower cover the hillsides in spring, and the yellow fiddleneck flourishes. In summer, intense heat and absence of rain cause the hills to turn golden brown. Wildlife includes the California ground squirrel, noisy blue-and-gray scrub jay, black bear, coyote, skunk, and gray fox.

At middle elevation (5,000–9,000 feet), where the giant sequoia belt resides, rock formations mix with meadows and huge stands of evergreens—red and white fir, incense cedar, and

ponderosa pines, to name a few. Wildflowers such as yellow blazing star and red Indian paintbrush bloom in spring and summer. The mule deer, golden-mantled ground squirrel, Steller's jay, and black bear (most active in fall) inhabit the area, as does the chickaree.

The high alpine section of the parks is extremely rugged, with a string of rocky peaks reaching above 13,000 feet to Mt. Whitney's 14,494 feet. Fierce weather and scarcity of soil make vegetation and wildlife sparse. Foxtail and whitebark pines have gnarled and twisted trunks, the result of high wind, heavy snowfall, and freezing temperatures. In summer you can see the yellow-bellied marmot, pika, weasel, mountain chickadee, and Clark's nutcracker.

DIFFICULT

Mineral King Trails. Many trails to the high country begin at Mineral King. The two most popular day hikes are Eagle Lake and Timber Gap, both of which are somewhat strenuous. At 7,800 feet, this is the highest point to which one can drive in either of the parks. Get a map and provisions, and check with rangers about conditions. ⊠ *Trailhead at end of Mineral King Rd., 25 miles east of Generals Hwy. (Rte. 198).*

HORSEBACK RIDING

Trips take you through redwood forests, flowering meadows, across the Sierra, or even up to Mt. Whitney. Costs per person range from $45 for a one-hour guided ride to around $275 per day for fully guided trips for which the packers do all the cooking and camp chores.

TOURS AND OUTFITTERS

Horse Corral Pack Station. Hourly, half-day, full-day, or overnight trips through Sequoia are available for beginning and advanced riders. ⊠ *Off Big Meadows Rd., 12 miles east of Generals Hwy. (Rte. 198) between Sequoia and Kings Canyon national parks* 🕾 *559/565–3404 in summer, 559/564–6429 year-round* ⌑ *$35–$145 day trips* ☉ *May–Sept.*

SLEDDING AND SNOWSHOEING

The Wolverton area, on Route 198 near Giant Forest, is a popular sledding spot, where sleds, inner tubes, and platters are allowed. You can buy sleds and saucers, starting at $10, at the Wuksachi Lodge (🕾 *559/565–4070*), 2 miles north of Lodgepole.

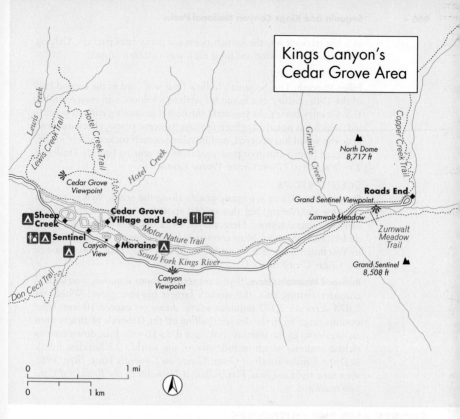

The Wuksachi Lodge also rents snowshoes for $18–$27. Naturalists lead snowshoe walks here and around Giant Forest, conditions permitting, on Saturdays and holidays. Snowshoes are provided for a $1 donation. Make reservations and check schedules at Giant Forest Museum (📞559/565–4480) or Wuksachi Lodge.

KINGS CANYON NATIONAL PARK

EXPLORING

SCENIC DRIVES

Kings Canyon Scenic Byway. About 10 miles east of Grant Grove Village is Jackson View, where you'll first see Kings River Canyon. Near Yucca Point, it's thousands of feet deeper than the much more famous Grand Canyon. Continuing through Sequoia National Forest past Boyden Cavern, you'll enter the larger portion of Kings Canyon National Park and, eventually, Cedar Grove Village. Past there, the U-shaped canyon becomes broader. Be sure to allow an hour to walk through Zumwalt Meadow. Also, be sure to park and take the less-than-five-minute walks to the base of Grizzly Falls and Roaring River Falls. The drive dead-ends at a big parking lot, the launch point for many backpackers. Driving the byway takes about one hour each way (without stops).

HISTORIC SITES

Fallen Monarch. This Sequoia's hollow base was used in the second half of the 19th century as a home for settlers, a saloon, and even to stable U.S. Cavalry horses. As you walk through it (assuming entry is permitted, which has not always been the case in recent years), check out how little the wood has decayed, and imagine yourself tucked safely inside, sheltered from a storm or protected from the searing heat. ⊠ *Trailhead 1 mile north of Grant Grove Visitor Center.*

SCENIC STOPS

Canyon View. There are many places along the scenic byway to pull over for sightseeing, but this special spot showcases evidence of the canyon's glacial history. Here, maybe more than anywhere else, you'll understand why John Muir compared Kings Canyon vistas with those in Yosemite. ⊠ *Kings Canyon Scenic Byway (Rte. 180), 1 mile east of the Cedar Grove turnoff.*

Redwood Mountain Grove. If you are serious about sequoias, you should consider visiting this, the world's largest big-tree grove. Within its 2,078 acres are 2,172 sequoias whose diameters exceed 10 feet. Your options range from the distant (pulling off the Generals Highway onto an overlook) to the intimate (taking a 6- to 10-mile hike down into its richest regions, which include two of the world's 25 heaviest trees). ⊠ *Drive 5 miles south of Grant Grove on Generals Hwy. (Rte. 198), then turn right at Quail Flat; follow it 1½ miles to the Redwood Canyon trailhead.*

SPORTS AND THE OUTDOORS

CROSS-COUNTRY SKIING

Roads to Grant Grove are accessible during heavy snowfall, making the trails here a good choice over Sequoia's Giant Forest when harsh weather hits.

HIKING

You can enjoy many of Kings Canyon's sights from your car, but the giant gorge of the Kings River Canyon and the sweeping vistas of some of the highest mountains in the United States are best seen on foot. Carry a hiking map—available at any visitor center—and plenty of water. Check with rangers for current trail conditions, and be aware of rapidly changing weather.

Road's End Permit Station. If you're planning to hike the backcountry, you can pick up a permit and information on the backcountry at Road's End Permit Station. You can also rent or buy bear canisters, a must for campers. When the station is closed, you can still complete a self-service permit form. ⊠ *6 miles east of Cedar Grove Visitor Center, at the end of Kings Canyon Scenic Byway* ☼ *Late May–late Sept., daily 7–3:30.*

Hiking in the Sierra Mountains is a thrilling experience, putting you amid some of the world's highest trees.

EASY

Fodor's Choice ★

Zumwalt Meadow Trail. Rangers say this is the best (and most popular) day hike in the Cedar Grove area. Just 1.5 miles long, it offers three visual treats: the South Fork of the Kings River, the lush meadow, and the high granite walls above, including those of Grand Sentinel and North Dome. ⊠ *Trailhead 4½ miles east of Cedar Grove Village turnoff from Kings Canyon Scenic Byway.*

MODERATE

Big Baldy. This hike climbs 600 feet and 2 miles up to the 8,209-feet summit of Big Baldy. Your reward is the view of Redwood Canyon. The round-trip hike is 4 miles. *Moderate.* ⊠ *Trailhead 8 miles south of Grant Grove on Generals Hwy. (Rte. 198).*

Redwood Canyon Trail. Avoid the hubbub of Giant Forest and its General Sherman Tree by hiking down to Redwood Canyon, the world's largest grove of sequoias. Opt for the trail toward Hart Tree, and you'll soon lose track of how many humongous trees you pass along the 6-mile loop. Count on spending four to six peaceful hours here—although some backpackers linger overnight (wilderness permit required). ⊠ *Trail begins off Quail Flat. Drive 5 miles south of Grant Grove on Generals Hwy. (Rte. 198), then turn right at Quail Flat; follow it 1½ miles to the Redwood Canyon trailhead.*

DIFFICULT

Hotel Creek Trail. For gorgeous canyon views, take this trail from the canyon floor at Cedar Grove up a series of switchbacks until it splits. Follow the route left through chaparral to the forested ridge and rocky outcrop known as Cedar Grove Overlook, where you can see the Kings

CLOSE UP

Mt. Whitney

At 14,494 feet, Mt. Whitney is the highest point in the contiguous United States and the crown jewel of Sequoia National Park's wild eastern side. The peak looms high above the tiny, high-mountain desert community of Lone Pine, where numerous Hollywood Westerns have been filmed. The high mountain ranges, arid landscape, and scrubby brush of the Eastern Sierra are beautiful in their vastness and austerity.

Despite the mountain's scale, you can't see it from the more traveled west side of the park because it is hidden behind the Great Western Divide. The only way to access Mt. Whitney from the main part of the park is to circumnavigate the Sierra Nevada via an eight-hour, nearly 300-mile drive outside the park. No road ascends the peak; the best vantage point from which to catch a glimpse of the mountain is at the end of Whitney Portal Road. The 13 miles of winding road leads from U.S. 395 at Lone Pine to the trailhead for the hiking route to the top of the mountain. Whitney Portal Road is closed in winter.

River Canyon stretching below. This strenuous 5-mile round-trip hike gains 1,200 feet and takes three to four hours to complete. For a longer hike, return via Lewis Creek Trail for an 8-mile loop. ⊠ *Trailhead at Cedar Grove pack station, 1 mile east of Cedar Grove Village.*

HORSEBACK RIDING

One-day destinations by horseback out of Cedar Grove include Mist Falls and Upper Bubb's Creek. In the backcountry, many equestrians head for Volcanic Lakes or Granite Basin, ascending trails that reach elevations of 10,000 feet. Costs per person range from $45 for a one-hour guided ride to around $275 per day for fully guided trips for which the packers do all the cooking and camp chores.

TOURS AND OUTFITTERS

Cedar Grove Pack Station. Take a day or overnight trip along the Kings River Canyon with Cedar Grove Pack Station. Popular routes include the Rae Lakes Loop and Monarch Divide. ⊠ *Kings Canyon Scenic Byway, 1 mile east of Cedar Grove Village* ☎ *559/565–3464 in summer, 559/337–2314 off-season* ✉ *Call for prices* ☻ *May–Oct.*

Grant Grove Stables. A one- or two-hour trip through Grant Grove leaving from Grant Grove Stables is a good way to get a taste of horseback riding in Kings Canyon. ⊠ *Rte. 180, ½ mile north of Grant Grove Visitor Center* ☎ *559/335–9292 mid-June–Sept., 559/594–9307 Oct.–mid-June* ✉ *$45–$70* ☻ *June–Labor Day, daily 8–6.*

SLEDDING AND SNOWSHOEING

In winter, Kings Canyon has a few great places to play in the snow. Sleds, inner tubes, and platters are allowed at both the Azalea Campground area on Grant Tree Road, ¼ mile north of Grant Grove Visitor Center, and at the Big Stump picnic area, 2 miles north of the lower Route 180 entrance to the park.

Snowshoeing is good around Grant Grove, where you can take naturalist-guided snowshoe walks on Saturdays and holidays mid-December through mid-March as conditions permit.

WHERE TO EAT

Prices in the reviews are the average cost of a main course at dinner or, if dinner is not served, at lunch.

SEQUOIA

$ ✕**Lodgepole Market and Snack Bar.** The choices here run the gamut from
CAFÉ simple to very simple, with the three counters only a few strides apart in a central eating complex. For hot food, venture into the snack bar. The deli sells prepackaged sandwiches along with ice cream scooped from tubs. You'll find other prepackaged foods and souvenirs in the market. $ *Average main: $6* ⊠ *Next to Lodgepole Visitor Center* ☎ *559/565–3301* ⊘ *Closed late Sept.–mid-Apr.*

$$$ ✕**Wolverton Barbecue.** Weather permitting, diners congregate on a
BARBECUE wooden porch that looks directly out onto a small but strikingly verdant meadow. In addition to the predictable meats such as ribs and chicken, the all-you-can-eat buffet has sides that include baked beans, corn on the cob, and potato salad. Following the meal, listen to a ranger talk and clear your throat for a campfire sing-along. Purchase tickets at Lodgepole Market, Wuksachi Lodge, or Wolverton Recreation Area's office. $ *Average main: $24* ⊠ *Wolverton Rd., 1½ miles northeast off Generals Hwy. (Rte. 198)* ☎ *559/565–4070, 559/565–3301* ⊘ *No lunch. Closed Mon.–Thurs. and early Sept.–mid-June.*

$$ ✕**Wuksachi Village Dining Room.** Huge windows run the length of the high-
AMERICAN ceilinged dining room, and a large fireplace on the far wall warms both the body and the soul. The diverse dinner menu—by far the best in the two parks—includes filet mignon, rainbow trout, and vegetarian pasta dishes, in addition to the ever-present burgers. The children's menu is economically priced. Breakfast and lunch also are served. $ *Average main: $21* ⊠ *Wuksachi Village* ☎ *559/565–4070* ⟅ *Reservations essential.*

KINGS CANYON

$ ✕**Cedar Grove Restaurant.** For a small operation, the menu here is sur-
AMERICAN prisingly extensive, with dinner entrées such as pasta, pork chops, and steak. For breakfast, try the biscuits and gravy, French toast, pancakes, or cold cereal. Burgers (including vegetarian patties) and hot dogs dominate the lunch choices. Outside, a patio dining area overlooks the Kings River. $ *Average main: $13* ⊠ *Cedar Grove Village* ☎ *559/565–0100* ⊘ *Closed Oct.–May.*

$$ ✕**Grant Grove Restaurant.** In a no-frills, open room, this restaurant offers
AMERICAN basic American fare such as pancakes for breakfast or hot sandwiches and chicken for later meals. Vegetarians and vegans will have to content themselves with a simple salad. Take-out service is available. $ *Average main: $19* ⊠ *Grant Grove Village* ☎ *559/335–5500.*

WHERE TO STAY

Prices in the reviews are the lowest cost of a standard double room in high season. For expanded hotel reviews, visit Fodors.com.

SEQUOIA

$$$
HOTEL
Fodor's Choice
★

Wuksachi Lodge. The striking cedar-and-stone main building here is a fine example of how a structure can blend effectively with lovely mountain scenery. **Pros:** best place to stay in the parks; lots of wildlife. **Cons:** rooms can be small; main lodge is a few minutes' walk from guest rooms. $ Rooms from: $185 ⊠ 64740 Wuksachi Way, Wuksachi Village ☎ 559/565–4070, 888/252–5757 ⊕ www.visitsequoia.com ⇨ 102 rooms.

KINGS CANYON

$$$
HOTEL

John Muir Lodge. This modern, timber-sided lodge is nestled in a wooded area in the hills above Grant Grove Village and offers year-round accommodations. **Pros:** common room stays warm; it's far enough from the main road to be quiet. **Cons:** check-in is down in the village. $ Rooms from: $195 ⊠ Kings Canyon Scenic Byway, ¼ mile north of Grant Grove Village ☎ 559/335–5500, 866/522–6966 ⊕ www.sequoia-kingscanyon.com ⇨ 24 rooms, 6 suites.

SACRAMENTO AND THE GOLD COUNTRY

WELCOME TO SACRAMENTO AND THE GOLD COUNTRY

TOP REASONS TO GO

★ **Rush to the past:** Marshall Gold Discovery State Park and Hangtown's Gold Bug & Mine conjure up California's mid-19th century boom.

★ **Capital connections:** Sedate Sacramento offers enough attractions to engage out-of-towners for a day or two, especially its Capitol, historic Old Sacramento, and dining scene.

★ **Bon appetit:** Sacramento is home to the California state fair in July and many ethnic food festivals. Nevada City and environs are known for summer mountain-music festivals and Victorian and Cornish winter-holiday celebrations.

★ **Vintage calm:** With bucolic scenery and friendly tasting rooms, the Shenandoah Valley is the Gold Country's laid-back answer to Napa.

★ **Ups and downs:** Calaveras Big Trees State Park is filled with giant sequoias, and Moaning Cavern's main chamber is big enough to hold the Statue of Liberty.

1 Sacramento and Vicinity. The gateway to the Gold Country, the seat of state government, and an agricultural hub, Sacramento plays many important contemporary roles. About 2.5 million people live in the metropolitan area, which offers up more sunshine and lower housing costs than coastal California.

2 The Gold Country— South. South of its junction with U.S. 50, Highway 49 traces in asphalt the famed Mother Lode. The peppy former gold-rush towns strung along the road have for the most part been restored and made presentable to visitors with an interest in one of the most frenzied episodes of American history.

3 The Gold Country— North. Highway 49 north of Placerville links the towns of Coloma, Auburn, Grass Valley, and Nevada City. Most are gentrified versions of once-rowdy mining camps, vestiges of which remain in roadside museums, old mining structures, and restored homes now serving as inns.

12

GETTING ORIENTED

The Gold Country is a largely laid-back and lower-tech destination for those seeking to escape Southern California and the Bay Area. Sacramento, Davis, and Woodland are in an enormous valley bordered to the east by the Sierra Nevada range. Foothill communities Nevada City, Placerville, and Sutter Creek were products of the gold rush.

Map labels:
Nevada City • Grass Valley • Colfax • Auburn • Rocklin • Coloma • Marshall Gold Discovery State Park • Hangtown's Gold Bug & Mine • Placerville • Folsom • Folsom Lake • Shenandoah Valley • Plymouth • Amador City • Sutter Creek • Ione • Jackson • San Andreas • Lockeford • Angels Camp • Murphys • Columbia • Calaveras Big Tree State Park • Arnold • Moaning Cavern • Jamestown • Sonora • Soulsbyville • Linden • Manteca • Ripon • Salida • Modesto • Oakdale • Waterford • Moccasin • Groveland • Mariposa • Lake Tahoe • Yosemite National Park • SIERRA NEVADA • SAN JOAQUIN VALLEY • Cosumnes • Stanislaus • Tuolumne • Merced • San Joaquin

0 — 25 mi
0 — 25 km

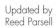
Updated by
Reed Parsell

A new era dawned for California when James Marshall turned up a gold nugget in the tailrace of a sawmill he was constructing along the American River. Before January 24, 1848, Mexico and the United States were still wrestling for ownership of what would become the Golden State. With Marshall's discovery, the United States tightened its grip on the region, and prospectors from all over the world came to seek their fortunes in the Mother Lode.

As gold fever seized the nation, California's population of 15,000 swelled to 265,000 within three years. The mostly young, mostly male adventurers who arrived in search of gold—the '49ers—became part of a culture that discarded many of the conventions of the eastern states. It was also a violent time. Yankee prospectors chased Mexican miners off their claims, and California's leaders initiated a plan to exterminate the local Native American population. Bounties were paid and private militias were hired to wipe out the Native Americans or sell them into slavery. California was to be dominated by the Anglo.

The gold-rush boom lasted scarcely 20 years, but it changed California forever. It produced 546 mining towns, of which fewer than 250 remain. The hills of the Gold Country were alive, not only with prospecting and mining but also with business, the arts, gambling, and a fair share of crime. Opera houses went up alongside brothels, and the California State Capitol, in Sacramento, was built with the gold dug out of the hills.

Today the Gold Country is one of California's less expensive destinations, a region of the Sierra Nevada foothills that is filled with natural and cultural pleasures. Visitors come to Nevada City, Auburn, Coloma, Sutter Creek, and Columbia not only to relive the past but also to explore art galleries, shop for antiques, and stay at inns full of character. Spring brings wildflowers, and in fall the hills are colored by bright red berries and changing leaves. Because it offers many outdoor activities, the Gold Country is a great place to take the kids.

Visiting Old Sacramento's museums is a good way to become immersed in history, but the Gold Country's heart lies along Highway 49, which winds the approximately 300-mile north–south length of the historic mining area. The highway, often a twisting, hilly, two-lane road, begs for a convertible with the top down.

12

PLANNING

WHEN TO GO

The Gold Country is most pleasant in spring, when the wildflowers are in bloom, and in fall. Summers can be hot: temperatures of 100°F are fairly common. Sacramento winters tend to be cool with occasionally foggy and/or rainy days; many Sacramentans drive to the foothills (or the coast) to get some winter sunshine. Throughout the year Gold Country towns stage community and ethnic celebrations. In December many towns are decked out for Christmas.

GETTING HERE AND AROUND

AIR TRAVEL

Sacramento International Airport (SMF) is served by Aeromexico, Alaska/Horizon, American, Delta, Hawaiian, JetBlue, Southwest, United, and US Airways. A private taxi from the airport to Downtown Sacramento costs about $40; the Super Shuttle fare is $25. Public buses (⇨ *see Bus and Light-Rail Travel*) are also an option.

Contacts Sacramento International Airport ✉ *6900 Airport Blvd., 12 miles northwest of Downtown off I–5, Sacramento* ☎ *916/929–5411* ⊕ *www.sacramento.aero/smf.* **Super Shuttle** ☎ *800/258–3826* ⊕ *www.supershuttle.com.*

BUS AND LIGHT-RAIL TRAVEL

Greyhound serves Sacramento from San Francisco and Los Angeles. Sacramento Regional Transit serves the capital area with buses and light-rail vehicles. Yolobus public buses nos. 42A and 42B connect SMF airport and Downtown Sacramento, West Sacramento, Davis, and Woodland.

Contacts Greyhound ☎ *800/231–2222* ⊕ *www.greyhound.com.* **Sacramento Regional Transit** ☎ *916/321–2877* ⊕ *www.sacrt.com.* **Yolobus** ☎ *530/666–2837, 916/371–2877* ⊕ *www.yolobus.com.*

CAR TRAVEL

Interstate 5 (north–south) and Interstate 80 (east–west) are the two main routes into and out of Sacramento. From Sacramento, three highways fan out toward the east, all intersecting with historic Highway 49: Interstate 80 heads northeast 34 miles to Auburn; U.S. 50 goes east 40 miles to Placerville; and Highway 16 angles southeast 45 miles to Plymouth. Highway 49 is an excellent two-lane road that winds and climbs through the foothills and valleys, linking the principal Gold Country towns. Traveling by car is the only practical way to explore the Gold Country.

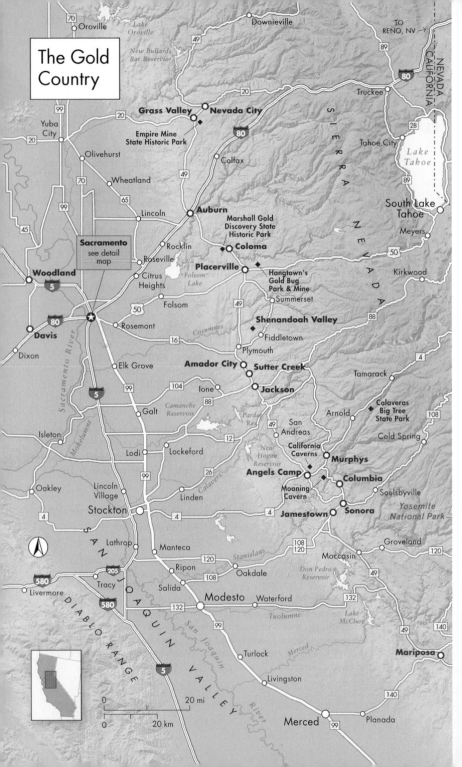

12

TRAIN TRAVEL

Amtrak trains serve Sacramento and Davis from San Jose, Oakland, and Emeryville (Amtrak buses transport passengers from San Francisco's Ferry Building to Emeryville). The trip takes 2½ hours. Amtrak also runs trains and connecting motor coaches from the Central Valley.

Contacts Amtrak ☎ 800/872-7245 ⊕ www.amtrak.com.

HEALTH AND SAFETY

In an emergency, dial 911.

Emergency Rooms Mercy Hospital of Sacramento ✉ 4001 J St., Sacramento ☎ 916/453-4545 ⊕ www.mercygeneral.org. Sutter General Hospital ✉ 2801 L St., Sacramento ☎ 916/733-8900 ⊕ www.suttermedicalcenter.org. Sutter Memorial Hospital ✉ 52nd and F Sts., Sacramento ☎ 916/733-1000 ⊕ www.suttermedicalcenter.org.

RESTAURANTS

American, Italian, and Mexican are common Gold Country fare, but chefs also prepare ambitious European, French, and California cuisine. Grass Valley's meat- and vegetable-stuffed *pasties*, introduced by 19th-century gold miners from Cornwall, are one of the region's more unusual treats. *Prices in the restaurant reviews are the average cost of a main course at dinner or, if dinner is not served, at lunch (excluding sales tax).*

HOTELS

Full-service hotels, budget motels, and small inns can be found in Sacramento. Larger towns along Highway 49—among them Auburn, Grass Valley, and Jackson—have chain motels and inns. Many Gold Country bed-and-breakfasts occupy former mansions, miners' cabins, and other historic buildings. *Prices in the reviews are the lowest cost of a standard double room in high season, excluding taxes. For expanded hotel reviews, visit Fodors.com.*

Contacts Amador Council of Tourism ☎ 209/267-9249, 877/868-7262 ⊕ www.touramador.com/accommodations. Gold Country Inns of Tuolumne County ⊕ www.goldbnbs.com. Historic Inns of Grass Valley and Nevada City ☎ 530/477-6634 ⊕ goldcountryinns.net.

VISITOR INFORMATION

Contacts Amador County Chamber of Commerce & Visitors Bureau ✉ 115 Main St., Jackson ☎ 209/223-0350 ⊕ www.amadorcountychamber.com. El Dorado County Visitors Authority ✉ 542 Main St., Placerville ☎ 530/621-5885, 800/457-6279 ⊕ visit-eldorado.com. Grass Valley/Nevada County Chamber of Commerce ✉ 212 W. Main St., Grass Valley ☎ 530/273-4667, 800/655-4667 ⊕ www.grassvalleychamber.com. Yosemite/Mariposa County Tourism Bureau ✉ 5158 Hwy. 140, Mariposa ☎ 209/742-4567 ⊕ www.yosemiteexperience.com. Tuolumne County Visitors Bureau ✉ 542 W. Stockton Rd., Sonora ☎ 209/533-4420, 800/446-1333 ⊕ www.tcvb.com.

SACRAMENTO AND VICINITY

California's capital is an ethnically diverse city, with sizable Mexican, Hmong, and Ukrainian populations, among many others.

SACRAMENTO

87 miles northeast of San Francisco; 384 miles north of Los Angeles.

All around the Golden State's seat of government you'll experience echoes of the gold-rush days, most notably in Old Sacramento, whose wooden sidewalks and horse-drawn carriages on cobblestone streets lend the waterfront district a 19th-century feel. The California State Railroad Museum and other venues hold artifacts of state and national significance, and historic buildings house shops and restaurants. River cruises and train rides are fun family diversions for an hour or two.

Due east of Old Sacramento is Downtown, where landmarks include the Capitol building and the surrounding Capitol Park. The convention center is also here. A persistent homeless problem and a scattering of boarded-up storefronts somewhat diminish the area's appeal.

Farther east, starting at about 15th Street, lies the city's most interesting neighborhood, Midtown, a mix of genteel Victorian edifices, ultramodern lofts, and innovative restaurants and cozy wine bars. The neighborhood springs to life on the second Saturday evening of the month, when art galleries hold open houses and the sidewalks are packed. A few intersections are jumping most evenings when the weather's good; they include the corner of 20th and L streets in what's known as Lavender Heights, the center of the city's gay and lesbian community.

GETTING HERE AND AROUND

Most people drive to Sacramento and get around by car. Yellow Cab is a reliable company.

Bus Travel Sacramento Regional Transit buses and light-rail vehicles serve the area. The No. 30 DASH shuttle bus links Old Sacramento, Midtown, and Sutter's Fort.

Car Travel Assuming that traffic is not a factor (though it can be), Sacramento is a 90-minute drive from San Francisco and a seven-hour drive from Los Angeles. Parking garages serve Old Sacramento and other tourist spots; on-street parking Downtown can be difficult to find.

ESSENTIALS

Transportation Contacts Sacramento Regional Transit ☏ 916/321–2877 ⊕ www.sacrt.com. **Yellow Cab Co. of Sacramento** ☏ 916/444–2222 ⊕ www.yellowcabsacramento.com.

Visitor Information Old Sacramento Visitor Information Center ✉ 1002 2nd St., at K St. ☏ 916/442–7644 ⊕ www.discovergold.org ☉ Daily 10–5. **Sacramento Convention and Visitors Bureau** ✉ 1608 I St., Suite 600 ☏ 916/808–7777, 800/292–2334 ⊕ www.discovergold.org.

The California State Railroad Museum is North America's most popular railroad museum.

EXPLORING
TOP ATTRACTIONS

American River Bicycle Trail. The Jedediah Smith Memorial Trail, as it's formally called, runs for 32 miles from Old Sacramento to Beals Point in Folsom. Walk or ride a bit of it and you'll see why local cyclists and pedestrians adore its scenic lanes, if not always each other: confrontations do occur between humorless speeders and meandering gawkers. It's pretty tame stuff, though worth being alert to as you enjoy great views of the American River and the bluffs overlooking it. ■TIP→ Bring lunch or a snack. Pretty parks and picnic areas dot the course.

California Automobile Museum. More than 150 vintage automobiles—including Model Ts, Hudsons, Studebakers, Pontiacs, and other bygone makes and models—are on display at this museum that pays tribute to automotive history and car culture. A 1920s roadside café and garage exhibit re-creates the early days of motoring, and the friendly docents are ready to explain everything you see. The museum is near Downtown and Old Sacramento, with ample free parking. ⊠ *2200 Front St., 1 block off Broadway, Downtown* ☎ *916/442–6802* ⊕ *www.calautomuseum. org* ⊠ *$8* ⊗ *Daily 10–6, Third Thurs. of the month, 10–9.*

Fodor's Choice **California State Railroad Museum.** Near what was the terminus of the
★ transcontinental and Sacramento Valley railroads, this 100,000-square-
FAMILY foot museum has 21 locomotives and railroad cars on display along with dozens of other exhibits. You can walk through a post-office car and peer into cubbyholes and canvas mailbags, enter a sleeping car that simulates the swaying on the roadbed and the flashing lights of a passing town at night, or glimpse inside the first-class dining car. The room

containing the gold "Last Spike," one of two cast in 1869 to commemorate the completion of the transcontinental railroad, is quietly compel-
ling. Kids have lots of fun at this museum, especially in the play area
upstairs. ■TIP→ **Don't miss the astounding exhibit of 1,000 vintage
toy trains.** ⊠ *125 I St., at 2nd St., Old Sacramento* ☎ *916/445–6645*
⊕ *www.csrmf.org* ⊠ *$10* ⊙ *Daily 10–5.*

Capitol. The lacy plasterwork of the Capitol's 120-foot-high rotunda
has the complexity and colors of a Fabergé egg. Underneath the
gilded dome are marble floors, glittering chandeliers, monumental
staircases, reproductions of century-old state offices, and legislative
chambers decorated in the style of the 1890s (the Capitol was built in
1869). Guides conduct tours of the building and the 40-acre Capitol
Park, which contains a rose garden, an impressive display of camellias (Sacramento's city flower), and the California Vietnam Veterans
Memorial. ■TIP→ **The photogenic front of the building is best captured in late-afternoon light.** ⊠ *Capitol Mall and 10th St., Downtown*
☎ *916/324–0333* ⊕ *www.statecapitolmuseum.com* ⊠ *Free* ⊙ *Daily
9–5; tours hourly 10–4.*

Fodor's Choice **Crocker Art Museum.** The oldest art museum in the American West has
★ a collection of art from Europe, Asia, and California, including *Sunday Morning in the Mines* (1872), a large canvas by Charles Christian
Nahl depicting the original mining industry, and the magnificent *Great
Canyon of the Sierra, Yosemite* (1871), by Thomas Hill. An expansion
completed in 2010 tripled the size of the Crocker, which hosts a bustling
mix of music and children's events. ⊠ *216 O St., at 3rd St., Downtown*
☎ *916/808–7000* ⊕ *www.crockerartmuseum.org* ⊠ *$10* ⊙ *Tues., Wed.,
and Fri.–Sun. 10–5; Thurs. 10–9.*

Governor's Mansion. This 15-room Italianate mansion was built in 1877
and used by the state's chief executives from the early 1900s until 1967,
when Ronald Reagan vacated it in favor of an upscale modern residence. Many of the interior decorations were ordered from the Huntington, Hopkins & Co. Hardware Store, one of whose partners, Albert
Gallatin, was the original occupant. Each of the seven marble fireplaces
has a petticoat mirror that ladies strolled past to see if their slips were
showing. ⊠ *1526 H St., at 16th St., Midtown* ☎ *916/323–3047* ⊕ *www.
parks.ca.gov* ⊠ *$5* ⊙ *Daily 10–5; tours hourly, last tour at 4.*

WORTH NOTING

FAMILY **California Museum.** Some of the exhibits at this celebration of all things
California are high-tech and interactive, but there are also scores
of archival drawers that you can pull out to see the real artifacts
of history and culture—from the California State Constitution to
surfing magazines. Board a 1949 cross-country bus to view a video
on immigration, visit a Chinese herb shop maintained by a holo-
graphic proprietor, or find familiar names inducted into the annually expanded California Hall of Fame. The museum's café is open
on weekdays until 2:30 pm. ⊠ *1020 O St., at 11th St., Downtown*
☎ *916/653–7524* ⊕ *www.californiamuseum.org* ⊠ *$8.50* ⊙ *Mon.–
Sat. 10–5, Sun. noon–5.*

12

FAMILY **Central Pacific Railroad Passenger Station.** At this reconstructed 1876 depot there's rolling stock to admire, a typical waiting room, and a small restaurant. Part of the year a train departs from the freight depot, south of the passenger station, making a 40-minute out-and-back trip between the Sacramento River and, less interestingly, Interstate 5. ⊠ *930 Front St., at J St., Old Sacramento* ☎ *916/445–6645* 🚇 *Station $4, free with same-day ticket from state railroad museum; train $10* ⊗ *Station daily 10–4; train Apr.–Sept. hourly on weekends, Oct.–Dec. days and hrs vary.*

Huntington, Hopkins & Co. Store. Picks, shovels, gold pans, and other paraphernalia used by gold-rush miners are on display at this re-creation of a 19th-century hardware store. Though it's named for two of the Big Four railroad barons, their store was far more elaborate. ⊠ *113 I St., at Front St., Old Sacramento* ☎ *916/323–7234* 🚇 *Free* ⊗ *Thurs.–Sun. 11–4.*

Leland Stanford Mansion. The painstakingly renovated Victorian mansion is distinguished by both the 19th-century paintings it houses as well as the home's general craftsmanship, both indoors and out. Stanford, a railroad baron, California governor, and U.S. senator, had this home built in 1856; additions were made in 1862 and the early 1870s. ⊠ *800 N St., at 8th St., Downtown* ☎ *916/324–0575* ⊕ *www.stanfordmansion.org* 🚇 *$5* ⊗ *Tours daily 10–4.*

QUICK
BITES

✕ **Tapa the World.** As the name implies, this cozy bar and restaurant serves tapas—small plates of meats, seafood, chicken, and veggies shared at the table—daily from 11:30 am until midnight in the heart of Midtown. ⑤ *Average main: $12* ⊠ *2115 J St., near 21st St., Midtown* ☎ *916/442–4353* ⊕ *www.tapatheworld.com.*

FAMILY   **Old Sacramento Schoolhouse Museum.** Sacramento's first school welcomed students in August 1849 and closed permanently four months later. Five years passed before another public school opened. Today it's a kid-friendly attraction that shows what one-room schoolhouses were like in the California Central Valley and foothills in the late 1800s. ⊠ *1200 Front St., at L St., Old Sacramento* ⊕ *www.scoe.net/ oldsacschoolhouse* ⊠ *Free* ⊙ *Mon.–Sat. 10–4, Sun. noon–4 (closed some weekends).*

State Indian Museum. Among the interesting displays at this museum near Sutter's Fort is one about Ishi, the last Yahi Indian to emerge from the mountains, in 1911. Ishi provided anthropologists with insight into his people's traditions and culture. Arts-and-crafts exhibits, a demonstration village, and an evocative 10-minute video also explore the lives and history of California's native peoples. ⊠ *2618 K St., at 27th St.* ☎ *916/324–0971* ⊕ *www.parks.ca.gov* ⊠ *$3* ⊙ *Wed.–Sun. 10–5.*

FAMILY   **Sutter's Fort.** German-born Swiss immigrant John Augustus Sutter founded Sacramento's earliest Euro-American settlement in 1839. Audio speakers give information at each stop along a self-guided tour that includes a blacksmith's shop, bakery, prison, living quarters, and livestock areas. Costumed docents sometimes reenact fort life, demonstrating crafts, food preparation, and firearms maintenance. ⊠ *2701 L St., at 27th St., Midtown* ☎ *916/445–4422* ⊕ *www.parks.ca.gov* ⊠ *$5 most days, $7 on interpretive program days* ⊙ *Tues.–Sun. 10–5.*

WHERE TO EAT

$$$
ITALIAN
Fodor's Choice
★

✕ **Biba.** Owner Biba Caggiano is a nationally recognized authority on Italian cuisine. The Capitol crowd flocks here for homemade ravioli, osso buco, grilled pork loin, and veal and rabbit specials. A pianist adds to the upscale ambience nightly. ⑤ *Average main: $28* ⊠ *2801 Capitol Ave., at 28th St., Midtown* ☎ *916/455–2422* ⊕ *www.biba-restaurant. com* ⚏ *Reservations essential* ⊙ *Closed Sun. No lunch Mon. or Sat.*

$$
AMERICAN

✕ **Cafeteria 15L.** A convenient perch across from Capitol Park, comfort-food haven 15L makes a great first impression on visitors and a lasting one on its many repeat local customers. Generous portions of sides such as macaroni and cheese and tater tots just might be the biggest hits, but entrées that include pork sliders and grilled-cheese sandwiches are also popular. The food here consistently receives high marks, and so does the attentive service. ⑤ *Average main: $18* ⊠ *1116 15th St., at L St., Downtown* ☎ *916/492–1960* ⊕ *www.cafeteria15l. com* ⊙ *No lunch weekends.*

$
MEXICAN

✕ **Ernesto's Mexican Food.** Customers often have to wait for a table on Friday and Saturday evenings at this popular restaurant. Fresh ingredients are stressed in the wide selection of entrées, and the margaritas are especially refreshing. Sister restaurant **Zocalo** (⊠ *1801 Capitol Ave.*

☎ 916/441–0303) has a striking indoor-outdoor atmosphere and is a popular launching spot for nights out on the town. $ *Average main: $14* ✉ *1901 16th St., at S St., Midtown* ☎ *916/441–5850* ⊕ *www. ernestosmexicanfood.com.*

$$$$
AMERICAN
Fodor'sChoice
★

✕ **The Firehouse.** Consistently ranked by local publications as one of the city's top restaurants, this formal and historic restaurant has a full bar, courtyard seating (its signature attraction), and creative American cooking, such as char-grilled spring rack of lamb served with roasted French fingerling potatoes and baby artichoke and fava bean succotash. Visitors who can afford to treat themselves to a fine and leisurely meal can do no better in Old Sacramento—although they might also opt for the less-pricey **Ten 22.** Located a block away and under the same ownership as the Firehouse, it serves pizza and other fancified comfort food. $ *Average main: $36* ✉ *1112 2nd St., at L St., Old Sacramento* ☎ *916/442–4772* ⊕ *www.firehouseoldsac.com* ⊗ *No lunch Sat.*

$$$
ECLECTIC

✕ **The Waterboy.** Rural French cooking and California cuisine, along with some Italian specialties, are the culinary influences at this upscale yet unfussy restaurant, which features such distinct dishes as veal sweetbreads, pan-seared scallops, and Sonoma Liberty duck breast. Organic produce and meats are used. $ *Average main: $25* ✉ *2000 Capitol Ave., at 20th St., Midtown* ☎ *916/498–9891* ⊕ *www.waterboyrestaurant. com* ⊗ *No lunch weekends.*

WHERE TO STAY
For expanded hotel reviews, visit Fodors.com.

$$$
B&B/INN

⌂ **Amber House Bed & Breakfast Inn.** About a mile from the Capitol, this B&B has rooms in a 1905 Craftsman-style home and an 1895 Dutch colonial–revival home. **Pros:** Midtown location; attentive service. **Cons:** freeway access isn't easy. $ *Rooms from: $179* ✉ *1315 22nd St., Midtown* ☎ *916/444–8085, 800/755–6526* ⊕ *www.amberhouse.com* ⇆ *10 rooms* ⊚ *Breakfast.*

$$$
HOTEL

⌂ **Citizen Hotel.** This luxury boutique hotel occupies the 1926 Cal Western Life building. **Pros:** modern amenities but with older-era charms; near the Capitol and Downtown attractions. **Cons:** pricey; smallish bathrooms. $ *Rooms from: $189* ✉ *926 J St., Downtown* ☎ *916/447–4460* ⊕ *www.jdvhotels.com* ⇆ *175 rooms, 23 suites* ⊚ *Breakfast.*

$$
HOTEL

⌂ **Delta King.** The best staterooms of this grand old riverboat, permanently moored on Old Sacramento's waterfront, are on the river side toward the back. **Pros:** intimate; historic sights nearby; creaky floors add to ambience. **Cons:** amenities aren't modern; creaky floors could keep you awake. $ *Rooms from: $165* ✉ *1000 Front St., Old Sacramento* ☎ *916/444–5464, 800/825–5464* ⊕ *www.deltaking.com* ⇆ *44 rooms* ⊚ *Breakfast.*

$$$
HOTEL

⌂ **Hyatt Regency Sacramento.** With a marble-and-glass lobby and luxurious rooms, this hotel across from the Capitol and adjacent to the convention center is arguably Sacramento's finest. **Pros:** beautiful Capitol Park is across the street; some rooms have small balconies. **Cons:** nearby streets can be dodgy at night; somewhat impersonal. $ *Rooms from: $195* ✉ *1209 L St., Downtown* ☎ *916/443–1234, 800/633–7313* ⊕ *www.hyatt.com* ⇆ *500 rooms, 24 suites.*

NIGHTLIFE AND THE ARTS
NIGHTLIFE

Blue Cue. A billiard lounge known for its selection of single-malt scotches, the Blue Cue is upstairs from the popular Mexican restaurant Centro. Wednesday night's trivia contest is a spirited event. ✉ *1004 28th St., at J St., Midtown* ☎ *916/441–6810* ⊕ *www.bluecue.com.*

Fox and Goose. This casual pub with live music serves fish-and-chips, Cornish pasties, and other traditional items—plus vegetarian/vegan fare—on weekdays until 9:30. ✉ *1001 R St., at 10th St., Downtown* ☎ *916/443–8825* ⊕ *www.foxandgoose.com.*

Harlow's. Harlow's restaurant draws a young-ish crowd to its art deco bar-nightclub for live music after 9 pm. ✉ *2708 J St., at 27th St., Midtown* ☎ *916/441–4693* ⊕ *www.harlows.com.*

Streets of London Pub. A favorite among Anglophiles, Streets is open after midnight every night. Darts and TV soccer, anyone? ✉ *1804 J St., at 18th St., Midtown* ☎ *916/498–1388* ⊕ *streetsoflondon.net.*

THE ARTS

California Musical Theatre. This group presents Broadway shows at the Sacramento Community Center Theater and the summer Music Circus offerings (think *Oklahoma, Annie*) at the theater-in-the-round Wells Fargo Pavilion. ✉ *1419 H St., at 14th St., Downtown* ☎ *916/557–1999* ⊕ *www.calmt.com.*

Crest Theatre. The art deco Crest is a beloved venue for classic and art-house films, along with concerts and other cultural events. ✉ *1013 K St., at 10th St., Downtown* ☎ *916/442–7378* ⊕ *www.thecrest.com.*

Sacramento Box Office. Tickets to major comedy, music, theater, and other cultural and sports events are sold through this online vendor. ✉ *Downtown* ☎ *888/583–6046* ⊕ *sacramentoboxoffice.com.*

SHOPPING

Greater Sacramento is filled with familiar shops. To try something new, wander through Midtown, especially J, K, and L streets between 16th and 26th streets.

The Beat. For more than 30 years this has been *the* place in Midtown to buy new and used records and CDs. Time has turned it into an antiques store for 20th-century electronics. ✉ *1700 J St., at 17th St.* ☎ *916/446–4402* ⊕ *thebeatsacramento.com.*

The Galleria at Roseville. The Sacramento region's largest shopping complex is a sprawling, heavily trafficked collection of chain stores and restaurants. It's always jumping. ✉ *1151 Galleria Blvd., north of Sacramento off I–80 Exit 105A, Roseville* ⊕ *www.westfield.com/galleriaatroseville.*

WOODLAND

20 miles northwest of Sacramento.

In its heyday, Woodland was among California's wealthiest cities. Established by gold seekers and entrepreneurs, it later became an agricultural gold mine. The legacy of the old land barons can be seen in the restored Victorian and Craftsman architecture downtown; the best examples can be found south of Main Street on College, Elm, 1st, and 2nd streets. The town's top attraction is the splendid Heidrick Ag History Center.

GETTING HERE AND AROUND

Yolobus (⊕ *www.yolobus.com*) serves downtown Woodland from Sacramento, though most visitors arrive by car via Interstate 5.

ESSENTIALS

Visitor Information Woodland Chamber of Commerce ✉ *307 1st St., at Dead Cat Alley* ☎ *530/662-7327* ⊕ *www.woodlandchamber.org.*

EXPLORING

FAMILY **Heidrick Ag History Center Tractor & Truck Museum.** This gigantic space provides a marvelous overview of the entire history of motorized agricultural vehicles. Souped-up and shiny, the antique threshers, harvesters, combines, tractors, and proto-tractors on display here look ready to service the farms of their eras all over again. And there's more. A separate wing surveys the evolution of the truck, with an emphasis on ones used for farm work. ✉ *1962 Hays La., off County Rd. 102* ☎ *530/666-9700* ⊕ *www.aghistory.org* 🖼 *$8* ⊙ *Mid-Mar.–early Nov. Wed.–Sun. 10–5; early Nov.–mid-Mar. 10–4.*

Woodland Opera House. This 1896 structure hosted minstrel shows, John Philip Sousa's marching band, and early vaudeville acts before closing for six decades (a sad saga that involved a penny-pinching Hershey's chocolate heir). Now restored, it hosts plays, musicals, and concerts. If the box office is open, ask for a backstage tour or a peek at the auditorium. ✉ *340 2nd St., at Main St.* ☎ *530/666-9617* ⊕ *www. woodlandoperahouse.org* ⊙ *Tours Tues. 1–4 or by appointment.*

WHERE TO EAT

$$ ✕ **Mojo's Kitchen428.** Woodland's dining scene turned a shade greener
AMERICAN when Mojo's opened with restored furnishings reportedly rescued from other businesses. The steaks, lamb shanks, and turkey pot pies all have their adherents, but if you're not into meat you'll find salmon and other seafood on the menu, along with vegetarian and even a few vegan items. A friendly, stylish place, Mojo's rewards customers for also adopting green practices: ride a bike here, and you'll receive 10% off your bill. $ *Average main: $20* ✉ *428 1st St., off Main St., Woodland* ☎ *530/661-0428* ⊕ *www.mojoskitchen428.com* ⊙ *No lunch Sun.*

DAVIS

10 miles west of Sacramento.

Davis began as a rich agricultural area and remains one, but it doesn't feel like a cow town. It's home to the University of California at Davis, whose students hang at downtown cafés, galleries, and bookstores (most of the action takes place between 1st and 4th and C and G streets), lending the city a vaguely cosmopolitan feel.

GETTING HERE AND AROUND

Most people arrive here by car via Interstate 80. Yolobus (⊕ *www. yolobus.com*) serves Davis from Sacramento. Downtown is walkable. Touring by bicycle is also an option—Davis is mostly flat.

ESSENTIALS
Visitor Information Davis Chamber of Commerce ⊠ *640 3rd St., at E St.* ☎ *530/756–5160* ⊕ *www.davischamber.com.*

EXPLORING
University of California, Davis. A top research university, UC Davis educates many of the Wine Country's vintners and grape growers. Campus tours depart from Buehler Alumni and Visitors Center. On a tour or not, worthy stops include the **Arboretum** (⊕ *arboretum.ucdavis.edu*)—this is a major agricultural school, and it shows—and the **Mondavi Center for the Performing Arts** (⊕ *www.mondaviarts.org*), a striking modern glass structure that presents top-tier artists. ⊠ *Visitor Center, Alumni La.* ☎ *530/752–8111* ⊕ *visit.ucdavis.edu* ☺ *Visitor Center, weekdays 8–5, Sat. 10–2; campus tours Sat. at 11:30.*

THE GOLD COUNTRY—SOUTH

This hilly region has an old-timey vibe. It's rich with antiques shops, quaint coffee shops, and delightfully appointed Victorian B&Bs.

PLACERVILLE

44 miles east of Sacramento.

It's hard to imagine now, but in 1849 about 4,000 miners staked out every gully and hillside in Placerville, turning the town into a rip-roaring camp of log cabins, tents, and clapboard houses. The area was then known as Hangtown, a graphic allusion to the nature of frontier justice. It took on the name Placerville in 1854 and became an important supply center for the miners. (*Placer* is defined roughly as valuable minerals found in riverbeds or lakes.) Mark Hopkins, Philip Armour, and John Studebaker were among the industrialists who got their starts here.

GETTING HERE AND AROUND
You'll need a car to get to and around Placerville; it's a 45-minute drive from Sacramento via U.S. 50.

EXPLORING
Apple Hill. During the fall harvest season (from September through December), the members of the Apple Hill Growers Association open their orchards and vineyards for apple and berry picking, picnicking, and wine and cider tasting. Many sell baked items and picnic food. At other times of the year, various roadside stands sell produce and other items. The association's website has maps you can download. ⚠ Traffic on October weekends is often backed up. ⊠ *About 5 miles east of Hwy. 49; take Camino exit from U.S. 50* ☎ *530/644–7692* ⊕ *www.applehill.com.*

FAMILY **Hangtown's Gold Bug Park & Mine.** Take a self-guided tour of this fully lighted mine shaft owned by the City of Placerville. The worthwhile audio tour (included) makes clear what you're seeing. ■TIP➔ A shaded stream runs through the park, and there are picnic facilities. ⊠ *2635 Goldbug La., off Bedford Ave., 1 mile off U.S. 50* ☎ *530/642–5207* ⊕ *www.goldbugpark.org* 🎫 *$5* ☺ *Apr.–Oct., daily 10–4; Nov.–Mar., weekends noon–4.*

WHERE TO EAT AND STAY

For expanded hotel reviews, visit Fodors.com.

$

VEGETARIAN

✕ **The Cozmic Cafe.** Crowds convene here for healthful wraps, burritos, sandwiches, salads, and the like, plus breakfast (served anytime), smoothies, and coffee drinks. Portions are big, prices are low, and the ambience is distinctive. The eatery is in the 1859 Pearson's Soda Works Building and extends back into the side of a mountain, into what used to be a mineshaft. The live music here is among the best in the foothills, and an upstairs pub beckons with local wines and microbrews. ⑤ *Average main: $9* ⊠ *594 Main St., at Bedford Ave.* ☎ *530/642–8481* ⊕ *www.ourcoz.com* ⊘ *Closed Mon.*

$$

B&B/INN

▦ **Seasons Bed & Breakfast.** One of Placerville's oldest homes has been transformed into a lovely and relaxing oasis. **Pros:** quiet setting; short walk to downtown; attentive hosts; great breakfasts. **Cons:** B&B environment not for everyone. ⑤ *Rooms from: $135* ⊠ *2934 Bedford Ave.* ☎ *530/626–4420* ⊕ *www.theseasons.net* ↪ *1 room, 2 suites, 1 cottage* ❙⊘❙ *Breakfast.*

SHENANDOAH VALLEY

20 miles south of Placerville.

The most concentrated Gold Country wine-touring area lies in the hills of the Shenandoah Valley, east of Plymouth. Robust Zinfandel is the primary grape grown here, but vineyards also produce other varietals. Most wineries are open for tastings at least on weekend afternoons; several have shaded picnic areas. ■**TIP**➔ **This region is gaining steam as a less-congested alternative to the Napa Valley.**

GETTING HERE AND AROUND

Reach the Shenandoah Valley by turning east on Fiddletown Road in Plymouth, between Placerville and Sutter Creek, and then north on Plymouth-Shenandoah Road. You will need a car to explore the valley and its vineyards.

EXPLORING

Shenandoah Vineyards. A plummy Barbera and an almost chocolaty Zinfandel top this winery's repertoire, but for a contrast you can also try a startlingly crisp Sauvignon Blanc. The Tempranillo is also good. An adjacent gallery sells contemporary art, pottery, photographs, and souvenirs. ■**TIP**➔ **Shenandoah is affiliated with the nearby Sobon Estate Winery, which has an engaging on-site museum about the area.** ⊠ *12300 Steiner Rd., Plymouth* ☎ *209/245–4455* ⊕ *www.sobonwine. com* ⊡ *Tasting $5* ⊘ *Daily 10–5.*

Sobon Estate. You can sip fruity, robust Zinfandels—old vine and new— and learn about wine making and Shenandoah Valley pioneer life at the museum here. This winery was established in 1856 and has been run since 1989 by the owners of Shenandoah Vineyards (whose wines you can also taste). ■**TIP**➔ **To sample the best of the Zins, pay the modest fee for the reserve tasting.** ⊠ *14430 Shenandoah Rd., east of Ostrom Rd., Plymouth* ☎ *209/245–4455* ⊕ *www.sobonwine.com* ⊡ *Tasting $5* ⊘ *Daily 9–5.*

Terre Rouge and Easton Wines. The winery of Bill and Jane Easton has two labels with two different wine-making styles: Terre Rouge focuses on Rhône-style wines, while Easton covers old-vine Zinfandel and Barbera. The winery has had good results with inky, soft Syrahs and Enigma, a blend of Marsanne, Viognier, and Roussane. ■TIP➔ You can picnic on the shaded patio here and there's a pétanque court nearby.

WORD OF MOUTH

"The Shenandoah Valley is what Napa was 30 years ago. Beautiful scenery, free tasting (for the most part), no appointments required (for the most part), really good wines, and a chance to talk to the actual winemakers."

—janisj

✉ *10801 Dickson Rd., at Shenandoah Rd., Plymouth* ☎ *209/245–4277* ⊕ *www.terrerougewines.com* ✉ *Tasting $5* ⊙ *Nov.–Aug., Thurs.–Mon. 11–4; Sept. and Oct., daily 11–4.*

Fodor'sChoice ★ **Vino Noceto.** This winery is an example of the benefits of focusing mostly on one varietal—in this case Sangiovese—and doing it well. Owners Suzy and Jim Gullett produce their Sangioveses in several different styles, from light and fruity to rich and heavy. They also produce small lots of wines from other varietals. ✉ *11011 Shenandoah Rd., at Dickson Rd., Plymouth* ☎ *209/245–6556* ⊕ *www.noceto.com* ✉ *Tasting free* ⊙ *Weekdays 11–4, weekends 11–5.*

WHERE TO EAT

$$$$
MODERN
AMERICAN
Fodor'sChoice
★

✕ **Taste.** An unexpected find on the dusty streets of tiny Plymouth, Taste serves eclectic modern cuisine centered around fresh, local produce. The choices range from phyllo-wrapped mushroom "cigars" to pan-seared scallops served with golden-beet risotto, kumquat, mint, fennel, and orange butter. Toss in tahini-grilled cauliflower with red-wine braised carrots and turnip greens, and even the vegetarians leave happy. ■TIP➔ Gold Country winemaking can be hit or miss, but with several sommeliers on staff, this is a terrific place to find out which producers are worth seeking out. There's also a great beer list. ⑤ *Average main: $35* ✉ *9402 Main St.* ☎ *209/245–3463* ⊕ *www.restauranttaste. com* ⊙ *Closed Tues. and Wed. No lunch weekdays.*

AMADOR CITY

6 miles south of Plymouth.

The history of tiny Amador City mirrors the boom-bust-boom cycle of many Gold Country towns. With an output of $42 million in gold, its Keystone Mine was one of the most productive in the Mother Lode. After all the gold was extracted, the miners cleared out, and the area suffered. Amador City now derives its wealth from tourists, who come to browse through its antiques and specialty shops, most of them on or just off Highway 49.

GETTING HERE AND AROUND

Park where you can along Old Highway 49 (a bypass diverts Highway 49 traffic around Sutter Creek and Amador City), and walk around.

Continued on page 494

EUREKA! CALIFORNIA'S GOLD RUSH

When James W. Marshall burst into John Sutter's Mill on January 24, 1848, carrying flecks of gold in his hat, the millwright unleashed the glittering California gold rush with these immortal words:

 "Boys, I believe I've found a gold mine!"

Before it was over, drowsy San Francisco had become the boomtown of the Golden West, Columbia's mines alone yielded $87,000,000, and California's Mother Lode—a vein of gold-bearing quartz that stretched 150 miles across the Sierra Nevada foothills—had been nearly tapped dry. Even though the gold rush soon became the gold bust, today you can still strike it rich by visiting the historic sites where it all happened.

Journey down the Gold Country Highway—a serpentine, nearly 300-mi-long two-lane route appropriately numbered 49—to find pure vacation treasure: fascinating mother lode towns, rip-roaring mining camps, and historic strike sites. In fact, in Placerville—as the former Hangtown, this spot saw so much new money and crime that outlaws were hanged in pairs—you can still pan the streams. And after you've seen the sights, the prospects remain just as golden: the entire region is a trove of gorgeous wineries, fun eateries, and Victorian-era hotels.

by: Reed Parsell and Robert I.C. Fisher

ALL THAT GLITTERED: '49ER FEVER

From imagination springs adventure, and perhaps no event in the 19th century provoked more wild adventures than the California gold rush of 1848 to 1855.

James Marshall

1856 U.S. quarter

John Sutter

GOLD IN THEM THAR HILLS California's golden lava was discovered purely by accident. Upon finding his cattle ranch had gone to ruin while he was away fighting in the Mexican-American War, New Jersey native James W. Marshall decided to build a sawmill, with John Sutter, outside the town of Coloma, 40 miles upstream of Sutter's Fort on the American River. To better power the mill, he had a wider siphon created to divert the river water and, one morning, spotted golden flakes in the trench. Rich fur magnate Sutter tried to keep the mother strike quiet, but his own staff soon decamped to pan the streams and the secret was out. The gold rush's impact was so profound that, practically overnight, it catapulted San Francisco into one of the nation's—and the world's—wealthiest cities.

BROTHER, CAN YOU SPARE AN INGOT? After Marshall, 37 at the time, saw his fledgling mill abandoned by workers who went to pan the streams, he left Coloma for almost a decade. During the 1860s he made some money as a vintner there—a dicey profession for a reported alcoholic. Eventually Marshall's wine business dried up, and he returned to prospecting in the 1870s. But without success. For six years starting in 1872, the state Legislature gave him a small pension as an acknowledgment of his gold rush importance, but for the last years of his life he was practically penniless. He died on Aug. 10, 1885, at age 74.w

THE GOLD CRUSH Before the gold rush ended, in 1855, it is estimated that it drew 300,000 people—Americans, Europeans, and Chinese—to the Sierra Nevada foothills to seek their fortune. Sadly, accidents, disease, and skirmishes with Native Americans took their toll on both the prospectors and the environment. In addition, the gold lust of '49er fever left more than a thousand murders in its wake (not counting the infamous "suspended" sentences meted out at Hangtown).

BOOM TO BUST

Jan. 24, 1848: James W. Marshall spies specks of bright rock in the streambed at his sawmill's site; Sutter certifies they are gold.

May, 1848: California's coastal communities empty out as prospectors flock to the hills to join the "forty-eighters."

Aug. 19, 1848: The *New York Herald* is the first East Coast newspaper to report a gold rush in California.

Oct. 13, 1849: California's state constitution is approved in Monterey. The state's new motto becomes "Eureka!"

1855: The California gold rush effectively ends, as digging for the precious mineral becomes increasingly difficult, and large corporations monopolize mining operations.

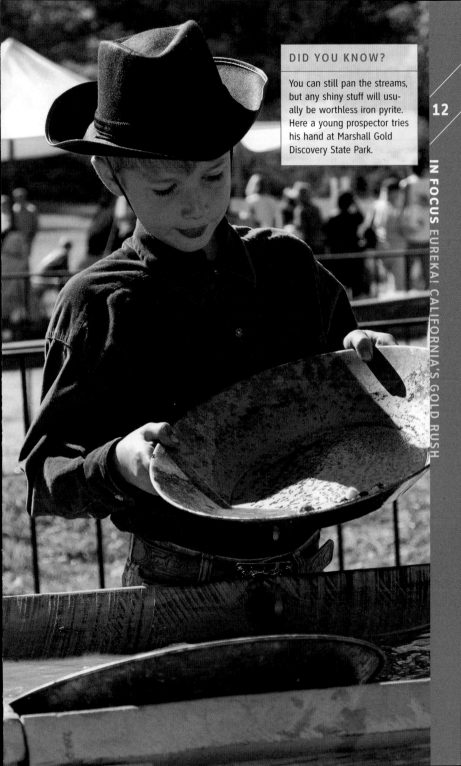

DID YOU KNOW?

You can still pan the streams, but any shiny stuff will usually be worthless iron pyrite. Here a young prospector tries his hand at Marshall Gold Discovery State Park.

GOING FOR THE GOLD

Marshall Gold Discovery State Park

If you want to go prospecting for the best sightseeing treasures in Gold Country, just follow this map.

Coloma

Empire Mine State Historic Park, Grass Valley:

During the century that it was operating, Empire Mine produced some 5.6 million ounces of gold. More than 350 miles of tunnels were dug, most under water. Operations ceased in 1956, but today visitors to the 800-acre park can go on 50-minute guided tours of the mines and enjoy great hiking trails and picnic spots.

Marshall Gold Discovery State Historic Park, Coloma:

Here's where it all began—a can't-miss gold rush site. See the stone cairn that marks the spot of James Marshall's discovery, the huge statue of him that rests on his grave site, and visit—together with crowds of schoolchildren—the updated museum, and more.

Hangtown's Gold Bug Park & Mine, Placerville:

Put on a hardhat and step into the 19th century at Gold Bug, located a few miles south of Marshall's jackpot site. Take a self-guided audio tour of a mine that opened in 1888, or a special tour of a mine opened in the 1850s, and do some "placering" (panning for gold) yourself, outside the gift shop. "Fool's gold" (used for billiard tables and chalkboards) was mostly found here before digging stopped in 1942.

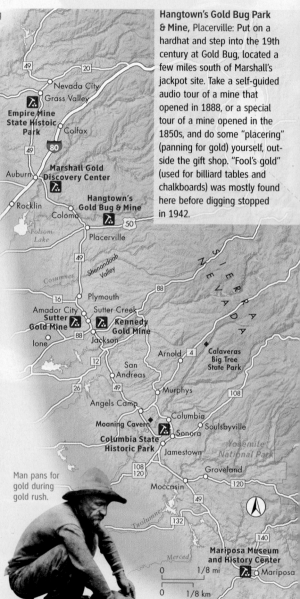

Man pans for gold during gold rush.

Empire Mine State Historic Park   Gold sifting pan   Columbia State Historic Park

Sutter Gold Mine: Between Amador City and Sutter Creek off Highway 49, this is the place to see how the so-called "Forty-Niner" individual prospectors were succeeded by large, deep-pocket mining companies. One-hour tours, offered daily April through most of October, take visitors deep into a hard-rock mine, where they can see ore veins that contain gold and learn the basics of hydraulic extraction.

Kennedy Gold Mine, Jackson: At 5,912 feet below ground, this is one of the world's deepest mines. Its head frame is one of the most dominant man-made sights along Highway 49's 295 miles. In operation from 1880 until World War II, the mine produced tens of millions of dollars of gold. One-hour tours, offered weekends and holidays from March through October, include a look inside the stately Mine Office.

Columbia State Historic Park

Columbia State Historic Park. Just north of Sonora, this is the best extant example of a gold rush-era town as it appeared in the mid-19th century. During its "golden" years, Columbia yielded more than $85 million in gold. Since World War II, the town has been restored. Fandango halls, Wells Fargo stage coaches, and a costumed staff bring a working 1850's mining town to life again.

Gold dollars

Mariposa Museum and History Center, Mariposa: Find all sorts of mining equipment, including a five-stamp ore mill, at this modest museum in the gold rush region's southernmost area. Also here is the fascinating California State Mining and Mineral Museum, home to a famous 13-pound golden nugget.

A PROSPECTING PRIMER

Grab any non-Teflon-coated pan with sloping sides and head up to "them thar hills." Find a stream—preferably one containing black sand—you can stoop beside, and then:

■ Scoop out sediment to fill your pan.

■ Add water, then gently shake the pan sideways, back and forth. This allows any gold to settle at the bottom.

■ Pick out and toss away any larger rocks.

■ Keep adding water, keep shaking the pan, and slowly pour the loosened waste gravel over the rim of the pan, making sure not to upend the pan while doing so.

■ If you're left with gold, yell "Eureka!" then put it in a glass container. Your findings may not make you rich, but will entitle you to bragging rights for as long as you keep the gold handy to show friends.

■ TIP→ If you'd rather not pan on your own, plenty of attractions and museums in the Gold Country will let you try your hand at prospecting. See listings in this chapter for more details on these historic sites.

WHERE TO STAY

For expanded hotel reviews, visit Fodors.com.

$$ **Imperial Hotel.** The whimsically decorated mock-Victorian rooms at
B&B/INN this 1879 hotel give a modern twist to the excesses of the era. **Pros:** comfortable; good restaurant and bar; tiny-town charm. **Cons:** no nightlife. ⑤ *Rooms from: $135* ⊠ *14202 Old Hwy. 49* ☎ *209/267–9172* ⊕ *www.imperialamador.com* ⇨ *6 rooms, 3 suites* ⑩| *Breakfast.*

SUTTER CREEK

2 miles south of Amador City.

Sutter Creek is a charming conglomeration of balconied buildings, Victorian homes, and neo–New England structures. The stores on Main Street (formerly part of Highway 49, which was rerouted) are worth visiting for works by the many local artists and craftspeople.

GETTING HERE AND AROUND

Arrive here by car on Highway 49. There's no public transit, but downtown is walkable. The visitor center organizes walking tours.

ESSENTIALS

Information Sutter Creek Visitor Center ⊠ *71A Main St.* ☎ *209/267–1344* ⊕ *www.suttercreek.org.*

EXPLORING

Monteverde Store Museum. This store, opened 1896, is a relic from the past: its final owner walked out more than four decades ago and never returned. These days you can peruse what he left behind, including typical wares from a century ago, an elaborate antique scale, and a chair-encircled potbellied stove. ⊠ *3 Randolph St.* ☎ *209/267–0493* ⊙ *Thurs.–Mon. if volunteers available, hrs vary.*

WHERE TO EAT AND STAY

For expanded hotel reviews, visit Fodors.com.

$$ ✗ **Susan's Place.** Fresh produce, prompt and attentive service, and a
AMERICAN lovely patio (especially so on warm summer evenings) distinguish this local favorite a half-block off the main drag. The serving of wine is a big deal here; there's even a "mystery wine" option that leaves the bottle (or glass) choice up to the owner. Try the eggplant and Portobello mushrooms on grilled panini bread. ⑤ *Average main: $20* ⊠ *15 Eureka St.* ☎ *209/267–0945* ⊕ *www.susansplace.com* ⊙ *Closed Mon.–Wed.*

$$ **Eureka Street Inn.** The leaded stained glass windows and the origi-
B&B/INN nal redwood paneling, wainscoting, and beams—and, oh yes, those gas-log fireplaces in most rooms—lend the Eureka Street Inn a cozy feel. **Pros:** quiet location; lovely porch; engaging owners; Wi-Fi; large bathrooms. **Cons:** only four rooms. ⑤ *Rooms from: $145* ⊠ *55 Eureka St.* ☎ *209/267–5500, 800/399–2389* ⊕ *www.eurekastreetinn.com* ⇨ *4 rooms* ⑩| *Breakfast.*

$$$ **The Foxes Inn of Sutter Creek.** The rooms in this 1857 white-clap-
B&B/INN board house are handsome, with high ceilings, antique beds, and armoires; five have gas fireplaces. **Pros:** lovely inside and out;

friendly owners. **Cons:** pricey. $ *Rooms from: $200* ⊠ *77 Main St.* ☎ *209/267–5882, 800/987–3344* ⊕ *www.foxesinn.com* ⇄ *5 rooms, 2 suites* ¶⊙¶ *Breakfast.*

$$

B&B/INN

⊞ **Grey Gables Inn.** Charming yet modern, this inn brings a touch of the English countryside to the Gold Country; the rooms, named after British poets, have gas-log fireplaces. **Pros:** English feel; tasteful interiors. **Cons:** hovers over main road; not much to do in town after dark. $ *Rooms from: $163* ⊠ *161 Hanford St.* ☎ *209/267–1039, 800/473–9422* ⊕ *www.greygables.com* ⇄ *8 rooms* ¶⊙¶ *Breakfast.*

$

HOTEL

⊞ **Sutter Creek Days Inn.** If you're on a budget, this hotel is a good choice; the rooms have coffeemakers, and most have queen-size beds. **Pros:** affordable; convenient; clean. **Cons:** can feel a bit impersonal. $ *Rooms from: $84* ⊠ *271 Hanford St.* ☎ *209/267–9177* ⊕ *www.daysinn.com/suttercreek* ⇄ *52 rooms* ¶⊙¶ *Breakfast.*

JACKSON

8 miles south of Sutter Creek.

Jackson wasn't the Gold Country's rowdiest town, but the party lasted longer here than most anywhere else: "girls' dormitories" (aka brothels) and nickel slot machines flourished until the mid-1950s. Jackson also had the world's deepest and richest gold mines, the Kennedy and the Argonaut, which together produced $70 million in gold. Most of the miners who worked the lode were of Serbian or Italian origin, and they gave the town a European character that persists to this day. Jackson has pioneer cemeteries whose headstones tell the stories of local Serbian and Italian families. The city's official website (⊕ *ci.jackson.ca.us*; click on "Visitor Center") has great cemetery and walking-tour maps; there are some interesting shops downtown.

GETTING HERE AND AROUND

Arrive by car on Highway 49. You can walk to downtown sights but otherwise will need a car.

EXPLORING

St. Sava Serbian Orthodox Church. The terraced cemetery on the grounds of the handsome church is an impressive sight. ⊠ *724 N. Main St.*

WHERE TO EAT

$

AMERICAN

✕ **Mel and Faye's Diner.** A local hangout famous for its "Moo Burger"— so big it still makes cow sounds, presumably—the diner is run by its namesakes' son, who has added slightly more sophisticated fare for breakfast, lunch, and dinner. $ *Average main: $10* ⊠ *31 Main St.* ☎ *209/223–0853* ⊕ *melandfayesdiner.com* ⊙ *Closed Tues.*

ANGELS CAMP

20 miles south of Jackson.

Angels Camp is famous chiefly for its May jumping-frog contest, based on Mark Twain's short story "The Celebrated Jumping Frog of Calaveras County." The writer reputedly heard the story of the jumping frog from Ross Coon, proprietor of Angels Hotel, which has been in operation since 1856.

GETTING HERE AND AROUND

Angels Camp is at the intersection of Highway 49 and Highway 4. You'll need a car to get here and around.

EXPLORING

Angels Camp Museum. Gold-rush relics are on display here: photos, rocks, petrified wood, blacksmith and mining equipment, even a horse-drawn hearse. The carriage house out back holds 31 carriages and impressive mineral specimens. ⊠ *753 S. Main St.* ☎ *209/736–2963* ⊕ *www.angelscampmuseumfoundation.org* ⊠ *$5* ⊙ *Dec.–Feb., weekends 10–4; Mar.–Nov., daily 10–4.*

FAMILY **California Cavern.** A ½-mile subterranean trail winds through large chambers and past underground streams and lakes. There aren't many steps to climb, but it's a strenuous walk with some narrow passageways and steep spots. The caverns, at a constant 55°F, contain crystalline formations not found elsewhere, and the 80-minute guided tour explains local history and geology. ⊠ *9 miles east of San Andreas on Mountain Ranch Rd., then about 3 miles on Cave City Rd.* ☎ *209/736–2708* ⊕ *www.caverntours.com* ⊠ *$14.95* ⊙ *Mar. and Apr., daily 10–4; May–Oct., daily 10–5; Nov.–Feb. weekends 10–4; hrs can vary, call to confirm.*

Fodor's Choice ★ FAMILY **Moaning Cavern.** A 235-step spiral staircase leads into this vast cavern. More adventurous sorts can rappel into the chamber—ropes and instruction are provided. Otherwise, the only way inside is via the 45-minute tour, during which you'll see giant (and still growing) stalactites and stalagmites and an archaeological site that holds some of the oldest human remains yet found in America. Outside there are three zip lines, starting at $39 per person. ⊠ *5350 Moaning Cave Rd., off Parrots Ferry Rd., about 2 miles south of Vallecito* ☎ *209/736–2708* ⊕ *www.caverntours.com* ⊠ *$14.95* ⊙ *May–Oct., daily 9–6; Nov.–Apr., weekdays 10–5, weekends 9–5; hrs can vary, call to confirm.*

MURPHYS

10 miles northeast of Angels Camp.

Murphys is the Gold Country's most compact, orderly town, with enough shops and restaurants to keep families busy for at least a half-day. A well-preserved town of white-picket fences, Victorian houses, and interesting shops, it exhibits an upscale vibe. Horatio Alger and Ulysses S. Grant came through here, staying at what's now called the Murphys Historic Hotel & Lodge when they, along with many other 19th-century tourists, came to investigate the giant sequoia groves in nearby Calaveras Big Trees State Park.

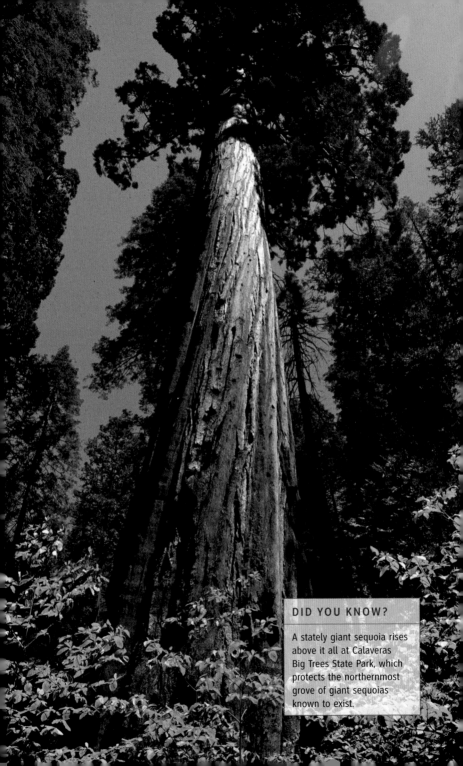

GETTING HERE AND AROUND

Murphys is 10 miles northeast of Highway 49 on Highway 4. You'll need to drive here. Parking can be difficult on summer weekends.

EXPLORING

Calaveras Big Tree State Park. The park protects hundreds of the largest and rarest living things on the planet—magnificent giant sequoia redwood trees. Some are 3,000 years old, 90 feet around at the base, and 250 feet tall. There are campgrounds and picnic areas; swimming, wading, fishing, and sunbathing on the Stanislaus River are popular in summer. ⊠ *Off Hwy. 4, 15 miles northeast of Murphys, 4 miles northeast of Arnold, Angels Camp* ☎ *209/795–2334* ⊕ *www.parks.ca.gov* ⧉ *$6 per vehicle day use; campsites $20* ⊘ *Park daily sunrise–sunset. Visitor center May–Oct., daily 11–3; Nov.–Apr., weekends 11–3.*

Ironstone Vineyards. Tours here take in spectacular gardens and underground tunnels cooled by a waterfall, and include the automated performance of a restored silent-movie-era pipe organ. On display near the tasting room is a 44-pound specimen of crystalline gold. The winery, known for Merlot, Cabernet Sauvignon, and Cabernet Franc, hosts concerts and other events. Its deli has picnic items. ■**TIP**➜ **Ironstone is worth a visit even if you don't drink wine.** ⊠ *1894 6 Mile Rd.* ⌖ *From Jones St. in town, head south on Scott St.* ☎ *209/728–1251* ⊕ *www.ironstonevineyards.com* ⧉ *Tastings $3–$6* ⊘ *Daily 10–5; open until 6 in summer.*

WHERE TO EAT AND STAY

For expanded hotel reviews, visit Fodors.com.

$$
AMERICAN
✕ **Grounds.** Light entrées, grilled vegetables, chicken, seafood, and steak are the specialties at this bustling bistro and coffee shop. Sandwiches, salads, and homemade soups are served for lunch. The crowd is friendly and the service attentive. ⑤ *Average main: $20* ⊠ *402 Main St.* ☎ *209/728–8663* ⊕ *www.groundsrestaurant.com.*

$$$
B&B/INN
▦ **Dunbar House 1880.** The oversize rooms in this elaborate Italianate-style home have brass beds, down comforters, gas-burning stoves, and claw-foot tubs. **Pros:** great breakfasts; lovely gardens; wonderful town. **Cons:** pricey. ⑤ *Rooms from: $199* ⊠ *271 Jones St.* ☎ *209/728–2897, 800/692–6006* ⊕ *www.dunbarhouse.com* ⥹*3 rooms, 2 suites* ⼉| *Breakfast.*

$
HOTEL
▦ **Murphys Historic Hotel & Lodge.** This 1855 stone hotel, whose register has seen the signatures of Mark Twain and the bandit Black Bart, figured in a Bret Harte short story. **Pros:** historical ambience; great bar; downtown. **Cons:** dated; creaky. ⑤ *Rooms from: $109* ⊠ *457 Main St.* ☎ *209/728–3444, 800/532–7684* ⊕ *www.murphyshotel.com* ⥹*29 rooms, 20 with bath* ⼉| *Breakfast.*

COLUMBIA

14 miles south of Angels Camp.

Columbia is the gateway for Columbia State Historic Park, one of the Gold Country's most visited sites. There are several inviting spots for a picnic in the area.

GETTING HERE AND AROUND

The only way to get here is by car, via either Highway 4 (the northern route) or Highway 49 (the southern) from Angels Camp.

EXPLORING

Fodor'sChoice
★
FAMILY

Columbia State Historic Park. Columbia comes as close to a gold-rush town in its heyday as any site in the Gold Country. Usually, you can ride a stagecoach, pan for gold, and watch a blacksmith working at an anvil. Street musicians perform in summer. Restored or reconstructed buildings include a Wells Fargo Express office, a Masonic temple, stores, saloons, a firehouse, churches, a school, and a newspaper office. At times, all are staffed to simulate a working 1850s town. The park also includes the **Historic Fallon House Theater,** where entertainment is presented much of the year. The town's two 19th-century historic lodgings, the Fallon Hotel ($) and City Hotel ($–$$) perch you in the past; find out more at ⊕ *www.cityhotel.com.* ⊠ *Fallon Hotel, 11175 Washington St.* ☎ *209/532–0150* ⊕ *www.parks.ca.gov* ⊠ *Free* ⊙ *Daily 9–5.*

12

SONORA

4 miles south of Columbia.

Miners from Mexico founded Sonora and made it the biggest town in the Mother Lode. Following a period of racial and ethnic strife, the Mexican settlers moved on, and Yankees built the commercial city visible today. Sonora's historic downtown section sits atop the Big Bonanza Mine, one of the richest in the state. Another mine, on the site of nearby Sonora High School, yielded 990 pounds of gold in a single week in 1879. Reminders of the gold rush are everywhere in Sonora, in prim Victorian houses, typical Sierra-stone storefronts, and awning-shaded sidewalks. Reality intrudes beyond the town's historic heart, with strip malls, shopping centers, and modern motels.

GETTING HERE AND AROUND

Arrive in Sonora by car via Highway 49 (if coming from Columbia, drive south on Parrots Ferry Road). Parking can be difficult on the busy main drag, Washington Street (Highway 49).

EXPLORING

Tuolumne County Museum and History Center. The small museum occupies a historic gold rush–era building that served as a jail until 1960. Vintage firearms and paraphernalia, gold specimens, and MiWuk baskets are among the many artifacts on display. ⊠ *158 W. Bradford St., at Lower Sunset Dr.* ☎ *209/532–1317* ⊕ *www.tchistory.org* ⊠ *Free* ⊙ *Weekdays 10–4, Sat. 10–3:30* ⊙ *Closed Sun.*

WHERE TO EAT AND STAY

For expanded hotel reviews, visit Fodors.com.

$
AMERICAN

✕ **Diamondback Grill and Wine Bar.** The bright decor and refined atmosphere suggest more ambitious fare, but burgers are what this place is about. Locals crowd the tables, especially after 6 pm, for the ground-meat patties, beer-battered onion rings, veggie burger, and fine wines. $ *Average main: $11* ⊠ *93 S. Washington St., at Linoberg St.* ☎ *209/532–6661* ⊕ *www.thediamondbackgrill.com* ⊙ *Closed Sun.*

$$ 🏨 **Barretta Gardens Bed and Breakfast Inn.** This inn is perfect for a roman-

B&B/INN tic getaway, with elegant Victorian rooms varying in size, all furnished with period pieces. **Pros:** lovely grounds; yummy breakfasts; romantic. **Cons:** only seven rooms. $ *Rooms from: $159* ⊠ *700 S. Barretta St.* ☎ *209/532–6039, 800/206–3333* ⊕ *www.barrettagardens.com* ➝ *7 rooms* |◎| *Breakfast.*

JAMESTOWN

4 miles south of Sonora.

Compact Jamestown supplies a touristy view of gold rush–era life. Shops in brightly colored buildings along Main Street sell antiques and gift items. You can try your hand at panning for gold here or explore a bit of railroad history.

GETTING HERE AND AROUND

Jamestown lies at the intersection of north–south Highway 49 and east–west Highway 108. You'll need a car to tour here.

EXPLORING

FAMILY **Gold Prospecting Adventures.** You'll get a real feel (sort of) for the life of a prospector on the three-hour gold-panning excursions led by this outfit's congenial, steeped-in-history tour guides. You might even strike gold at the Jimtown Mine. ⊠ *18170 Main St.* ☎ *209/984–4653, 800/596–0009* ⊕ *www.goldprospecting.com* ☞ *Call for hrs and fees.*

Railtown 1897. Have a look at the roundhouse, turntable, shop rooms, and old locomotives and rail cars at this mostly outdoor site, then—if it's operating—hop aboard a steam train for a 40-minute journey. Most children enjoy this low-tech change of pace. ⊠ *5th Ave. and Reservoir Rd.* ☎ *209/984–3953* ⊕ *www.railtown1897.org* ☜ *Roundhouse tour $5; train ride $13* ☉ *Apr.–Oct., daily 9:30–4:30; Nov.–Mar., daily 10–3; train ride weekends Apr.–Oct.*

WHERE TO STAY

For expanded hotel reviews, visit Fodors.com.

$$ 🏨 **National Hotel.** The National has been in business since 1859, and

HOTEL its furnishings—brass beds, regal comforters, and lace curtains—are authentic but not overly embellished. **Pros:** historic feel; great brunches. **Cons:** not much happens in town after dark. $ *Rooms from: $140* ⊠ *18183 Main St.* ☎ *209/984–3446, 800/894–3446 in CA* ⊕ *www. national-hotel.com* ➝ *9 rooms* |◎| *Breakfast.*

MARIPOSA

50 miles south of Jamestown.

Mariposa marks the southern end of the Mother Lode. Much of the land in this area was part of a 44,000-acre land grant Colonel John C. Fremont acquired from Mexico before gold was discovered and California became a state. Many people stop here on the way to Yosemite National Park, about an hour's drive east on Highway 140.

GETTING HERE AND AROUND

If driving, take Highway 49 or Highway 140. YARTS (⊕ *www.yarts.com*), the regional transit system, can get you to Mariposa from the Central Valley town of Merced (where you can also transfer from Amtrak) or from Yosemite Valley. Otherwise, you'll need a car to get here and around.

EXPLORING

California State Mining and Mineral Museum. Displays on gold-rush history here include a faux hard-rock mine shaft, a miniature stamp mill, and a 13-pound chunk of crystallized gold. In September 2012, thieves stole $1.3 million in gold and jewels; suspects were soon arrested, but only some of the items were recovered. ⊠ *5005 Fairground Rd., off Hwy. 49* ☎ *209/742–7625* ⊕ *www.parks.ca.gov* ⊠ *$4* ⊗ *May–Sept., daily 10–5; Oct.–Apr., Wed.–Mon. 10–4.*

WHERE TO EAT AND STAY

For expanded hotel reviews, visit Fodors.com.

$$$ ✕ **Charles Street Dinner House.** Though it recently changed hands, Charles
AMERICAN Street remains the classiest dinner joint in town. Another plus: it's centrally located. The extensive menu includes beef, chicken, pork, lamb, duck, lobster, and a few vegetarian options. ⑤ *Average main: $25* ⊠ *Hwy. 140 and 7th St.* ☎ *209/966–2366* ⊕ *www.charlesstreetdinnerhouse.net* ⊗ *No lunch Sat.–Mon.*

$$$ ✕ **Savoury's.** Some locals say they prefer Savoury's to the venerable
AMERICAN Charles Street Dinner House. The pasta and fresh bread receive especially enthusiastic praise; vegetarians and vegans can eat here. Everything about this place exudes competence and class. Kids might find it stuffy, though. ⑤ *Average main: $23* ⊠ *5034 Hwy. 140* ☎ *209/966–7677* ⊕ *savouryrestaurant.com* ⊗ *Closed Wed. No lunch.*

$$ ▦ **Mariposa Lodge.** Thoroughly modern and tastefully landscaped, the
HOTEL Mariposa is a solid option for those who want to stay within 30 miles of Yosemite National Park without spending a fortune. **Pros:** convenient; relatively inexpensive; clean. **Cons:** chain-like feel. ⑤ *Rooms from: $149* ⊠ *5052 Hwy. 140* ☎ *209/966–3607, 800/966–8819* ⊕ *www.mariposalodge.com* ⇨ *45 rooms* ⎮⊙⎮ *Breakfast.*

THE GOLD COUNTRY—NORTH

Gold has had a significant presence along this northern stretch of Highway 49, whose highlights include the bucolic Empire State Historic Park and Coloma, where the discovery of a few nuggets triggered the gold rush.

COLOMA

8 miles northwest of Placerville.

The California gold rush started in Coloma. "My eye was caught with the glimpse of something shining in the bottom of the ditch," James Marshall recalled. Marshall himself never found any more "color," as gold came to be called.

GETTING HERE AND AROUND

A car is the only practical way to get to Coloma, via Highway 49. Once parked, you can walk to all the worthwhile sights.

EXPLORING

FAMILY **Marshall Gold Discovery State Historic Park.** Most of Coloma lies within the historic park. Though crowded with tourists in summer, Coloma hardly resembles the mob scene it was in 1849, when 2,000 prospectors staked out claims along the streambed. The town's population grew to 4,000, supporting seven hotels, three banks, and many stores and businesses. But when reserves of the precious metal dwindled, prospectors left as quickly as they had come. A working reproduction of an 1840s mill lies near the spot where James Marshall first saw gold. A trail leads to a modest sign (considering the impact) marking his discovery. ■ TIP➜ Take a stroll up the surrounding hills for sublime views. ⊠ *310 Back St., off Hwy. 49* ☎ *530/622–3470* ⊕ *www.parks.ca.gov* ⊠ *$8 per vehicle* ☉ *Park daily 8–sunset. Museum Mar.–Oct., Tues.–Sat. 10–4; Nov.–Feb., daily 10–3.*

WHERE TO STAY

For expanded hotel reviews, visit Fodors.com.

$$ ⊡ **Coloma Country Inn.** Four of the rooms at this B&B on 2½ acres in the
B&B/INN   state historic park are inside an 1850s farmhouse, and two suites with kitchenettes occupy the carriage house. **Pros:** convenient to the park; quiet; leisurely ambience. **Cons:** no nightlife. ⑤ *Rooms from: $135* ⊠ *345 High St.* ☎ *530/622–6919* ⊕ *www.colomacountryinn.com* ⤙ *4 rooms, 2 suites* ⑩ *Breakfast.*

AUBURN

18 miles northwest of Coloma; 34 miles northeast of Sacramento.

Auburn is the Gold Country town most accessible to travelers on Interstate 80. An important transportation center during the gold rush, downtown Auburn has a small Old Town district with narrow climbing streets, cobblestone lanes, wooden sidewalks, and many original buildings. ■ TIP➜ Fresh produce, flowers, baked goods, and gifts are for sale at the farmers' market, held on Saturday morning year-round.

GETTING HERE AND AROUND

Amtrak serves Auburn, though most visitors arrive by car on Highway 49 or Interstate 80. Once downtown, you can tour on foot.

EXPLORING

Bernhard Museum Complex. Party like it's 1889 at this diverting complex, whose main structure opened in 1851 as the Traveler's Rest Hotel and for 100 years was the residence of the Bernhard family. The congenial docents, dressed in Victorian garb, describe the family's history and 19th-century life in Auburn. ⊠ *291 Auburn–Folsom Rd., at Fairgate Rd.* ☎ *530/889–6500* ⊠ *Free* ☉ *Tues.–Sun. 11–4.*

FAMILY **Gold Country Museum.** You'll get a feel for life in the mines at this museum whose highlights include a re-created mine tunnel, a gold-panning stream, and a reproduction saloon. ⊠ *1273 High St., off Auburn–Folsom Rd.* ☎ *530/889–6500* ⊠ *Free to museum, $3 to pan for gold* ☉ *Tues.–Sun. 11–4.*

12

Placer County Courthouse. Auburn's standout structure is the Placer County Courthouse. The classic gold-dome building houses the Placer County Museum, which documents the area's history—Native American, railroad, agricultural, and mining—from the early 1700s to 1900. ⊠ *101 Maple St., at Lincoln Way* ☎ *530/889–6500* 🖃 *Free* ⊙ *Daily 10–4.*

WHERE TO EAT AND STAY

For expanded hotel reviews, visit Fodors.com.

$ ✕ **Awful Annie's.** Big patio umbrellas (and outdoor heaters when neces-
AMERICAN sary) allow patrons to take in the Old Town view from this popular spot for lunch or breakfast—one specialty is a chili omelet. Another Annie's is at 490 G Street in nearby Lincoln. ⑤ *Average main: $10* ⊠ *160 Sacramento St., at Washington St.* ☎ *530/888–9857* ⊕ *www.awfulannies. com* ⊙ *No dinner.*

$$ ✕ **Latitudes.** Delicious multicultural cuisine is served in an 1870 Vic-
ECLECTIC torian. The menu (with monthly specials from diverse geographical regions) includes meat entrées prepared with the appropriate Mexican spices, curries, cheeses, or teriyaki sauce. Vegetarians and vegans have several inventive choices, including tofu and tempeh dishes. Sunday brunch is deservedly popular. ⑤ *Average main: $17* ⊠ *130 Maple St., at Auburn-Folsom Rd.* ☎ *530/885–9535* ⊕ *www.latitudesrestaurant. com* ⊙ *Closed Mon. and Tues.*

$$ 🏨 **Holiday Inn Auburn Hotel.** Above the freeway across from Old Town,
HOTEL this hotel has a welcoming lobby and chain-standard but nice rooms. **Pros:** convenient; clean; large rooms; loaner books. **Cons:** noise in rooms near parking lot. ⑤ *Rooms from: $127* ⊠ *120 Grass Valley Hwy.* ☎ *530/887–8787, 800/814–8787* ⊕ *www.auburnhi.com* ⌁ *96 rooms, 6 suites* ⦿ *Breakfast.*

GRASS VALLEY

24 miles north of Auburn.

More than half of California's total gold production was extracted from mines around Grass Valley, including the Empire Mine, which, along with the North Star Mining Museum, is among the Gold Country's most fascinating attractions.

GETTING HERE AND AROUND

You'll need a car to get here. Take Highway 20 east from Interstate 5 or west from Interstate 80. Highway 49 is the north–south route into town. Gold Country Stage vehicles (☎ *530/447–0103* ⊙ *Weekdays 7–6*) serve some attractions. Expect to wait, though.

EXPLORING

FAMILY **Empire Mine State Historic Park.** The hard-rock gold mine here was one of California's richest. An estimated 5.8 million ounces were extracted from its 367 miles of underground passages between 1850 and 1956. On a 50-minute tour you can walk into a mine shaft, peer into the mine's deeper recesses, and view the owner's "cottage," which has exquisite woodwork. ■**TIP**➜ With its shaded tables and gentle trails, this is a pleasant place for family picnics. ⊠ *10791 E. Empire St., south of Empire St. exit off Hwy. 49* ☎ *530/273–8522* ⊕ *www.parks.ca.gov*

Almost 6 million ounces of gold were extracted from the Empire Mine.

☎ *$7* ⏱ *May–Aug., daily 9–6; Sept.–Apr., daily 10–5. Tours May–Aug., daily on hr 11–4; Sept.–Apr., weekends at 1 (cottage only) and 2 (mine yard only), weather permitting.*

Holbrooke Hotel. The recently refurnished landmark hotel ($$), built in 1851, hosted entertainer Lola Montez and writer Mark Twain as well as Ulysses S. Grant and other U.S. presidents. Its restaurant-saloon ($$) is one of the oldest operating west of the Mississippi. ✉ *212 W. Main St., at N. Church St.* ☎ *530/273–1353, 800/933–7077* ⊕ *www. holbrooke.com.*

FAMILY **North Star Mining Museum.** Housed in a former powerhouse, the museum displays the 32-foot-high Pelton Water Wheel, said to be the largest ever built. It was used to power mining operations and was a forerunner of the modern turbines that generate hydroelectricity. Hands-on displays are geared to children. You can picnic nearby. ✉ *10933 Allison Ranch Rd., north of Empire St. exit off Hwy. 49* ☎ *530/273–4255* ⊕ *nevadacountyhistory.org* ☎ *Donation requested* ⏱ *May–mid-Oct., Tues.–Sun. 11–5.*

WHERE TO EAT AND STAY
For expanded hotel reviews, visit Fodors.com.

$ ✕ **Cousin Jack Pasties.** Meat- and vegetable-stuffed pasties are a taste of
BRITISH the region's history, having come across the Atlantic with Cornish miners and their families in the mid-19th century. The flaky crusts practically melt in your mouth. A simple food stand, Jack's is nonetheless a local landmark. $ *Average main: $8* ✉ *100 S. Auburn St., at Main St.* ☎ *530/272–9230* ▭ *No credit cards.*

$$ ✕ **Villa Venezia Restaurant.** Pasta and seafood are the specialties served
ITALIAN   up in a cozy, warm Victorian building with an intimate patio area. The
appetizers and salads very nearly outshine the outstanding main dishes.
⑤ *Average main: $22* ✉ *124 Bank St., at Stewart St.* ☎ *530/273–3555*
⊕ *www.villavenezia.info* ⊗ *No lunch Sat.–Thurs.*

$ ⊞ **Holiday Lodge.** This modest hotel is close to some Grass Valley attrac-
HOTEL   tions, and its staff can help arrange historical tours here and in Nevada
City and the small town of Washington. **Pros:** good price; friendly
staff. **Cons:** feels dated; exterior flirts with shabbiness. ⑤ *Rooms from:
$77* ✉ *1221 E. Main St.* ☎ *530/273–4406, 800/742–7125* ⊕ *www.
holidaylodge.biz* ⇶ *35 rooms* ⦿ *Breakfast.*

NEVADA CITY

4 miles north of Grass Valley.

Nevada City, once known as the Queen City of the Northern Mines,
is the most appealing of the northern Mother Lode towns. The iron-
shutter brick buildings that line the narrow downtown streets contain
antiques shops, galleries, boutiques, B&Bs, restaurants, and a winery.
Horse-drawn carriage tours add to the romance, as do gas street lamps.
At one point in the 1850s, Nevada City had a population of nearly
10,000—enough to support much cultural activity. Today, about 3,000
people live here.

GETTING HERE AND AROUND

You'll need a car to get here. Take Highway 20 east from Interstate 5
or west from Interstate 80. Highway 49 is the north–south route into
town. Gold Country Stage vehicles (☎ *530/447–0103* ⊗ *Weekdays 7–6*)
serve some attractions.

ESSENTIALS

Visitor Information Nevada City Chamber of Commerce ✉ *132 Main St.*
☎ *530/265–2692* ⊕ *www.nevadacitychamber.com.*

EXPLORING

Firehouse No. 1. With its gingerbread-trim bell tower, Firehouse No. 1
is one of the Gold Country's most distinctive buildings. A museum,
it houses gold-rush artifacts and the altar from a Chinese joss house
(temple). ✉ *214 Main St., at Coyote St.* ☎ *530/265–5468* ⊡ *Donation
requested* ⊗ *May–Nov., Tue.–Sun. 1–4.*

Miners Foundry. The foundry, erected in 1856, produced machines for
gold mining and logging. The Pelton Water Wheel, a power source for
the mines (the wheel also jump-started the hydroelectric power indus-
try), was invented here. ✉ *325 Spring St., at Bridge St.* ☎ *530/265–5040*
⊕ *www.minersfoundry.org.*

Nevada City Winery. Watch wine being created while you sip at this
winery whose tasting room overlooks the production area. Syrah and
Zinfandel are among the strengths here. ✉ *Miners Foundry Garage,
321 Spring St., at Bridge St.* ☎ *530/265–9463, 800/203–9463* ⊕ *www.
ncwinery.com* ⊡ *Tasting and tour free* ⊗ *Sun.–Thurs. noon–5, Fri. and
Sat. noon–6; tour on Sat. at 1:30.*

Nevada Theatre. This redbrick edifice, constructed in 1865, is California's oldest theater building. Mark Twain, Emma Nevada, and many other notable people appeared on its stage. These days, plays and old films are presented here. ⊠ *401 Broad St., at Commercial St.* ☎ *530/265–6161, 530/274–3456 for film showtimes* ⊕ *www.nevadatheatre.com.*

WHERE TO EAT AND STAY

For expanded hotel reviews, visit Fodors.com.

$$$ ✕ **Friar Tuck's.** Popular Friar Tuck's specializes in aromatic, interac-
ECLECTIC tive fondues and has an extensive seafood menu. The sparkling inte-
rior has a late-19th century ambience—it's one of Nevada City's best
indoor spaces. ⑤ *Average main: $25* ⊠ *111 N. Pine St., at Broad St.*
☎ *530/265–9093* ⊕ *friartucks.com* ⊗ *No lunch.*

$$$ ✕ **New Moon Cafe.** An attractively lighted room gives diners a cozy feel-
AMERICAN ing, though some patrons complain about the high noise level. Organic
flours and free-range meats are used when available. ⑤ *Average main:*
$25 ⊠ *203 York St., at Commercial St.* ☎ *530/265–6399* ⊕ *www.*
thenewmooncafe.com ⊗ *Closed Mon. No lunch weekends.*

$ ✕ **South Pine Cafe.** Locals flock here, especially for brunch. Lobster and
AMERICAN beef are on the menu, but the real attention-grabbers are vegetarian
entrées and side dishes, such as breakfast potatoes and apple-ginger
muffins. There's a branch in Grass Valley at 102 North Richardson
Street. ⑤ *Average main: $11* ⊠ *110 S. Pine St., at Spring St.* ☎ *530/265–*
0260 ⊕ *www.southpinecafe.com* ⊗ *No dinner.*

$$ ⚏ **Red Castle Historic Lodgings.** Antique furnishings and oriental rugs dec-
B&B/INN orate the rooms of this 1857 Gothic-revival mansion, a fine option for
Fodor'sChoice those who appreciate the finer points of Victorian design. **Pros:** friendly
★ owners; spectacular food; fascinating architecture; hillside setting over-
looking town. **Cons:** the walk uphill from downtown is a workout.
⑤ *Rooms from: $155* ⊠ *109 Prospect St.* ☎ *530/265–5135, 800/761–*
4766 ⊕ *www.redcastleinn.com* ⥽ *4 rooms, 3 suites* ⧉ *Breakfast.*

LAKE TAHOE

With Reno, Nevada

WELCOME TO LAKE TAHOE

TOP REASONS TO GO

★ **The lake:** Blue, deep, and alpine pure, Lake Tahoe is far and away the main reason to visit this high Sierra paradise.

★ **Snow, snow, snow:** Daring black-diamond runs or baby-bunny bumps—whether you're an expert, a beginner, or somewhere in between, there are many slopes to suit your skills at the numerous Tahoe-area ski parks.

★ **The great outdoors:** A ring of national forests and recreation areas linked by miles of trails makes Tahoe a nature lover's paradise.

★ **Dinner with a view:** You can picnic lakeside at state parks or dine in restaurants perched along the shore.

★ **A date with lady luck:** Whether you want to roll dice, play the slots, or hope the blackjack dealer goes bust before you do, you'll find round-the-clock gambling at the casinos on the Nevada side of the lake and in Reno.

1 **California Side.** With the exception of Stateline, Nevada—which, aside from its casino-hotel towers, seems almost indistinguishable from South Lake Tahoe, California—the California side is more developed than the Nevada side. Here you can find both commercial enterprises—restaurants, motels, lodges, resorts, residential subdivisions—and public-access facilities, such as historic sites, parks, campgrounds, marinas, and beaches.

2 **Nevada Side.** You don't need a highway sign to know when you've crossed from California into Nevada: the flashing lights and elaborate marquees of casinos announce legal gambling in garish hues. But you'll find more here than tables and slot machines. Reno, the Biggest Little City in the World, has a vibrant art scene and a serene downtown RiverWalk. And when you really need to get away from the chip-toting crowds, you can hike through pristine wilderness at Lake Tahoe–Nevada State Park, or hit the slopes near Incline Village.

GETTING ORIENTED

In the northern section of the Sierra Nevada mountain range, the Lake Tahoe area covers portions of four national forests, several state parks, and rugged wilderness areas with names like Desolation and Granite Chief. Lake Tahoe, the star attraction, straddles California and Nevada and is one of the world's largest, clearest, and deepest alpine lakes. The region's proximity to the Bay Area and Sacramento to the west and Reno to the east draws thrill seekers during ski season and again in summer when water sports, camping, and hiking are the dominant activities.

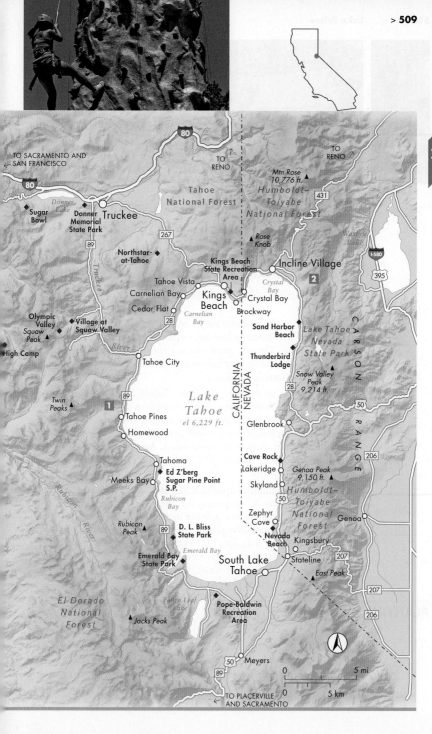

TO SACRAMENTO AND
SAN FRANCISCO

TO
RENO

TO
RENO

80

Tahoe
National Forest

Mtn Rose
10,776 ft.

Humboldt–
Toiyabe
National Forest

431

Washoe
Lake

I-580

Donner
Lake

**Sugar
Bowl**

**Donner
Memorial
State Park**

Truckee

Rose
Knob

89

267

**Northstar-
at-Tahoe**

**Kings Beach
State Recreation
Area**

Incline Village

2

395

Tahoe Vista

Carnelian Bay

Cedar Flat

28

**Kings
Beach**

Crystal
Bay

Crystal Bay

Brockway

Carnelian
Bay

**Sand Harbor
Beach**

Lake Tahoe
Nevada
State Park

C
A
R
S
O
N

**Olympic
Valley**

Squaw
Peak

**Village at
Squaw Valley**

River

**Thunderbird
Lodge**

R
A
N
G
E

High Camp

Tahoe City

Snow Valley
Peak
9,214 ft.

28

50

206

Twin
Peaks

89

1

Tahoe Pines

Homewood

*Lake
Tahoe*
el 6,229 ft.

CALIFORNIA
NEVADA

Glenbrook

50

Tahoma

Meeks Bay

**Ed Z'berg
Sugar Pine Point
S.P.**

Cave Rock

Lakeridge

Genoa Peak
9,150 ft.

Rubicon
Bay

Skyland

**Humboldt–
Toiyabe**

Rubicon
Peak

89

**D. L. Bliss
State Park**

Zephyr
Cove

*National
Forest*

Genoa

River

Emerald Bay

**Nevada
Beach**

Kingsbury

**Emerald Bay
State Park**

**South Lake
Tahoe**

Stateline

207

*El Dorado
National
Forest*

*Fallen Leaf
Lake*

**Pope-Baldwin
Recreation
Area**

East Peak

207

Jacks Peak

206

50

Meyers

0 ——— 5 mi

0 ——— 5 km

89

TO PLACERVILLE
AND SACRAMENTO

Updated
by Christine
Vovakes

Stunning Lake Tahoe is the largest alpine lake in North America, famous for its clarity, cobalt-blue water, and surrounding snowcapped peaks. Straddling the state line between California and Nevada, it lies 6,225 feet above sea level in the Sierra Nevada.

The border gives this popular resort region a split personality. About half its visitors are intent on low-key sightseeing, hiking, fishing, camping, and boating. The rest head directly for the Nevada side, where bargain dining, big-name entertainment, and the lure of a jackpot draw them into the glittering casinos.

The typical way to explore the Lake Tahoe area is to drive the 72-mile road that follows the shore through wooded flatlands and past beaches, climbing to vistas on the rugged southwest side of the lake and passing through busy commercial developments and casinos on its northeastern and southeastern edges. Another option is to actually go out *on* the 22-mile-long, 12-mile-wide lake on a sightseeing cruise or kayaking trip.

The lake, the communities around it, the state parks, national forests, and protected tracts of wilderness are the region's main draws, but other nearby destinations are gaining in popularity. Truckee, with an Old West feel and innovative restaurants, entices visitors looking for a relaxed pace and easy access to Tahoe's north shore and Olympic Valley ski parks. And today Reno, once known only for its casinos, attracts tourists with its buzzing arts scene, revitalized downtown riverfront, and campus events at the University of Nevada.

PLANNING

WHEN TO GO

A sapphire blue lake shimmering deep in the center of an ice white wonderland—that's Tahoe in winter. But those blankets of snow mean lots of storms that often close roads and force chain requirements on the interstate. In summer the roads are open, but the lake and lodgings are clogged with visitors seeking respite from valley heat. If you don't ski, the best times to visit are early fall—September and October—and late spring. The crowds thin, prices dip, and you can count on Tahoe being beautiful.

Most Lake Tahoe accommodations, restaurants, and even a handful of parks are open year-round, but many visitor centers, mansions, state parks, and beaches are closed from October through May. During those months, winter-sports enthusiasts swamp Tahoe's downhill resorts and cross-country centers, North America's largest concentration of skiing facilities. In summer it's cooler here than in the scorched Sierra Nevada foothills, the clean mountain air is bracingly crisp, and the surface temperature of Lake Tahoe is an invigorating 65°F to 70°F (compared with 40°F to 50°F in winter). This is also the time, however, when it may seem as if every tourist at the lake—100,000 on peak weekends—is in a car on the main road circling the shoreline (especially on Highway 89, just south of Tahoe City; on Highway 28, east of Tahoe City; and on U.S. 50 in South Lake Tahoe). Christmas week and July 4th are the busiest times, and prices go through the roof; plan accordingly.

GETTING HERE AND AROUND

AIR TRAVEL

The nearest airport to Lake Tahoe is Reno–Tahoe International Airport (RNO), in Reno, 50 miles northeast of the closest point on the lake. Airlines serving RNO include Alaska, Allegiant Air, American, Delta, Southwest, and United. Except for Allegiant Air, these airlines plus Aeromexico, Hawaiian, and JetBlue serve Sacramento International Airport (SMF), 112 miles from South Lake Tahoe. North Lake Tahoe Express runs buses ($45 one way, $85 round-trip) between RNO and towns on the lake's western and northern shores, plus Incline Village, Truckee, Squaw Valley, and Northstar. South Tahoe Express runs buses ($29.75 one-way, $53 round-trip) between Reno–Tahoe Airport and resort hotels in the South Lake Tahoe area.

Airports Reno–Tahoe International Airport ⊠ *2001 E. Plumb La., off U.S. 395/I–580, Exit 65B, Reno, Nevada* ☎ *775/328–6400* ⊕ *www.renoairport.com.* **Sacramento International Airport** ⊠ *6900 Airport Blvd., 12 miles northwest of downtown off I–5, Sacramento* ☎ *916/929–5411* ⊕ *www.sacramento.aero/smf.*

Transfers North Lake Tahoe Express ☎ *866/216–5222* ⊕ *www.northlaketahoeexpress.com.* **South Tahoe Express** ☎ *775/325–8944, 866/898–2463* ⊕ *www.southtahoeexpress.com.*

BUS TRAVEL

Greyhound stops in San Francisco, Sacramento, Truckee, and Reno. BlueGO ($2 per ride) provides year-round local service in South Lake Tahoe, Nifty 50 Trolley service to parks and other attractions during summer. On the north shore, Tahoe Area Regional Transit (TART; $1.75) operates buses between Tahoma and Incline Village and runs shuttles to Truckee. RTC RIDE buses ($2) serve the Reno area. All local rides require exact change.

In winter, BlueGO provides free ski shuttle service from South Lake Tahoe hotels and resorts to various Heavenly Mountain ski lodge locations. Most of the major ski resorts offer shuttle service to nearby lodging.

Bus Contacts Greyhound ☎ *800/231–2222* ⊕ *www.greyhound.com.*
BlueGO ☎ *530/541–7149* ⊕ *www.bluego.org.* **RTC RIDE** ☎ *775/348–7433*
⊕ *www.rtcwashoe.com.* **Tahoe Area Regional Transit (TART)** ☎ *530/550–1212,*
800/736–6365 ⊕ *www.laketahoetransit.com.*

CAR TRAVEL

Lake Tahoe is 198 miles northeast of San Francisco, a drive of less than four hours in good weather and light traffic—if possible avoid heavy weekend traffic, particularly leaving the San Francisco area for Tahoe on Friday afternoon and returning on Sunday afternoon. The major route is Interstate 80, which cuts through the Sierra Nevada about 14 miles north of the lake. From there Highway 89 and Highway 267 reach the west and north shores, respectively. U.S. 50 is the more direct route to the south shore, a two-hour drive from Sacramento. From Reno you can get to the north shore by heading south on U.S. 395/Interstate 580 for 10 miles, then west on Highway 431 for 25 miles. For the south shore, head south on U.S. 395/Interstate 580 through Carson City, and then turn west on U.S. 50 (56 miles total).

The scenic 72-mile highway around the lake is marked Highway 89 on the southwest and west shores, Highway 28 on the north and northeast shores, and U.S. 50 on the east and southeast. Sections of Highway 89 sometimes close during snowy periods, usually at Emerald Bay because of avalanche danger, which makes it impossible to complete the circular drive around the lake. Interstate 80, U.S. 50, and U.S. 395/Interstate 580 are all-weather highways, but there may be delays while snow is cleared during major storms. Interstate 80 is a four-lane freeway; much of U.S. 50 is only two lanes with no center divider. Carry tire chains from October through May, or rent a four-wheel-drive vehicle. Most rental agencies do not allow tire chains to be used on their vehicles; ask when you book.

Contacts California Highway Patrol ☎ *530/577–1001 South Lake Tahoe*
⊕ *www.chp.ca.gov.* **Caltrans Current Highway Conditions** ☎ *800/427–7623*
⊕ *www.dot.ca.gov.* **Nevada Department of Transportation Road Informa-**
tion ☎ *877/687–6237* ⊕ *www.safetravelusa.com/nv.* **Nevada Highway Patrol**
☎ *775/687–5300* ⊕ *www.nvdpspub.gov/nhp/roadhazard.aspx.*

TRAIN TRAVEL

Amtrak's cross-country rail service makes stops in Truckee and Reno. Amtrak also operates several buses daily between Reno and Sacramento to connect with coastal train routes.

Train Contact Amtrak ☎ *800/872–7245* ⊕ *www.amtrak.com.*

HEALTH AND SAFETY

In an emergency dial 911.

Hospital Contacts Barton Memorial Hospital ✉ *2170 South Ave., at 4th*
St., South Lake Tahoe ☎ *530/541–3420* ⊕ *www.bartonhealth.org.* **St. Mary's**
Regional Medical Center ✉ *235 W. 6th St., at Nevada St., Reno, Nevada*
☎ *775/770–3000 general information* ⊕ *www.saintmarysreno.org.* **Tahoe**
Forest Hospital ✉ *10121 Pine Ave., at Levon Ave., off Donner Pass Rd., Truckee*
☎ *530/587–6011* ⊕ *www.tfhd.com.*

OUTDOORS AND BACKCOUNTRY TIPS

If you're planning to spend any time outdoors around Lake Tahoe, whether hiking, climbing, skiing, or camping, be aware that weather conditions can change quickly in the Sierra. To avoid a life-threatening case of hypothermia, always bring a pocket-size, fold-up rain poncho (available in all sporting-goods stores) to keep you dry. Wear long pants and a hat. Carry plenty of water. Because you'll likely be walking on granite, wear sturdy, closed-toe hiking boots, with soles that grip rock. If you're going into the backcountry, bring a signaling device (such as a mirror), emergency whistle, compass, map, energy bars, and water purifier. When heading out alone, tell someone where you're going and when you plan to return.

13

If you plan to ski, be aware of resort elevations. In the event of a winter storm, determine the snow level before you choose the resort you'll ski. Often the level can be as high as 7,000 feet, which means rain at some resorts' base areas but snow at others.

BackCountry, in Truckee, operates an excellent website with current information about how and where to (and where not to) ski, mountain bike, and hike in the backcountry around Tahoe. The store also stocks everything from crampons to transceivers. For storm information, check the National Weather Service's website; for ski conditions, visit ⊕ *OntheSnow.com.* For reservations at campgrounds in California state parks, contact Reserve America. If you plan to camp in the backcountry of the national forests, you'll need to purchase a wilderness permit, which you can pick up at the forest service office or at a ranger station at any forest entrance. If you plan to ski the backcountry, check the U.S. Forest Service's recorded information for conditions.

Contacts and Information BackCountry ✉ *11400 Donner Pass Rd., at Meadow Way, Truckee* ☎ *530/582–0909 Truckee* ⊕ *www.thebackcountry. net.* **National Weather Service** ⊕ *www.wrh.noaa.gov/rev.* **OntheSnow. com** ⊕ *www.onthesnow.com/california/skireport.html.* **Reserve America** ☎ *800/444–7275* ⊕ *www.reserveamerica.com.* **U.S. Forest Service** ✉ *Office, 35 College Dr., South Lake Tahoe* ☎ *530/543–2600 general information, 530/587–3558 backcountry recording* ⊕ *www.fs.fed.us/r5/ltbmu.*

TOUR OPTIONS

The 312-passenger *Tahoe Queen,* a partially glass-bottomed paddle wheeler, departs from South Lake Tahoe daily for 2½-hour sightseeing cruises year-round by reservation and 3-hour dinner-dance cruises daily from late spring to early fall (weekly the rest of the year). The 520-passenger MS *Dixie II,* a stern-wheeler, sails year-round from Zephyr Cove to Emerald Bay on sightseeing, lunch, and dinner cruises. Fares for both boats range from $47 to $75.

Also in Zephyr Cove, Tahoe Boat Cruises operates the *Woodwind II,* a 50-passenger catamaran that sails on regular and champagne cruises from April through October. Fares range from $34 to $49. The company's *Safari Rose,* an 80-foot-long wooden motor yacht, departs from Tahoe Keys Marina for half-day cruises around the lake; $105, including lunch.

From May through September, the *Sierra Cloud*, a 41-passenger catamaran, departs from the Hyatt Regency beach at Incline Village and cruises the north shore area. The fare is $60.

Lake Tahoe Balloons flies over the lake from May through October; the hour-long trips cost $295. The entire experience takes four hours total.

Tour Contacts Lake Tahoe Balloons ☎ *530/544–1221, 800/872–9294* ⊕ *www.laketahoeballoons.com.* **MS Dixie II** ⊠ *Zephyr Cove Marina, 760 U.S. Hwy. 50, near Church St., Zephyr Cove, Nevada* ☎ *775/589–4906, 800/238–2463* ⊕ *www.zephyrcove.com/cruises.* **Sierra Cloud** ⊠ *Hyatt Regency Lake Tahoe, 111 Country Club Dr., Incline Village* ☎ *775/831–4386* ⊕ *www.awsincline.com.* **Tahoe Queen** ⊠ *Ski Run Marina, 900 Ski Run Blvd., off U.S. 50, South Lake Tahoe* ☎ *530/543–6191, 800/238–2463* ⊕ *www.zephyrcove.com/cruises.* **Tahoe Boat Cruises** ⊠ *Zephyr Cove Resort, 760 U.S. Hwy. 50, near Church St., Zephyr Cove* ☎ *775/588–1881, 888/867–6394* ⊕ *www.tahoecruises.com.*

RESTAURANTS

On weekends and in high season, expect a long wait at the more popular restaurants. And expect to pay resort prices almost everywhere. Some restaurants are only open 6 out of 12 months a year; during the "shoulder seasons" (from April to May and September to November), some places may close temporarily or limit their hours, so call ahead. Also, check local papers for deals and discounts during this time, especially two-for-one coupons. Many casinos use their restaurants to attract gamblers. Marquees often tout "$8.99 prime rib dinners" or "$1.99 breakfast specials." Some of these meals are downright lousy and they are usually available only in the coffee shops and buffets, but at those prices, it's hard to complain. The finer restaurants in casinos deliver pricier food, as well as reasonable service and a bit of atmosphere. Unless otherwise noted, even the most expensive area restaurants welcome customers in casual clothes. *Prices in the reviews are the average cost of a main course at dinner or, if dinner is not served, at lunch.*

HOTELS

Quiet inns on the water, suburban-style strip motels, casino hotels, slope-side ski lodges, and house and condo rentals throughout the area constitute the lodging choices at Tahoe. The crowds come in summer and during ski season; reserve as far in advance as possible, especially for holiday periods when prices skyrocket. Spring and fall give you a little more leeway and lower—sometimes significantly lower—rates. Check hotel websites for the best deals.

Head to South Lake Tahoe for the most activities and the widest range of lodging options. Heavenly Village in the heart of town has an ice rink, cinema, shops, fine dining restaurants, and simple cafés, plus a gondola that will whisk you up to the ski park. Walk two blocks south from downtown, and you can hit the casinos.

Tahoe City, on the west shore, has a small-town atmosphere and is accessible to several nearby ski resorts. A few miles northwest of the lake, Squaw Valley USA has its own self-contained upscale village, an aerial tram to the slopes, and numerous outdoor activities once the snow melts.

Looking for a taste of old Tahoe? The north shore with its woodsy backdrop is your best bet, with Carnelian Bay and Tahoe Vista on the California side. And across the Nevada border are casino resorts where Hollywood's glamour-stars once romped. *Prices in the reviews are the lowest cost of a standard double room in high season. For expanded hotel reviews, visit Fodors.com.*

SKIING AND SNOWBOARDING

The mountains around Lake Tahoe are bombarded by blizzards through-out most winters and sometimes in fall and spring; 10- to 12-foot bases are common. Indeed, the Sierras often have the deepest snowpack on the continent, but because of the relatively mild temperatures over the Pacific, falling snow can be very heavy and wet—it's nicknamed Sierra Cement for a reason. The upside is that you can sometimes ski and board as late as July (snowboarding is permitted at all Tahoe ski areas). The major resorts get extremely crowded on weekends. If you're going to ski on a Saturday, arrive early and quit early. Avoid moving with the masses: eat at 11 am or 1:30 pm, not noon. Also consider visiting the ski areas with few high-speed lifts or limited lodging and real estate at their bases: Alpine Meadows, Sugar Bowl, Homewood, Mt. Rose, Sierra-at-Tahoe, Diamond Peak, and Kirkwood. And to find out the true ski conditions, talk to waiters and bartenders—most of them are ski bums.

The Lake Tahoe area is also a great destination for Nordic skiers. "Skinny" (i.e., cross-country) skiing at the resorts can be costly, but you get the benefits of machine grooming and trail preparation. If it's bargain Nordic you're after, take advantage of thousands of acres of public forest and parkland trails.

VISITOR INFORMATION

Contacts Lake Tahoe Visitors Authority ⊠ *169 U.S. Hwy. 50, Stateline, Nevada* ☎ *775/588–5900, 800/288–2463* ⊕ *tahoesouth.com.* **U.S. Forest Service** ☎ *530/587–3558 backcountry recording* ⊕ *www.fs.usda.gov/tahoe.*

THE CALIFORNIA SIDE

The most hotels, restaurants, ski resorts, and state parks are on the California side of the lake, but you'll also encounter the most conges-tion and developed areas.

SOUTH LAKE TAHOE

50 miles south of Reno, 198 miles northeast of San Francisco.

The city of South Lake Tahoe's raison d'être is tourism: the casinos of adja-cent Stateline, Nevada; the ski slopes at Heavenly Mountain; the beaches, docks, bike trails, and campgrounds all around the south shore; and the backcountry of Eldorado National Forest and Desolation Wilderness. The main road into town, however, shows less attractive features: older motels, strip malls, and low-rise prefab-looking buildings that line both sides of U.S. 50. Though there are plenty of places to stay, we haven't recommended many because they're not top choices. The small city's saving grace is its convenient location and bevy of services, as well as its gorgeous lake views.

GETTING HERE AND AROUND

The main route into and through South Lake Tahoe is U.S. 50; signs say "Lake Tahoe Boulevard" in town. Arrive by car or, if coming from Reno Airport, take the South Tahoe Express bus. BlueGO operates daily bus service in the south shore area year-round, plus a ski shuttle from the large hotels to Heavenly Ski Resort in the winter.

ESSENTIALS

Visitor Information Lake Tahoe Visitors Authority ⊠ *Visitor Center, 169 U.S. Hwy. 50, at Kingsbury Grade, Stateline, Nevada* ☎ *775/588–5900, 800/288–2463* ⊕ *ltva.org* ⊠ *Visitor Center, 3066 Lake Tahoe Blvd., at San Francisco Ave.* ☎ *530/554–5050.*

EXPLORING

Fodor'sChoice
★
FAMILY

Heavenly Gondola. Whether you ski or not, you'll appreciate the impressive view of Lake Tahoe from the Heavenly Gondola. Its eight-passenger cars travel from the middle of town 2.4 miles up the mountain in 15 minutes. When the weather's fine, you can take one of three hikes around the mountaintop and then have lunch at Tamarack Lodge. Heavenly also offers day care for children. ⊠ *4080 Lake Tahoe Blvd.* ☎ *775/586–7000, 800/432–8365* ⊕ *www.skiheavenly.com* ⊡ *$36* ☉ *Summer daily 10–5; winter weekdays 9–4, weekends 8:30–4.*

Heavenly Village. The centerpiece of South Lake Tahoe's efforts to reinvent itself and provide a focal point for tourism, this complex at the base of the gondola has restaurants, some good shopping, a cinema, an arcade for kids, and the Heavenly Village Outdoor Ice Rink. ⊠ *1001 Heavenly Village Way, at U.S. 50* ⊕ *www.theshopsatheavenly.com.*

WHERE TO EAT

$
ECLECTIC

✕ **Blue Angel Café.** A favorite of locals, who fill the dozen or so wooden tables, this cozy spot with Wi-Fi serves basic sandwiches and salads along with internationally inspired dishes like chipotle shrimp tacos and Thai curry. ⑤ *Average main: $12* ⊠ *1132 Ski Run Blvd., at Larch Ave.* ☎ *530/544–6544* ⊕ *www.theblueangelcafe.com.*

$
MEXICAN

✕ **The Cantina.** A casual Tahoe favorite, the Cantina serves traditional Mexican dishes—huge burritos, enchiladas, and rellenos—as well as stylized Southwestern fare such as smoked-chicken polenta with grilled vegetables, and crab cakes in jalapeño cream sauce. The bartenders make great margaritas and serve 30 different kinds of beer. ⑤ *Average main: $13* ⊠ *765 Emerald Bay Rd., Hwy. 89, at 10th St.* ☎ *530/544–1233* ⊕ *www.cantinatahoe.com* ⚱ *Reservations not accepted.*

$$$$
ECLECTIC

✕ **Evan's American Gourmet Cafe.** Its excellent service, world-class food, and superb wine list make this the top choice for high-end dining in South Lake. Inside a converted cabin, the restaurant serves creative American cuisine that includes catch-of-the-day seafood offerings and meat dishes such as rack of lamb marinated with rosemary and garlic and served with raspberry demi-glace. Some diners find the table spacing a tad close. Evan's is intimate, to be sure, but the food always pleases. ⑤ *Average main: $31* ⊠ *536 Emerald Bay Rd., Hwy. 89, at 15th St.* ☎ *530/542–1990* ⊕ *www.evanstahoe.com* ☉ *No lunch.*

Continued on page 524

TAHOE A LAKE FOR ALL SEASONS

by Christine Vovakes

Best known for its excellent skiing, Lake Tahoe is a year-round resort and outdoor sports destination. All kinds of activities are available, from snowboarding some of the best runs in North America and gliding silently along the lakeshore on cross-country skis in winter, to mountain biking through lush forests and puttering around the alpine lake in a classic yacht in summer. Whatever you do—and whenever you visit—the sapphire lake is at the center of it all, pulling you out of your posh resort or rustic cabin rental like a giant blue magnet. There are many ways to enjoy and experience Lake Tahoe, but here are some of our favorites.

(top) Heavenly Mountain Resort,
(bottom) Sand Harbor Beach.

WINTER WONDERLAND

Home to a host of world-famous Sierra resorts, Tahoe is a premier ski destination. Add sledding, ice skating, cross-country skiing, and jingly sleigh rides under the stars to the mix, and you begin to get a glimpse of Tahoe's cold-weather potential.

DOWNHILL SKIING AND SNOWBOARDING

Even if you've never made it off the bunny hill before, you should definitely hit the slopes here at least once. The Lake Tahoe region has the deepest snowpack in North America, and you can ski from Thanksgiving until it melts—which is sometimes July.

One of the top-rated resorts in the country, Olympic Valley's **Squaw Valley USA** hosted the 1960 Winter Olympics that put Tahoe on the map. A great classic resort is **Sugar Bowl,** where you can revel in a bit of Disney nostalgia while you swoop down the slopes. Walt helped start the resort, which opened in 1939 and had Tahoe's first chair lift.

Even if you're not hitting the slopes at South Lake Tahoe's **Heavenly Mountain,** be sure to take a ride on their **Heavenly Gondola** so you can take in awe-inspiring views of the frozen circle of white ice that rings the brilliant lake.

(top) Skiing in Lake Tahoe,. (above left) Cross-country skiing, (above right) Snow boarding at Heavenly Mountain.

SKI RESORT	LOCATION	TRAILS	ACRES	BEGIN.	INTER.	ADV./EXP.
CALIFORNIA						
Alpine Meadows	Tahoe City	100	2,400	25%	40%	35%
Heavenly Mountain	South Lake Tahoe	94	4,800	20%	45%	35%
Homewood Mountain	Homewood	60	1,260	15%	50%	35%
Kirkwood	Kirkwood	72	2,300	15%	50%	35%
Northstar-at-Tahoe	Truckee	97	3,000	13%	60%	27%
Sierra-at-Tahoe	South Lake Tahoe	46	2,000	25%	50%	25%
Squaw Valley USA	Olympic Valley	170	4,000	25%	45%	30%
Sugar Bowl	Truckee	95	1,500	17%	45%	38%
NEVADA						
Diamond Peak	Incline Village	30	655	18%	46%	36%
Mt. Rose Ski Tahoe	Incline Village	61	1,200	20%	30%	50%

CROSS-COUNTRY SKIING

Downhill skiing may get all the glory here, but Lake Tahoe is also a premier cross-country (or Nordic) skiing destination. "Skinny" skiers basically have two options: pony up the cash to ski the groomed trails at a resort, or hit the more rugged (but cheaper—or free) public forest and parkland trails.

Beautiful **Royal Gorge** is the country's largest cross-country ski resort. Other resorts with good skinny skiing include **Kirkwood, Squaw Valley USA, Tahoe Donner,** and **Northstar-at-Tahoe.** Private operators **Spooner Lake Cross Country** and **Hope Valley Cross Country** will also have you shushing through pristine powder in no time.

For bargain Nordic on public trails, head to **Sugar Pine Point State Park.** Other good low-cost cross-country skiing locations include **Donner Memorial State Park, Lake Tahoe—Nevada State Park,** and **Tahoe Meadows** near Incline Village.

CAUTION⚠ Cross-country skiing is relaxing and provides a great cardiovascular workout—but it's also quite strenuous. If it's your first time out or you're not in great shape, start out slow.

SLEDDING AND TUBING

Kirkwood, Squaw Valley USA, Boreal, Soda Springs, and many other Tahoe resorts have areas where you can barrel down hills on inflatable tubes. Some good non-resort sledding spots are **Tahoe National Forest** and **Tahoe Meadows,** near Incline Village.

ICE SKATING

Want to work on your triple lutz? You can skate seasonally at **Heavenly Village Outdoor Ice Rink,** or year-round at the **South Tahoe Ice Arena.** Other great gliding spots include **Squaw Valley USA's Olympic Ice Pavilion.**

WARMING UP

To defrost your ski-stiff limbs, take a dip in a resort's heated pool, de-stress in a hotel spa…or enjoy a brandy by the fire at a cozy restaurant. Our favorite places to warm up and imbibe include Graham's of Squaw Valley and Soule Domain, near Crystal Bay.

Lake Tahoe
Outdoor Activities

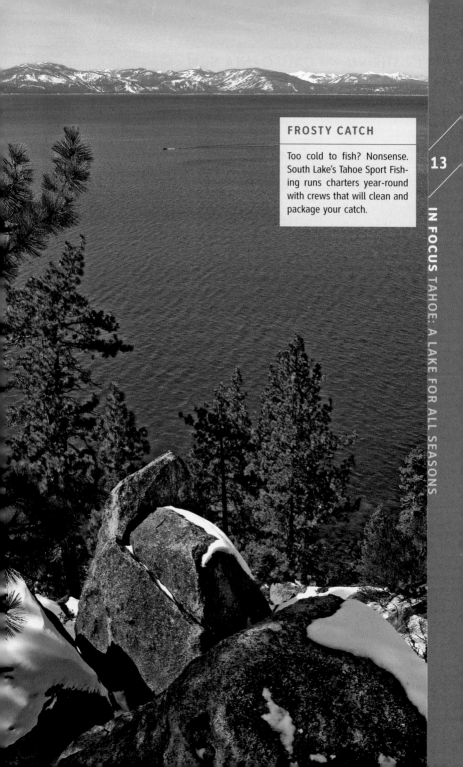

FROSTY CATCH

Too cold to fish? Nonsense. South Lake's Tahoe Sport Fishing runs charters year-round with crews that will clean and package your catch.

IN THE WARM CALIFORNIA SUN

Summer in Tahoe means diving into pure alpine waters, hiking a mountain trail with stunning lake views, or kayaking on glorious Emerald Bay. From tennis to golf to fishing, you can fill every waking moment with outdoor activity—or just stretch out on a sunny lakeside beach with a good book and a cool drink.

HIKING

The lake is surrounded by protected parkland, offering countless opportunities to take jaunts through the woods or rambles along lakeside trails.

One of the most unique hiking experiences in Tahoe is at Heavenly Mountain Resorts, where the **Heavenly Gondola** runs up to three nice trails. When you're done enjoying sky-high views of the lake, grab lunch at the nearby Tamarack Lodge.

Another out-of-the-ordinary option is a romantic moonlit trek. **Camp Richardson** has lots of trails and a long curve of lake to catch the moonlight.

In **Eldorado National Forest and Desolation Wilderness,** you can hike a small portion of the famous Pacific Crest Trail and branch off to discover beautiful backcountry lakes. Nearby **Eagle Falls** has stunning views of Emerald Bay.

One of Tahoe's best hikes is a 4½-mi trail at **D.L. Bliss State Park;** it has lovely views of the lake and leads to bizarre **Vikingsholm** (*see box on next page*).

Other great places to hike in Lake Tahoe include **Sugar Pines Point State Park, Olympic Valley's Granite Chief Wilderness, Squaw Valley USA's High Camp, Donner Memorial State Park,** and **Lake Tahoe—Nevada State Park.**

You can pick up hiking maps at the U.S. Forest Service office at the **Lake Tahoe Visitor Center.**

HIT THE BEACH

Lake Tahoe has some gorgeous lakeside sunbathing terrain; get to perennial favorite **Kings Beach State Recreation Area** early to snag a choice spot. Or, if you never want to be far from the water, reserve one of the prime beachside spots at **D.L. Bliss State Park Campground.**

(left) Fannette Island in Emerald Bay. (right) A young man leaps off a cliff into Lake Tahoe.

MOUNTAIN BIKING AND CYCLING

You don't need to be preparing for the Tour de France to join the biking fun. While there are myriad rugged mountain biking trails to choose from, the region is also blessed with many flat trails.

Truly intrepid cyclists take the lift up **Northstar-at-Tahoe** and hit the resort's 100 mi of trails. Another good option is **Sugar Pine Point State Park,** where you can hop on a 10-mi trail to Tahoe City.

Tahoe Sports in South Lake Tahoe is a good place for bike rentals and tips for planning your trip. **Cyclepath Mountain Bikes Adventures** in Truckee leads guided mountain biking tours, and **Flume Trail Bikes** on the Nevada side of the lake, near Glenbrook, rents bikes and operates a bike shuttle to popular trails.

LAKE TOURS AND KAYAKING

One of the best ways to experience the lake is by getting out on the water.

The *Tahoe Queen* is a huge glass-bottomed paddle-wheel boat that offers sightseeing cruises and dinner-dance cruises; in winter, it's the only water-borne ski shuttle in the world. The *Sierra Cloud, MS Dixie II,* and *Woodwind II* also ply the lake, offering a variety of enjoyable cruises. *(See Tour Options in the Planner section of this chapter for contact info.)*

Another enjoyable option is taking a throwback wooden cruiser from Tahoe Keys Marina in South Lake Tahoe to tour **Thunderbird Lodge,** the meticulously crafted stone mansion built in 1936 by socialite George Whittell.

For a more personal experience, rent a kayak and glide across **Emerald Bay. Kayak Tahoe** in South Lake Tahoe will have you paddling in no time.

VIKINGS?

As you kayak around Tahoe, you'll see many natural wonders...and a few manmade ones as well. One of the most impressive and strangest is **Vikingsholm,** a grand 1929 estate that looks like an ancient Viking castle. You can see it from **Emerald Bay** (which, appropriately, resembles a fjord), or hike to it via a steep one-mile trail.

(left top) Biking along the shore. (left bottom) Kayaking. (right) Steamboat cruise.

$$
SEAFOOD

✕ Fresh Ketch. Fish is the specialty at this dockside restaurant, where you can look out at the yachts in the Tahoe Keys marina. The upstairs dining room serves full dinners (no lunch) featuring fresh seafood and meats. The menu downstairs in the lively fireside seafood bar, beginning with lunch, is lighter and more eclectic, with reasonably priced hot and cold appetizers, salads, and sandwiches served through dinner. Have a hankering for something sweet? Stop by for dessert only and enjoy the view. There's live entertainment on Tuesday, Thursday, and Friday nights year-round, and on summer Saturdays. ⑤ *Average main: $22 ⊠ 2435 Venice Dr., off Tahoe Keys Blvd.* ☎ *530/541–5683 ⊕ thefreshketch.com.*

$
ECLECTIC

✕ Freshies. When you've had your fill of junk food, come here for delicious, healthful meals prepared with an "earth-friendly" attitude and commitment. Specialties include seafood and vegetarian dishes, but good grilled meats are always available, such as teriyaki steak and Hawaiian spare ribs with grilled pineapple. Freshies is in a minimall, and can be loud and crowded—try to snag a spot on the upstairs lakeview deck. ⑤ *Average main: $15 ⊠ Lakeview Plaza, 3330 Lake Tahoe Blvd., at Fremont Ave.* ☎ *530/542–3630 ⊕ www.freshiestahoe.com* ⌲ *Reservations not accepted ⊙ Closed Nov. until 4th Thurs.*

$$$$
ASIAN

✕ Kalani's. Fresh-off-the-plane seafood gets delivered from the Honolulu fish market to Heavenly Village's sexiest (and priciest) restaurant. The sleek, white-tablecloth dining room is decked out with carved bamboo, a burnt-orange color palette, and a modern-glass sculpture, all of which complement contemporary Pacific Rim specialties such as melt-from-the-bone baby back pork ribs with sesame-garlic soy sauce. Sushi selections with inventive rolls and sashimi combos, plus less expensive vegetarian dishes, add depth to the menu. ⑤ *Average main: $33 ⊠ 1001 Heavenly Village Way, #26, at U.S. 50* ☎ *530/544–6100 ⊕ www.kalanis.com ⊙ No lunch weekdays in winter.*

$
THAI

✕ Orchid's Thai. If you're hungry for Thai, stop here for good food at reasonable prices served in an attractive dining room. Tucked into a tiny mall, the restaurant isn't fantastic, but it's reliably good, and when every place in town is booked, this is a great backup. ⑤ *Average main: $10 ⊠ 2180 Lake Tahoe Blvd., at 3rd St.* ☎ *530/544–5541 ⊙ No lunch Sun.*

$
AMERICAN

✕ Red Hut Café. A vintage-1959 Tahoe diner, all chrome and red plastic, the Red Hut is a tiny place with a wildly popular breakfast menu: huge omelets; banana, pecan, and coconut waffles; and other tasty vittles. A second South Lake branch has a soda fountain and is the only one that serves dinner (average main $11). There's a third location in Stateline. ⑤ *Average main: $9 ⊠ 2723 Lake Tahoe Blvd., near Blue Lake Ave.* ☎ *530/541–9024 ⊕ www.redhutcafe.com ⌲ Reservations not accepted ⊙ No dinner at 2 locations* ⑤ *Average main: $9 ⊠ 3660 Lake Tahoe Blvd., at Ski Run Blvd.* ☎ *530/544–1595* ⑤ *Average main: $9 ⊠ 229 Kingsbury Grade, off U.S. 50, Stateline, Nevada* ☎ *775/588–7488.*

$$ ✕ **Scusa! Italian Ristorante.** This longtime favorite turns out big plates
ITALIAN of veal scallopine, chicken piccata, and linguine with clams—straight-
forward Italian-American food (and lots of it), served in an intimate
dining room warmed by a crackling fire on many nights. There's an out-
door patio that's open in warm weather. $ *Average main: $19* ✉ *2543
Lake Tahoe Blvd., near Silver Dollar Ave.* ☎ *530/542–0100* ⊕ *www.
scusalaketahoe.com* ☾ *No lunch.*

WHERE TO STAY
For expanded hotel reviews, visit Fodors.com.

13

$$$ 🛏 **Black Bear Inn Bed and Breakfast.** South Lake Tahoe's most luxurious
B&B/INN inn feels like one of the grand old lodges of the Adirondacks. **Pros:**
Fodor'sChoice intimate; serene, woodsy grounds; within walking distance of good res-
★ taurants. **Cons:** not appropriate for children under 16; pricey. $ *Rooms
from: $225* ✉ *1202 Ski Run Blvd.* ☎ *530/544–4451, 877/232–7466*
⊕ *www.tahoeblackbear.com* ⤳ *5 rooms, 4 cabins* ⊚ *Breakfast.*

$ 🛏 **Camp Richardson.** An old-fashioned family resort that is built
HOTEL around a 1920s lodge, this property features a few dozen cabins and
FAMILY a small inn, all tucked beneath giant pine trees on 80 acres fronting
Lake Tahoe. **Pros:** lakeside location; wide choice of lodgings. **Cons:**
dated style; no phone or TV in some rooms. $ *Rooms from: $105*
✉ *1900 Jameson Beach Rd.* ☎ *530/541–1801, 800/544–1801* ⊕ *www.
camprichardson.com* ⤳ *27 lodge rooms, 40 cabins, 7 inn rooms, 212
campsites; 100 RV sites.*

$$ 🛏 **Forest Suites Resort.** The location is excellent—5½ acres bordering a
HOTEL forest, right behind the Heavenly Village, a half block from the casinos,
and adjacent to a supermarket, cinema, and shops. **Pros:** as close to the
city center as pricier hotels; good bet for families. **Cons:** an older facility
with some rooms still being updated. $ *Rooms from: $147* ✉ *1 Lake
Pkwy.* ☎ *530/541–6655, 800/822–5950* ⊕ *www.forestsuites.com* ⤳ *17
rooms, 102 suites* ⊚ *Breakfast.*

$$ 🛏 **Inn by the Lake.** Across the road from a beach, the "inn" is essen-
HOTEL tially a high-end motel, with spacious, spotless rooms and suites. **Pros:**
great value; stellar service; short drive from Heavenly Mountain. **Cons:**
on busy Lake Tahoe Boulevard. $ *Rooms from: $170* ✉ *3300 Lake
Tahoe Blvd., at Fremont Ave.* ☎ *530/542–0330, 800/877–1466* ⊕ *www.
innbythelake.com* ⤳ *90 rooms, 10 suites* ⊚ *No meals.*

$$$ 🛏 **Marriott's Grand Residence and Timber Lodge.** You can't beat the loca-
RESORT tion of these two gigantic, modern condominium complexes right at
the base of Heavenly Gondola, smack in the center of town. **Pros:** cen-
tral location; great for families; near excellent restaurants. **Cons:** can
be jam-packed on weekends. $ *Rooms from: $175* ✉ *1001 Heavenly
Village Way* ☎ *530/542–8400, 800/845–5279* ⊕ *www.marriott.com*
⤳ *431 condos* ⊚ *No meals.*

$$ 🛏 **Sorensen's Resort.** Escape civilization by staying in a log cabin at this
RESORT woodsy 165-acre resort within the Eldorado National Forest, 20 min-
utes south of town. **Pros:** gorgeous, rustic setting. **Cons:** nearest nightlife
is 20 miles away. $ *Rooms from: $135* ✉ *14255 Hwy. 88, Hope Valley* ☎ *530/694–2203, 800/423–9949* ⊕ *www.sorensensresort.com* ⤳ *2
rooms with shared bath, 35 cabins, 5 houses* ⊚ *No meals.*

$$$ ⛰ **Tahoe Seasons Resort.** It's a 150-yard walk to California Lodge of
HOTEL Heavenly Mountain Resort from this all-suites time-share hotel, where
every room has a two-person sunken hot tub. **Pros:** steps from ski
resort; less touristy location. **Cons:** no restaurants or casinos within
walking distance. ⑤ *Rooms from: $180* ⊠ *3901 Saddle Rd.* ☎ *530/541–
6700 front desk, 800/540–4874 reservations* ⊕ *www.tahoeseasons.com*
↬ *160 suites* ⦿ *No meals.*

NIGHTLIFE

Most of the area's nightlife is concentrated in the casinos over the bor-
der in Stateline. To avoid slot machines and blinking lights, try the
California-side nightspots in and near Heavenly Village. The Marriott
Timber Lodge bars are always dependable.

The Fresh Ketch. The popular seafood restaurant's bar hosts bands on
Tuesdays, Thursdays, and Fridays year-round, and on Saturdays in
summer. ⊠ *2435 Venice Dr., off Tahoe Keys Blvd.* ☎ *530/541–5683*
⊕ *thefreshketch.com.*

Mc P's Irish Pub & Grill. You can hear live bands—rock, jazz, blues, alter-
native—on most nights at Mc P's, across the street from the Heavenly
Gondola. ⊠ *4093 Lake Tahoe Blvd., near Friday Ave.* ☎ *530/542–4435*
⊕ *www.mcpspubtahoe.com.*

SPORTS AND THE OUTDOORS

FISHING

Tahoe Sport Fishing. One of the area's largest and oldest fishing-charter
services offers morning and afternoon trips. Outings include all neces-
sary gear and bait, and the crew cleans and packages your catch. ⊠ *900
Ski Run Blvd., off U.S. 50* ☎ *530/541–5448, 800/696–7797 in CA*
⊕ *www.tahoesportfishing.com.*

GOLF

Lake Tahoe Golf Course. Set in a meadow with mountain views, this public
championship course was designed by William Bell. The Upper Truckee
River comes into play on several holes. Golf carts cost $20, and the twi-
light rate ($29) starts at 4 pm. ⊠ *2500 Emerald Bay Rd, Hwy. 89/U.S.
50* ☎ *530/577–0788* ⊕ *www.laketahoegc.com* ⛳ *Course: 18 holes. Par
71. 6741 yds. Slope 120. Greens fee: $65* ☞ *Facilities: Driving range,
putting green, pitching area, golf carts, rental clubs, pro shop, golf les-
sons, restaurant, bar.*

HIKING

The south shore is a great jumping-off point for day treks into nearby
Eldorado National Forest and Desolation Wilderness.

Desolation Wilderness. Trails at the 100-square-mile wilderness lead to
gorgeous backcountry lakes and mountain peaks. It's called Desolation
Wilderness for a reason, so bring a topographic map and compass, and
carry water and food. In summer, you can access this area by boarding
a boat taxi ($12 one way) at **Echo Chalet** (*9900 Echo Lakes Rd., off
U.S. 50, 530/659–7207;* ⊕ *www.echochalet.com*) and crossing Echo
Lake. The Pacific Crest Trail also traverses Desolation Wilderness. ⊠ *El
Dorado National Forest Information Center* ☎ *530/644–6048* ⊕ *www.
fs.usda.gov/eldorado.*

Pacific Crest Trail. Hike a couple of miles on this famous mountain trail that stretches from Mexico to Canada. ✉ *Echo Summit, about 12 miles southwest of South Lake Tahoe off U.S. 50* ☎ *916/285–1846, 888/728–7245* ⊕ *www.pcta.org.*

ICE SKATING

FAMILY **Heavenly Village Outdoor Ice Rink.** If you're here in winter, practice your jumps and turns at this rink between the gondola and the cinema. ✉ *1001 Heavenly Village Way* ☎ *530/542–4230* ⊕ *www. theshopsatheavenly.com* ✎ *$20; skate rental available* ☉ *Nov.–Mar., daily 10–8, weather permitting.*

13

South Tahoe Ice Arena. For year-round fun, head to this city-operated NHL regulation size indoor rink where you can rent equipment and sign up for lessons. In the evening the lights are turned low and a disco ball lights up the ice. ✉ *1176 Rufus Allen Blvd.* ☎ *530/542–6056* ⊕ *tahoearena.com* ✎ *$9, plus $3 skate rental* ☉ *Daily, hrs vary.*

KAYAKING

Kayak Tahoe. Sign up for lessons and excursions (to the south shore, Emerald Bay, and Sand Harbor), offered from May through September. You can also rent a kayak and paddle solo on the lake. ✉ *Timber Cove Marina, 3411 Lake Tahoe Blvd., at Balbijou Rd.* ☎ *530/544–2011* ⊕ *www.kayaktahoe.com.*

MOUNTAIN BIKING

Tahoe Sports Ltd. You can rent road and mountain bikes and get tips on where to ride from the friendly staff at this full-service sports store. ✉ *Tahoe Crescent V Shopping Center, 4000 Lake Tahoe Blvd.* ☎ *530/542–4000* ⊕ *www.tahoesportsltd.com.*

SKIING

If you don't want to pay the high cost of rental equipment at the resorts, you'll find reasonable prices and expert advice at Tahoe Sports (⇨ *see Mountain Biking, above*).

Fodor's Choice **Heavenly Mountain Resort.** Straddling two states, vast Heavenly Moun-
★ tain Resort—composed of nine peaks, two valleys, and four base-lodge areas, along with the largest snowmaking system in the western United States—has terrain for every skier. Beginners can choose wide, well-groomed trails, accessed from the California Lodge or the gondola from downtown South Lake Tahoe; kids have short and gentle runs in the Enchanted Forest area all to themselves. The Sky Express high-speed quad chair whisks intermediate and advanced skiers to the summit for wide cruisers or steep tree-skiing. Mott and Killebrew canyons draw experts to the Nevada side for steep chutes and thick-timber slopes. For snowboarders and tricksters, there are four different terrain parks.

The ski school is big and offers everything from learn-to-ski packages to canyon-adventure tours. Call about ski and boarding camps. Skiing lessons are available for children ages four and up; there's day care for infants older than six weeks. ✉ *Ski Run Blvd., off U.S. 50* ☎ *775/586–7000, 800/432–8365* ⊕ *www.skiheavenly.com* ☞ *97 trails on 4,800 acres, rated 20% beginner, 45% intermediate, 35% expert. Longest run 5½ miles, base 6,540 feet, summit 10,067 feet. Lifts: 30, including 1 aerial tram, 1 gondola, 2 high-speed 6-passenger lifts, and 8 high-speed quads.*

Hope Valley Cross Country. Operating from a yurt at Pickett's Junction, Hope Valley provides lessons and equipment rentals to prepare you for cross-country skiing and snowshoeing. The outfit has 60 miles of trails through Humboldt–Toiyabe National Forest, 10 of which are groomed. ⊠ *Hwy. 88, at Hwy. 89, Hope Valley* ☎ *530/721–2015* ⊕ *www.hopevalleyoutdoors.com.*

Kirkwood Ski Resort. Thirty-six miles south of Lake Tahoe, Kirkwood is the hard-core skiers' and boarders' favorite south-shore mountain, known for its craggy gulp-and-go chutes, sweeping cornices, steep-aspect glade skiing, and high base elevation. But there's also fantastic terrain for newbies and intermediates down wide-open bowls, through wooded gullies, and along rolling tree-lined trails. Tricksters can show off in the Stomping Grounds terrain park on jumps, wall rides, rails, and a half-pipe, all visible from the base area. The mountain gets hammered with more than 500 inches of snow annually, and often has the most in all of North America. If you're into out-of-bounds skiing, check out Expedition Kirkwood, a backcountry-skills program that teaches basic safety awareness. Kirkwood is also the only Tahoe resort to offer Cat-skiing. If you're into cross-country, the resort has 80 km (50 miles) of superb groomed-track skiing, with skating lanes, instruction, and rentals. Nonskiers can snowshoe, snow-skate, and go dogsledding or snow-tubing. The children's ski school has programs for ages 3 to 12. ⊠ *1501 Kirkwood Meadows Dr., off Hwy. 88, 14 miles west of Hwy. 89, Kirkwood* ☎ *800/967–7500 downhill, 209/258–7248 cross-country, 209/258–7293 lodging information, 877/547–5966 snow phone* ⊕ *www.kirkwood.com* ⚲ *72 trails on 2,300 acres, rated 15% beginner, 50% intermediate, 20% advanced, 15% expert. Longest run 2½ miles, base 7,776 feet, summit 9,800 feet. Lifts: 15, including 2 high-speed quads.*

Sierra-at-Tahoe. Often overlooked by skiers and boarders rushing to Heavenly or Kirkwood, Sierra-at-Tahoe has meticulously groomed intermediate slopes, some of the best tree-skiing in California, and gated backcountry access. Extremely popular with snowboarders, Sierra also has six terrain parks, including a super-pipe with 17-foot walls. For nonskiers there's a snow-tubing hill. Sierra has a low-key atmosphere that's great for families. Kids and beginners take the slow routes in the Mellow Yellow Zone. ⊠ *1111 Sierra-at-Tahoe Rd., 12 miles from South Lake Tahoe off U.S. 50, past Echo Summit, Twin Bridges* ☎ *530/659–7453 information, 530/659–7475 snow phone* ⊕ *www.sierraattahoe.com* ⚲ *46 trails on 2,000 acres, rated 25% beginner, 50% intermediate, 25% advanced. Longest run 2½ miles, base 6,640 feet, summit 8,852 feet. Lifts: 14, including 3 high-speed quads.*

POPE-BALDWIN RECREATION AREA

5 miles west of South Lake Tahoe.

To the west of downtown South Lake Tahoe, U.S. 50 and Highway 89 come together, forming an intersection nicknamed "the Y." If you head northwest on Highway 89, also called Emerald Bay Road, and follow the lakefront, commercial development gives way to national forests and state parks. One of these is Pope-Baldwin Recreation Area.

GETTING HERE AND AROUND

The entrance to the Pope-Baldwin Recreation Area is on the east side of Emerald Bay Road. In summer, BlueGO's Nifty 50 Trolley serves the area from South Lake Tahoe. From the northern and western communities, take a TART bus to Tahoma and transfer to the trolley. The area is closed to vehicles in winter, but you can cross-country ski here.

EXPLORING

Tallac Historic Site. Stroll or picnic lakeside, then explore **Pope House,** the magnificently restored 1894 mansion of George S. Pope, who made his money in shipping and lumber and played host to the business and cultural elite of 1920s America. There are two other estates here. One belonged to entrepreneur "Lucky" Baldwin; today it houses the **Baldwin Museum,** a collection of family memorabilia and Washoe Indian artifacts. The **Valhalla** (⊕ *www.valhallatahoe.com*), with a spectacular floor-to-ceiling stone fireplace, belonged to Walter Heller. Its Grand Hall and a lakeside boathouse, refurbished as a theater, host summertime concerts, plays, and cultural activities. Docents conduct tours of the Pope House in summer; call for tour times. In winter you can cross-country ski around the site. ⊠ *Hwy. 89* ☎ *530/541–5227 late May– Oct., 530/543–2600 year-round* ⊕ *www.tahoeheritage.org* 🖃 *Free, Pope House tour $5* ◷ *Grounds daily sunrise–sunset. Pope House and Baldwin Museum late May–late Sept., Thurs.–Tues. 10–4; call for Oct. hrs* ◷ *Closed Wed. and Nov.–late May.*

FAMILY **Taylor Creek Visitor Center.** At this center operated by the U.S. Forest Service you can visit the site of a Washoe Indian settlement; walk self-guided trails through meadow, marsh, and forest; and inspect the Stream Profile Chamber, an underground display with windows right into Taylor Creek. In fall you may see spawning kokanee salmon digging their nests. In summer Forest Service naturalists organize discovery walks and evening programs. ⊠ *Hwy. 89, 3 miles north of junction with U.S. 50* ☎ *530/543–2674 late May–Oct., 530/543–2600 year-round* ⊕ *www.fs.usda.gov/recmain/ltbmu/recreation* 🖃 *Free* ◷ *Late May–late Sept., Thurs.–Tues. 10–4; call for Oct. hrs* ◷ *Closed Wed. and Nov.–late May.*

Fjord-like Emerald Bay is quite possibly the prettiest part of Lake Tahoe.

EMERALD BAY STATE PARK

4 miles west of Pope-Baldwin Recreation Area.

GETTING HERE AND AROUND

The entrance to Emerald Bay State Park is on the east side of a narrow, twisting section of Highway 89. Caution is the keyword for both drivers and pedestrians. In summer, BlueGO's Nifty 50 Trolley serves the area from South Lake Tahoe. From the northern and western communities, take a TART bus to Tahoma and transfer to the trolley. The park is closed to vehicles in winter.

EXPLORING

Fodor's Choice ★ **Emerald Bay.** A massive glacier millions of years ago carved this 3-mile-long and 1-mile-wide fjordlike inlet. Famed for its jewel-like shape and colors, the bay surrounds Fannette, Tahoe's only island. Highway 89 curves high above the lake through Emerald Bay State Park; from the Emerald Bay lookout, the centerpiece of the park, you can survey the whole scene. This is one of the don't-miss views of Lake Tahoe. The light is best in mid- to late morning, when the bay's colors really pop. ✉ *Hwy. 89* ☎ *530/525–7232* ⊕ *www.parks.ca.gov.*

Vikingsholm. A steep 1-mile-long trail from the Emerald Bay lookout leads down to Vikingsholm, a 38-room estate completed in 1929. The original owner, Lora Knight, had this precise copy of a 1,200-year-old Viking castle built out of materials native to the area. She furnished it with Scandinavian antiques and hired artisans to build period reproductions. The sod roof sprouts wildflowers each spring. There are picnic tables nearby and a gray-sand beach for strolling. The hike back up is hard (especially if you're not yet acclimated to the elevation), but there are benches and stone culverts to rest on. At the 150-foot peak of Fannette Island are the ruins of a stone structure known as the Tea House, built in 1928 so that Knight's guests could have a place to enjoy afternoon refreshments after a motorboat ride. The island is

13

off-limits from February through June to protect nesting Canada geese. The rest of the year it's open for day use. ⊠ *Hwy. 89* ☎ *530/541–6498 summer, 530/525–3345 year-round* ⊕ *www.vikingsholm.com* ⊡ *Day-use parking fee $10, mansion tour $8* ⊙ *Late May–Sept., daily 10:30–4.*

SPORTS AND THE OUTDOORS
HIKING
Eagle Falls. Leave your car in the parking lot for Eagle Falls picnic area (near Vikingsholm; arrive early for a good spot), and head to these falls, a short but fairly steep walk up-canyon. You'll have a brilliant panorama of Emerald Bay from this spot near the boundary of Desolation Wilderness. For a strenuous full-day hike, continue 5 miles, past Eagle Lake, to Upper and Middle Velma Lakes. Pick up trail maps at Taylor Creek Visitor Center in summer, or year-round at the main U.S. Forest Service Office in South Lake Tahoe, at 35 College Drive. ⊠ *Hwy. 89, South Lake Tahoe.*

D.L. BLISS STATE PARK

3 miles north of Emerald Bay State Park, 17 miles south of Tahoe City.

GETTING HERE AND AROUND
The entrance to D.L. Bliss State Park is on the east side of Highway 89 just north of Emerald Bay. In summer, BlueGO's Nifty 50 Trolley serves the area from South Lake Tahoe. From the northern and western communities, take a TART bus to Tahoma and transfer to the trolley.

EXPLORING
D.L. Bliss State Park. This park takes its name from Duane LeRoy Bliss, a 19th-century lumber magnate. At one time Bliss owned nearly 75% of Tahoe's lakefront, along with local steamboats, railroads, and banks. The park shares 6 miles of shoreline with Emerald Bay State Park; combined the two parks cover 1,830 acres, 744 of which the Bliss family donated to the state. At the north end of Bliss is Rubicon Point, which overlooks one of the lake's deepest spots. Short trails lead to an old lighthouse and Balancing Rock, which weighs 250,000 pounds and balances on a fist of granite. The 4.5-mile Rubicon Trail—one of Tahoe's premier hikes—leads to Vikingsholm and provides stunning lake views. Two white-sand beaches front some of Tahoe's warmest water. ⊠ *Hwy. 89* ☎ *530/525–3345, 800/777–0369* ⊕ *www.parks.ca.gov* ⊡ *$8 per vehicle, day use* ⊙ *Late May–Sept., daily sunrise–sunset.*

ED Z'BERG SUGAR PINE POINT STATE PARK

8 miles north of D. L. Bliss State Park, 10 miles south of Tahoe City.

GETTING HERE AND AROUND

The entrance to Sugar Pine Point is on the east side of Highway 89, about a mile south of Tahoma. In summer, BlueGO's Nifty 50 Trolley serves the area from South Lake Tahoe. From the northern and western communities, take a TART bus to Tahoma and transfer to the trolley for the short ride to the entrance. There's also a bike trail that links Tahoe City to the park.

EXPLORING

Ehrman Mansion. The main attraction at Sugar Pine Point State Park is Ehrman Mansion, a 1903 stone-and-shingle summer home furnished in period style. In its day it was the height of modernity, with a refrigerator, an elevator, and an electric stove. Also in the park are a trapper's log cabin from the mid-19th century, a nature preserve with wildlife exhibits, a lighthouse, the start of the 10-mile biking trail to Tahoe City, and an extensive system of hiking and cross-country skiing trails. If you're feeling less ambitious, you can relax on the sun-dappled lawn behind the mansion and gaze out at the lake. ⊠ *Hwy. 89* ☎ *530/525–7982 mansion in season, 530/525–7232 year-round* ⊕ *www.parks.ca.gov* ⊡ *$10 per vehicle, day use; mansion tour $8* ⊘ *Mansion late May–early Sept., daily 11–3.*

Ed Z'Berg Sugar Pine Point State Park. Named for a state lawmaker who sponsored key conservation legislation, Lake Tahoe's largest state park has 2,000 acres of dense forests and nearly 2 miles of shore frontage. A popular spot during snow season, Sugar Pine provides cross-country trails and winter camping on a first-come, first-served basis. Rangers lead full-moon snowshoe tours from January to March. ⊠ *Hwy. 89, 1 mile south of Tahoma* ☎ *530/525–7982* ⊕ *www.parks.ca.gov.*

TAHOMA

1 mile north of Ed Z'berg Sugar Pine Point State Park, 23 miles south of Truckee.

With its rustic waterfront vacation cottages, Tahoma exemplifies life on the lake in its quiet early days before bright-lights casinos and huge crowds proliferated. In 1960 Tahoma was host of the Olympic Nordic-skiing competitions. Today there's little to do here except stroll by the lake and listen to the wind in the trees, making it a favorite home base for mellow families and nature buffs.

GETTING HERE AND AROUND

Approach Tahoma by car on Highway 89, called West Lake Boulevard in this section. In summer, BlueGO's Nifty 50 Trolley serves the area from South Lake Tahoe. From the northern and western communities, take a TART bus to Tahoma. A bike trail links Tahoe City to Tahoma.

WHERE TO STAY

For expanded hotel reviews, visit Fodors.com.

$$
B&B/INN
☒ **Tahoma Meadows B&B Cottages.** It's hard to beat this serene property for atmosphere and woodsy charm; it's a great retreat for families and couples. **Pros:** lovely setting; good choice for families; close to Homewood ski resort. **Cons:** far from the casinos. ⑤ *Rooms from: $159* ☒ *6821 W. Lake Blvd.* ☎ *530/525–1553, 866/525–1553* ⊕ *www. tahomameadows.com* ☞ *16 cabins* ⦿ *Breakfast.*

13

SPORTS AND THE OUTDOORS

SKIING

Homewood Mountain Resort. Schuss down these slopes for fantastic views—the mountain rises across the road from the Tahoe shoreline. This smaller, usually uncrowded resort is the favorite area of locals on a fresh-snow day, because you can find lots of untracked powder. It's also the most protected and least windy Tahoe ski area during a storm; when every other resort's lifts are on wind hold, you can almost always count on Homewood's to be open. There's only one high-speed chairlift, but there are rarely any lines, and the ticket prices are some of the cheapest around—kids 5 to 12 ski for $20, and those four and under are free. The resort may look small as you drive by, but most of it isn't visible from the road. ☒ *5145 W. Lake Blvd., Hwy. 89, 6 miles south of Tahoe City, Homewood* ☎ *530/525–2992* ⊕ *www.skihomewood. com* ☞ *64 trails on 1,260 acres, rated 15% beginner, 50% intermediate, and 35% advanced. Longest run 2 miles, base 6,230 feet, summit 7,880 feet. Lifts: 4 chairlifts, 4 surface lifts.*

TAHOE CITY

9 miles north of Tahoma, 14 miles south of Truckee.

Tahoe City is the only lakeside town with a charming downtown area good for strolling and window-shopping. Stores and restaurants are all within walking distance of the Outlet Gates, where water is spilled into the Truckee River to control the surface level of the lake. You can spot giant trout in the river from Fanny Bridge, so-called for the views of the backsides of sightseers leaning over the railing.

GETTING HERE AND AROUND

Tahoe City is at the junction of Highway 28, also called North Lake Boulevard, and Highway 89 where it turns northwest toward Squaw Valley and Truckee. TART buses serve the communities along the north and west shores, and connects them to Truckee.

ESSENTIALS

Visitor Information North Lake Tahoe Resort Association ☎ *530/583–3494, 888/434–1262* ⊕ *www.gotahoenorth.com.*

EXPLORING

Gatekeeper's Cabin Museum. This museum preserves a little-known part of the region's history. Between 1910 and 1968 the gatekeeper who lived on this site was responsible for monitoring the level of the lake, using a hand-turned winch system (still used today) to keep the water at the correct level. Also on this site, the fantastic Marian Steinbach Indian

Basket Museum displays 800 baskets from 85 tribes. ✉ *130 W. Lake Blvd.* ☎ *530/583–1762* ⊕ *www.northtahoemuseums.org* ✆ *$5* ⊙ *May– Sept., Wed.–Mon. 10–5; Oct.–Apr., Fri. and Sat. 10–4.*

Watson Cabin Living Museum. In the middle of town sits a 1909 log cabin built by Robert M. Watson and his son. Now a museum, it's filled with century-old furnishings and many reproductions. Docents are available to answer questions and will lead tours if you call ahead. ✉ *560 N. Lake Blvd.* ☎ *530/583–8717, 530/583–1762* ⊕ *www.northtahoemuseums. org* ✆ *$2* ⊙ *Late May–early Sept., Thurs.–Mon. 10–5.*

WHERE TO EAT

$$$
AMERICAN
✕ **Christy Hill.** Huge windows give diners here some of the best lake views in Tahoe. The menu features solid Euro–Cal preparations of fresh seafood, filet of beef, or vegetarian dishes. The extensive wine list and exceptionally good desserts earn accolades, as do the gracious service and casual vibe. If the weather is balmy, have dinner on the deck. In any season, this is a romantic choice for lake gazing and wine sipping. $ *Average main: $26* ✉ *115 Grove St., at N. Lake Blvd.* ☎ *530/583–8551* ⊕ *www.christyhill.com* ⊙ *Open daily. No lunch.*

$
AMERICAN
✕ **Fire Sign Café.** Watch the road carefully or you'll miss this great little diner 2 miles south of Tahoe City on Highway 89. There's often a wait for breakfast and lunch, but it's worth it. The pastries are made from scratch, the salmon is smoked in-house, the salsa is hand-cut, and there's real maple syrup for the many types of pancakes and waffles. Leave room for dessert; a fruit cobbler is almost always on the menu. $ *Average main: $10* ✉ *1785 W. Lake Blvd., at Fountain Ave.* ☎ *530/583–0871* ⊕ *www.firesigncafe.com* ⚠ *Reservations not accepted* ⊙ *No dinner.*

$
AMERICAN
✕ **Syd's Bagelry.** For breakfast bagels and pastries and lunchtime salads and sandwiches, locals head to Syd's, which brews good coffee and provides free Wi-Fi, too. Want the skinny on Tahoe City? Talk to Dean, the affable owner. $ *Average main: $7* ✉ *550 N. Lake Tahoe Blvd., at Grove St.* ☎ *530/583–2666* ⊙ *No dinner.*

$$$
ECLECTIC
✕ **Wolfdale's.** Consistent, inspired cuisine makes Wolfdale's one of the top restaurants on the lake. Seafood is the specialty on the changing menu; the imaginative entrées merge Asian and European cooking (drawing on the chef-owner's training in Japan) and lean toward the light and healthful, rather than the heavy and overdone. Everything from teriyaki glaze to smoked fish is made in-house. Request a window table, and book early enough to see the lake view from the elegantly simple dining room. $ *Average main: $27* ✉ *640 N. Lake Blvd., near Grove St.* ☎ *530/583–5700* ⊕ *www.wolfdales.com* ⚠ *Reservations essential* ⊙ *Closed Tues. No lunch.*

WHERE TO STAY

For expanded hotel reviews, visit Fodors.com.

$$
B&B/INN
🛏 **Cottage Inn.** Avoid the crowds by staying in one of these charming circa-1938 log cottages under the towering pines on the lake's west shore. **Pros:** romantic, woodsy setting; each room has a fireplace; full breakfast. **Cons:** no kids under 12. $ *Rooms from: $145* ✉ *1690 W. Lake Blvd.* ☎ *530/581–4073, 800/581–4073* ⊕ *www.thecottageinn. com* 🛏 *22 rooms* ⊙❘ *Breakfast.*

$$$$ ⬚ **Sunnyside Steakhouse and Lodge.** The views are superb at this pretty
HOTEL little lodge right on the lake, 3 miles south of Tahoe City. **Pros:** complimentary Continental breakfast and afternoon tea; most rooms have balconies overlooking the lake. **Cons:** can be pricey for families. ⑤ *Rooms from: $265* ✉ *1850 W. Lake Blvd.* ☎ *530/583–7200, 800/822–2754* ⊕ *www.sunnysideresort.com* ⇆ *18 rooms, 5 suites* ❍| *Breakfast.*

SPORTS AND THE OUTDOORS
GOLF
Tahoe City Golf Course. This 9-hole course, which opened in 1917, gives golfers views of Lake Tahoe. Rent a cart for $10. ■**TIP→ All greens break toward the lake.** ✉ *251 N. Lake Blvd.* ☎ *530/583–1516* ⊕ *www. playtcgc.com* ⚲ *Course: 18 holes. 5,261 yards. Par 66. Slope 108. Greens fees: $30 for 9 holes; $50 for 18* ⚲ *Facilities: Putting green, pitching area, golf carts, pull carts, rental clubs, pro shop, golf lessons, restaurant, bar.*

RAFTING
FAMILY **Truckee River Rafting.** In summer you can take a self-guided raft trip down a gentle 5-mile stretch of the Truckee River. This outfitter will shuttle you back to Tahoe City at the end of your two- to three-hour trip. On a warm day, this makes a great family outing. ✉ *175 River Rd., near W. Lake Blvd.* ☎ *530/583–1111* ⊕ *www.truckeeriverrafting.com.*

SKIING
Alpine Meadows Ski Area. The locals' favorite place to ski on the north shore is also the unofficial telemarking hub of the Sierra. With 450 inches of snow annually, Alpine has some of Tahoe's most reliable conditions. It's usually one of the first areas to open in November and one of the last to close in May or June. Alpine isn't the place for arrogant show-offs; instead, you'll find down-to-earth alpine fetishists. The two peaks here are well suited to intermediate skiers, with a number of runs for experts only. Snowboarders and hot-dog skiers will find a terrain park with a super-pipe, rails, and tabletops, as well as a boarder-cross course. Alpine is a great place to learn to ski and has a ski school that coaches those with physical and mental disabilities. On Saturday, because of the limited parking, there's more acreage per person than at other resorts. Lift tickets are good at neighboring Squaw Valley; a free shuttle runs all day between the two ski parks. ✉ *2600 Alpine Meadows Rd., off Hwy. 89, 6 miles northwest of Tahoe City and 13 miles south of Truckee* ☎ *530/583–4232, 800/403–0206, 530/452–4356 snow phone* ⊕ *www.skialpine.com* ⚲ *100 trails on 2,400 acres, rated 25% beginner, 40% intermediate, 35% advanced. Longest run 2½ miles, base 6,835 feet, summit 8,637 feet. Lifts: 13, including 1 high-speed 6-passenger lift and 2 high-speed quads.*

Tahoe Dave's Skis and Boards. You can rent skis, boards, and snowshoes at this shop, which has the area's best selection of downhill rental equipment. ✉ *590 N. Lake Blvd.* ☎ *530/583–6415* ⊕ *www.tahoedaves.com.*

OLYMPIC VALLEY

7 miles north of Tahoe City to Squaw Valley Road; 8½ miles south of Truckee.

Olympic Valley got its name in 1960, when Squaw Valley USA, the ski resort here, hosted the Winter Olympics. Snow sports remain the primary activity, but once summer comes, you can hike into the adjacent Granite Chief Wilderness, explore wildflower-studded alpine meadows, or lie by a swimming pool in one of the Sierra's prettiest valleys.

GETTING HERE AND AROUND

Squaw Valley Road, the only way into Olympic Valley, branches west off Highway 89 about 8 miles south of Truckee. TART connects the Squaw Valley ski area with the communities along the north and west shores, and Truckee, with year-round public transportation. Squaw Valley Ski Resort provides a free shuttle to many stops in those same areas.

EXPLORING

High Camp. You can ride the Squaw Valley Aerial Tram to this activity hub, which at 8,200 feet commands superb views of Lake Tahoe and the surrounding mountains. In summer, go for a hike, sit by the pool, or have a cocktail and watch the sunset. In winter, you can ski, ice-skate, or snow-tube. There's also a restaurant, a lounge, and a small Olympic museum. ⊠ *Aerial Tram Bldg., Squaw Valley* ☎ *800/403–0206* ⊕ *www. squaw.com/the-village* ⛷ *Aerial Tram, $29* ☉ *Daily; call for hrs.*

FAMILY **Village at Squaw Valley.** The centerpiece of Olympic Valley is a pedestrian mall at the base of several four-story ersatz Bavarian stone-and-timber buildings, where you'll find restaurants, high-end condo rentals, boutiques, and cafés. ⊠ *1750 Village East Rd.* ☎ *530/584–1000, 800/403– 0206 information, 800/731–8021 condo reservations* ⊕ *www.squaw. com/the-village.*

WHERE TO EAT

$$$ ✗**Graham's of Squaw Valley.** Sit by a floor-to-ceiling river-rock hearth
ECLECTIC   under a knotty-pine peaked ceiling in the intimate dining room in the Christy Inn Lodge. The southern European–inspired menu changes often, but expect hearty entrées such as fillet of beef with wild mushroom sauce, along with lighter-fare small plates like quail with red wine demi-glace. You can also stop in at the fireside bar for appetizers and wine from Graham's highly regarded wine list. ⑤ *Average main: $27* ⊠ *1650 Squaw Valley Rd.* ☎ *530/581–0454* ☉ *Closed Mon. No lunch.*

$$ ✗**Mamasake.** The hip sushi spot at Squaw serves stylized presentations.
JAPANESE   In the evening, sit at the bar and watch extreme ski movies, many of them filmed right outside the window. From 3 to 5 you can enjoy the afternoon special: a spicy-tuna or salmon hand roll and a can of Bud for five bucks. ⑤ *Average main: $16* ⊠ *1850 Village South Rd., off Squaw Valley Rd.* ☎ *530/584–0110* ⊕ *www.mamasake.com.*

$$$ ✗**PlumpJack Café.** The best restaurant in the entire Tahoe Basin is the
AMERICAN   epitome of discreet chic and a must-visit for serious foodies. The menu
Fodor'sChoice   changes seasonally, but look for roasted quail in an orange sauce, crispy
★   sweetbreads, and butter-poached lobster tail. Rather than complicated, heavy sauces, the chef uses simple reductions to complement a dish. The

Squaw Valley USA has runs for skiers of all ability levels—from beginner trails to cliff drops for experts.

result: clean, dynamic, bright flavors. The wine list is exceptional for its variety and reasonable prices. A less expensive but equally adventurous menu, including lunch, is served at the bar. ⑤ *Average main: $30* ✉ *1920 Squaw Valley Rd.* ☎ *530/583–1578, 800/323–7666* ⊕ *www.plumpjacksquawvalleyinn.com* ⚒ *Reservations essential.*

WHERE TO STAY

For expanded hotel reviews, visit Fodors.com.

$$$
HOTEL
Fodor's Choice
★
🏨 **PlumpJack Squaw Valley Inn.** If style and luxury are a must, make PlumpJack your first choice. **Pros:** small; intimate; lots of attention to details. **Cons:** not the best choice for families with small children. ⑤ *Rooms from: $220* ✉ *1920 Squaw Valley Rd.* ☎ *530/583–1576, 800/323–7666* ⊕ *www.plumpjacksquawvalleyinn.com* ⤳ *56 rooms, 8 suites* ⑩ *Breakfast.*

$$$$
RESORT
🏨 **Resort at Squaw Creek.** The rooms at this vast 650-acre resort-within-a-resort are done up in warm earth tones, with attractive wooden furnishings and rich fabrics. **Pros:** every conceivable amenity; private chairlift to Squaw Valley USA for ski-in, ski-out. **Cons:** very large; very pricey. ⑤ *Rooms from: $269* ✉ *400 Squaw Creek Rd.* ☎ *530/583–6300, 800/327–3353* ⊕ *www.squawcreek.com* ⤳ *203 rooms, 200 suites* ⑩ *No meals.*

$$$
HOTEL
🏨 **The Village at Squaw Valley USA.** Right at the base of the slopes, at the center point of Olympic Valley, the Village's condominiums were built in 2000 and still look fresh. **Pros:** family-friendly; near Village restaurants and shops. **Cons:** claustrophobia-inducing crowds on weekends. ⑤ *Rooms from: $179* ✉ *1750 Village East Rd.* ☎ *530/584–1000, 888/805–5022* ⊕ *www.squaw.com/the-village/lodging* ⤳ *198 suites* ⑩ *No meals.*

SPORTS AND THE OUTDOORS

GOLF

Resort at Squaw Creek Golf Course. For beautiful views of Squaw Valley's surrounding peaks, play this narrow, challenging championship course designed by Robert Trent Jones, Jr. Midrange twilight fees begin at noon for $78; the lowest rate, $60, starts at 3 pm. All fees include a golf cart plus valet parking. ⊠ *400 Squaw Creek Rd.* ☎ *530/583–6300* ⊕ *www. squawcreek.com* ⚑ *Course: 18 holes. 6,931 yards. Par 71. Slope 135. Greens fee: $98* ☞ *Facilities: Putting green, pitching area, golf carts, pull carts, rental clubs, pro shop, golf lessons, restaurant, bar.*

HIKING

High Camp. The Granite Chief Wilderness and the high peaks surrounding Olympic Valley are accessible by foot, but save yourself a 2,000-foot elevation gain by riding the Squaw Valley Aerial Tram to High Camp, the starting point for several hikes. Pick up trail maps at the tram building. High Camp offers sunset hikes in summer, and full-moon hikes in winter. ☎ *800/402–0206* ⊕ *www.squaw.com.*

ICE SKATING

FAMILY **Olympic Ice Pavilion.** Ice-skate here from late November to mid-March. A ride up the mountain in the Aerial Tram costs $29, plus $12 for skate rental and one hour of skate time. End your outing in the hot tub ($10). In summer, the pavilion converts into a roller-skating rink. Year-round, you get fabulous views of the lake and the Sierra Nevada. ⊠ *1960 Squaw Valley Rd., High Camp, Squaw Valley* ☎ *800/403–0206* ⊕ *www.squaw.com.*

MINIATURE GOLF

FAMILY **Squaw Valley Adventure Center.** Next to the Olympic Village Lodge, on the far side of the creek, this activities center has an 18-hole miniature golf course, a ropes course, and sometimes a bungee trampoline, a blast for kids. ⊠ *1960 Squaw Valley Rd.* ☎ *530/583–7673* ⊕ *www. squawadventure.com.*

ROCK CLIMBING

Headwall Climbing Wall. Before you rappel down a granite monolith, hone your skills at this challenging wall at the base of the Aerial Tram. ⊠ *Squaw Valley Adventure Center, 1960 Squaw Valley Rd.* ☎ *530/583–7673* ⊕ *www.squawadventure.com.*

SKIING

Resort at Squaw Creek. Cross-country skiers enjoy looping through the valley's giant alpine meadow. The resort rents equipment and provides trail maps. ⊠ *400 Squaw Creek Rd.* ☎ *530/583–6300* ⊕ *www. squawcreek.com.*

Fodor's Choice **Squaw Valley USA.** Known for some of the toughest skiing in the Tahoe ★ area, this park was the centerpiece of the 1960 Winter Olympics. Today it's the definitive North Tahoe ski resort and among the top-three megaresorts in California (the other two are Heavenly and Mammoth). Although Squaw has changed significantly since the Olympics, the skiing is still world-class and extends across vast bowls stretched between six peaks. Experts often head directly to the untamed terrain of the infamous KT-22 face, which has bumps, cliffs, and gulp-and-go chutes, or to the nearly vertical Palisades, where many famous Warren Miller extreme-skiing films have been shot. Fret not, beginners and intermediates: you have plenty of wide-open, groomed trails at High Camp (which sits at the *top* of the mountain) and around the more challenging Snow King Peak. Snowboarders and show-off skiers can tear up the six fantastic terrain parks, which include a giant super-pipe. On Fridays and Saturdays, lift prices include night skiing until 8 pm. Ski passes are good at neighboring Alpine Meadows; free shuttles run all day between the two ski parks. ⊠ *1960 Squaw Valley Rd., off Hwy. 89, 7 miles northwest of Tahoe City* ☎ *530/583–6985, 800/731–8021 lodging reservations, 530/452–4355 snow phone, 800/403–0206 information* ⊕ *www.squaw.com* ☞ *170 trails on 3,600 acres, rated 25% beginner, 45% intermediate, 30% advanced. Longest run 3.2 miles, base 6,200 feet, summit 9,050 feet. Lifts: 33, including a gondola-style funitel, a tram, 7 high-speed chairs, and 18 fixed-grip chairs.*

Tahoe Dave's Skis and Boards. If you don't want to pay resort prices, you can rent and tune downhill skis and snowboards at this shop. ⊠ *3039 Hwy. 89, at Squaw Valley Rd.* ☎ *530/583–5665* ⊕ *www.tahoedaves.com.*

TRUCKEE

13 miles northwest of Kings Beach, 14 miles north of Tahoe City.

Formerly a decrepit railroad town in the mountains, Truckee is now the trendy first stop for many Tahoe visitors. The town was officially established around 1863, and by 1868 it had gone from a stagecoach station to a major stopover for trains bound for the Pacific via the new transcontinental railroad. Freight trains and Amtrak's California Zephyr still stop every day at the depot right in the middle of town. Stop inside the depot for a walking-tour map of historic Truckee. Across from the station, where Old West facades line the main drag, you'll find galleries, gift shops, boutiques, old-fashioned diners, and several remarkably good restaurants. Look for outlet stores, strip malls, and discount skiwear shops along Donner Pass Road, north of the freeway. Because of its location on Interstate 80, Truckee is a favorite stopover for people traveling from the San Francisco Bay Area to the north shore of Lake Tahoe, Reno, and points east.

GETTING HERE AND AROUND

Truckee is just off Interstate 80 between highways 89 and 267. Greyhound and Amtrak stop here, Enterprise and Hertz provide car rentals, and TART buses serve Truckee and north shore communities.

ESSENTIALS

Visitor Information Truckee Donner Chamber of Commerce and the California Welcome Center ⊠ *Amtrak depot, 10065 Donner Pass Rd., near Spring St.* ☎ *530/587–8808* ⊕ *www.truckee.com.*

EXPLORING

Donner Memorial State Park and Emigrant Trail Museum. The park and museum commemorate the Donner Party, westward-bound pioneers—about 90; historians debate the exact number—who became trapped in the Sierra in the winter of 1846–47 in snow 22 feet deep. Barely more than half the pioneers survived, some by resorting to cannibalism. The Emigrant Trail Museum details the Donner Party's plight, and other displays explain railroad development through the Sierra. In the park, you can picnic, hike, camp, and go boating, fishing, and waterskiing in summer; winter brings cross-country skiing and snowshoeing on groomed trails. Slated for a 2014 debut, a new High Sierra Crossing Museum will contain exhibits about the Donner Party, regional Native Americans, and railroad and transportation development through Donner Pass. ⊠ *12593 Donner Pass Rd., off I–80, 2 miles west of Truckee* 🕾 *530/582–7892 museum, 800/444–7275 camping reservations* ⊕ *www.parks.ca.gov* 🖰 *$8 parking, day use* ⊙ *Museum late May–early Sept., daily 10–5; closed Tues. early Sept.–late May.*

OFF THE BEATEN PATH

Tahoe National Forest. Draped along the Sierra Nevada Crest north of Lake Tahoe, the national forest offers abundant outdoor recreation: hiking, picnicking, and camping in summer, and in winter, snowshoeing, skiing, and sledding over some of the deepest snowpack in the West. ⊠ *Truckee ranger station, 10811 Stockrest Springs Rd.* 🕾 *530/587–3558 Truckee ranger station, 530/265–4531 forest headquarters* ⊕ *www.fs.usda.gov/tahoe.*

WHERE TO EAT

$$$
ECLECTIC

✕ **Cottonwood.** Perched above town on the site of North America's first chairlift, this restaurant is an institution. The bar is decked out with old wooden skis, sleds, skates, and photos of Truckee's early days. The ambitious menu includes everything from grilled New York strip steak to baby back short ribs with Cajun spices to butternut-squash enchiladas—plus fresh-baked breads and desserts—but people come here mainly for the atmosphere and hilltop views. ⑤ *Average main: $23* ⊠ *10142 Rue Hilltop Rd., off Brockway Rd., ¼ mile south of downtown* 🕾 *530/587–5711* ⊕ *www.cottonwoodrestaurant.com* ⊙ *No lunch.*

$$$
ASIAN

✕ **Dragonfly.** Flavors are bold and zingy at this Cal-Asian spot, where every dish is well executed and stylishly presented. Southeast Asian cooking inspires most dishes, which you can savor in the bright, contemporary dining rooms—one for sushi—or, when the weather's nice, an outdoor terrace overlooking the busy street scene and the train depot. Lunch is a bargain, and there are many choices for vegetarians. Look for the staircase: the restaurant is on the second floor. ⑤ *Average main: $25* ⊠ *10118 Donner Pass Rd., at Spring St.* 🕾 *530/587–0557* ⊕ *www.dragonflycuisine.com.*

$$
AMERICAN

✕ **FiftyFifty Brewing Company.** In this Truckee brewpub, warm red tones and comfy booths, plus a pint of the Donner Party Porter, will take the nip out of a cold day on the slopes. The lunch-into-dinner menu includes salads, burgers, and the house specialty, a pulled-pork sandwich, plus barbecued ribs and pan-seared salmon. Order one of the inventive pizzas anytime. There's a full bar along with the brews, and lots of après-ski action. ⑤ *Average main: $19* ⊠ *11197 Brockway Rd.* 🕾 *530/587–2337* ⊕ *www.fiftyfiftybrewing.com.*

$$$
ECLECTIC

✕ **Moody's Bistro Bar & Beats.** Head here for contemporary-Cal cuisine in a sexy dining room with pumpkin-color walls, burgundy velvet banquettes, and art deco fixtures. The earthy, sure-handed cooking features organically grown ingredients: look for ahi poke, snazzy pizzas bubbling-hot from a brick oven, pan-roasted wild game, fresh seafood, and organic beef. Lunch fare is lighter. In summer dine alfresco surrounded by flowers. From Thursday through Saturday there's music in the borderline-raucous bar that gets packed with Truckee's bon vivants. $ *Average main: $24* ⊠ *10007 Bridge St., at Church St.* ☎ *530/587–8688* ⊕ *moodysbistro.com.*

WHERE TO STAY

For expanded hotel reviews, visit Fodors.com.

13

$$$

HOTEL

☷ **Cedar House Sport Hotel.** The clean, spare lines of the Cedar House's wooden exterior evoke a modern European feel, while energy-saving heating, cooling, and lighting systems emphasize the owners' commitment to sustainability. **Pros:** environmentally friendly; comfortable; hip. **Cons:** some bathrooms on the small side. $ *Rooms from: $190* ⊠ *10918 Brockway Rd.* ☎ *530/582–5655, 866/582–5655* ⊕ *www.cedarhousesporthotel.com* ⤳ *41 rooms* ❙❍❙ *Breakfast.*

$$$

RESORT

☷ **Northstar-at-Tahoe Resort.** The area's most complete destination resort entices families with its sports activities and concentration of restaurants, shops, and accommodations. **Pros:** array of lodging types; on-site shuttle; several dining options in Northstar Village. **Cons:** family accommodations are very pricey. $ *Rooms from: $229* ⊠ *5001 Northstar Dr., off Hwy. 267, 6 miles southeast of Truckee* ☎ *530/562–1010, 800/466–6784* ⊕ *www.northstarattahoe.com* ⤳ *250 units* ❙❍❙ *No meals.*

$$$$

RESORT

☷ **Ritz-Carlton Highlands Court, Lake Tahoe.** The first luxury hotel built in the Tahoe area in decades, the Ritz-Carlton opened in December 2009. **Pros:** superb service; gorgeous setting. **Cons:** prices as breathtaking as the views; must go off-site for golf and tennis. $ *Rooms from: $569* ⊠ *13031 Ritz-Carlton Highlands Court* ☎ *530/562–3000, 800/241–3333* ⊕ *www.ritzcarlton.com/laketahoe* ⤳ *153 rooms, 17 suites* ❙❍❙ *No meals.*

$$

B&B/INN

☷ **River Street Inn.** On the banks of the Truckee River, this 1885 wood-and-stone inn was at times a boardinghouse and a brothel. **Pros:** nice rooms; good value. **Cons:** parking is a half-block from inn. $ *Rooms from: $130* ⊠ *10009 E. River St.* ☎ *530/550–9290* ⊕ *www.riverstreetinntruckee.com* ⤳ *11 rooms* ❙❍❙ *Breakfast.*

SPORTS AND THE OUTDOORS

GOLF

Coyote Moon Golf Course. With towering pine trees lining the fairways and no houses to spoil the view, this course is as beautiful as it is challenging. Fees include a shared cart; the greens fee drops at 1 pm and dips again at 3. ⊠ *10685 Northwoods Blvd., off Donner Pass Rd.* ☎ *530/587–0886* ⊕ *www.coyotemoongolf.com* ⚑ *18 holes. 7,177 yds. Par 72. Slope 139. Greens fee: $149* ☽ *Closed late fall–late spring* ⚐ *Facilities: Driving range, putting green, pitching area, golf carts, rental clubs, pro shop, golf lessons, restaurant, bar.*

Northstar. The front nine holes here are open-links style, while the challenging back nine move through tight, tree-lined fairways. Fees include a cart. Twilight rates begin at 1 pm. You can play nine holes for $45; special teen rates encourage family outings. The restaurant serves breakfast and lunch only. ⊠ *168 Basque Dr., off Northstar Dr., west off Hwy. 267*

☎ *530/562–3290 pro shop* ⊕ *www.northstarattahoe.com/info/summer/ golf.asp* ⚑ *Course: 18 holes. 6,781 yds. Par 72. Slope 139. Greens fee: $80* ☞ *Facilities: Driving range, putting green, pitching area, golf carts, pull carts, rental clubs, pro shop, golf lessons, restaurant, bar.*

Old Greenwood. Beautiful mountain and forest views add to the pleasure of a round played at north Lake Tahoe's only Jack Nicklaus Signature Golf Course. The regular fees are high, but there's a $75 twilight rate beginning at 4 pm. ⊠ *12915 Fairway Dr., off Overland Trail Rd., off I–80, Exit 190* ☎ *530/550–7010* ⊕ *www.oldgreenwood.com* ⚑ *Course: 18 holes. 7,518 yards. Par 72. Slope 149. Greens fees: $160/$185.* ☞ *Facilities: driving range, putting green, pitching area, golf carts, rental clubs, pro shop, golf academy/lessons, restaurant, bar.*

MOUNTAIN BIKING

Northstar-at-Tahoe. In summer you can rent a bike and ride the lifts ($46, ages 13 and up) to the mountain-biking park for 100 miles of challenging terrain. The season extends from mid-June through September with varying hours. ⊠ *Northstar Dr., off Hwy. 267* ☎ *530/562–2268* ⊕ *www.northstarattahoe.com.*

Cyclepaths Mountain Bike Adventures. This combination full-service bike shop and bike-adventure outfitter offers instruction in mountain biking, guided tours, tips for self-guided bike touring, bike repairs, and books and maps on the area. ⊠ *10095 W. River St., by Bridge St.* ☎ *530/582– 1890* ⊕ *www.cyclepaths.net.*

SKIING

Several smaller resorts around Truckee offer access to the Sierra's slopes for less than half the price of the big resorts. Though you'll sacrifice vertical rise, acreage, and high-speed lifts, you can ski or ride and still have money left over for room and board. These are great places for first-timers and families with kids learning to ski.

Boreal. These slopes have 480 skiable acres and 500 vertical feet of terrain visible from the freeway; lift-served snow-tubing and night skiing go until 9. ⊠ *19749 Boreal Ridge Rd., at I–80, Boreal/Castle Peak exit, Soda Springs* ☎ *530/426–3666* ⊕ *www.rideboreal.com.*

Donner Ski Ranch. This ski park has 505 acres and 750 vertical feet and sits across from the more challenging Sugar Bowl (⇨ *below*). ⊠ *19320 Donner Pass Rd., Norden* ☎ *530/426–3635* ⊕ *www.donnerskiranch.com.*

Northstar-at-Tahoe. With two tree-lined, northeast-facing, wind-protected bowls, this park is the ideal place in a storm, and just may be the best all-around family ski resort at Tahoe. Hotshot experts unfairly call the mountain "Flatstar," but the meticulous grooming and long cruisers make it an intermediate skier's paradise. Boarders are especially welcome, with awesome terrain parks, including a 420-foot-long superpipe, a half-pipe, rails and boxes, and lots of kickers. Experts can ski the steeps and bumps off Lookout Mountain, where there's rarely a line for the high-speed quad. Northstar-at-Tahoe's cross-country center has 35 km (22 miles) of groomed trails, including double-set tracks and skating lanes. The school has programs for skiers ages three and up, and day care is available for tots two and older. The mountain gets packed on busy weekends but when there's room on the slopes, Northstar is loads of fun. *(⇨ See "When to Go" at the beginning of this chapter for alternatives on busy days.)* ⊠ *100 Northstar Dr., off Hwy. 267, 6 miles southeast of Truckee* ☎ *530/562–1010 information, 800/466–6784 lodging, 530/562–1330 snow phone* ⊕ *www.northstarattahoe.com* ⌂ *97 trails on 3,170 acres, rated 13% beginner, 60% intermediate, 27% advanced. Longest run 1.4 miles, base 6,330 feet, summit 8,610 feet. Lifts: 20, including 2 gondolas and 7 high-speed quads.*

Royal Gorge. If you love to cross-country, don't miss Royal Gorge, which serves up 200 km (124 miles) of track for all abilities, 75 trails on a whopping 6,000 acres, a ski school, and eight warming huts. Two trailside cafés and two lodges round out the facilities. Because the complex sits right on the Sierra Crest, the views are drop-dead gorgeous. ⊠ *9411 Pahatsi Dr., off I–80, Soda Springs/Norden exit, Soda Springs* ☎ *530/426–3871* ⊕ *www.royalgorge.com.*

Soda Springs. Along with 200 acres and 652 vertical feet, this ski park also has lift-served snow-tubing. ⊠ *10244 Soda Springs Rd., I–80 Soda Springs exit, Soda Springs* ☎ *530/426–3901* ⊕ *www.skisodasprings.com.*

Sugar Bowl. Opened in 1939 by Walt Disney, this is the oldest—and one of the best—resorts at Tahoe. Atop Donner Summit, it receives an incredible 500 inches of snowfall annually. Four peaks are connected by 1,500 acres of skiable terrain, with everything from gentle groomed corduroy to wide-open bowls to vertical rocky chutes and outstanding tree skiing. Snowboarders can hit two terrain parks with numerous boxes, rails, and jumps. Because it's more compact than some of the area's megaresorts, there's a gentility here that distinguishes Sugar Bowl from its competitors, making this a great place for families and a low-pressure, low-key place to learn to ski. It's not huge, but there's some very challenging terrain (experts: head to the Palisades). There's limited lodging at the base area. ⊠ *629 Sugar Bowl Rd., off Donner Pass Rd., 3 miles east of I–80 Soda Springs/Norden exit, 10 miles west of Truckee, Norden* ☎ *530/426–9000 information and lodging reservations, 530/426–1111 snow phone, 866/843–2695 lodging referral* ⊕ *www.sugarbowl.com* ⌂ *102 trails on 1,500 acres, rated 17% beginner, 45% intermediate, 38% advanced. Longest run 3 miles, base 6,883 feet, summit 8,383 feet. Lifts: 13, including 5 high-speed quads.*

Tahoe Dave's. You can save money by renting skis and boards at this shop, which has the area's best selection and also repairs and tunes equipment. ⊠ *10200 Donner Pass Rd., near Spring St.* ☎ *530/582–0900* ⊕ *www.tahoedaves.com.*

Tahoe Donner. Just north of Truckee, this park covers 120 acres and 600 vertical feet; the cross-country center includes 51 trails on 100 km (62 miles) of groomed tracks on 4,800 acres, with night skiing on Wednesdays in January and February. ⊠ *11509 Northwoods Blvd., at Muhlebach Way* ☎ *530/587–9444* ⊕ *www.tahoedonner.com.*

CARNELIAN BAY TO KINGS BEACH

5–10 miles northeast of Tahoe City.

The small lakeside commercial districts of Carnelian Bay and Tahoe Vista service the thousand or so locals who live in the area year-round and the thousands more who have summer residences or launch their boats here. Kings Beach, the last town heading east on Highway 28 before the Nevada border, is to Crystal Bay what South Lake Tahoe is to Stateline: a bustling town full of basic motels and rental condos, restaurants, and shops, used by the hordes of hopefuls who pass through on their way to the casinos.

GETTING HERE AND AROUND

To reach Kings Beach and Carnelian Bay from the California side, take Highway 89 north to Highway 28 north and then east. From the Nevada side, follow Highway 28 north and then west. TART provides public transportation in this area.

BEACHES

FAMILY **Kings Beach State Recreation Area.** The 28-acre Kings Beach State Recreation Area, one of the largest such areas on the lake, is open year-round. The 700-foot-long sandy beach gets very crowded in summer with people swimming, sunbathing, jet-skiing, riding in paddleboats, spiking volleyballs, and tossing Frisbees. If you're going to spend the day, come early enough to snag a table in the picnic area; there's also a good playground. **Amenities:** food and drink; parking (fee); toilets; water sports. **Best for:** sunrise; swimming; windsurfing. ⊠ *8318 N. Lake Blvd., Hwy. 28, Kings Beach* ☎ *530/546–7248* ⊕ *www.parks.ca.gov* ⊡ *$8 parking fee* ☉ *Daily.*

WHERE TO EAT AND STAY

For expanded hotel reviews, visit Fodors.com.

$$$ ✕ **Gar Woods Grill and Pier.** The view's the thing at this lakeside stalwart,
ECLECTIC where you can watch the sun shimmer on the water through the dining room's plate-glass windows or from the heated outdoor deck. Grilled steak and fish are menu mainstays, but be sure to try specialties like crab chilis rellenos and chipotle chicken salad. At all hours in season, the bar gets packed with boaters who pull up to the restaurant's private pier. ⑤ *Average main: $29* ⊠ *5000 N. Lake Blvd., Hwy. 28, Carnelian Bay* ☎ *530/546–3366* ⊕ *www.garwoods.com.*

$$ ✕ **Spindleshanks.** This handsome roadhouse, decorated with floor-to-
AMERICAN ceiling knotty pine, serves mostly classic American cooking—ribs, steaks, and seafood updated with adventurous sauces—as well as house-made ravioli. On cold nights request seating near the crackling fireplace and enjoy a drink from the full bar or choose a wine from the extensive list. ⑤ *Average main: $22* ⊠ *6873 N. Lake Blvd, Tahoe Vista* ☎ *530/546– 2191* ⊕ *www.spindleshankstahoe.com* ☉ *No lunch except summer.*

$ ⊡ **Ferrari's Crown Resort.** The family-owned and -operated Ferrari's
HOTEL has straightforward motel rooms in a resort setting, great for families
FAMILY with kids. **Pros:** family-friendly; lakeside location. **Cons:** older facility. ⑤ *Rooms from: $105* ⊠ *8200 N. Lake Blvd., Kings Beach* ☎ *530/546– 3388, 800/645–2260* ⊕ *www.tahoecrown.com* ⤳ *72 rooms* ⦿⧳ *Breakfast.*

$$$$
B&B/INN

Shore House. Every room has a gas fireplace, down comforter, and featherbed at this lakefront B&B in Tahoe Vista. **Pros:** waterfront honeymoon cottage; massage appointments available. **Cons:** pricey; not a good choice for children. *⑤Rooms from: $265 ⊠7170 N. Lake Blvd., Tahoe Vista ☎530/546–7270, 800/207–5160 ⊕www. shorehouselaketahoe.com ⇌8 rooms, 1 cottage ⑩Breakfast.*

THE NEVADA SIDE

13

The difference on the Nevada side of the lake is, of course, gambling, with all its repercussions.

CRYSTAL BAY

1 mile east of Kings Beach, 30 miles north of South Lake Tahoe.

Right at the Nevada border, Crystal Bay has a cluster of casinos that look essentially the same, but have a few minor differences. These casinos tend toward the tacky, and most of the lodging is lackluster.

GETTING HERE AND AROUND

From the California side, reach Crystal Bay via Highway 89 or 267 to Highway 28. TART serves the communities along the north and west shores.

EXPLORING

Cal-Neva Lodge. Bisected by the state line, the Cal-Neva Lodge opened in 1927 and has weathered many scandals. The largest involved former owner Frank Sinatra (he lost his gaming license in the 1960s for alleged mob connections). The secret tunnel that Frank built so that he could steal away unnoticed to Marilyn Monroe's cabin is definitely worth a look; call for tour times. ⊠*2 Stateline Rd. ☎800/225–6382 ⊕www. calnevaresort.com.*

Crystal Bay Club. Known for its classic steak and lobster dinner, the restaurant in this casino has a distinctive open-truss ceiling. ⊠*14 Hwy. 28, near Stateline Rd. ☎775/833–6333 ⊕ crystalbaycasino.com.*

Jim Kelley's Tahoe Nugget. Nearly 90 kinds of beer highlight the bar scene at Jim Kelley's Tahoe Nugget. In fact, they're the highlight of the entire casino, which has no table games, only slots and video poker. ⊠*20 Hwy. 28, near Stateline Rd. ☎775/831–0455.*

Tahoe Biltmore. A daily happy hour keeps this old favorite hopping. The circular Tahoe Biltmore sign is a 1962 "Googie-style" architectural riff off the Seattle Space Neeedle, which debuted the same year. ⊠*5 Hwy. 28, at Stateline Rd. ☎800/245–8667 ⊕www.tahoebiltmore.com.*

WHERE TO EAT

$$$
ECLECTIC

✕ **Soule Domain.** Rough-hewn wood beams and a vaulted wood ceiling lend high romance to this cozy 1927 pine-log cabin next to the Tahoe Biltmore. Chef-owner Charlie Soule's specialties include curried almond chicken, fresh sea scallops poached in champagne with a kiwi and mango cream sauce, and a vegan sauté with ginger, jalapeños, and tofu, but you'll find the chef's current passion in the roster of nightly specials. Some find Soule Domain pricey, but if you're looking for a place with a sterling menu where you can hold hands by candlelight, this is it. $ *Average main: $27* ✉ *9983 Cove Ave., ½ block up Stateline Rd. off Hwy. 28, Kings Beach* ☎ *530/546–7529* ⊕ *www.souledomain. com* ⊗ *No lunch.*

INCLINE VILLAGE

3 miles east of Crystal Bay.

Incline Village dates to the early 1960s when an Oklahoma developer bought 10,000 acres north of Lake Tahoe. His idea was to sketch out a plan for a town without a central commercial district, hoping to prevent congestion and to preserve the area's natural beauty. One-acre lakeshore lots originally fetched $12,000 to $15,000; today you couldn't buy the same land for less than several million.

GETTING HERE AND AROUND
From the California side, reach Incline Village via Highway 89 or 267 to Highway 28. From South Lake Tahoe, take U.S. 50 north to Highway 28 north. TART serves the communities along Lake Tahoe's north and west shores from Incline Village to Tahoma.

ESSENTIALS
Visitor Information Lake Tahoe Incline Village/Crystal Bay Visitors Bureau ✉ *969 Tahoe Blvd.* ☎ *775/832–1606, 800/468–2463* ⊕ *www.gotahoenorth.com.*

EXPLORING
Lakeshore Drive. Take this beautiful drive to see some of the most expensive real estate in Nevada. The route is discreetly marked: to find it, start at the Hyatt hotel and drive westward along the lake.

Fodor's Choice **Thunderbird Lodge.** George Whittell, a San Francisco socialite who once ★ owned 40,000 acres of property along the lake, built the lodge in 1936. You can tour the mansion and the grounds by reservation only, and though it's pricey to do so, you'll get a rare glimpse back to a time when only the very wealthy had homes at Tahoe. The lodge is accessible via a bus from the Incline Village Visitors Bureau, a catamaran from the Hyatt in Incline Village ($110), or a 1950 wooden cruiser from Tahoe Keys Marina in South Lake Tahoe, which includes Continental breakfast and lunch ($135). ☎ *775/832–8750 lodge info, 800/468– 2463 reservations, 775/588–1881, 888/867–6394 Tahoe Keys boat, 775/831–4386 Hyatt Incline catamaran* ⊕ *thunderbirdtahoe.org/tours* ✉ *$39 bus tour, $110 & 135 for boat tours* ⊗ *May–Oct., Tues.–Sat., call for tour times.*

BEACHES
Lake Tahoe–Nevada State Park and Sand Harbor Beach. Protecting much of the lake's eastern shore from development, the park comprises several sections that stretch from Incline Village to Zephyr Cove. Beaches and trails provide access to a wilder side of the lake, whether you're into cross-country skiing, hiking, or just relaxing at a picnic. With a gently sloping beach for lounging, crystal clear water for swimming and snorkeling, and a picnic area shaded by cedars and pines, **Sand Harbor Beach** is so popular that it sometimes fills to capacity by 11 am on

summer weekends. Boaters have two launch ramps. A handicap-accessible nature trail has interpretive signs and beautiful lake views. Pets are not allowed. **Amenities:** food and drink; parking ($12 mid-Apr.–mid-Oct., $7 rest of the year); toilets; water sports. **Best for:** snorkeling; sunset; swimming; walking. ⊠ *Sand Harbor Beach, Hwy. 28, 3 miles south of Incline Village* ☎ *775/831–0494* ⊕ *parks.nv.gov/parks/sand-harbor.*

WHERE TO EAT AND STAY

For expanded hotel reviews, visit Fodors.com.

13

$$$
ECLECTIC

✕**Fredrick's.** Copper-top tables lend a chic look to the dining room at this intimate bistro. The menu consists of a mélange of European and Asian dishes, most of them prepared with organic produce and free-range meats. Try the braised short ribs, roasted duck with caramel-pecan glaze, or the deliciously fresh sushi rolls. ■**TIP→ On cold nights ask for a table by the fire.** Ⓢ *Average main: $28* ⊠ *907 Tahoe Blvd., at Village Blvd.* ☎ *775/832–3007* ⊕ *fredricksbistro.com* ☉ *Closed Sun. and Mon. No lunch.*

$$$
FRENCH

✕**Le Bistro.** Incline Village's hidden gem serves expertly prepared French-country cuisine in a relaxed, romantic dining room. The chef-owner makes everything himself, using organically grown ingredients. Expect such dishes as pâté de campagne, escargot, herb-crusted roast lamb and fresh fish. Try the five-course prix-fixe menu ($51), which can be paired with award-winning wines. Service is gracious and attentive. ■**TIP→ This restaurant is hard to find, so ask for directions when you book.** Ⓢ *Average main: $30* ⊠ *120 Country Club Dr., #29, off Lake-shore Blvd.* ☎ *775/831–0800* ⊕ *www.lebistrorestaurant.net* ☉ *Closed Sun. and Mon. No lunch.*

$
SOUTHERN

✕**T's Rotisserie.** There's nothing fancy about T's (it looks like a small snack bar), but the mesquite-grilled chicken and tri-tip steaks are delicious and inexpensive—a rare combination in pricey Incline Village. It's mainly a take-out spot; seating is limited. Ⓢ *Average main: $8* ⊠ *901 Tahoe Blvd., at Village Blvd.* ☎ *775/831–2832* ▬ *No credit cards.*

$$$$
RESORT

▦ **Hyatt Regency Lake Tahoe.** A full-service destination resort on 26 acres of prime lakefront property, the Hyatt has a range of luxurious accommodations, from tower-hotel rooms to lakeside cottages. **Pros:** incredible views; first-class spa. **Cons:** pricey (especially for families). Ⓢ *Rooms from: $310* ⊠ *111 Country Club Dr.* ☎ *775/832–1234, 888/899–5019* ⊕ *www.laketahoe.hyatt.com* ⇱ *386 rooms, 36 suites* ⦿ *No meals.*

SPORTS AND THE OUTDOORS

GOLF

Incline Championship. Robert Trent Jones Sr. designed this challenging course of tightly cut, tree-lined fairways laced with water hazards that demand accuracy as well as distance skills. Greens fee includes a cart, except the 4:30 pm Super Twilight rate of $2 per hole (cart $25). ⊠ *955 Fairway Blvd., at Northwood Blvd., north off Hwy. 28* ☎ *866/925–4653* ⊕ *www.inclinegolf.com* ⚑ *Course: 18 holes. 7,106 yds. Par 72. Slope 146. Greens fee: $179* ☞ *Facilities: Driving range, putting green, pitching area, golf carts, rental clubs, pro shop, golf lessons, restaurant, bar.*

Get to Sand Harbor Beach in Lake Tahoe–Nevada State Park early; the park sometimes fills to capacity before lunchtime in summer.

Incline Mountain. Robert Trent Jones, Jr. designed this executive (shorter) course that requires accuracy more than distance skills. The green fee includes a cart. ⊠ *690 Wilson Way, at Golfer's Pass, south off Hwy. 431* ☎ *866/925–4653* ⊕ *www.inclinegolf.com* ⚑ *Course: 18 holes. 3519 yards. Par 58. Slope 104. Greens fees: $65/$75.* ☞ *Facilities: Driving range, putting green, pitching area, golf carts, rental clubs, pro shop, golf lessons, restaurant, bar.*

MOUNTAIN BIKING

Flume Trail Bikes. You can rent bikes and get helpful tips from this company that also operates a bike shuttle to popular trailheads. Ask about the secluded backcountry rental cabins for overnight rides. ⊠ *1115 Tunnel Creek Rd., at Ponderosa Ranch Rd., off Hwy. 28* ☎ *775/298–2501* ⊕ *www.theflumetrail.com.*

SKIING

Diamond Peak. A fun family mood prevails at Diamond Peak, which has affordable rates and many special programs. Snowmaking covers 75% of the mountain, and runs are groomed nightly. The ride up the 1-mile Crystal Express rewards you with fantastic views. Diamond Peak is less crowded than the larger areas and provides free shuttles to nearby lodgings. A great place for beginners and intermediates, it's appropriately priced for families. Though there are some steep-aspect black-diamond runs, advanced skiers may find the acreage too limited. For snowboarders there's a small terrain park. ⊠ *1210 Ski Way, off Country Club Dr.* ☎ *775/832–1177* ⊕ *www.diamondpeak.com* ☞ *30 trails on 655 acres, rated 18% beginner, 46% intermediate, 36% advanced. Longest run*

2½ miles, base 6,700 feet, summit 8,540 feet. Lifts: 6, including 2 high-speed quads.

Mt. Rose Ski Tahoe. At this park, ski some of Tahoe's highest slopes and take in bird's-eye views of Reno, the lake, and Carson Valley. Though more compact than the bigger Tahoe resorts, Mt. Rose has the

13

area's highest base elevation and consequently the driest snow. The mountain has a wide variety of terrain. The most challenging is the Chutes, 200 acres of gulp-and-go advanced-to-expert vertical. Intermediates can choose steep groomers or mellow, wide-open boulevards. Beginners have their own corner of the mountain, with gentle, wide slopes. Boarders and tricksters have three terrain parks to choose from, on opposite sides of the mountain, allowing them to follow the sun as it tracks across the resort. The mountain gets hit hard in storms; check conditions before heading up during inclement weather or on a windy day. ⊠ *22222 Mt. Rose Hwy., Hwy. 431, 11 miles north of Incline Village, Reno* ☎ *775/849–0704, 800/754–7673* ⊕ *www.skirose.com* ✆ *61 trails on 1,200 acres, rated 20% beginner, 30% intermediate, 40% advanced, 10% expert. Longest run 2½ miles, base 8,260 feet, summit 9,700 feet. Lifts: 8, including 2 high-speed 6-passenger lifts.*

Tahoe Meadows Snowplay Area. This is the most popular area near the north shore for noncommercial cross-country skiing, sledding, tubing, snowshoeing, and snowmobiling. ⊠ *Hwy. 431, between Incline Village and Mt. Rose.*

ZEPHYR COVE

22 miles south of Incline Village.

The largest settlement between Incline Village and the Stateline area is Zephyr Cove, a tiny resort. It has a beach, marina, campground, picnic area, coffee shop in a log lodge, rustic cabins, and nearby riding stables.

GETTING HERE AND AROUND

From the north shore communities, reach Zephyr Cove by following Highway 28 along the eastern side of the lake. From South Lake Tahoe, take U.S. 50 north and then west. Public transportation isn't available in Zephyr Cove.

EXPLORING

Cave Rock. Near Zephyr Cove, this 75 feet of solid stone at the southern end of Lake Tahoe–Nevada State Park is the throat of an extinct volcano. Tahoe Tessie, the lake's version of the Loch Ness monster, is reputed to live in a cavern below the impressive outcropping. Cave Rock towers over a parking lot, a lakefront picnic ground, and a boat launch. The views are some of the best on the lake; this is a good spot to stop and take a picture. However, this area is a sacred burial site for the Washoe Indians, and climbing up to the cave, or through it, is prohibited. ⊠ *U.S. 50, 4 miles north of Zephyr Cove* ☎ *775/831–0494.*

WHERE TO STAY

For expanded hotel reviews, visit Fodors.com.

$$$
RENTAL
FAMILY

⊡ **Zephyr Cove Resort.** Beneath towering pines at the lake's edge stand 28 cozy, modern vacation cabins with peaked knotty-pine ceilings. **Pros:** family-friendly. **Cons:** lodge rooms are very basic; can be noisy. ⑤ *Rooms from: $199* ⊠ *760 U.S. 50, 4 miles north of Stateline* ☎ *775/589–4907, 800/238–2463* ⊕ *www.zephyrcove.com* ↩ *28 cabins* ⦿| *No meals.*

STATELINE

5 miles south of Zephyr Cove.

Stateline is the archetypal Nevada border town. Its four high-rise casinos are as vertical and contained as the commercial district of South Lake Tahoe, on the California side, is horizontal and sprawling. And Stateline is as relentlessly indoors oriented as the rest of the lake is focused on the outdoors. This strip is where you'll find the most concentrated action at Lake Tahoe: restaurants (including typical casino buffets), showrooms with famous headliners and razzle-dazzle revues, tower-hotel rooms and suites, and 24-hour casinos.

GETTING HERE AND AROUND

From South Lake Tahoe take U.S. 50 north across the Nevada border to reach Stateline and its casinos. If coming from Reno's airport, take U.S. 395/Interstate 580 south to Carson City, and then head west on U.S. 50 to the lake and head south. Or take the South Tahoe Express bus. BlueGO operates daily bus service in the south shore area year-round, plus a ski shuttle from the large hotels to Heavenly in the winter.

BEACHES

Nevada Beach. Although less than a mile long, this is the widest beach on the lake and especially good for swimming (many Tahoe beaches are rocky). You can boat and fish here, and there are picnic tables, barbecue grills, and a campground beneath the pines. This is the best place to watch the July 4th or Labor Day fireworks, but most of the summer the subdued atmosphere attracts families and those seeking a less-touristy spot. **Amenities:** parking ($7 fee), water sports, toilets. **Best for:** sunrise, swimming, walking. ⊠ *Elk Point Rd., off U.S. 50, 3 miles north of Stateline* ☎ *530/543–2600* ⊕ *www.fs.usda.gov/ltbmu* ☉ *Open daily late May–Oct.* ↩ *No pets.*

WHERE TO EAT AND STAY

For expanded hotel reviews, visit Fodors.com.

$$$
FRENCH

✕ **Mirabelle.** Don't be put off by this restaurant's nondescript exterior. Inside there's an airy dining room with creamy yellow walls and white tablecloths. Enticing scents drift from the kitchen, where the Alsatian-born chef-owner, Camille Schwartz, prepares everything from puff pastry to meringues to homemade bread. Specialties include sautéed veal sweetbreads, garlicky escargot, and rack of lamb with fresh thyme. There's always a fresh fish entrée, plus a $33.50 prix-fixe "casual menu." ⑤ *Average main: $27* ⊠ *290 Kingsbury Grade,* *off U.S. 50* ☎ *775/586–1007* ⊕ *www.mirabelletahoe.com* ⊙ *Closed Mon. No lunch.*

$$ ⬚ **Harrah's Tahoe Hotel/Casino.** The hotel's major selling point is that
HOTEL   every room has two full bathrooms, each with a television and telephone, a boon if you're traveling with family. **Pros:** central location; great midweek values. **Cons:** can get noisy. ⑤ *Rooms from: $110* ⊠ *15 U.S. 50, at Stateline Ave.* ☎ *775/588–6611, 800/427–7247* ⊕ *www. harrahstahoe.com* ⊶ *470 rooms, 62 suites* ❑ *No meals.*

$ ⬚ **Harveys Resort Hotel/Casino.** The resort began as a cabin in 1944, and
HOTEL   now it's Tahoe's largest casino-hotel. **Pros:** hip entertainment; just a few blocks south of the Heavenly Gondola. **Cons:** can get loud at night. ⑤ *Rooms from: $80* ⊠ *18 U.S. 50, at Stateline Ave.* ☎ *775/588–2411, 800/648–3361* ⊕ *www.harveystahoe.com* ⊶ *705 rooms, 38 suites* ❑ *No meals.*

$ ⬚ **MontBleu.** The contemporary, slightly kitschy MontBleu has guest
HOTEL   rooms with oversize tubs, king-size beds, and views of Lake Tahoe and the surrounding mountains. **Pros:** indoor pool; first-class spa; great specials online. **Cons:** looking careworn in places; can get noisy; some rooms overlook parking lot's glaring lights. ⑤ *Rooms from: $99* ⊠ *55 U.S. 50* ☎ *775/588–3515, 800/648–3353* ⊕ *www.montbleuresort.com* ⊶ *328 rooms, 109 suites* ❑ *No meals.*

NIGHTLIFE

Each of the major casinos has its own showroom, featuring everything from comedy to magic acts to sexy floor shows to Broadway musicals.

Harveys Outdoor Summer Concert Series. The casino presents outdoor concerts on weekends in summer with headliners such as Sugarland, Brad Paisley, the Rascal Flats, and Toby Keith. ☎ *775/588–6611* ⊕ *www. harveystahoe.com.*

Peek. You can dance the night away with top-notch DJs, and often hear live performances, at this club that emulates a Vegas vibe. ⊠ *Harrah's, 15 U.S. 50* ☎ *775/588–6611* ⊕ *www.harrahstahoe.com.*

South Shore Room. Old-school (Rick Springfield) and really old-school (Eric Burdon) rockers play Harrah's big showroom, along with relatively less nostalgia-oriented headliners such as Los Lobos and—combining most of the above attributes—Chickenfoot. ⊠ *Harrah's, 15 U.S. 50* ☎ *775/588–6611* ⊕ *www.harrahstahoe.com.*

SPORTS AND THE OUTDOORS
GOLF

Edgewood Tahoe. Golfers of all skill levels enjoy this highly scenic lakeside course that has four sets of tees, offering a variety of course lengths. The greens fee includes an optional cart. ⊠ *100 Lake Pkwy., at U.S. 50* ☎ *775/588–3566, 866/761–4653* ⊕ *www.edgewood-tahoe. com* ⚐ *Course: 18 holes. 7,552 yards. Par 72. Slope 142. Greens fees: $220/$240* ⚲ *Facilities: Driving range, putting green, pitching area, golf carts, pull carts, caddies, rental clubs, pro shop, golf lessons, restaurant, bar.*

13

RENO

32 miles east of Truckee, 38 miles northeast of Incline Village.

Established in 1859 as a trading station at a bridge over the Truckee River, Reno grew along with the silver mines of nearby Virginia City and the transcontinental railroad that chugged through town. Train officials named it in 1868, but gambling—legalized in 1931—put Reno on the map. This is still a gambling town, with most of the casinos crowded into five square blocks downtown, but a thriving university scene and outdoor activities also attract tourists.

Parts of downtown are sketchy, but things are changing. Several defunct casinos are being converted into condominiums, and the riverfront is being reconceived. The town now touts family-friendly activities like kayaking on the Truckee, and new shops and excellent restaurants have sprung up outside the hotels. Temperatures year-round in this high-mountain-desert climate are warmer than at Tahoe, though it rarely gets as hot here as in Sacramento and the Central Valley, making strolling around town a pleasure.

GETTING HERE AND AROUND

Interstate 80 bisects Reno east–west, U.S. 395 north–south (south of town the road is signed U.S. 395/Interstate 580). Greyhound and Amtrak stop here, and several airlines fly into Reno-Tahoe International Airport. RTC Ride provides bus service in the greater Reno area.

ESSENTIALS

Bus Contact RTC Ride ⊠ *Transit Center, E. 4th and Lake Sts.* ☎ *775/348–7433* ⊕ *rtcwashoe.com.*

Visitor Information Reno-Sparks Convention and Visitors Authority ⊠ *4001 S. Virginia St.* ☎ *775/827–7650, 800/367–7366* ⊕ *www.visitrenotahoe.com.*

EXPLORING

TOP ATTRACTIONS

Fodor'sChoice
★
Riverwalk District. The makeover of Reno's waterfront has transformed this formerly dilapidated area into the toast of the town. The Riverwalk itself is a half-mile promenade on the north side of the Truckee River, which flows around lovely Wingfield Park, where outdoor festivals and other events take place. On the third Saturday of each month, local merchants host a **Wine Walk** between 2 and 5. For $20, you receive a wine glass and can sample fine wines at participating shops, bars, restaurants, and galleries. In July look for stellar outdoor art, opera, dance, and kids' performances as part of the monthlong **Artown festival** (⊕ *www.renoisartown.com*), presented mostly in Wingfield Park. Also at Wingfield is the **Truckee River Whitewater Park.** With activities for all skill levels, it's become a major attraction for water-sports enthusiasts. ⊠ *Riverwalk, north side of Truckee River between Lake and Ralston Sts.* ⊕ *www.renoriver.org.*

Eldorado. Action packed, with lots of slots and popular bar-top video poker, this casino also has good coffee-shop and food-court fare. Don't miss the Fountain of Fortune with its massive Florentine-inspired sculptures.

✉ *345 N. Virginia St., at W. 4th St.*
☏ *775/786–5700, 800/879–8879*
⊕ *www.eldoradoreno.com.*

FAMILY **Fleischmann Planetarium.** Digital star shows provide the glittering lights inside this facility that aims to make learning about astronomy entertaining for kids and adults. ✉ *University of Nevada, 1650 N. Virginia St., near E. 15th St.* ☏ *775/784–4811* ⊕ *www.planetarium.unr.nevada.edu* ✉ *Exhibits free; films and star shows $7* ◷ *Mon.–Thurs. noon–7; Fri. noon–9; Sat. 10–9, Sun. 10–7.*

RENO'S RIVERWALK

Stroll along the Truckee River and check out the art galleries, cinema, specialty shops, theater, and restaurants that line this lively refurbished section of town near Reno's casino district.

13

FAMILY **National Automobile Museum.** Antique and classic automobiles, including an Elvis Presley Cadillac, a Mercury coupe driven by James Dean in the movie *Rebel Without a Cause,* and the experimental and still futuristic-looking 1938 Phantom Corsair are all on display here. ✉ *10 S. Lake St., at Mill St.* ☏ *775/333–9300* ⊕ *www.automuseum.org* ✉ *$10* ◷ *Mon.–Sat. 9:30–5:30, Sun. 10–4.*

Nevada Museum of Art. A dramatic structure designed by Will Bruder houses this splendid museum's collection, which focuses on themes such as the Sierra Nevada/Great Basin and altered-landcape photography. Important traveling exhibitions often come here. ✉ *160 W. Liberty St., and Hill St.* ☏ *775/329–3333* ⊕ *www.nevadaart.org* ✉ *$10* ◷ *Wed. and Fri.–Sun. 10–5, Thurs. 10–8.*

Peppermill. A few miles from downtown, this casino is known for its excellent restaurants and neon-bright gambling areas. The Fireside cocktail lounge is a blast. ✉ *2707 S. Virginia St., at Peppermill La.* ☏ *775/826–2121, 866/821–9996* ⊕ *www.peppermillreno.com.*

WORTH NOTING

FAMILY **Circus Circus.** Families with kids head to this casino, where a midway above the floor has clowns, games, fun-house mirrors, and circus acts. ✉ *500 N. Sierra St., at W. 5th St.* ☏ *775/329–0711, 800/648–5010* ⊕ *www.circusreno.com.*

Harrah's. Occupying two city blocks, this landmark property has a sprawling casino and an outdoor promenade. ✉ *219 N. Center St., at E. 2nd St.* ☏ *775/786–3232, 800/427–7247* ⊕ *www.harrahsreno.com.*

Silver Legacy. A 120-foot-tall mining rig and video poker games draw gamblers to this razzle-dazzle casino. ✉ *407 N. Virginia St., at W. 4th St.* ☏ *775/329–4777, 800/687–8733* ⊕ *www.silverlegacyreno.com.*

WHERE TO EAT

$$$ ✕ **4th St. Bistro.** For deliciously simple, smart cooking, head to this
AMERICAN charming little bistro on the edge of town. The chef-owner uses organic produce and meats in her soulful preparations of dishes like grilled Moroccan spiced chicken breast with garbanzo beans and couscous. Ochre-color sponge-painted walls, tablecloths from Provence, and a roaring fireplace in winter warm the dining room. ⑤ *Average main: $30* ✉ *3065 W. 4th St.* ☏ *775/323–3200* ⊕ *www.4thstbistro.com* ◷ *Closed Sun. and Mon. No lunch.*

$ ✕**Bangkok Cuisine.** To eat well but not break the bank, come to this
THAI busy Thai restaurant and sample the delicious soups, salads, stir-fries, and curries. $ *Average main: $11* ✉ *55 Mt. Rose St., at S. Virginia St.* ☎ *775/322–0299* ⊕ *thaifoodreno.com* ☻ *No lunch Sun.*

$$$ ✕**Beaujolais Bistro.** This restaurant serves earthy, country-style French
FRENCH food with zero pretension—classics like beef bourguignon, roast duck,
Fodor's Choice escargots, and steak frites Béarnaise, all lovingly prepared and seasoned
★ just right. Less expensive small plates are also on the menu, or you can splurge on a sumptuous five-course $62 prix-fixe offering that changes nightly. The airy dining room has an inviting, casual vibe. $ *Average main: $28* ✉ *130 West St.* ☎ *775/323–2227* ⊕ *www.beaujolaisbistro. com* ☻ *Closed Mon. No lunch weekends.*

$ ✕**Chocolate Bar.** Part café, part cocktail bar, this hip little spot close to
CAFÉ the river makes truffles, chocolate fondue, fabulous fruity cocktails, gourmet appetizers, and hot chocolate, all served at a long wooden bar or at several tables and leather banquettes. Chocolate Bar is open late each night for those craving dessert, a chocolate cocktail, or a simple, unadorned cognac. $ *Average main: $13* ✉ *95 N. Sierra St., at W. 1st St.* ☎ *775/337–1122* ⊕ *www.thechocbar.com.*

WHERE TO STAY
For expanded hotel reviews, visit Fodors.com.

$ 🏨**Eldorado.** In the middle of glittering downtown, the resort's huge
HOTEL tower has rooms overlooking either the mountains or the lights of the city. **Pros:** fun; good food; amusingly kitschy decor. **Cons:** noisy. $ *Rooms from: $79* ✉ *345 N. Virginia St.* ☎ *775/786–5700, 800/879–8879* ⊕ *www.eldoradoreno.com* ⮌ *679 rooms, 137 suites* ⦿*No meals.*

$ 🏨**Harrah's.** Of the big-name casino hotels in downtown Reno, double-
HOTEL towered Harrah's does a good job, with no surprises. **Pros:** sets the standard for downtown Reno; great midweek rates. **Cons:** huge property. $ *Rooms from: $67* ✉ *219 N. Center St., at E. 2nd St.* ☎ *775/786–3232, 800/427–7247* ⊕ *www.harrahsreno.com* ⮌ *876 rooms, 52 suites* ⦿*No meals.*

$ 🏨**Peppermill.** A few miles removed from downtown Reno's flashy main
HOTEL drag, this property generates its own glitz with a dazzlilng neon-filled casino. **Pros:** luxurious rooms; casino decor; good (and inexpensive) coffee shop. **Cons:** deluge of neon may be off-putting to some. $ *Rooms from: $99* ✉ *2707 S. Virginia St., at Peppermill La.* ☎ *775/826–2121, 866/821–9996* ⊕ *www.peppermillreno.com* ⮌ *915 rooms, 720 suites* ⦿*No meals.*

THE FAR NORTH

With Lake Shasta, Mt. Shasta, and
Lassen Volcanic National Park

WELCOME TO THE FAR NORTH

TOP REASONS TO GO

★ **Mother Nature's wonders:** California's Far North has more rivers, streams, lakes, forests, and mountains than you'll ever have time to explore.

★ **Rock and roll:** With two volcanoes to entice you—Lassen and Shasta—you can learn first-hand what happens when a mountain blows its top.

★ **Fantastic fishing:** Whether you like casting from a riverbank or letting your line bob beside a boat, you'll find fabulous fishing in all the northern counties.

★ **Cool hops:** On a hot day there's nothing quite as inviting as a visit to Chico's world-famous Sierra Nevada Brewery. Take the tour and then savor a chilled glass on tap at the adjacent brewpub.

★ **Shasta:** Wonderful in all its forms: lake, dam, river, mountain, forest, and town.

1 **From Chico to Mt Shasta.** The Far North is bisected, south to north, by Interstate 5, which passes through several historic towns and state parks, as well as miles of mountainous terrain. Halfway to the Oregon border is Lake Shasta, a favorite recreation destination, and farther north stands the spectacular snowy peak of Mt. Shasta.

2 **The Backcountry.** East of Interstate 5, the Far North's main corridor, dozens of scenic two-lane roads crisscross the wilderness, leading to dramatic mountain peaks and fascinating natural wonders. Small towns settled in the second half of the 19th century seem frozen in time, except that they are well equipped with tourist amenities.

GETTING ORIENTED

The Far North is a vast area that stretches from the upper reaches of the Sacramento Valley north to the Oregon border and east to Nevada. The region includes all or part of eight counties with sparsely populated rural farming and mountain communities, as well as thriving small cities in the valley. Much of the landscape was shaped by two volcanoes—Mt. Shasta and Mt. Lassen—that draw amateur geologists, weekend hikers, and avid mountain climbers to their rugged terrain. An intricate network of high mountain watersheds feeds lakes large and small, plus streams and rivers that course through several forests.

14

Updated by Christine Vovakes

The wondrous landscape of California's northeastern corner, relatively unmarred by development, congestion, and traffic, is the product of volcanic activity. At the southern end of the Cascade Range, Lassen Volcanic National Park is the best place to witness the Far North's fascinating geology. Beyond the sulfur vents and bubbling mud pots, the park owes much of its beauty to 10,457-foot Mt. Lassen and 50 wilderness lakes.

The most enduring image of the region, though, is Mt. Shasta, whose 14,179-foot snowcapped peak beckons outdoor adventurers of all kinds. There are many versions of Shasta to enjoy—the mountain, the lake, the river, the town, the dam, and the forest—all named after the Native Americans known as the Shatasla, or Sastise, who once inhabited the region. The Far North's soaring mountain peaks, wild rivers teeming with trout, and almost unlimited recreational possibilities make it the perfect destination for sports lovers. You won't find many hot nightspots or cultural enclaves, but you will find superlative hiking and fishing.

PLANNING

WHEN TO GO

Heat scorches the valley in summer. Temperatures above 110°F are common, but the mountains provide cool respite. Fall throughout the Far North is beautiful, rivaled only by spring, when wildflowers and almond orchards bloom and mountain creeks fed by the snowmelt splash through the forests. Winter is usually temperate in the valley, but cold and snowy in high country. A few favorite tourist attractions are closed in winter.

GETTING HERE AND AROUND

AIR TRAVEL

For the cheapest fares, fly into Sacramento (⇨ *Chapter 22, Sacramento and the Gold Country*) and then rent a car—you'll need one anyway—and drive north. Chico and Redding, both served by United Express, have small airports. Neither has shuttle service, but you can take a taxi for about $30 to downtown Redding or $21 to downtown Chico.

Air Contacts Redding Municipal Airport ⊠ *6751 Woodrum Circle, off Airport Rd., Redding* ☎ *530/224-4320* ⊕ *www.ci.redding.ca.us/transeng/airports/rma.htm.*

Ground Transportation Taxi Service, Chico ☎ *530/893-4444, 530/342-2929.* **Taxi Service, Redding** ☎ *530/246-0577, 530/222-1234.*

BUS TRAVEL

Greyhound buses stop in Burney, Chico, Red Bluff, Redding, Susanville, and Weed. Various transit authorities provide local bus transportation *(see individual town listings for details)*, though few tourists avail themselves of it.

Bus Contact Greyhound ☎ *800/231-2222* ⊕ *www.greyhound.com.*

CAR TRAVEL

Interstate 5 runs up the center of California through Red Bluff and Redding. Chico is east of Interstate 5 on Highway 32. Lassen Volcanic National Park can be reached by Highway 36 from Red Bluff or (except in winter) Highway 44 from Redding. Highway 299 connects Weaverville, Redding and Alturas. U.S. 395 leads from Susanville to Alturas. Highway 89 will take you from Mt. Shasta to Quincy. Highway 36 links Chester and Susanville. Check weather reports and carry detailed maps, warm clothing, and tire chains whenever you head into mountainous terrain in winter.

Road Conditions Caltrans Current Highway Conditions ☎ *800/427-7623* ⊕ *www.dot.ca.gov.*

TRAIN TRAVEL

Amtrak serves Chico, Redding, and Dunsmuir.

Train Contacts Amtrak ☎ *800/872-7245* ⊕ *www.amtrak.com.*

RESTAURANTS

Redding, the urban center of the Far North, and college-town Chico have the greatest selection of restaurants. Cafés and simple eateries are the rule in the smaller towns, though trendy, innovative restaurants have been popping up. Dress is always informal. *Prices in the reviews are the average cost of a main course at dinner or, if dinner is not served, at lunch.*

HOTELS

Aside from the large chain hotels and motels in Redding and Chico, most accommodations in the Far North blend rustic appeal, simplicity, and coziness. Rooms in Redding, Chico, and Red Bluff usually are booked solid only during popular local events. Wilderness resorts close in fall and reopen after the snow season ends in May. For summer holiday weekends in towns such as Mt. Shasta, Dunsmuir, and Chester, and at camping sites within state or national parks, make lodging reservations well in advance. *Prices in the reviews are the lowest cost of a standard double room in high season. For expanded hotel reviews, visit Fodors.com.*

B&B Info California Association of Bed & Breakfast Inns ☎ 800/373-9251 ⊕ www.cabbi.com/region/Mount-Shasta.

VISITOR INFORMATION

Contacts Lassen County Chamber of Commerce ✉ 75 N. Weatherlow St., Susanville ☎ 530/257-4323 ⊕ www.lassencountychamber.com. **Shasta Cascade Wonderland Association** ✉ 1699 Hwy. 273, Anderson ☎ 530/365-7500, 800/474-2782 ⊕ www.shastacascade.com. **Visit Siskiyou** ☎ 800/926-4865 ⊕ visitsiskiyou.org.

FROM CHICO TO MT. SHASTA

From the blooming almond orchards of the fertile Sacramento River valley, through the forested mountains and to the dominating peak of a dormant volcano, this section of the Far North entices tourists in all seasons.

CHICO

180 miles from San Francisco, east on I–80, north on I–505 to I–5, and east on Hwy. 32; 86 miles north of Sacramento on Hwy. 99.

Chico (which is Spanish for "small") lies in the Sacramento Valley and offers a welcome break from the monotony of Interstate 5. The Chico campus of California State University, the scores of local artisans, and the area's agriculture (primarily almond orchards) all influence the culture here. Chico's true claim to fame, however, is the popular Sierra Nevada Brewery, which keeps beer drinkers across the country happy with its distinctive microbrews.

GETTING HERE AND AROUND

Both Highway 99, coming north from Sacramento or south off Interstate 5 at Red Bluff, and Highway 32, going east off Interstate 5 at Orland, intersect Chico. Amtrak and Greyhound stop here, and United Express flies into the Chico airport. Butte Regional Transit's B-Line buses serve Chico and nearby towns. Anchored by a robust university scene, the downtown neighborhoods are great for walking.

ESSENTIALS

Bus Contact B-Line ☎ 530/342-0221, 800/822-8145 ⊕ www.blinetransit.com.

Visitor Information Chico Chamber of Commerce ✉ 441 Main St., Ste. 150, near E. 5th St. ☎ 530/891-5556, 800/852-8570 ⊕ www.chicochamber.com.

EXPLORING

Bidwell Mansion State Historic Park. Built between 1865 and 1868 by General John Bidwell, the founder of Chico, this mansion was designed by Henry W. Cleaveland, a San Francisco architect. Bidwell and his wife welcomed many distinguished guests to their distinctive pink Italianate home, including President Rutherford B. Hayes, naturalist John Muir, suffragist Susan B. Anthony, and General William T. Sherman. A one-hour tour takes you through most of the mansion's 26 rooms. ✉ *525 The Esplanade, at Memorial Way* ☎ *530/895–6144* ⊕ *www.parks. ca.gov/parkindex* ☞ *$6* ⊗ *Mon. noon–5, weekends 11–5; last tour at 4* ⊗ *Closed Tues.–Fri.*

RED BLUFF ROUND-UP

Check out old-time rodeo at its best during the Red Bluff Round-Up. Held the third weekend of April, this annual event attracts some of the best cowboys in the country. For more information, visit ⊕ *www.redbluffroundup.com.*

14

Bidwell Park. The sprawling 3,670-acre Bidwell Park is a community green space straddling Big Chico Creek, where scenes from *Gone With the Wind* and the 1938 version of *Robin Hood* (starring Errol Flynn) were filmed. The region's recreational hub, it includes a golf course, swimming areas, and paved biking, hiking, and in-line skating trails. One of the largest city-run parks in the country, Bidwell starts as a slender strip downtown and expands eastward 11 miles toward the Sierra foothills. ✉ *300 S. Park Dr., off Hwy. 99* ☎ *530/896–7800* ⊕ *www.bidwellpark.org.*

Sierra Nevada Brewing Company. This pioneer of the microbrewery movement still has a hands-on approach to beer making. Tour the brew house and see how the beer is produced—from the sorting of hops through fermentation and bottling. You can also visit the gift shop and enjoy a hearty lunch or dinner in the brewpub where tastings are available (for a fee). ✉ *1075 E. 20th St., at Sierra Nevada St.* ☎ *530/345–2739, 530/899-4776* ⊕ *www.sierranevada.com* ☞ *Free* ⊗ *Tours daily, call for times.*

WHERE TO EAT

$$$
STEAKHOUSE

✕ **5th Street Steakhouse.** Hand-cut steak is the star in this refurbished early 1900s building, the place to come when you're craving red meat and a huge baked potato. Exposed redbrick walls warm the small dining area. A long mahogany bar catches the overflow crowds that jam the place on weekends. Lunch is served on Fridays only. No reservations for parties smaller than six persons are accepted on Fridays and Saturdays. ⑤ *Average main: $29* ✉ *345 W. 5th St., at Normal Ave.* ☎ *530/891–6328* ⊕ *www.5thstreetsteakhouse.com* ⊗ *No lunch Sat.–Thurs.*

$
AMERICAN

✕ **Madison Bear Garden.** This downtown favorite two blocks south of the Chico State campus is a great spot for checking out the vibrant college scene while enjoying a burger and a brew. ⑤ *Average main: $8* ✉ *316 W. 2nd St., at Salem St.* ☎ *530/891–1639* ⊕ *madisonbeargarden.com.*

$$$
MEDITERRANEAN

✕ **Red Tavern.** With its burgundy carpet, white linen tablecloths, and mellow lighting, this is one of Chico's coziest restaurants. The Mediterranean-influenced menu, inspired by fresh local produce, changes seasonally. There's a great California wine list, and also a full bar. ⑤ *Average main: $25* ✉ *1250 The Esplanade, at E. 3rd Ave.* ☎ *530/894–3463* ⊕ *www.redtavern.com* ⊗ *No dinner on Sunday, brunch only.*

WHERE TO STAY

For expanded hotel reviews, visit Fodors.com.

$$ $\boxdot$ **Hotel Diamond.** Crystal chandeliers and gleaming wood floors and
HOTEL banisters elegantly welcome guests into the foyer of this restored gem
in downtown Chico near the university. **Pros:** refined; great location;
breakfast voucher included in room rate. **Cons:** not a good choice
for families. $\boxed{\$}$ *Rooms from: $139* $\boxtimes$ *220 W. 4th St., near Broadway*
$\textcircled{\small{a}}$ *530/893–3100, 866/993–3100* $\oplus$ *www.hoteldiamondchico.com*
$\rightharpoondown$ *39 rooms, 4 suites* $\lvert\odot\rvert$ *Breakfast.*

SHOPPING

Made in Chico. This establishment sells locally made goods, including
pottery, olives, almonds, and Woof and Poof creations—whimsical
home decor items, such as stuffed Santas, elves, animals, and pillows.
$\boxtimes$ *127 W. 3rd St., between Main St. and Broadway* $\textcircled{\small{a}}$ *530/894–7009*
$\oplus$ *www.madeinchicostore.com.*

Needham Studios. Beautiful custom-made etched, stained, and bev-
eled glass is created at Needham Studios. $\boxtimes$ *237 Broadway, at 3rd St.*
$\textcircled{\small{a}}$ *530/345–4718* $\oplus$ *www.needhamstudios.com.*

Satava Art Glass Studio. Shop and watch demonstrations of glassblow-
ing at the Satava Art Glass Studio. $\boxtimes$ *819 Wall St.* $\textcircled{\small{a}}$ *530/345–7985*
$\oplus$ *satava.com.*

RED BLUFF

41 miles north of Chico on Hwy 99.

Historic Red Bluff is a gateway to Lassen Volcanic National Park.
Established in the mid-19th century as a shipping center and named for
the color of its soil, the town is filled with dozens of restored Victorians.
It's a great home base for outdoor adventures in the area.

GETTING HERE AND AROUND

Access Red Bluff via exits off Interstate 5, or by driving north on High-
way 99. Highway 36 is a long, twisting road that begins near the Pacific
Coast and goes to Red Bluff, then east to the towns near Lassen Vol-
canic National Park. Greyhound buses stop here and also provide con-
necting service to Amtrak. TRAX (Tehama Rural Area Express) serves
Red Bluff and neighboring towns.

ESSENTIALS

Bus Information TRAX $\textcircled{\small{a}}$ *530/385–2877* $\oplus$ *www.taketrax.com.*

Visitor Information Red Bluff–Tehama County Chamber of Commerce
$\boxtimes$ *100 Main St., at Rio St.* $\textcircled{\small{a}}$ *530/527–6220* $\oplus$ *www.redbluffchamber.com.*

EXPLORING

William B. Ide Adobe State Historic Park. Named for the first and only
president of the short-lived California Republic of 1846, William B.
Ide Adobe State Historic Park is on an oak-lined bank of the Sacra-
mento River. The Bear Flag Party proclaimed California a sovereign
nation, separate from Mexican rule, and the republic existed for 22
days before it was taken over by the United States. The republic's
flag has survived, with minor refinements, as California's state flag.

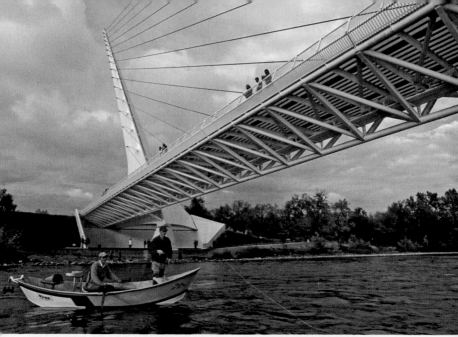
Fisherman under Santiago Calatrava's striking Sundial Bridge next to Turtle Bay Exploration Park

The park's main attraction is an adobe home built in the 1850s and outfitted with period furnishings. ⊠ *21659 Adobe Rd., at Park Pl.* ☎ *530/529–8599* ⊕ *www.parks.ca.gov/?page_id=458* 🖃 *$6 per vehicle* ⊙ *Park and picnic facilities; adobe home and historic sites open Fri.–Sun., varying hrs.*

WHERE TO EAT AND STAY
For expanded hotel reviews, visit Fodors.com.

$$
STEAKHOUSE
✕ **Green Barn Steakhouse.** You're likely to find cowboys sporting Stetsons and spurs feasting on sizzling porterhouse, baby back ribs, and prime rib at Red Bluff's premier steak house. For lighter fare, there's rainbow trout or clam fettuccine. Don't miss the bread pudding with rum sauce. The lounge is usually hopping, especially when there's an event at the nearby rodeo grounds. ⑤ *Average main: $19* ⊠ *5 Chestnut Ave., at Antelope Blvd.* ☎ *530/527–3161* ⌦ *Reservations not accepted* ⊙ *Closed Sun.*

$
HOTEL
🏨 **Sportsman Lodge.** On-site owners keep this small motel neat and inviting, with practical amenities like refrigerators, microwaves, cable TV, and free Wi-Fi. **Pros:** spacious rooms; helpful owners; pet-friendly. **Cons:** an older facility. ⑤ *Rooms from: $62* ⊠ *768 Antelope Blvd., near Trinity Ave.* ☎ *530/527-2888* ⊕ *www.redbluffsportsmanlodge.com* ⌦ *19 rooms.*

REDDING

32 miles north of Red Bluff on I–5.

As the largest city in the Far North, Redding is an ideal headquarters for exploring the surrounding countryside.

GETTING HERE AND AROUND

Reach Redding from exits off Interstate 5 or via Highway 299, which originates near coastal Eureka and crosses Weaverville and Redding before heading northeast to Burney and Alturas. Highway 44 stretches from Susanville past Lassen Park's north entrance before ending in Redding. United Express serves the Redding airport. Amtrak and Greyhound make stops here.

ESSENTIALS

Bus Information Redding Area Bus Authority ☎ *530/241–2877* ⊕ *www.rabaride.com.*

Visitor Information Redding Convention and Visitors Bureau ✉ *2334 Washington Ave., Ste. B* ☎ *530/225–4100, 800/874–7562* ⊕ *www.visitredding.com.*

EXPLORING

Fodor'sChoice
★
FAMILY

Turtle Bay Exploration Park. This park features walking trails, an arboretum and botanical gardens, and lots of interactive exhibits for kids, including a gold-panning area and the seasonal butterfly exhibit. The main draw is the stunning **Sundial Bridge**, which links the Sacramento River Trail and the park's arboretum and gardens. Access to the bridge and arboretum is free, but there's a fee for the museum. ✉ *844 Sundial Bridge Dr., off Hwy. 44* ☎ *530/243–8850* ⊕ *www.turtlebay.org* 🎟 *Museum $14* ⊗ *Apr.–Sept., Mon.–Sat. 9–5, Sun. 10–5; Oct.–Mar., Wed.–Sat. 9–4, Sun. 10–4.*

WHERE TO EAT AND STAY

For expanded hotel reviews, visit Fodors.com.

$$$
STEAKHOUSE

✕ **Jack's Grill.** Famous for its 16-ounce steaks, this popular bar and steak house also serves shrimp and chicken. A town favorite, the place is usually jam-packed and noisy. See Mike at the bar for a great martini. ⑤ *Average main: $24* ✉ *1743 California St., at Sacramento St.* ☎ *530/241–9705* ⊕ *www.jacksgrillredding.com* ⊗ *Closed Sun. No lunch.*

$
AMERICAN

✕ **Klassique Kafe.** Two sisters run this small, bustling restaurant that caters to locals looking for simple but hearty breakfast and lunch fare. The hot luncheon specials served daily might include butter beans and ham with corn bread, or chicken and dumplings. ⑤ *Average main: $9* ✉ *2427 Athens Ave., at Locust St.* ☎ *530/244–4939* ⊗ *Closed Sat. & Sun. No dinner.*

$$$
ITALIAN

✕ **Nello's Place.** Fine Italian dining and romantic ambience go hand-in-hand at one of Redding's best restaurants. You'll find a varied selection of veal, chicken, beef, and pasta dishes mixed with lighter fish and vegetarian fare. For special presentations, order a Caesar salad prepared tableside for two, and bananas flambé for dessert. There's a full bar in addition to an extensinve wine list. ⑤ *Average main: $24* ✉ *3055 Bechelli Ln., near Hartnell Ave., Redding* ☎ *530/223-1636* ⊕ *www. nellosrestaurant.net* ⊗ *Closed Mon.*

$ 🖭 **The Red Lion.** Close to Redding's convention center and regional rec-
HOTEL reation sites, this hotel is a top choice for both business and vacation
travelers. **Pros:** family-friendly; close to a major shopping and dining
area. **Cons:** on a noisy street. ⑤ *Rooms from: $119* ✉ *1830 Hilltop Dr.,
Hwy. 44/299 exit off I–5* ☎ *530/221–8700, 800/733–5466* ⊕ *www.
redlion.com* ⤻ *192 rooms, 2 suites.*

SPORTS AND THE OUTDOORS
FISHING
Fly Shop. This shop sells fishing licenses and has information about
guides, conditions, and fishing packages. ✉ *4140 Churn Creek Rd., at
Denton Way* ☎ *530/222–3555* ⊕ *www.flyshop.com.*

WEAVERVILLE

14

46 miles west of Redding on Hwy. 299.

A man known only as Weaver struck gold here in 1849, and the fledgling community that developed at the base of the Trinity Alps was
named after him. With its impressive downtown historic district, today
Weaverville is a popular headquarters for family vacations and biking,
hiking, fishing, and gold-panning excursions.

GETTING HERE AND AROUND
Highway 299 becomes Main Street down the center of Weaverville.
Take the highway either east from the Pacific Coast or west from Redding. Highway 36 from Red Bluff to Highway 3 heading north leads
to Weaverville. Trinity Transit provides minimal local bus service plus
a line that links Weaverville to Interstate 5 at Redding.

EXPLORING
Trinity County Courthouse. Trinity County Courthouse, built in 1856 as a
store, office building, and hotel, was converted to county use in 1865.
The Apollo Saloon, in the basement, became the county jail. It's the oldest courthouse still in use in California. ✉ *Court and Main Sts.*

Trinity County Historical Park. For a vivid sense of Weaverville's past, visit
the Trinity County Historical Park, especially its **Jake Jackson Memorial Museum,** which has a blacksmith shop and a stamp mill (where
ore is crushed) from the 1890s that is still in use. Also here are the
original jail cells of the Trinity County Courthouse. ✉ *780 Main St., at
Bartlett La.* ☎ *530/623–5211* ⊕ *trinitymuseum.org* 🕘 *Jan.–Mar., Wed.
and Sat. noon–4; Apr. and Oct., daily noon–4; May–Sept., daily 10–5;
Nov. and Dec., Wed.–Sat. 11–4.*

Fodor's Choice **Weaverville Joss House.** Weaverville's main attraction is the Joss House,
★ a Taoist temple built in 1874 and called Won Lim Miao ("the temple
of the forest beneath the clouds") by Chinese miners. The oldest continuously used Chinese temple in California, it attracts worshippers
from around the world. With its golden altar, antique weaponry, and
carved wooden canopies, the Joss House is a piece of California history that can best be appreciated on a guided 30-minute tour. The
original temple building and many of its furnishings—some of which
came from China—were lost to fire in 1873, but members of the
local Chinese community soon rebuilt it. ✉ *630 Main St., at Oregon*

St. ☎ 530/623–5284 ⊕ *www.parks.ca.gov/parkindex* 🖾 *Museum free; guided tour $4* ☉ *Thurs., Sat., and Sun. 10–5; last tour at 4.*

WHERE TO EAT AND STAY

For expanded hotel reviews, visit Fodors.com.

$ ✕ **La Casita.** A traditional selection of Mexican food is on the menu
MEXICAN here, including quesadillas (try the version with roasted chili peppers), tostadas, enchiladas, tacos, and tamales. Many dishes are available without meat. Open from late morning through dinner, this casual spot is great for a midafternoon snack. ⑤ *Average main: $9* ⊠ *252 Main St.* ☎ *530/623–5797* ☉ *Closed Sun.*

$$ ✕ **La Grange Café.** In two brick buildings dating from the 1850s (they're
AMERICAN among the oldest edifices in town), this eatery serves beef, buffalo, and other game meats, pasta, fresh fish, and farmers' market vegetables when they're available. There's a full premium bar, and the wine list is extensive. ⑤ *Average main: $20* ⊠ *520 Main St.* ☎ *530/623–5325* ☉ *Hours sometimes sporadic in winter.*

$ 🏨 **Red Hill Motel.** This 1940s-era property is popular with anglers, who
HOTEL appreciate the outdoor fish-cleaning area on the premises. **Pros:** close to popular bass fishing sites; inexpensive. **Cons:** older facility; some rooms need sprucing up. ⑤ *Rooms from: $53* ⊠ *50 Red Hill Rd.* ☎ *530/623– 4331* ⊕ *www.redhillresorts.com* 🛏 *4 rooms, 6 cabins, 2 duplexes.*

SPORTS AND THE OUTDOORS

Fly Stretch. Below the Lewiston Dam, east of Weaverville on Highway 299, is the Fly Stretch of the Trinity River, an excellent fly-fishing area.

Pine Cove Boat Ramp. This ramp on Lewiston Lake provides fishing access for those with disabilities—decks here are built over prime trout-fishing waters.

Weaverville Ranger Station. Check here for maps and information about hiking trails in the Trinity Alps Wilderness. ⊠ *360 Main St.* ☎ *530/623–2121.*

LAKE SHASTA AREA

12 miles north of Redding on I–5.

When you think of the Lake Shasta Area picture water, wilderness, dazzling stalagmites—and a fabulous man-made project in the midst of it all.

GETTING HERE AND AROUND

Interstate 5 north of Redding is the main link to the entire Lake Shasta area. Get to the dam by passing through tiny City of Shasta Lake. There is no local bus service.

ESSENTIALS

Shasta Cascade Wonderland Association ⊠ *1699 Hwy. 273, Anderson* ☎ *530/365–7500* ⊕ *www.shastacascade.com.*

EXPLORING

Lake Shasta. Twenty-one types of fish inhabit the lake, including rainbow trout and salmon. The lake region also has the largest nesting population of bald eagles in California. You can rent fishing boats, ski boats, sailboats, canoes, paddleboats, Jet Skis, and windsurfing boards at one of the many marinas and resorts along the 370-mile shoreline. ⊠ *Shasta Lake.*

Fodor's Choice **Lake Shasta Caverns.** Stalagmites, stalactites, flowstone deposits, and ★ crystals entice visitors to the Lake Shasta Caverns. To see this impressive spectacle, you must take the two-hour tour, which includes a catamaran ride across the McCloud arm of Lake Shasta and a bus ride up North Grey Rocks Mountain to the cavern entrance. The caverns are 58°F year-round, making them a cool retreat on a hot summer day. The most awe-inspiring of the limestone rock formations is the glistening Cathedral Room, which appears to be gilded. During peak summer months (June through August), tours depart every half hour; in April, May, and September it's every hour. A gift shop is open from 8 to 4:30. ⊠ *20359 Shasta Caverns Rd., off I–5, 17 miles north of Redding, Lakehead* ☎ *530/238–2341, 800/795–2283* ⊕ *lakeshastacaverns.com* ⊡ *$24* ⊙ *June–Aug., tours on the half hour, daily 9–4; Apr., May, and Sept., tours on the hour, daily 9–3; Oct.–Mar., tours at 10, noon, and 2.*

Shasta Dam. This is the second-largest concrete dam in the United States (only Grand Coulee in Washington is bigger). The visitor center has computerized photographic tours of the dam construction, video presentations, fact sheets, and historical displays. Hour-long guided tours inside the dam and its powerhouse leave from the center. ⊠ *16349 Shasta Dam Blvd., off Lake Blvd., Shasta Lake* ☎ *530/275– 1554* ⊕ *www.usbr.gov/mp/ncao* ⊡ *Free* ⊙ *Visitor center daily 8–5; call for tour times.*

WHERE TO EAT

$$ ✕ **Tail o' the Whale.** As its name suggests, this restaurant has a nautical
SEAFOOD theme. You can enjoy a panoramic view of Lake Shasta here while you savor house specials like charbroiled salmon, prime rib with prawns, and pasta dishes. This is a favorite spot for boaters, who anchor at a courtesy dock while they're dining. ⑤ *Average main: $19* ⊠ *10300 Bridge Bay Rd., Bridge Bay exit off I–5* ☎ *530/275–3021* ⊙ *No dinner Mon. and Tues. in winter months.*

SPORTS AND THE OUTDOORS

FISHING

The Fishen Hole. A couple of miles from the lake, this bait-and-tackle shop sells fishing licenses and provides information about conditions. ⊠ *3844 Shasta Dam Blvd., at Red Bluff St., Shasta Lake City* ☎ *530/275–4123.*

HOUSEBOATING

Houseboats here come in all sizes except small. As a rule, rentals are outfitted with cooking utensils, dishes, and most of the equipment you'll need—you supply the food and the linens. When you rent a houseboat, you receive a short course in how to maneuver your launch before you set out. You can fish, swim, sunbathe on the flat roof, or sit on the deck and watch the world go by. The shoreline of Lake Shasta is beautifully ragged, with countless inlets; it's not hard to find privacy.

14

Expect to spend a minimum of $350 a day for a craft that sleeps six. A three-day, two-night minimum is customary. Prices are often lower during the off-season (September through May). Bridge Bay Resort rents houseboats, fishing boats, ski boats, and patio boats. Shasta Cascade offers general information.

Bridge Bay Resort ⊠ 10300 Bridge Bay Rd., Redding ☎ 800/752–9669 ⊕ www.sevencrown.com/lakes/lake_shasta/bridge_bay/index.htm.

Shasta Cascade Wonderland Association ⊠ 1699 Hwy. 273, Anderson ☎ 530/365–7500, 800/474–2782 ⊕ www.shastacascade.com.

DUNSMUIR

10 miles south of Mt. Shasta on I–5.

Castle Crags State Park surrounds the tiny town of Dunsmuir, which was named for a 19th-century Scottish coal baron who offered to build a fountain if the town was renamed in his honor. The town's other major attraction is the Railroad Park Resort, where you can spend the night in restored railcars.

GETTING HERE AND AROUND

Reach Dunsmuir via exits off Interstate 5 at the north and south ends of town. When snow hasn't closed the route, you can take Highway 89 from the Lassen Park area toward Burney then northeast to Interstate 5 at Mt. Shasta. From there it's a 10-mile drive south to Dunsmuir. Amtrak stops here; Greyhound stops in Weed, 20 miles north. On weekdays, STAGE buses serve Dunsmuir.

ESSENTIALS

Bus Information STAGE ☎ 530/842–8295 ⊕ www.co.siskiyou.ca.us/GS/stageschedule.aspx.

Visitor Information Dunsmuir Chamber of Commerce ⊠ 5915 Dunsmuir Ave., Ste. 100 ☎ 530/235–2177 ⊕ dunsmuir.com.

EXPLORING

Fodor's Choice ★ **Castle Crags State Park.** Named for its 6,000-foot glacier-polished crags, which tower over the Sacramento River, this park offers fishing in Castle Creek, hiking in the backcountry, and a view of Mt. Shasta. The crags draw climbers and hikers from around the world. The 4,350-acre park has 28 miles of hiking trails, including a 2.75-mile access trail to **Castle Crags Wilderness**, part of the **Shasta-Trinity National Forest.** There are excellent trails at lower altitudes. Camping is allowed in winter on a first-come, first-served basis. ⊠ 6 miles south of Dunsmuir, Castella/Castle Crags exit off I–5 ☎ 530/235–2684 ⊕ www.parks.ca.gov/parkindex ⊠ $8 per vehicle, day use.

WHERE TO EAT AND STAY

For expanded hotel reviews, visit Fodors.com.

$$
MEDITERRANEAN
✕ **Café Maddalena.** The chef here gained experience working in top San Francisco restaurants before moving north to prepare adventurous Mediterranean fare with a French influence. Selections change seasonally but always feature a vegetarian dish, along with entrées such as Pacific salmon with Meyer lemon sauce, and lamb shoulder with

cassoulet. Wines from Spain, Italy, and France complement the meals. Ask about the daily prix fixe menu. $ *Average main: $19* ✉ *5801 Sacramento Ave.* ☎ *530/235–2725* ⊕ *www.cafemaddalena.com* ⊗ *Closed Mon.–Wed. and Jan.–mid-Feb. No lunch.*

$ 🛏 **Railroad Park Resort.** The antique
HOTEL cabooses here were collected over
FAMILY more than three decades and have been converted into cozy motel rooms in honor of Dunsmuir's railroad legacy. **Pros:** gorgeous setting; kitschy fun. **Cons:** cabooses can feel cramped; restaurant open mid-May through September. $ *Rooms from: $115* ✉ *100 Railroad Park Rd.* ☎ *530/235–4440* ⊕ *www.rrpark.com* ⇝ *23 cabooses, 4 cabins.*

> ### FINE FISHING
>
> The upper Sacramento River near Dunsmuir is consistently rated one of the best fishing spots in the country. Check with the chamber of commerce for local fishing guides.

14

MT. SHASTA

34 miles north of Lake Shasta on I–5.

GETTING HERE AND AROUND

Three exits off Interstate 5 lead to the town of Mt. Shasta. When snow hasn't closed the route, you can take Highway 89 from the Lassen Park area toward Burney then northeast to Mt. Shasta. The ski park is off Highway 89. Greyhound stops at Weed, 10 miles north; Amtrak stops at Dunsmuir, 10 miles south. There's no local bus system.

ESSENTIALS

Visitor Information Mt. Shasta Chamber of Commerce and Visitors Bureau ✉ *300 Pine St., at W. Lake St., Mt. Shasta* ☎ *530/926–4865, 800/926–4865* ⊕ *mtshastachamber.com.*

EXPLORING

Fodor'sChoice **Mt. Shasta.** The crown jewel of the 2.5-million-acre Shasta-Trinity
★ National Forest, Mt. Shasta, a 14,179-foot-high dormant volcano, is a mecca for day hikers. It's especially enticing in spring, when fragrant Shasta lilies and other flowers adorn the rocky slopes. The paved road reaches only as far as the timberline; the final 6,000 feet are a tough climb of rubble, ice, and snow (the summit is perpetually ice packed). Only a hardy few are qualified to make the trek to the top.

The town of Mt. Shasta has real character and some fine restaurants. Lovers of the outdoors and backcountry skiers abound, and they are more than willing to offer advice on the most beautiful spots in the region, which include out-of-the-way swimming holes, dozens of high mountain lakes, and a challenging 18-hole golf course with 360 degrees of spectacular views. ⊕ *mtshastachamber.com.*

WHERE TO EAT AND STAY

For expanded hotel reviews, visit Fodors.com.

$$ ✕**Lilys.** This restaurant in a white-clapboard home, framed by a picket
ECLECTIC fence and arched trellis, serves everything from steaks and pastas to Mexican and vegetarian dishes. Daily specials include prime rib and a fresh fish entrée. For innovative vegetarian fare try a *dal* burger, which

is made with walnuts, fresh veggies, garbanzo beans, and rice. Try their brunch on weekends. ⑤ *Average main: $20* ⊠ *1013 S. Mt. Shasta Blvd., at Holly St.* ☎ *530/926–3372* ⊕ *www.lilysrestaurant.com.*

$ ✕ **Seven Suns Coffee and Cafe.** A favorite gathering spot for locals, this
CAFÉ small coffee shop serves specialty wraps for breakfast and lunch, plus soup and salad selections. Pastries, made daily, include muffins and scones, and blackberry fruit bars in season. If the weather's nice, grab a seat on the patio. ⑤ *Average main: $9* ⊠ *1011 S. Mt. Shasta Blvd., at Holly St.* ☎ *530/926–9701* ⊕ *www.mtshastacoffee.com.*

$$ ⌂ **Best Western Tree House Motor Inn.** The clean, standard rooms at this
HOTEL motel less than a mile from downtown Mt. **Pros:** close to ski park; lobby's roaring fireplace is a big plus on winter days. **Cons:** not all lodging buildings have elevators. ⑤ *Rooms from: $145* ⊠ *111 Morgan Way* ☎ *530/926–3101, 800/545–7164* ⊕ *www.bestwestern.com* ⌁ *98 rooms, 7 suites* ⦿❘ *Breakfast.*

$$ ⌂ **Mount Shasta Resort.** Private chalets are nestled among tall pine trees
RENTAL along the shore of Lake Siskiyou, all with gas-log fireplaces and full kitchens. **Pros:** incredible views; romantic woodsy setting. **Cons:** kids may get bored. ⑤ *Rooms from: $169* ⊠ *1000 Siskiyou Lake Blvd.* ☎ *530/926–3030, 800/958–3363* ⊕ *www.mountshastaresort.com* ⌁ *65 units.*

SPORTS AND THE OUTDOORS
GOLF
Mount Shasta Resort. At a bit under 6,100 yards, the Mount Shasta Resort golf course isn't long, but it's beautiful and challenging, with narrow, tree-lined fairways and natural alpine terrain. Carts rent for $15; fabulous views are free. ⊠ *1000 Siskiyou Lake Blvd.* ☎ *530/926–3052* ⊕ *www.mountshastaresort.com* ⅃ *18 holes. 6035 yds. Par 70. Greens fees: $45/$60* ☞ *Facilities: driving range, putting green, pitching area, golf carts, pull carts, rental clubs, pro shop, golf lessons, restaurant, bar.*

HIKING
Mt. Shasta Forest Service Ranger Station. Check in here for current trail conditions and avalanche reports. ⊠ *204 W. Alma St., at Pine St.* ☎ *530/926–4511, 530/926–9613 avalanche conditions.*

MOUNTAIN CLIMBING
Fifth Season Mountaineering Shop. This shop rents bicycles and skiing and climbing equipment, and operates a recorded 24-hour climber-skier report. ⊠ *300 N. Mt. Shasta Blvd.* ☎ *530/926–3606, 530/926–5555 ski phone* ⊕ *www.thefifthseason.com.*

Shasta Mountain Guides. These guides lead hiking, climbing, and ski-touring groups to the summit of Mt. Shasta. ☎ *530/926–3117* ⊕ *shastaguides.com.*

SKIING
FAMILY **Mt. Shasta Board & Ski Park.** On the southeast flank of Mt. Shasta, this ski park has three triple-chair lifts and one surface lift on 425 skiable acres. Three-quarters of the trails are for beginning or intermediate skiers. The area's vertical drop is 1,435 feet, with a top elevation of 6,890 feet. The longest of the 32 trails is 1.75 miles. A package for beginners, available through the ski school, includes a lift ticket, ski rental, and a lesson. The school also runs ski and snowboard programs

for children. There's night skiing for those who want to see the moon rise as they schuss. The base lodge has a simple café, a ski shop, and a ski-snowboard rental shop. ✉ *Hwy. 89 exit east from I–5, south of Mt. Shasta* 🕿 *530/926–8610, 800/754–7427* ⊕ *www.skipark.com* ⊙ *Winter ski season schedule: Sun.–Wed. 9–4, Thurs.–Sat. 9–9.*

Mt. Shasta Nordic Center. This center, run by a nonprofit, maintains 15 miles of groomed cross-country ski trails. ✉ *Ski Park Hwy., off Hwy. 89 (take I–5's McCloud exit)* 🕿 *530/926–2142* ⊕ *mtshastanordic.org.*

THE BACKCOUNTRY

14

The Far North's primitive, rugged backcountry is arguably full of more natural wonders than any other region in California.

MCARTHUR–BURNEY FALLS MEMORIAL STATE PARK

Hwy. 89, 52 miles southeast of Mt. Shasta and 41 miles north of Lassen Volcanic National Park.

GETTING HERE AND AROUND

To see some stunning falls, head east off Interstate 5 on Highway 89 at Mt. Shasta. The drive is 52 miles. From Interstate 5 in Redding, head east 55 miles on Highway 299 to connect with Highway 89; follow signs 6 miles to the park. From Alturas, head west on Highway 299 for about 86 miles and hook up with Highway 89.

EXPLORING

Fodor's Choice
★
FAMILY

McArthur–Burney Falls Memorial State Park. Just inside the park's southern boundary, Burney Creek wells up from the ground and divides into two falls that cascade over a 129-foot cliff into a pool below. Countless ribbonlike streams pour from hidden moss-covered crevices; resident bald eagles are frequently seen soaring overhead. You can walk a self-guided nature trail that descends to the foot of the falls, which Theodore Roosevelt—according to legend—called "the eighth wonder of the world." On warm days, swim at Lake Britton; lounge on the beach; rent motorboats, paddleboats, and canoes; or relax at one of the campsites or picnic areas. The camp store is open from late April to the end of October. ✉ *24898 Hwy. 89, 6 miles north of Hwy. 299, Burney* 🕿 *530/335–2777* ⊕ *www.parks.ca.gov/parkindex* 🏷 *$8 per vehicle, day use.*

ALTURAS

86 miles northeast of McArthur–Burney Falls Memorial State Park on Hwy. 299.

Alturas is the county seat and largest town in Modoc County. The Dorris family arrived in the area in 1874, built Dorris Bridge over the Pit River, and later opened a small wayside stop for travelers. As in the past, travelers today come to see eagles and other wildlife, the Modoc National Forest, and active geothermal areas.

GETTING HERE AND AROUND

To get to Alturas from Susanville take Main Street/Highway 36 south for about 4 miles; turn left at U.S. 395 and stay on that highway for 99 miles. From Redding, take the Lake Blvd./299E exit off Interstate 5, head east and stay on Highway 299 for 140 miles. Sage Stage buses serve Alturas from Redding and Susanville.

ESSENTIALS

Bus Information Modoc County Sage Stage ☎ 530/233–3883, 530/233–6410 ⊕ www.sagestage.com.

Visitor Information Alturas Chamber of Commerce ✉ 600 S. Main St. ☎ 530/233–4434 ⊕ www.alturaschamberofcommerce.org.

EXPLORING

Modoc National Forest. Encompassing 1.6 million acres, Modoc National Forest protects 300 species of wildlife, including Rocky Mountain elk, wild horses, mule deer, and pronghorn antelope. In spring and fall, watch for migratory waterfowl as they make their way along the Pacific Flyway above the forest. Hiking trails lead to Petroglyph Point, one of the largest panels of rock art in the United States. ✉ *Park Headquarters, 800 W. 12th St.* ☎ *530/233–5811* ⊕ *www.fs.usda.gov/modoc.*

Modoc National Wildlife Refuge. The 7,021-acre Modoc National Wildlife Refuge was established in 1961 to protect migratory waterfowl. You might see Canada geese, sandhill cranes, mallards, teal, wigeon, pintail, white pelicans, cormorants, and snowy egrets. The refuge is open for hiking, bird-watching, and photography, but one area is set aside for hunters. Regulations vary according to season. ✉ *U.S. 395, 1½ miles south of Alturas, left on Rd. 56, then right on Rd. 115* ☎ *530/233–3572* ⊕ *www.fws.gov/refuge/modoc/* ▷ *Free* ☉ *Daily dawn–dusk.*

WHERE TO EAT

$$ ✕ **Brass Rail.** Prix-fixe dinners at this authentic Basque restaurant include
SPANISH wine, homemade bread, soup, salad, side dishes, coffee, and ice cream. Steak, lamb chops, fried chicken, shrimp, and scallops are among the best entrée selections. A lounge with a full bar adjoins the dining area. ⑤ *Average main: $21* ✉ *395 Lake View Dr., at Lake Rd.* ☎ *530/233–2906* ☉ *Closed Mon.*

SUSANVILLE

104 miles south of Alturas via U.S. 395; 65 miles east of Lassen Volcanic National Park via Highway 36.

Susanville, established as a trading post in 1854, tells the tale of its rich history through murals painted on buildings in the historic uptown area. You can take a self-guided tour around the original buildings and stop for a bite at one of the restaurants now housed within them. If you'd rather work up a sweat, you can hit the Bizz Johnson Trail and Eagle Lake recreation areas just outside town.

GETTING HERE AND AROUND

U.S. 395 connects Susanville and Alturas, about a 100-mile trip. From Red Bluff, take Interstate 5's Highway 36E/Fairgrounds exit and drive east for about 3 miles; turn left at Highway 36E and continue through the mountains for 103 miles. Lassen Rural Bus serves Susanville Monday through Saturday, and surrounding areas on weekdays only.

ESSENTIALS

Bus Information Lassen Rural Bus ☏ *530/252–7433* ⊕ *www.lassentransportation.org.*

Visitor Information Lassen County Chamber of Commerce ⊠ *75 N. Weatherlow St., off Main St.* ☏ *530/257–4323* ⊕ *www.lassencountychamber.com.*

EXPLORING

Bizz Johnson Trail. Bizz Johnson Trail follows a defunct line of the Southern Pacific Railroad for 25 miles. Known to locals as the Bizz, the trail is open for hikers, walkers, mountain bikers, horseback riders, and cross-country skiers. It skirts the Susan River through a scenic landscape of canyons, bridges, and forests abundant with wildlife. ⊠ *Trailhead, old railroad depot, 601 Richmond Rd., near N. Railroad Ave.* ☏ *530/257–0456* ⊕ *www.blm.gov/ca/eaglelake/bizztrail.html* ⊠ *Free.*

Eagle Lake. Anglers travel great distances to fish the waters of this large lake where the trout is prized for its size and fighting ability. Surrounded by high desert to the north and alpine forests to the south, Eagle Lake is also popular for picnicking, hiking, boating, waterskiing and windsurfing, and bird-watching—ospreys, pelicans, and many other waterfowl visit the lake. On land you might see mule deer, small mammals, and even pronghorn antelope—and be sure to watch for bald-eagle nesting sites. ⊠ *16 miles north of Susanville, Eagle Lake Rd. off Hwy. 139* ☏ *530/257–0456 for Eagle Lake Recreation Area, 530/825–3454 for Eagle Lake Marina* ⊕ *www.blm.gov/ca/eaglelake.*

WHERE TO EAT AND STAY

For expanded hotel reviews, visit Fodors.com.

$ ✕ **Mazatlan Grill.** The sauces are prepared on-site in this friendly, family-
MEXICAN run restaurant and lounge, which serves lunch and dinner daily. The dining room is simple and tidy, with comfortable upholstered booths. The extensive menu offers authentic, inexpensive Mexican fare ranging from fajitas and enchiladas to a vegetarian burrito. $ *Average main: $10* ⊠ *1535 Main St., at Park St.* ☏ *530/257–1800.*

$ ▦ **Best Western Trailside Inn Susanville.** This large, business-friendly motel
HOTEL is in the heart of Susanville but only a quick drive from the area's recreational sites. **Pros:** central location; seasonal pool; free breakfast. **Cons:** Main Street location can be noisy. $ *Rooms from: $85* ⊠ *2785 Main St., near Russell St.* ☏ *530/257–4123* ⊕ *www.bestwesterncalifornia.com* ⟿ *85 rooms* ⦿| *Breakfast.*

$ ▦ **High Country Inn.** Rooms are spacious in this colonial-style motel on
HOTEL the eastern edge of town. **Pros:** great mountain views; heated pool. **Cons:** lots of traffic in the area. $ *Rooms from: $84* ⊠ *3015 Riverside Dr., at Main St.* ☏ *530/257–3450, 866/454–4566* ⊕ *www.high-country-inn.com* ⟿ *66 rooms* ⦿| *Breakfast.*

Lassen Volcanic National Park

TO BURNEY

Cinder Cone

Butte Lake

Prospect Peak 8,338 ft.

Ash Butte

PAINTED DUNES

Snag Lake

FANTASTIC LAVA BEDS

Fairfield Peak

Crater Butte

Juniper Lake

Horseshoe Lake

GRASSY SWALE

Pacific Crest Trail

TO CHESTER AND SUSANVILLE

Warner Valley

Hat Mt.

DERSCH MEADOWS

Summit Lake North

Summit Lake South

CORRAL MEADOW

READING PEAK

Devil's Kitchen

DEVASTATED AREA

CHAOS CRAGS

Lassen Peak 10,457 ft.

Bumpass Hell

Kings Creek

TWIN MEADOWS

Entrance Station

Ranger Station

Manzanita Lake

BLUE LAKE CANYON

Sulphur Works

Kohm Yah-mah-nee Visitor Center

Entrance Station

TO REDDING

TO RED BLUFF AND CHICO

1/2 mi

1/2 km

0

0

LASSEN VOLCANIC NATIONAL PARK

45 miles east of Redding on Hwy. 44; 48 miles east of Red Bluff on Hwy. 36.

GETTING HERE AND AROUND

Whether coming from the west or the east, reach the park's southern entrance via Highway 36E, and turn onto Highway 89 for a short drive to the park. The northwest entrance is reached via Highway 44 from Redding and Susanville. No buses serve the area.

EXPLORING

Fodor's Choice ★ **Lassen Scenic Byway.** This 185-mile scenic drive begins in Chester and loops through the forests, volcanic peaks, geothermal springs, and lava fields of Lassen National Forest and Lassen National Park, providing for an all-day excursion into dramatic wilderness. From Chester, take Route 36 west to Route 89 north through the park, then Route 44 east to Route 36 west. Parts of the road are inaccessible in winter. ☎ *800/427–7623 CA Highway info service, 530/595–4480 Lassen Park visitor center.*

Fodor's Choice ★ **Lassen Volcanic National Park.** A dormant plug dome, Lassen Peak is the focus of Lassen Volcanic National Park's 165.6 square miles of distinctive landscape. The peak began erupting in May 1914, sending pumice, rock, and snow thundering down the mountain and gas and hot ash billowing into the atmosphere. Lassen's most spectacular outburst occurred in 1915 when it blew a cloud of ash some 7 miles into the stratosphere. The resulting mudflow destroyed vegetation for miles in some directions; the evidence is still visible today, especially in the Devastated Area. The volcano finally came to rest in 1921. Today, fumaroles, mud pots, lakes, and bubbling hot springs create a fascinating but dangerous landscape that can be viewed throughout the park, especially via a hiked descent into Bumpass Hell. Because of its significance as a volcanic landscape, Lassen became a national park in 1916. Several volcanoes—the largest of which is now Lassen Peak—have been active in the area for roughly 600,000 years. The four types of volcanoes found in the world are represented in the park, including shield (Prospect Peak), plug dome (Lassen Peak), cinder cone (Cinder Cone), and composite (Brokeoff Volcano). Lassen Park Road (the continuation of Highway 89 within the park) and 150 miles of hiking trails provide access to many of these volcanic wonders. ■**TIP**➔ **Caution is key here: heed signs that warn visitors to stay on the trails and railed boardwalks to avoid falling into boiling water or through dangerous thin-crusted areas of the park.** Although the park is closed to cars in winter, it's usually open to intrepid cross-country skiers and snowshoers. The Kohm Yah-mah-nee Visitor Center, at the southwest entrance to the park, is open year-round. ⊕ *www.nps.gov/lavo* 💲*$10 per car, $5 per person if not in a car.*

FAMILY **Sulphur Works Thermal Area.** Proof of Lassen Peak's volatility becomes evident shortly after you enter the park at the southwest entrance. Sidewalks skirt boiling springs and sulphur-emitting steam vents. This area is usually the last site to close because of snow. ⊠ *Lassen Park Rd., 1 mile from the southwest entrance ranger station.*

SPORTS AND THE OUTDOORS

HIKING

Fodor'sChoice
★
Bumpass Hell Trail. Boiling springs, steam vents, and mudpots highlight this 3-mile round-trip hike. Expect the loop to take about two hours. During the first mile of the hike there's a gradual climb of 500 feet before a steep 300-foot descent to the basin. You'll encounter rocky patches, so wear hiking boots. Stay on trails and boardwalks near the thermal areas, as what appears to be firm ground may be only a thin crust over scalding mud. *Moderate.* ⊠ *Trailhead at end of paved parking area off Lassen Park Rd., 6 miles from the southwest entrance ranger station.*

WORD OF MOUTH

"Lassen is one of those best-kept-secret spots. It has a little bit of everything: peaks, waterfalls, snow, trees, awesome flowers, a mini Yellowstone, and not tons of folks everywhere."

—spirobulldog

14

Fodor'sChoice
★
Lassen Peak Hike. This trail winds 2½ miles to the mountaintop. It's a tough climb—2,000 feet uphill on a steady, steep grade—but the reward is a spectacular view. At the peak you can see into the rim and view the entire park (and much of California's far north). Bring sunscreen, water, and a jacket since it's often windy and much cooler at the summit. ■TIP➜ **A multiyear restoration project means that all or part of the trail will be open only a few times during the year, so call ahead. Depending on funding, trail work is expected to be completed in 2015.** ⊠ *Trailhead past a paved parking area off Lassen Park Rd., 7 miles north of the southwest entrance ranger station* ☎ *530/595–4480.*

CHESTER

36 miles west of Susanville on Hwy 36.

The population of this small town on Lake Almanor swells from 2,500 to nearly 5,000 in summer as tourists come to visit. Chester serves as a gateway to Lassen Volcanic National Park.

GETTING HERE AND AROUND

Chester is on Highway 36E. When snow doesn't close Highway 89, the main road through Lassen Park, visitors can take Highway 44 from Redding to Highway 89 through the park and to Highway 36E and onto Chester and Lake Almanor. Plumas County Transit connects Chester to the Quincy area.

ESSENTIALS

Bus Information Plumas County Transit ☎ *530/283–2538*
⊕ *www.plumastransit.com.*

Visitor Information Lake Almanor Area Chamber of Commerce and Visitors Bureau ⊠ *162 Main St., near Stone Ave.* ☎ *530/258–2426*
⊕ *www.lakealmanorarea.com.*

Lassen Volcanic National Park's King Creek Falls Hike, which takes you through forests and meadows dotted with wildflowers, is a good hike for nature photographers.

EXPLORING

Lake Almanor. This lake's 52 miles of shoreline lie in the shadow of Mt. Lassen, and are popular with campers, swimmers, water-skiers, and anglers. At an elevation of 4,500 feet, the lake warms to above 70°F for about eight weeks in summer. ⊠ *Off Hwys. 89 and 36* ☎ *530/258–2426.*

WHERE TO EAT AND STAY

For expanded hotel reviews, visit Fodors.com.

$ ✕ **Kopper Kettle Cafe.** Locals return again and again to this tidy res-
AMERICAN taurant that serves home-cooked lunches and dinners. Head here for breakfast whenever you've got a hankering for scrambled eggs or biscuits and gravy. ⑤ *Average main: $14* ⊠ *243 Main St., at Myrtle St.* ☎ *530/258–2698.*

$ ✕ **Maria's Mexican Restaurant.** A festive atmosphere prevails in this
MEXICAN family-friendly restaurant and lounge, where traditional south-of-the-border fare is served. It's one of the few restaurants in the area with a full bar, a great place to enjoy a margarita at the end of a long day spent hiking. ⑤ *Average main: $10* ⊠ *159 Main St., at Willow Way* ☎ *530/258–2262* ☉ *Closed Sun.*

$ ⊡ **Best Western Rose Quartz Inn.** Down the road from Lake Almanor
HOTEL and close to Lassen Volcanic National Park, this small-town inn balances traditional decor and up-to-the-minute amenities like Wi-Fi. **Pros:** near national park; all beds have white duvet covers. **Cons:** standard rooms on the pricey side. ⑤ *Rooms from: $120* ⊠ *306 Main St., Chester* ☎ *530/258–2002, 888/571–4885* ⊕ *www.bestwesterncalifornia.com/ chester-hotels* ⇱ *51 rooms* ⦿ *Breakfast.*

$$ ▦ **Bidwell House.** Some guest rooms at this 1901 ranch house have
B&B/INN wood-burning stoves, claw-foot tubs, and antique furnishings; a sepa-
Fodor'sChoice rate cottage with a kitchen sleeps six. **Pros:** unique decor in each room;
★ beautiful wooded setting; near Lake Almanor. **Cons:** not ideal for kids.
⑤ *Rooms from: $125* ✉ *1 Main St., Chester* ☎ *530/258–3338* ⊕ *www.
bidwellhouse.com* ⮌ *14 rooms, 2 with shared bath* ⦿ *Breakfast.*

QUICY

67 miles southwest of Susanville via Hwys. 36 and 89.

A center for mining and logging in the 1850s, Quincy is nestled against the
western slope of the Sierra Nevada. The county seat and largest commu-
nity in Plumas County, the town is rich in historic buildings that have been
the focus of preservation and restoration efforts. The four-story court-
house on Main Street, one of several stops on a self-guided tour, was built
in 1921 with marble posts and staircases. The arts are thriving in Quincy,
too: catch a play or a bluegrass performance at the Town Hall Theatre.

GETTING HERE AND AROUND

Quincy is on Highway 70 and is accessible from all directions via moun-
tain roads. Highway 70 goes through the Feather River Canyon to
Highway 149, then Highway 99 to Chico and Red Bluff, a 198-mile
trip. From Quincy, Highway 70 connects to Highway 89 and then to
Highway 36E toward Susanville in the east, or westward toward Ches-
ter and Lassen Park. Plumas County Transit serves Chester and Quincy.
Lassen Rural Bus connects Quincy and Susanville.

ESSENTIALS

Bus Information Lassen Rural Bus ☎ *530/252–7433*
⊕ *www.lassentransportation.org.* **Plumas County Transit** ☎ *530/283–2538*
⊕ *www.plumastransit.com.*

Visitor Information Quincy Chamber of Commerce ✉ *464 W. Main St., at
Bradley St.* ☎ *530/283–0188* ⊕ *www.quincychamber.com.*

EXPLORING

Bucks Lake Recreation Area. The main recreational attraction in central
Plumas County is 17 miles southwest of Quincy at elevation 5,200 feet.
During warm months the lake's 17-mile shoreline, two marinas, and
eight campgrounds attract anglers and water-sports enthusiasts. Trails
through the tall pines beckon hikers and horseback riders. In winter
much of the area remains open for snowmobiling and cross-country
skiing. ✉ *Bucks Lake Rd.* ☎ *530/283–0188* ⊕ *www.plumascounty.org/
Communities/BucksLake.htm.*

Plumas County Museum. The cultural, home arts, and industrial history
displays at the Plumas County Museum contain artifacts dating to the
1850s. Highlights include collections of Maidu Indian basketry, pioneer
weapons, and rooms depicting life in the early logging and mining days
of Plumas County. Out in the Exhibit Yard are a working blacksmith
shop, a restored goldminer's cabin, and a railroad exhibit. ✉ *500 Jack-
son St., at Coburn St.* ☎ *530/283–6320* ⊕ *www.plumasmuseum.org*
🎫 *$2* ⊙ *Wed.–Sat. 8–5; closed noon-1 for lunch.*

14

Plumas National Forest. Plumas County is known for its wide-open spaces, and the 1.2-million-acre Plumas National Forest, with its high alpine lakes and crystal-clear woodland streams, is a beautiful example. Hundreds of campsites are maintained in the forest, and picnic areas and hiking trails abound. You can enter the forest along highways 70 and 89. ⊠ *U.S. Forest Service, 159 Lawrence St., near W. Main St.* ☎ *530/283–2050* ⊕ *www.fs.usda.gov/plumas* ⊗ *Office weekdays 8–4:30.*

WHERE TO EAT AND STAY
For expanded hotel reviews, visit Fodors.com.

$$
AMERICAN

✕ **Sweet Lorraine's.** Hearty fare served in this casual, bustling restaurant in Quincy's historic downtown area includes meaty dishes like St. Louis–style ribs as well as vegetarian options and lighter items; there's also a good selection of wines. If the weather is mild, dine alfresco on the patio. Counter seating is fast and friendly. ⑤ *Average main: $17* ⊠ *384 Main St., at Harbison Ave.* ☎ *530/283–5300* ⊗ *Closed Sun. and Mon.*

$
RENTAL
Fodor'sChoice
★

🔲 **Ada's Place.** This place is actually four uniquely beautiful cottages, secluded on a quiet street one block from the county courthouse and downtown Quincy. **Pros:** on-site owners' meticulous upkeep. **Cons:** not a good choice for children. ⑤ *Rooms from: $100* ⊠ *562 Jackson St., near Court St.* ☎ *530/283–1954, 877/234–2327* ⊕ *www.adasplace. com* ⟿ *4 cottages.*

$
B&B/INN

🔲 **Feather Bed.** The quaint romanticism of an 1893 Queen Anne Victorian plus proximity to Quincy's town center are the draws here. **Pros:** great location for exploring the town on foot. **Cons:** some rooms are small. ⑤ *Rooms from: $120* ⊠ *542 Jackson St.* ☎ *530/283–0102, 800/696–8624* ⊕ *www.featherbed-inn.com* ⟿ *5 rooms, 2 cottages* ⦿*Breakfast.*

$
HOTEL

🔲 **Lariat Lodge.** This small, single-story motel 2 miles east of downtown is a quiet haven surrounded by views of the Plumas National Forest. **Pros:** inexpensive rooms; lovely setting. **Cons:** older facility. ⑤ *Rooms from: $70* ⊠ *2370 E. Main St.* ☎ *530/283–1000, 800/999–7199* ⊟ *530/283–2164* ⊕ *www.lariatlodge.com* ⟿ *19 rooms.*

TRAVEL SMART
NORTHERN
CALIFORNIA

GETTING HERE AND AROUND

Wherever you plan to go in Northern California, getting there will likely involve driving, even if you fly. Major airports are usually far from main attractions. (In San Francisco, it's a 30-minute-plus trip between any Bay Area airport and downtown.) Northern California's major airport hub is SFO in San Francisco, but satellite airports can be found around most major cities. When booking flights, it pays to check these locations, as you may find more convenient times and a better location in relation to your hotel. Most small cities have their own commercial airports, with connecting flights to larger cities—but service may be extremely limited, and it may be cheaper to rent a car and drive from San Francisco.

■ AIR TRAVEL

Flying time to California is about 5½ hours from New York and 4 hours from Chicago. Travel from London to San Francisco is 11 hours and from Sydney approximately 14 ½. Flying between San Francisco and Los Angeles takes about 90 minutes.

AIRPORTS

California's gateways are Los Angeles International Airport (LAX), San Francisco International Airport (SFO), San Diego International Airport (SAN), Sacramento International Airport (SMF), and San Jose International Airport (SJC). Oakland International Airport (OAK) is another option in the Bay Area, and other Los Angeles airports include Long Beach (LGB), Bob Hope Airport (BUR), LA/Ontario (ONT), and John Wayne Airport (SNA).

Airport Information Bob Hope Airport ✉ Burbank ☎ 818/840–8840 ⊕ www. burbankairport.com. **John Wayne Airport** ☎ 949/252–5200 ⊕ www.ocair.com. **LA/ Ontario International Airport** ☎ 909/937– 2700 ⊕ www.flyontario.com. **Long Beach**

Airport ☎ 562/570–2600 ⊕ www.lgb.org. **Los Angeles International Airport** ☎ 310/646–5252 ⊕ www.lawa.org/lax. **Oakland International Airport** ☎ 510/563–3300 ⊕ www.flyoakland.com. **Sacramento International Airport** ☎ 916/929–5411 ⊕ www. sacramento.aero/smf. **San Diego International Airport** ☎ 619/400–2404 ⊕ www.san. org. **San Francisco International Airport** ☎ 650/821–8211, 800/435–9736 ⊕ www. flysfo.com. **San Jose International Airport** ☎ 408/392–3600 ⊕ www.flysanjose.com.

FLIGHTS

United, with hubs in San Francisco and Los Angeles, has the greatest number of flights into and within California. But most national and many international airlines fly to the state. Southwest Airlines connects smaller cities within California, often from satellite airports near major cities.

Airline Contacts Air Canada ☎ 888/247– 2262 ⊕ www.aircanada.com. **Alaska Airlines/ Horizon Air** ☎ 800/252–7522 ⊕ www. alaskaair.com. **American Airlines** ☎ 800/433– 7300 ⊕ www.aa.com. **British Airways** ☎ 800/247–9297 ⊕ www.britishairways.com. **Cathay Pacific** ☎ 800/233–2742 ⊕ www. cathaypacific.com. **Delta Airlines** ☎ 800/221– 1212 for U.S. reservations, 800/241–4141 for international reservations ⊕ www.delta. com. **Frontier Airlines** ☎ 800/432–1359 ⊕ www.flyfrontier.com. **Japan Air Lines** ☎ 800/525–3663 ⊕ www.jal.com. **JetBlue** ☎ 800/538–2583 ⊕ www.jetblue.com. **Qantas** ☎ 800/227–4500 ⊕ www.qantas.com. au. **Southwest Airlines** ☎ 800/435–9792 ⊕ www.southwest.com. **Spirit Airlines** ☎ 800/772–7117 ⊕ www.spirit.com. **United Airlines** ☎ 800/864–8331 for U.S. reservations, 800/538–2929 for international reservations ⊕ www.united.com. **US Airways** ☎ 800/428–4322 for U.S. and Canada reservations, 800/622–1015 for international reservations ⊕ www.usairways.com.

▮ BOAT TRAVEL

CRUISES

A number of major cruise lines offer trips that begin or end in California. Most voyages sail north along the Pacific Coast to Alaska or south to Mexico. California cruise ports include Los Angeles, San Diego, and San Francisco.

Cruise Lines Carnival Cruise Line
☎ 305/599–2600, 800/227–6482 ⊕ www. carnival.com. **Celebrity Cruises** ☎ 800/647–2251, 800/437–3111 ⊕ www.celebritycruises. com. **Crystal Cruises** ☎ 310/785–9300, 800/446–6620 ⊕ www.crystalcruises.com. **Holland America Line** ☎ 206/281–3535, 877/932–4259 ⊕ www.hollandamerica.com. **Norwegian Cruise Line** ☎ 305/436–4000, 866/234-7350 ⊕ www.ncl.com. **Princess Cruises** ☎ 661/753–0000, 800/774–6237 ⊕ www.princess.com. **Regent Seven Seas Cruises** ☎ 954/776–6123, 877/505-5370 ⊕ www.rssc.com. **Royal Caribbean International** ☎ 305/539–6000, 866/562-7625 ⊕ www.royalcaribbean.com. **Silversea Cruises** ☎ 954/522–4477, 877/276-6816 ⊕ www.silversea.com.

▮ BUS TRAVEL

Greyhound is the major bus carrier in California. Regional bus service is available in metropolitan areas.

Bus Information Greyhound ☎ 800/231–2222 ⊕ www.greyhound.com.

▮ CAR TRAVEL

There are two basic north–south routes in California: Interstate 5 runs inland most of the way from the Oregon border to the Mexican border; and U.S. 101 hugs the coast for part of the route from Oregon to Mexico. A slower but much more scenic option is to take California State Route 1, also referred to as Highway 1 and the Pacific Coast Highway, which winds along much of the California coast and provides an occasionally hair-raising, but breathtaking, ride.

From north to south, the state's east–west interstates are Interstate 80, Interstate 15, Interstate 10, and Interstate 8. Much of California is mountainous, and you may encounter winding roads, frequently cliffside, and steep mountain grades. In winter, roads crossing the Sierra from east to west may close at any time due to weather. Also in winter, Interstate 5 north of Los Angeles closes during snowstorms.

The flying and driving times in the accompanying charts represent best-case scenario estimates, but know that the infamous California traffic jam can occur at any time.

GASOLINE

Gasoline prices in California vary widely, depending on location, oil company, and whether you buy it at a full-service or self-serve pump. It's less expensive to buy fuel in the southern part of the state than in the north. If you're planning to travel near Nevada, you can save a bit by purchasing gas over the border. Gas stations are plentiful throughout the state. Most stay open late (24 hours along major highways and in big cities), except in rural areas, where Sunday hours are limited and where you may drive long stretches without a chance to refuel.

ROAD CONDITIONS

Rainy weather can make driving along the coast or in the mountains treacherous. Some of the smaller routes over mountain ranges and in the deserts are prone to flash flooding. When the rains are severe, coastal Highway 1 can quickly become a slippery nightmare, buffeted by strong winds and obstructed by falling debris from the cliffs above. When the weather is particularly bad, Highway 1 may be closed due to mud and rock slides.

Many smaller roads over the Sierra Nevada are closed in winter, and if it's snowing, tire chains may be required on routes that are open, most notably those to Yosemite and Lake Tahoe. From October through April, if it's raining along the coast, it's usually snowing at higher elevations. Consider renting a four-wheel-drive vehicle, or purchase chains before you get to the mountains. (Chains or cables generally cost $30 to $70, depending on tire size; cables are easier to attach than chains, but chains are more durable.) If you delay and purchase them in the vicinity of the chain-control area, the cost may double. Be aware that most rental-car companies prohibit chain installation on their vehicles. If you choose to risk it and do not tighten them properly, they may snap—your insurance likely will not cover any resulting damage. Uniformed chain installers on Interstate 80 and U.S. 50 will apply them at the checkpoint for $35 or take them off for less than that. Chain installers are independent business people, not highway employees, and set their own fees. They are not allowed to sell or rent chains. On smaller roads, you're on your own. Always carry extra clothing, blankets, water, and food when driving to the mountains in the winter, and keep your gas tank full to prevent the fuel line from freezing.

Road Conditions Caltrans Current Highway Conditions ☎ 800/427–7623 ⊕ www.dot.ca.gov.

WEATHER CONDITIONS

National Weather Service ☎ 707/443–6484 northernmost California, 831/656–1725 San Francisco Bay area and central California, 775/673–8100 Reno, Lake Tahoe, and northern Sierra, 805/988–6610 Los Angeles area, 858/675–8700 San Diego area ⊕ www.weather.gov.

ROADSIDE EMERGENCIES

Dial 911 to report accidents on the road and to reach the police, the California Highway Patrol (CHP), or the fire department. On some rural highways and on most interstates, look for emergency phones on the side of the road.

RULES OF THE ROAD

All passengers must wear seat belts at all times. It is illegal to leave a child six years of age or younger unattended in a motor vehicle. A child must be secured in a federally approved child passenger restraint system and ride in the back seat until at least eight years of age or until the child is at least 4 feet 9 inches tall. Children who are eight but don't meet the height requirement must ride in a booster seat or a car seat. Unless otherwise indicated, right turns are allowed at red lights after you've come to a full stop. Left turns between two one-way streets are allowed at red lights after you've come to a full stop.

Drivers with a blood-alcohol level higher than 0.08 who are stopped by police are subject to arrest, and those under 21 convicted of driving with a level of 0.01 or more can have their driving privileges revoked for a year. California's drunk-driving laws are extremely tough—violators may have their licenses immediately suspended, pay hefty fines, and spend the night in jail.

The speed limit on many interstate highways is 70 mph; unlimited-access roads are usually 55 mph. In cities, freeway speed limits are between 55 mph and 65 mph. Many city routes have commuter lanes during rush hour.

You must turn on your headlights whenever weather conditions require the use of windshield wipers.

Those 18 and older must use a hands-free device for their mobile phones while driving; those under 18 may not use mobile phones or wireless devices while driving. Texting on a wireless device is illegal for all drivers. Smoking in a vehicle where a minor is present is an infraction. For more information refer to the Department of Motor Vehicles driver's handbook at ⊕ www.dmv.ca.gov.

CAR RENTAL

When you reserve a car, ask about cancellation penalties, taxes, drop-off charges (if you're planning to pick up the car in one city and leave it in another), and surcharges (for being under or over a certain age, for additional drivers, or for driving across state or country borders or beyond a specific distance from your point of rental). All of these things can add substantially to your costs. Request car seats and extras such as GPS when you book.

Rates are sometimes—but not always—better if you book in advance or reserve through a rental agency's website. There are other reasons to book ahead, though: for popular destinations, during busy times of the year, or to ensure that you get certain types of cars (vans, SUVs, exotic sports cars).

■TIP→ Make sure that a confirmed reservation guarantees you a car. Agencies sometimes overbook, particularly for busy weekends and holiday periods.

A car is essential in most parts of California, though in compact San Francisco it's better to use public transportation to avoid parking headaches.

Rates statewide for the least expensive vehicle begin as low as $30 a day, usually on weekends, and less than $200 a week (though they increase rapidly from here). This does not include additional fees or the tax on car rentals, which is 9.00% in Los Angeles, 8.75% in San Francisco, and 8.00% in San Diego. Be sure to shop around—you can get a decent deal by carefully shopping the major car rental companies' websites. Compare prices by city before you book, and ask about "drop charges" if you plan to return the car in a city other than the one where you rented the vehicle. If you pick up at an airport, there may also be a facility charge of as much as $12 per rental; ask when you book.

In California, you must have a valid driver's license and be 21 to rent a car; rates may be higher if you're under 25. Some agencies will not rent to those under 25; check when you book. Non-U.S. residents must have a license with text that is in the Roman alphabet that is valid for the entire rental period. Though it need not be entirely written in English, it must have English letters that clearly identify it as a driver's license. In addition, most companies also require an international license; check in advance.

If you dream of driving down the coast with the top down, or you want to explore the desert landscape not visible from the road, consider renting a specialty vehicle. Agencies that specialize in convertibles and sport-utility vehicles will often arrange airport delivery in larger cities. Unlike most of the major agencies, the following companies guarantee the car class that you book.

Specialty Car Agencies Enterprise Exotic Car Rentals ☎ *800/400-8412, 866/458-9227 locations in San Francisco, Los Angeles, and other Southern California locations* ⊕ *exoticcars.enterprise.com.*

Major Rental Agencies
Alamo ☎ *800/462-5266* ⊕ *www.alamo. com.* **Avis** ☎ *800/331-1212* ⊕ *www.avis.com.* **Budget** ☎ *800/527-0700* ⊕ *www.budget. com.* **Hertz** ☎ *800/654-3131* ⊕ *www.hertz. com.* **National Car Rental** ☎ *877/222-9058* ⊕ *www.nationalcar.com.*

▌ TRAIN TRAVEL

One of the most beautiful train trips in the country, Amtrak's *Coast Starlight,* begins in Los Angeles and hugs the Pacific Coast to San Luis Obispo before it turns inland for the rest of its journey to Portland and Seattle. The *California Zephyr* travels from Chicago to Oakland via Denver; the *Pacific Surfliner* connects San Diego and San Luis Obispo via Los Angeles and Santa Barbara with multiple departures daily; and the *Sunset Limited* runs from Los Angeles to New Orleans via Arizona, New Mexico, and Texas.

Information Amtrak ☎ *800/872-7245* ⊕ *www.amtrak.com.*

ESSENTIALS

■ ACCOMMODATIONS

Most hotels require you to give your credit-card details before they will confirm your reservation. If you don't feel comfortable emailing this information, ask if you can fax it (some places even prefer faxes). However you book, get confirmation in writing and have a copy of it handy when you check in.

Be sure you understand the hotel's cancellation policy. Some places allow you to cancel without any kind of penalty—even if you prepaid to secure a discounted rate—if you cancel at least 24 hours in advance. Others require you to cancel a week in advance or penalize you the cost of one night. Small inns and B&Bs are most likely to require you to cancel far in advance. Most hotels allow children under a certain age to stay in their parents' room at no extra charge, but others charge for them as extra adults; find out the cutoff age for discounts.

Many B&Bs are entirely nonsmoking, and hotels and motels are decreasing their inventory of smoking rooms; if you require one, ask when you book if any are available.

BED-AND-BREAKFASTS

California has more than 1,000 bed-and-breakfasts. You'll find everything from simple homestays to lavish luxury lodgings, many in historic hotels and homes. The California Association of Bed and Breakfast Inns has about 300 member properties that you can locate and book through its website.

Reservation Services Bed & Breakfast.com ☎ 512/322–2710, 800/462–2632 ⊕ www. bedandbreakfast.com. **Bed & Breakfast Inns Online** ☎ 800/215–7365 ⊕ www.bbonline. com. **BnB Finder.com** ☎ 212/480–0414, 888/547–8226 ⊕ www.bnbfinder.com. **California Association of Bed and Breakfast Inns** ☎ 800/373–9251 ⊕ www.cabbi.com.

■ COMMUNICATIONS

INTERNET

Internet access is widely available in urban areas, but it's usually more difficult to get online in the state's rural areas. Most hotels offer some kind of connection—usually broadband or Wi-Fi. Many hotels charge a daily fee (about $10) for Internet access. Cybercafés are located throughout California.

Cybercafés ⊕ www.cybercafes.com.

■ EATING OUT

California has led the pack in bringing natural and organic foods to the forefront of American cooking. Though rooted in European cuisine, California cooking sometimes has strong Asian and Latin influences. Wherever you go, you're likely to find that dishes are made with fresh produce and other local ingredients.

The restaurants we list are the cream of the crop in each price category.

CUTTING COSTS

■ TIP➔ If you're on a budget, take advantage of the "small plates" craze sweeping California by ordering several appetizer-size portions and having a glass of wine at the bar, rather than having a full meal. Also, the better grocery and specialty-food stores have grab-and-go sections, with prepared foods on par with restaurant cooking, perfect for picnicking. At resort areas in the off-season (such as Lake Tahoe in October and May), you can often find two-for-one dinner specials at upper-end restaurants; check coupon apps or local papers or with visitor bureaus.

RESERVATIONS AND DRESS

Regardless of where you are, it's a good idea to make a reservation if you can. We only mention reservations specifically when they are essential (there's no other way you'll ever get a table) or when they are not accepted. For popular restaurants, book as far ahead as you can (often 30 days), and reconfirm as soon as you arrive. (Large parties should always call ahead to check the reservations policy.) We mention dress only when men are required to wear a jacket or a jacket and tie.

Online reservation services make it easy to book a table before you even leave home. OpenTable covers many California cities.

Contacts OpenTable ⊕ *www.opentable.com.*

WINES, BEER, AND SPIRITS

Throughout the state, most famously in the Napa and Sonoma valleys, you can visit wineries, many of which have tasting rooms and offer tours. Microbreweries are an emerging trend in the state's cities and in some rural areas in northern California. The legal drinking age is 21.

▌ HEALTH

Smoking is illegal in all California bars and restaurants, including on outdoor dining patios in some cities. If you have an existing medical condition that may require emergency treatment, be aware that many rural and mountain communities have only daytime clinics, not hospitals with 24-hour emergency rooms.

▌ HOURS OF OPERATION

Banks in California are typically open weekdays from 9 to 6 and Saturday morning; most are closed on Sunday and most holidays. Smaller shops usually operate from 10 to 6, with larger stores remaining open until 8 or later. Hours vary for museums, historical sites, and state parks, and many closed one or more days a week, or for extended periods during off-season months. It's a good idea to check before you visit a tourist site.

▌ MONEY

San Francisco tends to be an expensive city to visit, and rates at coastal resorts are almost as high. Hotel rates average $150 to $250 a night (though you can find cheaper places), and dinners at even moderately priced restaurants often cost $20 to $40 per person. Costs in the Gold Country and the Far North region are considerably less—many fine Gold Country bed-and-breakfasts charge around $100 a night, and some motels in the Far North charge $70 to $90.

CREDIT CARDS

It's a good idea to inform your credit-card company before you travel. Otherwise, the credit-card company might put a hold on your card owing to unusual activity—not a good thing halfway through your trip. Record all your credit-card numbers—as well as the phone numbers to call if your cards are lost or stolen—in a safe place, so you're prepared should something go wrong. Both MasterCard and Visa have general numbers you can call (collect if you're abroad) if your card is lost, but you're better off calling the number of your issuing bank, since MasterCard and Visa normally just transfer you to your bank; your bank's number is usually printed on your card.

Reporting Lost Cards American Express ☎ 800/992–3404 in U.S., 715/343–7977 *collect from abroad* ⊕ *www.americanexpress. com.* **Discover** ☎ 800/347–2683 in U.S., 801/902–3100 *collect from abroad* ⊕ *www.discovercard.com.*

Diners Club ☎ 800/234–6377 in U.S., 514/877–1577 collect from abroad ⊕ www.dinersclub.com. **MasterCard** ☎ 800/627–8372 in U.S., 636/722–7111 collect from abroad ⊕ www.mastercard.com. Visa ☎ 800/847–2911 in U.S., 303/967–1096 collect from abroad ⊕ www.visa.com.

▮ SAFETY

California is a safe place to visit, as long as you take the usual precautions. In large cities ask the concierge or desk clerk to point out areas on your map that you should avoid. Lock valuables in a hotel safe when you're not using them. (Some hotels have in-room safes large enough to hold a laptop computer.) Keep an eye on your handbag when you're out in public. Security is high (but mostly invisible) at theme parks and resorts.

▮ TAXES

Sales tax in California varies from about 7.5% to 10% and applies to all purchases except for food purchased in a grocery store; food consumed in a restaurant is taxed but take-out food purchases are not. Hotel taxes vary widely by region, from about 8% to 15.5%.

▮ TIME

California is in the Pacific time zone. Pacific daylight time (PDT) is in effect from mid-March through early November; the rest of the year the clock is set to Pacific standard time (PST).

▮ TIPPING

Most service workers in California are fairly well paid compared to those in the rest of the country, and extravagant tipping is not the rule here. Exceptions include wealthy enclaves such as Beverly Hills, La Jolla, and San Francisco as well as the most expensive resort areas.

TIPPING GUIDELINES FOR CALIFORNIA	
Bartender	$1 per drink, or 10%–15% of tab per round of drinks
Bellhop	$1–$5 per bag, depending on the level of the hotel
Hotel Concierge	$5 or more, if he/she performs a service for you
Hotel Doorman	$1–$2 if he/she helps you get a cab
Valet Parking Attendant	$2 when you get your car
Hotel Maid	$2–$3 per person, per day; more in high-end hotels
Waiter	15%–20% (20%-25% is standard in upscale restaurants); nothing additional if a service charge is added to the bill
Skycap at Airport	$1–$3 per bag
Hotel Room-Service Waiter	15%–20% per delivery, even if a service charge was added since that fee goes to the hotel, not the waiter
Taxi Driver	15%–20%, but round up the fare to the next dollar amount
Tour Guide	15% of the cost of the tour, more depending on quality

▮ TOURS

Guided tours are a good option when you don't want to do it all yourself. You travel along with a group (sometimes large, sometimes small), stay in prebooked hotels, eat with your fellow travelers (the cost of meals is sometimes included in the price of your tour, sometimes not), and follow a schedule.

But not all guided tours are an if-it's-Tuesday-this-must-be-Yosemite experience. A knowledgeable guide can take you places that you might never discover on your own, and you may be pushed to see more than you would have otherwise. Tours aren't for everyone, but they can be just the thing for trips to places where making travel arrangements is difficult or time-consuming.

Whenever you book a guided tour, find out what's included and what isn't. A "land-only" tour includes all your travel (by bus, in most cases) in the destination, but not necessarily your flights to and from or even within it. Also, in most cases prices in tour brochures don't include fees and taxes. And remember that you'll be expected to tip your guide (in cash) at the end of the tour.

SPECIAL-INTEREST TOURS

BIKING

Bicycling is a popular way to see the California countryside, and commercial tours are available throughout the state. Most three- to five-day trips are all-inclusive—you'll stay in delightful country inns, dine at good regional restaurants, and follow experienced guides. The Northern California Wine Country, with its flat valley roads, is one of the most popular destinations. When booking, ask about level of difficulty, as nearly every trip will involve some hill work. Tours fill up early, so book well in advance.

■TIP➔ Most airlines accommodate bikes as luggage, provided they're dismantled and boxed.

Contacts Napa and Sonoma Valley Bike Tours ✉ 6795 Washington St., Bldg. B, Yountville ☎ 707/251–8687, 707/996–2453 ⊕ www.napavalleybiketours.com. **Bicycle Adventures** ✉ 29700 S.E. High Point Way, Issaquah, Washington ☎ 800/443–6060, 425/250–5540 ⊕ www.bicycleadventures.com.

❚ VISITOR INFORMATION

The California Travel and Tourism Commission's website takes you to each region of California, with digital visitor guides in multiple languages, driving tours, maps, welcome center locations, information on local tours, links to bed-and-breakfasts, and a complete booking center. It also links you—via the Explore California menu—to the websites of city and regional tourism offices and attractions. ⇨ *For the numbers and websites of regional and city visitor bureaus and chambers of commerce see the "Planning" sections in each chapter.*

Contacts California Travel and Tourism Commission ✉ Sacramento ☎ 916/444–4429 information, 800/862–2543 brochures ⊕ www.visitcalifornia.com. **Carnival Cruise Line** ☎ 305/599–2600, 800/227–6482 ⊕ www.carnival.com. **Beverly Hills Rent a Car** ☎ 800/479–5996 San Francisco and several locations in Los Angeles, 310/274-6969 ⊕ www.bhrentacar.com. **Midway Car Rental** ☎ 866/717-6802 several locations in Los Angeles ⊕ www.midwaycarrental.com.

INDEX

PHOTO CREDITS

Front cover: Nick Elias [Description: Carneros, Napa Valley]. 1, Yuen Kwan, Fodors.com member. 2, Bryan Brazil/Shutterstock 5, Heavenly Mountain Resort. Chapter 1: Experience California: 8-9, Jay Anderson, Fodors.com member. 11, Helio San Miguel. 12 (top), Clinton Steeds/Flickr. 12 (bottom), Jose Vigano, Fodors.com member. 13, comfortablynirm, Fodors.com member. 15, vathomp, Fodors. com member. 16, Robert Holmes. 17 (left), sd_foodies, Fodors.com member. 17 (right), Lisa M. Hamilton. 18 (left), Christophe Testi/iStockphoto. 18 (top right), Corbis. 18 (bottom right), Warren H. White. 19 (top left), Alan A. Tobey/iStockphoto. 19 (bottom left), Janet Fullwood. 19 (right), Aaron Kohr/iStockphoto. 20, Warren H. White. 21, Thomas Kranzel/Venture Media. 22, Andrew Zarivny/ iStockphoto. 25, Robert Holmes. 26 (top), Janine Bolliger/iStockphoto. 26 (bottom), Lise Gagne/ iStockphoto. 27, iStockphoto. 28 (top), Evan Meyer/ iStockphoto. 28 (center), Kyle Maass iStockphoto. 28 (bottom left), iStockphoto. 28 (bottom right), Lise Gagne iStockphoto. 29, Tom Baker/Shutterstock. 30 (left), SuperStock/age fotostock. 30 (top right), CURAphotography/Shutterstock. 30 (bottom right), Michael Almond/iStockphoto. 31 (top), iStockphoto. 31(bottom), Lise Gagne/iStockphoto. 32 (top), Ross Stapleton-Gray/iStockphoto. 32 (center), Jay Spooner/iStockphoto. 32 (bottom), TebNad/Shutterstock. 33 (top), Jay Spooner/iStockphoto. 33 (bottom), Lise Gagne/iStockphoto. 34, John Elk III/Alamy. Chapter 2: The Central Coast: 35, TweetieV, Fodors.com member. 36, Stephen Walls/iStockphoto. 37 (top), Bart Everett/iStockphoto. 37 (bottom), Robert Holmes. 38, David M. Schrader/Shutterstock. 48, S. Greg Panosian/iStockphoto. 49, Ruben G. Mendoza. 50 (top), Richard Wong/www.rwongphoto.com/Alamy. 50 (bottom), Ruben G. Mendoza. 51 (top left), Witold Skrypczak/Alamy. 51 (top right), S. Greg Panosian/iStockphoto. 51 (bottom), Janet Fullwood. 52 (top left), GIPhotoStock Z/Alamy. 52 (top right), Craig Lovell/Eagle Visions Photography/Alamy. 52 (bottom) and 53 (top), S. Greg Panosian/iStockphoto. 53 (bottom), Eugene Zelenko/wikipedia.org. 59, David M. Schrader/Shutterstock. 67, Doreen Miller, Fodors.com member. 78, Robert Holmes. 96-97, Valhalla | Design & Conquer, Fodors.com member. Chapter 3: The Monterey Bay Area: 101, mellifluous, Fodors. com member. 102, Janet Fullwood. 103 (top), vittorio sciosia/age fotostock. 103 (bottom). Jeff Greenberg/age fotostock. 104, Brent Reeves/Shutterstock. 111, Robert Holmes. 118, Holger Mette/iStockphoto. 126, laurel stewart/iStockphoto. Chapter 4: San Francisco: 149-152,163, Brett Shoaf/Artistic Visuals Photography. 164 (top), Arnold Genthe. 164 (bottom), Library of Congress Prints and Photographs Division. 165 (left), Sandor Balatoni/SFCVB. 165 (right), Detroit Publishing Company Collection, Photography Collection, Miriam and Ira D. Wallach Division of Art, Prints and Photographs, The New York Public Library, Astor, Lenox and Tilden Foundation. 166, Brett Shoaf/Artistic Visuals Photography. 167 (top), Gary Soup/Flickr. 167 (bottom), Albert Cheng/Shutterstock. 168 (top), Sheryl Schindler/SFCVB. 168 (center), Ronen/Shutterstock. 168 (bottom), Robert Holmes. 177, travelstock44/ Alamy. 179, Brett Shoaf/Artistic Visuals Photography. 180, San Francisco Municipal Railway Historical Archives. 186, Lewis Sommer/SFCVB. 197, Robert Holmes. 203, aprillilacs, Fodors.com member. 207, Rafael Ramirez Lee/iStockphoto. 214, yummyporky/Flickr. 215 (top and bottom), Lisa M. Hamilton. 234 (top), Fairmont Hotels, Resorts. 234 (center left), The Huntington Hotel. 234 (center right), David Phelps/Argonaut Hotel. 234 (bottom), Cesar Rubio/Joie de Vivre Hospitality. 235 (top), The Ritz-Carlton, San Francisco. 235 (center left & center right), Joie de Vivre Hospitality. 235 (bottom), Cris Ford/Union Street Inn. 236, Queen Anne Hotel. 242, Rough Guides/Alamy. 247, Robert Holmes. Chapter 5: The Bay Area: 251 and 252, Robert Holmes. 253, Jyeshern Cheng/iStockphoto. 254, Brett Shoaf/Artistic Visuals Photography. 260, Caro/Alamy. 265, 273, 280, Robert Holmes. 287, Mark Rasmussen/iStockphoto. 289, Robert Holmes. 294, S. Greg Panosian/iStockphoto. Chapter 6: The Wine Country: 303, Robert Holmes. 304, iStockphoto. 305, Robert Holmes. 306, Warren H. White. 314, Robert Holmes. 315 (top), kevin miller/iStockphoto. 315 (bottom), Far Niente+Dolce+Nickel & Nickel. 316 (top and bottom) Robert Holmes. 317 (top) Domaine Carneros. 317 (bottom), star5112/ Flickr. 318 (top left), Rubicon Estate. 318 (top right and bottom) and 319 (top and bottom), Robert Holmes. 320 (top), Philippe Roy/Alamy. 320 (center), Agence Images/Alamy. 320 (bottom), Cephas Picture Library/Alamy. 321 (top), Napa Valley Conference Bureau. 321 (second and third from top), Wild Horse Winery (Forrest L. Doud). 321 (fourth from top), Napa Valley Conference Bureau. 321 (fifth from top), Panther Creek Cellars (Ron Kaplan). 321 (sixth from top), Clos du Val (Marvin Collins). 321 (seventh from top), Panther Creek Cellars (Ron Kaplan). 321 (bottom), Warren H. White. 322, courtesy of the di Rosa Collection. 324, Robert Holmes. 334, Far Niente+Dolce+Nickel & Nickel. 336, Terry Joanis/Frog's Leap. 344, Chuck Honek/Schramsberg Vineyard. 347, Castello di Amorosa. 359, 360, 366-367, and 371, Robert Holmes. Chapter 7: The North Coast: 377, Thomas Barrat/Shutterstock. 378 (all), Robert Holmes. 379 (top), Russ Bishop/age fotostock. 379 (bottom), Robert Holmes. 380, Janet Fullwood. 387, 393, and 397, Robert Holmes. Chapter 8: Redwood National Park: 405, iStockphoto. 406 (top), Michael Schweppe/wikipedia.org. 406 (center), Agnieszka Szymczak/

iStockphoto. 406 (bottom), Natalia Bratslavsky/Shutterstock. 408, WellyWelly/Shutterstock. Chapter 9: The Southern Sierra: 413, Randall Pugh, Fodors.com member. 414, Craig Cozart/iStockphoto. 415 (top), David T Gomez/iStockphoto. 415 (bottom left and bottom right), Robert Holmes. 416, christinea78, Fodors.com member. 421, moonjazz/Flickr. 428, Douglas Atmore/iStockphoto. Chapter 10: Yosemite National Park: 431, Sarah P. Corley, Fodors.com member. 432, Yosemite Concession Services. 433 (top), Andy Z./Shutterstock. 431 (bottom), Greg Epperson/age fotostock. 434, Doug Lemke/Shutterstock. 438, Rebalyn, Fodors.com member. 443, Nathan Jaskowiak/Shutterstock. 446, Greg Epperson/age fotostock. 450-51, Katrina Leigh/Shutterstock. Chapter 11: Sequoia and Kings Canyon National Parks: 453 and 454, Robert Holmes. 455 (top), Greg Epperson/age fotostock. 455 (bottom) and 456, Robert Holmes. 463, urosr/Shutterstock. 467, Robert Holmes. Chapter 12: Sacramento and the Gold Country: 471 and 473 (top and bottom), Robert Holmes. 474, Andy Z./Shutterstock. 479, Marcin Wichary/Flickr. 489, Image Asset Management/age fotostock. 490 (left) and 490 (right), wikipedia.org. 490 (center), Charles Danek. 491, Ambient Images Inc./Alamy. 492 (top), Trailmix.Net/Flickr. 492 (center), oger jones/Flickr. 492 (bottom), L. C. McClure/wikipedia.org. 493 (top left), Russ Bishop/age fotostock. 493 (top center), vera bogaerts/iStockphoto. 493 (top right and bottom left), Walter Bibikow/age fotostock. 493 (bottom right), Charles Danek. 497, Janet Fullwood. 504, RickC/Flickr. Chapter 13: Lake Tahoe: 507, Tom Zikas/North Lake Tahoe. 508 (top), Rafael Ramirez Lee/iStockphoto. 508 (bottom) and 509, Janet Fullwood. 510, Jay Spooner/iStockphoto. 517 (top), Heavenly Mountain Resort. 517 (bottom), Jake Foster/iStockphoto. 518 (top), Lake Tahoe Visitors Authority. 518 (bottom left), iStockphoto. 518 (bottom right), Heavenly Mountain Resort. 521 and 522 (left), Andrew Zarivny/iStockphoto. 522 (right), Harry Thomas/iStockphoto. 523 (top left), Joy Strotz/Shutterstock. 523 (bottom left), iStockphoto. 523 (right), Jennifer Stone/Shutterstock. 530, Jay Spooner/iStockphoto. 537, Tom O'Neill. 548, Christopher Russell/iStockphoto. Chapter 14: The Far North: 555, NPS. 556 (top and bottom), Robert Holmes. 557 (top), Andy Z./Shutterstock. 557 (bottom), NPS. 558, ThreadedThoughts/Flickr. 563, Robert Holmes. 572, kathycsus/Flickr. 578, NPS. Back cover (from left to right): Celso Diniz/Shutterstock; Dan Harmeson/iStockphoto; Robert Holmes. Spine: S. Greg Panosian/iStockphoto.

NOTES

NOTES

ABOUT OUR WRITERS

San Francisco writer **Michele Bigley** spends most of her days exploring her favorite city with her two sons and husband. When not hunting for sand dollars, hiking through eucalyptus groves, or munching on Italian pastries, she writes articles, books, iPhone apps, and essays about her travels around the globe. Michele helped update our San Francisco chapter.

Christine Ciarmello is a freelance food and travel writer who was previously deputy editor at the West Coast's regional lifestyle magazine, *Sunset*. There, she explored food, wine, and cocktails—as well as travel. She has an obsession with out-the-box hotels, which you can follow on Twitter @cciarm. Previously she was editor-in-chief at *ISLANDS* magazine, where she explored the foods of Asia, Europe, and the Caribbean. A native New Orleanian who spent her formative years eating gumbo and char-grilled oysters, Christine eats out most nights in San Francisco and contributed to our San Francisco chapter.

Native Californian **Cheryl Crabtree**—who updated the Central Coast and Monterey Bay chapters—has worked as a freelance writer since 1987. She has contributed to Fodor's California since 2003 and has written for Fodor's Complete Guide to the National Parks of the West. Cheryl is editor of Montecito Magazine. Her articles have appeared in many regional and national publications, including US Airways in-flight magazine and Santa Barbara Seasons, and annual visitor magazines in Santa Barbara and Ventura.

Longtime Fodor's writer, editor, and contributor to our San Francisco chapter, **Denise M. Leto** roams the city out of sheer love for SF, peeking down overgrown alleyways and exploring tucked-away corners from the Tenderloin to the Richmond, often with her three homeschooled kids in tow.

Daniel Mangin returned to California, where he's maintained a home for three decades, after two stints at the Fodor's editorial offices in New York City, the second one as the Editorial Director of Fodors.com and the Compass American Guides. While at Compass he was the series editor for the California Wine Country guide and commissioned the Oregon Wine Country and Washington Wine Country guides. With several dozen wineries less than a half-hour's drive from home, he often finds himself transported as if by magic to a tasting room bar, communing with a sophisticated Cabernet or savoring the finish of a smooth Pinot Noir. For this edition, Daniel updated our Wine Country chapter.

Fiona G. Parrott is a Californian native. She spent her childhood exploring the raw wilderness of Marin County and her later years exploring the culinary and musical delights of San Francisco. At present she divides her adventure time between wilderness and cityscape, writing about the Bay Area's cutting edge hot spots. She has worked as a veterinarian, actor, watermelon picker, latrine builder, and university lecturer, but writing for Fodor's is one of her most exciting jobs. She helped update our San Francisco chapter.

For more than 20 years **Reed Parsell** has written travel stories, for newspapers and magazines, about destinations throughout the world. Recently he has written mostly about California attractions, and has updated the Mojave, Southern Sierra, and Sacramento and the Gold Country chapters for several years. He is the principal author of *Fodor's In Focus: Yosemite, Sequoia and Kings Canyon National Parks*, and frequently visits Death Valley. Reed, who lives in Sacramento with his wife and daughter, would like to thank David S. Williams for being an invaluable companion on Fodor's research trips through the Central Valley, Mojave Desert, and up and down the Eastern Sierra.

Jerry James Stone has been eating and drinking his way through San Francisco for years now where he focuses on the sustainable food and wine movement. You can find all his vegan and vegetarian recipes at Cooking Stoned (www.cookingstoned.tv) and others on the back of eco-friendly wines. Jerry helped update the San Francisco chapter in this year's guide. Follow him on Twitter @ jerryjamesstone for mouth-watering recipe ideas.

Freelance writer **Christine Vovakes**—who updated the North Coast, Lake Tahoe, Far North, the Redwoods, and Travel Smart chapters—has contributed to Fodor's California since 2004, and also has written for Fodor's Complete Guide to the National Parks of the West, Fodor's Pacific Northwest, and Fodor's Essential USA. Her travel articles and photographs have appeared in many publications, including *The Washington Post, The Christian Science Monitor, The Sacramento Bee,* and the *San Francisco Chronicle.*

Bobbi Zane—who updated Experience California for this edition—grew up in Southern California. She now lives in historic Julian in San Diego County. Her articles on Palm Springs have appeared in the *Orange County Register* and *Westways* magazine. She has contributed to Fodor's *Complete Guide to the National Parks of the West* and Fodor's *San Diego*. She has also contributed to *Escape to Nature Without Roughing It.*